Antonin Artaud
SELECTED WRITINGS

*Edited, and with
an introduction, by*

SUSAN SONTAG

Translated from the French by

HELEN WEAVER

Notes by

SUSAN SONTAG
and DON ERIC LEVINE

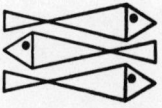

Antonin Artaud
Antonin Artaud
Antonin Artaud
SELECTED WRITINGS

Farrar, Straus and Giroux

NEW YORK

Translation copyright © 1976 by Farrar, Straus and Giroux, Inc.

All rights reserved
First printing, 1976
Printed in the United States of America
Designed by Loretta Li

Translated from the French, *Oeuvres complètes*,
© Editions Gallimard 1956, 1961, 1964, 1966, 1967, 1969, 1970, 1971, 1974

Introduction © 1973, 1976 by Susan Sontag

> Acknowledgment is made to *The New Yorker*, in whose pages Susan Sontag's Introduction originally appeared in somewhat different form
>
> "On the Balinese Theater," "*Mise en scène* and Metaphysics," "The Marx Brothers," "The Theater of Cruelty," "An End to Masterpieces," "An Emotional Athleticism," "Oriental Theater and Western Theater," from *The Theater and Its Double*, by Antonin Artaud, copyright © 1958 by Grove Press, Inc. Reprinted by permission of Grove Press, Inc.

Library of Congress Cataloging in Publication Data

Artaud, Antonin, 1896–1948.
    Selected writings.

PQ2601.R677A28   1976.   841'.9'12   79–143303

Contents

Artaud
    AN ESSAY BY SUSAN SONTAG   xvii

I Five early poems
    "THE MYSTIC SHIP" (1913)   3
    "VERLAINE DRINKS" (1921)   3
    "BLACK GARDEN" (1921/1922)   4
    "THE POEM OF ST. FRANCIS OF ASSISI"   4
    (1922)
    "LOVE" (1923)   5

II Two early essays
    "THE DEPARTMENT STORE POISON"   9
    (UNDATED)
    "PICTORIAL VALUES AND THE LOUVRE"   10
    (1921)

III Letters from 1921–23
    TO MADAME TOULOUSE (LATE JULY 1921)   15
    TO MAX JACOB (OCTOBER 1921)   15
    TO YVONNE GILLES (OCTOBER 1921)   17
    TO YVONNE GILLES (JUNE 1922)   18
    TO GÉNICA ATHANASIOU (AUGUST 17,   18
    1922)
    TO YVONNE GILLES (NOVEMBER 1922)   20
    TO GÉNICA ATHANASIOU (MAY 6, 1923)   20
    TO GÉNICA ATHANASIOU (OCTOBER 24,   21
    1923)

IV From *Bilboquet* (1923)
    "THERE AREN'T ENOUGH MAGAZINES . . ."   25
    "RIMBAUD & THE MODERNS"   26
    "A MENTAL PAINTER"   27

V *Correspondence with Jacques Rivière*   31
    (1923–24)

Contents

VI **Two essays from 1924**
- "The Evolution of Décor" — 53
- "Picasso Exhibit" — 56

VII ***The Umbilicus of Limbo* (1925)**
- "Where others present their works . . ." — 59
- "A great fervor . . ." — 59
- "With me god-the-hound . . ." (poem) — 60
- Letter to a doctor — 61
- "Paul the Birds" — 61
- Letter — 64
- "Description of a Physical State" — 64
- "A slender belly . . ." — 65
- "Dark Poet" (poem) — 67
- "Letter to the Legislator of the Law on Narcotics" — 68
- "The poets lift up hands . . ." (poem) — 71
- "There is an acid and murky anguish . . ." — 71
- "The Spurt of Blood" (play) — 72

VIII **From *The Nerve Meter* (1925)**
- "I really felt . . ." — 79
- "An actor is seen . . ." — 80
- "I have aspired no further . . ." — 80
- "In sleep . . ." — 80
- "It must be understood . . ." — 80
- "To find oneself again . . ." — 81
- "To think without the slightest breaking off . . ." — 81
- "A kind of constant leakage . . ." — 82
- "Under this crust of skin and bone . . ." — 82
- "A powerlessness . . ." — 82
- "What is difficult . . ." — 82
- "Do you know . . ." — 82

Contents

	Letter	83
	"Here is someone . . ."	83
	"I am an idiot . . ."	83
	"If only one could . . ."	84
	"What I lack . . ."	84
	"All writing is garbage . . ."	85
IX	***Fragments of a Diary from Hell* (1925)**	91
X	**More prose texts from 1925**	
	"General Security: The Liquidation of Opium"	99
	"Inquiry . . . Is Suicide a Solution?"	102
	"Dinner Is Served"	103
	"Letter to the Buddhist Schools"	104
	"The Activity of the Surrealist Research Bureau"	105
	"Manifesto in Clear Language"	108
	"Situation of the Flesh"	109
XI	***Eighteen Seconds*, a screenplay (1925–26)**	115
XII	**From *Art and Death* (1925–27)**	
	"Who, in the depths . . ." (probably 1927)	121
	"Letter to the Clairvoyant" (1926)	125
	"Héloïse and Abelard" (1925)	129
	"Clear Abelard" (1927)	132
	"Uccello the Hair" (1926)	135
XIII	**"In Total Darkness, or The Surrealist Bluff" (1927)**	139
XIV	**On *The Seashell and the Clergyman***	
	"Cinema and Abstraction" (1927)	149
	"Cinema and Reality" (1927)	150

Contents

XV	**On the Alfred Jarry Theater**	
	"The Alfred Jarry Theater" (1926)	155
	"Alfred Jarry Theater. First Season: 1926–27" (1926)	157
	"Manifesto for a Theater That Failed" (1926/1927)	159
	"Strindberg's Dream Play" (1928)	163
XVI	**Letters from 1927–30**	
	to Génica Athanasiou (September 16, 1927)	167
	to Abel Gance (November 27, 1927)	167
	to René Allendy (November 30, 1927)	168
	to Yvonne Allendy (June 7, 1928)	171
	to Yvonne Allendy (March 26, 1929)	172
	to Yvonne Allendy (June 5, 1930)	174
	to René Allendy (July 12, 1930)	175
XVII	**Questions and answers on the cinema**	
	"Reply to a Questionnaire" (undated)	181
	Interview for Cinémonde (1929)	182
XVIII	**Excerpts from notebooks and private papers (1931–32)**	189
XIX	**Letters from 1931**	
	incomplete draft of a letter, addressee unknown	199
	to Louis Jouvet (April 15, 1931)	200
	to Jean-Richard Bloch (April 23, 1931)	202
	to Louis Jouvet (April 27, 1931)	203
	draft of a letter to René Daumal (July 14, 1931)	205
	to Jean Paulhan (August 5, 1931)	208

Contents

	TO JEAN PAULHAN (SEPTEMBER 23, 1931)	209
	TO LOUIS JOUVET (OCTOBER 20, 1931)	210

XX **For *The Theater and Its Double* (1931–36)**

"ON THE BALINESE THEATER" (1931)	215
"MISE EN SCÈNE AND METAPHYSICS" (1932)	227
"THE MARX BROTHERS" (1932)	240
"THE THEATER OF CRUELTY: FIRST MANIFESTO" (1932)	242
"AN END TO MASTERPIECES" (1933)	252
"AN EMOTIONAL ATHLETICISM" (1935)	259
"ORIENTAL THEATER AND WESTERN THEATER" (1935)	267
"THE THEATER OF THE SERAPHIM" (1936)	271

XXI **Letters from 1932–33**

TO JEAN PAULHAN (JANUARY 22, 1932)	279
TO JEAN PAULHAN (JANUARY 30, 1932)	284
TO GEORGE SOULIÉ DE MORANT (FEBRUARY 17, 1932)	286
TO GEORGE SOULIÉ DE MORANT (FEBRUARY 19, 1932)	291
TO LOUIS JOUVET (MARCH 1, 1932)	296
TO JEAN PAULHAN (AUGUST 3, 1932)	297
TO ANDRÉ GIDE (AUGUST 7, 1932)	298
TO JEAN PAULHAN (AUGUST 23, 1932)	302
TO JEAN PAULHAN (SEPTEMBER 12, 1932)	303
TO JEAN PAULHAN (NOVEMBER 27, 1932)	304
TO JEAN PAULHAN (DECEMBER 16, 1932)	307
TO ANAÏS NIN (APRIL 1933)	308

XXII **"The Premature Old Age of the Cinema" (1933)** — 311

XXIII	From *Heliogabalus, or The Anarchist Crowned* (1934)	317
XXIV	**Letters and drafts from 1934–35**	
	TO JEAN PAULHAN (JUNE 1, 1934)	337
	"APPEAL TO YOUTH: INTOXICATION-DISINTOXICATION" (LATE 1934)	338
	TO ANDRÉ GIDE (FEBRUARY 10, 1935)	340
	TO JEAN-LOUIS BARRAULT (JUNE 14, 1935)	342
	DRAFT OF A LETTER TO THE INTERNATIONAL CONFERENCE OF WRITERS FOR THE DEFENSE OF CULTURE (LATE JUNE 1935)	344
	DRAFT OF A LETTER TO THE DIRECTOR OF THE ALLIANCE FRANÇAISE (DECEMBER 14, 1935)	347
XXV	**Excerpts from notebooks and private papers (1935)**	353
XXVI	**The trip to Mexico (1936)**	
	"MAN AGAINST DESTINY"	357
	LETTER TO JEAN PAULHAN (MARCH 26, 1936)	364
	"FIRST CONTACT WITH THE MEXICAN REVOLUTION"	366
	"WHAT I CAME TO MEXICO TO DO"	370
	LETTER TO JEAN-LOUIS BARRAULT (JULY 10, 1936)	374
XXVII	**From *A Voyage to the Land of the Tarahumara***	
	"THE MOUNTAIN OF SIGNS" (1936)	379
	"THE PEYOTE DANCE" (LATE 1936 OR EARLY 1937)	382
XXVIII	**Letters from 1937**	
	TO CÉCILE SCHRAMME (FEBRUARY 7, 1937)	395

Contents

	TO CÉCILE SCHRAMME (FEBRUARY 19, 1937)	395
	TO CÉCILE SCHRAMME (APRIL 16, 1937)	396
	TO CÉCILE SCHRAMME (APRIL 30, 1937)	398
	TO RENÉ ALLENDY (JUNE 1937)	399
	TO ANDRÉ BRETON (JULY 30, 1937)	400
	TO ANNE MANSON (SEPTEMBER 8, 1937)	403
	TO ANDRÉ BRETON (SEPTEMBER 14, 1937)	405
XXIX	From *The New Revelations of Being* (1937)	413
XXX	**Letters from 1940 (Ville-Evrard)**	
	TO GÉNICA ATHANASIOU (NOVEMBER 10, 1940)	417
	TO GÉNICA ATHANASIOU (NOVEMBER 24, 1940)	418
XXXI	**Letters from 1943–45 (Rodez)**	
	TO JACQUES LATRÉMOLIÈRE (MARCH 25, 1943)	423
	TO GASTON FERDIÈRE (MARCH 29, 1943)	424
	TO GASTON FERDIÈRE (OCTOBER 18, 1943)	429
	TO GHYSLAINE MALAUSSÉNA (JANUARY 9, 1944)	433
	TO GASTON FERDIÈRE (FEBRUARY 5, 1944)	435
	TO EUPHRASIE ARTAUD (JUNE 22, 1944)	436
	TO JACQUES LATRÉMOLIÈRE (JANUARY 6, 1945)	437
	TO MARIE-ANGE MALAUSSÉNA (JANUARY 30, 1945)	440
	TO HENRI PARISOT (SEPTEMBER 7, 1945)	441
	TO HENRI PARISOT (SEPTEMBER 17, 1945)	443
	TO HENRI PARISOT (SEPTEMBER 20, 1945)	446

Contents

	TO HENRI PARISOT (SEPTEMBER 22, 1945)	448
	TO HENRI PARISOT (OCTOBER 6, 1945)	451
	TO HENRI PARISOT (OCTOBER 9, 1945)	456
	TO HENRI PARISOT (NOVEMBER 27, 1945)	463
XXXII	**Two letters from 1946**	
	"LETTER ABOUT LAUTRÉAMONT"	469
	LETTER TO HENRI PARISOT (NOVEMBER 17, 1946), KNOWN AS "COLERIDGE THE TRAITOR"	473
XXXIII	***Van Gogh, the Man Suicided by Society* (1947)**	483
XXXIV	**Letter to Pierre Loeb (April 23, 1947)**	515
XXXV	**From *Artaud le Momo* (1947)**	
	"THE RETURN OF ARTAUD, LE MÔMO"	523
	"INSANITY AND BLACK MAGIC"	529
XXXVI	***Indian Culture* and *Here Lies* (1947)**	537
XXXVII	***To Have Done with the Judgment of God*, a radio play (1947)**	555
XXXVIII	**Last letters**	
	TO FERNAND POUEY (DECEMBER 11, 1947)	575
	TO FERNAND POUEY (JANUARY 16, 1948)	577
	TO WLADIMIR PORCHÉ (FEBRUARY 4, 1948)	578
	TO FERNAND POUEY (FEBRUARY 7, 1948)	580
	TO RENÉ GUILLY (FEBRUARY 7, 1948)	581
	TO FERNAND POUEY AND RENÉ GUIGNARD (FEBRUARY 17, 1948)	583

Contents

           TO PAULE THÉVENIN (FEBRUARY 24,   584
              1948)

Writings about Artaud   589
Notes   593

Illustrations

[follow page 204]

At age five, with his sister Marie-Ange

Around 1920, at twenty-four

Around 1920

At his sister's wedding

As Cecco, in Marcel Vandal's film *Graziella* (1925)

As Gringalet, in Luitz-Morat's film *Le Juif Errant* (1926)

As Marat, in Abel Gance's *Napoleon* (1926–27)

As Marat

As the Intellectual, in Léon Poirier's film *Verdun, Visions d'Histoire* (1928)

As the monk Massieu, in Carl Dreyer's *The Passion of Joan of Arc* (1928)

As the father in his play, *The Cenci*, produced in 1935 by the Theater of Cruelty

On the grounds of the asylum in Rodez, with Dr. Ferdière in May 1946

Self-portrait (December 17, 1946)

His room in the clinic in Ivry-sur-Seine

In his room, shortly before his death

Artaud

SUSAN SONTAG

THE MOVEMENT TO DISESTABLISH the "author" has been at work for over a hundred years. From the start, the impetus was—as it still is—apocalyptic: vivid with complaint and jubilation at the convulsive decay of old social orders, borne up by that worldwide sense of living through a revolutionary moment which continues to animate most moral and intellectual excellence. The attack on the "author" persists in full vigor, though the revolution either has not taken place or, wherever it did, has quickly stifled literary modernism. Gradually becoming, in those countries not recast by a revolution, the dominant tradition of high literary culture instead of its subversion, modernism continues to evolve codes for preserving the new moral energies while temporizing with them. That the historical imperative which appears to discredit the very practice of literature has lasted so long—a span covering numerous literary generations—does not mean that it was incorrectly understood. Nor does it mean that the malaise of the "author" has now become outmoded or inappropriate, as is sometimes suggested. (People tend to become cynical about even the most appalling crisis if it seems to be dragging on, failing to come to term.) But the longevity of modernism does show what happens when the prophesied resolution of drastic social and psychological anxiety is postponed—what unsuspected capacities for ingenuity and agony, and the domestication of agony, may flourish in the interim.

In the established conception under chronic challenge, literature is fashioned out of a rational—that is, socially accepted—language into a variety of internally consistent types of discourse (e.g., poem, play, epic, treatise, essay, novel) in the form of individual "works" that are judged by such norms as veracity, emotional power, subtlety, and relevance. But more than a century of literary modernism has made clear the contingency of once stable genres and undermined the very notion of an autonomous work. The standards used to appraise literary works now seem by no means self-evident, and a good deal less than universal. They are a particular culture's confirmations of its notions of rationality: that is, of mind and of community.

Being an "author" has been unmasked as a role that, whether

conformist or not, remains inescapably responsible to a given social order. Certainly not all pre-modern authors flattered the societies in which they lived. One of the author's most ancient roles is to call the community to account for its hypocrisies and bad faith, as Juvenal in the *Satires* scored the follies of the Roman aristocracy, and Richardson in *Clarissa* denounced the bourgeois institution of property-marriage. But the range of alienation available to the pre-modern authors was still limited— whether they knew it or not—to castigating the values of one class or milieu on behalf of the values of another class or milieu. The modern authors are those who, seeking to escape this limitation, have joined in the grandiose task set forth by Nietzsche a century ago as the transvaluation of all values, and redefined by Antonin Artaud in the twentieth century as the "general devaluation of values." Quixotic as this task may be, it outlines the powerful strategy by which the modern authors declare themselves to be no longer responsible—responsible in the sense that authors who celebrate their age and authors who criticize it are equally citizens in good standing of the society in which they function. The modern authors can be recognized by their effort to disestablish themselves, by their will not to be morally useful to the community, by their inclination to present themselves not as social critics but as seers, spiritual adventurers, and social pariahs.

Inevitably, disestablishing the "author" brings about a redefinition of "writing." Once writing no longer *defines* itself as responsible, the seemingly common-sense distinction between the work and the person who produced it, between public and private utterance, becomes void. All pre-modern literature evolves from the classical conception of writing as an impersonal, self-sufficient, freestanding achievement. Modern literature projects a quite different idea: the romantic conception of writing as a medium in which a singular personality heroically exposes itself. This ultimately private reference of public, literary discourse does not require that the reader actually know a great deal about the author. Although ample biographical information is available about Baudelaire and next to nothing is known about the life of Lautréamont, *The Flowers of Evil* and *Maldoror* are equally dependent as literary works upon the idea of the author as a tormented self raping its own unique subjectivity.

In the view initiated by the romantic sensibility, what is produced by the artist (or the philosopher) contains as a regulating internal structure an account of the labors of subjectivity. Work derives its credentials from its place in a singular lived experience; it assumes an inexhaustible personal totality of which "the work" is a by-product, and inadequately expressive of that totality. Art becomes a statement of self-awareness—an awareness that presupposes a disharmony between the self of the artist and the community. Indeed, the artist's effort is measured by the size of its rupture with the collective voice (of "reason"). The artist is a consciousness trying to be. "I am he who, in order to be, must whip his innateness," writes Artaud—modern literature's most didactic and most uncompromising hero of self-exacerbation.

In principle, the project cannot succeed. Consciousness as given can never wholly constitute itself in art but must strain to transform its own boundaries and to alter the boundaries of art. Thus, any single "work" has a dual status. It is both a unique and specific and already enacted literary gesture, and a meta-literary declaration (often strident, sometimes ironic) about the insufficiency of literature with respect to an ideal condition of consciousness and art. Consciousness conceived of as a project creates a standard that inevitably condemns the "work" to be incomplete. On the model of the heroic consciousness that aims at nothing less than total self-appropriation, literature will aim at the "total book." Measured against the idea of the total book, all writing, in practice, consists of fragments. The standard of beginnings, middles, and ends no longer applies. Incompleteness becomes the reigning modality of art and thought, giving rise to anti-genres—work that is deliberately fragmentary or self-canceling, thought that undoes itself. But the successful overthrow of old standards does not require denying the failure of such art. As Cocteau says, "the only work which succeeds is that which fails."

The career of Antonin Artaud, one of the last great exemplars of the heroic period of literary modernism, starkly sums up these revaluations. Both in his work and in his life, Artaud failed. His work includes verse; prose poems; film scripts; writings on cinema, painting, and literature; essays, diatribes, and polemics on the theater; several plays, and notes for many unrealized theater projects, among them an opera; a historical novel; a four-part dramatic monologue written for radio; essays on the peyote cult of the Tarahumara Indians; radiant appearances in two great films (Gance's *Napoleon* and Dreyer's *The Passion of Joan of Arc*) and many minor ones; and hundreds of letters, his most accomplished "dramatic" form—all of which amount to a broken, self-mutilated corpus, a vast collection of fragments. What he bequeathed was not achieved works of art but a singular presence, a poetics, an aesthetics of thought, a theology of culture, and a phenomenology of suffering.

In Artaud, the artist as seer crystallizes, for the first time, into the figure of the artist as pure victim of his consciousness. What is prefigured in Baudelaire's prose poetry of spleen and Rimbaud's record of a season in hell becomes Artaud's statement of his unremitting, agonizing awareness of the inadequacy of his own consciousness to itself—the torments of a sensibility that judges itself to be irreparably estranged from thought. Thinking and using language become a perpetual calvary.

The metaphors that Artaud uses to describe his intellectual distress treat the mind either as a property to which one never holds clear title (or whose title one has lost) or as a physical substance that is intransigent, fugitive, unstable, obscenely mutable. As early as 1921, at the age of twenty-five, he states his problem as that of never managing to possess his mind "in its *entirety*." Throughout the nineteen-twenties, he laments that his ideas "abandon" him, that he is unable to "discover" his ideas, that he cannot "attain" his mind, that he has "lost" his understanding of words and "forgotten" the forms of thought. In more direct metaphors, he rages against the chronic erosion of his ideas, the way his thought crumbles beneath him or leaks away; he describes his mind as fissured, deteriorating, petrifying, liquefying, coagulating, empty, impenetrably dense: words rot. Artaud suffers not from doubt as to whether his "I" thinks but from a conviction that he does not possess his own thought. He does not say that he is unable to think; he says that he does not "have" thought—which he takes to be much more than having correct ideas or judgments. "Having thought" means that process by which thought sustains itself, manifests itself to itself, and is answerable "to all the circumstances of feeling and of life." It is in this sense of thought, which treats thought as both subject and object of itself, that Artaud claims not to "have" it. Artaud shows how the Hegelian, dramatistic, self-regarding consciousness can reach the state of total alienation (instead of detached, comprehensive wisdom)—because the mind remains an object.

The language that Artaud uses is profoundly contradictory. His imagery is materialistic (making the mind into a thing or object), but his demand on the mind amounts to the purest philosophical idealism. He refuses to consider consciousness except as a process. Yet it is the process character of consciousness—its unseizability and flux—that he experiences as hell. "The real pain," says Artaud, "is to feel one's thought shift within oneself." The *cogito*, whose all too evident existence seems hardly in need of proof, goes in desperate, inconsolable search of an *ars cogitandi*. Intelligence, Artaud observes with horror, is the purest contingency. At the antipodes of what Descartes and Valéry relate in their great optimistic epics about the quest for clear and distinct ideas, a Divine Comedy of thought, Artaud reports the unending misery and bafflement of consciousness seeking itself: "this intellectual tragedy in which I am always vanquished," the Divine Tragedy of thought. He describes himself as "in constant pursuit of my intellectual being."

The consequence of Artaud's verdict upon himself—his conviction of his chronic alienation from his own consciousness—is that his mental deficit becomes, directly or indirectly, the dominant, inexhaustible subject of his writings. Some of Artaud's accounts of his Passion of thought are almost too painful to read. He elaborates little on his emotions—panic, confusion, rage, dread. His gift was not for psychological understanding (which, not being good at it, he dismissed as trivial) but for a more original mode of description, a kind of physiological phenomenology of his unending desolation. Artaud's claim in *The Nerve Meter* that no one has ever so accurately charted his "intimate" self is not an exaggeration. Nowhere in the entire history of writing in the first person is there as tireless and detailed a record of the microstructure of mental pain.

Artaud does not simply record his psychic anguish, however. It constitutes his work, for while the act of writing—to give form to intelligence—is an agony, that agony also supplies the energy for the act of writing. Although Artaud was fiercely disappointed when the relatively shapely poems he submitted to the *Nouvelle Revue Française* in 1923 were rejected by its editor, Jacques Rivière, as lacking in coherence and harmony, Rivière's strictures proved to be liberating. From then on, Artaud denied that he was simply creating more art, adding to the storehouse of "literature." The contempt for literature—a theme of modernist literature first loudly sounded by Rimbaud—has a different inflection as Artaud expresses it in the era when the Futurists, Dadaists, and Surrealists had made it a commonplace. Artaud's contempt for literature has less to do with a diffuse nihilism about culture than with a specific experience of suffering. For Artaud, the extreme mental—and also physical—pain that feeds (and authenticates) the act of writing is necessarily falsified when that energy is transformed into artistry: when it attains the benign status of a finished, literary product. The verbal humiliation of literature ("All writing is garbage," Artaud declares in *The Nerve Meter*) safeguards the dangerous, quasi-magical status of writing as a vessel worthy of bearing the author's pain. Insulting art (like insulting the audience) is an attempt to head off the corruption of art, the banalization of suffering.

The link between suffering and writing is one of Artaud's leading themes: one earns the right to speak through having suffered, but the necessity of using language is itself the central occasion for suffering. He describes himself as ravaged by a "stupefying confusion" of his "language in its relations with thought." Artaud's alienation from language presents the dark side of modern poetry's successful verbal alienations—of its creative use of language's purely formal possibilities and of the ambiguity of words and the artificiality of fixed meanings. Artaud's problem is not what language is in itself but the relation language has to what he calls "the intellectual apprehensions of the flesh." He can barely afford the traditional complaint of all the great mystics that words tend to petrify living thought and to turn the immediate, organic, sensory stuff of experience into something inert, merely verbal. Artaud's fight is only secondarily with the deadness of language; it is mainly with the refractoriness of his own inner life. Employed by a consciousness that defines itself as paroxysmic, words become knives. Artaud appears to have been afflicted with an extraordinary inner life, in which the intricacy and clamorous pitch of his physical sensations and the convulsive intuitions of his nervous system seemed permanently at odds with his ability to give them verbal form. This clash between facility and impotence, between extravagant verbal gifts and a sense of intellectual paralysis, is the psychodramatic plot of everything Artaud wrote; and to keep that contest dramatically valid calls for the repeated exorcising of the respectability attached to writing.

Thus, Artaud does not so much free writing as place it under permanent suspicion by treating it as the mirror of consciousness—so that the range of what can be written is made coextensive with consciousness itself, and the truth of any statement is made to depend on the vitality and wholeness of the consciousness in which it originates. Against all hierarchical, or Platonizing, theories of mind, which make one part of consciousness superior to another part, Artaud upholds the democracy of mental claims, the right of every level, tendency, and quality of the mind to be heard: "We can do anything in the mind, we can speak in any tone of voice, *even one that is unsuitable.*" Artaud refuses to exclude any perception as too trivial or crude. Art should be able to report from anywhere, he thinks—although not for the reasons that justify Whitmanesque openness or Joycean license. For Artaud, to bar any of the possible transactions between different levels of the mind and the flesh amounts to a dispossession of thought, a loss of vitality in the purest sense. That narrow tonal range which makes up "the so-called literary tone"—literature in its traditionally acceptable forms—becomes worse than a fraud and an instrument of intellectual repression. It is a sentence of mental death. Artaud's notion of truth stipulates an exact and delicate concordance between the mind's "animal" impulses and the highest operations of the intellect. It is this swift, wholly unified consciousness that Artaud invokes in the obsessive accounts of his own mental insufficiency and in his dismissal of "literature."

The quality of one's consciousness is Artaud's final standard.

He unfailingly attaches his utopianism of consciousness to a psychological materialism: the absolute mind is also absolutely carnal. Thus, his intellectual distress is at the same time the most acute physical distress, and each statement he makes about his consciousness is also a statement about his body. Indeed, what causes Artaud's incurable pain of consciousness is precisely his refusal to consider the mind apart from the situation of the flesh. Far from being disembodied, his consciousness is one whose martyrdom results from its seamless relation to the body. In his struggle against all hierarchical or merely dualistic notions of consciousness, Artaud constantly treats his mind as if it *were* a kind of body—a body that he could not "possess," because it was either too virginal or too defiled, and also a mystical body by whose disorder he was "possessed."

It would be a mistake, of course, to take Artaud's statement of mental impotence at face value. The intellectual incapacity he describes hardly indicates the limits of his work (Artaud displays no inferiority in his powers of reasoning) but does explain his project: minutely to retrace the heavy, tangled fibers of his body-mind. The premise of Artaud's writing is his profound difficulty in matching "being" with hyper-lucidity, flesh with words. Struggling to embody live thought, Artaud composed in feverish, irregular blocks; writing abruptly breaks off and then starts again. Any single "work" has a mixed form; for instance, between an expository text and an oneiric description he frequently inserts a letter—a letter to an imaginary correspondent or a real letter that omits the name of the addressee. Changing forms, he changes breath. Writing is conceived of as unleashing an unpredictable flow of searing energy; knowledge must explode in the reader's nerves. The details of Artaud's stylistics follow directly from his notion of consciousness as a morass of difficulty and suffering. His determination to crack the carapace of "literature"—at least, to violate the self-protective distance between reader and text—is scarcely a new ambition in the history of literary modernism. But Artaud may have come closer than any other author to actually doing it—by the violent discontinuity of his discourse, by the extremity of his emotion, by the purity of his moral purpose, by the excruciating carnality of the account he gives of his mental life, by the genuineness and grandeur of the ordeal he endured in order to use language at all.

The difficulties that Artaud laments persist because he is thinking about the unthinkable—about how body is mind and how mind is also a body. This inexhaustible paradox is mirrored in Artaud's wish to produce art that is at the same time anti-art. The latter paradox, however, is more hypothetical than real. Ignoring Artaud's disclaimers, readers will inevitably assimilate his strategies of discourse to art whenever those strategies reach (as they often do) a certain triumphant pitch of incandescence. And three small books published between 1925 and 1929—*The Umbilicus of Limbo*, *The Nerve Meter*, and *Art and Death*—which may be read as prose poems, more splendid than anything that Artaud did formally as a poet, show him to be the greatest prose poet in the French language since the Rimbaud of *Illuminations* and *A Season in Hell*. Yet it would be incorrect to separate what is most accomplished as literature from his other writings.

Artaud's work denies that there is any difference between art and thought, between poetry and truth. Despite the breaks in exposition and the varying of "forms" within each work, everything he wrote advances a line of argument. Artaud is always didactic. He never ceased insulting, complaining, exhorting, denouncing—even in the poetry written after he emerged from the insane asylum in Rodez, in 1946, in which language becomes partly unintelligible; that is, an unmediated physical presence. All his writing is in the first person, and is a mode of address in the mixed voices of incantation and discursive explanation. His activities are simultaneously art and reflections on art. In an early essay on painting, Artaud declares that works of art "are worth only as much as the conceptions on which they are founded, whose value is exactly what we are calling into question anew." Just as Artaud's work amounts to an *ars poetica* (of which his work is no more than a fragmentary exposition), so he takes art-making to be a trope for the functioning of all consciousness—of life itself.

This trope was the basis of Artaud's affiliation with the Surrealist movement, between 1924 and 1926. As Artaud understood

ANTONIN ARTAUD

Surrealism, it was a "revolution" applicable to "all states of mind, to all types of human activity," its status as a tendency within the arts being secondary and merely strategic. He welcomed Surrealism—"above all, a state of mind"—as both a critique of mind and a technique for improving the range and quality of the mind. Sensitive as he was in his own life to the repressive workings of the bourgeois idea of day-to-day reality ("We are born, we live, we die in an environment of lies," he wrote in 1923), he was naturally drawn to Surrealism by its advocacy of a more subtle, imaginative, and rebellious consciousness. But he soon found the Surrealist formulas to be another kind of confinement. He got himself expelled when the majority of the Surrealist brotherhood were about to join the French Communist Party—a step that Artaud denounced as a sellout. An actual social revolution changes nothing, he insists scornfully in the polemic he wrote against "the Surrealist bluff" in 1927. The Surrealist adherence to the Third International, though it was to be only of short duration, was a plausible provocation for his quitting the movement, but his dissatisfaction went deeper than a disagreement about what kind of revolution is desirable and relevant. (The Surrealists were hardly more Communist than Artaud was. André Breton had not so much a politics as a set of extremely attractive moral sympathies, which in another period would have brought him to anarchism, and which, quite logically for his own period, led him in the nineteen-thirties to become a partisan and friend of Trotsky.) What really antagonized Artaud was a fundamental difference of temperament.

It was on the basis of a misunderstanding that Artaud had fervently subscribed to the Surrealist challenge to the limits that "reason" sets upon consciousness, and to the Surrealists' faith in the access to a wider consciousness afforded by dreams, drugs, insolent art, and asocial behavior. The Surrealist, he thought, was someone who "despairs of attaining his own mind." He meant himself, of course. Despair is entirely absent from the mainstream of Surrealist attitudes. The Surrealists heralded the benefits that would accrue from unlocking the gates of reason, and ignored the abominations. Artaud, as extravagantly heavyhearted as the Surrealists were optimistic, could, at most, apprehensively concede legitimacy to the irrational. While the Surrealists proposed exquisite games with consciousness which no one could lose, Artaud was engaged in a mortal struggle to "restore" himself. Breton sanctioned the irrational as a useful route toward a new mental continent. For Artaud, bereft of the hope that he was traveling anywhere, it was the terrain of his martyrdom.

By extending the frontiers of consciousness, the Surrealists expected not only to refine the rule of reason but to enlarge the yield of physical pleasure. Artaud was incapable of expecting any pleasure from the colonization of new realms of consciousness. In contrast to the Surrealists' euphoric affirmation of both physical passion and romantic love, Artaud regarded eroticism as something threatening, demonic. In *Art and Death* he describes "this preoccupation with sex which petrifies me and rips out my blood." Sexual organs multiply on a monstrous, Brobdingnagian scale and in menacingly hermaphrodite shapes in many of his writings; virginity is treated as a state of grace, and impotence or castration is presented—for example, in the imagery generated by the figure of Abelard in *Art and Death*—as more of a deliverance than a punishment. The Surrealists appeared to love life, Artaud notes haughtily. He felt "contempt" for it. Explaining the program of the Surrealist Research Bureau in 1925, he had favorably described Surrealism as "a certain order of repulsions," only to conclude the following year that these repulsions were quite shallow. As Marcel Duchamp said in a moving eulogy of his friend Breton in 1966, when Breton died, "the great source of Surrealist inspiration is love: the exaltation of elective love." Surrealism is a spiritual politics of joy.

Despite Artaud's passionate rejection of Surrealism, his taste was Surrealist—and remained so. His disdain for "realism" as a collection of bourgeois banalities is Surrealist, and so are his enthusiasms for the art of the mad and the non-professional, for that which comes from the Orient, for whatever is extreme, fantastic, gothic. Artaud's contempt for the dramatic repertory of his time, for the play devoted to exploring the psychology of individual characters—a contempt basic to the argument of the manifestos in *The Theater and Its Double*, written between 1931 and 1936—starts from a position identical with the one from which Breton dismisses the novel in the first "Manifesto of Surrealism" (1924). But Artaud makes a wholly different use of the enthusiasms and the aesthetic prejudices he shares with Breton. The Surrealists are connoisseurs of joy, freedom, pleasure. Artaud is a connoisseur of despair and moral struggle. While the Surrealists explicitly refused to accord art an autonomous value, they perceived no conflict between moral longings and aesthetic ones, and in that sense Artaud is quite right in saying that their program is "aesthetic"—merely aesthetic, he means. Artaud does perceive such a conflict, and demands that art justify itself by the standards of moral seriousness.

From Surrealism, Artaud derives the perspective that links his own perennial psychological crisis with what Breton calls (in the "Second Manifesto of Surrealism," of 1930) "a general crisis of consciousness"—a perspective that Artaud kept throughout his writings. But no sense of crisis in the Surrealist canon is as bleak as Artaud's. Set alongside Artaud's lacerated perceptions, both cosmic and intimately physiological, the Surrealist jeremiads seem tonic rather than alarming. (They are not in fact addressing the same crises. Artaud undoubtedly knew more than Breton about suffering, as Breton knew more than Artaud about freedom.) A related legacy from Surrealism gave Artaud the possibility of continuing throughout his work to take it for granted that art has a "revolutionary" mission. But Artaud's idea of revolution diverges as far from that of the Surrealists as his devastated sensibility does from Breton's essentially wholesome one.

Artaud also retained from the Surrealists the romantic imperative to close the gap between art (and thought) and life. He begins *The Umbilicus of Limbo,* written in 1925, by declaring himself unable to conceive of "work that is detached from life," of "detached creation." But Artaud insists, more aggressively than the Surrealists ever did, on that devaluation of the separate work of art which results from attaching art to life. Like the Surrealists, Artaud regards art as a function of consciousness, each work representing only a fraction of the whole of the artist's consciousness. But by identifying consciousness chiefly with its obscure, hidden, excruciating aspects he makes the dismembering of the totality of consciousness into separate "works" not merely an arbitrary procedure (which is what fascinated the Surrealists) but one that is self-defeating. Artaud's narrowing of the Surrealist view makes a work of art literally useless in itself; insofar as it is considered as a thing, it is dead. In *The Nerve Meter,* also from 1925, Artaud likens his works to lifeless "waste products," mere "scrapings of the soul." These dismembered bits of consciousness acquire value and vitality only as metaphors for works of art; that is, metaphors for consciousness.

Disdaining any detached view of art, any version of that view which regards works of art as objects (to be contemplated, to enchant the senses, to edify, to distract), Artaud assimilates all art to dramatic performance. In Artaud's poetics, art (and thought) is an action—and one that, to be authentic, must be brutal—and also an experience suffered, and charged with extreme emotions. Being both action and passion of this sort, iconoclastic as well as evangelical in its fervor, art seems to require a more daring scene, outside the museums and legitimate showplaces, and a new, ruder form of confrontation with its audience. The rhetoric of inner movement which sustains Artaud's notion of art is impressive, but it does not change the way he actually manages to reject the traditional role of the work of art as an object—by an analysis and an experience of the work of art which are an immense tautology. He sees art as an action, and therefore a passion, of the mind. The mind produces art. And the space in which art is consumed is also the mind—viewed as the organic totality of feeling, physical sensation, and the ability to attribute meaning. Artaud's poetics is a kind of ultimate, manic Hegelianism in which art is the compendium of consciousness, the reflection by consciousness on itself, and the empty space in which consciousness takes its perilous leap of self-transcendence.

Closing the gap between art and life destroys art and, at the same time, universalizes it. In the manifesto that Artaud wrote for the Alfred Jarry Theater, which he founded in 1926, he welcomes "the disrepute into which all forms of art are successively falling." His delight may be a posture, but it would be inconsistent for him to regret that state of affairs. Once the leading criterion for an art becomes its merger with life (that is, everything, including other arts), the existence of separate art forms ceases to be defensible. Furthermore, Artaud assumes that one of the existing arts must soon recover from its failure of nerve and become the total art form, which will absorb all the others. Artaud's lifetime of work may be described as the sequence of his efforts to formulate and inhabit this master art, heroically following out his conviction that the art he sought could hardly be the one—involving language alone—in which his genius was principally confined.

The parameters of Artaud's work in all the arts are identical with the different critical distances he maintains from the idea of an art that is language only—with the diverse forms of his lifelong "revolt against poetry" (the title of a prose text he wrote in Rodez in 1944). Poetry was, chronologically, the first of the many arts he practiced. There are extant poems from as early as 1913, when he was seventeen and still a student in his native Marseilles; his first book, published in 1923, three years after he moved to Paris, was a collection of poems; and it was the unsuccessful submission of some new poems to the *Nouvelle Revue Française* that same year which gave rise to his celebrated correspondence with Rivière. But Artaud soon began slighting poetry in favor of other arts. The dimensions of the poetry he was capable of writing in the twenties were too small for what Artaud intuited to be the scale of a master art. In the early poems, his breath is short; the compact lyric form he employs provides no outlet for his discursive and narrative imagination. Not until the great outburst of writing in the period between 1945 and 1948, in the last three years of his life, did Artaud, by then indifferent to the idea of poetry as a closed lyric statement, find a long-breathed voice that was adequate to the range of his imaginative needs—a voice that was free of established forms and open-ended, like the poetry of Pound. Poetry as Artaud conceived it in the twenties had none of these possibilities or adequacies. It was small, and a total art had to be, to feel, large; it had to be a multi-voiced performance, not a singular lyrical object.

All ventures inspired by the ideal of a total art form—whether in music, painting, sculpture, architecture, or literature—manage in one way or another to theatricalize. Though Artaud need not have been so literal, it makes sense that at an early age he moved into the explicitly dramatic arts. Between 1922 and 1924, he acted in plays directed by Charles Dullin and the Pitoëffs, and in 1924 he also began a career as a film actor. That is to say, by the mid-nineteen-twenties Artaud had two plausible candidates for the role of total art: cinema and theater. However, because it was not as an actor but as a director that he hoped to advance the candidacy of these arts, he soon had to renounce one of them—cinema. Artaud was never given the means to direct a film of his own, and he saw his intentions betrayed in a film of 1928 that was made by another director from one of his screenplays, *The Seashell and the Clergyman*. His sense of defeat was reinforced in 1929 by the arrival of sound, a turning point in the history of film aesthetics which Artaud wrongly prophesied—as did most of the small number of moviegoers who had taken films seriously throughout the nineteen-twenties—would terminate cinema's greatness as an art form. He continued acting in films until 1935, but with little hope of getting a chance to direct his own films and with no further reflection upon the possibilities of cinema (which, regardless of Artaud's discouragement, remains the century's likeliest candidate for the title of master art).

From late 1926 on, Artaud's search for a total art form centered upon the theater. Unlike poetry, an art made out of one material (words), theater uses a plurality of materials: words, light, music, bodies, furniture, clothes. Unlike cinema, an art using only a plurality of languages (images, words, music), theater is carnal, corporeal. Theater brings together the most diverse means—gesture and verbal language, static objects and movement in three-dimensional space. But theater does not become a master art merely by the abundance of its means, however. The prevailing tyranny of some means over others has to be creatively subverted. As Wagner challenged the convention of alternating aria and recitative, which implies a hierarchical relation of speech, song, and orchestral music, Artaud denounced the practice of making every element of the staging serve in some way the words that the actors speak to each other. Assailing as false the priorities of dialogue theater which have subordinated theater to "literature," Artaud implicitly upgrades the means that characterize such other forms of dramatic performance as dance, oratorio, circus, cabaret, church, gymnasium, hospital operating room, courtroom. But annexing these resources from other arts and from quasi-theatrical forms will not make theater a total art form. A master art cannot be constructed by a series of additions; Artaud is not urging mainly that the theater add to its means. Instead, he seeks to purge the theater of what is extraneous or easy. In calling for a theater in which the verbally oriented actor of Europe would be retrained as an "athlete" of the heart, Artaud shows his inveterate taste for spiritual and physical effort—for art as an ordeal.

Artaud's theater is a strenuous machine for transforming the mind's conceptions into entirely "material" events, among which are the passions themselves. Against the centuries-old priority that the European theater has given to words as the means for conveying emotions and ideas, Artaud wants to show the organic basis of emotions and the physicality of ideas—in the bodies of the actors. Artaud's theater is a reaction against the state of underdevelopment in which the bodies (and the voices, apart from talking) of Western actors have remained for generations, as have the arts of spectacle. To redress the imbalance that so favors verbal language, Artaud proposes to bring the training of actors close to the training of dancers, athletes, mimes, and singers, and "to base the theater on spectacle before everything else," as he says in his "Second Manifesto of the Theater of Cruelty," published in 1933. He is not offering to replace the charms of language with spectacular sets, costumes, music, lighting, and stage effects. Artaud's criterion of spectacle is sensory violence, not sensory enchantment; beauty is a notion he never entertains. Far from considering the spectacular to be in itself desirable, Artaud would commit the stage to an extreme austerity—to the point of excluding anything that stands for something else. "Objects, accessories, sets on the stage must be apprehended directly . . . not for what they represent but for what they are," he writes in a manifesto of 1926. Later, in *The Theater and Its Double*, he suggests eliminating sets altogether. He calls for a "pure" theater, dominated by the "physics of the absolute gesture, which is itself idea."

If Artaud's language sounds vaguely Platonic, it is with good reason. Like Plato, Artaud approaches art from the moralist's point of view. He does not really like the theater—at least, the theater as it is conceived throughout the West, which he accuses of being insufficiently serious. His theater would have nothing to do with the aim of providing "pointless, artificial diversion," mere entertainment. The contrast at the heart of Artaud's polemics is not between a merely literary theater and a theater of strong sensations but between a hedonistic theater and a theater that is morally rigorous. What Artaud proposes is a theater that Savonarola or Cromwell might well have approved of. Indeed, *The Theater and Its Double* may be read as an indignant attack on the theater, with an animus reminiscent of the *Letter to d'Alembert* in which Rousseau, enraged by the character of Alceste in *The Misanthrope*—by what he took to be Molière's sophisticated ridiculing of sincerity and moral purity as clumsy fanaticism—ended by arguing that it lay in the nature of theater to be morally superficial. Like Rousseau, Artaud revolted against the moral cheapness of most art. Like Plato, Artaud felt that art generally lies. Artaud will not banish artists from his Republic, but he will countenance art only insofar as it is a "true action." Art must be cognitive. "No image satisfies me unless it is at the same time *knowledge*," he writes. Art must have a beneficial spiritual effect on its audience—an effect whose power depends, in Artaud's view, on a disavowal of all forms of mediation.

It is the moralist in Artaud that makes him urge that the theater be pared down, be kept as free from mediating elements as possible—including the mediation of the written text. Plays tell lies. Even if a play doesn't tell a lie, by achieving the status of a "masterpiece" it *becomes* a lie. Artaud announces in 1926 that he does not want to create a theater to present plays and so perpetuate or add to culture's list of consecrated masterpieces. He judges the heritage of written plays to be a useless obstacle and the playwright an unnecessary intermediary between the audience and the truth that can be presented, naked, on a stage. Here, though, Artaud's moralism takes a distinctly anti-Platonic turn: the naked truth is a truth that is wholly material. Artaud defines the theater as a place where the obscure facets of "the spirit" are revealed in "a real, material projection."

To incarnate thought, a strictly conceived theater must dispense with the mediation of an already written script, thereby ending the separation of author from actor. (This removes the most ancient objection to the actor's profession—that it is a form of psychological debauchery, in which people say words that are not their own and pretend to feel emotions that are functionally insincere.) The separation between actor and audience must be reduced (but not ended), by violating the boundary between the stage area and the auditorium's fixed rows of seats. Artaud, with his hieratic sensibility, never envisages a form of theater in which the audience actively participates in the performance, but he wants to do away with the rules of theatrical decorum which permit the audience to dissociate itself from its own experience. Implicitly answering the moralist's charge that the theater distracts people from their authentic selfhood by leading them to concern themselves with imaginary problems, Artaud wants the theater to address itself neither to the spectators' minds nor to their senses but to their "total existence." Only the most passionate of moralists would have wanted people to attend the theater as they visit the surgeon or the dentist. Though guaranteed not to be fatal (unlike the visit to the surgeon), the operation upon the audience is "serious," and the audience should not leave the theater "intact" morally or emotionally. In another medical image, Artaud compares the theater to the plague. To show the truth means to show archetypes rather than individual psychology; this makes the theater a place of risk, for the "archetypal reality" is "dangerous." Members of the audience are not supposed to identify themselves with what happens on the stage. For Artaud, the "true" theater is a dangerous, intimidating experience—one that excludes placid emotions, playfulness, reassuring intimacy.

The value of emotional violence in art has long been a main tenet of the modernist sensibility. Before Artaud, however, cruelty was exercised mainly in a disinterested spirit, for its aesthetic efficacy. When Baudelaire placed "the shock experience" (to borrow Walter Benjamin's phrase) at the center of his verse and his prose poems, it was hardly to improve or edify his readers. But exactly this was the point of Artaud's devotion to the aesthetics of shock. Through the exclusiveness of his commitment to paroxysmic art, Artaud shows himself to be as much of a moralist about art as Plato—but a moralist whose hopes for art deny just those distinctions in which Plato's view is grounded. As Artaud opposes the separation between art and life, he opposes all theatrical forms that imply a difference between reality and representation. He does not deny the existence of such a difference. But this difference can be vaulted, Artaud implies, if the spectacle is sufficiently—that is, excessively—violent. The "cruelty" of the work of art has not only a directly moral function but a cognitive one. According to Artaud's moralistic criterion for knowledge, an image is true insofar as it is violent.

Plato's view depends on assuming the unbridgeable difference between life and art, reality and representation. In the famous imagery in Book VII of the *Republic*, Plato likens ignorance to living in an ingeniously lit cave, for whose inhabitants life is a spectacle—a spectacle that consists of only the shadows of real events. The cave is a theater. And truth (reality) lies outside it, in the sun. In the Platonic imagery of *The Theater and Its Double*, Artaud takes a more lenient view of shadows and spectacles. He assumes that there are true as well as false shadows (and spectacles), and that one can learn to distinguish between them. Far from identifying wisdom with an emergence from the cave to gaze at a high noon of reality, Artaud thinks that modern consciousness suffers from a lack of shadows. The remedy is to remain in the cave but devise better spectacles. The theater that Artaud proposes will serve consciousness by "naming and directing shadows" and destroying "false shadows" to "prepare the way for a new generation of shadows," around which will assemble "the true spectacle of life."

Not holding a hierarchical view of the mind, Artaud overrides the superficial distinction, cherished by the Surrealists, between the rational and the irrational. Artaud does not speak for the familiar view that praises passion at the expense of reason, the flesh over the mind, the mind exalted by drugs over the prosaic mind, the life of the instincts over deadly cerebration. What he advocates is an alternative relation to the mind. This was the well-advertised attraction that non-Occidental cultures held for Artaud, but it was not what brought him to drugs. (It was to calm the migraines and other neurological pain he suffered from all his life, not to expand his consciousness, that Artaud used opiates, and got addicted.)

For a brief time, Artaud took the Surrealist state of mind as a model for the unified, non-dualistic consciousness he sought. After rejecting Surrealism in 1926, he reproposed art—specifically, theater—as a more rigorous model. The function that Artaud gives the theater is to heal the split between language and flesh. It is the theme of his ideas for training actors: a training antithetical to the familiar one that teaches actors neither how to move nor what to do with their voices apart from talk. (They can scream, growl, sing, chant.) It is also the subject of his ideal dramaturgy. Far from espousing a facile irrationalism that polarizes reason and feeling, Artaud imagines the theater as the place where the body would be reborn in thought and thought would be reborn in the body. He diagnoses his own disease as a split *within* his mind ("My conscious aggregate is broken," he writes) that internalizes the split between mind and body. Artaud's writings on the theater may be read as a psychological manual on the reunification of mind and body. Theater became his supreme metaphor for the self-correcting, spontaneous, carnal, intelligent life of the mind.

Indeed, Artaud's imagery for the theater in *The Theater and Its Double,* written in the nineteen-thirties, echoes images he uses in writings of the early and mid-nineteen-twenties—such as *The Nerve Meter,* letters to René and Yvonne Allendy, and *Fragments of a Diary from Hell*—to describe his own mental pain. Artaud complains that his consciousness is without boundaries and fixed position; bereft of or in a continual struggle with language; fractured—indeed, plagued—by discontinuities; either without physical location or constantly shifting in location (and extension in time and space); sexually obsessed; in a state of violent infestation. Artaud's theater is characterized by an absence of any fixed spatial positioning of the actors vis-à-vis each other and of the actors in relation to the audience; by a fluidity of motion and soul; by the mutilation of language and the transcendence of language in the actor's scream; by the carnality of the spectacle; by its obsessively violent tone. Artaud was, of course, not simply reproducing his inner agony. Rather, he was giving a systematized, positive version of it. Theater is a projected image (necessarily an *ideal* dramatization) of the dangerous, "inhuman" inner life that possessed him, that he struggled so heroically to transcend and to affirm. It is also a homeopathic technique for treating that mangled, passionate inner life. Being a kind of emotional and moral surgery upon consciousness, it must of necessity, according to Artaud, be "cruel."

When Hume expressly likens consciousness to a theater, the image is morally neutral and entirely ahistorical; he is not thinking of any particular kind of theater, Western or other, and would have considered irrelevant any reminder that theater evolves. For Artaud, the decisive part of the analogy is that theater—and consciousness—can change. For not only does consciousness resemble a theater but, as Artaud constructs it, theater resembles consciousness, and therefore lends itself to being turned into a theater-laboratory in which to conduct research in changing consciousness.

Artaud's writings on the theater are transformations of his aspirations for his own mind. He wants theater (like the mind) to be released from confinement "in language and in forms." A liberated theater liberates, he assumes. By giving vent to extreme passions and cultural nightmares, theater exorcises them. But Artaud's theater is by no means simply cathartic. At least in its intention (Artaud's practice in the nineteen-twenties and thirties is another matter), his theater has little in common with the anti-theater of playful, sadistic assault on the audience which was conceived by Marinetti and the Dada artists just before and after World War I. The aggressiveness that Artaud proposes is controlled and intricately orchestrated, for he assumes that sensory violence can be a form of embodied intelligence. By insisting on theater's cognitive function (drama, he writes in 1923, in an essay on Maeterlinck, is "the highest form of mental activity"), he rules out randomness. (Even in his Surrealist days, he did not join in the practice of automatic writing.) Theater, he remarks occasionally, must be "scientific," by which he means that it must not be random, not be merely expressive or spontaneous or personal or entertaining, but must embrace a wholly serious, ultimately religious purpose.

Artaud's insistence on the seriousness of the theatrical situation also marks his difference from the Surrealists, who thought of art and its therapeutic and "revolutionary" mission with a good deal less than precision. The Surrealists, whose moralizing impulses were considerably less intransigent than Artaud's, and who brought no sense of moral urgency at all to bear on art-making, were not moved to search out the limits of any single art form. They tended to be tourists, often of genius, in as many of the arts as possible, believing that the art impulse remains the same wherever it turns up. (Thus, Cocteau, who had the ideal Surrealist career, called everything he did "poetry.") Artaud's greater daring and authority as an aesthetician result partly from the fact that although he, too, practiced several arts, refusing, like the Surrealists, to be inhibited by the distribution of art into different media, he did not regard the various arts as equivalent forms of the same protean impulse. His own activities, however dispersed they may have been, always reflect Artaud's quest for a total art form, into which the others would merge—as art itself would merge into life.

Paradoxically, it was this very denial of independence to the different territories of art which brought Artaud to do what none of the Surrealists had even attempted: completely rethink one art form. Upon that art, theater, he has had an impact so profound that the course of all recent serious theater in Western Europe and the Americas can be said to divide into two periods—before Artaud and after Artaud. No one who works in the theater now is untouched by the impact of Artaud's specific ideas about the actor's body and voice, the use of music, the role of the written text, the interplay between the space occupied by the spectacle and the audience's space. Artaud changed the understanding of what was serious, what was worth doing. Brecht is the century's only other writer on the theater whose importance and profundity conceivably rival Artaud's. But Artaud did not succeed in affecting the conscience of the modern theater by himself being, as Brecht was, a great director. His influence derives no support from the evidence of his own productions. His practical work in the theater between 1926 and 1935 was apparently so unseductive that it has left virtually no trace, whereas the idea of theater on behalf of which he urged his productions upon an unreceptive public has become ever more potent.

From the mid-nineteen-twenties on, Artaud's work is animated by the idea of a radical change in culture. His imagery implies a medical rather than a historical view of culture: society is ailing. Like Nietzsche, Artaud conceived of himself as a physician to culture—as well as its most painfully ill patient. The theater he planned is a commando action against the established culture, an assault on the bourgeois public; it would both show people that they are dead and wake them up from their stupor. The man who was to be devastated by repeated electric-shock treatments during the last three of nine consecutive years in mental hospitals proposed that theater administer to culture a kind of shock therapy. Artaud, who often complained of feeling paralyzed, wanted theater to renew "the sense of life."

Up to a point, Artaud's prescriptions resemble many programs of cultural renovation that have appeared periodically during the last two centuries of Western culture in the name of simplicity, *élan vital*, naturalness, freedom from artifice. His diagnosis that we live in an inorganic, "petrified culture"—whose lifelessness he associates with the dominance of the written word—was hardly a fresh idea when he stated it; yet, many decades later, it has not exhausted its authority. Artaud's argument in *The Theater and Its Double* is closely related to that of the Nietzsche who in *The Birth of Tragedy* lamented the shriveling of the full-blooded archaic theater of Athens by Socratic philosophy—by the introduction of characters who reason. (Another parallel with Artaud: what made the young Nietzsche an ardent Wagnerian was Wagner's conception of opera as the *Gesamtkunstwerk*—the fullest statement, before Artaud, of the idea of total theater.)

Just as Nietzsche harked back to the Dionysiac ceremonies that preceded the secularized, rationalized, verbal dramaturgy of Athens, Artaud found his models in non-Western religious or magical theater. Artaud does not propose the Theater of Cruelty as a new idea within Western theater. It "assumed . . . another form of civilization." He is referring not to any specific civilization, however, but to an idea of civilization that has numerous bases in history—a synthesis of elements from past societies and from non-Western and primitive societies of the present. The preference for "another form of civilization" is essentially eclectic. (That is to say, it is a myth generated by certain moral needs.) The inspiration for Artaud's ideas about theater came from Southeast Asia: from seeing the Cambodian theater in Marseilles in 1922 and the Balinese theater in Paris in 1931. But the stimulus could just as well have come from observing the theater of a Dahomey tribe or the shamanistic ceremonies of the Patagonian Indians. What counts is that the other culture be genuinely other; that is, non-Western and non-contemporary.

At different times, Artaud followed all three of the most

frequently traveled imaginative routes from Western high culture to "another form of civilization." First came what was known just after World War I, in the writings of Hesse, René Daumal, and the Surrealists, as the Turn to the East. Second came the interest in a suppressed part of the Western past—heterodox spiritual or outright magical traditions. Third came the discovery of the life of so-called primitive peoples. What unites the East, the ancient antinomian and occult traditions in the West, and the exotic communitarianism of pre-literate tribes is that they are elsewhere, not only in space but in time. All three embody the values of the past. Though the Tarahumara Indians in Mexico still exist, their survival in 1936, when Artaud visited them, was already anachronistic; the values that the Tarahumara represent belong as much to the past as do those of the ancient Near Eastern mystery religions that Artaud studied while writing his historical novel *Heliogabalus,* in 1933. The three versions of "another form of civilization" bear witness to the same search for a society integrated around overtly religious themes, and flight from the secular. What interests Artaud is the Orient of Buddhism (see his "Letter to the Buddhist Schools," written in 1925) and of Yoga; it would never be the Orient of Mao Tse-tung, however much Artaud talked up revolution. (The Long March was taking place at the very time that Artaud was struggling to mount his productions of the Theater of Cruelty in Paris.)

This nostalgia for a past often so eclectic as to be quite unlocatable historically is a facet of the modernist sensibility which has seemed increasingly suspect in recent decades. It is an ultimate refinement of the colonialist outlook: an imaginative exploitation of non-white cultures, whose moral life it drastically oversimplifies, whose wisdom it plunders and parodies. To that criticism there is no convincing reply. But to the criticism that the quest for "another form of civilization" refuses to submit to the disillusionment of accurate historical knowledge, one can make an answer. It never sought such knowledge. The other civilizations are being used as models and are available as stimulants to the imagination precisely because they are *not* accessible. They are both models and mysteries. Nor can this quest be dismissed as fraudulent on the ground that it is insensitive to the political forces that cause human suffering. It consciously opposes such sensitivity. This nostalgia forms part of a view that is deliberately *not* political—however frequently it brandishes the word "revolution."

One result of the aspiration to a total art which follows from denying the gap between art and life has been to encourage the notion of art as an instrument of revolution. The other result has been the identification of both art and life with disinterested, pure playfulness. For every Vertov or Breton, there is a Cage or a Duchamp or a Rauschenberg. Although Artaud is close to Vertov and Breton in that he considers his activities to be part of a larger revolution, as a self-proclaimed revolutionary in the arts he actually stands between the two camps—not interested in satisfying either the political or the ludic impulse. Dismayed when Breton attempted to link the Surrealist program with Marxism, Artaud broke with the Surrealists for what he considered to be their betrayal, into the hands of politics, of an essentially "spiritual" revolution. He was anti-bourgeois almost by reflex (like nearly all artists in the modernist tradition), but the prospect of transferring power from the bourgeoisie to the proletariat never tempted him. From his avowedly "absolute" viewpoint, a change in social structure would not change anything. The revolution to which Artaud subscribes has nothing to do with politics but is conceived explicitly as an effort to redirect culture. Not only does Artaud share the widespread (and mistaken) belief in the possibility of a cultural revolution unconnected with political change but he implies that the *only* genuine cultural revolution is one that has nothing to do with politics.

Artaud's call to cultural revolution suggests a program of heroic regression similar to that formulated by every great *anti*political moralist of our time. The banner of cultural revolution is hardly a monopoly of the Marxist or Maoist left. On the contrary, it appeals particularly to apolitical thinkers and artists (like Nietzsche, Spengler, Pirandello, Marinetti, D. H. Lawrence, Pound) who more commonly become right-wing enthusiasts. On the political left, there are few advocates of cultural revolution. (Tatlin, Gramsci, and Godard are among those who come to mind.) A radicalism that is purely "cultural" is either illusory or, finally, conservative in its implications. Artaud's plans for subverting and revitalizing culture, his longing for a new type of human personality illustrate the limits of all thinking about revolution which is anti-political.

Cultural revolution that refuses to be political has nowhere to go but toward a theology of culture—and a soteriology. "I aspire to another life," Artaud declares in 1927. All Artaud's work is about salvation, theater being the means of saving souls which he meditated upon most deeply. Spiritual transformation is a goal on whose behalf theater has often been enlisted in this century, at least since Isadora Duncan. In the most recent and solemn example, the Laboratory Theater of Jerzy Grotowski, the whole activity of building a company and rehearsing and putting on plays serves the spiritual reeducation of the actors; the presence of an audience is required only to witness the feats of self-transcendence that the actors perform. In Artaud's Theater of Cruelty, it is the audience that will be twice-born—an untested claim, since Artaud never made his theater work (as Grotowski did throughout the nineteen-sixties in Poland). As a goal, it seems a good deal less feasible than the discipline for which Grotowski aims. Sensitive as Artaud is to the emotional and physical armoring of the conventionally trained actor, he never examines closely how the radical retraining he proposes will affect the actor as a human being. His thought is all for the audience.

As might have been expected, the audience proved to be a disappointment. Artaud's productions in the two theaters he founded, the Alfred Jarry Theater and the Theater of Cruelty, created little involvement. Yet, although entirely dissatisfied with the quality of his public, Artaud complained much more about the token support he got from the serious Paris theater establishment (he had a long, desperate correspondence with Louis Jouvet), about the difficulty of getting his projects produced at all, about the paltriness of their success when they were put on. Artaud was understandably embittered because, despite a number of titled patrons, and friends who were eminent writers, painters, editors, directors—all of whom he constantly badgered for moral support and money—his work, when it was actually produced, enjoyed only a small portion of the acclaim conventionally reserved for properly sponsored, difficult events attended by the regulars of high-culture consumption. Artaud's most ambitious, fully articulated production of the Theater of Cruelty, his own *The Cenci*, lasted for seventeen days in the spring of 1935. But had it run for a year he would probably have been equally convinced that he had failed.

In modern culture, powerful machinery has been set up whereby dissident work, after gaining an initial semi-official status as "avant-garde," is gradually absorbed and rendered acceptable. But Artaud's practical activities in the theater barely qualified for this kind of cooptation. *The Cenci* is not a very good play, even by the standards of convulsive dramaturgy which Artaud sponsored, and the interest of his production of *The Cenci*, by all accounts, lay in ideas it suggested but did not actually embody. What Artaud did on the stage as a director and as a leading actor in his productions was too idiosyncratic, narrow, and hysterical to persuade. He has exerted influence through his ideas about the theater, a constituent part of the authority of these ideas being precisely his inability to put them into practice.

Fortified by its insatiable appetite for novel commodities, the educated public of great cities has become habituated to the modernist agony and well skilled in outwitting it: any negative can eventually be turned into a positive. Thus, Artaud, who urged that the repertory of masterpieces be thrown on the junk pile, has been extremely influential as the creator of an alternative repertory, an adversary tradition of plays. Artaud's stern cry "No more masterpieces!" has been heard as the more conciliatory "No more of *those* masterpieces!" But this positive recasting of his attack on the traditional repertory has not taken place without help from Artaud's practice (as distinct from his rhetoric). Despite his repeated insistence that the theater should dispense with plays, his own work in the theater was far from playless. He named his first company after the author of *King Ubu*. Apart from his own projects—*The Conquest of Mexico* and *The Capture of Jerusalem* (unproduced) and *The Cenci*—there were a number of then unfashionable or obscure masterpieces that Artaud wanted to revive. He did get to stage the two great "dream plays" by Calderón and Strindberg (*Life Is a Dream* and *A Dream Play*), and over the years he hoped also to direct productions of Euripides (*The Bacchae*), Seneca (*Thyestes*), *Arden of Feversham*, Shakespeare (*Macbeth, Richard II, Titus Andronicus*), Tourneur

(*The Revenger's Tragedy*), Webster (*The White Devil, The Duchess of Malfi*), Sade (an adaptation of *Eugénie de Franval*), Büchner (*Woyzeck*), and Hölderlin (*The Death of Empedocles*). This selection of plays delineates a now familiar sensibility. Along with the Dadaists, Artaud formulated the taste that was eventually to become standard serious taste—Off-Broadway, Off-Off-Broadway, in university theaters. In terms of the past, it meant dethroning Sophocles and Corneille and Racine in favor of Euripides and the dark Elizabethans; the only dead French writer on Artaud's list is Sade. In the last fifteen years, that taste has been represented in the Happenings and the Theater of the Ridiculous; the plays of Genet, Jean Vauthier, Arrabal, Carmelo Bene, and Sam Shepard; and such celebrated productions as the Living Theater's *Frankenstein,* Eduardo Manet's *The Nuns* (directed by Roger Blin), Michael McClure's *The Beard,* Robert Wilson's *Deafman Glance,* and Heathcote Williams's *ac/dc*. Whatever Artaud did to subvert the theater, and to segregate his own work from other, merely aesthetic currents in the interests of establishing its spiritual hegemony, could still be assimilated as a new theatrical tradition, and mostly has been.

If Artaud's project does not actually transcend art, it presupposes a goal that art can sustain only temporarily. Each use of art in a secular society for the purposes of spiritual transformation, insofar as it is made *public,* is inevitably robbed of its true adversary power. Stated in directly, or even indirectly, religious language, the project is notably vulnerable. But atheist projects for spiritual transformation, such as the political art of Brecht, have proved to be equally cooptable. Only a few situations in modern secular society seem sufficiently extreme and uncommunicative to have a chance of evading cooptation. Madness is one. What surpasses the limit of suffering (like the Holocaust) is another. A third is, of course, silence. One way to stop this inexorable process of ingestion is to break off communication (even anti-communication). An exhaustion of the impulse to use art as a medium of spiritual transformation is almost inevitable—as in the temptation felt by every modern author when confronted with the indifference or mediocrity of the public, on the one hand, or the ease of success, on the other, to stop writing altogether. Thus, it was not just for lack of money or support within the profession that, after putting on *The Cenci,* in 1935, Artaud abandoned the theater. The project of creating in a secular culture an institution that can manifest a dark, hidden reality is a contradiction in terms. Artaud was never able to found his Bayreuth—though he would have liked to—for his ideas are the kind that cannot be institutionalized.

The year after the failure of *The Cenci,* Artaud embarked on a trip to Mexico to witness that demonic reality in a still existing "primitive" culture. Unsuccessful at embodying this reality in a spectacle to impose on others, he became a spectator of it himself. From 1935 onward, Artaud lost touch with the promise of an ideal art form. His writings, always didactic, now took on a prophetic tone and referred frequently to esoteric magical systems, like the Cabala and tarot. Apparently, Artaud came to believe that he could exercise directly, in his own person, the emotional power (and achieve the spiritual efficacy) he had wanted for the theater. In the middle of 1937, he traveled to the Aran Islands, with an obscure plan for exploring or confirming his magic powers. The wall between art and life was still down. But instead of everything being assimilated into art, the movement swung the other way; and Artaud moved without mediation into his life—a dangerous, careering object, the vessel of a raging hunger for total transformation which could never find its appropriate nourishment.

Nietzsche coolly assumed an atheist theology of the spirit, a negative theology, a mysticism without God. Artaud wandered in the labyrinth of a specific type of religious sensibility, the Gnostic one. (Central to Mithraism, Manichaeism, Zoroastrianism, and Tantric Buddhism, but pushed to the heretical margins of Judaism, Christianity, and Islam, the perennial Gnostic thematics appear in the different religions in different terminologies but with certain common lines.) The leading energies of Gnosticism come from metaphysical anxiety and acute psychological distress—the sense of being abandoned, of being an alien, of being possessed by demonic powers which prey on the human spirit in a cosmos vacated by the divine. The cosmos is itself a battlefield, and each human life exhibits the conflict between the repressive, persecuting forces from without and the feverish, afflicted individual spirit seeking redemption. The demonic forces of the cosmos exist as physical matter. They also exist as "law," taboos, prohibitions. Thus, in the Gnostic metaphors the spirit is abandoned, fallen, trapped in a body, and the individual is repressed, trapped by being in "the world"—what we would call "society." (It is a mark of all Gnostic thinking to polarize inner space, the psyche, and a vague outer space, "the world" or "society," which is identified with repression—making little or no acknowledgment of the importance of the mediating levels of the various social spheres and institutions.) The self, or spirit, discovers itself in the break with "the world." The only freedom possible is an inhuman, desperate freedom. To be saved, the spirit must be taken out of its body, out of its personality, out of "the world." And freedom requires an arduous preparation. Whoever seeks it must both accept extreme humiliation and exhibit the greatest spiritual pride. In one version, freedom entails total asceticism. In another version, it entails libertinism—practicing the art of transgression. To be free of "the world," one must break the moral (or social) law. To transcend the body, one must pass through a period of physical debauchery and verbal blasphemy, on the principle that only when morality has been deliberately flouted is the individual capable of a radical transformation: entering into a state of grace that leaves all moral categories behind. In both versions of the exemplary Gnostic drama, someone who is saved is beyond good and evil. Founded on an exacerbation of dualisms (body-mind, matter-spirit, evil-good, dark-light), Gnosticism promises the abolition of all dualisms.

Artaud's thought reproduces most of the Gnostic themes. For example, his attack on Surrealism in the polemic written in 1927 is couched in a language of cosmic drama, in which he refers to the necessity of a "displacement of the spiritual center of the world" and to the origin of all matter in "a spiritual deviation." Throughout his writings, Artaud speaks of being persecuted, invaded, and defiled by alien powers; his work focuses on the vicissitudes of the spirit as it constantly discovers its lack of liberty in its very condition of being "matter." Artaud is obsessed with physical matter. From *The Nerve Meter* and *Art and Death*, written in the nineteen-twenties, to *Here Lies* and the radio play

ANTONIN ARTAUD

To Have Done with the Judgment of God, written in 1947–48, Artaud's prose and poetry depict a world clogged with matter (shit, blood, sperm), a defiled world. The demonic powers that rule the world are incarnated in matter, and matter is "dark." Essential to the theater that Artaud conceives—a theater devoted to myth and magic—is his belief that all the great myths are "dark" and that all magic is black magic. Even when life is encrusted by petrified, degenerate, merely verbal language, Artaud insists, the reality lies just underneath—or somewhere else. Art can tap these powers, for they seethe in every psyche. It was in search of these dark powers that Artaud went to Mexico in 1936 to witness the Tarahumara peyote rites. The individual's salvation requires making contact with the malevolent powers, submitting to them, and suffering at their hands in order to triumph over them.

What Artaud admires in the Balinese theater, he writes in 1931, is that it has nothing to do with "entertainment" but, rather, has "something of the ceremonial quality of a religious rite." Artaud is one of many directors in this century who have sought to re-create theater as ritual, to give theatrical performances the solemnity of religious transactions, but usually one finds only the vaguest, most promiscuous idea of religion and rite, which imputes to a Catholic mass and a Hopi rain dance the same artistic value. Artaud's vision, while perhaps not any more feasible in modern secular society than the others, is at least more specific as to the kind of rite involved. The theater Artaud wants to create enacts a secularized Gnostic rite. It is not an expiation. It is not a sacrifice, or, if it is, the sacrifices are all metaphors. It is a rite of transformation—the communal performance of a violent act of spiritual alchemy. Artaud summons the theater to renounce "psychological man, with his well-dissected character and feelings, and social man, submissive to laws and misshapen by religions and precepts," and to address itself only "to total man"—a thoroughly Gnostic notion.

Whatever Artaud's wishes for "culture," his thinking ultimately shuts out all but the private self. Like the Gnostics, he is a radical individualist. From his earliest writings, his concern is with a metamorphosis of the "inner" state of the soul. (The self is, by definition, an "inner self.") Mundane relations, he assumes, do not touch the kernel of the individual; the search for redemption undercuts all social solutions.

The one instrument of redemption of a possibly social character which Artaud considers is art. The reason he is not interested in a humanistic theater, a theater about individuals, is that he believes that such a theater can never effect any radical transformation. To be spiritually liberating, Artaud thinks, theater has to express impulses that are larger than life. But this only shows that Artaud's idea of freedom is itself a Gnostic one. Theater serves an "inhuman" individuality, an "inhuman" freedom, as Artaud calls it in *The Theater and Its Double*—the very opposite of the liberal, sociable idea of freedom. (That Artaud found Breton's thinking shallow—that is, optimistic, aesthetic—follows from the fact that Breton did not have a Gnostic style or sensibility. Breton was attracted by the hope of reconciling the demands of individual freedom with the need to expand and balance the personality through generous, corporate emotions; the anarchist view, formulated in this century with the greatest subtlety and authority by Breton and Paul Goodman, is a form of conservative, humanistic thinking—doggedly sensitive to everything repressive and mean while remaining loyal to the limits that protect human growth and pleasure. The mark of Gnostic thinking is that it is enraged by *all* limits, even those that save.) "All true freedom is dark," Artaud says in *The Theater and Its Double*, "and is infallibly identified with sexual freedom, which is also dark, although we do not know precisely why."

Both the obstacle to and the locus of freedom, for Artaud, lie in the body. His attitude covers the familiar Gnostic thematic range: the affirmation of the body, the revulsion from the body, the wish to transcend the body, the quest for the redeemed body. "Nothing touches me, nothing interests me," he writes, "except what addresses itself *directly* to my flesh." But the body is always a problem. Artaud never defines the body in terms of its capacity for sensuous pleasure but always in terms of its electric capacity for intelligence and for pain. As Artaud laments, in *Art and Death*, that his mind is ignorant of his body, that he lacks ideas that conform to his "condition as a physical animal," so he complains that his body is ignorant of his mind. In Artaud's imagery of distress, body and spirit prevent each other from being intelligent. He speaks of the "intellectual cries" that come from his flesh, source of the only knowledge he trusts. Body has a mind. "There is a mind in the flesh," he writes, "a mind quick as lightning."

It is what Artaud expects intellectually from the body that leads to his recoil from the body—the ignorant body. Indeed, each attitude implies the other. Many of the poems express a profound revulsion from the body, and accumulate loathsome evocations of sex. "A true man has no sex," Artaud writes in a text published in December 1947. "He ignores this hideousness, this stupefying sin." *Art and Death* is perhaps the most sex-obsessed of all his works, but Artaud demonized sexuality in everything he wrote. The most common presence is a monstrous, obscene body—"this unusable body made out of meat and crazy sperm," he calls it in *Here Lies*. Against this fallen body, defiled by matter, he sets the fantasied attainment of a pure body—divested of organs and vertiginous lusts. Even while insisting that he is nothing but his body, Artaud expresses a fervent longing to transcend it altogether, to abandon his sexuality. In other imagery, the body must be made intelligent, respiritualized. Recoiling from the defiled body, he appeals to the redeemed body in which thought and flesh will be unified: "It is through the skin that metaphysics will be made to reenter our minds"; only the flesh can supply "a definitive understanding of Life." The Gnostic task of the theater that Artaud imagines is nothing less than to create this redeemed body—a mythic project that he explains by referring to that last great Gnostic systematics, Renaissance alchemy. As the alchemists, obsessed with the problem of matter in classically Gnostic terms, sought methods of changing one kind of matter into another (higher, spiritualized) kind of matter, so Artaud sought to create an alchemical arena that operates on the flesh as much as on the spirit. Theater is the exercise of a "terrible and dangerous act," he says in "Theater and Science"—"THE REAL ORGANIC AND PHYSICAL TRANSFORMATION OF THE HUMAN BODY."

Artaud's principal metaphors are classically Gnostic. Body is mind turned into "matter." As the body weighs down and deforms the soul, so does language, for language is thought turned into "matter." The problem of language, as Artaud poses it to himself, is identical with the problem of matter. The disgust for the body and the revulsion against words are two forms of the same feeling. In the equivalences established by Artaud's imagery, sexuality is the corrupt, fallen activity of the body, and "literature" is the corrupt, fallen activity of words. Although Artaud never entirely stopped hoping to use activities in the arts as a means of spiritual liberation, art was always suspect—like the body. And Artaud's hope for art is also Gnostic, like his hope for the body. The vision of a total art has the same form as the vision of the redemption of the body. ("The body is the body/ it is alone/ it has no need of organs," Artaud writes in one of his last poems.) Art will be redemptive when, like the redeemed body, it transcends itself—when it has no organs (genres), no different parts. In the redeemed art that Artaud imagines, there are no separate works of art—only a total art environment, which is magical, paroxysmic, purgative, and, finally, opaque.

Gnosticism, a sensibility organized around the idea of knowing (gnosis) rather than around faith, sharply distinguishes between exoteric and esoteric knowledge. The adept must pass through various levels of instruction to be worthy of being initiated into the true doctrine. Knowledge, which is identified with the capacity for self-transformation, is reserved for the few. It is natural that Artaud, with his Gnostic sensibility, should have been attracted to numerous secret doctrines, as both an alternative to and a model for art. During the nineteen-thirties, Artaud, an amateur polymath of great energy, read more and more about esoteric systems—alchemy, tarot, the Cabala, astrology, Rosicrucianism. What these doctrines have in common is that they are all relatively late, decadent transformations of the Gnostic thematics. From Renaissance alchemy Artaud drew a model for his theater: like the symbols of alchemy, theater describes "philosophical states of matter" and attempts to transform them. Tarot, to give another example, supplied the basis of *The New Revelations of Being*, written in 1937, just before his seven-week trip to Ireland; it was the last work he wrote before the mental breakdown that resulted in his confinement when he was returned to France. But none of these already formulated, schematic, historically fossilized secret doctrines could contain the convulsions of the living Gnostic imagination in Artaud's head.

Only the exhausting is truly interesting. Artaud's basic ideas are crude; what gives them their power is the intricacy and eloquence of his self-analysis, unequaled in the history of the Gnostic imagination. And, for the first time, the Gnostic themes can be seen in evolution. Artaud's work is particularly precious as the first complete documentation of someone *living through* the trajectory of Gnostic thought. The result, of course, is a terrible smash.

The last refuge (historically, psychologically) of Gnostic thought is in the constructions of schizophrenia. With Artaud's return from Ireland to France began nine years of imprisonment in mental hospitals. Evidence, mainly from letters he wrote to his two principal psychiatrists at Rodez, Dr. Gaston Ferdière and Dr. Jacques Latrémolière, shows how literally his thought followed the Gnostic formulas. In the ecstatic fantasies of this period, the world is a maelstrom of magical substances and forces; his consciousness becomes a theater of screaming struggle between angels and demons, virgins and whores. His horror of the body now unmodulated, Artaud explicitly identifies salvation with virginity, sin with sex. As Artaud's elaborate religious speculations during the Rodez period may be read as metaphors for paranoia, so paranoia may be read as a metaphor for an exacerbated religious sensibility of the Gnostic type. The literature of the crazy in this century is a rich religious literature—perhaps the last original zone of genuine Gnostic speculation.

When Artaud was let out of the asylum, in 1946, he still considered himself the victim of a conspiracy of demonic powers, the object of an extravagant act of persecution by "society." Although the wave of schizophrenia had receded to the point of no longer swamping him, his basic metaphors were still intact. In the two years of life that remained to him, Artaud forced them to their logical conclusion.

In 1944, still in Rodez, Artaud had recapitulated his Gnostic complaint against language in a short text, "Revolt Against Poetry." Returning to Paris in 1946, he longed to work again in the theater, to recover the vocabulary of gesture and spectacle;

but in the short time left to him he had to resign himself to speaking with language only. Artaud's writings of this last period—virtually unclassifiable as to genre: there are "letters" that are "poems" that are "essays" that are "dramatic monologues"—give the impression of a man attempting to step out of his own skin. Passages of clear, if hectic, argument alternate with passages in which words are treated primarily as material (sound): they have a magical value. (Attention to the sound and shape of words, as distinct from their meaning, is an element of the Cabalistic teaching of the *Zohar*, which Artaud had studied in the nineteen-thirties.) Artaud's commitment to the magical value of words explains his refusal of metaphor as the principal mode of conveying meaning in his late poems. He demands that language directly express the physical human being. The person of the poet appears in a state beyond nakedness: flayed.

As Artaud reaches toward the unspeakable, his imagination coarsens. Yet his last works, in their mounting obsession with the body and their ever more explicit loathing of sex, still stand in a direct line with the early writings, in which there is, parallel to the mentalization of the body, a corresponding sexualization of consciousness. What Artaud wrote between 1946 and 1948 only extends metaphors he used throughout the nineteen-twenties—of mind as a body that never allows itself to be "possessed," and of the body as a kind of demonic, writhing, brilliant mind. In Artaud's fierce battle to transcend the body, everything is eventually turned into the body. In his fierce battle to transcend language, everything is eventually turned into language. Artaud, describing the life of the Tarahumara Indians, translates nature itself into a language. In the last writings, the obscene identity of the flesh and the word reaches an extremity of loathing—notably in the play commissioned by French radio, *To Have Done with the Judgment of God*, which was then banned on the eve of its projected broadcast in February 1948. (Artaud was still revising it a month later, when he died.) Talking, talking, talking, Artaud expresses the most ardent revulsion against talk—and the body.

The Gnostic passage through the stages of transcendence implies a move from the conventionally intelligible to what is conventionally unintelligible. Gnostic thinking characteristically reaches for an ecstatic speech that dispenses with distinguishable words. (It was the adoption by the Christian church in Corinth of a Gnostic form of preaching—"speaking in tongues"—that provoked Paul's remonstrations in the First Epistle to the Corinthians.) The language Artaud used at the end of his life, in passages in *Artaud le Mômo, Here Lies,* and *To Have Done with the Judgment of God,* verges on an incandescent declamatory speech beyond sense. "All true language is incomprehensible," Artaud says in *Here Lies.* He is not seeking a universal language, as Joyce did. Joyce's view of language was historical, ironic, whereas Artaud's view is medical, tragic. The unintelligible in *Finnegans Wake* not only is decipherable, with effort, but is meant to be deciphered. The unintelligible parts of Artaud's late writings are supposed to remain obscure—to be directly apprehended as sound.

The Gnostic project is a search for wisdom, but a wisdom that cancels itself out in unintelligibility, loquacity, and silence. As Artaud's life suggests, all schemes for ending dualism, for a unified consciousness at the Gnostic level of intensity, are eventually bound to fail—that is, their practitioners collapse into what society calls madness or into silence or suicide. (Another example: the vision of a totally unified consciousness expressed in the gnomic messages Nietzsche sent to friends in the weeks before his complete mental collapse in Turin in 1889.) The project transcends the limits of the mind. Thus, while Artaud still desperately reaffirms his effort to unify his flesh and his mind, the terms of his thinking imply the annihilation of consciousness. In the writings of this last period, the cries from his fractured consciousness and his martyred body reach a pitch of inhuman intensity and rage.

Artaud offers the greatest *quantity* of suffering in the history of literature. So drastic and pitiable are the numerous descriptions he gives of his pain that readers, overwhelmed, may be tempted to distance themselves by remembering that Artaud was crazy.

In whatever sense he ended up being mad, Artaud had been mad all his life. He had a history of internment in mental hospitals from mid-adolescence on—well before he arrived in Paris from Marseilles, in 1920, at the age of twenty-four, to begin his career in the arts; his lifelong addiction to opiates, which may have aggravated his mental disorder, had probably begun before this date. Lacking the saving knowledge that allows most people to be conscious with relatively little pain—the knowledge of what Rivière calls "the blessed opacity of experience" and "the innocence of facts"—Artaud at no time in his life wholly got out from under the lash of madness. But simply to judge Artaud mad—reinstating the reductive psychiatric wisdom—means to reject Artaud's argument.

Psychiatry draws a clear line between art (a "normal" psychological phenomenon, manifesting objective aesthetic limits) and symptomatology: the very boundary that Artaud contests. Writing to Rivière in 1923, Artaud insists on raising the question of the autonomy of his art—of whether, despite his avowed mental deterioration, despite that "fundamental flaw" in his own psyche which sets him apart from other people, his poems do nevertheless exist *as poems*, not just as psychological documents. Rivière replies by expressing confidence that Artaud, despite his mental distress, will one day become a good poet. Artaud answers impatiently, changing his ground: he wants to close the gap between life and art implicit in his original question and in Rivière's well-intentioned but obtuse encouragement. He decides to defend his poems as they are—for the merit they possess just because they don't quite make it as art.

The task of the reader of Artaud is not to react with the distance of Rivière—as if madness and sanity could communicate with each other only on sanity's own ground, in the language of reason. The values of sanity are not eternal or "natural," any more than there is a self-evident, common-sense meaning to the condition of being insane. The perception that some people are crazy is part of the history of thought, and madness requires a historical definition. Madness means not making sense—means saying what doesn't have to be taken seriously. But this depends entirely on how a given culture defines sense and seriousness; the definitions have varied widely through history. What is called insane denotes that which in the determination of a particular society must not be thought. Madness is a concept that fixes limits; the frontiers of madness define what is "other." A mad person is someone whose voice society doesn't want to listen to, whose behavior is intolerable, who ought to be suppressed. Different societies use different definitions of what constitutes madness (that is, of what does not make sense). But no definition is less provincial than any other. Part of the outrage over the current practice in the Soviet Union of locking up political dissenters in insane asylums is misplaced, in that it holds not only that doing so is wicked (which is true) but that doing so is a fraudulent use of the concept of mental illness; it is assumed—naïvely—that there is a universal, correct, scientific standard of sanity (the one enforced in the mental-health policies of, say, the United States, England, and Sweden, rather than the one enforced in those of a country like Morocco). This is simply not true. In every society, the definitions of sanity and madness are arbitrary—are, in the largest sense, political.

Artaud was extremely sensitive to the repressive function of the concept of madness. He saw the insane as the heroes and martyrs of thought, stranded at the vantage point of extreme social (rather than merely psychological) alienation, volunteering for madness—as those who, through a superior conception of honor, prefer to go mad rather than forfeit a certain lucidity, an extreme passionateness in presenting their convictions. In a letter to Jacqueline Breton from the hospital in Ville-Evrard in April 1939, after a year and a half of what was to be nine years of confinement, he wrote, "I am a fanatic, I am not a madman." But any fanaticism that is not a group fanaticism is precisely what society understands as madness.

Madness is the logical conclusion of the commitment to individuality when that commitment is pushed far enough. As Artaud puts it in the "Letter to the Medical Directors of Lunatic Asylums" in 1925, "all individual acts are anti-social." It is an unpalatable truth, perhaps quite irreconcilable with the humanist ideology of capitalist democracy or of social democracy or of liberal socialism—but Artaud is right. Whenever behavior becomes sufficiently individual, it will become objectively anti-social and will seem, to other people, mad. All human societies agree on this point. They differ only on how the standard of madness is applied, and on who are protected or partly exempted (for reasons of economic, social, sexual, or cultural privilege) from the penalty of imprisonment meted out to those whose basic antisocial act consists in not making sense.

The insane person has a dual identity in Artaud's works: the ultimate victim, and the bearer of a subversive wisdom. In his preface, written in 1946, to the proposed Gallimard collected edition of his writings, he describes himself as one of the mentally underprivileged, grouping lunatics with aphasiacs and illiterates. Elsewhere in the writings of his last two years, he repeatedly situates himself in the company of the mentally hyper-endowed who have gone mad—Hölderlin, Nerval, Nietzsche, and van Gogh. Insofar as the genius is simply an extension, and intensification, of the individual, Artaud suggests the existence of a natural affinity between genius and madness in a far more precise sense than the romantics did. But while denouncing the society that imprisons the mad, and affirming madness as the outward sign of a profound spiritual exile, he never suggests that there is anything liberating in losing one's mind.

Some of his writings, particularly the early Surrealist texts, take a more positive attitude toward madness. In "General Security: The Liquidation of Opium," for instance, he seems to be defending the practice of a deliberate derangement of the mind and senses (as Rimbaud once defined the poet's vocation). But he never stops saying—in the letters to Rivière, to Dr. Allendy, and to George Soulié de Morant in the nineteen-twenties and nineteen-thirties, in the letters written between 1943 and 1945 from Rodez, and in the essay on van Gogh written in 1947, some months after his release from Rodez—that madness is confining, destroying. Mad people may know the truth—so much truth that society takes its revenge on these unhappy seers by outlawing them. But being mad is also unending pain, a state to be transcended—and it is that pain which Artaud renders, imposing it on his readers.

To read Artaud through is nothing less than an ordeal. Understandably, readers seek to protect themselves with reductions and applications of his work. It demands a special stamina, a special sensitivity, and a special tact to read Artaud properly. It is not a question of giving one's assent to Artaud—this would be shallow—or even of neutrally "understanding" him and his relevance. What is there to assent to? How could anyone assent to Artaud's ideas unless one was already in the demonic state of siege that he was in? Those ideas were emitted under the intolerable pressure of his own situation. Not only is Artaud's position not tenable; it is not a "position" at all.

Artaud's thought is organically part of his singular, haunted, impotent, savagely intelligent consciousness. Artaud is one of the great, daring mapmakers of consciousness *in extremis*. To read him properly does not require believing that the *only* truth that art can supply is one that is singular and is authenticated by extreme suffering. Of art that describes other states of consciousness—less idiosyncratic, less exalted, perhaps no less profound—it is correct to ask that it yield general truths. But the exceptional cases at the limit of "writing"—Sade is one, Artaud is another—demand a different approach.

What Artaud has left behind is work that cancels itself, thought that outbids thought, recommendations that cannot be enacted. Where does that leave the reader? Still with a body of work (which will run to about fifteen volumes in the Gallimard collected edition in French), even though the character of Artaud's writings forbids their being treated simply as "literature." Still with a body of thought, even though Artaud's thought forbids assent—as his aggressively self-immolating personality forbids identification. Artaud shocks, and, unlike the Surrealists, he remains shocking. (Far from being subversive, the spirit of the Surrealists is ultimately constructive and falls well within the humanist tradition, and their stagy violations of bourgeois proprieties were not dangerous, truly asocial acts. Compare the behavior of Artaud, who really was impossible socially.) To detach his thought as a portable intellectual commodity is just what that thought explicitly prohibits. It is an event, rather than an object.

Forbidden assent or identification or appropriation or imitation, the reader can only fall back on the category of inspiration. "INSPIRATION CERTAINLY EXISTS," as Artaud affirms in capital letters in *The Nerve Meter*. One can be inspired by Artaud. One can be scorched, changed by Artaud. But there is no way of applying Artaud.

Even in the domain of the theater, where Artaud's presence

can be decanted into a program and a theory, the work of those directors who have most benefited from his ideas (like Roger Blin, Judith Malina and Julian Beck, Joseph Chaikin, Charles Marowitz, Peter Brook, Jerzy Grotowski, Eugenio Barba, Andrei Serban, Richard Schechner, Jorge Lavelli, Luca Ronconi, Victor Garcia) shows there is no way to use Artaud that stays true to him. Not even Artaud himself found the way; by all accounts, his own stage productions were far from being up to the level of his ideas. And for the many people not connected with the theater—mainly the anarchist-minded, for whom Artaud has been especially important—the experience of his work remains profoundly private. Artaud is someone who has made a spiritual trip for us—a shaman. It would be presumptuous to reduce the geography of Artaud's trip to what can be colonized. Its authority lies in the parts that yield nothing for the reader except intense discomfort of the imagination.

Artaud's work becomes usable according to our needs, but the work vanishes behind our use of it. When we tire of using Artaud, we can return to his writings. "Inspiration in stages," he says. "One mustn't let in too much literature."

All art that expresses a radical discontent and aims at shattering complacencies of feeling risks being disarmed, neutralized, drained of its power to disturb—by being admired, by being (or seeming to be) too well understood, by becoming relevant. Most of the once exotic themes of Artaud's work have within the last decade become loudly topical: the wisdom (or lack of it) to be found in drugs, Oriental religions, magic, the life of North American Indians, body language, the insanity trip; the revolt against "literature," and the belligerent prestige of non-verbal arts; the appreciation of schizophrenia; the use of art as violence against the audience; the necessity for obscenity. Artaud in the nineteen-twenties had just about every taste (except enthusiasms for comic books, science fiction, and Marxism) that was to become prominent in the American counterculture of the nineteen-sixties, and what he was reading in that decade—the *Tibetan Book of the Dead*, books on mysticism, psychiatry, anthropology, tarot, astrology, Yoga, acupuncture—is like a prophetic anthology of the literature that has recently surfaced as popular reading among the advanced young. But the current relevance of Artaud may be as misleading as the obscurity in which his work lay until now.

Unknown outside a small circle of admirers ten years ago, Artaud is a classic today. He is an example of a willed classic—an author whom the culture attempts to assimilate but who remains profoundly indigestible. One use of literary respectability in our time—and an important part of the complex career of literary modernism—is to make acceptable an outrageous, essentially forbidding author, who becomes a classic on the basis of the many interesting things to be said about the work that scarcely convey (perhaps even conceal) the real nature of the work itself, which may be, among other things, extremely boring or morally monstrous or terribly painful to read. Certain authors become literary or intellectual classics because they are *not* read, being in some intrinsic way unreadable. Sade, Artaud, and Wilhelm Reich belong in this company: authors who were jailed or locked up in insane asylums because they were screaming, because they were out of control; immoderate, obsessed, strident authors who repeat themselves endlessly, who are rewarding to quote and read bits of, but who overpower and exhaust if read in large quantities.

Like Sade and Reich, Artaud is relevant and understandable, a cultural monument, as long as one mainly refers to his ideas without reading much of his work. For anyone who reads Artaud through, he remains fiercely out of reach, an unassimilable voice and presence.

Five early poems

I

The Mystic Ship

It will be lost, that archaic ship
In seas that will bathe my desperate dreams;
And its towering masts will dissolve in the mist
Of a biblical and hymning sky.

It will not be a pastoral, that air that plays
Mysteriously among the naked trees;
And the holy ship will never sell
Its rare cargo in exotic lands.

A stranger to the genial harbors of earth,
It knows only God and eternally alone
Cleaves the glorious waves of the infinite.

The tip of its bowsprit pierces the unknown.
Each night atop its darkened masts trembles the pure
And mystic silver of the polar star.

Verlaine Drinks

There will always be whores on street corners,
Lost shells stranded on the stellar shores
Of a blue dusk which is neither of here nor of earth
Where taxis roll by like bewildered bugs.

But roll less than in my whirling head
The green gem of absinthe deep in the glass
Where I drink perdition and the thunder
Of the Lord's judgment to roast my naked soul.

Ah! how the tangled spindles of the streets
Turn and spin the fabric of men and women,
As if a spider were weaving her web
With the filaments of discovered souls.

Black Garden

They have blossomed from the lands of death,
These flowers which a long-wrought dream has poured
With ashes and the unearthly vapor
Of a bed of night iris shedding petals
One by one, like the hours of darkness,
Through the tide-race of a terrible last season
Into the black water. The slow diamonds
Of the luminous hour glittered, strange
Illumination of a capsized sun.
The lilies have squandered the whole dark horde
Of the lovely garden pounded by the sea
And the hardened metal of your sacred columns
Has trembled, O stems. Behold the night, offering
The key that opens wide her gates of horn
To the emanations of delivered souls.

The Poem of St. Francis of Assisi

I am the saint, I am he who was
A man, very small among other men;
And I have only a few thoughts that crown me
And flow from me with a confused sound.

I am that eternal absent from himself
Who always walks beside his own path.
And one day my souls left me, tomorrow
I shall awake in an ancient town.

I tell you, I am the wanderer who has come
To offer you the image of a humble example.
For this I left myself on an old Sunday
Following the evangelical flight of the Angelus bells.

And behold, I arrived at the circle of souls,
They rushed down a circus ring of little hills;
And the grasses were droning muted psalms
At the feet of donkeys bearing souls who smiled at me.

Five early poems

I am no longer ashamed of my robe or of my hands
Which belong to me and to you, my brothers;
And on that day I unbound myself from earth
And waves passed through my transparent body.

Around me lies a city of rigging
Whose ramparts are like the water of boundless seas,
And behold, I recovered that which begins
And the word that ends, and the land beyond.

I have only a face of wax and I am an orphan
And yet wherever I go Angels come
To show me the path of that strange Father
Whose heart is softer than a human father's heart.

Seek me out, I come from the kingdom of peace,
That peace that penetrates the very stones,
And I have pity on this incessant dust
Of human bones returning to the burned ground.

I am he who can dissolve the terror
Of being a man and going among the dead,
For is not my body the miraculous ash
Whose earth is the voice of the speaking dead?

Love

Love? We must purge ourselves
Of this hereditary slime
In which our stellar vermin
Continue to strut

The organ, the organ that grinds the wind
The undertow of the raging sea
Are like the hollow melody
Of this disconcerting dream

ANTONIN ARTAUD

She, we, or this soul
That we seat at the banquet—
Tell us which one is deceived,
O Inspirer of the infamous

She who lies in my bed
And shares the air of my room
Can throw dice on the table
The very ceiling of my mind

Two early essays

II

The Department Store Poison

The large department store bears an enormous share of responsibility for the general debasement of taste in France.

It is the department store, with its moderate prices and its delivery facilities, that has virtually imposed on the middle-class home and even on the country cottage the stupid color reproduction, the idiotic sideboard, the phony antique brass lamp, and all the other hideous furnishings of the modern apartment.

It has promoted the universal deterioration of taste by bringing about the extinction of those isolated centers of individual initiative, the small stores.

Whereas in the cities of certain great foreign countries—in Vienna, for example—each interior bears an unmistakable personal stamp, the total standardization of decorative poverty drives the visitor away from the French home.

People are stupid, people are blind. They do not know that one does not furnish simply to furnish, that furniture is designed to serve a useful function, and that it can deviate from strict functionalism only when it has unquestionable artistic and aesthetic interest. The most unpretentious painted white cupboard, which simply shelters those objects most necessary to daily life, is a thousand times more beautiful than some mass-produced Bon Marché pedestal table that vaguely refers to styles of which only the caricature remains.

For in offering such merchandise Mr. Boucicaut* is interested only in filling his cash registers with as much money as possible. It makes no difference to him if by his fault such a tide of ugliness has spread over the world that modern man may be said to be steeped in ugliness from the hour of his birth to the hour of his death.

Martine, Mare, and Francis Jourdain may vie with one another in ingenuity and create furnishings whose harmony is a true enchantment to the eye and almost to the ear, but they will reach only the moneyed aristocracy, who pay dearly for the privilege of living in beautiful surroundings.

---

* The name Boucicaut is being used here as a symbol and could just as well represent the director of the Bon Marché, the Louvre, the Galeries Lafayette, or any other house of perdition.

Boucicaut, because of the size of his business, will remain the great invader of the home and the poisoner of the aesthetic well-being of the public.

Pictorial Values and the Louvre

Value has become for us primarily a question of metaphysics. Our first duty is to find the fundamental principles on which works of art must rest, as well as those which apply to every existing work. We can gain some insight into Cubist art from Cubist tendencies in contemporary poetry.

These poets can neither imagine nor invent anything which is outside the repertoire of our hearts.

To demonstrate the distribution of states of consciousness into separate and unrelated levels, they practice a divisionism which produces a mosaic of unconscious images based on an irrational disorder—and after all, who can say that there really is a connection, and that we have not arbitrarily associated these states as if they were causally interdependent, and that this is the way consciousness proceeds; I myself, in my most obvious moments of disorder, have comparable conceptions.

Our judgments are clouded by a measure of sensual emotion (owing to the sometimes rudimentary education of our senses).

Example: the shoemaker who, on seeing a Detaille, experiences an emotion that is just as concentrated and intense as the emotion we would experience in the presence of an Odilon Redon. (Considering the influence of the time of day, the quality of the light, of a memory, of a regret, of indigestion, of our mood, is the absolute merely an average?)

If the absolute exists by itself, are we not therefore authorized to seek an art liberated from the conditions of the senses, a new art which would consummate the divorce of the sensations from reason, a geometric art which would admit only sensations of a purely intellectual order (if such exist), which would owe nothing to the contribution of the senses properly speaking, that is, of our nerves?

Two early essays

Thus the examples of art shut up in the Louvre are worth only as much as the principles according to which they were constructed, principles whose value is precisely what is being called into question.

I hasten to say that some convention will always be necessary. Since artists work on a flat surface and use lines, they will not, even in the face of pure reason, be able to avoid a certain coordination, a certain legibility; for, being human, it is only hypothetically that we can create relationships between planes and lines that will not be recognized by our senses.

In the last analysis, since we are unable to imagine for our reason anything tangible outside the forms presented to us by our senses, we shall be obliged to come back to representational painting and also to poetry, but with stricter attention to the exigencies of reason.

Letters from 1921–23

III

TO MADAME TOULOUSE

[Marseilles, late July 1921]

My Mind is very troubled these days; I won't bother to go into the reasons. I haven't bought the *Cahiers d'Aujourd'hui* since the second issue, but there was no point loading myself down with them for the trip. However, if you could get me the issues of *Crapouillot* that have come out since the first of June they would make good reading for this Vacation, as well as Chesterton's novel *The Man Who Was Thursday* published by *La Nouvelle Revue Française* and perhaps Conrad's *Typhoon* by the same publisher. There is nothing of this kind here. And I don't feel like reading anything but novels of adventure, which does not mean that they are devoid of intellectuality: they have more of it than other novels, but it is intellectuality in action.

No, it is not familiarity with Rimbaud that shows through in what I am doing; the similarity is there because I have identical preoccupations. Contrary to what one might think, I have read Rimbaud only once, and for poems like his, especially the prose poems, that is nothing. How different it is with Poe. It can certainly be said that he has influenced me. Anyway, we must wait until I have really written something. So far I have done only one or two poems that give any indication of what I might become. Besides, one must be in possession of the TOTALITY of one's mind, something which I have never achieved.

I shall be at Evian around the third of August.

Antonin Artaud

TO MAX JACOB

[October 1921]

Dear Max Jacob,

Your influence has helped me, and you have certainly had a large part in the fortunate change that is taking place in my life. Recently I managed to get an audition with Gémier, who after hearing me thought that what I was doing might well interest your friend Dullin. I had already written to Dullin, giving your name, but without waiting for his reply I went to see him, saying that Gémier had sent me. Dullin heard me and immediately made me a member of his little group. I identified myself as the author of the letter, and your name helped to establish an understanding between us, since it provided us with yet another connection.

I am very enthusiastic about his work. It seems to me by far the most interesting project that exists in contemporary theater. The whole thing is based on such a desire for moral *integrity*, from the point of view of morality as well as of the acting profession, and on such serious and well-conceived artistic principles, that this venture can pass in our day for an *innovation*. To hear Dullin teach is to feel that one is rediscovering old secrets and a whole forgotten mystique of theatrical production. It is both a theater and a school. A few plays will be performed in the course of this season by a company trained in Dullin's methods, of which each actor is a student. I need not tell you that among these students some have arrived at a level of development that would arouse the envy of many well-known actors. We act from the deepest stratum of our hearts, we act with our hands, with our feet, with all our muscles and all our limbs. We feel the object, we smell it, we touch it, we see it, we listen to it—and there is nothing, there are no props. The Japanese are our masters and our inspiration, together with Edgar Allan Poe. It is *admirable*.

Moreover, Gabory is being *marvelous*. He has just accepted two of my poems for *Action*, and he has been extremely kind to me. There is only one false note. I am still living off my family and I don't know how long this can go on; but how could you have thought that I was asking you for money? No, Max Jacob, I am only too aware of your own financial troubles. But I would like to find some way of supplementing my income outside my working hours. Painting is not very practical—I have a dark room where it is difficult to work. Besides, I am too engrossed—I could do only a few watercolors, a few sketches.

Thank you for writing to *Action* for me. The success of your letter has been complete, as you see. And I am happy to be working with a friend of yours. As a person I find him delightful. I don't need to tell you that I have always admired him greatly as an artist.

My very best wishes, and thanks.
Shall we see each other soon? And where?

Antonin Artaud

TO YVONNE GILLES

[October 1921]

All this week I have been extremely occupied and *preoccupied*. Gémier had given me an appointment for an audition on Monday afternoon, but he postponed it to Wednesday. The ordeal went off as well as possible, and he sent me to Charles Dullin, the actor who was with him last year at the Comédie Montaigne and whom you must have seen in *Le Simoun,* in which he played the leading role with extraordinary skill. This actor has started a small group, something like L'Oeuvre or the Vieux-Colombier but even more special, if possible. It is both a theater and a school which applies principles of instruction that were invented by him and whose purpose is to *internalize* the actor's performance. For in addition to the purification of the stage he is also interested in its *renovation* or, more accurately, its total originality. In other words, he wants his productions to give a constant impression of something that has *never been seen before.* All the action takes place in the soul. The sets are even more stylized and symbolic than at the Vieux-Colombier. His ideal is the Japanese actor who performs without props. Vividly painted masks with black hair are hung on the walls, some in black leather or made to look like old wood. The gods of the school are not Tolstoy, Ibsen, or Shakespeare, but Hoffmann and Poe. The first production will be a play of harsh frenzy and abnormal acuity. Dullin himself will play the leading role with the intensity for which he is known.
It is curious, to say the least, that I with my tastes have fallen into something so congenial to my own mentality.

It's only a beginning and it's very small. The room is barely a third the size of the Vieux-Colombier. It's almost chamber theater. At its most crowded, the room can hold a hundred people.

So after Gémier heard me he said that what I was doing might interest Dullin and sent me to him. Dullin heard me on Thursday and I was immediately made a member of his company. But there is a great deal of work. Besides rehearsals, there are several hours of practice every day: improvisation, rhythmic gymnastics, diction, etc. I shall very likely be in the second production, since the first has been in rehearsal for some time.

I shall not be able to come for lunch, since I am busy. I don't yet know when my free time will be, but I will be able to come some afternoon. I shall write you later.

Antonin Artaud

TO YVONNE GILLES

[June 1922]

I am overwhelmed with work. We are putting on a wonderful play: Calderón's *Life Is a Dream*. And I have a role of tremendous range, something on the order of *King Lear*, if I myself were playing the part of the king. There is another extraordinary role which Dullin plays. For this production I have also designed the costumes and the sets. So you can imagine how busy I am. On the 22nd of June we will be at the Vieux-Colombier, where we will give a series of performances; after that, we will perform in the Roman theater in Orange and the one in Carcassonne.

With kind regards,
Antonin Artaud

TO GÉNICA ATHANASIOU

[Cavalaire, August 17, 1922]

No, Génica, no, I am not angry with you. I know too well what an effort I have to make myself just to get to the *state of mind* in which I can write. But the soul of man is not in words. Besides, I trust you. Your letter, your cards reveal to me feelings not only of an intensity but above all of a *quality* so rare that they put me in possession at last of the ideal of perfect, *celestial* love of which I had dreamed. And this kind of love is not experienced twice. I believe in you. There are in your soul and in my soul things that need to come together. And if ever life divided us, our souls would be able to heal, with time, but they would remain *diminished*. Yes, you allow me to taste things which few men are privileged to taste, things of which the majority are unaware. And after the soul of my mind, you are the soul of my life, so different from yourself that you cannot imagine how profoundly you are this soul. Therefore, be at peace, be silent if silence gives you pleasure, we love each other better when we do not write, for all words are a lie. When we speak we betray our soul. To look at each other would be enough. One feels things, but merely the *effort* that one makes to express them is already a betrayal.

This morning a little while before I received your letter a feeling of calm came over me, of certainty, of sweetness, I was staring into space, at the underside of a thatched roof with the sea in front of me, and I saw your face in me and above me, I sensed it with the eyes of my soul, for several seconds it did not move, I saw the expression of your mouth, the subdued color of your skin, and your eyes like a lake shining through the fresh, brilliant leaves, so that I was amazed when I read in your note that you had seen me in the same way as I saw you. Usually when one stares at a vision it disappears, but you remained.

One evening, the 14th of August, I watched a wonderful moonrise, very Japanese, over the sea, with pines that were dead black as in Japan, the moon huge, sad, and gentle, a little sick, yellow, dirty, a calm upon the darkened waters and this great flower of light—sick, autumnal—which had bloomed over the waters. My mind was very sick for five days, a recurrence of my nervous disease in which I was robbed of all tangible expression of my consciousness, I could no longer read, or write, or think, I had no material thought, so to speak, for within myself I was more profound, but incapable of expressing myself, paralyzed, now my material soul has returned, and to think that madness causes even the spiritual soul to be lost. Difficult problem. I am being a little obscure, perhaps it is difficult for you to understand me.

Nothing from Dullin either. I too feel that the Atelier must be finished. What will become of me? Will I even be able to find

work in Paris? Agonizing question, for how will we be able to see each other? Well, you always know where to write me.
Always. I am with you.
My soul on your lips.

Nanaqui

TO YVONNE GILLES

[November 1922]

I met André Fraye at the exhibit of his work at Marcel Bernheim's on the rue Caumartin. He informed me that he was not on the jury of the Salon d'Automne this year. This is the reason why nothing has been done about your paintings, which deserve a better fate. I found the paintings of Dunoyer de Segonzac surprisingly powerful, full of very unusual effects. Other works that contribute a new or personal note are Jean Marchand's portrait, the works of Hélène Perdriat, Fraye's landscapes, and the portrait of a young girl by Théophile Robert. And Zadkine's wood sculptures of nudes are in a class by themselves, but the rest is more worthless than usual.

At the moment we are rehearsing an *Antigone* by Jean Cocteau, freely adapted from Sophocles and restored to its true level of eternal modernism. I play the role of the soothsayer Tiresias. The sets and the masks will be by Picasso. Here is one production that will not be lacking in originality.

Cordially,
Antonin Artaud

TO GÉNICA ATHANASIOU

[Paris, May 6, 1923]

Génica, dearest. I want to answer your letter immediately. Not that I was waiting for it to write you, but so that you won't have to wait any longer. I wanted to tell you only certain special things, very good things, and I wanted to be equal to it. I am going to write you more fully, VERY fully tomorrow. I feel you more than ever, I experience again the same quality of atmosphere, the same warmth, the same thoughts in the air as when we were together. It's been a year already. A year of complete, absolute love. It is beautiful. I am happy and it is because of you.

Until tomorrow. I hold you tight in my arms. I take you into me.

NAKY

Notice how my handwriting resembles yours.

TO GÉNICA ATHANASIOU

Twenty-FOUR—October 24, 1923

You must be calm, darling, angel. Already I am better. Already my mind is recovering. I am still alive. If there is one of us who needs to be cured, it is you and not me. With all my soul, with all that is purest in me I swear to you once and for all that you have always exaggerated the trouble. Ask my mother if you know her. She will tell you that I have always been merciless with my intimates, and this well before opium, that I have never been able to tolerate any contradiction. I wish you had known me three years ago, five years ago, ten years ago, I was a raging demon because of the evil which smoldered within me, and which was not opium. Whatever you may think, I have not gone back on opium again since my return. Your deductions are false. To be sure, I take opium from time to time, but not out of habit, I swear to you on the life to come, on *the higher reality of my mind*, which is the thing that is most important to me in the world. You are obsessed, Génica, you must make up your mind to be cured. In your case, happily, you have only to want it and to reflect. I love you. You have never been able, you have never been willing to believe me because YOUR OBSESSION was stronger than the truth. What is the question, Génica? You have never been willing to consider the real question. Understand at last that the primordial thing, the thing which is the question is the INTENSITY of suffering. You are always talking about my life, about being cured someday, but you must understand that *the idea of suffering* is stronger than the idea of healing, the idea of life. And the question for me is to relieve this suffering; the very intensity of this suffering *prevents* me from thinking of anything else. You have never tried the weight of the intensity of this suffering. You talk to me of waiting, of being patient, as if the horror of my life could allow me to wait. Your brain which is healthy, your body which does not feel my pain, allow you to believe that I could wait, but my twisted body, my broken body, my hacked brain do not give me time to wait. Stop going over and over the same arguments. You have driven me to despair for the last two days. Come back to yourself. You can see from this letter that I am MUCH more lucid than you.

Dear soul.

Naky

From *Bilboquet* (1923)

IV

THERE AREN'T ENOUGH MAGAZINES, or if you will, all existing magazines are useless. We are appearing because we believe we are responding to something. We are *real*. This excuses us from being necessary. There should be as many magazines as there are valid *states of mind*. The amount of printed matter would then be reduced to very little, but this little would give the abstract and total of what should be thought, or what is worth publishing.

All magazines are slaves to a *way of thinking* and as a result they despise *thought*. They all have the serious defect of being edited by several people. Thus they imagine that they are reflecting a state of opinion, when they are really only a grab bag. For there is no such thing as a state of opinion, there are various opinions which are more or less worthy of being expressed. But humanity is incurable. No one will ever prevent people from being sure of their own thought and suspicious of someone else's; if someone who has a valid point of view wants to give it an audience, he has no choice but to start a magazine. We have a point of view that is worth expressing. Circumstances external to the fact of thinking correctly or incorrectly prevent existing magazines from accepting this point of view in its absolute nakedness. There are no free magazines; all magazines have what amounts to a creed. Thus we are choosing the only means of being ourselves and of being ourselves totally.

We will appear when we have something to say. When we think that we have an interesting view on a false way of thinking, or when an aesthetic or moral phenomenon seems to lend itself to discussion. This magazine will therefore be a *personal* magazine, interesting in that it will be the creation of a single individual, but we will welcome as guests those artists and writers whose work seems to accord with our state of mind, to illustrate it, or to relate to it in some way.

ENO DAILOR

Rimbaud & the Moderns

New events in thought, stirrings, vitality of relations—not relations of feelings, of the inside of one feeling to the inside of another feeling, but of the outside of a feeling, its place, its status, of the *importance* of one feeling to the *importance* of another feeling, the external, figurative value of one thought in relation to another thought—and of his reactions to these things, their acceptance within him, their twists and turns—this is the contribution of Rimbaud.

Rimbaud taught us a new way of being, a new way of maintaining ourselves in the midst of things.

Plundered by the moderns solely for his obscurities, for the interplay of relationships invented by him and not even for the nature of the things he discussed—which he himself for that matter treats only from the outside (feeling this outside externally), and if he digs, it is only to extract still other exteriors; the inner essence of phenomena always remained unknown to him—and the moderns have not even retained these phenomena but only ways of discussing them. Is this not true of Raval, Fierens, and the other followers? Another mind is at the source of certain tics of the contemporary style, soon just as outmoded as all the affectations of the decadents: this is the Mallarmé of *Divagations*.

Rimbaud, in his eagerness to give each word its full burden of meaning, classified his words as if they were values existing outside the thought that conditions them, and performed those strange inversions of syntax in which each syllable seems to be objectified and to become preponderant. But Mallarmé was difficult in the face of his thought where Paul Fierens is difficult only for those who read him, and with an insignificant subject. I hasten to say that Paul Fierens writes perfect little poems, which I find to be successful elucidations of contemporary thought. I object only to his reviews.

From *Bilboquet* (1923)

A MENTAL PAINTER

In the fetus genre, Paul Klee (German) organizes some interesting visions.

I rather like some of his nightmares, his mental syntheses conceived as architectural structures (or his architectural structures with a mental quality), and some cosmic syntheses in which all the secret objectivity of things is made tangible, more so than in the syntheses of George Grosz. When the two artists are considered together, the profound difference in their inspiration appears. George Grosz screens the world and reduces it to his vision; in Paul Klee the things of the world are organized—and he seems merely to be writing at their dictation. Organization of visions, of forms; fixation, stabilization of thoughts, inductions and deductions of images, with the conclusion that flows from these. Organization of images, search for the underlying meaning of certain images, clarifications of visions of the mind: such seems to me to be this art. The dryness, the precision of Grosz become very obvious in the presence of these organized visions which retain their appearance of visions, their quality of mental objects.

Correspondence with Jacques Rivière (1923–24)

V

JACQUES RIVIÈRE TO ANTONIN ARTAUD

May 1, 1923

Sir,

I regret that I am unable to publish your poems in *La Nouvelle Revue Française*. But I am interested enough in them to want to make the acquaintance of their author. If it were possible for you to stop by the review some Friday between four and six, I would be happy to see you.

Cordially yours,
Jacques Rivière

ANTONIN ARTAUD TO JACQUES RIVIÈRE

June 5, 1923

Sir,

At the risk of imposing on you, I should like to ask you to reconsider a few points of our conversation this afternoon.

The question of the acceptability of these poems is a problem which concerns you as much as it does me. I am speaking, of course, of their absolute acceptability, of their literary existence.

I suffer from a horrible sickness of the mind. My thought abandons me at every level. From the simple fact of thought to the external fact of its materialization in words. Words, shapes of sentences, internal directions of thought, simple reactions of the mind—I am in constant pursuit of my intellectual being. Thus as soon as *I can grasp a form,* however imperfect, I pin it down, for fear of losing the whole thought. I lower myself, I know, and I suffer from it, but I consent to it for fear of dying altogether.

All this, which is very badly expressed, threatens to introduce a dangerous ambiguity into your judgment of me.

This is why, out of respect for the central feeling which dictates my poems to me and for those strong images or figures of speech which I have been able to find, in spite of everything I propose these poems for existence. These figures of speech, these awkward expressions for which you reproach me, I have noticed and accepted. Remember: I did not contest them. They stem from the profound uncertainty of my thought. I consider myself fortunate indeed when this uncertainty is not replaced by the absolute nonexistence from which I suffer at times.

Here again I fear an ambiguity. I would like you to understand that it is not a question of that greater or lesser degree of existence which is commonly called inspiration, but of a total absence, a real extinction.

This is also why I told you that I had nothing, no work in progress, the few things that I showed you constituting those scraps which I was able to rescue from utter nothingness.

It is very important to me that the few manifestations of *spiritual* existence which I have been able to give myself not be regarded as nonexistent because of the blemishes and awkward expressions they contain.

In showing you the poems, it seemed to me that their faults, their unevennesses were not sufficiently flagrant to destroy the overall impression of each poem.

You must believe, sir, that I have in mind no immediate or selfish goal, I wish only to settle a desperate problem.

For I cannot hope that time or effort will remedy these obscurities or these failings; this is why I lay claim with so much insistence and anxiety to this existence, aborted though it be. And the question I would like to have answered is this: Do you think that one can allow less literary authenticity and effectiveness to a poem which is imperfect but filled with powerful and beautiful things than to a poem which is perfect but without much internal reverberation? I am aware that a magazine like *La Nouvelle Revue Française* requires a certain formal level and a great purity of content, but granting this, is the substance of my thought so confused, then, and its overall beauty rendered so ineffective by the impurities and hesitations scattered through it that it fails, from the point of view of *literature,* to exist? It is the whole problem of my thinking that is at stake. The question for me is nothing less than knowing whether or not I have the right to continue to think, in verse or in prose.

One of these Fridays I shall take the liberty of presenting to you with my compliments the little pamphlet of poems which Kahnweiler has just published and which is called *Tric Trac du Ciel,* as well as the small volume, *Douze Chansons,* in the series

"Les Contemporains." You will then be able to give me your *definitive* judgment of my poems.

Antonin Artaud

JACQUES RIVIÈRE TO ANTONIN ARTAUD

June 23, 1923

Dear Sir,

I have read carefully what you were kind enough to submit for my consideration, and it is in all sincerity that I think I can reassure you about the anxieties which your letter betrayed and which I was so touched that you chose to confide to me. There are in your poems, as I told you from the beginning, awkwardnesses and above all oddities which are disconcerting. But they seem to me to correspond to a certain studied effort on your part rather than to a lack of control over your ideas.

Obviously (and this is what prevents me for the moment from publishing any of your poems in *La Nouvelle Revue Française*) you do not usually succeed in creating a sufficient unity of impression. But I have had enough experience in reading manuscripts to feel that this concentration of your resources on a simple poetic object is not at all ruled out by your temperament and that with a little patience, even if it entails only the elimination of divergent images or touches, you will succeed in writing poems that are perfectly coherent and harmonious.

I shall always be delighted to see you, to chat with you, and to read anything you would like to submit to me. Do you want me to send back the copy you brought me?

Very cordially yours,
Jacques Rivière

ANTONIN ARTAUD

ANTONIN ARTAUD TO JACQUES RIVIÈRE

Paris, January 29, 1924

Sir,

You have reason to have forgotten me. It was last May that I made you a little mental confession. And I asked you a question. With your permission, I would like to finish that confession today, to go on with it, to go to the very end of myself. I do not seek to justify myself in your eyes, it is a matter of indifference to me whether I seem to exist in the eyes of anyone at all. I have, to cure me of the judgment of others, the whole of the distance that separates me from myself. Please do not regard this as insolence, but rather as the very accurate confession, the painful disclosure of a distressing state of mind.

I resented your reply for a long time. I had presented myself to you as a mental case, a genuine psychic anomaly, and you answered me with a literary judgment on some poems which I did not value, which I could not value. I flattered myself that you had not understood me. I see today that I may not have been sufficiently explicit, and for this too I ask your forgiveness.

I had imagined that I could hold your interest, if not by the stylistic perfection of my verses, at least by the rarity of certain mental phenomena which actually made it impossible for these verses to be any different, whereas I had within me precisely what was needed to bring them to the uttermost point of perfection. A conceited statement, I am exaggerating, but deliberately.

My question may in fact have been specious, but it was to you that I put it, to you and no one else, because of the extreme sensitivity, the almost unhealthy acuteness of your mind. I flattered myself that I was bringing you a case, a distinctive mental case, and curious as I thought you were about all mental distortions, about all those obstacles that are destructive of thought, I thought thereby to draw your attention to the *real* value, the initial value of my thought, and of the productions of my thought.

This scattered quality of my poems, these defects of form, this constant sagging of my thought, must be attributed not to a lack of practice, a lack of control over the instrument I was handling, a lack of *intellectual development;* but to a central collapse of the soul, to a kind of erosion, both essential and fleeting, of the thought, to a temporary non-possession of the material benefits of my development, to an abnormal separation of the elements of thought (the impulse to think, at each of the terminal stratifications of thought, passing through all the stages, all the bifurcations of thought and of form).

There is something which destroys my thought; something which does not prevent me from being what I might be, but which leaves me, so to speak, in suspension. Something furtive which robs me of the words *that I have found*, which reduces my mental tension, which is gradually destroying in its substance the body of my thought, which is even robbing me of the memory of those idioms with which one expresses oneself and which translate accurately the most inseparable, the most localized, the most living inflections of thought. I shall not go on. I do not need to describe my state.

I only want to say enough about it to be at last understood and believed by you.

And so I ask you to trust me. Accept, I beg you, the reality of these phenomena, accept their furtiveness, their eternal recurrence, accept the fact that I would have written this letter before today if I had not been in this state. So once again here is my question:

You are familiar, are you not, with the subtlety, the fragility of the mind? Haven't I told you enough about it to prove to you that I have a mind which exists *literarily*, as T. exists, or E., or S., or M.? Restore to my mind the concentration of its forces, the cohesion that it lacks, the constancy of its tension, the consistency of its own substance. (And all this objectively is so little.) And tell me whether that which is missing in my poems (the old ones) could not be restored to them in a flash?

Do you believe that in a well-organized mind apprehension is accompanied by extreme weakness, and that one can simultaneously astonish and disappoint? Finally, though I may be a good judge of my mind, I can judge the productions of my mind only insofar as they merge with it in a kind of happy unconsciousness. This will be my criterion.

To conclude, I am therefore sending you the latest product of my mind. In relation to myself it is worth little, although it is still better than nothing. It is a makeshift. But the question for me is whether it is better to write this than to write nothing at all.

It is you who will give the answer by accepting or rejecting this little attempt. You will judge it, of course, from the point of view of the absolute. But I shall tell you that it would be a very great consolation for me to think that even though I am not *all* of myself, not as tall, not as dense, not as wide as myself, I can still be something. For this reason, monsieur, be truly absolute. Judge this prose without regard to any questions of trends, of principles, of personal taste, judge it with the charity of your soul, the characteristic lucidity of your mind, reconsider it with your heart.

It probably indicates a brain and a soul which exist, and which deserve a certain place. In the interest of the palpable expansion of this soul, do not brush it aside unless your conscience protests with all its strength, but if you have a doubt, let it be resolved in my favor.

I surrender myself to your judgment.

Antonin Artaud

Postscript to a Letter in Which Certain Literary Principles of Jacques Rivière Were Discussed

You will tell me: to give an opinion on such matters requires another mental cohesion and another acuity. Well, it is my peculiar weakness and my *absurdity* to want to write no matter what the cost, and to express myself.

I am a man who has suffered much from the mind, and as such I have the *right* to speak. I know how business is done in there. I have agreed once and for all to give in to my inferiority. And yet I am not stupid. I know that it is possible to think further than I think, and perhaps differently. All I can do is wait for my brain to change, wait for its upper drawers to open. An hour from now, tomorrow perhaps, I will have changed my mind, but this present thought exists, I will not allow my thought to be lost.

A.A.

Correspondence with Jacques Rivière (1923–24)

CRY

The little celestial poet
Opens the shutters of his heart.
The skies collide. Oblivion
Uproots the symphony.

Stableboy, the crazy house
Which gives you wolves to guard
Does not guess the rage
Smoldering under the great alcove
Of the vault that hangs over us.

Therefore silence and night
Muzzle all impurity
The sky with giant strides
Moves in on the crossroads of noise.

The star eats. The slanting sky
Soars toward the summit
Night sweeps away the remains
Of our satisfying meal.

On earth a slug walks
Greeted by ten thousand white hands
A slug crawls to the place
Where the earth has vanished.

Some angels were returning in peace
Summoned by no obscenity
When there rose the real voice
Of the spirit that summoned them.

The sun lower than the day
Turned the whole sea to steam.
A dream strange but clear
Was born on the earth gone mad.

ANTONIN ARTAUD

The little lost poet
Leaves his celestial place
With an idea from beyond the earth
Pressed to his long-haired heart.

*

Two traditions met.
But our padlocked thoughts
Did not have room:
Experiment to be repeated.

A.A.

ANTONIN ARTAUD TO JACQUES RIVIÈRE

March 22, 1924

My letter deserved at least a reply. Return, sir, letters and manuscripts.

I would like to have found something intelligent to say to you to indicate clearly what divides us, but it is useless. I am a mind not yet formed, an idiot: think of me what you will.

Antonin Artaud

JACQUES RIVIÈRE TO ANTONIN ARTAUD

Paris, March 25, 1924

Dear Sir,

Of course, I agree with you completely, your letters deserved a reply. I simply haven't been able to write one yet: that's all. Please forgive me.

One thing strikes me: the contrast between the extraordinary precision of your self-diagnosis and the vagueness, or at least the formlessness, of your creative efforts.

I was wrong no doubt, in my letter of last year, to try to reassure you at all costs: I acted like those doctors who think they can cure their patients by refusing to believe them, by denying the strangeness of their case, by forcing them back into the normal. It is a bad method. I regret it.

Even if I had no other evidence, your handwriting—tormented, wavering, collapsing, as if sucked in here and there by secret whirlpools—would be sufficient guarantee of the reality of the phenomena of mental "erosion" of which you complain.

But how do you escape them so well when you try to define your sickness? Is one to believe that anguish gives you this strength and this lucidity which fail you when you yourself are not at issue? Or is it the proximity of the object which you are struggling to grasp which suddenly affords you such a solid grip? In any case, you achieve, in the analysis of your own mind, total and remarkable successes which must give you confidence in this mind itself, since it is also the instrument which obtains these successes for you.

Other considerations may also help you, not, perhaps, to hope for a cure, but at least to bear your illness with patience. They are of a general nature. You speak somewhere in your letter of the "fragility of the mind." This fragility is superabundantly borne out by the mental disorders studied and catalogued by psychiatry. But it has not, perhaps, been sufficiently shown to what degree so-called normal thought is the product of chance mechanisms.

That the mind has an existence of its own, that it has a tendency to live on its own substance, that it grows over the personality with a kind of egoism and with no concern for keeping the personality in harmony with the world, is something which apparently can no longer, in our time, be debated. Paul Valéry dramatized this autonomy of the thinking function in human beings in a marvelous way in his famous *Evening with Monsieur Teste*. Regarded in itself, the mind is a kind of canker; it reproduces, it advances constantly in all directions; you note yourself as one of your torments "the impulse to think, at each of the terminal stratifications of thought"; the outlets of the mind are unlimited in number; no idea obstructs it; no idea brings it fatigue or satisfaction; even those temporary releases which our physical functions find in exercise are denied it. The man who thinks spends himself totally. Romanticism aside, there is no other escape from pure thought but death.

There is a whole body of literature—I know that it preoccupies you as much as it interests me—which is the product of the immediate and, so to speak, animal functioning of the mind. It has the appearance of a vast field of ruins; those columns which are standing are supported only by chance. Chance reigns there, and a kind of dreary multiplicity. One can say that it is the most accurate and direct expression of that monster which every man carries within him but which he usually seeks instinctively to chain with the bonds of facts and experience.

But, you will tell me, is this really what is meant by the "fragility of the mind"? While I complain of weakness, you describe to me another sickness which comes from an excess of force, an overflow of power.

Here is my idea at closer range: the mind is fragile in that it has need of obstacles—obstacles not of its own making. When left to itself, it is lost, it is destroyed. It seems to me that this mental "erosion," these internal thefts, this "destruction" of the thought "in its substance" which afflict your mind are the result of the excessive freedom you allow it. It is the absolute that unhinges it. To be taut, the mind needs a boundary and it needs to come up against the blessed opacity of experience. The only cure for madness is the innocence of facts.

As soon as you accept the mental level, you accept all the troubles and especially all the lapses of the mind. If by thought one means *creation,* as you seem to most of the time, it must at all costs be relative; one will find security, constancy, strength, only by engaging the mind in something.

I know: there is a kind of intoxication in the instant of its pure emanation, in that moment when its fluid flows directly from the brain and encounters a quantity of spaces, a quantity of stages and levels into which to spread. It is this totally subjective impression of complete freedom and even of complete intellectual license which our "Surrealists" have tried to convey in the dogma of a fourth poetic dimension. But the punishment for this flight is close at hand: the universal possibility turns into concrete impossibilities; the captured phantom finds to avenge him twenty internal phantoms which paralyze us, which devour our spiritual substance.

Is this to say that the normal functioning of the mind must

consist in a slavish imitation of the given and that thinking is nothing more than reproducing? I do not think so; one must choose what one wishes to "render" and it must always be not only something definite, not only something knowable, but also something unknown; for the mind to find all its power, the concrete must serve as the mysterious. Every striking idea, every memorable utterance, the words by which one later recognizes the writer, are always the result of a compromise between a current of intelligence that comes out of him and an ignorance that comes over him, a surprise, an obstacle. The rightness of an expression always involves a remnant of hypothesis; language must have hit upon a noiseless object, and sooner than reason would have reached it. But where the object, the obstacle are completely lacking, the mind keeps on going, unswerving and exhausted; and everything falls apart in an immense contingency.

It may be that I am judging you both from too abstract a point of view and on the basis of too personal preoccupations: however, it seems to me that your case can be explained in large part by the considerations which I have just discussed, a little too fully, and that it fits into the general structure that I have tried to define. As long as you let your intellectual force pour out into the absolute, it is tormented by eddies, riddled with helplessness, exposed to predatory winds that disorganize it; but as soon as, driven back by anguish to your own mind, you direct it at this immediate and enigmatic object, it condenses, intensifies, becomes useful and penetrating and brings you positive benefits; that is, truths expressed with all the three-dimensionality that can make them communicable, accessible to others, in short, something which transcends your suffering, your very existence, something which enlarges and consolidates you, which gives you the only reality that man can reasonably hope to conquer by his own forces, the reality in others.

I am not habitually an optimist; but I refuse to despair of you. My sympathy for you is very great; I was wrong to leave you waiting so long without a word.

I am keeping your poem. Send me everything you write.

With warm regards,
Jacques Rivière

ANTONIN ARTAUD

ANTONIN ARTAUD TO JACQUES RIVIÈRE

Paris, May 7, 1924

Very dear Sir,

To return to a discussion which is already old, one need only realize for a moment that this impossibility of expressing myself applies to the most basic needs of my life, to my most urgent contingencies—and to the suffering which ensues—to understand that it is not for want of desperate effort that I have given up on myself. I am on leave from poetry. It is only because of circumstances that are fortuitous and external to my real possibilities that I do not realize myself. I ask only that someone believe that I have within me the potentiality for the crystallization of things, in forms and with the right words.

I had to wait all this time to be in a position to send you this short note which is clear at the expense of being well written. You can draw from it the obvious conclusions.

One thing in your letter remains a little unclear to me: and that is the use that you intend to make of the poem I sent you. You have put your finger on an aspect of myself; literature properly speaking interests me rather little. But if by chance you should decide to publish it, please send me the proofs, as I must change two or three words.

With all best wishes,
Antonin Artaud

JACQUES RIVIÈRE TO ANTONIN ARTAUD

May 24, 1924

Dear Sir,

An idea has occurred to me which I have resisted for some time but which I find extremely attractive. I want you to think about it too. I hope it pleases you. In any case, it would have to be worked out in detail.

Why shouldn't we publish the letter, or rather letters that you have written me? I have just reread again the one you wrote on the 29th of January. It is really altogether remarkable.

There would be only a little work of transposition to be done. I mean that we would give the addressee and the writer fictitious names. Perhaps I could draft a reply based on the one that I sent you, but more developed and less personal. Perhaps we could also include a bit of your poetry or of your essay on Uccello? The whole would make up a little epistolary novel which would be rather unusual.

Give me your opinion, and in the meantime believe me sincerely yours,

Jacques Rivière

ANTONIN ARTAUD TO JACQUES RIVIÈRE

May 25, 1924

Dear Sir,

Why lie, why try to put on a literary level something which is the cry of life itself, why give an appearance of fiction to that which is made of the ineradicable substance of the soul, which is like the wail of reality? Yes, your idea pleases me, it delights me, it overwhelms me, but only provided we give the reader the impression that he is not involved with something fabricated. We have the right to lie, but not about the essence of the thing. I do not insist on signing the letters with my name. But it is absolutely necessary for the reader to feel that he has in his hands the elements of a true story. We would have to publish my letters from the first to the last and to do this we would have to go back to June 1923. The reader must be given all the elements of the discussion.

A man possesses himself in flashes, and even when he possesses himself, he does not reach himself completely. He does not realize that constant cohesion of his forces without which all true creation is impossible. Nevertheless, this man exists. I mean to say that he has a distinct reality which redeems him. Should he be condemned to oblivion simply because he can give only fragments of himself? You yourself do not think so, and the proof of this is the importance which you attach to these fragments. For a long time I have been meaning to suggest to you that we put them together. I did not dare, and now your letter answers my desire. This is to tell you with what satisfaction I welcome the idea that you propose.

I am perfectly aware of the sudden stops and starts in my poems, they are related to the very essence of inspiration and proceed from my chronic inability to concentrate on an object. Because of a physiological weakness, a weakness which affects the very substance of that which is usually called the soul and which is the emanation of our nervous force coagulated around objects. But this weakness afflicts the whole age, as witness Tristan Tzara, André Breton, Pierre Reverdy. But in their case the soul is not physiologically damaged, it is not damaged substantially, but it is damaged at all the points where it joins something else, it is not damaged *outside of thought;* what, then, is the source of the trouble, is it really the atmosphere of the age, a miracle floating in the air, a cosmic and evil anomaly, or the discovery of a new world, an actual expansion of reality? The fact nevertheless remains that they do not suffer and that I do suffer, not only in the mind but in the flesh and in my everyday soul. This lack of connection to the object which characterizes all of literature is in me a lack of connection to life. As for myself, I can truly say that I am not in the world, and this is not merely an attitude of the mind. My last poems seemed to me to show serious progress. Are they really so unpublishable in their totality? But what does it matter, I would rather show myself as I am, in my nonexistence and my rootlessness. One could in any case publish large fragments of them. I believe that most of the stanzas, taken separately, are good. It is only putting them together that destroys their value. You will choose these fragments yourself, you will arrange the letters. *In this area I can no longer judge.* But my primary concern is that no ambiguity arise as to the nature of the phenomena which I call to my defense. The reader must believe in a real sickness and not in a phenomenon of the age, a sickness which touches the essence of the being and its central possibilities of expression, and which applies to a whole life.

A sickness which affects the soul in its most profound reality, and which infects its manifestations. The poison of being. A veritable *paralysis.* A sickness which deprives you of speech, memory, which uproots your thought.

I have said enough, I think, to be understood, publish this last letter. I realize as I finish it that it can serve as a clarification and conclusion to the discussion as far as I am concerned.

With affectionate gratitude,
Antonin Artaud

ANTONIN ARTAUD TO JACQUES RIVIÈRE

June 6, 1924

Dear Sir,

. . . .

My mental life is shot through with petty doubts and peremptory certainties which express themselves in lucid and coherent words. And my weaknesses are of a more precarious structure, they are themselves nebulous and badly formulated. They have living roots, roots of anguish which touch the heart of life; but they do not possess the disorder of life, one does not feel in them that cosmic breath of a soul shaken to its foundations. They are of a mind which cannot conceive of its weakness, otherwise it would translate it into dense and powerful words. And here, monsieur, is the whole problem: to have within oneself the inseparable reality and the physical clarity of a feeling, to have it to such a degree that it is impossible for it not to be expressed, to have a wealth of words, of acquired turns of phrase capable of joining the dance, coming into play; and the moment the soul is preparing to organize its wealth, its discoveries, this revelation, at that unconscious moment when the thing is on the point of coming forth, a superior and evil will attacks the soul like a poison, attacks the mass consisting of word and image, attacks the mass of feeling, and leaves me panting as if at the very door of life.

And now suppose that I feel this will physically passing through me, that it jolts me with a sudden and unexpected electricity, a repeated electricity. Suppose that each of my thinking moments is on certain days shaken by these profound tempests which nothing outside betrays. And tell me whether any literary work whatsoever is compatible with states of this kind. What brain could withstand them? What personality would not break down? If I only had the strength, I would occasionally indulge in the luxury of mentally subjecting to the mortification of so insistent a pain some well-known thinker, some old or young writer who is producing, and whose emerging views are winning respect, to see what would be left of him. One must not be too quick to judge men, one must trust them to the point of absurdity, to the dregs. These ventured works which often seem to you the product of a mind which is not yet in possession of itself, and which perhaps will never be, who knows what a brain they conceal, what power of life, what mental fever which only the circumstances have reduced. But enough about myself and my works to be, I no longer ask anything but to feel my brain.

Antonin Artaud

JACQUES RIVIÈRE TO ANTONIN ARTAUD

Paris, June 8, 1924

Dear Sir,

Perhaps I rather indiscreetly substituted myself, with my ideas and my prejudices, for your suffering and your singularity. Perhaps I chattered on, where I should have understood and sympathized. I wanted to reassure you, to cure you. This is no doubt because of the kind of rage with which I always react, where I am concerned, in the direction of life. In my own struggle to live, I shall not admit defeat as long as I can breathe.

Your last letters, in which the word "soul" occurs several times in place of the word "mind," awaken in me a sympathy even graver, but more embarrassed, than the first ones. I sense, I touch upon a profound and private misery; I remain immobilized in the presence of sufferings which I can only dimly glimpse. But perhaps this attitude of bewilderment will provide you with more help and encouragement than my previous ratiocinations.

And yet! Am I totally incapable of understanding your torments? You say that "a man possesses himself in flashes, and even when he possesses himself, he does not reach himself completely." This man is you; but I can tell you that it is also myself. I know nothing that resembles your "tempests" or that "evil will" which "attacks the soul from without" and its powers of expression. But the sensation that I sometimes have of being unworthy of myself is no less distinct for being more general, less painful.

Like you, I reject the convenient symbol of inspiration to explain the alternate states through which I pass. It is a question of something more profound, something more "substantial," if I may twist the meaning of this word, than a fair wind which may or may not come to me from the depths of my mind; it is a question of gradations which I pass through in my own reality. Not voluntarily, alas! but in a purely accidental manner.

One thing that is remarkable is that the very fact of my existence is never for me, as you observe in yourself, the object of serious doubt; there always remains something of myself, but it is very often something poor, clumsy, weak, and almost suspect. At such moments I do not lose all idea of my complete reality; but sometimes I do lose all hope of ever recovering it. It is like a roof over me which hangs in the air by a miracle, and to which I see no way of raising myself.

My feelings, my ideas—the same ones as usual—pass through me with a faint air of unreality; they are so diminished, so hypothetical that they seem to belong to pure philosophical speculation, they are still there, however, but they look at me as if to make me admire their absence.

Proust described the "intermittences of the heart"; someone should describe the intermittences of being.

Obviously, there are in the case of these disappearances of the soul physiological causes which can often be rather easily determined. You speak of the soul as "the coagulation of our nervous force," you say that it can be "physiologically damaged." I agree with you that the soul is very much dependent on the nervous system. And yet its crises are so capricious that I sometimes understand how one might be tempted to turn, as you do, to the mystical explanation of an "evil will" working relentlessly from without to reduce it.

In any case, it is a fact, I believe, that a whole category of men is subject to oscillations in the level of their being. How many times have we mechanically assumed a familiar psychological attitude only to discover suddenly that it was beyond us, or rather that we had secretly become unequal to it! How many times has our most habitual personality suddenly appeared to us as artificial, and even fictitious, for want of the spiritual or "essential" resources that should nourish it!

Where does it go, and where does it return from, our being which all psychology down to our day has pretended to regard as a constant? It is a problem that is almost insoluble unless one resorts to a religious dogma like that of grace, for example. I am surprised that our age (I am thinking of Pirandello, of Proust, in whom it is implicit) has dared to raise it and leave it unanswered, confining itself to anxiety.

"A soul physiologically damaged." That is a terrible heritage. And yet I believe that from a certain point of view, from the point of view of insight, it can also be a privilege. It is the only means we have of understanding ourselves a little, or at least of seeing ourselves. Someone who does not know depression, who has never felt the soul encroached upon by the body, invaded by its weakness, is incapable of perceiving any truth about the nature of man; one must go beneath the surface, one must look at the underside; one must lose the ability to move, or hope, or believe, in order to observe accurately. How are we to distinguish our intellectual or moral mechanisms unless we are temporarily deprived of them? It must be the consolation of those who experience death in small doses this way that they are the only ones who know anything about how life is made.

And then "the mortification of so insistent a pain" prevents the ridiculous fog of vanity from rising in them. You wrote me: "I have, to cure me of the judgment of others, the whole of the distance that separates me from myself." Here is the function of this "distance": it "cures us of the judgment of others"; it prevents us from doing anything to bribe this judgment, or accommodate ourselves to it; it keeps us pure, and in spite of the variations in our reality, it assures us a greater degree of identity.

Of course, health is the only acceptable ideal, the only one to which anyone I call a man has the right to aspire; but when it is given to someone from the outset, it blinds him to half the world.

I have allowed myself to comfort you again, in spite of

myself, by trying to show you how precarious, even with respect to existence, the so-called normal state can be. I hope with all my heart that the stages I have described are accessible to you, in the upward as well as in the other direction. Why, after all, should a moment of plenitude, of being equal to yourself, be denied you, seeing that you already have the courage to desire it? There is no absolute danger except for him who abandons himself; there is no complete death except for him who acquires a taste for dying.

Affectionately,
Jacques Rivière

Two essays from 1924

VI

THE EVOLUTION OF DÉCOR

We must ignore *mise en scène** and the theater.

All the great dramatists, the model dramatists, thought outside the theater.

Look at Aeschylus, Sophocles, Shakespeare.

On another level, look at Racine, Corneille, Molière. The latter eliminate, or almost eliminate, external staging, but they exploit to the utmost the internal movements, that kind of perpetual coming and going in their protagonists' souls.

Subservience to the author, dependence on the text, what a dismal tradition! Each text has infinite possibilities. The spirit of the text, not the letter! A text requires more than analysis and perception.

We must reestablish a kind of magnetic intercommunication between the spirit of the author and the spirit of the director. The director must even set aside his own logic and his own understanding. Those who have claimed up to now to base their productions solely on texts may have succeeded in ridding themselves of the pious mimicry of certain traditions, but they have failed to transcend the theater and their own understanding. They have simply replaced certain Molièresque or Odéonian traditions with new traditions originating in Russia or elsewhere. And although they were trying to get rid of the theater as such, they persisted in thinking in terms of the theater. They were working with the stage, with décor, with actors.

They conceive each work in relation to the theater. Retheatricalize the theater: this is their monstrous new slogan. But the theater must be thrust back into life.

Which does not mean that the theater must be lifelike. As if one could simply imitate life. What we must do is rediscover *the life of the theater*, in all its freedom.

This life exists intact in the texts of the great tragedians, when one hears them with all their color, when one sees them in their full dimensions and at their level, with their volumes, their perspective, their peculiar density.

---

* *Mise en scène:* literally, putting on the stage. There is no satisfactory English equivalent for this term, which refers to all that is meant by staging, direction, production, stagecraft, and stage setting.—*Ed.*

But we lack the capacity for mysticism. What good is a director who is not in the habit of looking within himself, who does not possess the ability to withdraw and be released from himself? This discipline is indispensable. It is only through purification and oblivion that we can recover the purity of our initial reactions and learn to restore to each theatrical gesture its indispensable human meaning.

For the moment, let us look above all for plays which are like a transubstantiation of life. One goes to the theater to escape from oneself or, if you will, to rediscover in oneself, not necessarily one's best qualities, but those qualities that are rarest and most carefully *screened*. In the theater everything is permissible except barrenness and banality. Just look at painting. There are young painters around now who have rediscovered the meaning of real painting. They are painting chess players or card players who look like gods.

What is the source of this attraction which the circus and the music hall have for our modern world? I would be inclined to use the word "fantasy" if I did not feel that it has been prostituted, at least in the sense in which it is understood today, and if it did not lead one inevitably toward that *retheatricalization* of the theater which is the battle cry of the contemporary ideal. On the contrary, I say that we must intellectualize the theater, we must place the feelings and gestures of the characters on the level of their rarest and most essential meaning. We must make the atmosphere of the theater more rarefied. Which does not require any lofty metaphysical operation—witness the circus—but simply a sense of the values of the mind. This eliminates and rules out at least three quarters of current productions, but it forces the theater to return to its source and in so doing saves it. To save the theater I would even banish Ibsen, because of all those discussions of points of philosophy or morality which do not sufficiently affect the souls of his protagonists *in relation to us*.

Sophocles, Aeschylus, and Shakespeare made up for certain pangs of the soul that were a little too much on the level of ordinary life by that kind of divine terror which weighed upon the gestures of their heroes and to which audiences were more sensitive than they are today.

Two essays from 1924

What we have lost on the strictly mystical side we can make up on the intellectual side.

But in order to do this we must learn to be mystics again, at least in a certain sense, and by concentrating on a text, forgetting ourselves, forgetting the theater, we must wait and seize the images that arise in us, naked, natural, excessive, and follow these images to the very end.

We must rid ourselves not only of all reality, all verisimilitude, but even of all logic, if at the end of illogic we can still catch a glimpse of life.

In practical terms, and since in spite of everything one must have principles, here are a few concrete ideas:

There is no doubt that everything about the theater which is visibly false contributes to the error from which we are suffering. Look at clowns. They construct the stage with the direction of a glance. There should be nothing on the stage that is not real. But all this has been said. The audience will not tolerate three-dimensional actors moving around in flat perspectives with painted masks. Illusion does not exist for the front-row orchestra. We must either push back the stage or eliminate the whole visual side of the spectacle.

Moreover, in order to make the mental gradations more perceptible, we must establish between Shakespeare and ourselves a kind of physical bridge. An ordinary actor in a costume which will distinguish him from normal life without projecting him into the past will appear to be watching the spectacle without taking part in it. A character in a top hat without makeup who by his appearance would stand out from the crowd. We would have to change the structure of the room so that the stage could be moved according to the needs of the action. We would also have to do away with the strictly spectacle side of the spectacle. People would come not so much to see as to participate.

The audience must have the feeling that they could, without specialized training, do what the actors are doing.

Given these few principles, the rest is up to the skill of the director, who must find the elements of suggestion and style, the architecture or the essential line most likely to evoke the atmosphere and plausibility of the work.

Picasso Exhibit

"I paint my canvases in the future. I compose them in the style which time will confer on them. I am three centuries ahead. I paint future images. I paint them with the eyes of the future. I give them the style I hope they will acquire in the future."

But for the moment Picasso evokes for us only the past. His art is a residue, a "decantation" of painting. It has far too much the quality of end rather than of means. Picasso is straining to think in classifiable, determined forms. And he is classifying them for the future. He defines himself much more than he expresses himself. He expresses himself while contemplating himself. His art now belongs to the past. His last Cubist paintings moved us much more. They were their own manner. They defined only themselves and that small part of the world which they re-created to their liking. Less immediately accessible, they disclosed their secrets gradually. A prodigious life force crackled through their dense lines, an unknown and profound reality in which the whole soul recognized itself.

De profundis, Picasso.

The Umbilicus of Limbo (1925)

VII

WHERE OTHERS PRESENT THEIR WORKS, I claim to do no more than show my mind.
Life consists of burning up questions.
I cannot conceive of work that is detached from life.
I do not like detached creation. Neither can I conceive of the mind as detached from itself. Each of my works, each diagram of myself, each glacial flowering of my inmost soul dribbles over me.

I am as much myself in a letter written to explain the inner contraction of my being and the senseless castration of my life as in an essay which is external to myself and which appears to me as an indifferent pregnancy of my mind.

I suffer because the Mind is not in life and life is not the Mind; I suffer from the Mind as organ, the Mind as interpreter, the Mind as intimidator of things to force them to enter the Mind.

I suspend this book in life, I want it to be eaten away by external things, and above all by all the rending jolts, all the thrashings *of my future self.*

All these pages float around like pieces of ice in my mind. Excuse my absolute freedom. I refuse to make a distinction between any of the moments of myself. I do not recognize any structure in the mind.

We must get rid of the Mind, just as we must get rid of literature. I say that the Mind and life communicate on all levels. I would like to write a Book which would drive men mad, which would be like an open door leading them where they would never have consented to go, in short, a door that opens onto reality.

And this is no more the preface to a book than the poems which are scattered here and there, or the enumeration of all the rages of ill-being.

This is only a piece of ice which is also stuck in my throat.

A GREAT FERVOR, conscious and teeming, bore my soul like a filled abyss. A carnal and resonant wind was blowing, and even the sulphur was thick with it. And tiny rootlets filled this wind like a network of veins, and their intersections flashed. Space was measurable and grating, but without penetrable form. And the center was a mosaic of explosions, a kind of hard cosmic hammer of distorted weight which kept falling like a brow in space, but with a sound that seemed distilled. And the woolly wrapping of the sound had the dull immediacy and the penetration of a living gaze. Yes, space was yielding its whole mental padding in which no thought was yet clear or had replenished its load of objects. But little by little the mass turned like a slimy and powerful nausea, a sort of vast influx of blood, vegetal and thundering. And the rootlets which were trembling at the corners of my mind's eye detached themselves with vertiginous speed from the wind-contracted mass. And all space trembled like a vagina being pillaged by the globe of the burning sky. And something like the beak of a real dove pierced the confused mass of states, all profound thinking at this moment formed layers, resolved itself, became transparent and reduced.

And now we needed a hand which would become the very organ of comprehension. And two or three times more the whole vegetable mass heaved, and each time my eye shifted to a more precise position. The very darkness became profuse and without object. The total frost gained clarity.

With me god-the-hound, and his tongue
which like an arrow pierces the crust
of the double vaulted dome
of the earth that itches him.

And here is the triangle of water
crawling forward like a bug,
but which under the burning bug
returns as a stab.

Under the breasts of horrid earth
god-the-bitch has hidden,
breasts of earth and frozen water
which rot her hollow tongue.

The Umbilicus of Limbo (1925)

And here is the virgin-with-the-hammer
to pound the caves of earth
which the skull of the stellar dog
feels hideously rise.

Doctor,

    There is one point I wanted to stress: that is the importance of the thing on which your injections act; that sort of fundamental slackening of my being, that sinking of my mental level which does not, as one might think, signify any sort of diminution of my morality (of my moral soul) or even of my intelligence but, if you will, of my utilizable intellectuality, of my conceptual abilities, and which has more to do with my own sense of myself than with the part of myself that I show to others.

    That secret and multiform crystallization of thought which chooses its form at a *given moment*. There is an immediate and direct crystallization of the self among all the possible forms, all the modes of thought.

    And now, Doctor, that you are fully aware of the part of me that can be reached (and cured by drugs), of the litigious point of my life, I hope that you will be able to give me a sufficient quantity of subtle liquids, specious agents, mental morphine to raise my sinking, to balance what falls, to reunite what is separated, to rebuild what is destroyed.

    My thought salutes you.

PAUL THE BIRDS, OR THE PLACE OF LOVE

    Paolo Uccello is struggling in the middle of a vast mental web in which he has lost all the pathways of his soul, and even the form and the suspension of his reality.

    Leave your tongue, Paolo Uccello, leave your tongue, my tongue, my tongue, shit, who is speaking, where are you? Beyond, beyond, Mind, Mind, fire, tongues of fire, fire, fire, eat your tongue, old dog, eat his tongue, eat, etc. I tear out my tongue.

    YES.

Meanwhile, Brunelleschi and Donatello are tearing at themselves like the damned. The heavy and poised point of the litigation is nevertheless Paolo Uccello, but he is on another level from them.

There is also Antonin Artaud. But an Antonin Artaud in labor, and on the other side of all mental windows, who makes every effort to think himself elsewhere than there (at the house of André Masson, for example, who has the same physical appearance as Paolo Uccello, the layered appearance of an insect or an idiot, and who is caught like a fly in painting, in *his* painting, which as a consequence is layered).

And besides, it is in him (Antonin Artaud) that Uccello conceives himself, but when he conceives himself he is no longer really in him, etc., etc. The fire in which his panes are steeped has been transmuted into a beautiful fabric.

And Paolo Uccello continues the ticklish operation of this desperate wrenching.

It's a question of a problem which was presented to the mind of Antonin Artaud, but Antonin Artaud doesn't need problems, he's already pissed off enough at his own thoughts, and among other things because he confronted himself and discovered that he was a bad actor, for example, yesterday, at the movies, in *Surcouf*, without having this grub of Little Paul come and eat his tongue.

The theater was built and conceived by him. He stuck in a lot of arcades and levels on which all his characters fling themselves about like dogs.

There is a level for Paolo Uccello, and a level for Brunelleschi and Donatello, and a little level for Selvaggia, Paolo's wife.

Two, three, ten problems crisscrossed suddenly with the zigzagging of their spiritual tongues and all the planetary shiftings of their levels.

As the curtain rises, Selvaggia is dying.

Paolo Uccello enters and asks her how she feels. The question has the knack of exasperating Brunelleschi, who breaks the solely mental atmosphere of the play with a clenched and physical fist.

The Umbilicus of Limbo (1925)

BRUNELLESCHI—Pig, madman.
PAOLO UCCELLO, *sneezing three times*—Idiot.

But first let us describe the characters. Let's give them each a physical form, a voice, a costume.

Paul the Birds has an inaudible voice, the walk of an insect, and a robe which is too big for him.

Brunelleschi, however, has a real stage voice, resonant and substantial. He looks like Dante.

Donatello is somewhere between: St. Francis of Assisi before the Stigmata.

The action takes place on three levels.

It goes without saying that Brunelleschi is in love with the wife of Paul the Birds. He reproaches him, among other things, for letting her starve to death. Does one starve to death in the Mind?

For we are *solely* in the Mind.

The drama exists on several levels and has several aspects, it consists as much in the stupid question of whether Paolo Uccello will finally acquire enough human compassion to give Selvaggia something to eat as it does in knowing which of the three or four characters will remain on his level the longest.

For Paolo Uccello represents the Mind, not exactly *pure*, but *detached*.

Donatello is the Mind exalted. He no longer looks at the earth, but he is still connected to it with his feet.

Brunelleschi, however, is completely rooted in the earth, and it is in an earthy and sexual way that he desires Selvaggia. He thinks only of copulating.

Paolo Uccello, though, is not unaware of sexuality, but he sees it as glazed and mercurial, and as cold as ether.

And as for Donatello, he has stopped missing it.

Paolo Uccello has nothing under his robe. He has only a bridge in place of a heart.

At Selvaggia's feet there is a plant which should not be there.

All of a sudden Brunelleschi feels his cock swell and become enormous. He cannot hold it back and out flies a great white bird, like sperm which turns and spirals in the air.

Dear Sir,

Don't you think this might be the time to try to connect the Cinema with the intimate reality of the brain? I am sending you some excerpts from a screenplay which I hope you will like. You will see that its mental level, its inner conception give it a place in written language. And to make the transition less abrupt, I have prefaced it with two essays which tend progressively—I mean as they develop—to break down into images that are less and less disinterested.

This screenplay is inspired, if remotely, by a book which is certainly poisoned and exhausted, but I am still grateful to it for helping me to find images. And since I am not telling a story but simply giving a series of images, no one will mind that I present only fragments. I also have at your disposal two or three pages in which I make an attempt at surreality, try to make it yield its soul, give up its marvelous venom. These pages could preface the whole, and if you like I will send them to you soon.

I am, etc.

Description of a Physical State

a sharp burning sensation in the limbs,

muscles twisted, as if flayed, the sense of being made of glass and breakable, a fear, a recoiling from movement and noise. An unconscious confusion in walking, gestures, movements. A will that is perpetually strained to make the simplest gestures,

renunciation of the simple gesture,

a staggering and central fatigue, a kind of gasping fatigue. Movements must be recomposed, a sort of deathlike fatigue, a fatigue of the mind in carrying out the simplest muscular contraction, the gesture of grasping, of unconsciously clinging to something,

must be sustained by a constant effort of the will.

A fatigue as old as the world, the sense of having to carry

The Umbilicus of Limbo (1925)

one's body around, a feeling of incredible fragility which becomes a shattering pain,

a state of painful numbness, a kind of numbness localized in the skin which does not inhibit any movement but which changes the internal sensation of a limb and gives the simple act of standing up straight the value of a victorious effort.

Probably localized in the skin, but felt as the radical elimination of a limb, and presenting to the brain only images of limbs that are threadlike and woolly, images of limbs that are far away and not where they should be. A sort of internal fracturing of the whole nervous system.

A shifting vertigo, a sort of oblique bewilderment which accompanies every effort, a coagulation of heat which grips the entire surface of the skull or is cut into pieces, shifting patches of heat.

A painful exacerbation of the skull, a sharp pressure of the nerves, the nape of the neck straining after its pain, temples turning to glass or marble, a head trampled by horses.

One must speak now of the disembodiment of reality, of that sort of rupture that seems determined to multiply itself between things and the feeling they produce in our mind, the place they should take.

This instantaneous classification of things in the cells of the mind, not so much in their logical order as in their emotional or affective order

(which no longer holds):

things have no more odor, no more sex. But their logical order is also sometimes broken precisely because of their lack of emotional aroma. Words rot at the unconscious summons of the brain, all the words for any kind of mental operation, and especially those operations which affect the most habitual, most active responses of the mind.

A SLENDER BELLY. A belly of fine powder, as in a picture. At the foot of the belly, an exploded grenade.

The grenade deploys a flaky network which rises like tongues of fire, cold fire.

The network takes the belly and turns it over. But the belly does not turn.

These are veins of winy blood, blood mixed with saffron and sulphur, but a sulphur sweetened with water.

Above the belly one can see breasts. And higher up, and in depth, but on another level of the mind, a sun burns, but in such a way that it seems to be the breast that burns. And at the foot of the grenade, a bird.

The sun has a kind of look. But a look that would look at the sun. The look is a cone that is overturned on the sun. And all space is like a frozen music, but a vast, profound music, well constructed and secret, and full of congealed ramifications.

And all this held together with columns and with a kind of architect's watercolor wash which connects the belly with reality.

The canvas is hollow and layered. The painting is well enclosed in the canvas. It is like a closed circle, a kind of abyss which turns and divides into two parts at the middle. It is like a mind that sees itself and grows hollow, it is kneaded and shaped incessantly by the clenched hands of the mind. But the mind sows its phosphorus.

The mind is firm. It has a foothold in the world. The grenade, the belly, the breasts, are like testimonial proofs of reality. There is a dead bird, there is the foliage of columns. The air is full of pencil strokes, pencil strokes like knife slashes, like the scratches of a magic fingernail. The air is adequately stirred.

And now it is arranging itself in cells in each of which grows a grain of unreality. The cells settle each in its place, in the shape of a fan,

around the belly, in front of the sun, beyond the bird, and around this network of sulphured water.

But the architecture is indifferent to the cells, it supports and does not speak.

Each cell carries an egg in which gleams what germ? In each cell an egg is suddenly born. In each there is a swarming that is inhuman but limpid, the stratifications of an arrested universe.

Each cell carries its egg and presents it to us; but it matters little to the egg whether it is chosen or rejected.

Not all the cells carry an egg. In some appears a whorl. And

The Umbilicus of Limbo (1925)

in the air a larger whorl hangs, but as if already sulphurated, or still made of phosphorus and wrapped in unreality. And this whorl has all the importance of the most powerful thought.

The belly evokes surgery and the Morgue, the construction yard, the public square, and the operating table. The body of the belly seems made of granite or marble or plaster, but a plaster that has set. There is a compartment for a mountain. The sky's foam surrounds the mountain with a cool, translucent ring. The air around the mountain is loud, pious, legendary, forbidden. Access to the mountain is forbidden. The mountain has its own place in the soul. It is the horizon of something that constantly recedes. It gives the feeling of an eternal horizon.

As for me, I have described this painting with tears, for this painting touches me to the heart. In it I feel my thought unfold as in an ideal, absolute space, but a space whose form could be brought into reality. I fall into it from heaven.

And each of my fibers uncurls and finds its place in fixed compartments. I return to it as to my source; in it I sense the place and the arrangement of my mind. The person who painted this picture is the greatest painter in the world. To André Masson, his due.

Dark Poet

Dark poet, the breast of a virgin
haunts you,
bitter poet, life boils
and the city burns,
and the sky sucks up its rain,
your pen scratches at the heart of life.

Forest, forest, eyes swarm
over the multiple pine seeds;
hair of the storm, poets
ride off on horses, on dogs.

Eyes rage, tongues curl,
the sky rushes into nostrils
like a nourishing blue milk;
women, hard vinegar hearts,
I am hanging from your mouths.

Letter to the Legislator of the Law on Narcotics

Dear legislator,
    Legislator of the law of 1916, supplemented by the decree of July 1917 on narcotics, you are an ass.
    Your law serves only to annoy druggists all over the world without lowering the level of drug addiction in the nation, because:
    1. The number of drug addicts who obtain their supplies from drugstores is negligible.
    2. The real addicts don't get their supplies from drugstores.
    3. Addicts who get their supplies from drugstores are *all* sick.
    4. The number of addicts who are sick is negligible in comparison with the number of addicts who are seeking pleasure.
    5. Pharmaceutical restrictions on drugs will never bother pleasure-seeking and organized addicts.
    6. There will always be pushers.
    7. There will always be people who become addicts through weakness, through passion.
    8. Sick addicts have an inalienable right within society, which is that they be left the hell alone.
    It is above all a question of conscience.
    The law on narcotics places in the hands of the inspector-usurper of public health the right to have control over human suffering; it is a pretension peculiar to modern medicine to try to dictate to the individual conscience. All the bleatings of the official charter are powerless against this phenomenon of conscience: namely, that I am the master of my pain, even more than of my death. Every man is the judge, and the exclusive judge, of

The Umbilicus of Limbo (1925)

the quantity of physical suffering or of mental emptiness that he can honestly stand.

Whether I am lucid or not, there is a lucidity which no sickness will ever take from me, that is the lucidity which dictates to me the sense of my physical life.* And if I have lost my lucidity,

---

* I am aware that there exist serious disturbances of the personality which may even lead the conscious self to the loss of its own individuality: consciousness remains intact but no longer recognizes itself as belonging to itself (and no longer recognizes itself on any level).

There are disturbances that are less serious, or rather less fundamental, but much more painful and more important to the individual and somehow more *damaging* to vitality. These occur when consciousness appropriates, truly recognizes as belonging to it, a whole series of phenomena of dislocation and dissolution of its forces in the midst of which its substance is destroyed.

These are the disturbances I have in mind.

But the important question is whether life is not more damaged by a disembodiment of thought which preserves a portion of consciousness than by the projection of this consciousness into an indefinable elsewhere which strictly preserves its thought. The point is not that this thought makes mistakes, that it does not make sense; the point is that it is produced, that it throws off sparks, mad though they may be. The point is that it exists. And I maintain that I, among others, have no thought.

This makes my friends laugh.

And yet!

For by *having thought* I do not mean seeing correctly or even *thinking* correctly; having thought to me means *sustaining* one's thought, being able to manifest it to oneself and to have it respond to all the circumstances of feeling and of life. But mainly to have it *respond to oneself.*

For here there arises that indefinable and murky phenomenon which I despair of making anyone understand, especially my friends (or better still, my enemies, those who take me for the shadow *I feel myself to be*—and they do not think to say correctly, shadows twice over, because of them and because of me).

As for my friends, I have never seen them like me, with their tongues hanging out and their minds horribly stalled.

Yes, my thought knows itself and it now despairs of reaching itself. It knows itself, by which I mean that it suspects itself; and in any case it no longer feels itself.—I am talking about the physical life, the substantial life of thought (and this brings me back to my point), I am talking about that minimal and crude version of conceptual life—which has not yet reached language but is capable of reaching it when required—without which the soul cannot go on living and life is as if extinguished.—Those

there is only one thing for medicine to do, and that is to give me those substances which permit me to recover the use of that lucidity.

You gentlemen who are the dictators of the pharmaceutical profession in France, you are a pack of impotent curs. There is one thing which you had better take into account: that is that opium is that inviolable and despotic substance which allows those who have had the misfortune to lose the life of their souls the possibility of recovering it.

There is a disease against which opium is sovereign, and that disease is called Anguish—mental, medical, physiological, logical, or pharmaceutical, as you like.

Anguish which drives men mad.
Anguish which drives men to suicide.
Anguish which condemns them to hell.
Anguish which medicine does not know.
Anguish which your doctor does not understand.
Anguish which violates life.
Anguish which constricts the umbilical cord of life.

By your iniquitous law you place in the hands of persons in whom I have no confidence whatsoever—medical asses, druggists

---

who complain of the inadequacies of human thought and of their own inability to be satisfied with what they call their thought are confusing and erroneously placing on the same level clearly differentiated states of thought and of form, the lowest of which is no more than language, whereas the highest is still mind.

If what I know to be my thought were available to me, I might perhaps have written *The Umbilicus of Limbo*, but I would have written it in a completely different way. People tell me that I think, because I have not completely stopped thinking and because in spite of everything my mind sustains itself at a certain level and occasionally gives proofs of its existence which no one is willing to recognize as feeble and devoid of interest. But thinking means something more to me than not being completely dead. It means being in touch with oneself at every moment; it means not ceasing for a single moment to feel oneself in one's inmost being, in the unformulated mass of one's life, in the substance of one's reality; it means not feeling in oneself an enormous hole, a crucial absence; it means always feeling one's thought equal to one's thought, however inadequate the form one is able to give it. But my thinking sins not only because of its weakness, but also because of its quantity. I always think at an inferior rate.

The Umbilicus of Limbo (1925)

of dung, dishonest judges, doctors, midwives, pedantic inspectors —the authority over my anguish, an anguish which in me is as acute as the needles of all the compasses of hell.

Whether the tremors are of the body or of the soul, the human seismograph does not exist that would enable someone looking at me to reach a more precise evaluation of my suffering than the lightning flash of my own mind!

All the fortuitous scientific knowledge of mankind is not superior to the direct knowledge that I can have of my being. I am the only judge of what is within me.

Get back to your attics, medical vermin, and you too, Monsieur Sheeplike Legislator, it is not love of mankind that makes you rave, but a tradition of idiocy. Your ignorance of what a man is is equaled only by your stupidity in limiting him. May your law be visited on your father, your mother, your wife, your children, and all your descendants. And now choke on your law.

The poets lift up hands
where living acids tremble,
on tables the idol sky
is braced, and the subtle sex

dips an icy tongue
into each hole, each space
which the sky leaves in its wake.

The ground is fouled with souls
and women with pretty cunts
whose miniature corpses
uncurl their mummies.

THERE IS AN ACID AND MURKY ANGUISH, as powerful as a knife, whose torments have the weight of the earth, an anguish that comes in flashes, that is punctuated by abysses as dense and serried as insects, like a kind of tough vermin whose every motion is arrested, an anguish in which the mind strangles and cuts itself off—kills itself.

This anguish consumes nothing that does not belong to it; it is born of its own asphyxiation.

It is a *congealing* of the marrow, an absence of mental fire, a failure of the circulation of life.

But the anguish of opium has another hue, it does not have this metaphysical flavor, this marvelous imperfection of tone. I imagine it as full of echoes, caves, labyrinths, and turns; full of speaking tongues of fire, of mental eyes in action, and of the clapping of a thunder that is dark and full of reason.

But I imagine the soul under opium as well centered and yet infinitely divisible, and transportable like a *thing which exists*. I imagine the soul as feeling, I see it struggle and consent at the same time, and turn its tongues in all directions, multiply its sex—and kill itself.

One must experience the real unraveled void, the void that no longer has an organ. The void of opium contains as it were the shape of a brow that thinks, that has located the position of the black pit.

I am talking about the absence of a pit, about a kind of suffering that is cold and without images, without feeling, and which is like an indescribable collision of failures.

The Spurt of Blood

THE YOUNG MAN
    I love you and life is wonderful.
THE GIRL, *with a tremor of intensity in her voice*
    You love me and life is wonderful.
THE YOUNG MAN, *in a lower tone*
    I love you and life is wonderful.
THE GIRL, *in an even lower tone than his*
    You love me and life is wonderful.
THE YOUNG MAN, *suddenly turning away*
    I love you.
        A silence.

The Umbilicus of Limbo (1925)

Come here where I can see you.
THE GIRL, *same business, moves so that she is facing him*
There.
THE YOUNG MAN, *in an excited, high-pitched voice*
I love you, I am tall, I am clear, I am full, I am dense.
THE GIRL, *in the same high-pitched voice*
We love each other.
THE YOUNG MAN
We are intense. Oh, what a well-made world.
A silence. There is heard the sound of a huge wheel turning and making a wind. A hurricane divides them in two.

Then one sees two stars collide and a series of legs of living flesh falling together with feet, hands, heads of hair, masks, colonnades, porticoes, temples, and alembics which fall, but more and more slowly, as if they were falling in space, then three scorpions one after the other, and finally a frog, and a scarab which lands with exasperating, nauseating slowness.
THE YOUNG MAN, *shouting at the top of his lungs*
Heaven has gone mad.
He looks at the sky.
Let's get out of here.
He pushes THE GIRL *in front of him.*
Enter a medieval KNIGHT *in an enormous suit of armor, followed by a wet nurse who supports her bosom with both hands and pants because of her swollen breasts.*
THE KNIGHT
Leave your tits alone. Give me my papers.
THE WET NURSE, *giving a shrill scream*
Oh! Oh! Oh!
THE KNIGHT
What the hell is the matter with you?
THE WET NURSE
Our girl over there, with him.
THE KNIGHT
Shut up, there's no girl!

THE WET NURSE
  I tell you, they're fucking.
THE KNIGHT
  I don't give a shit if they're fucking.
THE WET NURSE
  Lecher.
THE KNIGHT
  Cow.
THE WET NURSE, *thrusting her hands into her pockets, which are as enormous as her breasts*
  Pimp.
    Quickly she throws him his papers.
THE KNIGHT
  Phiote, let me eat.
    The WET NURSE *runs off.*
    He gets up, and out of each paper he produces an enormous slice of Swiss cheese.
    Suddenly he coughs and chokes.
THE KNIGHT, *with his mouth full*
  Unh. Unh. Show me your breasts. Show me your breasts. Where did she go?
    He runs off. The YOUNG MAN *returns.*
THE YOUNG MAN
  I saw, I knew, I understood. Here are the main square, the priest, the shoemaker, the vegetable market, the threshold of the church, the lantern of the brothel, the scales of justice. I can't stand it any more!
    A PRIEST, *a* SHOEMAKER, *a* BEADLE, *a* BAWD, *a* JUDGE, *a fruit and vegetable* PEDDLER *enter like shadows.*
THE YOUNG MAN
  I have lost her, give her back.
ALL, *in different voices*
  Who, who, who, who.
THE YOUNG MAN
  My wife.
THE BEADLE, *very self-important*
  Your wife, eh? Joker!
THE YOUNG MAN
  Joker! She may be yours!

The Umbilicus of Limbo (1925)

THE BEADLE, *slapping his brow*
> It may be true.
>> *He runs off.*
>> *The* PRIEST *now breaks away from the group and puts his arm around the* YOUNG MAN's *neck.*

THE PRIEST, *as if confessing someone*
> To what part of her body did you most often allude?

THE YOUNG MAN
> To God.
>> *The* PRIEST, *discountenanced by his reply, immediately adopts a Swiss accent.*

THE PRIEST, *with a Swiss accent*
> But that's out of date. We don't look at it that way. For that you must go to volcanoes, to earthquakes. As for us, we must be content with the little obscenities of man in the confessional. And that's it, that's life.

THE YOUNG MAN, *very impressed*
> So that's life! Well, everything is a mess.

THE PRIEST, *still in a Swiss accent*
> Of course.
>> *Suddenly it becomes night on the stage. The earth trembles. Thunder rages, lightning zigzags in all directions, and during the lightning flashes you see all the characters begin to run, get in each other's way, fall down, pick themselves up, and run around like madmen.*
>> *At a certain point an enormous hand seizes the* BAWD's *hair, which catches fire and expands visibly.*

A GIGANTIC VOICE
> Bitch, look at your body!
>> *The* BAWD's *body appears absolutely naked and hideous under her blouse and skirt, which become like glass.*

THE BAWD
> Leave me alone, God.
>> *She bites God on the wrist. A huge spurt of blood slashes across the stage, and by the light of a particularly large flash of lightning the* PRIEST *can be seen making the sign of the cross.*
>> *When the lights come on again, all the characters are*

dead and their bodies are lying all over the ground. The only ones left are the YOUNG MAN *and the* BAWD, *who are looking at each other hungrily.*
 The BAWD *falls into the* YOUNG MAN's *arms.*
THE BAWD, *sighing and as if at the height of orgasm*
 Tell me how it happened.
 The YOUNG MAN *buries his face in his hands.*
 The WET NURSE *returns, carrying the* GIRL *under her arm like a package. The* GIRL *is dead. She drops her on the ground, where she collapses and becomes as flat as a pancake.*
 The WET NURSE *has lost her breasts. Her chest is completely flat.*
 At this point the KNIGHT *enters, seizes the* WET NURSE, *and shakes her violently.*
THE KNIGHT, *in a terrible voice*
 Where did you put it? Give me my Swiss cheese.
THE NURSE, *gaily*
 Here.
 She lifts her skirts.
 The YOUNG MAN *tries to run, but he freezes like a petrified marionette.*
THE YOUNG MAN, *who looks suspended in midair, in the voice of a ventriloquist*
 Don't hurt Mama.
THE KNIGHT
 Damn her.
 He covers his face in horror.
 Now an enormous number of scorpions emerge from under the WET NURSE's *skirts and begin to swarm in her vagina, which swells and splits, becomes vitreous, and flashes like the sun.*
 The YOUNG MAN *and the* BAWD *flee like victims of brain surgery.*
THE GIRL, *getting up in a daze*
 The virgin! So that's what he was looking for.

CURTAIN

From *The Nerve Meter* (1925)

. . . .

I REALLY FELT that you were breaking up the atmosphere around me, that you were clearing the way to allow me to advance, to provide room for an impossible space for that in me which was as yet only potential, for a whole virtual germination which must be sucked into life by the space that offered itself.

I often put myself into this state of impossible absurdity in order to try to generate thought in myself. There are a few of us in this era who have tried to get hold of things, to create within ourselves spaces for life, spaces which did not exist and which did not seem to belong in actual space.

I have always been struck by that obstinacy of the mind in wanting to think in terms of dimensions and spaces, and in fixing on arbitrary states of things in order to think, in thinking in segments, in crystalloids, so that each mode of being remains fixed at a starting point, so that thought is not in immediate and uninterrupted communication with things—this fixation and this immobilization, this tendency of the soul to construct monuments occurring, as it were, BEFORE THOUGHT. Evidently this is the right condition for creativity.

But I am even more struck by that inexhaustible, that meteoric illusion which inspires in us those predetermined, circumscribed conceptual structures, those crystallized segments of soul, which seem to form a great plastic page in osmotic relation to the rest of reality. And surreality is like a contracting of the osmosis, a kind of reversed communication. Far from seeing it as a lessening of control, I see it, on the contrary, as a greater control, but a control which, instead of acting, doubts: a control which inhibits contacts with ordinary reality and allows more subtle and rarefied contacts, contacts pared down to a cord which ignites but never breaks.

I imagine a soul that is worked upon and, as it were, sulphured and phosphorated by these contacts, as the only acceptable state of reality.

But I know not what nameless, unknown lucidity gives me the tone and the cry of these contacts and makes me experience them myself. I experience them with a certain insoluble totality, I mean a totality about whose emotional impact I have not the slightest doubt. And I, in relation to these disturbing contacts, am in a state of minimal tremor, I would have you imagine an arrested void, a mass of mind buried somewhere, become virtuality.

AN ACTOR IS SEEN as if through crystals.
    Inspiration in stages.
    One mustn't let in too much literature.

I HAVE ASPIRED NO FURTHER than the clockwork of the soul, I have transcribed only the pain of an abortive adjustment.
    I am a total abyss. Those who believed me capable of a whole pain, a beautiful pain, a dense and fleshy anguish, an anguish which is a mixture of objects, an effervescent grinding of forces rather than a suspended point
    —and yet with restless, uprooting impulses which come from the confrontation of my forces with these abysses of offered finality
    (from the confrontation of forces of powerful size),
    and there is nothing left but the voluminous abysses, the immobility, the cold—
    in short, those who attributed to me more life, who thought me at an earlier stage in the fall of the self, who believed me immersed in a tormented noise, in a violent darkness with which I struggled
    —are lost in the shadows of man.

IN SLEEP, nerves tensed the whole length of my legs.
    Sleep came from a shifting of belief, the pressure eased, absurdity stepped on my toes.

IT MUST BE UNDERSTOOD that all of intelligence is only a vast contingency, and that one can lose it, not like a lunatic who is dead, but like a living person who is in life and who feels working

From *The Nerve Meter* (1925)

on himself its attraction and its inspiration (of intelligence, not of life).
The titillations of intelligence and this sudden reversal of contending parties.
Words halfway to intelligence.
This possibility of thinking in reverse and of suddenly reviling one's thought.
This dialogue in thought.
The ingestion, the breaking off of everything.
And all at once this trickle of water on a volcano, the thin, slow falling of the mind.

To FIND ONESELF AGAIN in a state of extreme shock, clarified by unreality, with, in a corner of oneself, some fragments of the real world.

To THINK WITHOUT THE SLIGHTEST BREAKING OFF, without pitfalls in my thought, without one of those sudden disappearances to which my marrow is accustomed as a transmitter of currents.
My marrow is sometimes amused by these games, sometimes takes pleasure in these games, takes pleasure in these furtive abductions over which the sense of my thought presides.
At times all I would need is a single word, a simple little word of no importance, to be great, to speak in the voice of the prophets: a word of witness, a precise word, a subtle word, a word well steeped in my marrow, gone out of me, which would stand at the outer limit of my being,
and which, for everyone else, would be nothing.
I am the witness, I am the only witness of myself. This crust of words, these imperceptible whispered transformations of my thought, of that small part of my thought which I claim has already been formulated, and which miscarries,
I am the only person who can measure its extent.

ANTONIN ARTAUD

A KIND OF CONSTANT LEAKAGE of the normal level of reality.

UNDER THIS CRUST OF SKIN AND BONE which is my head there is a persistence of anguish, not like a moral point, not like the ratiocinations of a ridiculously fastidious nature, or a nature inhabited by a leaven of anxieties which are constantly rising to the top, but like a (decantation)
    within,
    like the dispossession of my vital substance,
    like the physical and essential loss
    (I mean loss from the standpoint of essence)
                          of a sense.

A POWERLESSNESS to crystallize unconsciously the broken point of the mechanism to any degree at all.

WHAT IS DIFFICULT is to find one's place and to reestablish communication with one's self. Everything depends on a certain flocculation of things, on the clustering of all these mental gems around a point which has yet to be found.
    Here, then, is what I think about thought:
    INSPIRATION CERTAINLY EXISTS.
    And there is a phosphorescent point at which all reality is recovered, but changed, transformed—and by what??—a point of magical utilization of things. And I believe in mental meteorites, in private cosmogonies.

DO YOU KNOW what it means to have a suspended sensibility, this kind of tremendous vitality split in two, this point of necessary cohesion to which being can no longer rise, this place of terror, this place of prostration?

From *The Nerve Meter* (1925)

Dear Friends,

What you mistook for my works were merely the waste products of myself, those scrapings of the soul that the normal man does not welcome.

What concerns me is not whether my illness has retreated or advanced but the suffering and the persistent blasting of my mind.

Here I am back at M., where I am experiencing again the sensation of sluggishness and dizziness, this sudden and insane need for sleep, this abrupt loss of strength accompanied by a feeling of profound suffering, of instantaneous stupefaction.

HERE IS SOMEONE in whose mind no place becomes inured, and who does not suddenly feel his soul on the left, where the heart is. Here is someone for whom life is a point, and for whom the soul has no edges and the mind no beginnings.

I AM AN IDIOT by the suppression of thought, by the malformation of thought; I am vacant by the stupefaction of my tongue.

Malformation, disorganization of a certain number of those vitreous corpuscles of which you make such unconsidered use. A use which you do not know, at which you have never been present.

All the terms in which I choose to think are for me TERMS in the literal sense of the word, that is, true terminations, borders of my mental   ,* of all the states to which I have subjected my thinking. I am truly LOCALIZED by my terms, and if I say that I am LOCALIZED by my terms, I mean that I do not recognize them as valid in my thought. I am truly paralyzed by my terms, by a series of terminations. And however ELSEWHERE my thought may be at these moments, I have no choice but to bring it out through these terms, however contradictory to itself,

---

* Blank space in the original French.—*Trans.*

however parallel, however ambiguous they may be, or pay the penalty of no longer being able to think.

IF ONLY ONE COULD taste one's void, if one could really rest in one's void, and this void were not a certain kind of being but not quite death either.
    It is so hard to no longer exist, to no longer be in something. The real pain is to feel one's thought shift within oneself. But thought as a fixed point is certainly not painful.
    I have reached the point where I am no longer in touch with life, but still have all the appetites and the insistent titillation of being. I have only one occupation left: to remake myself.

WHAT I LACK is words that correspond to each minute of my state of mind.
    "But that's normal, everyone at times is at a loss for words, you're too hard on yourself, no one would think so to hear you, you express yourself perfectly in French, you attach too much importance to words."
    You are asses, from the intelligent to the dimwitted, from the perceptive to the obtuse, you are asses, I mean that you are dogs, I mean that you bark in the streets, that you are determined not to understand. I know myself, and that is enough for me, and that should be enough, I know myself because I watch myself, I watch Antonin Artaud.
    "You know yourself, but we see you, we see very well what you are doing."
    "Yes, but you cannot see my thought."
    At each of the stages of my thinking mechanism there are gaps, halts—understand me, I do not mean in time, I mean in a certain kind of space (I know what I mean); and I do not mean a series of thoughts, I do not mean a full sequence of thoughts, I mean a SINGLE thought, only one, and an INNER thought; I do not mean one of Pascal's thoughts, a philosopher's thought, I mean a contorted fixation, the sclerosis of a certain state. Take that!

From *The Nerve Meter* (1925)

I consider myself in my minutiae. I put my finger on the precise point of the fault, the unadmitted slide. For the mind is more reptilian than you yourselves, messieurs, it slips away snakelike, to the point where it damages our language, I mean it leaves it in suspense.

I am the man who has most felt the stupefying confusion of his speech in its relations with thought. I am the man who has most accurately charted the moment of his most intimate, his most imperceptible lapses. I lose myself in my thought, actually, the way one dreams, the way one suddenly slips back into one's thought. I am the man who knows the inmost recesses of loss.

ALL WRITING IS GARBAGE.

People who come out of nowhere to try to put into words any part of what goes on in their minds are pigs.

The whole literary scene is a pigpen, especially today.

All those who have points of reference in their minds, I mean on a certain side of their heads, in well-localized areas of their brains, all those who are masters of their language, all those for whom words have meanings, all those for whom words have meanings, all those for whom there exist higher levels of the soul and currents of thought, those who represent the spirit of the times, and who have named these currents of thought, I am thinking of their meticulous industry and of that mechanical creaking which their minds give off in all directions,

—are pigs.

Those for whom certain words have meaning, and certain modes of being, those who are so precise, those for whom emotions can be classified and who quibble over some point of their hilarious classifications, those who still believe in "terms," those who discuss the ranking ideologies of the age, those whom women discuss so intelligently and the women themselves who speak so well and who discuss the currents of the age, those who still believe in an orientation of the mind, those who follow paths, who drop names, who recommend books,

—these are the worst pigs of all.

You are quite unnecessary, young man!

ANTONIN ARTAUD

No, I am thinking of bearded critics.

And I have already told you: no works, no language, no words, no mind, nothing.

Nothing but a fine Nerve Meter.

A kind of incomprehensible stopping place in the mind, right in the middle of everything.

And do not expect me to name this everything, to tell you how many parts it is divided into, don't expect me to tell you its weight, don't think that you can get me to discuss it, and that while discussing I will forget myself and that I will thus begin, without realizing it, to THINK—and that it will be illuminated, that it will live, that it will deck itself in a multitude of words, all with well-polished meanings, all different, and able to express all the attitudes and nuances of a very sensitive and penetrating thought.

Ah, these states that are never named, these eminent positions of the soul, ah, these intermissions of the mind, ah, these minuscule failures which are the nourishment of my hours, ah, this population teeming with facts—I always use the same words and really I don't seem to advance very much in my thinking, but actually I am advancing more than you, bearded asses, pertinent pigs, masters of the false word, wrappers of portraits, serial writers, groundlings, cattle raisers, entomologists, plague of my speech.

I told you that I have lost my speech, but that is no reason for you to persist in speaking.

Enough, I shall be understood in ten years by people who will be doing what you do today. Then my geysers will be known, my ice floes will be seen, the secret of adulterating my poisons will have been learned, the games of my soul will be revealed.

Then all my hairs, all my mental veins will be buried in lime, then my bestiary will be perceived and my mystique will have become a hat. Then they will see the joints of the stones steam, and arborescent bouquets of mental eyes will be crystallized in glossaries, then they will see stone meteors fall, then they will see ropes, then they will understand a geometry without space, they will learn what is meant by the configuration of the mind, and they will understand how I lost my mind.

Then they will understand why my mind is not here, then they

From *The Nerve Meter* (1925)

will see all language drain away, all minds run dry, all tongues shrivel up, human faces will flatten and deflate as if sucked in by hot-air vents, and this lubricating membrane will continue to float in the air, this lubricating caustic membrane, this double-thick, many-leveled membrane of infinite crevices, this melancholy and vitreous membrane, but so sensitive, so pertinent itself, so capable of multiplying, dividing, turning with a flash of crevices, senses, drugs, penetrating and noxious irrigations,
    then all this will be accepted,
    and I shall have no further need to speak.

Fragments of a
Diary from Hell (1925)

IX

for André Gaillard

NEITHER MY CRY nor my fever belongs to me. This disintegration of my secondary forces, of these concealed elements of thought and of the soul, try to imagine merely their constancy.

This thing which is halfway between the color of my typical atmosphere and the pinnacle of my reality.

I am in need not so much of nourishment as of a kind of elementary consciousness.
This nucleus of life to which the emission of thought clings.
A nucleus of central asphyxia.

Simply to settle on a clear truth, that is, one that has a single edge.

This problem of the emaciation of my self no longer appears solely under the aspect of pain. I feel that new factors are intervening in the adulteration of my life and that I have a kind of new consciousness of my inner leakage.

I see in the act of throwing the dice and of risking the affirmation of some intuitively felt truth, however uncertain, my whole reason for living.

I remain for hours under the impression of one idea, one sound. My emotion does not develop in time, does not have a temporal sequence. The ebbing of my soul is in perfect accord with the absolute ideality of mind.

To confront the metaphysics which I have created for myself as a result of this emptiness I carry within.

This pain driven into me like a wedge at the center of my purest reality, at that region of the sensibility where the two worlds of body and mind come together—I have learned to distract myself from it by means of a false suggestion.
For the space of that minute which is marked by the illumination of a lie, I concoct an idea of escape, I rush down a false trail

prompted by my blood. I close the eyes of my intelligence and, giving voice to the unformulated within me, I offer myself the illusion of a system whose terms elude me. But this moment of error leaves me with the sense of having wrested from the unknown something real. I believe in spontaneous conjurations. On the paths along which my blood draws me it cannot be that one day I will not discover a truth.

The paralysis overtakes me and hinders me more and more from coming back to myself. I no longer have any support, any base . . . I look for myself I know not where. My thought can no longer go where my emotions and the images that rise within me drive it. I feel castrated even in my slightest impulses. I finally manage to see the daylight through the barrier of myself by dint of renunciations in every phase of my intelligence and my sensibility. It must be understood that what is damaged in me is the living man, and that this paralysis that chokes me is at the center of my ordinary personality and not of my sense of being a man of destiny. I am definitively apart from life. My torment is as subtle and refined as it is bitter. It is necessary for me to make insane efforts of the imagination, multiplied tenfold by the grip of this strangling asphyxia, in order to succeed in *thinking* my disease. And if I persist in this pursuit, in this need to pin down once and for all the state of my suffocation . . .

You are quite wrong to allude to this paralysis which threatens me. It does threaten me and it gains ground from one day to the next. It exists already like a horrible reality. To be sure, I still have the use of my limbs (but for how long?), but I have long since ceased to be in control of my mind, and my unconscious governs me completely with impulses which arise from the depths of my nervous rages and from the whirling of my blood. Hurried and rapid images, which speak to my mind only words of anger and blind hatred, but which pass as quickly as the stabs of a knife or flashes of lightning in a congested sky.

I am stigmatized by a living death in which real death holds no terrors for me.

Fragments of a Diary from Hell (1925)

These terrifying forms which advance on me, I feel that the despair they bring is alive. It slips into this nucleus of life beyond which the paths of eternity extend. It is truly an eternal separation. They slip their knives into this center where I feel myself a man, they sever those vital ties which bind me to the dream of my lucid reality.

Forms of a fundamental despair (truly vital),
crossroads of separation,
crossroads of the sensation of my flesh,
abandoned by my body,
abandoned by all possible human feeling.
I can compare it only to the state in which one finds oneself in the throes of a delirium brought on by fever during a serious illness.

It is this contradiction between my inner facility and my exterior difficulty which creates the torment of which I am dying.

Time may pass and the social upheavals of the world may devastate the ideas of men, I am safe from all ideas steeped in phenomena. Leave me to my extinguished clouds, to my immortal impotence, to my unreasonable hopes. But let it be known that I renounce none of my errors. If I have made mistakes, it is the fault of my flesh, but these lights which my mind allows to filter through from one hour to the next are my flesh whose blood is sheathed in lightning.

He talks to me about Narcissism, I retort that it is a question of my life. I worship not the self but the flesh, in the palpable sense of the word. All things touch me only insofar as they affect my flesh, insofar as they coincide with it, and only at that point where they arouse my flesh, not beyond. Nothing touches me, nothing interests me except what addresses itself *directly* to my flesh. And now he talks to me about the other. I retort that the Self and the Other are two distinct terms which should not be confused, and are precisely the two opposing terms that maintain the equilibrium of the flesh.

I feel the ground under my thought crumble, and I am led to consider the terms I use without the support of their inner meaning, their personal substratum. And even more than that, the point at which this substratum seems to connect with my life suddenly becomes strangely sensitive and potential. I have the notion of a space that is unforeseen and fixed, where normally all is movement, communication, interference, passage.

But this erosion which attacks the very foundations of my thought, in its most urgent communications with intelligence and with the instinctiveness of the mind, does not occur in some intangible abstract realm where only the higher faculties of the intelligence participate. Rather than the mind, which remains intact, although bristling with barbs, it is the neurological pathways of thought which this erosion damages and diverts. It is in the limbs and the blood that this absence and this standstill make themselves particularly felt.

A great cold,
an excruciating abstinence,
the limbo of a nightmare of bones and muscles, with the sensation of the gastric functions snapping like a flag in the phosphorescence of the storm.
Larval images that are pushed about as if with a finger and bear no relation to any substance.

I am a man by virtue of my hands and my feet, my belly, my heart of meat, my stomach whose knots reunite me to the putrefaction of life.

People talk to me of words, but it is not a question of words, it is a question of the duration of the mind.
This husk of words that falls away, it must not be imagined that the soul is not involved in it. Beside the mind there is life, there is the human being in the circle around which this mind revolves, bound to it by a multitude of fibers . . .

No, all bodily uprootings, all diminutions of physical activity and this discomfort in feeling oneself dependent in one's body, and this body itself, weighed down with marble and lying on a

Fragments of a Diary from Hell (1925)

hard board, do not equal the pain of being deprived of physical knowledge and of the sense of one's inner equilibrium. That the soul deserts language or language deserts the mind, and that this rupture plows in the fields of the senses a vast furrow of despair and blood, this is the great pain which undermines not the outer skin or the framework, but the STUFF of the body. What one must lose is this wandering spark which one felt WAS an abyss that enclosed the whole extent of the possible world, and a sense of futility so overpowering that it is like the heart of death. This futility is like the moral color of this abyss and of this intense stupefaction, and its physical color is the taste of a blood that gushes in cascades through the orifices of the brain.

There is no use telling me that this death trap is inside me. I am part of life, I represent the fatality that chooses me, and it is not possible that all the life in the world counts me with it at a given moment, since by its very nature it threatens the principle of life.

There is something which is higher than all human activity: this is the example of this monotonous crucifixion, this crucifixion in which the soul destroys itself without end.

The cord which I allow to be penetrated by the intelligence which preoccupies me and by the unconscious which nourishes me reveals more and more subtle fibers in the heart of its treelike tissue. And it is a new life that is reborn, a life that is more and more profound, eloquent, deeply rooted.

No precise information can ever be given by this soul that is choking; for the torment that is killing it, flaying it fiber by fiber, is occurring below the level of thought, below the level that language can reach, since it is the very union of what creates the soul and holds it together spiritually that breaks down at exactly those times when life summons it to a consistent clarity. No clarity is ever possible concerning this passion, this sort of cyclical and fundamental martyrdom. And yet the soul lives, but its duration is subject to eclipses in which the fleeting is perpetually mingled with the fixed, and the confused with this incisive language whose clarity does not last. This curse is highly instructive for the depths that it inhabits, but the world will not understand the lesson.

The emotion that attends the hatching of a form, the adaptation of my humors to the possibility of a speech of no duration, is for me a state that has another value besides the completion of my activity.
It is the touchstone of certain spiritual lies.
This sort of backward step which the mind takes when consciousness outstares it, to go in search of the emotion of life. This emotion, which lies outside the particular point where the mind seeks it and which emerges with its rich density of freshly molded forms, this emotion which brings the mind the overwhelming sound of matter—the whole soul flows toward it and passes through its ardent fire. But more than the fire, what ravishes the soul is the limpidity, the facility, the naturalness, and the glacial candor of this too-fresh matter which exudes both hot and cold.
The soul knows what the appearance of this matter signifies and of what subterranean massacre its birth is the reward. This matter is the standard of a void which does not know itself.

When I think about myself, my thought seeks itself in the ether of a new space. I am on the moon as others are on their balconies. I participate in planetary gravitation in the fissures of my mind.

Life will go on, events will unfold, spiritual conflicts will be resolved, and I shall not participate in any of it. I have nothing to expect either from the physical or the psychological point of view. For me there is perpetual pain and darkness, the night of the soul, and I have no voice to cry out.
Squander your riches far from this unfeeling body to which no season, either spiritual or sensual, makes any difference.
I have chosen the realm of pain and darkness as others have chosen that of radiance and the accumulation of matter.
I do not work within the confines of any realm.
I work in the unique moment of duration.

More prose texts from 1925

GENERAL SECURITY
THE LIQUIDATION OF OPIUM

It is my undisguised intention to exhaust the subject once and for all, so they will leave us the hell alone with the so-called dangers of the drug.

My point of view is clearly anti-social.

There is only one reason to attack opium. This is the danger that its use can inflict on society as a whole.

BUT THIS DANGER IS NONEXISTENT.

We are born rotten in body and soul, we are congenitally maladjusted; do away with opium, you will not do away with the need for crime, the cancers of the body and the soul, the propensity to despair, inborn cretinism, hereditary syphilis, the instability of the instincts, you will not prevent the fact that there are souls predestined for poison, in whatever form—the poison of morphine, the poison of reading, the poison of loneliness, the poison of onanism, the poison of sexual overindulgence, the poison of the congenital weakness of the soul, the poison of alcohol, the poison of tobacco, the poison of anti-sociability. There are souls that are incurable and lost to the rest of society. Deprive them of one means of folly, they will invent ten thousand others. They will create subtler, wilder methods, methods that are absolutely DESPERATE. Nature herself is fundamentally anti-social, it is only by a usurpation of powers that the organized body of society opposes the *natural* inclination of humanity.

Let the lost destroy themselves, we have better ways to occupy our time than to attempt a regeneration which is not only impossible but also pointless, ODIOUS, AND HARMFUL.

So long as we have failed to eliminate any of the causes of human despair, we do not have the right to try to eliminate those means by which man tries to cleanse himself of despair.

For it would first be necessary to do away with that natural and hidden impulse, that *specious* inclination of man which makes him seek a solution, which gives him *the idea* of seeking a solution to his troubles.

For the lost are lost by nature, all your ideas of moral regeneration will make no difference, there is AN INNATE DETERMINISM, there is an undeniable incurability in suicide, crime, idiocy, madness, there is an invincible cuckoldry in man, there is a congenital weakness of the character, a castration of the mind.

Aphasia exists, locomotor ataxia exists, syphilitic meningitis, theft, usurpation. Hell is of this world and there are men who are unhappy escapees from hell, escapees destined ETERNALLY to reenact their escape. But enough of that.

Man is miserable, the soul is weak, there are men who will always destroy themselves. It matters little how they do it; THIS IS NOT THE BUSINESS OF SOCIETY.

We have demonstrated, have we not, that society can do nothing about this, that it is wasting its time, and that it is only becoming further entrenched in its own stupidity.

And finally, HARMFUL.

Those of us who dare to face the truth know, do we not, the results of the prohibition of alcohol in the United States.

An overproduction of folly: beer with the alcoholic content of ether, alcohol spiked with cocaine and sold under the counter, increased drunkenness, a kind of general intoxication. IN SHORT, THE LAW OF THE FORBIDDEN FRUIT.

The same for opium.

Prohibition, which causes increased public curiosity about the drug, has so far profited only the pimps of medicine, journalism, and literature. There are people who have built fecal and industrious reputations on their alleged indignation against the inoffensive and insignificant sect of the damned of the drug (inoffensive because insignificant in size and because always an exception), this minority of those damned by the mind, by the soul, by the disease.

Ah! How neatly tied, in these people, is the umbilical cord of morality! Since they left their mothers they have never sinned, have they? They are apostles, they are the descendants of priests; one can only wonder from what source they draw their indignation, and above all how much they have pocketed to do this, and in any case what it has done for them.

But this is not the point.

In reality, this furor over drugs and the stupid laws that result from it:

1. *Are powerless against the need for the drug* which, whether or not it is satisfied, is intrinsic to the soul and would

More prose texts from 1925

drive it to deliberately anti-social gestures, EVEN IF THE DRUG DID NOT EXIST.

2. *Aggravate the social need for the drug*, and change it into a secret vice.

3. *Aggravate the real disease*, for this is the real question, the central issue, the dangerous point:
UNFORTUNATELY FOR MEDICINE, THE DISEASE EXISTS.

All the laws, all the restrictions, all the campaigns against narcotics will only succeed in depriving all the most destitute cases of human suffering, who possess over society certain inalienable rights, of the solvent for their miseries, a sustenance for them more wonderful than bread, and the means of finally re-entering life.

Better the plague than morphine, proclaims official medicine, better hell than life. Only an idiot like Jean-Pierre Liausu (who is, moreover, an ignorant nonentity) would claim that we should let the *sick stew in their own sickness.*

And all the boorishness of the person betrays itself and indulges itself fully: IN THE NAME, HE CLAIMS, OF THE GENERAL WELFARE.

Destroy yourselves, you who are desperate, and you who are tortured in body and soul, abandon all hope. There is no more solace for you in this world. The world lives off your rotting flesh.

And you, lucid madmen, spastics, cancer patients, chronic meningitis cases, you are the misunderstood. There is a point in you which no doctor will ever understand, and for me this is the point which saves you and makes you august, pure, wonderful: you are outside life, you are above life, you have miseries which the ordinary man does not know, you exceed the normal level, and it is for this that men refuse to forgive you, you poison their peace of mind, you undermine their stability. You have irrepressible pains whose essence is to be inadaptable to any known state, indescribable in words. You have repeated and shifting pains, incurable pains, pains beyond imagining, pains which are neither of the body nor of the soul, *but which partake of both.* And I share your suffering, and I ask you: who dares to ration our relief? In the name of what superior lucidity that usurps our very souls, we who are at the very root of knowledge and lucidity?

And this because of our desire, because of our determination to suffer. We whom pain has sent traveling through our souls in search of a calm place to cling to, seeking stability in evil as others seek stability in good. We are not mad, we are wonderful doctors, we know the dosage of soul, of sensibility, of marrow, of thought. You must leave us alone, you must leave the sick alone, we ask nothing of mankind, we ask only for the relief of our suffering. We have evaluated our lives well, we know what restrictions they impose on others and above all on ourselves. We know what willed deterioration, what renunciation of ourselves, what paralyses of subtle functions our disease inflicts on us each day. We are not going to kill ourselves just yet. In the meantime, leave us the hell alone.

January 1, 1925

Inquiry

ONE LIVES, ONE DIES. WHAT IS THE ROLE OF WILL IN ALL THIS? PEOPLE SEEM TO KILL THEMSELVES THE WAY THEY DREAM. IT IS NOT A MORAL QUESTION THAT WE ARE RAISING:

IS SUICIDE A SOLUTION?

No, suicide is still a hypothesis. I claim the right to doubt suicide as I do all the rest of reality. For the moment and until further notice *it is necessary* to be tormented by doubt, not of existence itself, which is within reach of anyone, but of the internal vibration and the profound sensibility of things, of acts, of reality. I believe in nothing to which I am not joined by the sensibility of a thinking and meteoric cord, and yet I am a little too lacking in meteors in action. The constructed and sentient existence of every man is a burden to me, and I resolutely abhor all reality. Suicide is merely the fabulous and remote victory of men who think well, but the state of suicide proper is to me incomprehensible. The suicide of a neurasthenic is without any representational value whatsoever, but simply the state of soul of a man who has carefully planned his suicide, the material circumstances, and the moment of wondrous release. I know nothing about things, I know nothing of any human state, no part of the world turns for me, turns in me. I suffer hideously from life. There is no state that I can attain. And it is certain that I have been dead for a long time, I have already committed suicide. They have suicided me, so to speak. But what would you say to an *anterior suicide*, a suicide which made us retrace our steps, but to the other side of existence, not to the side of death. This is the only suicide that would have value for me. I have no appetite for death, I have an appetite *for not existing*, for never having fallen into this interlude of imbecilities, abdications, renunciations, and obtuse encounters which is the self of Antonin Artaud, much weaker than he is. The self of this wandering invalid which from time to time presents its shadow on which he himself has spat, and long since, this crippled and shuffling self, this virtual, impossible self which nevertheless finds itself in reality. No one has felt its weakness as strongly as he, it is the principal, essential weakness of humanity. To destroy, to not exist.

DINNER IS SERVED

Leave the caves of being. Come. The mind breathes outside the mind. The time has come to abandon your lodgings. Surrender to the Universal Thought. The Marvelous is at the root of the mind.

We are of the inside of the mind, of the interior of the head. Ideas, logic, order, Truth (with a capital T), Reason, we throw them all into the nothingness of death. Look to your logic, sirs, look to your logic, you do not know how far our hatred of logic can lead us.

It is only by a diverting of the flow of life, by a paralysis imposed on the mind, that one can fix life in its so-called real physiognomy, but reality is not under this surface. This is why we who aspire to a certain surreal eternity, we who have long since ceased to consider ourselves in the present and who are, as it were, the real shadows of ourselves, will not permit your coming and annoying us in the mind.

Whoever judges us is not born to the mind, to that mind which we wish to experience and which is for us outside of what you call mind. You must not draw our attention too often to the chains that bind us to the petrifying imbecility of mind. We have laid our hands on a new beast. The heavens respond to our attitude of senseless absurdity. This habit that you have of turning your backs on questions will not prevent the heavens from opening on the appointed day and a new language from taking root in the midst of your idiotic machinations, we mean the idiotic machinations of your thought.

There are signs in Thought. Our attitude of absurdity and death is the attitude of greatest receptivity. Through the fissures of a reality that is henceforth unviable, there speaks a deliberately sibylline world.

LETTER TO THE BUDDHIST SCHOOLS

You who are not in the flesh, and who know at what point in its carnal trajectory, in its senseless coming and going, the soul finds the absolute logos, the new word, the inner ground, you who know how one can turn in one's thinking, and how the mind can be saved from itself, you who are inside yourselves, you whose minds are no longer on the level of the flesh: there are hands here for whom taking is not everything, brains that see beyond a forest of roofs, a blossoming of façades, a nation of wheels, an activity of fire and of marble. Let them come, this nation of iron, these words written with the speed of light, let the sexes come toward each other with the force of bullets; what will be changed in the pathways of the soul? In the spasms of the heart, in the dissatisfaction of the mind.

You must throw them into the sea, all these whites who arrive with their small minds and their tamed spirits. We must make these dogs understand, we are not talking about the old disease of humanity. Our spirits suffer from other needs than those inherent in life. We suffer from a rottenness, from the rottenness of Reason.

Logical Europe crushes the mind endlessly between the hammer blows of two extremes, she opens the mind only to close it again. But now the suffocation is at its peak, we have suffered too long under the yoke. The mind is greater than the mind, the metamorphoses of life are many. Like you, we reject progress: come, tear down our houses.

Let our hacks continue to write a little longer, let our journalists continue to babble, our critics to drone, our Jews to flow into their molds of plunder, our politicians to declaim, and our legal assassins to hatch their crimes in peace. *We* know what life is really like. Our writers, our thinkers, our doctors, our fools are conspiring to ruin life. Let all these hacks rail against us, let them rail out of habit or mania, let them rail from castration of the mind, from their inability to catch the nuances, to reach those glassy alluvia, those revolving planets where the exalted mind of man renews itself without end, we have won over the best thought. Come. Save us from these larvae. Design us new houses.

THE ACTIVITY OF THE SURREALIST RESEARCH BUREAU

The fact of a Surrealist revolution in things is applicable to all states of mind,
to all types of human activity,
to all conditions in the world within the mind,
to all established facts of morality,
to all orders of mind.

This revolution aspires to a general devaluation of values, a depreciation of the mind, a demineralizing of the obvious, an absolute and perpetual confusion of languages,
an unleveling of thought.

It aspires to the rupture and disqualification of logic, which it will hunt down until it has rooted out its oldest defenses.

It aspires to a spontaneous reclassification of things according to an order that is more profound and more subtle, and impossible to elucidate by the methods of ordinary reason, but an order all the same, and one that is perceptible to some unknown sense . . . but perceptible all the same, and an order which does not belong entirely to death.

Between the world and ourselves the rupture is complete. We do not speak to make ourselves understood, but only inside ourselves, with the plowshares of anguish, with the cutting edge of a fierce obstinacy, we turn thought over, we make thought uneven.

The Surrealist Research Bureau is devoting all its efforts to this reclassification of life.

There is a whole philosophy of Surrealism, or what can take the place of a philosophy, to be instituted.

It is not a question, strictly speaking, of establishing canons or precepts, but

1. of finding means of Surrealist investigation in the heart of Surrealist thought;

2. of locating landmarks, means of reconnaissance, channels, islands.

Up to a certain point, one can and should acknowledge a Surrealist mystique, a certain order of beliefs which elude ordinary reason but which are nevertheless well defined, which bear on clearly determined points of the mind.

Surrealism registers not so much beliefs as a certain order of repulsions.

Surrealism is above all a state of mind, it does not advocate formulas.

The most important point is to put oneself in the right frame of mind.

No Surrealist is in the world, or thinks of himself in the present, or believes in the effectiveness of the mind as spur, the mind as guillotine, the mind as judge, the mind as doctor, and he resolutely hopes to be apart from the mind.

The Surrealist has judged the mind.

He has no feelings which are a part of himself, he does not recognize any thought as his own. His thought does not fashion for him a world to which he *reasonably* assents.

He despairs of attaining his own mind.

But after all he is in the mind, it is from within that he judges himself, and in comparison with his thought the world does not carry much weight. But during the interval of some loss, some departure from himself, some instantaneous reabsorption of the mind, he will see the white beast appear, the vitreous beast that thinks.

This is why he is a Head, he is the only Head which is emerging into the present. In the name of his inner freedom, in the name of the exigencies of his peace, his perfection, his purity, he spits on you, world given over to desiccating reason, to the imprisoning mimicry of the ages, world who have built your houses of words and established your tables of precepts in a place where the Surreal mind, the only mind strong enough to uproot us, must finally explode.

*

These notes, which the stupid will judge from the point of view of seriousness and the clever from the point of view of language, are one of the first examples, one of the first aspects of what I mean by the Confusion of my speech. They are addressed to the confused in mind, to those rendered speechless by a paralysis of the tongue. Here, nevertheless, are a great many notes which are central to their purpose. Here thought fails, here the mind reveals its anatomy. Here are idiotic notes, notes that are primitive, as that other says, "in the articulation of their thought." But notes that are really subtle.

What well-balanced mind will not discover in them a perpetual correction of language, and the tension after the absence, the knowledge of indirectness, the acceptance of the badly expressed? These notes which despise language, which spit upon thought.

And yet between the fissures of a thought which is badly constructed in human terms, a thought which is unequally crystallized, there gleams a desire for meaning. The desire to bring to light the deviations of a thing that is still badly done, a desire for belief.

At this point there enters a certain Faith,

but let all coproloquists listen, all aphasiacs, and in general all the disinherited of language and of the word, the pariahs of Thought.

I speak only for them.

ANTONIN ARTAUD

Manifesto in Clear Language

for Roger Vitrac

If I believe neither in Evil nor in Good, if I feel such a strong inclination to destroy, if there is nothing in the order of principles to which I can reasonably accede, the underlying reason is in my flesh.

I destroy because for me everything that proceeds from reason is untrustworthy. I believe only in the evidence of what stirs my marrow, not in the evidence of what addresses itself to my reason. I have found levels in the realm of the nerve. I now feel capable of evaluating the evidence. There is for me an evidence in the realm of pure flesh which has nothing to do with the evidence of reason. The eternal conflict between reason and the heart is decided in my very flesh, but in my flesh irrigated by nerves. In the realm of the affective imponderable, the image provided by my nerves takes the form of the highest intellectuality, which I refuse to strip of its quality of intellectuality. And so it is that I watch the formation of a concept which carries within it the actual fulguration of things, a concept which arrives upon me with a sound of creation. No image satisfies me unless it is at the same time *Knowledge,* unless it carries with it its substance as well as its lucidity. My mind, exhausted by discursive reason, wants to be caught up in the wheels of a new, an absolute gravitation. For me it is like a supreme reorganization in which only the laws of Illogic participate, and in which there triumphs the discovery of a new Meaning. This Meaning which has been lost in the disorder of drugs and which presents the appearance of a profound intelligence to the contradictory phantasms of sleep. This Meaning is a victory of the mind over itself, and although it is irreducible by reason, it exists, but only *inside the mind.* It is order, it is intelligence, it is the signification of chaos. But it does not accept this chaos as such, it interprets it, and because it interprets it, it loses it. It is the logic of Illogic. And this is all one can say. My lucid unreason is not afraid of chaos.

I renounce nothing of that which is the Mind. I want only to transport my mind elsewhere with its laws and its organs. I do not surrender myself to the sexual mechanism of the mind, but on the contrary within this mechanism I seek to isolate those discoveries which lucid reason does not provide. I surrender to the fever of dreams, but only in order to derive from them new laws. I seek multiplication, subtlety, the intellectual eye in delirium, not rash vaticination. There is a knife which I do not forget.

But it is a knife which is halfway into dreams, which I keep inside myself, which I do not allow to come to the frontier of the lucid senses.

That which belongs to the realm of the image is irreducible by reason and must remain within the image or be annihilated.
Nevertheless, there is a reason in images, there are images which are clearer in the world of image-filled vitality.
There is in the immediate teeming of the mind a multiform and dazzling insinuation of animals. This insensible and *thinking* dust is organized according to laws which it derives from within itself, outside the domain of clear reason or of *thwarted* consciousness or reason.

In the exalted realm of images, illusion properly speaking, or material error, does not exist, much less the illusion of knowledge; but this is all the more reason why the meaning of a new knowledge can and must descend into the reality of life.
The truth of life lies in the impulsiveness of matter. The mind of man has been poisoned by concepts. Do not ask him to be content, ask him only to be calm, to believe that he has found his place. But only the Madman is really calm.

SITUATION OF THE FLESH

I think about life. All the systems that I shall ever construct will never equal my cries: the cries of a man engaged in remaking his life.

I imagine a system in which all of man would participate, man with his physical flesh and the heights, the intellectual projection of his mind.

For me the first consideration is the incomprehensible magnetism of man, what for lack of a more striking expression I am obliged to call his life force.

These unformulated forces which besiege me, the day will come when my reason will have to accept them, the day will come when they will replace higher thought, these forces which from the outside have the shape of a cry. There are intellectual cries, cries born of the *subtlety* of the marrow. This is what I mean by Flesh. I do not separate my thought from my life. With each vibration of my tongue I retrace all the pathways of my thought in my flesh.

One must have been deprived of life, of the nervous irradiation of existence, of the conscious wholeness of the nerves, in order to realize that the Sense, and the Science, of all thought is hidden in the nervous vitality of the marrow, to realize how mistaken those persons are who put all their faith in Intelligence or in absolute Intellectuality. Above all else there is the wholeness of the nerves. A wholeness that includes all of consciousness, and the secret pathways of the mind in the flesh.

But what am I in relation to this theory of the Flesh or, more accurately, of Existence? I am a man who has lost his life and who is seeking by every means to restore it to its place. I am in some sense the Generator of my own vitality: a vitality which is more precious to me than consciousness, for that which in other men is merely the way to be a Man is in me all of Reason.

In the course of this secret quest into the limbo of my consciousness, I have thought I felt explosions, like the colliding of hidden stones or the sudden petrification of flames. Flames that are like imperceptible truths miraculously come to life.

But one must proceed slowly along the road of dead stones, especially when one has lost the *understanding of words*. It is an indescribable science and one that expands in slow thrusts. And he who possesses it does not understand it. But even the Angels do not understand, for all real understanding is *obscure*. The clear Mind belongs to matter. I mean the Mind that is clear at a given moment.

But I must inspect this meaning of flesh which is to give me a metaphysics of Being, and the definitive understanding of Life.

For me the word Flesh means above all *apprehension*, hair standing on end, flesh laid bare with all the intellectual profundity of this spectacle of pure flesh and all its consequences for the senses, that is, for the sentiments.

And sentiment means presentiment, that is, direct understanding, communication turned inside out and illumined from within. There is a mind in the flesh, but a mind quick as lightning. And yet the excitement of the flesh partakes of the high substance of the mind.

And yet whoever says flesh also says sensibility. Sensibility, that is, assimilation, but the intimate, secret, profound, absolute assimilation of my own pain, and consequently the solitary and unique knowledge of that pain.

Eighteen Seconds, a screenplay (1925–26)

XI

A STREET CORNER, AT NIGHT, under a lamppost, a man dressed in black, his face immobile, fidgeting with his cane, a watch hanging from his left hand. The hand marks the seconds.
Close-up of the watch marking the seconds.
The seconds pass with infinite slowness on the screen.
When the hand reaches the eighteenth second, the drama will be over.
The time which is going to unfold on the screen is a time inside the man's mind.
It is not the normal time. The normal time is eighteen real seconds. The events which will be seen flowing by on the screen will consist of images inside the man. The whole interest of the screenplay lies in the fact that the time it takes for the events described to occur is really eighteen seconds, whereas the description of these events will require an hour or two to be projected on the screen.
The spectator will see unfolding before him those images which, at a given moment, will start to pass through the mind of the man.
This man is an actor. He is on the point of becoming famous, or at least very well known, and he is also about to win the heart of a woman he has loved for a long time.
He has been stricken with a bizarre malady. He has become incapable of reaching his thoughts; he has retained all his lucidity, but no matter what thought occurs to him, he can no longer give it external form, that is, translate it into appropriate gestures and words.
The necessary words desert him, they no longer answer his summons, he is reduced to watching a procession of images, an enormous number of contradictory images without very much connection from one to the next.
This renders him incapable of participating in the lives of others, or of devoting himself to any activity.
View of the man at the doctor's. His arms crossed, his hands clenched on them. The doctor towering above him. The doctor pronounces his sentence.
Again we find the man under the lamppost just as he is having an intense realization of his state. He curses heaven, he

thinks: Just when I was about to start living! And to win the heart of the woman I love, who has resisted so long.

View of the woman, very beautiful, enigmatic, her face severe and closed.

View of the soul of the woman as the man pictures it to himself.

Landscape, flowers, lavishly illuminated.

Gesture of malediction by the man:

Oh, to be anyone at all! To be that miserable hunchbacked news vendor who sells his papers in the evening, but to really possess the full extent of one's mind, to really be the master of one's mind, in short, to think!

Quick shot of the news vendor in the street. Then in his room, his head in his hands, as if he were holding the world. He really possesses his mind. This man, at least, really possesses his mind. He can hope to conquer the world and he has a right to think that he will actually succeed in conquering it one day.

For he also possesses INTELLIGENCE. He does not know the limitations of his being, he can hope to possess everything: love, fame, power. And in the meantime he works and he searches.

View of the news vendor gesticulating at his window: cities moving and trembling beneath his feet. Once again, at his table. With books. His finger outstretched. Flocks of women in the air. Piles of thrones.

If he can only find the central problem, the one on which all the others depend, then he can hope to conquer the world.

If only he can find not even the solution to the problem but simply what this central problem is, what it consists of, if only he can find out how to state it.

Yes, but what about his hump? Perhaps even his hump will disappear.

View of the news vendor in the center of a crystal ball. Rembrandt lighting. And in the center a luminous point. The ball becomes the globe. The globe becomes opaque. The news vendor disappears in the middle and pops out like a jack-in-the-box with his hump on his back.

Now we see him embark in search of the problem. We find him in smoky dens, in groups where people are seeking some ideal or other. Ritual gatherings. Men giving vehement speeches. The hunchback at a table listening. Shaking his head, disillusioned. In the middle of the groups, a woman. He recognizes her: it is She! He screams: Ah! arrest her! She is a spy, he says. Uproar. Everyone gets up. The woman escapes. He is beaten up and thrown into the street.

What have I done? I have betrayed her, I love her! he says.

View of the woman at home. At the feet of her father: I recognized him. He is mad.

He travels on, continuing to search. View of the man on a road with a stick. Then at his table, looking through books. Close-up of the cover of a book: the Cabala. Suddenly there is a knock at the door. Some cops come in. They seize him and put him in a straitjacket: he is taken to the madhouse. He goes mad. View of the man shaking the bars. I shall find the central problem, he screams, the one that all the others hang from like grapes on a cluster, and then:

No more madness, no more world, no more mind, above all no more anything.

But a revolution clears out the prisons, the asylums, the doors of the asylums are opened; he is freed. It's you, the mystic, they shout at him, you are the Master of us all, come. Humbly he says no. But they drag him. Be king, they tell him, mount the throne. And trembling, he mounts the throne.

They withdraw and leave him alone.

Vast silence. Magical amazement. And suddenly he thinks: I am master of everything, I can have everything.

He can have everything, yes, everything, except the possession of his mind. He still is not the master of his mind.

But actually, what is the mind? Of what does it consist? If only one could be the master of one's physical person. To have all power, to be able to do anything with one's hands, with one's body. Meanwhile, the books pile up on his table. He puts his head on the books and falls asleep.

This mental reverie is interrupted by a new Dream.

Yes, to be able to do everything, to be an orator, a painter, an actor, yes, but isn't he already an actor? Yes, he is an actor. And now he sees himself on stage with his hump, at the feet of his mistress who is performing with him. And his hump is false too:

it is contrived. And his mistress is his real mistress, his mistress in life.

A magnificent hall, overflowing with people, and the King in his box. But it is also he who plays the character of the king. He is the king, he listens and sees himself at the same time on the stage. And the king has no hump. He has found out: the hunchbacked man on the stage is only an effigy of himself, a traitor who has taken away his wife, who has robbed him of his mind. He gets up and shouts: Arrest him. Uproar. Vast confusion. The actors challenge him. The woman yells at him: It's not you any more, you don't have your hump, I don't recognize you. He is mad! And just then the two characters melt into each other on the screen. The entire room trembles with its columns and its candelabra. The trembling grows more and more violent. And against this trembling background pass all the images, also trembling, of the king, the news vendor, the hunchbacked actor, the madman, the insane asylum, the crowds, and he is back on the sidewalk under the lamppost, with his watch hanging from his left hand and his cane moving in the same way.

Barely eighteen seconds have passed; he takes one last look at his miserable destiny. Then, without hesitation or the slightest emotion, he takes a revolver out of his pocket and puts a bullet in his head.

From *Art and Death* (1925–27)

XII

WHO, IN THE DEPTHS of certain kinds of anguish, at the bottom of certain dreams, has not known death as a shattering and marvelous sensation unlike anything else in the realm of the mind? One must have known this suctionlike rise of anguish whose waves cover you and fill you to bursting as if driven by some intolerable bellows. An anguish which approaches and withdraws, each time more vast, each time heavier and more swollen. It is the body itself that has reached the limit of its distension and its strength and which must nevertheless go further. It is a kind of suction cup placed on the soul, whose bitterness spreads like an acid to the furthest boundaries of perception. And the soul does not even possess the ability to burst. For this distension itself is false. Death is not satisfied so cheaply. In the physical sphere, this distension is like the reverse image of a contraction which must occupy the mind *over the whole extent of the living body*.

This breath which is suspended is the last, truly the last. It is time to settle one's accounts. The moment so long feared, so long dreaded, so long imagined, is here. And it is true that one is going to die. One observes and measures one's breath. And the vast time completely unfurls to its limit in a resolution it cannot fail to dissolve in without a trace.

Die, miserable bones! And it is well known that your thought is not completed, finished, and that no matter what way you turn, you have not yet *begun* to think.

No matter.—The fear that swoops down on you tears you apart to the very limit of the impossible, for you know very well that you must cross to that other side for which nothing in you is ready, not even this body, above all this body which you will leave behind without forgetting either its substance, or its density, or its impossible asphyxia.

And it will be like a bad dream where you are outside the situation of your body, having dragged it that far anyway and making yourself suffer in it and enlightening yourself with its deafening impressions, where space is always smaller or larger than you, where no part of the feeling you bring with you of an ancient terrestrial orientation can any longer be satisfied.

And this is what it is, and it is this forever. At the feeling of this desolation and this unnamable malaise, what cry, worthy of the baying of a hound in a dream, makes your skin crawl, makes you gag in the bewilderment of a senseless drowning? No, it is not true. It is not true.

But the worst is that it is true. And along with this feeling of desperate veracity in which it seems to you that you are going to die again, that you are going to die for the second time (You say to yourself, you say aloud that you are going to die. You are going to die: *I am going to die for the second time*)—just then some unknown moisture from a lake of iron or stone or wind refreshes you incredibly and consoles your mind, and you flow, you create yourself by flowing to your death, to your new state of death. This water that flows is death, and from the moment that you contemplate yourself with tranquillity, that you register your new sensations, it means that the great identification is beginning. You were dead and now once again you find yourself alive—ONLY THIS TIME YOU ARE ALONE.

I have just described a sensation of anguish, a dream sensation in which the anguish slips into the dream almost as I imagine the agony must slip in and finally culminate in death.

In any case, dreams like these cannot lie. They do not lie. And these sensations of death placed end to end, this suffocation, this despair, this torpor, this desolation, this silence, don't we see them in the magnified suspension of a dream, with this feeling that one of the faces of the new reality is perpetually behind one?

But at the bottom of death or of the dream, the anguish begins again. This anguish, like a rubber band that is stretched and suddenly hits you in the throat, is neither unknown nor new. The death into which one slipped without being aware, the fetal contraction of the body, that head—it had to pass, that head that carried consciousness and life and consequently the supreme suffocation, and consequently the most excruciating pain—it also had to pass through the smallest possible opening. But it torments to the limit of the pores, and this head, by dint of shaking and writhing with terror, has as it were the idea, the feeling that it is swollen and that its terror has taken shape, that it has burgeoned under the skin.

And since, after all, death is not new, but on the contrary only too well known, for at the end of this distillation of viscera does one not perceive the image of a panic that has already been

From *Art and Death* (1925-27)

experienced? The very force of despair seems to re-create certain childhood situations in which death appeared clearly in the form of an uninterrupted confusion. Childhood knows sudden awakenings of the mind, intense prolongations of thought which are lost with advancing age. In certain panics known to childhood, certain monumental and unreasonable terrors which are haunted by the sense of an extra-human menace, it is incontestable that death appears

like the tearing of a nearby membrane, like the lifting of a veil which is the world, as yet formless and insecure.

Who has no memory of extraordinary enlargements which belonged to a wholly mental reality and which therefore were hardly astonishing, which were presented, or rather abandoned, to the forest of his childhood senses? Prolongations permeated with a perfect understanding, permeating everything, crystallized, eternal.

But what strange thoughts this understanding selects, from what disintegrated meteor it recombines the human atoms.

The child sees recognizable processions of ancestors in which he notes the origins of all known resemblances of man to man. The world of appearances rises and overflows into the imperceptible, the unknown. Then the darkening of life takes place and henceforth states of this kind never recur except by the grace of an absolutely abnormal lucidity, such as that brought about by narcotics.

Whence the immense utility of drugs in liberating, in heightening the mind. Whether or not they are lies from the point of view of a reality which is not known for its great value, this reality being merely one of the most transitory and least recognizable aspects of the infinite reality, this reality being equivalent to matter and destined to rot along with it, from the point of view of the mind drugs take on a higher dignity which makes them the closest and most useful auxiliaries of death.*

---

* I affirm—and I cling to the idea that death is not outside the realm of the mind, that it is within certain limits knowable and approachable by a certain sensibility.

Everything in the order of the written that abandons the realm of clear and orderly perception, everything that seeks to bring about an overthrow of appearances, to introduce a doubt concerning the relative

This manacled death in which the soul writhes, straining to regain a state that is at last complete and permeable,

in which everything would not be shock, the sharpness of a delirious confusion that ratiocinates endlessly upon itself, tangled in the fibers of a mixture that is both intolerable and melodious,

in which everything would not be sickness,

in which the smallest place would not be constantly reserved for the greatest hunger for a space that is absolute and this time definitive,

in which this pressure of paroxysms would suddenly be pierced by the feeling of a new level,

in which from the bottom of a nameless confusion this stirring, snorting soul would sense the possibility, as in dreams, of awakening to a clearer world, after boring through it no longer knows what barrier—and would find itself in a luminosity where at last its limbs would unfold and where the world's partitions would seem infinitely fragile.

---

positions of the images of the mind, everything that promotes confusion without destroying the surging force of thought, everything that upsets the relations between things by giving the subverted mind an even greater vision of truth and violence, all these things provide access to death, put us in touch with those more refined states of mind which are the proper ambiance of death.

This is why all those who dream without mourning their dreams, without coming away from these immersions into a fertile unconsciousness with a sense of unbearable nostalgia, are pigs. Dreams are true. All dreams are true. I have a sense of asperities, of landscapes that seem sculptured, of undulating stretches of ground covered with a kind of cool sand, whose meaning is:

"regret, disillusionment, abandonment, separation, when shall we meet again?"

Nothing resembles love so much as the appeal of certain landscapes seen in dreams, as the encircling of certain hills, of a kind of material clay whose shape is as if molded to the thought.

When shall we meet again? When will the earthy taste of your lips come again to brush the anxiety of my mind? The earth is like a whirlpool of mortal lips. Life digs before our eyes the gulf of all the caresses that have not been. What are we to do with this angel at our side who has not been able to appear? Will all our sensations remain forever intellectual, and will not our dreams succeed in igniting one soul whose feeling will help us to die? What is this death in which we are forever alone, in which love does not show us the way?

This soul could be reborn; yet it is not reborn; for although soothed, it feels that it is still dreaming, that it still is not used to that dream state with which it does not manage to identify itself.

At this instant in his mortal reverie the living man, having arrived at the impasse of an impossible identification, withdraws his soul with a violent gesture.

There he is, thrown back on the bare level of the senses, in a bottomless light.

Outside the infinite musicality of nerve waves, exposed to the boundless hunger of the atmosphere, to the absolute cold.

. . . .

Letter to the Clairvoyant

for André Breton

Madam,

You live in a poor room, involved with life. It would be useless to expect to hear heaven murmuring in your windows. Nothing, neither your appearance nor the air, separates you from us; but some childishness more profound than experience compels us to slash away endlessly and to drive away your face, and even the attachments of your life.

My soul torn and soiled, you know that I sit before you no more than a shadow, but I am not afraid of this terrible knowledge. I know you in all the vital centers of my self, and much closer to me than my mother. And I am as if naked before you. Naked, immodest and naked, upright and like an apparition of myself, but without shame, for in your eye that races vertiginously through my fibers, evil is really without sin.

Never have I felt so precise, so unified, so confident even beyond scruples, beyond all malice that might come from others or myself, and also so discerning. You added the tip of fire, the starry tip to the trembling thread of my hesitation. Neither judged nor judging *myself,* whole without effort, complete without forcing myself; except for life, it was happiness. And finally no more fear that my tongue, my great awkward thick tongue, my insignificant tongue would become forked; I scarcely needed to stir my thoughts.

Meanwhile, I entered your room without terror, without a trace of the most ordinary curiosity. And yet you were the mistress and the oracle, you could have appeared to me as the very soul and the God of my appalling destiny. To be able to see and to tell me! That nothing foul or secret remain dark, that everything buried be uncovered, that the repressed be spread out at last before the fine steady eye of an absolutely pure judge. The eye of one who discerns and disposes but who does not even know that she can overwhelm you.

The mild and perfect light in which one no longer suffers from one's soul, however infested with evil. A light without cruelty or passion in which only a single atmosphere is now revealed, the atmosphere of a serene and pious, of a precious fatality. Yes, coming to you, Madam, I was no longer afraid of my death. Death or life, I saw only a great calm space in which the shadows of my destiny dissolved. I was truly safe, liberated from all misery, for even my misery to come was sweet to me, if by some *impossible* chance I had misery to fear in my future.

My destiny no longer appeared to me as this covered road which could only harbor evil. I had lived in eternal apprehension of this destiny and, although *at a distance,* I felt it very near, and I felt that all along it had been hidden in me. No violent eddy overwhelmed my fibers in advance, I had already been too afflicted and overwhelmed by misfortune. My fibers now registered only a great mass of uniform sweetness. And I hardly cared that the most terrible gates opened before me; the terrible was already behind me. And even if bad, my impending future affected me only as a harmonious discord, a series of peaks reversed, blunted, and absorbed within me. All you could prophesy, Madam, was the leveling of my life.

But what reassured me above all was not this profound certainty, embedded in my flesh, but rather the sense of the uniformity of all things. A magnificent absolute. I had no doubt learned to draw nearer to death, and this was why all things, even the most cruel, now appeared to me only from the point of view of equilibrium, an equilibrium in which their meaning was a matter of complete indifference.

But there was still something else. This meaning, which was a matter of indifference in terms of its immediate effect on my person, was still imbued with something good. I came to you with undiluted optimism. An optimism that was not a natural inclination of my mind but came from this profound understanding of the equilibrium in which my whole life was immersed. My life to come, balanced by my terrible past, flowing smoothly into death. I *knew* my death in advance as the completion of a life that was at last level, and sweeter than my best memories. And before my eyes reality swelled, was amplified until it became that supreme knowledge in which the value of present life falls apart under the blows of eternity. It could no longer be that eternity would not avenge me for this relentless sacrifice of myself, one in which I myself did not participate. And my immediate future, my future starting from the minute I first entered your circle, that future also belonged to death. As for you, your appearance impressed me from the first moment as favorable.

The emotion of knowing was dominated by a sense of the infinite mildness of existence.* No harm could come to me from that steady blue eye with which you examined my destiny.

---

* I cannot help it. I had this feeling in Her presence. Life was good because this clairvoyant existed. The presence of this woman was like opium to me: purer, lighter, although less *substantial* than opium, but deeper, more vast, and opening other portals in the cells of my mind. This active state of spiritual communication, this conflagration of neighboring and tiny worlds, this imminence of infinite lives that this woman afforded me a view of, showed me at last a way out of life and a reason for the world's existence. For one cannot accept Life unless one is *large*, unless one feels at the source of phenomena, at least a certain number of them. Without the power of expansion, without a certain domination over things, life is indefensible. Only one thing is exalting in the world: contact with the powers of the mind. But in the presence of this clairvoyant a rather paradoxical phenomenon occurs. I no longer feel the need to be powerful or vast. The seduction that she exerted on me is more violent than my pride; a certain curiosity is enough for the moment. In her presence I am ready to renounce everything: pride, will, intelligence. Especially intelligence. This intelligence which is all my pride. I am not speaking, of course, of a certain logical agility of mind, of the ability to think rapidly or to make quick diagrams in the margins of memory. I am speaking of

All life became for me that blessed landscape in which our shifting dreams turn toward us with the face of our self. The idea of absolute knowledge merged with the idea of the absolute similarity of life and of my own consciousness. And from this double similarity I derived a sense of an impending birth in which, although apart from my destiny, you were the good and indulgent mother. I no longer found anything mysterious in the fact of this abnormal clairvoyance in which the gestures of my past and future existence were depicted for you with their full burden of warnings and relationships. I felt that my mind had entered into communication with yours with regard to the *form* of these warnings.

But what of you, Madam, what is this fiery vermin that suddenly steals into you, and by the artifice of what unimaginable atmosphere? For after all you *see*, and yet the same stretch of space surrounds us.

The horror, Madam, is in the immobility of these walls, these things, in the familiarity of the furniture that surrounds you, the accessories of your divination, in the quiet indifference of the life in which you participate as I do.

And your clothes, Madam, those clothes that touch *someone who sees*. Your flesh, all your functions. I cannot accept this idea that you are subject to the conditions of Space and Time, that you are burdened by the necessities of the body. You must be much too light to exist in space.

Then again you seemed to me so pretty, and graceful in so human, so ordinary a way. As pretty as any of the women from whom I expect bread and the spasm, and who boost me up toward a physical threshold.

---

a subterranean understanding of the world and of things, an understanding which often requires a long time to mature, which need not take material form in order to be satisfied, and which affords profound insights into the mind. It is on the pledge of this understanding, halting and more often than not without substance (and which I *myself* do not possess), that I have always asked people to give me credit, even if they must wait a hundred years and be satisfied in the meantime with silence. I know in what limbo I can find this woman again. I am mining a problem which is bringing me close to gold, to all subtle matter, a problem as abstract as pain, which has no form and which trembles and evaporates at a human touch.

In my mind's eye you are without limits or boundaries, absolutely, deeply incomprehensible. For how do you adjust to life, you who have the gift of second sight? And that long level road down which your soul walks like a tightrope walker, and where I, I would read so clearly the future of my death.

Yes, there are still men who know the distance from one feeling to another, who know how to create levels and stops in their desires, who know how to stand aloof from their desires and their souls only to reclaim them later falsely as victors. And there are these thinkers who painfully circumscribe their thoughts, who introduce sham into their dreams, these scholars who unearth laws with sinister pirouettes!

But you, dishonored, despised, soaring, you set fire to life. And behold the wheel of Time is all at once aflame with the force that made the heavens screech.

You come upon me, tiny, swept aside, rejected, and just as desperate as yourself; and you lift me up, you take me away from this place, this false space in which you no longer deign to make the gesture of living, since you have already attained the membrane of your repose. And this eye, this eye gazing at me, this single desolate gaze which is all my existence, you magnify it and turn it in on itself, and behold, a luminous burgeoning makes a bliss without shadows, revives me like a mysterious wine.

Héloïse and Abelard

Life dwindled before his eyes. Whole regions of his brain rotted. The phenomenon was known, but even so it was not simple. Abelard did not present his state as a discovery, but finally he wrote:

Dear friend,

I am enormous. I cannot help it, I am a high place where the tallest masts acquire breasts instead of sails, while the women feel their sexual organs become hard as pebbles. For my part, I cannot prevent myself from feeling all these eggs rolling and pitching under the dresses as the hour and the spirit moves them. Life comes and goes and grows small across the pavement of the breasts. From one minute to the next the face of the world has changed. Wound around the fingers are the souls with their cracks of mica, and into the mica Abelard passes, for above everything is the erosion of the mind.

All the mouths of dead males laugh at the risk of their teeth, through the arcade of their virgin teeth or through teeth coated with hunger and plated with filth, like the armature of Abelard's mind.

But here Abelard falls silent. Only his esophagus continues to function. Not, of course, the appetite of the vertical passage with its pressure of famine, but the splendid upright silver tree with its ramifying veinlets designed for air, surrounded by foliage of birds. In short, a strictly vegetal and rustling life in which the legs move with their mechanical step and the thoughts like tall boats with their sails reefed. The passage of bodies.

The mummified mind breaks loose. Life, highly constricted, lifts its head. Has the great thaw come at last? Will the bird burst through the gate of tongues, will the breasts branch out and the small mouth resume its place? Will the seed tree break through the obdurate granite of the hand? Yes, in my hand there is a rose, and my tongue shifts of itself. Oh, oh, oh! how light my thought is. My mind is as slender as a hand.

But the fact is that Héloïse also has legs. The best part is that she has legs. She also has that thing shaped like a sailor's sextant, around which all magic revolves and grazes, that thing like a sheathed sword.

But above all, Héloïse has a heart. A beautiful heart erect and full of branches, straining, firm, full of grain, braided by me, abundant delight, catalepsy of joy!

She has hands that surround books with their cartilage of honey. She has breasts of uncooked meat, so small, whose pressure drives one mad; her breasts are a network of fibers. She has a thought that belongs to me, a thought that is insidious and twisted, that unwinds as from a cocoon. She has a soul.

In her thought I am the flashing needle and it is her soul that

From *Art and Death* (1925-27)

accepts the needle and lets it in, and I am better with my needle than all the others in their beds, for in my bed I roll the thought and the needle in the sinuosities of her sleeping cocoon.

For it is always to her that I find my way back along the thread of this love without limits, this love that is scattered to the world. And in my hands grow craters, grow networks of breasts, grow explosive loves which my life wins over from my sleep.

But by way of what trances, what sudden starts, what gradual glidings has he arrived at this idea of the enjoyment of his mind? For the fact is that at this moment Abelard is enjoying his mind. He is enjoying it fully. He no longer thinks of himself either to the right or to the left. He is here. Everything that is happening in him belongs to him. And in him at this moment things are happening. Things that make it unnecessary for him to look for himself. This is the important point. He no longer has to stabilize his atoms. They combine of themselves, they arrange themselves into a point. His whole mind is reduced to a series of ascents and descents, but the descent is always to the center. He has things.

His thoughts are beautiful leaves, level surfaces, successions of centers, clusters of contacts among which his intelligence glides without effort: it goes. For this is what intelligence is: to walk around oneself. The question no longer arises whether to be shrewd or slight and to come back to oneself from a distance, to embrace, to reject, to separate.

He glides from one state to the next.

He lives. And things inside him shift like grain in a sieve.

The question of love becomes simple.

What does it matter whether he is less or more, since he can move about, glide, change, find himself, and survive.

He has rediscovered the game of love.

But how many books there are between his thought and the dream!

How many losses. And all this while, what was he doing with his heart? It is amazing that he has any heart left.

He is really there. He is there like a living medallion, like a bush of petrified metal.

Look at him, the essential knot.

As for Héloïse, she is wearing a dress, she is beautiful outside and inside.

He feels in himself the exaltation of roots, the massive, terrestrial exaltation, and his foot on the body of the turning earth feels the mass of the firmament.

And Abelard, become like a dead man, and feeling his skeleton crack and vitrify, Abelard cries out, at the vibrating point and climax of his effort:

"Here is where God is sold, now the plains of sex, the stones of flesh are mine. No pardon, I do not ask for pardon. Your God is no more than a cold weight, dunghill of the body, brothel of the eyes, virgin of the stomach, dairy of the sky!"

Now the celestial dairy is exalted. He is seized with nausea.

His flesh within him turns its scaly shaft, he feels his hair bristle, his stomach blocked, he feels his penis melt. Night rises studded with needles and suddenly with a snip of shears THEY eradicate his manhood.

And over there, Héloïse pulls up her dress and makes herself quite naked. Her skull is white and milky, her breasts disreputable, her legs spindly, her teeth make the noise of paper. She is stupid. And this is the wife of Abelard the eunuch.

CLEAR ABELARD

The murmuring armature of heaven traces on the window of his mind always the same amorous signs, the same cordial correspondences which might perhaps save him from being a man if he would agree to save himself from love.

He must surrender. He cannot hold out any longer. He surrenders. This melodious agitation is upon him. His sex throbs: a tormenting wind murmurs, whose sound is higher than heaven. The river rolls the corpses of women. Are they Ophelia, Beatrice, Laura? No, ink, no, wind, no, reeds, banks, shores, foam, flakes. The floodgate is down. Out of his desire Abelard has made a floodgate. At the confluence of the terrible and melodious surge. It is Héloïse being rolled, borne toward him—AND WHO WANTS HIM.

From *Art and Death* (1925–27)

Behold in the sky the hand of Erasmus sowing the mustard seed of madness. Ah! curious harvest. The motion of the Bear fixes the time in the sky, fixes the sky in Time, from that inverted side of the world to which the sky offers its face. Vast releveling.

It is because the sky has a face that Abelard has a heart in which so many stars sprout supreme and make his penis grow. At the end of metaphysics is this love all paved with flesh, all burning with gems, born in the sky after so many sowings of the seed of madness.

But Abelard chases the sky like bluebottle flies. Strange rout. Where can we go? God! Quick, the eye of a needle. The tiniest eye of a needle through which Abelard cannot come and get us.

The weather is strangely fine. For it has to be fine now. From today on, Abelard is no longer chaste. The narrow chain of books has been broken. He has renounced the chaste and *permissible* coitus of God.

What a sweet thing is coitus! Even when human, even when using the body of a woman, what intimate and seraphic pleasure! Heaven within the reach of earth, less beautiful than earth. Paradise embedded in his fingernails.

But the charm of sidereal lights, even seen from the top of the tower, is not worth the space of a woman's thigh. Is not Abelard the priest for whom love is so clear?

How clear is coitus, how clear is sin. So clear. What seeds, how sweet are these flowers with their swooning sexes, how avid are the heads of pleasure, how lavishly at the highest point of joy pleasure spreads her poppies. Her poppies of sound, her poppies of light and music, swiftly, like a magnetic rise of birds. Pleasure plays a piercing and mystical music on the cutting edge of a slender dream. Oh! this dream in which love consents to reopen her eyes! Yes, Héloïse, it is in you that I walk with all my philosophy, in you that I renounce the ornaments, and I give you in their place the men whose minds tremble and flash within you.
—How the Mind admires itself, since Woman admires Abelard at last. Let this foam gush against the deep and radiant walls. The trees. The vegetation of Attila.

He has her. He possesses her. She smothers him. And each page draws its bow and advances. This book in which one turns over the pages of the brain.

Abelard has cut his hands. To that terrible paper kiss, what symphony can henceforth compare. Héloïse eats fire. Opens a door. Climbs a stairway. Someone rings. Her soft crushed breasts rise. Her skin is much fairer on her breasts. Her body is white but tarnished, for no woman's belly is pure. Their skins are the color of mildew. The belly smells good, but how pathetic. And so many generations dream about this one. It is here. Abelard possesses it as a man. Famous belly. It is this and it is not this. Eat straw, eat fire. The kiss opens her caverns where the sea comes to die. Here is this spasm in which the heavens conspire, toward which a spiritual coalition hurls itself, AND IT COMES FROM ME. Ah! how I feel myself to be only viscera, without the bridge of the mind above me. Without all those magic meanings, without all those secrets superimposed. She and I. We are really here. I hold her. I kiss her. A final pressure restrains me, freezes me. I feel between my thighs the Church stopping me, complaining, will it paralyze me? Am I going to withdraw? No, no, I push aside the final barrier. St. Francis of Assisi, who was guarding my sex, steps aside. St. Bridget unclenches my teeth. St. Augustine undoes my belt. St. Catherine of Siena puts God to sleep. It is over, it is really over, I am no longer a virgin. The wall of heaven is overthrown. The universal madness overtakes me. I scale my pleasure to the highest summit of the ether.

But now St. Héloïse hears him. Later, infinitely later, she hears him and speaks to him. A kind of night fills his teeth. Enters, moaning, into the caverns of his skull. She lifts the lid of his sepulcher with her insect-bony hand. Her voice sounds like a she-goat in a dream. She trembles, but he trembles much more than she. Poor man! Poor Antonin Artaud! For it is indeed he, this impotent wretch who scales the stars, who tries to pit his weakness against the cardinal points of the elements, who, out of each of the subtle or solid faces of nature, tries to create a thought that will hold, an image that will stand. If he could create as many elements, provide at least a metaphysics of disaster, the beginning would be the fall!

Héloïse regrets that she did not have instead of her belly a wall like the one against which she was leaning when Abelard harassed her with an obscene dart. For Artaud, privation is the

From *Art and Death* (1925-27)

beginning of this death he desires. But what a beautiful image is a eunuch!

UCCELLO THE HAIR

for Génica

Uccello, my friend, my chimera, you lived with this myth of hair. The shadow of this great lunar hand with which you record the monsters of your brain will never reach the vegetation of your ear, which turns and swarms to the left with every breeze from your heart. On the left the hair, Uccello, on the left dreams, on the left nails, on the left the heart. It is on the left that all the shadows open, the naves, like human orifices. With your head lying on this table where all humanity is capsized, what do you see other than the vast shadow of a hair? A hair like two forests, a hair like three fingernails, like a meadow of eyelashes, like a rake in the grass of heaven. The world is strangled and suspended and eternally staggering on the plains of this flat table on which you rest your heavy head. And when you question the faces of those around you, what do you see but a circulation of branches, a network of veins, the tiny path of a wrinkle, the floral pattern of a sea of hair? Everything is turning, everything is vibratile, and what is the eye worth, stripped of its lashes? Wash, wash the lashes, Uccello, wash the lines, wash the trembling trace of the hairs and wrinkles on these hanging faces of dead men who look at you like eggs, and in your monstrous palm, filled with moonlight like an illumination of spleen, here again is the august trace of your hairs which emerge with their lines as fine as the dreams in your drowned man's brain. From one hair to the next, how many secrets and how many surfaces. But two hairs right next to each other, Uccello. The ideal line of the hairs, inexpressibly fine and twice repeated. There are wrinkles that run all the way around the face and extend into the neck, but under the hair there are also wrinkles, Uccello. Also, you can go all the way around this egg which hangs between the stones and the stars, and which alone possesses the double animation of eyes.

When you painted your two friends and yourself in a careful study, you left on the canvas something like the shadow of a strange fluff in which I discern your regrets and your sorrow, Paolo Uccello, badly illuminated. Wrinkles are traps, Paolo Uccello, but hairs are tongues. In one of your paintings, Paolo Uccello, I saw the light of a tongue in the phosphorescent shadow of the teeth. It is through the tongue that you restore living expression in inanimate canvas. And it is thus that I live, Uccello all swaddled in your beard, it is thus that you understood and defined me in advance. Bless you, you who had a rocky and earthy preoccupation with depth. You lived with this idea as if in a moving poison. And you writhe eternally in the circles of this idea, and I follow you in the dark, feeling my way toward the light of that tongue that calls me from the depths of a miraculous mouth. An earthy and rocky preoccupation with depth—I who lack earth on all levels. Did you really assume I would descend into this lower world with my mouth open and my mind perpetually astonished? Did you really imagine these screams in all the senses of the world and of language, as from a thread madly unwound? The long patience of wrinkles is what saved you from a premature death. For I know that you were born with a mind as hollow as mine, but you were able to fix this mind on something even smaller than the outline and the origin of a lash. By the breadth of a hair you are balanced over a formidable abyss from which, however, you are eternally divided.

But I also bless, Uccello, little boy, little bird, little ragged light, I bless your well-placed silence. Apart from those lines that sprout from your head like a foliation of messages, nothing remains of you but the silence and the secrecy of your fastened robe. Two or three signs in the air, where is the man who pretends to be more alive than these three signs and from whom, throughout the hours that cover him, one would think of asking more than the silence that precedes or follows them? I feel all the stones of the world and the phosphorus of space that are attracted by my passing, making their way through me. They form the words of a black syllable in the pastures of my brain. You, Uccello, are learning to be only a line and the heightened level of a secret.

"In Total Darkness, or The Surrealist Bluff" (1927)

XIII

The question of whether the Surrealists drove me out or whether I walked out on their grotesque parody has long since ceased to be relevant.* I withdrew because I had had enough of a masquerade that had gone on all too long. Besides, I was quite certain that in the new context they had chosen, just as in any other, the Surrealists would do nothing. Time and the facts have not failed to prove me right.

As to the question of whether Surrealism is in accord with the Revolution or whether the Revolution must be made outside the Surrealist adventure, one wonders what difference it can make to the world when one considers how little influence the Surrealists have managed to gain over the manners and ideas of the times.

Indeed, one wonders if there is still a Surrealist adventure, or if Surrealism did not die on the day when Breton and his adepts decided to join the Communist movement and to seek in the realm of facts and of immediate matter the culmination of an action that could normally develop only within the inmost confines of the brain.

They believe they can permit themselves to mock me when I speak of a metamorphosis of the interior conditions of the soul,**

---

* *I will not dwell on the fact that the Surrealists,* in their effort to destroy me, have found nothing better than to make use of my own writings. It must be clearly understood that the footnote which appears on pages 6 and 7 of the pamphlet "Au grand jour" and which is designed to undermine the very foundations of my activity is simply the wholesale reproduction, the thinly disguised copy of fragments taken from manuscripts which I sent to them in which I was concerned with placing their activities, riddled as they are with miserable hatreds and aimlessness, in their true light. I had made these fragments the substance of an article that was rejected by two or three magazines, including the *N.R.F.*, as too compromising. It does not matter through the services of what informer this article fell into their hands. What matters is that they found it sufficiently embarrassing to feel the need of counteracting its effect. As for those accusations which I directed at them and which they are turning back at me, I leave it to those who know me well, and not to their base methods, to decide who is right.

The whole root, all the exacerbations of our quarrel, turn on the word "Revolution."

** As if a man who has experienced once and for all the limits of his action, who refuses to drive himself beyond what he believes in conscience these limits to be, were less worthy of interest from the revolutionary

as if I understood soul in the disgusting sense in which they understand it, and as if from the viewpoint of the absolute there could be the slightest interest in seeing the social armature of the world change or in seeing power pass from the hands of the bourgeoisie into those of the proletariat.

point of view than some deluded noisemaker who in the stifling world we live in, a world that is closed and forever motionless, assigns to some insurrectional state the responsibility for deciding between acts and gestures that everyone knows he will not perform.

This is precisely what made me sick of Surrealism: the consideration of the native impotence, the congenital weakness of these gentlemen, contrasted with their perpetually ostentatious attitude, with their threats in the air, their blasphemings into the void. And what are they doing today but once again flaunting before us their impotence, their invincible sterility? It is for refusing to commit myself beyond my self, for demanding silence around me, and for being faithful in thought and action to what I felt to be my deep and incurable powerlessness, that these gentlemen judged my presence among them to be inconvenient. But what they found most reprehensible and blasphemous was that I refused to assign to anyone but myself the responsibility for determining my limitations, that I insisted on being free and the master of my own action. But what does all the Revolution in the world mean to me if I know that I will remain in endless pain and misery in the charnel house of myself? For each man to refuse to consider anything beyond his own deepest sensibility, beyond his inmost self, this for me is the point of view of the complete Revolution. No revolution is good unless it benefits me and people like me. The revolutionary forces of any movement are those capable of shifting the present foundations of things, of changing the angle of reality.

But in a letter to the Communists they admit their total lack of preparation for the realm they have just entered. Better, they admit that the kind of activity asked of them is incompatible with their own mentality.

And it is here that they and I, whatever they may think, share at least in part an inhibition that is similar in essence, although it is the result of causes whose gravity and significance are very different for them and for me. In the last analysis they admit that they are incapable of doing what I have always refused to attempt. As for the Surrealist action itself, I am not worried. They can scarcely do more than spend their time preparing it—polishing and perfecting themselves like some Stendhal, these Amiels of the Communist revolution. The idea of the Revolution will never be anything for them but an idea which is in no danger of acquiring, even with age, the slightest bit of effectiveness.

But don't they see that they are revealing the emptiness of the Surrealist movement itself, of Surrealism untouched by any contamination,

"In Total Darkness" (1927)

If, moreover, the Surrealists were really looking for this, they would at least be excusable. Their goal would be banal and limited, but at least it would exist. But have they the slightest goal toward which to undertake an action, and when did they ever give a damn about formulating one?

Are they even working toward a goal? Are they working with motives? Do the Surrealists believe they can justify their expectation by the mere fact that they are aware of it? Expectation is not a state of mind. When one does nothing, one runs no risk of falling on one's face. But this is not sufficient reason to get oneself talked about.

I have too much contempt for life to think that any sort of change that might develop in the realm of appearances could in any way change my detestable condition. What divides me from the Surrealists is that they love life as much as I despise it. To enjoy themselves on every occasion and through every pore, this is the center of their obsessions. But is not asceticism an integral part of the true magic, even the blackest, even the most foul? Even the diabolical hedonist has an ascetic side, a certain spirit of mortification.

---

when they feel the need to interrupt its internal development, its true development, and shore it up with a commitment in principle or in fact to the French Communist Party? Is this what has become of that movement of revolt, that conflagration at the base of all reality? Did Surrealism, in order to survive, need to take the form of a material revolt, to identify itself with various demands concerning the eight-hour day or the readjustment of wages or the struggle against the high cost of living? What a farce, or what baseness of soul. And yet this is what they seem to be saying, that this commitment to the French Communist Party seemed to them the logical outcome of the development of the Surrealist idea and its only ideological safeguard!!!

But I deny that the logical development of Surrealism has led it to this clearly defined form of revolution known as Marxism. I have always thought that a movement as independent as Surrealism was not amenable to the procedures of ordinary logic. But this is a contradiction which is not likely to bother the Surrealists much, inclined as they are not to overlook anything that might be to their advantage, anything that might temporarily be of use to them.—Talk to them of Logic and they will answer you with Illogic, but talk to them of Illogic, Disorder, Incoherence, Freedom, and they will answer you with Necessity, Law, Obligations, Strictness. This fundamental bad faith is basic to their machinations.

I am not talking about their writings, which are brilliant, although negated by the point of view from which they are presented. I am talking about their central attitude, about the example of their lives as a whole. I do not hate them as individuals. I reject and condemn them as a group, giving each of them all the respect and even admiration he deserves for his works or for his mind. In any case I shall not, like them, be childish enough to execute a complete about-face and to deny them all talent the moment they cease to be my friends. But fortunately this is not the point.

The point is this displacement of the spiritual center of the world, this breaking up of appearances, this transfiguration of the possible which Surrealism was to help bring about. All matter begins with a spiritual deviation. To depend on things and on their transformations for guidance is the attitude of an obscene brute, of a metaphysical opportunist. Nobody has ever understood anything and the Surrealists themselves do not understand and cannot foresee where their desire for Revolution will lead them. Incapable of imagining, of conceiving a Revolution which did not evolve within the hopeless limitations of matter, they resort to fatality, to a certain accident of debility and impotence which is peculiar to them, in order to explain their inertia, their eternal sterility.

Surrealism has never meant anything to me but a new kind of magic. The imagination, the dream, that whole intense liberation of the unconscious whose purpose is to raise to the surface of the soul all that it is in the habit of keeping concealed, must necessarily introduce profound transformations in the scale of appearances, in the value of signification and the symbolism of the created. The whole of concrete reality changes its garb or shell and ceases to correspond to the same mental gestures. The beyond, the invisible, replace reality. The world no longer holds.

It is then that one can begin to screen out illusions, to eliminate frauds.

May the thick walls of the occult collapse once and for all on these impotent talkers who waste their lives in rebukes and empty threats, on these revolutionaries who revolutionize nothing.

These brutes whom it would suit me to be converted by. I would certainly need it. But at least I recognize that I am weak

"In Total Darkness" (1927)

and impure. I aspire to another life. And all things considered, I would rather be in my position than in theirs.*

What remains of the Surrealist adventure? Little besides a great disappointed hope, but in the domain of literature itself they may, in fact, have contributed something. This anger, this scathing disgust poured on the written word constitutes a fertile attitude and one which may be useful someday, later on. It has already purified literature, brought it closer to the essential truth of the brain. But that is all. Of positive conquests outside literature or images there are none, and yet this was the only thing that mattered. Out of the right use of dreams could be born a new way of guiding one's thought, a new way of relating to appearances. Psychological truth was stripped of all parasitic, useless excrescence, was much closer to being captured than before. We were alive then, to be sure, but perhaps it is a law of the spirit that the abandonment of reality can only lead to illusion. Within the narrow framework of our tangible domain we are pressured and solicited from every direction. We have seen this clearly in that aberration which has led revolutionaries on the highest possible level to literally abandon this level and to attach to this word "revolution" its utilitarian and practical meaning, the social meaning that is alleged to be the only valid one, since no one

---

* This bestiality which I am talking about and which revolts them so much is, however, what best distinguishes them. Their love of immediate pleasure, that is, of matter, has caused them to lose their original orientation, that magnificent power of escape whose secret we believed they were going to reveal to us all. A spirit of disorder, of petty wrangling, compels them to tear each other apart. Yesterday it was Soupault and I who left in disgust. Before that, it was Roger Vitrac, whose exclusion was one of their first dirty tricks.

They can howl in their corner all they like and deny it, I shall reply that for me Surrealism has always been an insidious extension of the invisible, the unconscious made accessible. The treasures of the invisible unconscious become palpable, guiding speech directly, with a single impulse.

For me Ruysbroeck, Martínez Pasqualis, Böhme are sufficient justification. Any spiritual act, if it is right, materializes when necessary. The internal conditions of the soul! But they carry with them their sacred commitment of stone, of real action. This is an established and self-evident fact, irremediably implied.

wants to be taken in by words. Curious reversal of position, curious leveling process.

Merely to advance a psychological attitude: does anyone believe that this can be enough, if this attitude is wholly characterized by inertia? The inner spirit of Surrealism leads it to Revolution. This is the positive fact. The only effective conclusion which is possible (so they say) and which a large number of Surrealists have refused to endorse; but as for the others, what has this espousal of Communism given them, what has it cost them? It has not made them take one step forward. This morality of becoming on which the Revolution is said to depend—never have I felt its necessity within the closed circle of my person. I place above any material necessity the logical exigencies of my own reality. This is the only logic that seems valid to me, and not some higher logic whose radiations affect me only insofar as they touch my sensibility. There is no discipline to which I feel forced to submit, however rigorous the reasoning that would persuade me to embrace it.

Two or three principles of life and death are for me higher than any precarious allegiance. And I have never encountered a logic that seemed to me anything but borrowed.

*

Surrealism has died of the idiotic sectarianism of its adepts. What remains is a kind of hybrid mass to which the Surrealists themselves are incapable of putting a name. Perpetually on the fringe of appearances, incapable of gaining a foothold on life, Surrealism is still at the stage of seeking its outlet, of marking time. Powerless to choose, to decide either totally in favor of the lie or totally in favor of the truth (the true lie of the illusory spiritual, the false truth of the immediate but destructible real), Surrealism hunts for that unfathomable, that indefinable interstice of reality in which to insert its once powerful lever, which has now fallen into the hands of eunuchs. But my well-known mental debility and cowardice refuse to take the slightest interest in upheavals which would affect only this external, immediately perceptible aspect of reality. External metamorphosis is, in my opinion, something which can only be given as a bonus. The social level, the material level toward which the Surrealists direct

"In Total Darkness" (1927)

their pathetic attempts at action, their forever ineffectual hatreds, is for me no more than a useless and obvious illusion.

I know that in the present dispute I have with me all free men, all true revolutionaries who think personal freedom is a good higher than any conquest achieved on a relative level.

*

My scruples in the face of all real action?

These scruples are absolute and they are of two kinds. Strictly speaking, they are based on a deep-rooted sense of the profound futility of any action whatsoever, whether spontaneous or unspontaneous.

This is the point of view of total pessimism. But a certain form of pessimism carries with it its own kind of lucidity. The lucidity of despair, the lucidity of senses that are exacerbated and as if on the edge of the abyss. And alongside the horrible relativity of any human action, this unconscious spontaneity which drives one, in spite of everything, to action.

And also in the equivocal, unfathomable realm of the unconscious: signals, perspectives, insights, a whole life that grows when one confronts it and reveals itself as capable of continuing to trouble the mind.

Here, then, are the scruples we hold in common. But with the Surrealists these scruples seem to have been resolved in favor of action. But once the necessity of this action has been acknowledged, they hasten to declare themselves incapable of it. It is a realm from which they are forever alienated by the configuration of their minds. And is this not exactly what I have always said about myself? Although I, of course, have in my favor psychological and physiological circumstances which are desperately abnormal and of which they would never know how to avail themselves.

On The Seashell and the Clergyman

CINEMA AND ABSTRACTION

Pure cinema is an error, just as in any art it is an error to try to reach the principle of that art to the detriment of its objective means of representation. It is a peculiarly terrestrial principle that things can act on the mind only by way of a certain state of matter, a minimum of substantial forms that are adequately realized. There may be a kind of abstract painting which dispenses with objects, but the pleasure that is derived from it retains a certain hypothetical quality which may, it is true, be satisfying to the mind. The foundation of cinematographic thought seems to be the utilization of existing objects and forms which can be made to say everything, for the patterns of nature are profound and truly infinite.

The Seashell and the Clergyman manipulates created nature and tries to make it yield a little of the mystery of its most secret combinations. One must not, therefore, try to find in it a logic or a sequence that does not exist in things; one must interpret the images that follow one another in terms of their essential, intimate significance, an inner significance that goes from the outside to the inside. *The Seashell and the Clergyman* does not tell a story but develops a series of states of mind which are derived from one another just as one thought is derived from another without this thought reproducing the reasonable sequence of events. From a collision of objects and gestures are derived real psychic situations among which the cornered mind seeks some subtle means of escape. Nothing exists except in terms of forms, volumes, light, air—but above all in terms of the sense of a detached and naked emotion that slips in between the paved roads of images and reaches a kind of heaven where it bursts into full bloom.

The characters are merely brains or hearts. The woman displays her animal desire, she has the shape of her desire, the spectral glitter of the instinct that drives her to be one and constantly different in her repeated metamorphoses.

Génica Athanasiou has succeeded in identifying herself with a role which is entirely instinctive and in which a very curious sexuality acquires an air of fatality that goes beyond the character as a human being and reaches the universal. Similarly, I have nothing but praise for Alex Alin and Bataille. And finally,

I want to address a very special thanks to Germaine Dulac, who was able to appreciate a screenplay that seeks to penetrate the very essence of the cinema and is not concerned with any allusion either to art or to life.

Cinema and Reality

Two paths seem to be open to the cinema right now, neither of which, undoubtedly, is the right one.

On the one hand there is pure or absolute cinema, and on the other there is that kind of venial hybrid art which insists on translating into more or less suitable images psychological situations that would be perfectly at home on the stage or in the pages of a book but not on the screen, since they are merely the reflection of a world that depends on another source for its raw material and its meaning.

It is clear that everything we have seen up to now that passes for abstract or pure cinema is very far from meeting what seems to be one of the essential requirements of cinema. For although the mind of man may be able to conceive and accept abstraction, no one can respond to purely geometric lines which possess no significative value in themselves and which are not related to any sensation that the eye of the screen can recognize or classify. No matter how deeply we dig into the mind, we find at the bottom of every emotion, even an intellectual one, an affective sensation of a nervous order. This sensation involves the recognition, perhaps on an elementary level, but at least on a tangible one, of something substantial, of a certain vibration that always recalls states, either known or imagined, that are clothed in one of the myriad forms of real or imagined nature. Thus the meaning of pure cinema would lie in the re-creation of a certain number of forms of this kind, it would lie in a movement and follow a rhythm which is the specific contribution of this art.

Between a purely linear visual abstraction (and the play of light and shadow is similar to the play of lines) and the fundamentally psychological film which relates the development of a story that may or may not be dramatic, there is room for an

On *The Seashell and the Clergyman*

attempt at true cinema, of whose substance or meaning nothing in the films that have been presented to date gives any suggestion.

In heavily plotted films, all the emotion and all the humor depend solely on the text, to the exclusion of the images; with a few rare exceptions, all the thought in a film is in the subtitles, and even in films without subtitles the emotion is verbal, it requires the clarification or support of words, for the situations, the images, the actions all turn on a clear meaning. We have yet to achieve a film with purely visual situations whose drama would come from a shock designed for the eyes, a shock drawn, so to speak, from the very substance of our vision and not from psychological circumlocutions of a discursive nature which are merely the visual equivalent of a text. It is not a question of finding in visual language an equivalent for written language, of which the visual language would merely be a bad translation, but rather of revealing the very essence of language and of carrying the action onto a level where all translation would be unnecessary and where this action would operate almost intuitively on the brain.

In the screenplay that follows, I have tried to carry out this idea of a visual cinema in which even psychology is engulfed by actions. No doubt this screenplay does not achieve the absolute image of all that can be done in this direction; but at least it points the way. Not that the cinema must renounce all human psychology: that is not its principle—on the contrary—but it must give psychology a form that is much more vital and active, and without those connections that try to reveal the motives for our actions in an absolutely stupid light instead of spreading them before us in their original and profound barbarity.

This screenplay is not the re-creation of a dream and should not be considered as such. I shall not attempt to excuse its apparent incoherence by the facile subterfuge of dreams. Dreams have more than their logic. They have their life, in which there appears an intelligent and somber truth. This screenplay seeks the somber truth of the mind in images which have issued solely from themselves and which do not derive their meaning from the situation in which they develop but from a kind of powerful inner necessity that casts them in a light of inescapable clarity.

The human skin of things, the epidermis of reality: this is the primary raw material of cinema. Cinema exalts matter and reveals it to us in its profound spirituality, in its relations with the spirit from which it has emerged. Images are born, are derived from one another purely as images, impose an objective synthesis more penetrating than any abstraction, create worlds which ask nothing of anyone or anything. But out of this pure play of appearances, out of this so to speak transubstantiation of elements is born an inorganic language that moves the mind by osmosis and without any kind of transposition in words. And because it works with matter itself, cinema creates situations that arise from the mere collision of objects, forms, repulsions, attractions. It does not detach itself from life but rediscovers the original order of things. The films that are most successful in this sense are those dominated by a certain kind of humor, like the early Buster Keatons or the less human Chaplins. A cinema which is studded with dreams, and which gives you the physical sensation of pure life, finds its triumph in the most excessive sort of humor. A certain excitement of objects, forms, and expressions can only be translated into the convulsions and surprises of a reality that seems to destroy itself with an irony in which you can hear a scream from the extremities of the mind.

On the Alfred Jarry Theater

XV

The Alfred Jarry Theater

The theater shares the disrepute into which all forms of art are successively falling. Amid the confusion, the *absence*, the distortion of all human values, in this agonizing uncertainty we live in regarding the necessity or value of this art or that form of mental activity, the idea of theater is probably the most gravely afflicted. It would be useless to search in the mass of spectacles presented every day for something that corresponded to any idea one might have of an absolutely pure theater.

If the theater is an amusement, too many serious problems demand our attention for us to be able to divert the least particle of it to anything so ephemeral. If the theater is not an amusement, if it is an authentic reality, then how are we to restore its rank as reality, how are we to make each spectacle a kind of event? This is the problem we must solve.

Our inability *to believe*, to accept illusion, is immense. Dramatic ideas no longer have for us the brilliance, the bite, that quality of something unique, unprecedented, *whole*, that continue to characterize certain ideas in literature or painting. The moment we introduce this idea of pure theater and try to give it concrete form, one of the first questions we must face is the question whether we will be able to find an audience capable of giving us the necessary minimum of confidence and trust, capable, in short, of *joining forces* with us. For, unlike writers or painters, we cannot do without an audience; indeed, the audience becomes an integal part of our undertaking.

. . . .

Theater is the one thing in the world most impossible to save. An art based entirely on a power of illusion which it is incapable of obtaining has no choice but to disappear.

. . . Words either do or do not have their power of illusion. They have their own value. But sets, costumes, gestures, and false cries will never take the place of the reality we are waiting for. This is the crux of the matter: the creation of a reality, the unprecedented eruption of a world. The theater must give us this ephemeral but real world, this world tangential to objective reality. Either the theater will become this world, or we will do without the theater.

Is there anything more contemptible and at the same time more ominously terrible than the spectacle of the police going into action? Society is familiar with these performances, which are based on the serenity with which it controls the lives and liberty of the people. When the police are preparing to make a raid, their movements resemble the choreography of a ballet. Policemen come and go. The dismal sound of police whistles tears the air. A kind of painful solemnity emanates from all movements. Little by little the circle closes in. These movements which on first glance seemed insignificant gradually become meaningful—as does that point of space which has served up to now as their pivot. It is an ordinary-looking house whose doors suddenly open, and from inside the house there emerges a group of women walking single file, like beasts to the slaughter. The plot thickens: the police net was intended not for a gang of criminals but only for a group of women. Our emotion and our amazement are at their peak. Never has a more effective stage setting been followed by such a denouement. For surely we are just as guilty as these women and just as cruel as these policemen. It is really a complete spectacle. Well, this spectacle is ideal theater. This anguish, this feeling of guilt, this victory, this satiety give the tone and feeling of the mental state in which the spectator must leave our theater. He will be shaken and antagonized by the internal dynamic of the spectacle, and this dynamic will be in direct relation to the anxieties and preoccupations of his whole life.

The illusion will no longer depend on the probability or improbability of the action but on its communicative power and its reality.

Is it clear now what we are driving at? What we are driving at is this: that with each performance we put on we are playing a serious game, that the whole point of our effort resides in this quality of seriousness. It is not to the minds or the senses of the spectators that we address ourselves but to their whole existence. Their existence and ours. We stake our own lives on the spectacle that unfolds on the stage. If we did not have the very clear and very profound sense that an intimate part of our lives was involved in that spectacle, we would see no point in pursuing the experiment. The spectator who comes to our theater knows that he is to undergo a real operation in which not only his mind but his senses and his flesh are at stake. Henceforth he will go to the theater the way he goes to the surgeon or the dentist. In the same state of mind—knowing, of course, that he will not die, but that it is a serious thing, and that he will not come out of it unscathed. If we were not convinced that we would reach him as deeply as possible, we would consider ourselves inadequate to our most absolute duty. He must be totally convinced that we are capable of making him scream.

ALFRED JARRY THEATER
FIRST SEASON: 1926–27

Theatrical conventions have had their day. As we are today, we cannot accept a theater that continues to deceive us. We need to believe in what we see. A performance that repeats itself every evening according to rites that are always the same, always identical to what they were the night before, can no longer win our support. The spectacle we are watching must be unique, it must give the impression that it is as unprecedented, as incapable of repeating itself as any action in life, any event brought on by circumstances.

With this theater, in short, we reestablish communication with life instead of cutting ourselves off from it. Neither the spectator nor we can take ourselves seriously unless we feel very clearly that part of our inner life is engaged in this action unfolding on the stage. Whether comic or tragic, our performance will be of the kind that sooner or later produces a forced smile. This is the purpose of our undertaking.

This is the kind of *human* anguish the spectator must feel as he leaves our theater. He will be shaken and antagonized by the internal dynamic of the spectacle that will unfold before his eyes. And this dynamic will be in direct relation to the anxieties and preoccupations of his whole life.

Such is the fatality that we evoke, and the spectacle will be this fatality itself. The illusion that we seek to create will depend not on the degree of verisimilitude of the action but on the communicative power and the reality of this action. Each spectacle will by its very nature become a kind of event. The spectator must have the sense that what is being performed in front of him is a scene from his own life, and an important scene at that.

In short, we ask of our audience an intimate and profound involvement. Discretion is not our concern. With each spectacle we put on, we are playing a serious game. Unless we are determined to follow our principles wherever they may lead us, we do not feel the game is worth playing. The spectator who comes to our theater will know that he is about to undergo a real operation in which not only his mind but his senses and his flesh are at stake. If we were not convinced that we could reach him as deeply as possible, we would consider ourselves inadequate to our most absolute duty. He must be totally convinced that we are capable of making him scream.

This necessity we are under of being as real and as alive as possible is sufficient indication of the contempt we have for all theatrical devices properly speaking, for all that constitutes what is traditionally known as *mise en scène*, like lighting, sets, costumes, etc. There is a whole picturesque quality which can be made to order and which has nothing to do with our concerns. It would take very little to make us go back to candles. The essence of theater lies for us in an imponderable quality that does not accommodate itself in any way to progress.

What will give the spectacles we put on their value of reality and clarity will usually depend on some imperceptible discovery that is capable of creating the maximum illusion in the mind of the spectator. Suffice it to say that as far as *mise en scène* and principles go, we entrust ourselves bravely to chance. In the theater that we want to create, chance will be our god. We fear no failure, no catastrophe. If we did not have faith in a possible miracle, we would not embark on such a risky course. But a single miracle would be sufficient reward for our efforts and our patience. We count on this miracle.

The director, who does not work according to any principle but who follows his own inspiration, may or may not make the find that we need. Depending on the play he has to put on, he may or may not hit upon a striking and ingenious invention, he may or may not find the *disturbing element capable of throwing the spectator into the desired state of doubt*. Our whole success depends on this alternative.

Still, it is quite obvious that we shall be working with specific texts; the works that we shall be performing belong to literature, such as it is. How can we reconcile our desire for freedom and independence with the necessity of conforming to certain directives imposed by texts?

For the purposes of this definition that we are trying to give of the theater, only one thing seems to us unassailable, only one thing seems real: the text. But the text as a distinct reality, existing in itself, sufficient unto itself, not in terms of its spirit, for which we have very little respect, but simply in terms of the displacement of air created by its enunciation. This is all we care about.

For what strikes us as essentially restrictive in the theater, and above all essentially destructible, is what distinguishes theatrical art from pictorial art and literature, all that odious and cumbersome apparatus that turns a written play into a spectacle instead of remaining within the limits of words, images, and abstractions.

It is this apparatus, this visual display that we wish to reduce to an impossible minimum and to overlay with the seriousness and disturbing quality of the action.

Manifesto for a Theater That Failed

In the age of confusion in which we live, an age filled with blasphemies and with the phosphorescent gleams of an infinite denial, an age in which all values, artistic as well as moral, seem to be dissolving into an abyss that nothing in any previous age of the mind can give an idea of, I was foolish enough to think that I could create a theater, that I could at least initiate this attempt to revive the universally despised value of the theater, but the stupidity of some and the bad faith and base vulgarity of others have dissuaded me from it forever.

Of this attempt the manifesto that follows is all that remains.

On January —, 1927, the A. . . Theater will present its first production. Its founders have the keenest awareness of the kind of despair the launching of such a theater implies. And it is not without a sort of remorse that they have made this decision. Let there be no mistake. The A. . . Theater is not a business, as everyone suspects. But it is an attempt on which a certain number of minds are staking their all. We do not believe, we can no longer believe that there is something in the world that can be called a theater, we see no reality to which such an appellation might be applied. A terrible confusion weighs on our lives. No one would think of denying that from the spiritual point of view we live in a critical period. We believe in all the threats of the invisible. And it is against the invisible itself that we are struggling. We are totally dedicated to unearthing certain secrets. And what we want to bring to light is precisely the mass of desires, dreams, illusions, and beliefs that have given rise to this lie which no one any longer believes in, and which is known, derisively it would seem, as theater. We want to revive certain images, but images that are evident and tangible, images that are not tainted with an eternal disillusionment. We are creating a theater not in order to put on plays but so that all that is obscure, hidden, and unrevealed in the mind will be manifested in a kind of material, objective projection. We do not seek, as has been done before, as has always been characteristic of the theater, to give the illusion of what is not, but on the contrary, to present to the eye certain tableaux, certain indestructible, undeniable images that will speak directly to the mind. The objects, the props, even the scenery which will appear on the stage will have to be understood in an immediate sense, without transposition; they will have to be taken not for what they represent but for what they really are. *Mise en scène* properly speaking, the movements of the actors, must be regarded solely as the visible signs of an invisible or secret language. There will not be a single theatrical gesture that will not carry behind it all the fatality of life and the mysterious encounters of dreams. Whatever in life has a prophetic, divinatory meaning, whatever corresponds to a presentiment or proceeds from a fertile error of the mind, will sooner or later appear upon our stage.

Obviously, our undertaking is all the more dangerous because it is highly ambitious. But it is important that people grasp the idea that we are not afraid of nothingness. There is no empty space in nature which we do not believe that, at one time or

On the Alfred Jarry Theater

another, the human mind can fill. It is clear what a terrible task we have undertaken; we aim to do no less than return to the sources, human or inhuman, of the theater, and raise it from the dead.

All that partakes of the obscurity and the magnetic fascination of dreams, those dark strata of consciousness which are all that concern us in the mind, we want to see all this radiate and triumph on the stage, even if it means destroying ourselves and exposing ourselves to the ridicule of a colossal failure. Nor are we afraid of the kind of commitment our effort represents.

We conceive of the theater as an authentic performance of magic. We do not address ourselves to the eyes, or to the direct emotion of the soul; what we are trying to create is a certain *psychological* emotion in which the inmost motives of the heart will be laid bare.

We do not think that life should be represented in itself, or that it is worthwhile to pursue this direction.

Toward this ideal theater we ourselves are groping blindly. We know in part what we want to do and how we could do it on a material level, but we have faith in an accident, a miracle which will reveal all that we still do not know, and which will impart all its profound higher life to this poor matter that we insist on kneading.

Regardless of the degree of success of our performances, those who attend them will understand that they are participating in a mystical experiment by which an important part of the domain of the mind and consciousness may be definitively saved or lost.

Antonin Artaud

November 13, 1926

P.S. These toilet-paper revolutionaries would have us believe that to start a theater today (as if *literature* were worth bothering with, as if it were of any consequence, as if it were not *elsewhere* that we had always fixed our lives), this filthy scum would have us believe that to start a theater today is a counterrevolutionary effort, as if Revolution were a taboo idea which has always been untouchable.

ANTONIN ARTAUD

Well, I do not recognize any idea as taboo.

For me there are several ways of understanding Revolution, and among them the Communist way seems by far the worst, the most limited. A lazy man's revolution. It makes no difference to me, I proclaim it in a loud voice, whether the power passes from the hands of the bourgeoisie into those of the proletariat. For me this does not constitute Revolution. Revolution does not lie in a simple transfer of power. A Revolution which is primarily concerned with the necessities of production and which therefore persists in relying on mechanization as a means of improving the lot of the workers is for me a revolution of eunuchs. And I get no nourishment from that grain. On the contrary, I think that one of the principal reasons for the disease from which we suffer is the insane externalization and the infinite proliferation of force; also, an abnormal facility that has entered into human relations which does not allow our thoughts the time to take root. We are all driven to despair by mechanization at every stage of our meditation. But the real roots of the disease are deeper, it would take a whole volume to analyze them. For the moment I will confine myself to saying that the Revolution most urgently needed consists of a kind of regression into time. Let us return to the mentality or even simply to the way of life of the Middle Ages, but really and by a kind of essential metamorphosis, and then I shall consider that we have accomplished the only revolution worth talking about.

If anything should be blown up, it is the foundations of most of the habits of modern thinking, European or otherwise. By these habits the Surrealists are far more affected than I, I assure you, and their respect for certain fetishes in human form and their reverence for Communism is the best proof of this.

If I had created a theater, what I would have done would have borne as little relation to what is commonly known as theater as an obscene performance bears to an ancient mystery play.

A.A.

January 8, 1927

On the Alfred Jarry Theater

Strindberg's Dream Play

Strindberg's *Dream Play* belongs to the repertoire of an ideal theater, as one of those model plays whose staging is for a director the crowning achievement of his career. The range of emotions expressed within this one work is infinite. In it one finds both the inside and the outside of a thought that is varied and vibrantly alive. In it the highest problems are represented, evoked in a form that is concrete as well as mysterious. It is truly the universality of the mind and of life whose magnetic shudder is offered us and grips us where we are most specifically and most productively human. The success of a performance of this kind inevitably blesses a director. The Alfred Jarry Theater owed it to itself to put on a play of this kind. The *raison d'être* and founding principle of this new company are known. The Alfred Jarry Theater wants to reintroduce into the theater the sense, not of life, but of a certain truth that inhabits the deepest strata of the mind. Between real life and the life of dreams there exists a certain interplay of mental associations, relationships between gestures or events that can be translated into actions, which constitute precisely that theatrical reality which the Alfred Jarry Theater has undertaken to revive. The sense of the true reality of the theater has been lost. The notion of theater has been erased from the human brain. And yet it still exists, halfway between reality and dreams. But until it has been rediscovered in its most absolute and most fertile wholeness, the theater will not cease to be in danger. The theater of today represents life, it seeks by the use of more or less realistic scenery and lighting to re-create for us the ordinary truth of life, or else it cultivates *illusion*—and that is the worst of all. Nothing is less capable of taking us in than the illusion of phony props, pasteboard, and painted backdrops which the modern stage presents. One must take one's choice and not try to compete with life. There is in the mere exposition of the objects of the real world, in their combinations, in their order, in the relationship of the human voice to light, a whole reality which is sufficient unto itself and which has no need of the other reality in order to live. It is this false reality which is theater, it is this reality which must be cultivated.

The production of the *Dream Play* obeys this necessity to

offer nothing to the eyes of the audience which cannot be utilized immediately and as is by the actors. Three-dimensional characters who will be seen moving about amid props, objects, a whole reality that is likewise three-dimensional. The false amid the real: that is the ideal definition of this production. A meaning, a function of a new spiritual order given to the ordinary objects and things of life.

Letters from 1927–30

XVI

TO GÉNICA ATHANASIOU

[Paris, September 16, 1927]

Génica, no matter what you do for me you will always be Life and Death

I have suffered to find similar inclinations in the being whom I regarded as my wife and whom I revered profoundly

if you had something to reproach me for you should have explained yourself candidly instead of making these painful insinuations

this is the cause of everything

I desire neither to break with you nor to abandon you

I believed you totally incapable of these base preoccupations which you scorned in others

hence my anger

when I think of what you used to be

and what you have suddenly become!!!

it is impossible for me to believe that it is my fault

anyway you can be sure that I regret it profoundly

will you also make me regret having believed in you, having had a confidence that I hoped would be eternal!!!!

TO ABEL GANCE

Paris, November 27, 1927

Dear Abel Gance,

You will soon be receiving a copy of my correspondence with Rivière, which will show you that I am concerned with the highest questions of the mind. The highest, and the most remote. I know that under your direction Jean Epstein is going to film Edgar Allan Poe's "The Fall of the House of Usher." I do not make many claims in this world, but I do claim to understand Poe and to be myself a man very much like the Master of Usher. If I don't have this character in my bones, *no one in the world does.* I am his physical and psychological embodiment. I'm not telling you that I'm interested in this part, I'm telling you that I demand it. John Barrymore, who is the only other man capable of playing the part, would do so magically, I admit, but he would be playing it from the outside, whereas I shall play it from the inside. My life is the life of Usher and of his sinister hovel. I have the plague in the marrow of my nerves and I suffer from it. There is a *quality* of nervous suffering which the greatest actor in the world cannot *project on the screen* unless he has experienced it himself. I have experienced it. I think like Usher. All my writings prove it—and I won't even mention my professional experience. If I haven't won the game it is because the game is truly lost, but this time lost for everyone.

Your infinitely devoted,
Antonin Artaud

58 rue La Bruyère, Paris IX

TO RENÉ ALLENDY

Paris, November 30, 1927

Dear friend,
   Have I told you that those psychoanalytic sessions I finally agreed to undergo made an unforgettable impression on me? You are aware of the sort of primarily instinctive and nervous repugnance I showed for this type of treatment when I met you. You succeeded in making me change my mind, not from an intellectual point of view, for there is in this curiosity, in this probing of my consciousness by an alien intelligence a kind of prostitution, a kind of immodesty which I shall always reject, but from an experimental point of view I have observed the benefits I derived from it, and if necessary I will lend myself again to an attempt of this kind. But from the very depths of my being I continue to flee psychoanalysis, I shall always flee it as I shall flee every attempt to circumscribe my consciousness with precepts or formulas, with any kind of verbal organization. In spite of everything, I shall testify to the charge your treatment has produced in me. However, and this is the reason I am writing you, there is in those around me, and especially in you, a tendency to believe me *cured*, to think that I have returned to normal life and that my case has

ceased to come under the jurisdiction of medicine. This is not true. I still have a great need, a fundamental need of someone like you, provided you are willing to revise your opinion of my case. I see very clearly the tendency that people have to believe that I have recovered all the ground I lost and that I am in a glorious period of my life, that the fates are smiling on me and showering me with gifts and favors. And indeed on the surface everything seems to indicate that this is true. I seem to be blessed by the gods from the material as well as the moral and spiritual point of view. Well, there is something rotten in me, there is a sort of fundamental flaw in my psyche that prevents me from enjoying the things that destiny offers me. I tell you this so that you will not lose interest in me and so that you will believe that I continue to have need of your help. My lucidity is total, keener than ever, what I lack is an object to which to apply it, an inner substance. This is more serious and more painful than you think. I would like to get beyond this point of absence, of emptiness. This marking time that weakens me and makes me inferior to everyone and everything. I have no life, I have no life!!! My inner enthusiasm is dead. It has been years now since I lost it, since I lost this inner surge that saves me. This spontaneity of images that sustain the self. In which my personality recovers itself, explores itself. Finds its density, its precious resonance. Apathy has taken possession of my mind. Whatever I find in the way of images or ideas seems to come to me as if by chance, seems to be an old memory that clings, that has only the appearance of new life—and the quality *suffers* accordingly. This is not a fantasy, an impression. It is a fact that I am no longer myself, that my real self is asleep. I go after my images. I pull them up a handful at a time, they do not come to me or compel my attention. Under these conditions I no longer have any criterion. These images, whose value lies in their authenticity, have lost their value, they are only effigies, reflections of thoughts previously pondered or pondered by others, not presently and personally THOUGHT. Understand me. It is not even a question of the quality of the images, or the quantity of the thoughts. It is a question of fulgurating *vitality*, of truth, of reality. There is no more life. Life does not inform, does not illumine what I think. I said LIFE. I did not say the appearance of life, I said real life, the essential illumination: being, the original spark from which every thought is ignited—that center. I feel that my center is dead. And I suffer. I suffer at each of my spiritual expirations, I suffer from their absence, from the state of uncertainty through which all my thoughts *inexorably* pass, by which MY THOUGHT is diluted and diverted. The trouble is always the same. Try as I may, I cannot *think*. Try to understand this hollowness, this intense and lasting emptiness. This vegetation. How horribly I am vegetating. I can neither advance nor retreat. I am fixed, localized around a point which is always the same and which all my books describe. But my books I have left behind me now. But I have not gone beyond them, for in order to go beyond them I would first have to *live*. And I refuse to live. This is what I have tried to make you understand. The point is that my thought no longer develops either in space or in time. I am nothing. I have no self. For in the presence of anything at all, conception or circumstance, I think nothing. My mind suggests nothing to me. There is no use looking. And neither from the intellectual side nor from the emotional or purely imaginary side do I possess anything. I am without any kind of reserve. Without any kind of possibility.

There is no point in my looking for images. I KNOW that I shall never find my images. That nothing in me will ever rise to the degree of mental firmness, of inner compression that would enable me to meet or recover myself. As long as I have not recovered my own electricity, an intensity of vision, a *range* of conceptions born easily, I mean born rather than forced or fabricated, all my works will be unreliable, because they will be born under false conditions, conditions that no man knows except myself. Nothing I write is created, or participates in creation; everything has the appearance of a last resort, is done not haphazardly but without necessity, and always for lack of something better. Dear friend, I swear to you that it is serious, very serious. I am vegetating in the worst kind of moral idleness. I never work. What comes out of me is drawn out as if by chance. And I could just as well write or say or think something completely different from what I say or think and it would represent me just as well. That is to say, just as badly. That is to say, not at all. I am not here. I am not here, and I never will be. It is serious because it is not a question of the gratuitous work of writing, or of images for their own sake, but rather of the thought itself, that is to say, the life. The same vacuity possesses me in relation to every circumstance of life. The same business as in the letters to Rivière. I am quite aware that I bore everyone, that no one is interested—but what am I to do, since I am alive? Short of *dying*, there is no solution. Shall I die, or will you, having understood me and realizing *the low value* of my present life, which deceives so many people, will you find the medical means of saving me?

Your devoted friend,
Artaud

P.S. Thank you for the pills, but I used them up two weeks ago. In Cannes I'll need enough for three weeks. I would need at least forty strong ones, for as you suspect I have fallen right back on laudanum.
Alas!!!!

TO YVONNE ALLENDY

[Paris, June 7, 1928]

Dear Madam,

I simply *do not understand* your interpretation of my attitude toward Breton. I did not get angry with him right away because I did not really want to, because I was hoping that he would change his mind, and because I did not believe that emotional factors should enter into it, but as for my attitude toward the play and *the future of what I am doing*, you can be sure, and you do me wrong when you doubt it (that was why I was so annoyed on the telephone), that my mind is made up once and for all to break with Breton *the moment he comes to sabotage the play*. There is no doubt on this point. The performance will take place in spite of him and, of course, against him, since this is the meaning he wants to give to it.

As for inviting him, no. I had not really considered what I was doing in inviting him and that if I did invite him I would no longer have the right to throw him out. Not only will he not be invited, but if he comes he will not be seated. As for the question of whether we can *refuse* him admission, maybe you would be good enough to talk this over with Aron. Since it appears that we do not have the legal right to prevent anyone from entering the theater, I do not see what measures can be taken other than to force him to pay for his seat. Nor do I see any way to prevent him from entering unless we went to the police, which would be disgraceful.

I hope you will forgive me for getting so annoyed just now, but you must understand how upset I am after the series of blows I have suffered. After I left you the other night I had a terrible experience. I'll tell you about it, but you'll see that you must forgive me and that you cannot hold it against me.

I am your friend. But I must beg you not to say, not even to think, that my attitude is not clear. I shall stop at nothing to defend my play, I beg you to believe it. As for you, to tell your friends not to come would be a terrible thing and one which could do us grave harm. It goes without saying that I shall do all that must be done to spare you the necessity of taking such an extreme step.

Antonin Artaud

TO YVONNE ALLENDY

Nice, March 26, 1929

Dear friend,

1. To make a talking film now or ever strikes me as a bad idea. The Americans, who have invested a great deal in the talking film, are digging their own graves, as are all companies that produce bad films on the pretext that they are more salable; the talking Cinema is a piece of folly, an absurdity. Indeed, the very negation of Cinema. That someone may *possibly* succeed in synchronizing the sounds of a countryside, the noise of a scene chosen purely for its visual quality, I admit, and I see very well what could be done in this direction. But there is no difference between this and the imitative sounds of an orchestra. The sound is produced by a loudspeaker, a recording, instead of by the orchestra, but there is no difference in *value*. For, however well *synchronized* it may be, it does not come from the screen, from

that potential, absolute space which the screen spreads before us. No matter what they do, our ear will always hear it *in the theater*, whereas our eye sees *outside of the theater* what goes on on the screen.

One would have to invent a completely talking screen which would create auditory perspectives in all three *dimensions,* just as the visual screen creates perspectives for the eye. But this is science and does not interest me.

If I have an idea for a film involving possibilities for sound or music, and I'm going to think about it, I'll tell you about it. BUT I WON'T PUT ANY WORDS IN IT.

2. There is no bearable producer in Nice, or IN FRANCO-FILM right now, to whom I would entrust a screenplay. So all you can do is offer that gentleman in Paris one of the screenplays I'm going to send you.

3. I'll give it my first consideration. But you know that for me to do a commercial screenplay would be to destroy myself. Worse than that, it would be an immoral act. The sinister thing about concessions is that they diminish and discredit a man and this is so *essentially* because this man is going against his nature and consequently against the functioning of his mind. The great American successes like *Lonesome* or *Underworld* are not what are usually meant by commercial movies.

FINALLY

I shall not be able to do anything until I have recovered.

I had ceased to believe that I was ill, but with ALL MY LUCIDITY,

the horrible pressure in the head and at the top of the spinal column, the constriction in the chest, the ideas of blood and murder, the torpors, the nameless spells of faintness, the general horror in which I find myself immersed together with a mind that is fundamentally sound, make that mind unusable.

You understand that I would long since have accepted the inevitable and stopped boring the world if all that had not constituted an ABSOLUTE obstacle in its petty and ridiculous RELATIVITY.

Best wishes,
Artaud

ANTONIN ARTAUD

TO YVONNE ALLENDY

June 5, 1930

Dear friend,
 I have just spent the whole afternoon going around in the hope of finding work. I was very badly received at the first place I went to and better received elsewhere. I must admit that this was when I knew the people personally. Here is what I think you might say to Marinetti:

 "Some time ago I mentioned a friend of ours, Antonin Artaud, some of whose rather Surrealistic literary efforts you have read, including *The Umbilicus of Limbo.*
 "I don't know whether I told you that Mr. Artaud is also an actor in the cinema and the theater. I think you must have seen in Italy Abel Gance's *Napoleon,* in which Mr. Artaud played the part of Marat, and perhaps Carl Dreyer's *The Passion of Joan of Arc,* in which Mr. Artaud played Massieu, the young monk who defends Joan of Arc. He also played the part of the Intellectual in Léon Poirier's *Verdun,* and other parts in numerous films, including Marcel L'Herbier's *L'Argent,* Raymond Bernard's *Tarakanova,* etc.
 "I know that Italy is making great efforts right now in the field of cinema and that the Pittaluga Company, among others, has just refurbished its Studios in order to produce talking and sound films in several languages. I would like to suggest that for the French versions of its films it might be advisable for Pittaluga to use actors who are already well known for their performances here. Mr. Artaud is one of this group. You know that, in addition to his gifts as a writer, he has experimented with theatrical production, and since 1927 his Alfred Jarry Theater has presented four plays.
 "I enclose some photographic documents that will give you an idea of the stark and forceful style that he introduced into his work in staging, whose effect is sometimes agonizing, compelling, and very contemporary. Some of these photographs illustrate his attempts to make a short experimental film based on the English Gothic novel *The Monk* by Matthew Gregory Lewis.

I need not go into the difficulties Mr. Artaud has encountered here in Paris in introducing his ideas. Dr. Allendy and myself would be grateful for anything you could do to enable Mr. Artaud to play any unusual character parts in the French versions of films to be made in Rome in the near future. Once he is there, Mr. Artaud could personally tell you his ideas regarding the talking or sound film. And perhaps it would be possible to arrange to have him make a few short films of his own, which will have an acute and compact interest.

"I am, etc.

"P.S. The enclosed documents will already give you an idea of the movement he would be able to introduce into a film and of certain lighting techniques of his own which tend to give the movement and the general ambiance a kind of psychic value that reveals all the secrets of the unconscious."

There, dear friend, is a rough version of what I think you might say. I enclose the documents, but I am very anxious that this letter be mailed tonight special delivery. With my apologies for your trouble and my gratitude for your continued kindnesses in my behalf, I beg you to believe in my most *sincere* friendship.

Please convey my most affectionate greetings to the doctor.

Antonin Artaud

TO RENÉ ALLENDY

Berlin, July 12 [1930]

Dear doctor and friend,

I have already written from here to Ruttmann about the screenplay. But I must clarify for you the subject of my relations with Pathé-Nathan. All I did was send a letter to one of the directors indicating that I had several screenplays ready to be produced, and I received in reply a letter asking me to send the screenplays, along with a printed questionnaire asking my name and qualifications, and what director I had in mind. In response to this last question I gave the name of Walter Ruttmann for the screenplay of *The 32*. And that's all. This does not mean that things have progressed very far. My health continues to bother me in every possible way. The pressure on the back of the neck is still overwhelming every time I try to begin to work. Indeed, I have no desire to work. It is very hard for me to do what I have to do here at the Studio, which is not amusing, and the difficulty is increased by the sudden disappearance of the elementary reflexes, which hinders me terribly in my profession. One discovers long afterward that one has not made a certain gesture which the circumstances dictated, that one has not had a certain reaction, or even a certain recoil, that one has not reacted and that one is inert in a situation where normally one would have jumped. And when one observes this profound inertia which weighs one down like lead, one feels a physical indifference which is powerful and complete, which even leads one to forget what one might have *been*.

There are quite a few homeopathic pharmacies here. Perhaps, if you think of it, you could tell me a medicament that might control these particular symptoms. I saw Professor Sachs, who put me in touch with a great German director, G. W. Pabst. The latter seemed very interested in my case, and I am to see him again to talk at length, he said. I have also seen Raffaello Busoni, who is certainly an extremely charming man and a talented painter, although rather classical. I missed an appointment with him, where I was to have met an important politician and a well-known journalist, because of the cinema, but I have been invited again for Monday evening.

If I were not perpetually tormented by the pain in my head, I would keenly enjoy the life of Berlin, which is a city of astonishing luxury and bewildering license. I am constantly dazed by what I see. They carry their obsession with eroticism everywhere, even to the store windows, where all the mannequins thrust out their pelvises. And everything is gold, red, green, and black, with mauve lighting. The food actually overflows, and everywhere there are visions of cakes drowning in whipped cream and ice cream laden with fruit. On the other hand, the coffee is undrinkable and the tobacco unsmokable. The Germans are gentle, polite, obsequious, nervous, and sometimes a little servile, on the whole. Sometimes I pass soldiers of the Reichswehr who give me withering looks out of the corners of their eyes and mutter that I am French, without my even opening my mouth.

There is an amazing building here called the Vaterland—Paris contains nothing like it. It is a kind of pleasure house five stories high. On each story there are one or two café-restaurants, each evoking a different country, and at the back of each café is a theatrical landscape in relief, representing in one the Bosporus (the Turkish café), in another the mountains of the Tyrol, in a third Vienna, in another Spain, in another Hungary, in another America. And each serves the drinks and dishes of that country. The most amazing is the café of the Rhine, which contains a kind of overhanging balustrade with a view of the Rhine and its castles. And suddenly the sky covers over with clouds, thunder growls, it grows dark, and a torrential rain falls while lighting effects simulate a thunderstorm with absolute realism. The thunder especially bears no relation to theatrical thunder. You hear the slightest rumbles with meticulous precision. It's extraordinary.

I did not think when I started this letter that it would be so long. I was forced to abandon it this morning at the second page because of the horrible pains I felt, but this evening I feel a little better.

Please give my fondest wishes to Mrs. Allendy.

Very cordially,
Antonin Artaud

Passauer Strasse 10, Berlin

P.S. I am also writing Pathé-Nathan telling them that Walter Ruttmann has already chosen Génica Athanasiou for the part, in case the film is made, information which I had not given them the first time.

Questions and answers on the cinema

XVII

REPLY TO A QUESTIONNAIRE

1. *What kind of films do you like?*
2. *What kind of films would you like to see made?*

1. I like *the cinema*.
I like any kind of films.
But all the kinds of films have yet to be created.

I believe that the cinema can only allow a certain kind of films: the kind in which all the means of sensual action available to the cinema are utilized.

The cinema involves a total reversal of values, a complete revolution in optics, perspective, and logic. It is more exciting than phosphorus, more captivating than love. One cannot go on indefinitely destroying its galvanizing power by the use of subjects that neutralize its effects, subjects that really belong to the theater.

2. So I demand phantasmagorical films, films that are *poetic* in the accurate, philosophical meaning of the word, psychic films.

Which excludes neither psychology, nor love, nor the display of any of the human feelings.

But films in which there is a pulverizing, a recombining of the things of the heart and the mind in order to give them a cinematographic quality *which is yet to be found*.

The cinema calls for extravagant subjects and a detailed psychology. It requires speed, but above all it requires repetition, insistence, recapitulation. The human soul in all its aspects. In the cinema we are all *—and cruel. It is the superiority and the powerful law of this art that its rhythm, its speed, its quality of remoteness from life, its illusory aspect require a close screening and a distillation of all its elements. This is why it calls for extraordinary subjects, climactic states of mind, an atmosphere of vision. The cinema is a remarkable stimulant. It acts directly on the gray matter of the brain. When the flavor of art has been blended in sufficient proportion with the psychic ingredient it contains, it will go far beyond the theater,

---

* Word missing in the French manuscript.—*Trans.*

which we will then relegate to the attic with our souvenirs. For the theater is by its very nature a betrayal. We go to the theater much more to see actors than to see plays, at least it is primarily the actors who affect us. In the cinema the actor is merely a living sign. He alone provides the setting, the idea of the author, and the sequence of events. This is why we do not think about him. Chaplin plays Chaplin, Pickford plays Pickford, Fairbanks plays Fairbanks. They are the film. One could not conceive of it without them. They are in the foreground where they get in no one's way. This is why they do not exist. So nothing comes between the work and ourselves. Above all, the cinema has the power of a poison that is harmless and direct, a subcutaneous injection of morphine. This is why the subject of the film cannot be inferior to its effectiveness—and why it must have an element of magic.

INTERVIEW FOR CINÉMONDE

When the editors of Cinémonde *gave me the assignment of interviewing Antonin Artaud, I began looking for him at once. It was not easy, Antonin Artaud was not to be found. Wherever I asked for him, I was told that he had not been seen in a long time. And yet I was sure that after completing his role in* Tarakanova, *Antonin Artaud had returned to Paris. I had almost given up hope of meeting him when one day, in a bar near Place Clichy, I heard behind me a voice that sounded familiar. I turned around: it was Antonin Artaud. You can imagine my delight.*

"You! I don't believe it!" *I exclaimed, very surprised.* "My dear friend, I have you and I won't let you go until you give me an interview."

Antonin Artaud smiled.

"Ah! These journalists, always so tenacious. But do you really think that what I have to say will interest your readers?"

"*Why of course, otherwise I wouldn't have pursued you.*"

At last Antonin Artaud agreed to an interview.

"My service record," *he began.* "First of all a juvenile lead in *Faits Divers,* an avant-garde film which was shown at the Ursulines and which contained a slow-motion strangling scene that in those days passed for an innovation. A few small parts in various films, *Surcouf, Le Juif Errant, Graziella*. Finally Abel Gance's *Napoleon*, in which I played Marat. This was the first role where I was able to feel natural on the screen, where I had an opportunity not only to try to be realistic but to express my own conception of a figure, a character who seemed the incarnation of a force of nature, disinterested and indifferent to everything that was not the force of his passions.

"After Marat, I played the monk Massieu in Carl Dreyer's *Joan of Arc*. This time I played a saint who was no longer seething, full of outbursts, and perpetually at war with himself, but, on the contrary, calm.

"I do not wish to concern myself with what this film and my role in this film have become in the so-called commercial version. I know that I have unforgettable memories of my work with Dreyer. This time I was working with a man who was able to make me believe in the rightness, the beauty, and the human interest of his conception. And whatever ideas I may have had about the cinema, about poetry, about life, for once I realized that I was no longer dealing with an aesthetic, a bias, but with a work of art, with a man determined to elucidate one of the most agonizing problems that exist. Dreyer was determined to show Joan of Arc as a victim of one of the most painful distortions there are: the distortion of a divine principle passing into the brains of men, whether they are called the Government or the Church or by some other name.

"And the modalities, the pure technique of this work were fascinating, for although I found Dreyer a demanding person, I also found in him not a director but a man, in the most sensitive, the most human, and the fullest sense of the word. Dreyer insistently demanding from the actor, instilling in the actor the spirit of a scene, and then giving him the latitude to direct it, to give it any sort of personal inclination, provided he remain faithful to the spirit required. In the final scene of the moral martyrdom of Joan, before the execution, before the communion, when Brother Massieu asks Joan whether she still believes that she has been sent by heaven, Dreyer knew that the kind of exaltation communicated to Massieu by Joan, by the situation and by the scene may not have been indispensable, but it was dictated by the emotion of the facts themselves, and he would not have thought of preventing it.

"There are a great many things I could still say about Carl Dreyer's film. I am only glad that the presentation of the uncut version has changed the general opinion of this overwhelming film.

"After *Joan of Arc*, I played the Intellectual in Léon Poirier's *Verdun, Visions d'Histoire*; Mazaud in Marcel L'Herbier's *L'Argent*, and the part of a Bohemian lover in *Tarakanova*, which I have just finished under the direction of Raymond Bernard.

"Although I haven't had the opportunity, in these last films, to create such strong characters as in *Napoleon* and *Joan of Arc*, I am sure that now that I've made contact with several directors I'll finally have the opportunity to create a complete character.

"The cinema is a terrible profession. Too many obstacles prevent one's expressing oneself or carrying out an idea. Too many commercial or financial contingencies hamper the directors I know. One defends too many people, too many things, too many blind necessities. For this reason the cinema is a profession which I shall certainly abandon if I'm given a role that makes me feel restricted, disabled, cut off from myself, from what I think and what I feel.

"For mercy's sake, my dear friend, don't compare me to Conrad Veidt, as many people do. This actor has a special inclination toward the convulsive, the excessive, which I am trying more and more to avoid.

"One last word on the profession of being an actor. Every day I hear directors who are deficient in real dramatic sense extol, at the expense of the professional actor, the non-professional actor who, as in *Finis Terrae*, for example, can be made to play any life-like scene better than a professional.

"The discussion rests on a misunderstanding, and that is all there is to it.

"The non-professional actor does on the screen the same thing that he does in life, and which with a little patience one can make him perform; but the professional film actor, I mean the good actor, the real actor who, although he is placed in an artificial realm, the realm of art or poetry, feels and thinks directly, spontaneously, without performing; this actor does something that no one else could do, something that he himself in his normal state does not do.

"This is the whole question, dear friend; and I would be very grateful if in your article you would devote more space to the ideas I am talking about than to my roles. The former are more likely to interest your readers than the latter."

"*But why, Artaud? There's no reason.*"

And on this note I took my leave of this excellent actor. It was late, but I did not care; at last I had my interview.

Excerpts from notebooks and private papers (1931–32)

XVIII

That which is true in life always gives the feeling of intelligence.

*

No longer to be in command of one's anger,
to be reduced to looking for the reactions that punctuate our minds,
the terrible inertia of real thought, after verbal memory and vocabulary have disappeared,
the mind living amid the collapse of language, the mind reduced to looking for its forms, makes its way toward adverse, fictitious forms which replace it very badly.

The mind can no longer locate the sources capable of fleshing out its anger and is reduced to looking for bursts and *flashes* which would represent it [the mind].

That terrible thing of *appearing to oneself* inferior to what one really is and of no longer recognizing oneself except in revelations.

*

All problems are incomprehensible.
There is no longer any fixed level if the mind collapses metaphysically from the bottom and cannot concentrate on aspects of the concrete.

If one could think of everything.

Encounter with syphilis.

What are the cases in which the physical encounter does not occur.

*

Metaphysical feelings to be unearthed, to be condensed in states which presuppose certain classes of images just as the color of certain skies presupposes the flight of certain birds.

Ideas about Becoming and possibility.

To free oneself from a utilitarian and everyday psychology which regards a certain number of fundamental ideas as innate.

We have lost all contact with certain symbols that have been reduced, emaciated, even with their miraculous unity.

Fear is poetry.

Religious forces of nature.

*

I am miserable like a man who has lost the best of himself.
I can no longer reach all my beautiful ideas, but not like a man who suffers from a temporary drying up of consciousness on certain rare and precious points which may be representative but are still exceptional, and with whom it is a certain formal acuity, a certain brilliance of expression, a rich and brilliant way of grasping ideas, and the art and the force or the bite of these ideas that are missing rather than the idea itself, however stringently it may be reduced to everything which is it and separated from that which is not it. No, it is the idea itself, the idea and its memory, it is *forgotten*, forgotten, gone out of me, it has abandoned me, it and the others, so completely that I shall never be able to call it back to me, to recall it, to name it and distinguish it, if only in its forms and its cutting edge, and in its distinct separations. Once again I have lost the feeling of the thinkable. So that even to name ideas in connection with which one can begin to think something is to reveal something to me, is to recall to my memory things of a forgotten world from which I have been banished. In the literal sense I am poor in mind, for the thoughts that I attain, the points of mind that I am capable of reaching are infinitely restricted.

*

Our Western world, full of material concerns, is turning away from Metaphysics.

From notebooks and private papers (1931-32)

A phobia about Metaphysics seems even to be one of the dominant characteristics of our mind; and to be involved with Metaphysics seems in the West to be the prerogative of a very limited number of individuals.

One could define the East as the only part of the world where Metaphysics is part of the daily practice of life.

*

The wound, the dreadful hollowness of the paralyzed self, when it is a question of rousing it on the few points about which it thinks something, about which it has, as they say, "its opinion."
Not only is it no longer able to express this opinion, but it has forgotten what it refers to, and even from a distance it no longer knows what it was about.

*

In the strange pursuit of something which no one cares about and which, if I did find it, could never be of any real utility. For it so happens that it is a question of utility, and utility of the most essential kind, since what I pursue amid the misery and pain of desperate confusion is no less than the *fact of absolute thought*. What I seek to isolate and surround, what I want to confront at least once in my life, is that *point of thought* where, having cast off the commonest illusions and temptations of language, I find myself confronting a utilization of my mind which is absolutely naked, absolutely clear and without ambiguity or possible confusion. I realize that in so doing I am already deceiving myself, for in periods of normalcy I should *feel* in possession of this point by the simple fact of desiring it. If the profound confusion in which my whole mind is bathed is sufficient reason that I must seek to provoke, by means of trickery, patience, painful effort, a spiritual attitude into which I should be transported quite naturally, this attitude of simple clarity, this kind of new beginning manufactured out of whole cloth whose purpose is to allow me to find out how far I have come, does momentarily stave off the anguish that descends on me by the mere fact that I am thinking or trying to think. And even in the state in which I find myself right now and which evokes what is really the simplest mental operation there is, it is only by proceeding step by step and by sneaking up on myself at every moment, by measuring my interior mental gestures at each of these steps, by doing nothing that might lead the fatalities that spy on me and threaten me to believe that I am really trying to think further than I say, that I avoid the intrusion of grave anxieties created to deprive me of the usage of all intellectuality. I realize, moreover, that all these ruses and stratagems would be useless and that I am at this moment much more rich and powerful than I really am, or else even this portion of intellectual reflection directed toward very simple and very insignificant objects would be completely denied me, for I have learned to appreciate how much stronger destiny was than myself, and that I was without shelter and without defense against it; truly the poorest and most disarmed of spirits created. This is why I only wish to describe the full extent and the full desolation of my misery which is, I believe, without precedent and without any kind of comparison possible. For I believe that no one has ever seen a *living* mind, I say living, that is, still conscious, lucid, capable of observing and measuring its own life, capable, if necessary and at certain moments, of weighing and judging its own thought, the innumerable creations of this thought—and which nevertheless is as if dead and which has become, truly and literally, incapable of thinking, of *what is called thinking,* for even those thoughts which at long intervals it still formulates, those judgments which escape it under the stimulus of a sudden excitement, are the exception that proves the uniformity of its void. For the terrible part is that, in the throes of an impotence that is established in its own eyes and a thousand times demonstrated, it has to contend with the almost unanimous incredulity of others, an incredulity that prevents it from receiving the help it deserves. It is also true that this impotence, these blasts from the abyss which overwhelm it pass, proceed, and occur in cycles, but it is also true that since my mind is present at the profound decline and non-manifestation of its own powers, it judges and knows better than another how far it has come and the value, in terms of its real thought, its discernible self, of a given internal explosion, a given coagulation of real thought. It knows, for example, in the presence of the throbbing of universal and contemporary thought, how little it feels itself and how much its profound consciousness responds; it knows, in the inertia and the solitude of an inert self, of what sudden leaps, of what constant wrenchings, of what serious disharmonies between a keen sensibility and a contracted, inoperative intelligence, its inner consciousness is the theater—and *the result*. There is, first of all, the inner dialogue between consciousness and mind, that kind of soliloquy to which everything is reduced and by which everything is ultimately measured in the inner domain, which sees its words burst, its phrases abort, its stability scattered, curiously undermined, full of flight, full of a horrible suspended absence; at this point, in the face of this disaster which is more than uncomfortable and which at whatever degree condemns it to anguish, the most physical anguish, consciousness, ceasing to struggle with a clarity, a lucidity which are however necessary, and knowing the inexplicable miscarriages that threaten it, falls back upon itself, tries to let itself live, tries *not to think*. Don't think, say the stupid, says the vulgar herd, *why try to think?* As if without this it were possible to live, and I defy anyone to imagine that absolutely unthinkable thing, a mind that could really exist without thinking.

And yet it is to this, to this sort of internal inactive inertia of a mind that forbids itself all self-expression that *my* mind condescends, reduces itself. In the face of this failure of internal speech it resorts to a kind of pure consciousness, but this is precisely where the malaise begins, an insane wrenching, a suspension mingled with sensibility, with forms, with words, with directions, with sensations, with accents. For if this inertia, this silence were natural, all would be well, but this consciousness which cannot normally surround with forms, with words, shows its absolute confusion by revealing itself as empty, *deprived of its substance*.

All normal repose is denied it. Its states are not whole, it cannot rest on anything, it has no complete sense of anything, any feeling that it has that is fixed or established is immediately destroyed, it shows that it truly has no resilience. Thus it is not speech, it is not the mind that is sick, it is the being, the whole being, for after the silence of speech, the need to include something, no matter what, rushes up from the depths of the unconscious and this something dries up, demineralizes immediately. And this maladjustment of consciousness is the result of life.

But this lucidity which is in me and which observes these perpetual defeats registers each of these failures as an ineluctable anguish.

Until now I have contemplated this somber and highly tormented life which was given me in the inertia and solitude of myself, beyond any particular duty, beyond all intimacy with others as beyond all real activity.

The collision with other consciousnesses, the necessity of maintaining certain relationships, of keeping up a problematical rank, by obliging me to practice this impotence publicly, will help me to take its real measure.

*

It is a question of giving me back a life,

and it should be easy for him to know if I am worth the trouble of dragging me out of the hell in which I have been revolving year after year without possible escape or termination.

*

The only real poetry is cosmic,
the elements of density, breadth, transparency, opacity,
the rage for being, and its dissimulation on the greatest possible scale,

the poetry of seasons, dawns, sun suspended in a certain light that verges on green, mauve, orange, a certain haze,
the lyricism of the social or personal passions, all this is merely accidental,
presupposes a state of things that is perfect, collected, stabilized.

But even if there is a poetry of joy, it cannot exist in resignation, for the praise, the happiness, the exaltation of this imperfect order which is ours is an exaltation which mistakes its object,

From notebooks and private papers (1931–32)

one should define this fear, which is similar to an immense space, to that void which is found in the center of a whirlpool.

*

The total forgetting of ideas.

In matters of feeling I can't even find anything that would correspond to feelings.
And I have nothing to say either.

Letters from 1931

XIX

INCOMPLETE DRAFT OF A LETTER, ADDRESSEE UNKNOWN

Thursday evening

Dear friend,

    I detest literature more than you do. But how far from literature are these so-called messages that you mention, as well as this letter of bookish vatication—no, not even that: journalistic vatication—of which you sent me an excerpt. It is the letter of an apprentice magus, a naïf, a charlatan among charlatans. Everything that this beginner writes, or stammers in his infantile way, we read long ago and in a better form in the books of René Guénon, who never mistook theosophists for initiates, and who does not confuse literati with magi or those who sweep out the Temple with the priests. This letter has nothing to say to me or to anyone else, and I only regret that a man as truly gifted as yourself is taken in by words, and mistakes for real coin all the counterfeit currency palmed off by every quack of the High and true Science, which is not, thank God, so easy to prostitute. A few words by you about what I have tried to do in *The Monk* would have compromised you far less than that world of watered-down allusions, of false, commercialized giddiness which surrounds you and which is gradually gaining on you instead of it being you who are gaining on yourself after carrying out one of those intellectual revolutions whose secret I like to think you possess. For example, you could have said sensational things about the illnesses and the magnetic collapses of the black sorcerers, to which this sudden trickle, this quasi-menstrual flow of my forces outside their *personal* and secret conduits and contexts bears a diabolical resemblance. *The Monk* is a laying on of magic, an absorption of fictional reality by the hallucinatory and real poetry of the high spheres, the profound circles of the invisible. It is worth remarking this indifference to the real, the everyday, the ordinary which Lewis betrays throughout his pages, which are perpetually inspired by the breath of unreality. He never bothers to show us the boundary, and there is none; and at no moment in the writing of this unbeliever, this enemy of priests, does humor come to disturb or *dilute* the supernatural. One can say what one wants, his characters leave an impression in the mind, a *wake* that does not fade. And compared with Bernanos their superhuman psychology is *dated*, drawn, determined, motivated in all its reactions, all its consequences in this world——and perhaps in the next. One can pretend to despise the novel, but one cannot rebel against the characters created by novelists, when they have been able to arm them to live. It doesn't bother me at all when a writer says that "the countess went out at three" if I have been convinced that she exists and that she did go out, just as I might know about some mistress of mine—that she went out at a certain time if I had her followed and if I had somebody report to me what she did with her time.—The fact that a man such as you is not impressed that someone was able to write a book which does not observe the customary demarcations between the real and the surreal detracts in no way from the profound authenticity of this book, nor does it prevent the book from taking its place among all the manifestations of a state of mind which is our own, and which wants that the things of pure intellect also regain their rank among appearances, and at a choice place, the first, among everything that exists. Everything that in a work like *The Golden Ass*, for example, is presented in the guise of fiction and above all of Symbol is presented here in its full meaning. In short, one can say that the author was overtaken by his subject. *The Monk* is not the first novel of the great romantic tradition, but it is the most significant.

It lacks nothing [. . .]

TO LOUIS JOUVET

Paris, April 15, 1931

Dear Sir,

Although the Alfred Jarry Theater is no more, I am still alive, unfortunately for me, and I find myself right now in a painful situation. I have an urgent need for work and I thought you could not refuse me a helping hand. You can see from my work in the cinema what type of roles could be assigned to me without risk, but this is not what I have in mind.

You know, because you have had occasion to criticize them harshly, my efforts as a director! Whatever people may think of them, they intended to demonstrate a state of mind which is *contemporary*, and similar to the one I express in my writings. This state of mind exists, it has dominated and nourished all the literature of the last ten years. I do not ask you to provide me with the means to put on a play in your theater using techniques that have been criticized because they are too modern. All I ask is an opportunity to utilize, *in a limited sphere*, my experience in staging. Here is how I would visualize this in practical terms. I would not expect to put on plays in your theater as a director. I can see from here the smile of derision, the shrug of the shoulders that the mere idea produces in you. I need to eat; my inaction weighs on me, and it strikes me as somewhat monstrous to be restricted to the position of a mere performer: I will take the roles that are assigned me, but in addition I am sure that if you really tried you would find an interesting job for me *in your theater*. You could put me to work laying out the broad lines of productions, doing the initial groundwork on plays. Then during rehearsals perhaps I could make observations that would turn out to be useful, could exercise critical faculties that would contribute to the final form of a work. Merely suggestions. To this end, therefore, and to give you an idea of what I can do, I am sending you:

    a) a production outline for Strindberg's *Ghost Sonata*.

    b) a short *talking pantomime*. This pantomime, which has already been sold to someone, no longer belongs to me, although I am the author, but it is unpublished and it needs a production. I think it gives a rather accurate image of my conception, not of pantomime, but of the theater. I think it would make an interesting curtain raiser.

    Looking forward to your reply and hoping that you will take my request into consideration at your earliest possible convenience, I am very sincerely yours,

Antonin Artaud

45 rue Pigalle, Hôtel Saint-Charles

P.S. I hope you will read the outlines I am submitting to you carefully and give me your reactions.

ANTONIN ARTAUD

Please understand *the spirit* in which I write you. It is a question of giving me a helping hand, of allowing an ability which I daresay is not without interest to be used, and, granting that I have something to say, *of allowing me to begin to stammer it out.* I am much more accommodating than people say and I ask only to be understood and finally I ask you *to believe in the urgency of my need for assistance.* In any case, *thanks.*

TO JEAN-RICHARD BLOCH

April 23, 1931

Dear Sir,

Couldn't you find a way, if you thought about it seriously, of launching a project involving the founding of a new kind of theater? A careful reading of your *Destin du Théâtre* shows me that we think alike on quite a few essential points, and you must not judge me on the basis of the performances—rushed and improvised from makeshift materials—of the Alfred Jarry Theater. Those performances did not give a very accurate impression either of my real inclinations or of my ability to carry them out from a purely technical and professional point of view. My inclinations are pushing me toward "interior theater," theater as the incarnation of dreams, of thoughts projected onto the stage as if in a pure and uninhibited state, that is, without indication of origin!!! A theater that turns its back on life, on the real world, that allows no limitation, no visible transposition. A theater not based on the human, habitual psychology of characters, a theater that takes a visible position. A theater not based on psychology, a theater in which conflicts find their resolution in a collision of physical forces, of feelings elevated to the stature of real persons, of organic hallucinations struggling with men and objectified. In short, a theater in which freedom of thought finds absolute expansion in all possible forms: was classical theater interested in rigorously determining the psychology of its gods??? This theater would reintegrate for its audience the conception of the absolute spectacle, it would provide the equivalent of a kind of intellectual music hall in which all the senses and all the faculties would be satisfied at the same time. I can't go into the subject any further in a letter, but I am much preoccupied with the idea of carrying out this project. The most difficult part would be finding plays: the repertoire might include Hölderlin's *The Death of Empedocles* and Shelley's *Cenci,* in spite of their human and brutal quality (but Shelley's original idea as a poet would be restored by plastic means), a play by Jean-Richard Bloch, a play by Byron, Cyril Tourneur's *The Revenger's Tragedy,* etc., etc.

Real theater does not exist in France.

It seems to me that it would be easy to arouse the interest of certain milieux, certain groups, perhaps even certain fortunes, by proposing this idea of founding a theater that might turn out to be a national theater with results and ramifications throughout Europe and repercussions throughout the world. A theater that would establish the notion of a style of *mise en scène* invented *here.* Because for me the point of departure and touchstone of real theater is *mise en scène,* if the term is understood in its profound sense of the visual, auditory, and spatial power of the theatrical style of a written work.

I am still feeling my way with great difficulty, like a man who is hunted down by life; the launching of a project like this would enable me to find it.

Cordially,
Antonin Artaud

45 rue Pigalle, Hôtel Saint-Charles, Paris

TO LOUIS JOUVET

Paris, April 27, 1931

Dear Sir,

At our last meeting you mentioned your plan to expand during the coming season. Although I did not exactly have the

ANTONIN ARTAUD

impression that you were considering me as a possible collaborator, I am sending you a second production outline, this time for a modern play.

Your program demonstrates that you intend to give priority to a certain modern school of the theater. And yet all the plays you have presented so far do not go beyond certain limits, remain *faithful* to a certain vision, a certain tradition. You certainly agree with me and with everyone else today that one can go further, that the real theater we are all waiting for presupposes a total reversal of level, context, orientation, that its center of gravity is elsewhere. It seems to me that it must be part of your program, no matter how few productions you give, to supplement these *conventional* plays with other plays that are more deliberately, more essentially revolutionary. This can be done only if one has some completely solid productions to help support the new ones. For that matter, there is no reason why plays that are revolutionary in my sense of the word cannot become financially sound in a short period of time, because they will suddenly be regarded as the only ones that correspond to the altered viewpoint of a public starved for the new and unexpected. The modern theater is waiting for its form, one that will be in accord with the moral, intellectual, and emotional vision of the time. As soon as we begin to discover this form, the public will no longer be satisfied with any other. In other words, I think it's very smart to be revolutionary these days: it's the only way to become commercial!!!

I'm not sending you the play on which my outline is based as a model of the genre. This play restores only one aspect of the theater we are hoping for, which as far as I am concerned must be intellectually much freer, more liberated from heaviness—morally, physically, and in every sense.

Cordially,
Antonin Artaud

45 rue Pigalle

At age five, with his sister Marie-Ange

Around 1920, at twenty-four

Around 1920

At his sister's wedding

As Cecco, in Marcel Vandal's film
Graziella (1925)

As Gringalet, in Luitz-Morat's film *Le Juif Errant* (1926)

As Marat, in Abel Gance's *Napoleon* (1926–27)

As Marat

As the Intellectual, in Léon Poirier's film
Verdun, Visions d'Histoire (1928)

As the monk Massieu, in Carl Dreyer's
The Passion of Joan of Arc (1928)

As the father in *The Cenci* (1935)

Collection Dr. Ferdière

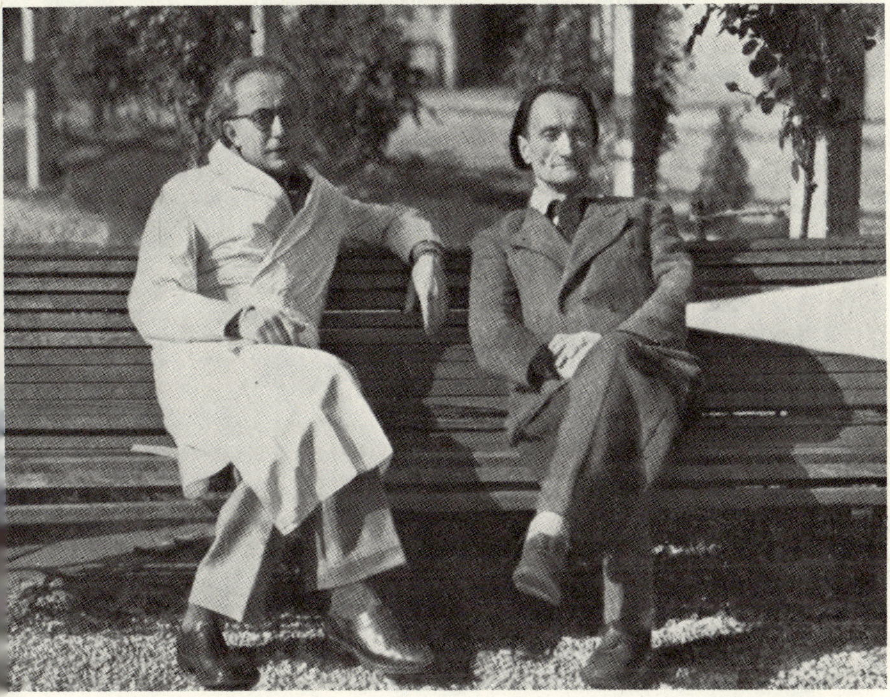

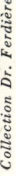

On the grounds of the asylum in Rodez, with Dr. Ferdière, in May 1946

Self-portrait

Photo Denise Colomb

His room in the clinic in Ivry-sur-Seine

Photo Denise Colomb

In his room, shortly before his death

DRAFT OF A LETTER TO RENÉ DAUMAL

Paris, July 14, 1931

STATEMENT

Dear friend,
   I am still wondering about the objection you made regarding the question I had raised about bringing in the notion of duality in   *
   But you do agree with me that this manifesto that we must draft together to explain the goals of the theater I want to start must be based on absolutely concrete considerations, must begin with the case against the present state of the theater in France and in Europe, and must say something to this effect:
   that the state of total degeneracy in which the French theater has been floundering since the war has recently been aggravated by a kind of economic crisis which has just forced a large percentage of Paris theaters out of business.
   However, it is very significant for the future of the theater in France that during this same period a number of movie theaters continue to do capacity business. We do not believe that the comparatively low price of a cinematic spectacle is enough to explain this sudden drop in the public's interest in the theater and its sudden alienation from a form of expression the demand for which was once, especially in times of crisis, comparable to the demand for staple commodities; but it does seem that the taste of the public for spectacles, the taste of that part of the public that only went to the theater in search of relaxation of a strictly digestive kind, must find a cinematic presentation equally entertaining. For although one can easily see in what way the theater as it now exists in France shows its inferiority to any film, even a very ordinary one, one cannot see either intellectually speaking or above all from the viewpoint of spectacle in what way it might show its superiority. And the public, by emptying as a body those halls in which a written theater with literary pretensions and a doubtful psychological observation is outliving itself, is spon-

---

* Blank in manuscript.—*Trans.*

taneously giving a genre long since outmoded exactly what it deserves.

If the theater is designed to distill a system of life, if it is supposed to constitute a kind of heroic synthesis of the age in which it was conceived, if one can define it as the concrete residue and reflection of the morals and habits of an age, it is clear that the cinema gives us a dynamic and complete image of modern life in its most varied aspects which the theater does not even approach.

The theater as it has existed not only in France but throughout Europe for almost a century is limited to the psychological and verbal portrait of individual man. All specifically theatrical means of expression have gradually been replaced by the text, which in turn has absorbed the action so completely that in the final analysis we have seen the entire theatrical spectacle reduced to a single person delivering a monologue in front of a backdrop.

This conception, however valid in itself, confirms in the minds of Westerners the supremacy of spoken language, which is both more precise and more abstract, over all other languages; and it has also had the unforeseen result of making the cinema, the art of images, a substitute for the spoken theater!

If in its rivalry with the theater the cinema has won the first round, it seems to have lost the second. Which, however, is not enough to breathe into a theater that has become hopelessly passive a life that it has lost.

But although the theater in France seems unable to free itself from the atmosphere of a brothel or to be more interesting than a civil-court hearing, an effort was being made even before the war in some countries of Europe, especially in Germany, and since the war in Russia, to restore to the art of *mise en scène* and spectacle the luster they had lost. The Ballets Russes are bringing a sense of color back to the stage. And from now on, in mounting a production, one must take into account the necessities of visual harmony, just as after Piscator one must take into account the dynamic and plastic necessities of movement, just as after Meyerhold and Appia one must take into account an architectural conception of scenery utilizing not only depth but height, and employing perspective in terms of masses and volumes rather than merely flat surfaces and *trompe l'oeil*.

Finally, the psychological conception, the old classical conception of the theater of manners and the theater of character, in which man is studied with what might be called a photographic—at any rate inert, prematurely dead, essentially anti-heroic—interest in his passions, studied in an everyday and habitual context, so that every play is like a game of chess or a game of psychological construction and gives us only a flat and depressing image of reality; and when an innovation appears, it replaces the habitual conception of man as all of a piece and acting as a unit, and flinging himself about like a wild boar, with a fragmented and multiform conception of man divided in a play full of mirrors, as one can catch a glimpse of him in the masterpieces of Pirandello, and here we leave the civil-court room or at best the floor of the court of assizes for the psychoanalyst's office, which brings us down one more notch in our psychological and demoralizing experience of man who, no matter what monsters he brings forth and frequents, is nevertheless everyday man; this conception, then, of man entranced before his personal monsters, is now under attack, and this attack is the only truly theatrical attempt, in Russia under the Revolution, to bring about a theater of action and a mass theater.

*

An era of the theater is over and we do not believe we should bother to condemn a genre which is condemned by history.

Insofar as the theater is   ,* the cinema has taken its place.

There is a place now for a theater that . . .

That there is a poetry of the cinema is possible, but
1. economic necessities will usually force the cinema to reject it.
2. when it does exist, it can never be placed on the level of theater, since it is physiological, animal, mechanical in nature.
3. [it is] crude, without magnetism; it is incorrect to speak of the magnetism of images.

---

* Blank in the original French.—*Trans.*

ANTONIN ARTAUD

TO JEAN PAULHAN (unfinished letter)

Paris, August 5, 1931

Dear friend,

I want to try, outside the stylistic limitations that are necessarily imposed by a formal magazine article, even one written with all the required sincerity, to describe for you as a friend, with an intense feeling of intellectual sympathy, the strange intellectual quality—this, too, eminently and above all intellectual—that I experienced at the sight and sound (at that kind of simultaneous stimulation of all the senses, of all the faculties of the mind at the same time, which is so total that in the end one is unable to make any distinction) of the beneficent, the miraculous spectacle of the Balinese Theater. To say the least, it constitutes an affront to our old Western conceptions of theater. It does more than present us with an astonishing production, an astonishing exploitation of all the means that can be employed in the reduced and limited space of a stage. The Balinese Theater reveals the secret existence of a kind of authentic theatrical language of such power that it seems to eliminate the very mental gestures that seem to have given birth to it, that it renders all translation into words impossible and useless. This language consists of a kind of orchestra of vocal modulations and gestures similar to the instrumental orchestra that serves as its fabric or backdrop. *There is an absolute quality about these spatial constructions, a quality of true physical absoluteness, of which only Orientals could possibly conceive. It is in this, it is in the nobility and the total audacity of their intentions that the conceptions of the Balinese Theater differ from our European conceptions of theater, much more than in the strange perfection of their productions.*

Those who believe in the division and compartmentalization of genres of art may pretend to see the magnificent performers of the Balinese Theater merely as dancers, dancers entrusted with embodying some mysterious high myths whose grandeur makes the general level of our Western theater seem revoltingly and inexpressibly crude, childish, and trivial; the truth is that the Balinese Theater offers us in finished form themes of pure theater on which the stage effects confer a dense equilibrium, a gravitational solidity that is fully materialized. This impression is extraordinary. It is so strong that [. . .]

TO JEAN PAULHAN

Paris, September 23, 1931

My very dear friend,

In the near future I am planning to start teaching a course in dramatic and cinematographic art. I shall hold my classes in the conference room of Editions Denoël & Steele at 19 rue Amélie.

Do you think you'll be able to send me some students?

In any case, I hope that you'll be good enough to tell people about it and that you can do me the favor of putting a short announcement to this effect in the *N.R.F.* All you have to say is that Antonin Artaud will be giving classes in dramatic and cinematographic art. This is part of a whole campaign of mine. In other words, these classes will have more than a merely didactic interest, and I think they are likely to interest a great many beginners.

Do you think the announcement could appear in the next issue? I shall also talk to the advertising department of the *N.R.F.* to see if they couldn't give me a good price on a quarter page for the same purpose.

If you're back I'll be in to see you soon. I'm very impatient to see you again.

Your devoted friend,
Antonin Artaud

58 rue La Bruyère

P.S. Prospective students should simply send me a note c/o Denoël & Steele at 19 rue Amélie, or to my address.
My thanks and apologies.

ANTONIN ARTAUD

TO LOUIS JOUVET

Tuesday evening, October 20, 1931

Dear friend,

    Do you think you could let me keep the manuscript of *Roi des Enfants* a little longer? My personal opinion of the value of the play is unimportant, as is any prediction I might make about its success. All I wanted to know was whether it was definite that this play would be performed, whether you, Louis Jouvet, were personally counting on a success in presenting it, and what kind of success you expected to have. I also wanted to know whether the date of the performance was more or less set. All this to avoid wasting my efforts. This being understood, if you sincerely think I could be useful to you in some way, I should be delighted, whether or not the play is to be performed, to go to work on it and to give you my personal suggestions about it. I shall write you a kind of report that will be as complete as possible, and you will utilize it as you see fit.

    I think you will agree with me that there is no performable play, no matter how fine, that cannot be improved and even corrected and remade by means of a skillful *mise en scène*. But I do not believe that *mise en scène* is a matter of writing or can be done on paper. Indeed, it is the distinctive quality of theatrical effects that they cannot be contained in words or even in sketches. A *mise en scène* is created *on* stage. And either one is a man of the theater or one is not. It seems to me absolutely impossible to describe a movement, a gesture, or above all a theatrical *intonation* without actually performing it. To describe a *mise en scène* by verbal or graphic means is like trying to make a drawing of a certain kind of pain. The production outlines for the *Ghost Sonata* or the *Coup de Trafalgar*, which seemed a little literary to you, seemed to me actually the maximum of what can be *written* and *described*, if one limits oneself to the language of words. The same words intended to describe a gesture or tone of voice can be realized on the stage in ten thousand different ways. All this is incommunicable and must be demonstrated on the spot. Any idea of staging that I can communicate to you will become valid only when it is furnished with movements, gestures, whispers, and cries. I have an idea for a whole sonic and visual technique which, if I tried to describe it in words, would require volumes crammed with verbal ratiocination all revolving around the same point repeated a hundred times. And all this would be pointless, since a single real intonation would achieve the same purpose in an instant. Which means that any suggestions I could give you would be of value only if I were in a position to control the *mise en scène* physically and line by line, with the corresponding movements. Indeed, physically, objectively, I see the *mise en scène* limited to a few indispensable and significant objects and props, together with a certain number of stories or levels whose dimensions and perspectives are part of the structure of the scenery. I see these stories or levels partaking of a *quality* of light which is for me the primordial element of the world of the stage. But I also see the range of the voices and the degree of the intonations as constituting another kind of level, and in any case a concrete element having the same importance as the scenery or the range of lighting effects. In addition to all this, the movements, gestures, and attitudes should be controlled with the same discipline as the movements of a ballet, although in a way that is more imperceptible, less obvious. For me it is this discipline governing all possible forms of expression on a stage that constitutes theater, whereas in our European theater all that matters is the text, if that. And also that truly paradoxical idea taken from Diderot that on stage the actor does not *really* feel what he is saying, that he retains absolute control over his actions, and that he can act and think about something else at the same time, like what he's going to have for dinner.—I have a great deal to say about this, but I shall stop for now. All this will be the subject of a lecture on the theater which I shall be giving soon at the Sorbonne along with the reading of a play. I would be happy if you would read my article on the Balinese Theater in the October issue of *La Nouvelle Revue Française* and tell me your reactions. I am *wholeheartedly* and cheerfully at your disposal with regard to *Roi des Enfants*. I would be very happy to do a careful job on it. I am not in a position to refuse work right now, since I no longer want to work in the cinema as an actor, and in fact I am asking you to give me an opportunity to work.

With my warmest best wishes,
Antonin Artaud

58 rue La Bruyère, Paris IX

For *The Theater and Its Double*
(1931–36)

On the Balinese Theater

The first performance of the Balinese Theater, which draws mainly on dancing, singing, pantomime, and music—and very little on psychological theater as we understand it here in Europe —restores the theater to its level of pure and autonomous creation, under the sign of hallucination and of fear.

It is quite remarkable that the first of the short plays that make up the program, which presents the admonishments of a father to a daughter who is rebelling against tradition, begins with an entrance of ghosts. The male and female characters who are going to serve the development of a dramatic but familiar subject appear to us first as personages in their spectral state, in that hallucinatory guise which is the attribute of every theatrical character, even before the situations in this sort of symbolic sketch are allowed to develop. And indeed, the situations in this play are merely a pretext. The drama does not develop as a conflict of feelings but of states of mind, which are themselves ossified and reduced to gestures—to structures. In short, the Balinese are carrying out with the utmost rigor the idea of pure theater, in which everything, conception and realization alike, has value or existence only in terms of its degree of objectification *on the stage*. They demonstrate triumphantly the absolute preponderance of the director, whose creative power *eliminates words*. The situations are vague, abstract, extremely general. What brings them to life is the complex profusion of all the artifices of the stage, which impose on our minds, as it were, the idea of a metaphysics derived from a new utilization of gesture and voice.

What is really curious about all these gestures, these angular and abruptly broken attitudes, these syncopated modulations formed at the back of the throat, these musical phrases that break off short, these flappings of insect wings, these rustlings of branches, these sounds of hollow drums, these creakings of robots, these dances of animated puppets, is this: that out of their labyrinth of gestures, attitudes, and sudden cries, out of gyrations and turns that leave no portion of the space on the stage unused, there emerges the sense of a new physical language based on signs rather than words. These actors with their geometric robes seem like animated hieroglyphs. And it is not merely the shape of their robes which, shifting the axis of the human figure, creates next to the clothing of these warriors in a state of trance and of perpetual war a kind of symbolic or second clothing, which inspires an intellectual idea and which is related by all the intersecting lines to all the intersections of the spatial perspective. No, these spiritual signs have a precise meaning which impresses us only intuitively, but with enough violence to render useless any translation into logical or discursive language. And for lovers of realism at any price, who would tire of these perpetual allusions to secret and unusual attitudes of the mind, there is still the eminently realistic performance of the double who is terrified by these apparitions from the beyond. These tremblings, this childish yelping, this heel that strikes the ground rhythmically in time to the mechanism of the liberated unconscious, this double who at a certain point hides behind its own reality, offers us a portrayal of fear which is valid in every latitude and which shows us that in the human as well as the superhuman the Orientals have something to teach us in matters of reality.

The Balinese, who have a repertoire of gestures and mimetic devices for every circumstance of life, restore the superiority of theatrical convention; they demonstrate the power and the supremely effective force of a certain number of conventions that are well learned and above all masterfully executed. One reason for the pleasure we take in this flawless performance lies in the use these actors make of a precise number of unfailing gestures, tested bits of mimicry occurring on schedule, but above all in the spiritual ambiance, in the profound and subtle study that has governed the elaboration of these dramatic expressions, these powerful signs which give the impression that after many ages their power has not been exhausted. These mechanically rolling eyes, these pouts, these recurrent muscular contractions, whose studiously calculated effects rule out any recourse to spontaneous improvisation, these horizontally moving heads which seem to slide from one shoulder to the other as if on rollers—all this, which corresponds to immediate psychological necessities, also corresponds to a kind of spiritual architecture made up not only of gestures and sign language but also of the evocative power of a rhythm, the musical quality of a physical movement, the parallel and admirably fused harmony of a tone. All this may shock our European sense of theatrical freedom and spontaneous inspiration, but let no one say that this mathematics makes for sterility or monotony. The amazing thing is that a sense of richness, fantasy, and lavish abundance is created by this performance, which is governed by an attention to detail and a conscious control that are overwhelming. And the most compelling correspondences are constantly fusing sight with sound, intellect with sensibility, the gesture of a character with the evocation of the movements of a plant, across the scream of an instrument. The sighing of a wind instrument prolongs the vibrations of vocal chords with such a sense of identity that one cannot tell whether it is the voice itself that is being sustained or the senses that have absorbed the voice from the beginning. A frolicking of joints, the musical angle which the arm makes with the forearm, a foot that falls, a knee that bends, fingers that seem to fly off the hand—all this is like a perpetual play of mirrors in which the parts of the human body seem to send each other echoes, musical phrases, in which the notes of the orchestra, the whispers of the wind instruments evoke the idea of a violent aviary where the actors themselves provide the beating wings. Our theater, which has never conceived of this metaphysics of gesture, or known how to use music for such immediate and concrete dramatic purposes, our purely verbal theater which is ignorant of everything that constitutes theater, that is, everything that exists in the air of the stage, everything that is measured and surrounded by air, everything that has density in space—movements, forms, colors, vibrations, attitudes, cries—our theater would do well, in regard to what cannot be measured and what depends on the mind's power of suggestion, to ask the Balinese Theater for a lesson in spirituality. This purely popular and non-sacred theater gives us an extraordinary idea of the intellectual level of a culture that bases its civic festivals on the struggles of a soul in the grips of the specters and phantoms of the beyond. For it is a purely internal conflict that is going on in the last part of the spectacle. And, in passing, one may remark the degree of theatrical sumptuousness which the Balinese have been able to give it. Their sense of the plastic necessities of the stage is equaled only by their understanding of physical fear and of the means of releasing it. And there is in the truly terrifying appearance of their devil (probably of Tibetan origin) a striking similarity to a certain puppet within our memory, with swollen hands of white gelatin and nails of green foliage, which was the finest ornament of one of the first plays performed by the Alfred Jarry Theater.

We cannot approach this spectacle head on; it assails us with a superabundance of impressions, each richer than the last, but in a language to which it seems that we no longer possess the key. And this kind of irritation created by the impossibility of finding the thread, tracking down the beast, putting one's ear to the instrument in order to hear better, is only one more of its charms. And by language I do not mean the idiom that cannot be grasped on first hearing, but a kind of theatrical language which is external to all *spoken language* and which seems to contain a vast experience of the stage, an experience in comparison with which our productions, based exclusively on dialogue, seem like mere stammerings.

What is most impressive about this spectacle—so calculated to upset our Western conceptions of the theater that many people will deny that it has any theatrical quality at all, whereas it is the finest example of pure theater that we have been privileged to see—what is impressive and disconcerting for us Europeans is the admirable intellectuality that one feels sparkling throughout, in the dense and subtle fabric of the gestures, in the infinitely varied modulations of the voice, in that downpour of sound, as of a vast forest dripping and coming to life, and in the equally sonorous interlocking of the movements. From a gesture to a cry or a sound there is no transition: everything corresponds, as if through mysterious passageways etched right into the brain!

There is here a whole collection of ritual gestures to which we do not have the key and which seem to obey extremely precise musical indications, with something more which does not usually belong to music and which seems designed to surround thought, to pursue it, and to lead it into an inextricable and certain web. Indeed, everything about this theater is calculated in exquisite and mathematical detail. Nothing is left to chance or to personal initiative. It is a kind of superior dance in which the dancers are, above all, actors.

Time and again you see them perform a kind of recovery with measured steps. Just as you think they are lost in an inextricable maze of measures, just as you feel them about to fall into confusion, they have a characteristic way of recovering their balance, a special way of propping up the body, the twisted legs, that gives the impression of a wet rag being wrung out in time—and in three final steps, which always lead inexorably toward the middle of the stage, the suspended rhythm is over and the beat is resolved.

Everything about these dancers is just as disciplined and impersonal; there is not a movement of a muscle, not a rolling of an eye that does not seem to belong to a kind of studied mathematics which governs everything and through which everything happens. And the strange thing is that in this systematic depersonalization, in these purely muscular facial movements that are superimposed on the features like masks, everything works, everything has the maximum effect.

A kind of terror grips us as we contemplate these mechanized beings, whose joys and sorrows do not really seem to belong to them but rather to obey established rites that were dictated by higher intelligences. In the last analysis, it is certainly this impression of a Life that is higher and prescribed that impresses us most in this spectacle, which is like some rite that one might profane. And it has the solemnity of a sacred rite—the hieratic quality of the costumes gives each actor something like a double body, a double set of limbs—and the actor stiffly encased in his costume seems only the effigy of himself. There is also the broad, pounding rhythm of the music—an extremely insistent, droning, and fragile music, in which the most precious metals seem to be ground, in which springs of water seem to gush up as if in their natural state, and armies of insects march through vegetation, in which one seems to hear captured the very sound of light, in which the sound of deep solitudes seems to be reduced to flights of crystals, etc., etc.

Furthermore, all these sounds are connected to movements, as if they were the natural fulfillment of gestures that have the same quality they have; and this is done with such a sense of musical analogy that ultimately the mind is forced to confuse the two elements and to attribute to the articulated gestures of the performers the sonorities of the orchestra—and the reverse.

An impression of inhumanity, of divinity, of miraculous revelation is also created by the exquisite beauty of the women's headdresses: that series of luminous circles piled one on the other, composed of combinations of multicolored feathers or pearls so rich and beautiful that the total effect has a quality of *revelation*, whose crests sway rhythmically, responding *consciously*, it seems, to the slightest movements of their bodies.—There are also those other headdresses with a sacerdotal look, shaped like tiaras crowned with tufts of stiff flowers in oddly contrasting pairs of colors.

This dazzling blend of explosions, escapes, passages, and detours in all the directions of external and internal perception constitutes a supreme idea of theater, one which seems to have been preserved down through the ages in order to teach us what the theater should never have ceased to be. And this impression is reinforced by the fact that this spectacle—which is apparently popular and secular in its own country—is, as it were, the daily bread of the artistic feelings of these people.

Aside from the prodigious mathematics of the spectacle, what to me seems calculated to surprise and to astonish us most is this *revelatory aspect of matter*, which seems suddenly to scatter into signs in order to teach us the metaphysical identity of the concrete and the abstract, and to teach it to us *in gestures designed to last*. For the realistic aspect of matter is known in Western theater, but here it is carried to the nth power and definitively stylized.

In this theater all creation arises from the stage and finds its expression and even its origins in a secret psychic impulse which is Speech anterior to words.

It is a theater which eliminates the playwright in favor of what we in our Western theatrical jargon would call the director; but the director becomes a kind of magical conductor, a master of sacred ceremonies. And the raw material with which he works,

the themes he brings to quivering life are not of himself but of the gods. They seem to come from the primitive connections of Nature which a double Spirit has favored.
What he sets in motion is the MANIFESTED.
It is a kind of primary Physics from which the Spirit has never been separated.

In a spectacle like that of the Balinese Theater there is something that eliminates entertainment, that quality of a pointless artificial game, an evening's diversion, which is the distinguishing characteristic of our theater. Its productions are carved directly from matter, from life, from reality. They possess some of the ceremonial quality of a religious rite, in that they extirpate from the mind of the spectator any idea of pretense, of the grotesque imitation of reality. This intricate gesticulation which we watch has a purpose, an immediate purpose toward which it moves by powerful means, means whose effectiveness we are in a position to experience directly. The ideas to which it aspires, the states of mind it seeks to create, the mystical solutions it offers are awakened, heightened, and attained without delay or equivocation. All this seems to be an exorcism to make our demons FLOW.

There is in this theater a low humming of the things of instinct, but brought to a point of transparency, intelligence, and malleability where they seem to offer us in physical form some of the most secret perceptions of the mind.
The situations presented may be said to have originated on stage. They have reached such a point of objective materialization that one cannot possibly imagine them outside of this dense perspective, this closed and limited sphere of the stage.
This spectacle gives us a marvelous complex of pure theatrical images for the comprehension of which a whole new language seems to have been invented: the actors with their costumes form true hieroglyphs that live and move around. And these three-dimensional hieroglyphs are in turn embellished with a certain number of gestures—mysterious signs which correspond to some fabulous and obscure reality that we Westerners have definitively repressed.
There is something that partakes of the spirit of a magical

trick in this intense liberation of signs that are at first held back and then suddenly thrown into the air.

A chaotic turbulence, full of familiar landmarks, and at times strangely well organized, seethes in this effervescence of painted rhythms in which the single tone of the background is sustained throughout and comes through like a well-planned silence.

This idea of pure theater, which in the West is purely theoretical and which no one has ever tried to invest with the slightest reality, is realized in the Balinese Theater in a way that is astonishing, because it eliminates all possibility of resorting to words to elucidate the most abstract subjects; and because it has invented a language of gestures which are designed to move in space and which can have no meaning outside of it.

The space of the stage is utilized in all its dimensions and one might say on all possible levels. For in addition to a keen sense of plastic beauty these gestures always have as their ultimate purpose the elucidation of a mental state or a mental conflict.

At least this is the way they appear to us.

No point of space and at the same time no possible suggestion is lost. And there is an almost philosophical sense of the power that nature possesses of suddenly hurling everything into chaos.

One senses in the Balinese Theater a pre-verbal state, a state which can choose its own language: music, gestures, movements, words.

There is no doubt that this quality of pure theater, this physics of the absolute gesture which is itself idea and which forces the conceptions of the mind to pass, in order to be perceived, through the fibrous mazes and networks of matter—all this gives us a new idea of what properly belongs to the realm of forms and of manifested matter. These people who manage to give a mystical meaning to the mere shape of a robe and who, not content to place beside man his Double, attribute to each clothed man his double of clothing, who pierce these illusory or secondary garments with a sword that makes them resemble huge butterflies impaled on air, these people possess to a much greater degree than we the innate sense of the absolute and magical symbolism of nature, and offer us a lesson which it is only too sure that our theatrical technicians will be powerless to take advantage of.

This intellectual space, this psychic interplay, this silence ridden with thoughts which exists between the elements of a written sentence, is here traced in the space of the stage, between the parts of the body, the air, and the perspectives of a certain number of cries, colors, and movements.

In the productions of the Balinese Theater the mind has the feeling that the conception first collided with the gestures, that it first took root amid a whole fermentation of visual or auditory images, conceived as if in their pure state. In other words, something rather similar to the conditions for composing music must have existed for this *mise en scène* in which everything that is a conception of the mind is merely a pretext, a potentiality whose double has produced this intense poetry of the stage, this language of space and color.

This perpetual play of mirrors which goes from a color to a gesture and from a cry to a movement, is constantly leading us over paths that are steep and difficult for the mind, and plunging us into that state of uncertainty and ineffable anguish which is the domain of poetry.

From these strange gestures of hands that flutter like insects in the green evening, there emanates a kind of horrible obsession, a kind of inexhaustible mental ratiocination, like a mind desperately trying to find its way in the maze of its unconscious.

And it is much less matters of feeling than of intelligence that this theater makes palpable for us and surrounds with concrete signs.

And it is by intellectual paths that it leads us to the reconquest of the signs of reality.

From this point of view, the gesture of the lead dancer who is always touching himself on the same place on the head as if to mark the location and the life of some mysterious central eye, some intellectual egg, is highly significant.

What is a colorful allusion to the physical impressions of nature is repeated on the level of sound, and sound is in turn merely the nostalgic representation of something else, of a kind of magical state in which sensations have become so rarefied that they are capable of being visited by the mind. And even the imitative harmonies, the sound of the rattlesnake, the clicking of insect carapaces against each other, evoke some clearing in a teeming landscape which is about to be hurled into chaos. And these dancers clad in dazzling garments, whose bodies underneath seem to be wrapped in swaddling clothes! There is something umbilical, something larval in their movements. At the same time one must note the hieroglyphic aspect of their costumes, whose horizontal lines extend beyond the body in all directions. They are like huge insects covered with lines and segments designed to connect them to some natural perspective of which they seem to be no more than a detached geometry.

These costumes which surround their abstract gliding when they walk, and the strange crossings of their feet!

Each of their movements traces a line in space, completes some unknown but precise figure, of a very calculated hermeticism—a figure to which an unexpected gesture of the hand adds the final touch.

And these robes that flare out above the hips and hold the dancers as if suspended in air, as if pinned to the backdrop of the theater, and prolong each of their leaps into a flight.

These cries from the entrails, these rolling eyes, this continual abstraction, these sounds of branches, of chopping wood and rolling logs, all this in a vast space where sounds are magnified and come from several sources, all this combines to arouse and crystallize in our minds a new and, so to speak, concrete conception of the abstract.

And it must be noted that when this abstraction, which departs from a marvelous theatrical edifice before returning to thought, when this abstraction encounters in its flight impressions of the world of nature, it always grasps them at that point where they undermine their molecular unity; which means that there is no more than a gesture still separating us from chaos.

The last part of the spectacle is, in comparison with all the filth, brutality, and degradation that is endlessly masticated on our European stages, a divine anachronism. And I do not know any other theater that would dare to pin down in this way, *as if in their natural state,* the horrors of a soul possessed by the specters of the Beyond.

They dance, and these metaphysicians of natural disorder who give us back each atom of sound, each fragmentary perception as if ready to return to its source, have been able to create a juncture between movement and sound so perfect that these sounds of hollow wood, resounding drums, and empty instruments seem to be made by dancers with arms and legs of hollow wood.

All at once we are in the midst of a metaphysical struggle, and the rigidity of the body in trance, stiffened by the surge of the cosmic forces invading it, is admirably expressed in this dance, both frenzied and full of rigidity and angles, in which one suddenly senses the beginning of the headlong fall of the mind.

It is like waves of matter breaking one on top of the other, and rushing from all sides of the horizon to enter into an infinitesimal space of trembling, of trance—and to cover over the void with fear.

There is an absolute in these constructed perspectives, a quality of true physical absoluteness which only Orientals could possibly conceive of—it is in this, it is in the nobility and in the studied audacity of their intentions, that these conceptions differ from our European conceptions of theater much more than in the strange perfection of their productions.

Those who believe in the division and compartmentalization of art forms may pretend to see the magnificent performers of the Balinese Theater merely as dancers, dancers entrusted with embodying some mysterious lofty Myths whose grandeur makes the level of our modern Western theater seem inexpressibly crude and infantile. The truth is that the Balinese Theater offers us in finished form themes of pure theater upon which the stage performance confers a dense equilibrium, a gravitational solidity that is fully materialized.

All this is bathed in a profound intoxication which restores to us the very elements of ecstasy, and in this ecstasy we rediscover the dry teeming and mineral rustle of plants, ruins, blasted trees illumined from the front.

All bestiality, all animality is reduced to its bare gesture: mutinous sounds of the earth splitting, the freezing of trees, the bleats of animals.

The feet of the dancers, in the gesture of parting their robes, dissolve thoughts and sensations and return them to their pure state.

And always this confrontation of the head, this Cyclopean eye, the inner eye of the mind for which the right hand gropes.

Mimicry of mental gestures which mark, cut, fix, divide, and subdivide feelings, states of mind, metaphysical ideas.

This theater of quintessence in which things perform strange about-faces before returning to abstraction.

So accurately do their gestures fall on this rhythm of wood, of hollow drums, so surely and from such heights do they scan it and seize it from the air, that it seems to be the very emptiness of their hollow limbs that will be accented by this music.

The stratified, lunar eyes of the women.

This dreamlike eye which seems to absorb us and before which we ourselves appear as *phantoms*.

The total satisfaction afforded by these dance gestures, these turning feet which combine states of the soul, these little fluttering hands, these dry and precise tappings.

We are present at a mental alchemy which turns a state of mind into a gesture, the dry, bare, linear gesture that all our actions could have if they moved toward the absolute.

It happens that this mannerism, this excessive hieraticism with its sliding alphabet, its screams like splitting rock, its sounds of branches, its sounds of wood being chopped and logs being rolled, creates in the air, in space, visually as well as aurally, a kind of physical and animated drone. And after a moment the magical identification has been made: WE KNOW THAT IT IS WE WHO ARE SPEAKING.

For *The Theater and Its Double* (1931-36)

Who, after witnessing the formidable battle between Arjuna and the Dragon, will dare to maintain that all theater is not on the stage, that is to say, outside of situations and words?

Dramatic and psychological situations have passed here into the very pantomime of combat, which is a function of the athletic and mystical interplay of bodies—and of what I would almost call the undulatory use of the stage, whose enormous spiral is revealed one level at a time.

The warriors enter the mental forest with glidings of fear; they are seized by a vast shudder, a voluminous and as if magnetic rotation in which one feels the rush of animal or mineral meteors.

It is more than a physical tempest, it is a crushing of the mind that is signified by the scattered trembling of their limbs and of their rolling eyes. The sonorous pulsation of their bristling heads is at times excruciating—as is this music behind them which sways and which at the same time nourishes some unknown space in which physical pebbles roll to a stop.

And behind the Warrior, bristling from the formidable cosmic tempest, is the Double, who struts about, indulging the childishness of his schoolboy sarcasms, and who, roused by the aftereffects of the surging storm, moves unaware through charms of which he has understood nothing.

MISE EN SCÈNE AND METAPHYSICS

In the Louvre there is a work by a Primitive painter who may or may not be well known, I do not know, but in any case his name will never be representative of an important period in the history of art. This Primitive is Lucas van Leyden, and in my opinion he makes the four or five hundred years of painting that came after him useless and invalid. The painting I am talking about is entitled *Lot and His Daughters*, a biblical subject which was fashionable in his day. Of course the Bible in the Middle Ages was not understood the way we understand it today, and this painting is a strange example of the mystical deductions that can be drawn from it. Its emotion, in any case, is visible even from a distance; it strikes the mind with a kind of visual harmony that is electrifying, a harmony whose effectiveness acts as a whole and is communicated in a single glance. Even before one has had a chance to determine what is going on, one senses that it is something of great importance, and one almost feels that the ear is moved at the same time as the eye. A drama of high intellectual significance seems to have been concentrated here like a sudden gathering of clouds which the wind or some much more compelling force has brought together to measure their thunder.

And in fact the sky of the painting is black and overcast, but even before one notices that the drama has originated in the sky, and is taking place in the sky, the peculiar lighting of the painting, the way the forms are clustered together, the impression that emanates from it even at a distance—all this announces a kind of drama of nature which is unequaled by anything in the productions of the Great Masters.

A tent has been pitched at the edge of the sea, and before it Lot sits wearing a breastplate and a fine red beard, watching his daughters parade before him as if he were attending a banquet of whores.

And in fact they are strutting, some depicted as mothers, others as Amazons, combing their hair or fencing, as if they had never had any other purpose than to charm their father, to serve as his plaything or instrument. Thus we see the profoundly incestuous quality of the old theme which the painter develops here in passionate images—proof that he has understood it absolutely as if he were a modern man, that is, as we would understand it ourselves, in all its profound sexuality. Proof that its quality of profound but poetic sexuality has not escaped him any more than it escapes us.

On the left side of the painting and a little more in the background, there rises to prodigious heights a black tower that is supported at the base by a whole network of rocks, shrubs, and winding roads marked by milestones and dotted here and there with houses. By a fortunate effect of perspective, one of these roads emerges at a given point from the thicket through which it was winding, crosses a bridge, and finally receives a shaft of that ominous light that is spilling out from between the clouds and irregularly bathing the countryside. The sea in the background of the painting is extremely high but extremely calm, considering that skein of fire that is seething in one corner of the sky.

Sometimes while we are watching a display of fireworks it happens that, through the nocturnal bombardment of shooting stars, sky rockets, and Roman candles, we suddenly see revealed before our eyes in a hallucinatory light, standing out in relief against the darkness, certain details of the landscape: trees, tower, mountains, houses, whose illumination and whose appearance will always remain associated in our minds with the idea of those ear-splitting sounds. It is impossible to express better this subordination of the various elements of the landscape to the fire manifested in the sky than by saying that although they possess their own light, they nevertheless remain like so many muted echoes of the fire, like glowing points of reference born of the fire and put there to permit it to exert its full force of destruction.

There is, moreover, something terrifyingly energetic and disturbing in the way the painter presents this fire, as an element that is still active and mobile in an immobilized form. It does not matter how this effect is achieved, it is real; one has only to see the painting to be convinced.

However this may be, this fire, which no one will deny creates an impression of intelligence and malice, serves, by its very violence, to counterbalance in the mind the physical solidity and weight of the rest.

Between the sea and the sky, but to the right and on the same plane of perspective as the Black Tower, there is a narrow spit of land crowned by a ruined monastery.

This spit of land, although it seems close to the bank where Lot's tent is pitched, nevertheless leaves room for an enormous gulf in which an unprecedented maritime disaster seems to have occurred. Ships which have been broken in two but have not yet gone down are leaning on the sea as if on crutches, with their uprooted masts and spars floating around them in all directions.

It would be difficult to say why the impression of disaster created by the sight of only one or two ruined ships is so total.

The painter seems to have possessed certain secrets of linear harmony and the means of making this harmony act directly on the brain like a physical agent. In any case, this impression of an intelligence permeating external nature, especially the way in which it is represented, is visible in several other details of the painting, such as that bridge, high as an eight-story house, rising over the sea, and across which figures are parading single file like the Ideas in Plato's cave.

It would be false to pretend that the ideas that are conveyed by this painting are clear. But they are of a grandeur to which we have become unaccustomed as a result of that kind of painting which only knows how to apply paint, that is, all the painting of the last few centuries.

There is also an idea about sexuality and reproduction, with Lot seemingly placed there to live off his daughters, like a pimp. This is almost the only social idea that the painting contains.

All the other ideas are metaphysical. I am reluctant to use that word, but it is accurate; and I should even say that their poetic grandeur, their physical power over us, arises from the fact that they are metaphysical, and that their spiritual profundity is inseparable from the formal and visual harmony of the painting.

There is also an idea about Becoming which the various details of the landscape and the way they are painted, the way their planes either cancel each other or correspond to each other, introduce into our minds in precisely the same manner as does a piece of music.

There is another idea, about Fatality, which is conveyed not so much by the apparition of this sudden fire as by the solemn way in which all the forms are organized or disorganized beneath it, some as if bending beneath an irresistible wind of panic, others motionless and almost ironic, all obeying a powerful intellectual harmony which seems the very spirit of nature in external form.

There is also an idea about Chaos, and there are ideas about the Miraculous, and Equilibrium; there are even one or two ideas about the impotences of Speech, whose uselessness seems to be demonstrated by this supremely physical and anarchic painting.

In any case, I submit that this painting is what the theater should be, if the theater knew how to speak the language that belongs to it.

And I raise this question:

Why is it that in the theater, at least in the theater as we know it in Europe, or rather in the West, why is it that everything specifically theatrical, that is, everything that defies expression in speech, in words, or, if you will, everything that is not contained in dialogue (and even dialogue itself regarded in terms of its possibilities for sound effects on the stage, and of the *requirements* of these sound effects), is relegated to the background?

And why is it that Western theater (I say Western because fortunately there are others, like Oriental theater, which have managed to retain intact the idea of theater, whereas in the West this idea—like everything else—has been *prostituted*), why is it that Western theater cannot conceive of the theater except as a theater of dialogue?

Dialogue—something that is written and spoken—does not belong specifically to the stage, it belongs to books; and the proof of this is that in manuals of literary history there is always space reserved for drama regarded as a subdivision of the history of the spoken language.

I say that the stage is a physical and concrete place which demands to be filled and which must be made to speak its own concrete language.

I say that this concrete language, intended for the senses and independent of speech, must first satisfy the senses, that there is a poetry of the senses as there is a poetry of language, and that this physical and concrete language to which I allude is truly theatrical only insofar as the thoughts it expresses transcend spoken language.

The question will be raised, what are these thoughts which speech cannot express and which could find their ideal expression not in speech but in the concrete and physical language of the stage?

I shall answer this question a little later.

It seems more urgent to determine the nature of this physical language, this material and substantial language by which theater may be differentiated from speech.

It consists of everything that occupies the stage, everything that can be manifested and expressed physically on a stage, and that addresses itself first to the senses instead of addressing itself first to the mind, like the language of speech. (I am quite aware that words themselves have their own potential as sound, that they have various ways of being projected into space, which are called *intonations*. And there is a great deal that could be said about the concrete value of intonation in the theater, about this quality that words have—apart from their concrete meaning—of creating their own music according to the way in which they are uttered, which can even go against that meaning—of creating beneath language an undercurrent of impressions, correspondences, analogies. But this theatrical way of regarding language is itself a subordinate *aspect* of language for the playwright and one which, especially nowadays, he no longer takes into account in creating his plays. So I shall not consider it.)

This language designed for the senses must be concerned from the beginning with satisfying them. This does not prevent it from later developing all its intellectual potentialities on all possible levels and in all directions. And this permits the replacement of the poetry of language by a poetry of space which will be resolved precisely in the realm of all that does not belong strictly to words.

To clarify what I mean, it would no doubt be helpful to have a few examples of this poetry of space which is capable of creating kinds of physical images that are equivalent to verbal images. I shall give these examples a little further on.

This very difficult and complex poetry assumes many guises, and first among these are all the means of expression that can be utilized on a stage,* such as music, dance, plastic art, pantomime, mimicry, gesture, intonation, architecture, lighting, and sets.

Each of these means has its own intrinsic poetry, as well as a kind of ironic poetry which arises from the way it is combined with the other means of expression; and the consequences of these combinations, and of the way they react on each other and against each other, are easy to perceive.

I shall return presently to the subject of this poetry which can be fully effective only when it is concrete, that is, when it objectively produces something by virtue of its *active* presence on the stage;—when a sound, as in the Balinese Theater, is equivalent to

---

* Insofar as they prove capable of exploiting the immediate physical possibilities that the stage offers and of replacing the fixed forms of art with those living and threatening forms through which the meaning of the old ceremonial magic can find new reality on the level of theater; insofar as they yield to what might be called the *physical temptation* of the stage.

a gesture and, instead of serving as decoration, as the accompaniment of a thought, helps to develop it, guides it, destroys it, or changes it definitively, etc.

One form of this poetry of space—apart from the poetry that can be created by combinations of lines, forms, colors, objects in their natural state, as one finds them in all the arts—is the language of signs. And I would like to speak for a moment about that other aspect of pure theatrical language which has nothing to do with speech, that language of signs, gestures, and attitudes which have an ideographic value as they exist in certain pantomimes that have not been corrupted.

By "pantomime that has not been corrupted" I mean direct Pantomime in which the gestures—instead of representing words or sentences as in our European pantomime, which is only fifty years old and which is merely a distortion of the silent parts of Italian *commedia*—represent ideas, mental attitudes, aspects of nature, in an effective, concrete manner, that is, by always evoking natural objects or details, like that Oriental language in which night is represented by a tree on which a bird has already closed one eye and starts to close the other. Another abstract idea or mental attitude might be illustrated by one of the innumerable symbols from Scripture, for example, the eye of the needle through which the camel cannot pass.

It is clear that these signs constitute true hieroglyphs in which man, insofar as he helps to compose them, is merely one form among others, hieroglyphs to which, by virtue of his double nature, he nevertheless contributes a peculiar prestige.

This language, which evokes in the mind images of an intense natural (or spiritual) poetry, gives an idea of what it might mean for the theater to have a poetry of space independent of spoken language.

However this may be, I note that in our theater, which lives under the exclusive dictatorship of speech, this language of signs and mimicry, this silent pantomime, these attitudes, these gestures in space, these objective intonations—in short, everything I regard as specifically theatrical in the theater—all these elements, when they exist outside the text, are universally regarded as the inferior aspect of theater, are dismissed as "stage business," and are confused with what is referred to as *mise en scène* or "staging," *mise en scène* often being erroneously used to designate that artistic and external display of lavishness which is the province of costumes, lighting, and sets.

In opposition to this point of view, which strikes me as altogether Western or rather Latin, that is, obstinate, I maintain that insofar as this language begins with the stage, draws its power from its spontaneous creation on stage, and struggles directly with the stage without resorting to words (and why not conceive of a play composed directly on stage, produced on stage?), it is *mise en scène* that is theater, much more than the written and spoken play. No doubt I shall be asked to state what is Latin about this point of view opposed to my own. What is Latin is the need to use words in order to express ideas that are clear. Because for me clear ideas, in the theater as in everything else, are ideas that are dead and finished.

The idea of a play created directly on stage, by encountering the obstacles of production and of the stage, compels the discovery of a language that is active, active and anarchic, in which the habitual boundaries of feelings and words are abandoned.

In any case, and I hasten to say so at once, a theater that subordinates *mise en scène* and production—that is, everything that is specifically theatrical—to the script is a theater for idiots, madmen, perverts, grammarians, grocers, anti-poets, and positivists, in short, a theater for Westerners.

I am quite aware that the language of gesture and attitude, that dance and music are less capable of elucidating a character, relating a person's thoughts, or exposing clear and precise states of consciousness than verbal language, but who ever said that the theater was created to elucidate a character, or to resolve the kind of human and emotional, contemporary and psychological conflicts with which our modern theater is filled?

To look at the theater as we see it here, one would think that there is nothing more to life than knowing whether we will make love well, whether we will make war or will be cowardly enough to make peace, how we learn to live with our little anxieties, and whether we will become aware of our "complexes" (to use technical language) or whether on the contrary our "complexes" will do us in. It is rarely that the conflict rises to the social level or that our social and moral system is put on trial. Our theater never goes so far as to wonder whether by chance this social and moral system might be unjust.

Well, I say that the present state of society is unjust and should be destroyed. If it is the business of the theater to be concerned about this, it is even more the business of the machine gun. Our theater is not even capable of raising the question in the inflammatory and powerful way that is required; but even if it did raise the question, it would still be deviating from its purpose, which I consider higher and more mysterious.

All the preoccupations enumerated above stink unbelievably of man, transitory and physical man, I will even go so far as to say *carrion man*. These preoccupations with personal matters disgust me, they disgust me to the highest degree, as does almost all contemporary theater, which is as human as it is anti-poetic and which, with the exception of three or four plays, seems to me to stink of decadence and pus.

Contemporary theater is in a state of decadence because it has lost feeling on the one hand for seriousness and on the other for laughter. Because it has broken with gravity, with efficacity that is immediate and pernicious—in short, with Danger.

Because it has also lost the sense of true humor and of the physical and anarchic, dissociative power of comedy.

Because it has broken with that spirit of profound anarchy which is at the root of all poetry.

It must be granted that everything about the purpose of an object, about the meaning or use of a natural form, is a matter of convention.

When nature gave a tree the form of a tree, she could just as well have given it the form of an animal or a hill; we would have thought *tree* when we looked at the animal or the hill, and the trick would have worked.

It is agreed that a pretty woman has a melodious voice; yet, if since the world began we had heard all pretty women trumpet like elephants, we would for eternity have associated the idea of trumpeting with the idea of a pretty woman, and some part of our inner vision of the world would have been radically transformed.

This helps us to understand that poetry is anarchic insofar as it calls into question all relationships between objects and all relationships between forms and their meanings. It is also anarchic insofar as its appearance is the consequence of a disorder that brings us closer to chaos.

I shall not give further examples. They could be multiplied to infinity, and not just with humorous examples like those I have just used.

Theatrically these inversions of form, these displacements of meaning could become the essential element of that poetry of humor and space which is the exclusive domain of *mise en scène*.

In one of the Marx brothers' films, a man who thinks he is about to embrace a woman puts his arms around a cow, which moos. And through a conjunction of circumstances which it would take too long to relate, this moo, at this moment, takes on an intellectual dignity equal to that of any woman's cry.

A situation of this kind, which is possible in the cinema, is no less possible in the theater as it is today. One would not have to do much—for example, replace the cow with an animated puppet, a kind of monster endowed with speech, or with a man dressed as an animal—to rediscover the secret of an objective poetry based on humor which the theater renounced and abandoned to the Music Hall, and which the Cinema later adopted.

A moment ago I mentioned danger. The best way I can think of to carry out this idea of danger on stage is the unforeseen which is objective, the unforeseen not in situations but in things, the sudden unexpected transition from a mental image to a real image; for example, a man who blasphemes sees suddenly materialize before his eyes, realistically depicted, the image of his blasphemy (on the condition, I should add, that this image is not entirely gratuitous, that it gives rise in turn to other images in the same spiritual vein, etc.).

Another example would be the appearance of an imaginary Creature made of wood and cloth, wholly fabricated, corresponding to nothing, and yet intrinsically disturbing, capable of bringing back to the stage some faint breath of that great metaphysical fear that underlies all ancient theater.

The Balinese with their imaginary dragon, like all Orientals, have retained the sense of that mysterious fear which they know to be one of the most effective and indeed essential elements of theater, when it is restored to its proper level.

True poetry, whether we like it or not, is metaphysical, and I would even go so far as to say that it is its metaphysical range, its degree of metaphysical power, which is the measure of its real value.

This is the second or third time I have brought up the subject of metaphysics. In speaking of psychology just now, I mentioned dead ideas, and I am sure that many people will be inclined to say that if there is an inhuman idea in the world, an ineffectual and dead idea that conveys almost nothing, even to the mind, it is the idea of metaphysics.

This is the result, as René Guénon says, of "our purely Western manner, our anti-poetic and truncated manner of considering first principles (apart from the energetic and total spiritual state that corresponds to them)."

In the Oriental theater with its metaphysical bent, as opposed to the Western theater with its psychological bent, this whole compact mass of gestures, signs, postures, and sounds that makes up the language of production and of the stage, this language that develops all its physical and poetic consequences on all levels of consciousness and in all directions, inevitably leads the mind to adopt profound attitudes which might be called *metaphysics in action*.

I shall come back to this point presently. For the moment let us return to theater as we know it.

A few days ago I attended a discussion on the theater. There I saw that species of human snake, otherwise known as playwrights, explain how to go about introducing a play to a producer, like those men in history who introduced poisons into the ears of their rivals. The point of the discussion, I believe, was to determine the future orientation of the theater, in other words, its destiny.

They determined nothing at all, and at no point did anyone touch on the true destiny of the theater, that is, what by definition and by nature the theater is intended to represent, or the methods it has at its disposal. On the contrary, the theater appeared as some sort of frozen world in which the actors are cramped by gestures that will never be of any use to them, the air is filled with congealed intonations that are already falling to pieces, music is reduced to a kind of numbered list whose figures are starting to fade, and there are flashes of light which have also solidified and which correspond to traces of movement—and all around, an extraordinary fluttering of men in black suits arguing over receipts at the foot of a white-hot cash register. As if the theatrical machine were henceforth reduced to everything that surrounds it; and it is because it is reduced to everything that surrounds it, and because the theater is reduced to everything that is no longer theater, that its atmosphere stinks in the nostrils of people of taste.

For me the theater is identified with its possibilities of realization when the most extreme poetic results are derived from them, and the possibilities of realization of the theater belong entirely to the domain of *mise en scène* when the latter is regarded as a language of space and of movement.

But to derive extreme poetic results from the means of realization is to make them the basis of a metaphysics, and I think no one will object to this way of considering the matter.

And to create a metaphysics of language, gestures, attitudes, sets, and music from the point of view of theater is, I think, to consider them in terms of all the ways they can have of encountering time and movement.

To give objective examples of this poetry that results from the various ways a gesture, a sound, or an intonation may have of laying more or less stress on a given area of space at a given moment of time, seems as difficult as it would be to communicate in words a sense of the particular quality of a sound or of the degree and quality of a physical pain. It all depends on the production and can only be determined on stage.

This would be the proper place to review all the means of expression available to the theater (or to *mise en scène*, which, in the system I have just expounded, is identified with the theater). But this would take me too far, and I shall limit myself to one or two examples.

First, spoken language.

To make a metaphysics out of spoken language is to make

language express what it does not usually express. It is to use it in a new, exceptional, and unaccustomed way, to restore its possibilities for physical shock, to divide it and distribute it actively in space, to use intonations in an absolutely concrete manner and to restore their power to hurt as well as really to manifest something, to turn against language and its basely utilitarian —one might almost say alimentary—sources, against its origins as a trapped animal, and finally, to consider language as *Incantation*.

Everything about this poetic and active way of regarding expression on stage leads us away from the human, contemporary, and psychological meaning of the theater and back to the religious and mystical acceptation of which our theater has lost all sense.

And if one has only to utter the word *religious* or *mystical* to be taken for a sacristan or for a profoundly illiterate bonze outside a Buddhist temple who at best can only turn prayer wheels, this is simply a measure of our inability to derive the full meaning from a word and our profound ignorance of the spirit of synthesis and analogy.

This may mean that we have reached the point where we have lost all contact with true theater, since we limit it to the realm of what can be reached by everyday thought, to the realm, whether known or unknown, of consciousness;—and if we do address ourselves theatrically to the unconscious, it is only to steal from it what it has managed to collect (or conceal) in the way of accessible and everyday experience.

It is said that one reason for the physical power over the mind, for the immediate and imaginative force of certain productions of the Oriental theater, like those of the Balinese theater, is that this theater is based on age-old traditions, that it has retained intact the secrets of using gestures, intonations, and harmony in relation to the senses and on all possible levels. This does not condemn Oriental theater, but it condemns us, and along with us it condemns the state of things in which we live and which must be destroyed, destroyed with diligence and with malice, on every level and at every point where it hinders the free exercise of thought.

The Marx Brothers

Animal Crackers, the first film by the Marx brothers that we have seen here, impressed me, as it did everyone, as an *extraordinary thing:* the liberation by means of the screen of a special magic which the customary relationships between words and images do not usually reveal, and if there is a characteristic state, a distinct poetic level of the mind that can be called *Surrealism, Animal Crackers* belongs to it.

It is difficult to say what this kind of magic consists in. It is probably something that is not peculiar to the cinema, but which does not belong to the theater either, something which could only be compared to certain successful Surrealist poems, if any such existed. The poetic quality of a film like *Animal Crackers* might correspond to the definition of humor, if this word had not long since lost its meaning of total liberation, of the destruction of all reality in the mind.

In order to understand the powerful, total, definitive, absolute originality (I am not exaggerating, I am simply trying to define, and if I am carried away by enthusiasm, I can't help it) of a film like *Animal Crackers,* and at times (at least throughout the finale) of a film like *Monkey Business,* one would have to add to the notion of humor the notion of something disturbing and tragic, a fatality (neither fortunate nor unfortunate, but difficult to express) which slips in behind it, like the revelation of a dreadful illness on a profile of absolute beauty.

In *Monkey Business* we find the Marx brothers, each with his own style, sure of themselves and ready, one feels, to come to grips with circumstances. But whereas in *Animal Crackers* each character was losing face from the beginning, here for the first three quarters of the film one watches the antics of clowns amusing themselves and playing tricks, some of them very successful, and it is only at the end that things get out of hand and that objects, animals, sounds, master and servants, host and guests, everything comes to a boil, goes mad, and revolts, amid the ecstatic and lucid comments of one of the Marx brothers, excited by the spirit which he has finally managed to unleash and of which he seems to be the dazed and temporary commentator.

For *The Theater and Its Double* (1931-36)

Nothing could be at once so hallucinatory or so terrible as this kind of manhunt, this final showdown, this chase in the twilight of a cattle barn, a stable with spider webs hanging everywhere, when men, women, and animals go berserk and land in the middle of a pile of incongruous objects whose *movements* or *sounds* will each be used in turn.

In *Animal Crackers* when a woman suddenly falls over backward on a sofa with her legs in the air and for a split second shows us everything we might want to see, when a man suddenly grabs a woman in a drawing room, does a few dance steps with her, and slaps her on the behind in time to the music, a kind of intellectual freedom is exercised in which the unconscious of each character, repressed by customs and conventions, avenges itself and our unconscious at the same time. But in *Monkey Business* when a man wanted by the police grabs a beautiful woman and dances with her, *poetically*, with a kind of serious pursuit of the charm and grace of attitude, here the claim made on our sensibility seems double, and demonstrates all that is poetic and perhaps even revolutionary in the jokes of the Marx brothers.

But the fact that the music to which the couple consisting of the wanted man and the beautiful woman dance is a music of nostalgia and escape, *a music of deliverance,* sufficiently indicates the dangerous side of all these funny jokes, and shows that when the poetic spirit is exercised, it always moves toward a kind of seething anarchy, a total breakdown of reality by poetry.

If the Americans, to whose spirit this genre of film belongs, refuse to see these films as anything but humorous, and if they insist on limiting themselves to the superficial and comical connotations of the word "humor," so much the worse for them, but this will not prevent us from regarding the finale of *Monkey Business* as a hymn to anarchy and total rebellion, that finale which puts the bray of a calf on the same intellectual level and attributes to it the same quality of lucid pain as the scream of a frightened woman, that finale in which in the darkness of a dirty barn two lecherous servants happily paw the bare shoulders of their master's daughter, and chat casually with their helpless master, all this amid the intoxication, also intellectual, of the pirouettes of the Marx brothers. And the triumph of all this is in the kind of exaltation, both visual and auditory, that all these events acquire in the half light, in the degree of vibration they achieve and in the kind of powerful disturbance that their total effect ultimately produces in the mind.

The Theater of Cruelty
(first manifesto)

We cannot go on prostituting the idea of the theater, whose only value lies in its excruciating, magical connection with reality and with danger.

Stated this way, the question of the theater must arouse general attention, since theater, because of its physical aspect and because it requires *expression in space* (the only real expression, in fact), allows the magical means of art and speech to be practiced organically and as a whole, like renewed exorcisms. From all this it follows that we shall not restore to the theater its specific powers of action until we have restored its language.

That is to say: instead of relying on texts that are regarded as definitive and as sacred we must first of all put an end to the subjugation of the theater to the text, and rediscover the notion of a kind of unique language halfway between gesture and thought.

This language can only be defined in terms of the possibilities of dynamic expression in space as opposed to the expressive possibilities of dialogue. And what theater can still wrest from speech is its potential for expansion beyond words, for development in space, for a dissociative and vibratory effect on our sensibilities. This is the function of intonations, the particular way a word is uttered. And beyond the auditory language of sounds, this is the function of the visual language of objects, movements, attitudes, gestures, but provided their meaning, their physiognomy, their combinations, are extended until they become signs and these signs become a kind of alphabet. Once the theater has become aware of this language in space, which is a language of sounds, cries, lights, onomatopoeia, it must organize it by making the characters and the objects true hieroglyphs, and by utilizing their symbolism and their correspondences in relation to all organs and on all levels.

The question for the theater, then, is to create a metaphysics of speech, gesture, and expression, in order to rescue it from its psychological and human stagnation. But all this can be of use only if there is behind such an effort a kind of real metaphysical temptation, an appeal to certain unusual ideas which by their very nature cannot be limited, or even formally defined. These ideas, which have to do with Creation, with Becoming, with Chaos, and are all of a cosmic order, provide an elementary notion of a realm from which the theater has become totally estranged. These ideas can create a kind of passionate equation between Man, Society, Nature, and Objects.

It is not a question, however, of putting metaphysical ideas directly on the stage, but of creating various kinds of temptations, of indrafts of air around these ideas. And humor with its anarchy, poetry with its symbolism and its images, provide a kind of elementary notion of how to channel the temptation of these ideas.

We must now consider the purely material aspect of this language. That is, of all the ways and means it has of acting on the sensibility.

It would be meaningless to say that this language relies on music, dance, pantomime, or mimicry. Obviously it utilizes movements, harmonies, and rhythms, but only insofar as they can converge in a kind of central expression, without favoring any particular art. This does not mean, either, that it does not make use of ordinary events, ordinary passions, but it uses them only as a springboard, just as HUMOR-AS-DESTRUCTION, through laughter, can serve to win over to its side the habits of reason.

It is with an altogether Oriental sense of expression that this objective and concrete language of the theater serves to corner and surround the organs. It flows into the sensibility. Abandoning Western uses of speech, it turns words into incantations. It extends the voice. It utilizes vibrations and qualities of the voice. It wildly stamps in rhythms. It pile-drives sounds. It seeks to exalt, to benumb, to charm, to arrest the sensibility. It releases the sense of a new lyricism of gesture which, by its rapidity or its spatial amplitude, ultimately surpasses the lyricism of words. In short, it ends the intellectual subjugation to language by conveying the sense of a new and more profound intellectuality which hides itself under the gestures and signs, elevated to the dignity of particular exorcisms.

For all this magnetism and all this poetry and these direct means of seduction would be nothing if they were not designed to put the mind physically on the track of something, if the true theater could not give us the sense of a creation of which we possess only one face, but whose completion exists on other levels.

And it does not matter whether these other levels are really conquered by the mind, that is, by the intelligence; this is to diminish them and that has no interest or meaning. What matters is that by reliable means the sensibility be put in a state of subtler and more profound perception, and this is the very purpose of that magic and those rites, of which the theater is only a reflection.

Technique

It is a question, therefore, of making the theater, in the proper sense of the word, a function; something as localized and as precise as the circulation of the blood in the arteries, or the apparently chaotic development of dream images in the brain, and this by a powerful linkage, a true enslavement of the attention.

The theater cannot become itself again—that is, it cannot constitute a means of true illusion—until it provides the spectator with the truthful precipitates of dreams, in which his taste for crime, his erotic obsessions, his savagery, his fantasies, his utopian sense of life and of things, even his cannibalism, pour out on a level that is not counterfeit and illusory but internal.

In other words, the theater must seek by every possible means to call into question not only the objective and descriptive external world but the internal world, that is, man from a metaphysical point of view. It is only thus, we believe, that we may once again be able to speak in connection with the theater about the rights of the imagination. Neither Humor, nor Poetry, nor Imagination means anything unless, by an anarchic destruction generating a fantastic flight of forms which will constitute the whole spectacle,

For *The Theater and Its Double* (1931–36)

they succeed in organically calling into question man, his ideas about reality, and his poetic place in reality.

But to regard theater as a second-hand psychological or moral function, and to believe that dreams themselves have only a replacement function, is to diminish the profound poetic bearing of both dreams and theater. If the theater, like dreams, is bloody and inhuman, it is in order to manifest and to root unforgettably in us the idea of a perpetual conflict and a spasm in which life is constantly being cut short, in which everything in creation rises up and struggles against our condition as already formed creatures, it is to perpetuate in a concrete and immediate way the metaphysical ideas of certain Fables whose very atrociousness and energy are enough to demonstrate their origin and their content of essential principles.

This being so, one sees that, by its proximity to the principles that transfuse it poetically with their energy, this naked language of the theater, a language that is not virtual but real, must make it possible, by utilizing the nervous magnetism of man, to transgress the ordinary limits of art and speech, in order to realize actively, that is magically, *in real terms*, a kind of total creation in which man can only resume his place between dreams and events.

Themes

We have no intention of boring the audience to death with transcendent cosmic preoccupations. That there may be profound keys to thought and action with which to read the spectacle as a whole, does not generally concern the spectator, who is not interested in such things. But they must be there all the same; and this concerns us.

THE SPECTACLE. Every spectacle will contain a physical and objective element, perceptible to all. Cries, groans, apparitions, surprises, theatrical tricks of all kinds, the magical beauty of costumes taken from certain ritual models, dazzling lighting effects, the incantatory beauty of voices, the charm of harmony, rare notes of music, the colors of objects, the physical rhythm of movements whose crescendo and decrescendo will blend with the rhythm of movements familiar to everyone, concrete apparitions of new and surprising objects, masks, puppets larger than life, sudden changes of lighting, physical action of light which arouses sensations of heat and cold, etc.

MISE EN SCÈNE. It is in terms of *mise en scène*, regarded not merely as the degree of refraction of a text on the stage but as the point of departure of all theatrical creation, that the ideal language of the theater will evolve. And it is in the utilization and handling of this language that the old duality between author and director will disappear, to be replaced by a kind of unique Creator who will bear the double responsibility for the spectacle and the plot.

THE LANGUAGE OF THE STAGE. It is not a question of eliminating spoken language but of giving words something of the importance they have in dreams.

Also, one must find new methods of transcribing this language, which might be related to the methods of musical notation, or might make use of some sort of code.

As for ordinary objects, or even the human body, elevated to the dignity of signs, it is obvious that one can derive inspiration from hieroglyphic characters, not only in order to transcribe these signs in a legible way that enables one to reproduce them at will, but also in order to compose on the stage symbols that are precise and immediately legible.

This code language and this musical notation will also be invaluable as a means of transcribing voices.

Since it is fundamental to this language to make a specialized use of intonations, these intonations must constitute a kind of harmonic balance, a kind of secondary distortion of speech that must be reproducible at will.

Similarly, the ten thousand and one facial expressions captured in the form of masks will be labeled and catalogued, so that they can participate directly and symbolically in this concrete language of the stage; and this independently of their particular psychological utilization.

Furthermore, these symbolic gestures, these masks, these attitudes, these individual or group movements whose innumerable meanings constitute an important part of the concrete language of the theater—evocative gestures, emotive or arbitrary attitudes, frenzied pounding out of rhythms and sounds—will be reinforced and multiplied by a kind of reflection of gestures and attitudes that consists of the mass of all the impulsive gestures, all the failed attitudes, all the slips of the mind and the tongue which reveal what might be called the impotences of speech, and in which there is a prodigious wealth of expressions, to which we shall not fail to have recourse on occasion.

There is, besides, a concrete idea of music in which sounds make entrances like characters, in which harmonies are cut in two and are lost in the precise entrances of words.

From one means of expression to another, correspondences and levels are created; and even the lighting can have a specific intellectual meaning.

MUSICAL INSTRUMENTS. They will be used for their qualities as objects and as part of the set.

Also, the need to act directly and profoundly upon the sensibility through the sense organs invites research, from the point of view of sound, into qualities and vibrations of sounds to which we are absolutely unaccustomed, qualities which contemporary musical instruments do not possess and which compel us to revive ancient and forgotten instruments or to create new ones. They also compel research, beyond the domain of music, into instruments and devices which, because they are made from special combinations or new alloys of metals, can achieve a new diapason of the octave and produce intolerable or ear-shattering sounds or noises.

LIGHT.—LIGHTING. The lighting equipment currently in use in theaters is no longer adequate. In view of the peculiar action of light on the mind, the effects of luminous vibrations must be investigated, along with new ways of diffusing light in waves, or sheets, or in fusillades of fiery arrows. The color range of the equipment currently in use must be completely revised. In order to produce particular tone qualities, one must reintroduce into light an element of thinness, density, opacity, with a view to producing heat, cold, anger, fear, etc.

COSTUMES. As for costumes, and without suggesting that there can be any such thing as a standard theatrical costume that is the same for all plays, we shall insofar as possible avoid modern dress—not because of any fetishistic and superstitious taste for the old, but because it seems absolutely obvious that certain age-old costumes intended for ritual use, although they were once of their time, retain a beauty and appearance that are revelatory, by virtue of their closeness to the traditions that gave them birth.

THE STAGE.—THE AUDITORIUM. We are eliminating the stage and the auditorium and replacing them with a kind of single site, without partition or barrier of any kind, which will itself become the theater of the action. A direct communication will be reestablished between the spectator and the spectacle, between the actor and the spectator, because the spectator, by being placed in the middle of the action, is enveloped by it and caught in its cross fire. This envelopment is the result of the very shape of the room.

For this reason we shall abandon existing theater buildings and use some kind of hangar or barn, which we shall have reconstructed according to techniques that have resulted in the architecture of certain churches or certain sacred buildings, and certain Tibetan temples.

In the interior of this construction, special proportions of height and depth will prevail. The room will be enclosed by four walls, without any kind of ornament, and the audience will be seated in the middle of the room, below, on movable chairs, to allow them to follow the spectacle that will go on all around them. In effect, the absence of a stage in the ordinary sense of the word will allow the action to spread out to the four corners of the room. Special areas will be set aside, for the actors and the action, at the four cardinal points of the room. The scenes will be played in front of whitewashed walls designed to absorb the light. In addition, overhead galleries will run around the entire periphery of the hall, as in certain Primitive paintings. These galleries will enable the actors to pursue each other from one part of the room to another whenever the action requires, and will permit the action to spread out on all levels and in all perspectives of height and depth. A cry uttered at one end of the room can be transmitted from mouth to mouth, with successive amplifications and modulations, to the other end of the room. The action will unfold, will extend its trajectory from level to level, from point to point; paroxysms will suddenly break out, flaring up like fires in different places; and the quality of true illusion of the spectacle, like the direct and immediate hold of the action on the spectator, will not be an empty phrase. For this diffusion of the action over an immense space will mean that the lighting of a scene and the various lighting effects of a performance will seize the audience as well as the characters;—and several simultaneous actions, several phases of an identical action in which the characters, clinging together in swarms, will withstand all the assaults of the situations, and the external assaults of the elements and the storm, will have their counterpart in physical means of lighting, thunder, or wind, whose repercussions the spectator will undergo.

Nevertheless, a central area will be set aside which, without serving as a stage properly speaking, will enable the main part of the action to be concentrated and brought to a climax whenever necessary.

OBJECTS.—MASKS.—PROPS. Puppets, enormous masks, objects of unusual proportions will appear by the same right as verbal images to emphasize the concrete aspect of every image and every expression—and the counterpart of this will be that things which usually require their objective representation will be treated summarily or disguised.

SETS. There will be no sets. This function will be adequately served by hieroglyphic characters, ritual costumes, puppets thirty feet high representing the beard of King Lear in the storm, musical instruments as tall as men, objects of strange shape and unknown purpose.

IMMEDIACY. But, people will say, a theater so removed from life, from facts, from current preoccupations . . . From the present and events, yes! From profound preoccupations which are the prerogative of the few, no! In the *Zohar*, the Story of Rabbi Simeon, who burns like fire, is as immediate as fire.

WORKS. We shall not perform any written plays, but shall attempt to create productions directly on stage around subjects, events, or known works. The very nature and arrangement of the room require spectacle and there is no subject, however vast, that can be denied us.

SPECTACLE. There is an idea of total spectacle that must be revived. The problem is to make space speak, to enrich and furnish it; like mines laid in a wall of flat rocks which suddenly give birth to geysers and bouquets.

THE ACTOR. The actor is at once an element of prime importance, since it is on the effectiveness of his performance that the success of the spectacle depends, and a kind of passive and neutral element, since all personal initiative is strictly denied him. It is an area in which there are no precise rules; and between the actor from whom one requires the mere quality of a sob and the actor who must deliver a speech with his own personal qualities of persuasion, there is the whole margin that separates a man from an instrument.

INTERPRETATION. The spectacle will be calculated from beginning to end, like a language. In this way there will be no wasted movement and all the movements will follow a rhythm; and since each character will be an extreme example of a type, his gesticulation, his physiognomy, his costume will appear as so many rays of light.

THE CINEMA. To the crude visualization of what is, the theater through poetry opposes images of what is not. From the point of view of action, moreover, one cannot compare a cinematic image which, however poetic, is limited by the properties of celluloid, to a theatrical image, which obeys all the exigencies of life.

CRUELTY. Without an element of cruelty at the foundation of every spectacle, the theater is not possible. In the state of degeneracy, in which we live, it is through the skin that metaphysics will be made to reenter our minds.

THE PUBLIC. First of all this theater must exist.

THE PROGRAM. We shall stage, without taking account of the text:

1. An adaptation of a work from the period of Shakespeare that is entirely relevant to our present state of mental confusion, whether it be one of Shakespeare's apocryphal plays, like *Arden of Feversham*, or an altogether different play from the same period.

2. A play of extreme poetic freedom by Léon-Paul Fargue.

3. An excerpt from the *Zohar:* The Story of Rabbi Simeon, which has the violence and the ever present force of a conflagration.

4. The story of Bluebeard reconstructed from historical documents, with a new idea of eroticism and cruelty.

5. The Fall of Jerusalem, according to the Bible and History; with the blood-red color that trickles from it, and with the feeling of despair and panic in people's minds visible even in the light; and on the other hand, the metaphysical disputes of the prophets, with the frightful intellectual agitation they create, whose repercussions fall physically on the King, the Temple, the Populace, and Historical Events.

6. A Tale by the Marquis de Sade in which the eroticism will be transposed, represented allegorically and clothed, resulting in a violent externalization of cruelty and a concealment of the rest.

7. One or more romantic melodramas in which improbability will become an active and concrete element of poetry.

8. Büchner's *Woyzeck*, in a spirit of reaction against our principles, and to illustrate what can be derived theatrically from a formal text.

9. Works of the Elizabethan theater stripped of their texts, of which we shall retain only trappings of the period, situations, characters, and plots.

ANTONIN ARTAUD

An End to Masterpieces

One reason for the asphyxiating atmosphere in which we live without possible escape or recourse—and for which we are all responsible, even the most revolutionary among us—is this respect for what has already been written, formulated, or painted, what has been given form, as if all expression were not finally exhausted and had not reached the point where things must fall apart if they are to begin again.

We must put an end to this idea of masterpieces reserved for a so-called elite, and which the mass of people do not understand; we must realize that the mind has no restricted districts like those set apart for clandestine sexual encounters.

The masterpieces of the past are good for the past: they are not good for us. We have a right to say what has been said and even what has not been said in a way which pertains to us, which is immediate and direct, which corresponds to present modes of feeling, and which everyone will understand.

It is idiotic to blame the masses for having no sense of the sublime, when we confuse the sublime with one of its formal manifestations, which are always dead manifestations. And if, for example, the modern mass audience no longer understands *Oedipus Rex*, I would go so far as to say that this is the fault of *Oedipus Rex* and not the fault of the audience.

In *Oedipus Rex* there is the theme of Incest and the idea that nature ridicules morality, and that there are forces at large somewhere which we would do well to beware of, whether we call these forces *destiny* or something else.

There is also the presence of an epidemic of the plague which is a physical embodiment of these forces. But all this is in costumes and in language which have lost all contact with the crude and epileptic rhythm of our time. Sophocles speaks grandly perhaps, but in a manner that is no longer relevant to the age. He speaks too subtly for this age, as if he were speaking beside the point.

However, a mass audience that trembles at train wrecks, that is familiar with earthquakes, plague, revolution, war, that is sensitive to the disorderly throes of love, is capable of reaching all these high ideas and asks only to be made aware of them, provided one speaks to them in their own language, and provided these ideas do not come to them by way of costumes and an overrefined language which belong to dead ages, ages that will never be brought to life again.

Today, as in the past, the masses are hungry for mystery: they ask only to become aware of the laws according to which destiny is revealed and perhaps to guess the secret of its manifestations.

Let us leave textual criticism to academic drudges and formal criticism to aesthetes, and recognize that what has been said need not be said again; that an expression does not work twice, does not live twice; that all words, once uttered, are dead and are effective only at the moment when they are uttered; that a form that has been used has no function but to urge us to look for another; and that the theater is the only place in the world where a gesture, once made, can never be exactly duplicated.

If the masses do not come to literary masterpieces it is because these masterpieces are literary, that is, fixed; and fixed in forms that no longer respond to the needs of the time.

Far from blaming the masses and the public, we should blame the formal screen which we interpose between ourselves and the masses, and this new form of idolatry, this idolatry of fixed masterpieces which is one of the aspects of bourgeois conformity.

This conformity which causes us to confuse sublimity, ideas, things with the forms they have assumed down through the ages and in ourselves—in our mentalities, the mentalities of snobs, fops, and aesthetes whom the public no longer understands.

There is no point in accusing the bad taste of a public that slakes its thirst with nonsense, as long as one has not shown the public a valid spectacle; and I defy anyone to show me *here* a valid spectacle, valid in the highest sense of theater, since the last great romantic melodramas, that is, in the past hundred years.

The public which takes the false for the true has a feeling for the true, and always responds to it when it does appear. However, it is not on the stage that one must look for truth today, but in the street; and if one offers the crowd in the streets an opportunity to show its human dignity, it will always do so.

If the masses have lost the habit of going to the theater; if we have all come to regard the theater as an inferior art, a means of vulgar distraction, and to use it as an outlet for our bad instincts —this is because we have been told too often that it was theater, that is, lies and illusion. It is because for four hundred years, that is, since the Renaissance, we have become accustomed to a purely descriptive and narrative theater, a theater that tells us about psychology.

It is because much ingenuity has been exerted to bring to life on the stage creatures that are plausible but detached, with the spectacle on one side and the audience on the other—and because the masses are no longer shown anything but the mirror image of what they are.

Shakespeare himself is responsible for this aberration and for this decay, for this disinterested idea of the theater according to which a theatrical performance leaves the audience intact, without one image thrown off that produces its vibration in the organism, leaving an impression that will never be erased.

If in Shakespeare man is sometimes preoccupied by that which transcends him, ultimately it is always a question of the consequences of this preoccupation for man, that is, of psychology.

Psychology, with its relentless effort to reduce the unknown to the known, that is, the daily and the ordinary, is the cause of this decline and this terrible loss of energy, which seems to me to have reached its lowest point. And it seems to me that both the theater and we ourselves must have done with psychology.

Indeed, I believe that on this point we are all in agreement and that there is no need to descend to the revolting level of modern French theater in order to condemn psychological theater.

Stories about money, money anxieties, social climbing, throes of love untouched by altruism, sexuality sprinkled with an eroticism lacking in mystery, may be psychology, but they are not theater. These anxieties, this lechery, these ruttings in the presence of which we are reduced to lip-smacking voyeurs, turn to revolution and to vinegar: we must become aware of this.

But this is not the most serious aspect.

If Shakespeare and his imitators have gradually instilled in us an idea of art for art's sake, with art on one side and life on the other, one could rely on this ineffectual and lazy idea as long as

For *The Theater and Its Double* (1931–36)

life outside held together. But it is now clear from too many signs that everything that once sustained our lives is coming apart, that we are all mad, desperate, and sick. And I urge *us* to react.

This idea of a detached art, of poetry as something charming that exists only to beguile our leisure time, is a decadent idea, and it demonstrates loudly our capacity for castration.

Our literary admiration for Rimbaud, Jarry, Lautréamont, and a few others, which drove two men to suicide but which for others turned into café gossip, is related to this idea of literary poetry, of detached art, of a neuter spiritual activity which does nothing and produces nothing; and I observe that it was at a time when personal poetry, which involves only the person who writes it at the moment he is writing it, was at its peak that the theater was most despised by poets who have never had a sense either of direct and concerted action, or of efficacity, or of danger.

We must put an end to this superstition of texts and of *written* poetry. Written poetry is valuable once, and after that it should be destroyed. Let the dead poets make way for the others. And we should be able to see that it is our veneration for what has already been done, however beautiful and valuable it may be, that petrifies us, that immobilizes us and keeps us from making contact with the underlying force, whether you call it mental energy, the life force, the determinism of exchanges, the lunar menses, or whatever you like. Beneath the poetry of texts there is poetry pure and simple, without form and without text. And just as the efficacity of those masks that are used in the magical rites of certain tribes is exhausted—and the masks are then good for nothing but to be put in museums—so the poetic efficacity of a text is exhausted; but the poetry and efficacity of the theater are exhausted least quickly, since they include the action of what is expressed in gestures and in speech, and which never occurs twice in the same way.

It is a question of knowing what we want. If we are all prepared for war, plague, famine, and slaughter, we do not even need to say so, we have only to go on as we are. Go on behaving like snobs, flocking to hear some singer or other, some admirable performance which does not go beyond the realm of art (and even the Ballets Russes, at the height of their glory, never went beyond the realm of art), some exhibit of easel painting in which striking forms flash out here and there, but at random and without any true consciousness of the forces they could stir up.

This empiricism, this randomness, this individualism, and this anarchy must cease.

Enough of personal poems which benefit those who write them much more than those who read them.

Enough, once and for all, of these manifestations of a closed, egotistical, and personal art.

Our anarchy, our mental confusion is a function of the anarchy of everything else—or rather, everything else is a function of this anarchy.

I am not one of those who believe that civilization must change so that the theater can change; but I do believe that the theater, utilized in the highest and most difficult possible sense, has the power to influence the aspect and formation of things: and the encounter on the stage of two passionate manifestations, two living centers, two nervous magnetisms is something as whole, as true, and as decisive, even, as in life the encounter of two epidermises in a momentary lust.

This is why I propose a theater of cruelty.—With that mania for depreciating everything that we all have today, as soon as I uttered the word "cruelty" everyone immediately took it to mean "blood." But *"theater of cruelty"* means a theater that is difficult and cruel first of all for myself. And on the level of representation it is not a question of that cruelty which we can practice on each other by cutting up each other's bodies, by sawing away at our personal anatomies, or, like Assyrian emperors, by sending each other packages of human ears, noses, or neatly severed nostrils through the mail, but of that much more terrible and necessary cruelty which things can practice on us. We are not free. And the sky can still fall on our heads. And the theater has been created to teach us, first of all, that.

Either we shall be able to return by modern and present-day means to this superior idea of poetry and of poetry through theater which is behind the Myths told by the great ancient tragedians, either we shall be able once again to entertain a religious idea of the theater, that is, without meditation, without useless contemplation, without vague dreams, to arrive at a consciousness and a mastery of certain dominant forces, certain notions that govern everything; and since notions, when they are effective, carry their own energy, to recover within ourselves those energies which ultimately create order and heighten the value of life, or we might just as well give up without a struggle and at once, and recognize that we are no longer good for anything but disorder, famine, blood, war, and epidemics.

Either we shall bring all the arts back to one central attitude and necessity, finding an analogy between a gesture made in painting or the theater and a gesture made by lava in a volcanic eruption, or we must stop painting, babbling, writing, and doing anything at all.

I propose to return to the theater that elementary magical idea, taken up by modern psychoanalysis, which consists of curing a patient by having him assume the external attitude of the state one would like to restore him to.

I propose to renounce this empiricism of images which the unconscious furnishes at random and which we throw off also at random, calling them poetic and therefore hermetic images, as if that kind of trance that poetry provides did not have its reverberation throughout the whole sensibility, in all the nerves, and as if poetry were some vague force that did not vary its movements.

I propose to return by way of the theater to an idea of the physical understanding of images and of the means of inducing trances, as in Chinese medicine, which knows, over the whole extent of the human anatomy, what points must be punctured in order to regulate even the subtlest functions.

For someone who has forgotten the communicative power and magical mimicry of gesture, the theater can reinstruct, because a gesture carries its energy with it, and because, after all, there are human beings in the theater who can manifest the force of the gesture that is made.

To create art is to deprive a gesture of its reverberation in the organism, whereas if the gesture is made under the necessary conditions and with the necessary force, this reverberation invites the organism, and through it the whole individual personality, to assume attitudes that correspond to the gesture that has been made.

The theater is the only place in the world and the last collective means we still have of reaching the organism directly and, in periods of neurosis and base sensuality like the one in which we are immersed, of attacking this base sensuality by physical means which it cannot resist.

If music has an effect on snakes, it is not because of the spiritual notions it offers them, but because snakes are long, because they lie coiled on the ground, because their bodies touch the ground at almost every point; and the musical vibrations which are communicated to the ground reach their bodies like a very subtle and prolonged massage; well, I propose that we treat the spectators like snakes that are being charmed, and that we lead them by way of the organism to the subtlest notions.

At first by crude means which are gradually refined. These crude immediate means hold their attention from the beginning.

This is why in the "theater of cruelty" the spectator is in the middle and the spectacle surrounds him.

In this spectacle, sound effects are constant: sounds, noises, cries are chosen first for their vibratory quality, then for what they represent.

Among these means, which are gradually refined, lighting also plays a part. Lighting which is not designed merely to add color or to illuminate, and which contributes its force, its influence, its suggestions. And the light of a green cavern does not have the same sensual effect on the organism as the light of a windy day.

After sound and light there is action, and the dynamism of action: it is here that theater, far from copying life, enters into communication, if it can, with pure forces. And whether one accepts or denies them, it is still permissible to speak of forces when referring to whatever it is that engenders energizing images in the unconscious, and gratuitous crime in the outside world.

A violent and concentrated action is a metaphor of lyricism: it evokes supernatural images, a bloodline of images, a bloody gush of images in the poet's mind as well as the spectator's.

Whatever conflicts may haunt the mind of an age, I defy the spectator to whom violent scenes have transferred their blood, who has felt a superior action passing through his own body, who has seen the extraordinary and essential movements of his thought suddenly illuminated in extraordinary events—violence and bloodshed having been placed at the service of the violence of thought—I defy this spectator to indulge outside the theater in ideas of war, rioting, or random murders.

Stated in this way, the idea seems pretentious and childish. And it will be argued that one example leads to another, that the attitude of healing leads to healing, and the attitude of murder leads to murder. Everything depends on the style and the purity with which things are done. There is a risk. But it should not be forgotten that although a theatrical gesture may be violent, it is disinterested; and that what the theater teaches us is precisely the uselessness of the action which, once done, is no longer necessary, and the superior usefulness of that state which is not made use of by action but which, *restored*, produces sublimation.

Therefore, I propose a theater in which violent physical images pound and hypnotize the sensibility of the spectator, who is caught in the theater as if in a whirlwind of higher forces.

A theater which, abandoning psychology, recounts the extraordinary, puts on the stage natural conflicts, natural and subtle forces, and which presents itself first of all as an exceptional force of redirection. A theater which produces trances, as the dances of the Dervishes and the Isawas produce trances, and which addresses itself to the organism by precise means, and with the same means as the healing music of certain tribes which we admire on records but which we are incapable of originating among ourselves.

There is a risk involved, but under the circumstances I feel the risk is worth taking. I do not believe that we can ever revitalize our present way of life and I do not believe it is even worthwhile holding on to it; but I do propose something to get us out of our stagnation, instead of continuing to groan about it, and about the boredom, inertia, and stupidity of everything.

An Emotional Athleticism

We must recognize that the actor has a kind of emotional musculature which corresponds to certain physical localizations of feelings.

The actor is like a real physical athlete, but with this surprising qualification, that he has an emotional organism which is analogous to the athlete's, which is parallel to it, which is like its double, although it does not operate on the same level.

The actor is an athlete of the heart.

For him too there is this division of total man into three worlds; and the sphere of the emotions is his peculiar domain.

It belongs to him organically.

The muscular movements of physical effort are like the effigy of another identical effort, which in the movements of dramatic performance is localized at the same points.

The place from which the athlete draws the strength to run is the place from which the actor draws the strength to hurl a spasmodic curse, whose path, however, is turned back toward the inside.

All the sudden movements of boxing, wrestling, the hundred-yard dash, the high jump, have analogous organic foundations in the movement of the passions; they have the same physical points of support.

With this further qualification, however, that the movement is reversed and that with respect to breathing, for example, whereas in the actor the body is supported by the breath, in the boxer, in the physical athlete, it is the breath that is supported by the body.

This question of breathing is, in fact, primary; it is related inversely to the importance of the external movement.

The more restrained and internalized the movement, the fuller and heavier the breathing, the more substantial and full of resonance.

Whereas when the movement is sweeping, broad, and externalized, the corresponding breathing is characterized by short and labored puffs.

It is certain that for every feeling, every movement of the mind, every leap of human emotion, there is a breath that belongs to it.

And the rhythms of the breath have names which are taught to us by the Cabala; it is these rhythms that give the human heart its form, and give the movements of the passions their sex.

The actor is merely a crude empiricist, an amateur doctor guided by an obscure instinct.

And yet the point is not, whatever people may think, to teach him to rave.

The point is to do away with this sort of wild-eyed ignorance in which all of contemporary theater advances as if in darkness, this ignorance in which it stumbles endlessly. The gifted actor finds in his instinct the wherewithal to catch and project certain forces; but although these forces have their physical pathways within the body and *within the organs,* he would be completely amazed if someone revealed to him that they exist, for their existence has never occurred to him for a moment.

In order to make use of one's emotionality the way a wrestler utilizes his musculature, one must see the human being as a Double, as the Ka of Egyptian Mummies, as a perpetual specter illuminated by the forces of emotionality.

A specter who is fluid and never finished, whose forms the true actor apes, a specter on whom he imposes the forms and image of his sensibility.

It is on this double that the theater has its influence, it is this spectral effigy that it shapes, and like all specters, this double has a long memory. The memory of the heart is durable and of course it is with his heart that the actor thinks, but here the heart predominates.

This means that in the theater more than anywhere else it is the world of emotion that the actor must become aware of, but he must attribute to this world virtues which are not those of an image, virtues which have a physical meaning.

It does not matter whether or not the hypothesis is correct, what matters is that it is verifiable.

One can physiologically reduce the soul to a maze of vibrations.

One can see this specter of a soul as if intoxicated by the cries it produces, otherwise how explain Hindu mantras, those consonances, those mysterious rhythms in which the physical undersides of the soul, hunted down to their hiding places, come out and tell their secrets in the light of day.

Belief in a fluid materiality of the soul is indispensable to the profession of actor. To know that a passion is composed of matter, that it is subject to the plastic fluctuations of matter, gives us a dominion over the passions which extends our area of power.

To reach the passions by means of their forces instead of regarding them as pure abstractions confers a mastery on the actor which makes him the equal of a true healer.

To know that there is a physical outlet for the soul enables one to reach this soul from the other direction, and to rediscover its being by certain mathematical analogies.

To know the secret of the *rhythm* of the passions, of that kind of musical *tempo* that governs their harmonic pulsation: this is an aspect of theater which our modern psychological theater has certainly not dreamed of for a long time.

But this *tempo* can be discovered by analogy; and it is discovered in the six ways of distributing and retaining the breath like a precious element.

Every breath has three rhythms, just as there are underlying all creation three principles which find their corresponding image even in the breath.

The Cabala divides the human breath into six principal arcana of which the first, known as the Great Arcanum, is that of creation:

ANDROGYNOUS	MALE	FEMALE
BALANCED	EXPANSIVE	ATTRACTIVE
NEUTER	POSITIVE	NEGATIVE

I have had the idea of employing a knowledge of breathing not only in the actor's work but in his professional training. For if a knowledge of breathing illuminates the color of the soul, there is all the more reason why it can arouse the soul, facilitate its expansion.

It is obvious that if breathing accompanies effort, the mechanical production of the breath will generate in the working organism a corresponding quality of effort.

The effort will have the color and rhythm of the artificially produced breath.

The effort accompanies the breath sympathetically, and according to the quality of the effort to be produced, a preparatory emission of breath will make this effort easy and spontaneous. I insist on the word "spontaneous," for the breath rekindles life, it inflames its very substance.

What voluntary breathing brings about is a spontaneous reappearance of life. Like a voice of infinite colors at the edges of which soldiers lie sleeping. The alarm clock or the military trumpet has the effect of throwing them regularly into the fray. But let a child suddenly cry "wolf" and the same soldiers would wake up. They wake up in the middle of the night. False alarm: the soldiers are about to come back. But no: they run into hostile groups, they have fallen into a real hornets' nest. It was in a dream that the child cried out. His unconscious, more sensitive and floating, came upon a troop of enemies. Thus by indirect means the artificial lie of the theater falls upon a reality more formidable than the other, a reality which life had not suspected.

Thus, by means of the sharpened penetration of breathing, the actor probes the depths of his personality.

For that breath which nourishes life enables one to retrace its stages one by one. And the actor can invoke a feeling he does not have by means of breath, provided he judiciously combines its effects, and provided he does not mistake its sex. For breath is either male or female; and it is less often androgynous. But one may have to portray precious states of suspension.

The breath accompanies the feeling and one can enter the feeling by means of the breath, provided one has correctly chosen the particular breath that is proper to that feeling.

There are, as we have said, six principal combinations of breaths:

NEUTER	MASCULINE	FEMININE
NEUTER	FEMININE	MASCULINE
MASCULINE	NEUTER	FEMININE
FEMININE	NEUTER	MASCULINE
MASCULINE	FEMININE	NEUTER
FEMININE	MASCULINE	NEUTER

And a seventh state which is higher than the breaths and which through the door of the highest Guna, the state of Sattva, joins the manifest to the non-manifest.

If someone claims that since the actor is not primarily a metaphysician, he need not concern himself with this seventh state, we reply that according to us, although the theater is the perfect and most complete symbol of universal manifestation, the actor carries within him the principle of this state, this path of blood by which he enters all the other states each time his potential organs awaken from their sleep.

Of course, most of the time instinct is there to compensate for this absence of a notion that can be defined; and there is no need to fall from so high in order to emerge among the median passions like those with which contemporary theater is filled. And the system of breathing was certainly not designed for the median passions. It is not for a declaration of adulterous love that we are being prepared by the intensive training of the breath according to an ancient system.

It is for a subtle quality of scream, it is for desperate demands of the soul that we are predisposed by an emission repeated over and over again.

And we localize this breath, we divide it into states of contraction and relaxation combined. We use our body as a screen through which will and the release of will pass in turn.

No sooner do we think of desiring than we forcefully project a male beat, followed with no perceptible break in continuity by a prolonged female beat.

No sooner do we think of not desiring or even of not thinking than a weary female breath makes us inhale the suffocating heat of a cave, the damp breath of a forest; and on the same prolonged beat we make a heavy exhalation; meanwhile, the muscles of our entire body, vibrating by regions, have not ceased to function.

The important thing is to become aware of these localizations of emotional thought. One means of recognition is effort; and the same points on which the physical effort falls are also those touched by the emanation of emotional thought. They serve as springboards for the emanation of feelings.

It should be noted that all that is feminine, all that is surrender, anguish, appeal, invocation, all that reaches toward something in a gesture of supplication, rests also on the points where effort is felt, but it does so the way a diver digs his heels into the ocean floor in order to rise to the surface: there is a sudden vacuum where before there was tension.

But in this case the masculine returns to haunt the place of the feminine like a ghost; whereas when the emotional state is male, the inner body composes a kind of inverse geometry, an image of the state reversed.

To become aware of the physical obsession, of the muscles grazed by the emotion is enough, as in the control of the breath, to release this potential emotion, to give it a resonance that is silent but profound, and of unusual violence.

Thus it appears that any actor, even the least gifted, can by this physical skill augment the inner density and volume of his feeling, and a full-bodied expression follows this organic mastery.

It is not irrelevant to this end to know a few points of localization.

The man who lifts weights lifts them with his loins, it is with a movement of the lower back that he supports and reinforces the strength of his arms; and it is rather curious to observe that inversely in every feminine and hollowing feeling—sobbing, desolation, spasmodic panting, fear—it is in the small of the back that the vacuum is physically expressed, in the very place where Chinese acupuncture relieves congestion of the kidneys. Because Chinese medicine proceeds only by means of the empty and the full. Convex and concave. Tension and relaxation. *Yin and Yang.* Masculine feminine.

Another point of radiation: the point of anger, aggression, biting, is the center of the solar plexus. It is from here that the head draws the force to discharge its psychological venom.

The point of heroism and sublimity is also the seat of guilt. The place where one beats one's breast. The place where anger boils, anger that rages and does not advance.

But where anger advances, guilt retreats; this is the secret of the empty and the full.

A high-pitched anger which is taken apart begins with a loud neuter and is localized in the plexus by means of a sudden, feminine void; then, obstructed at the shoulder blades, it bounces back like a boomerang and gives off male sparks which are consumed without advancing. In order to lose their biting tone, they retain the correlation of the male breath: they exhale violently.

These are merely examples illustrating the few fertile principles which make up the substance of the literature on this subject. Others who have the time to do so will construct the complete anatomy of the system. There are 380 points in Chinese acupuncture, of which 73 principal ones are used in current therapy. There are many fewer crude outlets for our human emotionality.

Many fewer supports which can be indicated and on which to base the athleticism of the soul.

The secret is to exacerbate these supports like a musculature that is being flayed.

The rest is achieved by screams.

*

In order to reforge the chain, the chain of a time when the spectator sought his own reality in the spectacle, we must allow the spectator to identify himself with the spectacle, breath for breath and beat for beat.

It is not enough for the spectator to be captivated by the magic of the spectacle, he will not be captivated unless we know *where to reach him.* We have had enough of a haphazard magic, a poetry that no longer has the support of science.

In the theater, poetry and science must henceforth be one.

Every emotion has organic bases. It is by cultivating his emotion in his body that the actor recharges its voltaic density.

To know in advance the points of the body that must be touched is to throw the spectator into magical trances. And it is from this precious kind of science that poetry in the theater has long been estranged.

To know the points of localization in the body is, therefore, to reforge the magic chain.

And with the hieroglyph of a breath I can rediscover an idea of sacred theater.

N.B. No one knows how to scream any more in Europe, least of all, actors. In a hypnotic trance, they can no longer utter a cry. People in the theater who can do nothing but talk and who have forgotten that they had a body have also forgotten the use of their throats. The atrophied windpipe is not even an organ but a monstrous abstraction that talks: actors in France can no longer do anything but talk.

ORIENTAL THEATER AND WESTERN THEATER

The revelation of the Balinese Theater had been to provide us with a physical and non-verbal idea of theater in which theater is contained within the limits of everything that can happen on a stage independently of the written text, whereas theater as we conceive it in the West is closely related to the text and limited by it. In our Western theater the Word is everything and there is nothing outside of the Word. Theater is a branch of literature, a kind of high-sounding variety of language, and although we may admit that there is a difference between the text as performed on a stage and the text as we read it, although we may confine theater within the limits of what goes on between the lines, we cannot succeed in separating theater from the idea of a performed text.

This idea of the supremacy of speech in the theater is so deeply rooted in us and we are so accustomed to regarding theater as the mere physical reflection of the text that everything in the theater that goes beyond the text, everything that is not contained within its limits and strictly conditioned by it, seems to us to come under the heading of *mise en scène*, which is regarded as something inferior in comparison with the text.

This subjugation of the theater to speech gives one reason to wonder whether by chance the theater might not possess a language of its own, whether it would be totally fantastic to regard it as an independent and autonomous art on a level with music, painting, dance, etc.

One finds in any case that if this language does exist, it is necessarily related to *mise en scène*, regarded:

1. As the visual and plastic materialization of speech.

2. As the language of everything that can be said and signified on a stage independently of speech, everything that finds its expression in space, or everything that can be touched or taken apart by space.

Once we regard this language of *mise en scène* as the pure

language of theater, we must discover whether it can achieve the same inner purpose as speech, whether mentally and theatrically it can lay claim to the same intellectual power as spoken language. In other words, we must ask ourselves not whether it can state thoughts clearly but whether it can *make us think*, whether it can lead the mind to assume profound attitudes which are effective from its own point of view.

In short, to raise the question of the intellectual power of expression through objective forms, the intellectual power of a language that uses only forms, or sounds, or gestures, is to raise the question of the intellectual power of art.

If we have reached the point where we regard art merely as a source of pleasure and entertainment, and confine it to a purely formal utilization of forms within the harmony of certain external relationships, this in no way diminishes its profound expressive value; but the spiritual weakness of the West, which is the place par excellence where people have confused art and aestheticism, is to think that there could be painting which would be an end in itself, dancing which would be purely plastic, as if we had set out to cut off the forms of art, to sever their ties with all the mystical attitudes they are capable of assuming as they confront the absolute.

It is clear, then, that the theater, insofar as it remains enclosed within its language and in correlation with it, must break away from the present, that its function is not to resolve social or psychological conflicts, to serve as a battlefield for moral passions, but to give objective expression to secret truths, to bring to light by means of forceful gestures that portion of truth which has been buried under the forms in their encounters with Becoming.

To do this, to connect the theater with the expressive possibilities of forms, and of everything in the way of gestures, sounds, colors, movements, etc., is to restore it to its original function, to place it once again in its religious and metaphysical context, to reconcile it with the universe.

It will be objected that words have their own metaphysical properties, that it is not forbidden to conceive of speech as well as gesture on the universal level, and that it is on this level, moreover, that speech acquires its major power, as a dissociative force brought to bear on physical appearances, on all states in which the mind has become stabilized and tends to remain fixed. It is clear, though, that this metaphysical way of regarding speech is not the way in which Western theater uses it, that it uses speech not as an active force which starts with the destruction of appearances in order to reach the mind but on the contrary, as a final stage of thought which is lost when it is externalized.

Speech in Western theater is only used to express psychological conflicts peculiar to man and his situation in the daily reality of life. His conflicts lend themselves perfectly to the spoken word, and whether they remain in the psychological domain or pass over into the social domain, the moral interest of the drama will always depend on the way its conflicts attack and break down the characters. And the drama will always take place in a domain in which the verbal resolutions of speech will retain their advantage. But these moral conflicts, by their very nature, have absolutely no need of the stage to be resolved. To give predominance on stage to spoken language or verbal expression, over the objective expression of gestures and everything that reaches the mind by means of the senses in space, is to turn one's back on the physical necessities of the stage and to reject its possibilities.

The domain of the theater is not psychological but plastic and physical. And the point is not whether the physical language of the theater is capable of arriving at the same psychological resolutions as the language of words, whether it can express feelings and passions as well as words; the point is whether there are not in the domain of thought and intelligence attitudes which words are incapable of capturing and which gestures, and everything that partakes of the language of space, express with greater precision than words.

Before giving an example of the relationship between the physical world and profound states of mind, I hope you will excuse me if I quote myself:

> Every true feeling is in reality untranslatable. To express it is to betray it. But to translate it is to *conceal* it. True expression hides what it manifests. It confronts the mind with the real emptiness of nature by creating as a reaction a kind of fullness in the thought. Or, if you prefer, to counter the manifestation-illusion of nature, it creates an emptiness in the thought. Every powerful

emotion awakens in us the idea of emptiness. And the clear language which prevents this sense of emptiness also prevents poetry from appearing in the mind. This is why an image, an allegory, a figure of speech which disguises what it wants to reveal has more meaning for the mind than the clarity provided by the analytical properties of speech.

This is why true beauty never impresses us directly, and why a setting sun is beautiful because of everything it takes away from us.

The nightmares of Flemish painting make an impression on us because of the juxtaposition to the real world of what has become a caricature of this world. They present us with phantoms which we might have encountered in our dreams. They have their source in those semi-conscious states which give rise to abortive gestures and absurd slips of the tongue. Next to an abandoned child they place a leaping harp; next to a human embryo swimming in subterranean waterfalls they show a formidable fortress below which a veritable army advances. Next to dreamlike uncertainty the march of certainty, and beyond a yellow underground light the orange glow of a huge autumn sun about to disappear.

The point is not to do away with speech in the theater but to change its function, and above all to reduce its role, to regard it as something other than a means of guiding human characters to their external goals, since the theater is concerned only with the way feelings and passions conflict with one another and differ from one person to the next in life.

To change the function of speech in the theater is to use it in a concrete and spatial sense, and in combination with everything in the theater that is spatial and of significance in the concrete realm; it is to manipulate it like a solid object that sets things in motion, first in the air, next in a realm which is infinitely more mysterious and more secret but which also admits of extension, and this secret but extended realm will be identified without much difficulty as that of formal anarchy on the one hand but also of continuous formal creation on the other.

And this identification of the function of theater with all the possibilities of formal and extended manifestation gives rise to the idea of a certain poetry of space which is in turn identified with sorcery.

In Oriental theater with its metaphysical tendencies, in contrast to Western theater with its psychological tendencies, there is a possession by the forms of their meanings and their significations on all possible levels; or if you prefer, their vibrations are not received on a single level but on all levels of the mind at the same time.

And it is because the forms can be regarded from so many aspects that they acquire their power to disturb and charm and that they are a constant stimulation for the mind. It is because Oriental theater does not consider the external aspects of things on a single level, because it does not confine itself to the single obstacle or to the physical impact of these aspects on the senses, but always considers the degree of mental possibility from which these aspects have emerged, that it participates in the intense poetry of nature and retains its magical relationship with all the objective degrees of the universal magnetism.

It is from this viewpoint of magical utilization and sorcery that we must consider *mise en scène,* not as the reflection of a written text and of all that projection of physical doubles that is derived from the written work, but as the burning projection of all the objective consequences that can be derived from a gesture, a word, a sound, a piece of music, and from various combinations of these. This active projection can only occur on the stage and its effects can only be discovered in front of the stage and on the stage; and the writer who relies exclusively on written words has no function and must yield to specialists in this objective and animated sorcery.

The Theater of the Seraphim

for Jean Paulhan

There are enough details to make it understandable.
To be more precise would spoil the poetry of the thing.

NEUTER
FEMININE
MASCULINE

I want to attempt a terrible feminine. The cry of the revolt that is trampled underfoot, of anguish armed for war, of the demand for justice.

It is like the groan of an abyss that is opened: the wounded earth cries out, but voices are raised, deep as the bottom of the abyss, voices which are the bottom of the abyss crying.

Neuter. Feminine. Masculine.

In order to utter this cry I empty myself.

Not of air, but of the very power of sound. I raise up in front of myself my human body. And having cast on it "THE EYE" of a horrible measurement, part by part I force it to reenter me.

First the belly. It is with the belly that silence must begin, on the right, on the left, on the spot of hernial obstructions, the place where surgeons operate.

The *Masculine,* in order to force out the cry of strength, would first press on the area of obstructions, would command the irruption of the lungs in the breath and of the breath in the lungs.

Here, alas! it is just the opposite, and the war I want to make comes from the war that is made on me.

And there is in my *Neuter* a massacre! You understand, it is the blazing image of a massacre that nourishes my own war. My war is nourished by a war, and it spits out its own war.

NEUTER. *Feminine. Masculine.* There is in this neuter a gathering, the will which lies in wait for war, and which will bring forth war from the force of its shock.

Sometimes the Neuter is nonexistent. It is a Neuter of respite, of light, finally of space.

Between two breaths, the void *extends,* but then it is like a space that extends.

Here it is an asphyxiated void. The constricted void of a throat in which the very violence of the death rattle has blocked respiration.

It is in the belly that the breath descends
and creates its void
from which it hurls it TO THE TOP OF THE LUNGS.

This means: in order to scream I do not need strength, I only need weakness, and the desire will come out of weakness, but will live, and will recharge weakness with all the force of the demand for justice.

And yet, and this is the secret, *just as* IN THE THEATER, the force will not come out. The active masculine will be repressed. And it will retain the energetic will of the breath. It will retain it for the whole body, and on the outside there will be a scene of the *disappearance* of force at which the SENSES WILL BELIEVE THEY ARE PRESENT.

Now, from the void of my belly I have reached the void which menaces the top of the lungs.

From there with no perceptible break in continuity the breath falls on the lower back, first on the left it is a feminine cry, then on the right, at the point where Chinese acupuncture treats nervous fatigue, when this indicates a malfunctioning of the spleen or the viscera, when it reveals intoxication.

Now I can fill my lungs with the sound of a cataract whose rush would destroy them, if the cry I chose to utter were not a dream.

Gathering the two points of the void on the belly, and then without passing to the lungs, gathering the two points *just above* the kidneys, they brought forth in me the image of that scream armed for war, that terrible subterranean cry.

For this scream I must fall.

It is the scream of the wounded warrior who brushes past the broken walls with a drunken sound of glass.

I fall.
I fall but I am not afraid.
I give up my fear in the sound of rage, in a solemn roaring.

NEUTER. *Feminine. Masculine.*

The Neuter was heavy and fixed. The Feminine is thundering and terrible, like the baying of an incredible mastiff, squat as the cavernous columns, dense as the air that immures the gigantic vaults of the underground cavern.

ANTONIN ARTAUD

I cry out in the dream,
but I know that I am dreaming,
and over BOTH SIDES OF THE DREAM
I make my will prevail.

I scream in an armature of bone, in the caverns of my thoracic cage which in the paralyzed eyes of my head takes on immoderate importance.

But with this stricken scream, to scream I must fall.
I fall into a tunnel and I cannot get out, I can never get out.
Never again *into the Masculine*.

I have said so: the Masculine is nothing. It retains force, but it shrouds me in force.
As for the outside it is a slap, a larva of air, a globule of sulphur that explodes in water, this masculine, the sigh of a closed mouth at the moment that it closes.
When all the air has passed into the scream and there is nothing left for the face. From this thunderous baying of a mastiff, the feminine and closed face has just turned away in time.

And it is here that the cataracts begin.
This scream that I have just uttered *is* a dream.
But a dream that eats away the dream.
I really am in a tunnel, I am breathing, with the appropriate breaths, O miracle, and I am the actor.
The air around me is vast, but blocked, for the cavern is walled in.
I play the part of a petrified warrior, who has fallen all alone into the caverns of the earth and who cries out, stricken with fear.
Now the scream I have just uttered calls forth first a hole of silence, a silence that shrinks, then the sound of a cataract, a sound of water, this is in order, for the sound is related to theater. For in all real theater things follow a rhythm that is clearly understood.

THE THEATER OF THE SERAPHIM:

This means that once again there is *magic in living;* that the air of the tunnel which is drunk is driven back like an army from my closed mouth to my wide-open nostrils, with a terrible warrior's sound.

This means that when I act my scream has ceased to turn upon itself, but that it awakens its double from sources in the walls of the tunnel.

And this double is more than an echo, it is the memory of a language whose secret the theater has lost.

Big as a conch, it can be held in the hollow of the hand, this secret; it is thus that Tradition speaks.

All the magic of existence will have passed into a single chest when Time has been locked away again.

And this will be very close to a great cry, the source of a human voice, a single and isolated human voice, like a warrior who has lost his army.

To describe the cry that I dreamed, to describe it in living words, with the appropriate words, and mouth to mouth and breath to breath, to make it pass not into the ear but into the chest of the spectator.

Between the person who stirs in me when, as an actor, I move forward on a stage and the one I am when I move forward in reality, there is a difference of degree, to be sure, but the difference is in favor of theatrical reality.

When I live I do not feel myself live. But when I act, it is then that I feel myself exist.

What is to prevent me from believing in the dream of the theater when I believe in the dream of reality?

When I dream I am doing something and in the theater I am doing something.

The events of the dream, directed by my deep inner consciousness, teach me the meaning of the events of the waking state in which a naked fatality directs me.

But the theater is like one long waking state in which it is I who direct the fatality.

But in this theater in which I govern my personal fate and which is based on breathing, and which after breathing is founded on the sound or the scream, we must, in order to reforge the chain, the chain of a time when the spectator sought his own reality in the spectacle, we must allow the spectator to identify himself with the spectacle, breath for breath and beat for beat.

It is not enough for the spectator to be captivated by the magic of the spectacle, he will not be captivated unless we know where to reach him. We have had enough of a haphazard magic, a poetry that no longer has the support of science.

In the theater, poetry and science must henceforth be one.
Every emotion has organic bases. It is by cultivating his emotion in his body that the actor recharges its voltaic density.
To know in advance the points of the body that must be touched is to throw the spectator into magical trances.
And it is from this precious kind of science that poetry in the theater has long been estranged.
To know the points of localization in the body is, therefore, to reforge the magic chain.
And with the hieroglyph of a breath I want to rediscover an idea of sacred theater.

Mexico, April 5, 1936

Letters from 1932–33

XXI

TO JEAN PAULHAN

Friday, January 22, 1932

Dear friend,

I have the impression—and I beg you to be *absolutely frank* with me—that in the end you were a little disappointed in my lecture. Unlike Jean Cocteau, I am not afraid of reservations when they are justified and fair—on the contrary. I prefer to be precisely aware of a fault or omission so that I can correct it the next time, rather than delude myself over qualities that all too often, alas! do not exist. So I would regard it as an act of friendship if you would answer frankly and bluntly the question I ask you.

I think that when you read my lecture to yourself it did not make the violent, dazzling impression that it had made on you at the Sorbonne.

For my own part, I still feel that this lecture is excellent, and even rather important in some respects, but I suspect that certain formal imperfections, occasionally glaring and above all numerous, which my delivery *succeeded* in hiding completely, became noticeable and distracting once you had it in front of you. Am I right? If not, how do you explain why this lecture, which you said you wanted to present as the manifesto of the theatrical ideas of the *N.R.F.*, did not appear at the beginning of the issue? And indeed, how do you explain the fact that you even hesitated to put it in the February issue at all, when it was you yourself who asked me, the day after I read it at the Sorbonne, whether February was not too soon *for me,* so urgent did its appearance seem to you then? Please understand the spirit in which I ask you all these questions. They all proceed from a certain anxiety, the anxiety of an author who is unsure of the value of his work.

Ah! To be sure, I do not write with joy. My old obstacles are not yet completely overcome. Everything I write is the result of a real victory over myself, an excruciating inner conflict in which my mind rarely has the upper hand. You were telling me that all poets go through this! But you know very well that this is not true, at least not in the same way, not to the same degree. I have a *sick* mind, as you are aware.

My conflicts are not those of a healthy brain. A healthy brain, in a man who knows his language, does not suddenly experience these gaps, these repeated lapses which by their very nature are irreparable, because *correcting* them would entail a reexamination of the thought itself in all its profundity. So tell me the *truth*, Jean Paulhan. I won't be so petty as to hold it against you. One would have to have the contemptible spirit of a Surrealist to resent sincere and just criticism, for their so-called pride is merely the withdrawal of a mind which is alarmed by its own weakness and which rears in terror. Someday I shall write something about all that scum. For there is nothing that gives me such violent nausea, a nausea of the mind, as the continued activity of a group which has long been exhausted and which no longer has anything to say, this kind of indefensible activity, this obstinate lie, this desperate determination to maintain the mind, the organs of thought, in an inhuman posture that has long since ceased to correspond to anything either in the realm of the mind or in the realm of life. The old quarrel between Cocteau and the Surrealists is absurd. For at bottom they are all the same and I assure you that anyone who was not aware of their petty bickering would put a film like *L'Age d'Or* and a film like *The Blood of a Poet* on the same level, would throw them into the same bag, for one is just as irrelevant and pointless as the other. Cocteau has been very kind to me and I shall not say publicly, at least for the moment, what I think of his film. So I beg you in all friendship to keep all this strictly to yourself. It is confidential. But of all these films I think that *The Seashell and the Clergyman* has directly inspired other films and that they all belong to the same spiritual vein, but that what was of interest in 1927—for *The Seashell* was the first of its kind and a historically important film—is no longer of interest in 1932, or five years later.

I do not believe that human beings are capable of justice, and intellectual honesty is only a word today, a dirty word that makes us uncomfortable, but in all justice criticism, if it still existed, would have to recognize the kinship of all these films and say that they ALL come from *The Seashell and the Clergyman,* except, of course, for the *spirit*, which has eluded them all.—Films like these, even and *especially* those composed in a sleepless state, belong to the somber and secret logic of the dream, but what has eluded them is the intellectual current, the organizing principle of these dream images, whose necessity impresses the mind only through the force of this organizing and underlying current. It is little enough to say that they must be *understood* like music. What is the opposite of music is the arbitrary, the foolish, and the gratuitous. But however beautiful each of the images may be, taken separately—and there are some beautiful images in *The Blood of a Poet*, just as there were here and there some beautiful images in *L'Age d'Or*—what gives them value and meaning (and by meaning one must understand not some significance that can be elucidated clearly, but their *raison d'être*, their analogical and discriminative power) is the way they are integrated, the way they relate to a kind of intellectual background music, a music which is totally absent in *L'Age d'Or* as well as in *The Blood of a Poet!* You can't throw in images the way you throw in a fishhook, at random! These obedient images are, in a film constructed according to the dark and mysterious rules of the unconscious, *necessary* images, imperious and tyrannical images, and we are far from that in every case.

Anyway, I think the time for this sort of intellectual exercise is long since over!—It can be useful for a while to rediscover by methods that are unusual, excessive, arbitrary, methods that are primitive, direct, and stripped of non-essentials, polished to the bone, the laws of eternal poetry, but these laws are always the same, and the goal of poetry cannot be simply to play *with the laws by which it is made*. But for the past ten years this has been the central preoccupation of the cinema, as well as of literature, painting, and all the arts. Just because with the help of psychoanalysis the rules of the game have become infinitely clear, and because the technique of poetry has revealed its secrets, the point is not to show that we are extraordinarily intelligent and that we now know how to go about it, the point is finally to produce the exemplary works of this poetry of the unconscious, this profound analogical poetry which I call poetry of the unconscious for lack of a better term, but which is the only poetry possible, the only true and possible poetry with metaphysical tendencies, on which films like *The Blood of a Poet* resolutely turn their back. As well as *L'Age d'Or*, as well as every Surrealist poem ever written. There is a great deal to be said about all this. Someday I shall try to write what I think about it, when my own mind is free, liberated from its profound unconscious obstacles. For all day long this mind is bogged down and fettered; when it escapes a little I write, for example my lecture on the theater, with those occasional lapses of expression, those formal problems which indicate the persistence of a profound and terrifying disease that distorts and poisons my whole life. I impatiently await a letter from you which will give me your *real opinion,* in full, of my lecture and the rest.

Your devoted friend,
Antonin Artaud

P.S. I have not sent you the article you asked me for on *The Threepenny Opera*, for several reasons:
    1. In the first place, I haven't had time.
    2. I hadn't *seen* the film and was not able to see it until Wednesday afternoon. That was too late.
    3. What I had to say about it was too important to be limited to just one page. For after "viewing" it, as they say in the jargon of the cinema, I felt that the reflections it generated were so important that an ordinary review would not be adequate. For me they are of the first importance, for it is the very life and *raison d'être* of the cinema that are called into question by a film of this kind. And in view of the extraordinary success it has had, the question arises of the general value of *Opinion,* or what is called *Opinion,* as well as the intellectual level of our age, which proves its baseness and its complete *disorientation.* I insist on the word. *Disorientation.* Absence of landmarks. People are really losing their sense of direction. Intellectually speaking, of course.
    4. I myself acted in this film which I mean to criticize and I intend to make some very serious *criticisms* of it, criticisms which in other circumstances, and if I was talking about something else, I would call *accusations.* But having acted in it makes it delicate. I can only criticize it effectively if I am provided with the official authority which I would have, for example, if I were the regular critic of a magazine or newspaper. I can see you smile and look surprised at what look like the beginnings of a kind of petty ambition that you would not have expected to find in me. But

after all, the *N.R.F.* has no regular column on the cinema. Wouldn't it be possible to start one in which critiques of films would appear every month, in each issue? This column would be carefully kept up to date. Of course, there won't be a film worth talking about every month, but the existence of this regular column could provide an opportunity for some interesting reflections on the state of the cinema. Naturally, I would retain complete independence, I would be able to speak my mind freely. No doubt my career as an actor would suffer, but I really don't care. I have long since given up making a career as an actor, even for economic reasons, in a field that is rotten to the core. And it would be good and refreshing for me and for everyone else if I said that the profession and the world of the cinema are more rotten than anyone could imagine. A practical detail is not without value: writing this column would enable me to have a press card and to attend all screenings and all important premières of films without paying. Besides, I think that from a commercial point of view it could be a good thing for the *N.R.F.* if people knew that it had a regular column on films. It would bring the review a whole audience which loves good cinema and which doesn't know where to turn. You'll say that there is the *Revue du Cinéma,* but that's not the same thing. And it can always be said that the point of view of the *N.R.F.* is much more literary and that of the *Revue du Cinéma* more technical; but all this is just between us!

Getting back to *The Threepenny Opera,* I found this film that for so many months has been arousing the enthusiasm of the cultivated masses rather mediocre and ordinary. And even the ban from which it has profited contributes to my dislike, for there is nothing in the bitter human salt of the story it tells that can justify such *direct* and excessive severity, when it all seems so irrelevant to OUR OWN TIME. And both the censors who were able to find something pernicious in this film and the literary and artistic elite who by protesting the stupid decision of the censors believed they were defending a work of high moral and intellectual quality seem to me to have adopted attitudes that are ridiculous, inappropriate, and irrelevant. Naturally, the eighteenth-century English opera *The Beggar's Opera,* like the German adaptation of this unique work, *Die Dreigroschenoper*, is worthy of all enthusiasm and all defense, but not the screen version of G. W. Pabst.

*

Dialectics is the art of considering ideas from every conceivable point of view—it is a method of distributing ideas.

TO JEAN PAULHAN

Saturday evening, January 30, 1932

But, dear friend, the only reason I allowed myself to make that remark about my article was that you yourself had suggested it be placed at the beginning, in order to give it the quality of a Manifesto. And the reason I wrote you about this was not, certainly, to complain about the change, but because it seemed to me that this change of physical sequence indicated a more serious change of a moral nature in your own attitude toward and evaluation of my article.

And this made me anxious, because I am anxious by nature and uncertain of the value of what I write. In spite of your letter, I cannot help thinking that although you attribute to my article a certain interest and significance, you have recovered from your original enthusiasm; otherwise your unconscious would not have forgotten your promise and your suggestion.

I attach no importance to the sequence of articles in the magazine, but we cannot prevent the public and the readers from doing so and from regarding the placement of this lecture almost at the end of the magazine (the text section) and AFTER everyone else, as a judgment on its value.

I gave you complete freedom with the corrections, but two or three of them do more than correct mistakes or grammatical errors or strengthen a shaky syntax; they adulterate my thought, and that is rather serious.

Thus, the sentence that begins:

"There is secondarily an idea about sexuality and reproduction, with Lot placed there, etc."

ACTUALLY READS:

"There is also an idea about sexuality and reproduction *at the origins,* with Lot placed there."

This is very serious, for the elimination of those three words not only takes away the poetry of the sentence but takes away its underlying meaning, and adulterates my whole argument. I will confess that I am grieved by it.

And there are other similar substitutions or omissions of words which bother me a great deal, not because through some foolish pride of authorship I am attached to my text, but I am attached to my thought, and it pains me to see it weakened and eroded in this way.

And now I would like to ask you a question:

"Do you really think syntax is so important?"

In the few details that you asked me to correct it is clear that my mind was at an impasse, that to deprive it of *a word* was in reality to deprive it of *a thought,* for it could not have invented another phrase and it would have been necessary to rewrite enormous sections of text. I do not believe in crushing or emasculating language, but I don't think it matters if a writer who obviously respects syntax makes enormous mistakes on occasion if one feels that they are inseparable from the *shape* of the movement, the special fire, the strangely lit facet of a particular thought, which needed this perversion in order to catch this secret fire, this illumination of one of its hidden facets.

This is true of the sentence:

"It seems to me impossible to better express *in this painting* the relationships, etc."

The sentence left my brain with a flow that was turbid but firm.—To rearrange it was to reason, to cut the flow.

By now I obey the rules of language intuitively, and so much the worse for language when my intuition or my sense of intellectual harmony deceives me.

Well, I wanted to go over all these little details with you. Tell me what you have decided or what you have been able to do about my proposal to write a regular column on films in the *N.R.F.* The very fact of continuity would enable me to say things that I could never say in discussing a single film! For the choice necessarily obliges me to restrict myself, to individualize my critiques; whereas a regular column makes it possible to take a position.

Theoretically the rehearsals of *Woyzeck* should begin any day now, but it's no longer a secret to anyone that things at the Atelier are in a terrible state, so much so that it is impossible for Dullin to undertake any new project. And nothing will be decided before seeing what happens with Steve Passeur's play *Les Tricheurs*, the dress rehearsal of which took place yesterday.

I don't know what happened with this play. But reading it made a violent, dazzling impression on me, and yet at the performance I felt that I was in the presence of a *technician*, a clockmaker, a mechanic of the things of the mind. It was a well-constructed mechanism that functioned before me, without excessive mystery and indeed without any mystery at all.

In short, I had seen a rigor and an intellectual power where there had been only a rather artificial mental game. And the actor who played the lead was able to bring if off only by playing his role in a human and sensual manner, that is, by going against the role as it was written.

I'll write and tell you what happens or come to see you very soon.

Your friend,
Antonin Artaud

TO GEORGE SOULIÉ DE MORANT

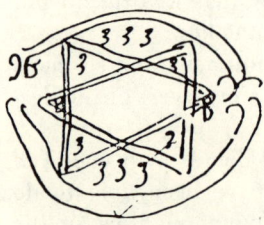

February 17, 1932
Thursday morning

Dear Sir,

I was surprised and filled with admiration at the way you *divined* my condition, at the precision and the uncanny accuracy with which you located the profound, disarming, demoralizing troubles with which I have so long been afflicted, and at the same time I envied you for the synthetic way you had of presenting them in their proper light, having SENSED them as they present themselves and in their place, a faculty of which I am preeminently deprived.

So I am writing you simply out of my anxiety at having *nevertheless* forgotten a characteristic phenomenon which would enable you to see even more deeply and clearly into my horrible condition. A horribly cruel condition, which I really have no words to characterize because I can neither see nor reveal anything definite in myself in my uncertainty, whatever my condition, regarding

1. my internal perceptions and observations.
2. the effectiveness of the means given me to define and express them.

If the mind is damaged, it is damaged, of course, in all circumstances and on all levels.

Anyway, nothing is so odious and painful, nothing so agonizing for me as doubt cast on the reality and nature of the phenomena I describe.

People sometimes see me as too brilliant in the expression of my inadequacies, my profound deficiency and the helplessness I describe, to believe that it is not imaginary and pure fabrication.

They do not doubt the reality of my subjective troubles and the state of pain in which I am immersed; they doubt their objectivity and, above all, their *range*.

But, and I can never insist on this enough, my condition undergoes infinite fluctuations which pass from the very worst to a relative improvement. In these improved states I become again somewhat capable of thinking, *feeling*, and writing, and you can be very sure that I would not have undertaken a letter of this kind if I were not somewhat *recovered*, just as usually people do not notice that at those moments when I speak and describe my disease the fact is that it has partly disappeared.

All this is elementary and I am not saying it for your benefit, of course, but usually I have to say it over and over again.

I have been, as I told you, much more seriously ill than I am right now, at the mercy of a kind of terrifying crushing and tearing of consciousness, truly *baffled* with respect to my most elementary perceptions, unable to connect anything, to assemble anything in my mind or still less to express anything, since nothing could be retained.

Psychically it was the same kind of collapse as occurs physiologically when the stomach or the intestines can no longer retain anything. And physically I found myself oppressed by an extreme exhaustion, torn between a sensation of emptiness, a total lack of nervous energy, and a sensation of magnetic compression, a sensation of burning heaviness which was also carried to extremes.

At the mercy of this double, this multiple sensation, the mind, which could not apply itself to anything, also found itself deprived of the continuity of its inner life, to the point where the images that were born, just as the subconscious connects them and automatically starts to give them form, these images, these representations, these forms *took pleasure* in tantalizing the mind by disappearing or disintegrating too soon, maddening the mind that was trying to grasp them.

The characteristic *pattern* of my condition is currently the same, the only difference being one of intensity and degree. And with the additional fact that whereas when these troubles, these singular phenomena first began I believed myself to be completely incapacitated, I nevertheless observed that I was sometimes capable of doing something, and the torture is now worse when I am unable to express myself.

This state of exhaustion and physical pressure which is unchanged, though reappearing with diminished intensity (may the gods grant that certain burning states I have known never return again), reinforced by a sensation of physical withdrawal from myself, as if I were about to lose control of my limbs, my reflexes, my most spontaneous motor reactions, is combined with another sensation of rigidity and horrible physical fatigue of the tongue when I speak, for *the effort of thinking* always has a physical effect on my whole musculature, and the stuttering from which I suffer in varying degrees and which sometimes disappears completely fatigues me enormously (I have noted from my earliest childhood, between the ages of six and eight, these periods of stuttering and of a horrible physical contraction of the facial nerves and the tongue, following periods of calm and perfect facility), and all this is complicated by corresponding psychic troubles which did not appear *dramatically* until about the age of nineteen.

There is a certain sensation of emptiness in the facial nerves, but an active emptiness, so to speak, which physically took the form of a kind of vertiginous magnetization of the front of the face. These are not images and this should be taken almost literally. For this physical vertigo was horribly distressing and this sensation that I am describing reached its climax two or three years after the onset of my disease. This sensation was sometimes replaced by a kind of psychological spasm, a violent distress that rolled me as if in a wave of ruin which, no matter where I was, made me want not to weep but to sob with horror, to howl with despair. For a long time now, fortunately, none of this has returned, and there remain certain shifting or localized physical pains, and a profound clouding of the consciousness which attacks me periodically, robs me of my private symbols and my ideas, deprives me of the benefit of the intellectual system that I have developed.

I now suffer primarily

1. intellectually, on the one hand,
2. sentimentally and emotionally, on the other.

1. Since the mechanism of the mind has been destroyed in its continuity, I can no longer think except in fragments. When I do think, the major part of the stock of terms and vocabulary which I have personally accumulated is unusable, being rusty and *forgotten* somewhere, but even after the term has appeared, the underlying thought collapses, the contact is suddenly broken, the underlying nervous response no longer corresponds to the thought, the mechanism has broken down—and *I am talking about the times when I am thinking!!!* If I am not thinking, it is quite useless to try to call on my private vocabulary. Then, whether someone asks me something, or whether I observe my own emptiness and attempt to produce a thought, the drama begins, the intellectual drama in which I am perpetually defeated.

For I find it impossible that I do not have something to say, besides, I know that in some sense or another I once had a personal style of thinking, and conceptions have come to me in a confused way, but woe be to me if I attempt to elucidate them, to make them concrete. It seems to me that I have even forgotten *how to think*. Yes, it is the notion of this private intellectual vacuum which I should like to *illuminate* once and for all. It seems to me the dominant characteristic of my condition. It is the thing which no one can pretend to share with me, to possess along with me, this *forgetting* of the forms of thought. It is this which is characteristic. And along with the forms of thought, there is also a forgetting of oneself, of the forms of one's intellectual or moral sensibility, one's sensibility in the presence of ideas. In these states, it is a question of nothing less than forgetting the intellectual content of the mind, of losing contact with all those first assumptions which are at the foundation of thought.

And

2. the affective or emotional confusion which I mentioned earlier is intimately related to this disappearance, this catastrophe at the higher level, for it is quite clear that the destructive element which demineralizes the mind and deprives it of its first assumptions is not concerned with knowing whether the mind will keep its sorrows for its personal use or apply them to something more impersonal which in other circumstances might have served as the basis of some kind of work, some kind of *product!* No one will ever really know what makes the mind decide in favor of creation. The same thoughts, the same voluntary impulses could, after all, just as well serve only to inflate the ego, to nourish it more intimately, to increase its internal density, and so much the worse for works and creativity, since psychically the result is the same; but in my case, this obscuring, this uprooting of the higher levels of consciousness and thought holds true, unfortunately, for all the circumstances of life, if intellectually my brain has become inoperative, can no longer function, the moments during which this void possesses me, fills me with anguish and sorrow, and makes me feel that my life is wasted, unusable, have an emotional value as well, they are expressed in the soul as a coloration of nothingness, an affect of total despair well designed in my own image, but as for this affect, on the other hand, it is its lack of resonance, its coagulation [. . .]

TO GEORGE SOULIÉ DE MORANT
Nunc salmavat

Friday evening, February 19, 1932

Dear doctor,

Something which has almost disappeared from the field of my observation and which no longer characterizes my condition is that impression of incredible fatigue, of total exhaustion, an exhaustion which seems to undermine the resistance, the muscular coordination of the organism on all levels and in all senses. And this sensation of monstrous, horrible fatigue, this vast, extraordinary pressure on the top of the skull and the back of the neck, a pressure whose force and whose volume, seemingly, is so great that it feels like the weight of the world on one's shoulders, is accompanied by one knows not what cosmic emotion, is combined with the tactile sensitivity, the vast feel of interstellar space, and the proof of this is that when I am lying in bed the sensation, far from disappearing, grows worse, is transformed into an impression of painful emptiness, operating magnetically, which presses on the limbs and the whole length of the spinal column and surrounds the pelvis. When I am in these states, a number of unconscious images persist, they themselves are not sick, but the malady seems to manifest itself the moment an image becomes conscious, however slightly, the moment it is invested with sensibility, emotion, will. As soon as the slightest suggestion of an intellectual desire appears to help some image or idea take a body by taking a form, as soon as one tries to pronounce in a clear and lucid manner any one of those unspoken words which the mind associates endlessly, the disease manifests its presence, its continuity; it is as if the mind need only decide to enjoy an internal idea or image for this enjoyment to be taken away from it: the spoken image regularly miscarries, and to try to bring this idea or image out into the world is even more difficult, and only serves to reveal more flagrantly and more rapidly the lack of continuity, the lack of nervous density which is fundamental to my present personality.

The fluctuations in my condition are roughly indicated, first, by the greater or lesser number of times that I have to complain about a thought that miscarries in this way!—and second, by the degree of stratification and evolution or development of the thought in which the fissure occurs.

That is to say:

granting that every idea or image arising in the unconscious constitutes, with the intervention of will, an unspoken word, the question is at what moment in its formation the fissure will occur, and whether it is certain that the intervention or manifestation of the will is a cause of trouble, an occasion for fissure, and whether the fissure will occur in this thought or in the following one.

In order to delay the fissure until the following thought, the thought or the sentence that expresses it must be fiendishly short, for I am not in a condition that allows me to dwell on any thought, no matter how briefly.

A lack of continuity, a lack of development, a lack of persistence in my thoughts is, therefore, one of the essential characteristics of my condition. But this lack of persistence, which has appeared in connection with this or that secondary manifestation of consciousness in thoughts that are more or less colorless and uninteresting, is the very thing which, by preventing me from being validly and lastingly aware of who I am, or what I think, or of any judgments that I might make on this basis, also prevents me from keeping present in the mind a number of archetypical images corresponding to my personal sensations and representations, and consequently from becoming aware and staying aware of *myself*—and it does not matter whether my vitality and my latent lucidity have been aroused by an association that is private, silent, and static when I am alone, by an external spectacle, a question asked by someone else, a conversation overheard, or a discussion at which I am present, I know that the fissure, the cutting off, the break will not fail to occur. They will occur more or less quickly according to the day, the mood, the phase I am in, and they let me say more or less, and they are inevitable and terribly *abnormal,* by which I mean that it is valid to maintain that this is manifestly pathological, for the objection has often been put to me that these breaks in thought, these impediments to intellectual manifestation happen to everyone, as they say—yes, but infinitely less often in the first place, and in the second place there is also a difference of quality and degree: the break does not impair consciousness and manifestation to the same degree, and then too it is, so to speak, only one stitch in the fabric that gives way, whereas with me it is the whole fabric, the break temporarily destroys all of consciousness, the mechanism of the brain which in other people recovers what has been lost does not do so in me since it is its *operation* which is damaged and its functioning which is arrested. And on this point there is another observation to be made: this inability to form or develop thoughts might in some sense be regarded as analogous to the stammering which possesses my outward elocution almost every time I want to speak. It is as if each time my thought tries to manifest itself it contracts, and it is this contraction that shuts off my thought from within, makes it rigid as in a spasm; the thought, the expression stops because the flow is too violent, because the brain wants to say too many things which it thinks of all at once, ten thoughts instead of one rush toward the exit, the brain sees the whole thought at once with all its circumstances, and it also sees all the points of view it could take and all the forms with which it could invest them, a vast juxtaposition of concepts, each of which seems more necessary and also more dubious than the others, which all the complexities of syntax would never suffice to express and expound; but if one really analyzes a state of this kind it is not by being too full that consciousness errs at these moments but by being too empty, for this prolific and above all unstable and shifting juxtaposition is an illusion. Originally there was no juxtaposition, for it seems that in every state of consciousness there is always a dominant theme, and if the mind has not *automatically* decided on a dominant theme it is through weakness and because at that moment nothing dominated, nothing presented itself with enough force or continuity in the field of consciousness to be recorded. The truth is, therefore, that rather than an overflow or an excess there was a deficiency; in the absence of some precise thought that was able to develop, there was slackening, confusion, fragility.

It so happens that this slackening, this confusion, this fragility express themselves in an infinite number of ways and correspond to an infinite number of new impressions and sensations, the most characteristic of which is a kind of disappearance or disintegration or collapse of first assumptions which even causes me to wonder why, for example, red (the color) is considered red and affects me as red, why a judgment affects me as a judgment and not as a pain, why I feel a pain, and why this particular pain, which I feel without understanding it and which I must continue to suffer so violently and so bitterly that I struggle to analyze it in an attempt to pry it loose from me, for after all there is no reason why what is simply a perverse and perverted way of being and feeling should be the cause of a state that makes me miserable. No doubt that idiotic and crude reaction of people who, when confronted by someone else's pain, say, Don't think about it, is right, but they are metaphysically right and do not know it, and they little suspect through what strange channels they would have to force their sensibility and the reflection of this sensibility in the accumulated images of the self in order to arrive at the detachment to which that other philosophical maxim alludes when it says:

"Pain, you are only a word."

The point of all this is that in those periods when I have something to say I am bothered by an abnormal haste but that the periods in which I have something to say are exceptional. It would also be necessary to stop looking at thought from an intellectual viewpoint, and as if the object of each of your thoughts had to be a written work. Which need not prevent you from thinking in a rare way, rare, that is to say essential, more selective than other ways.

But the state that you complain of is not a difficulty in expressing oneself, and contrary to what you think, dear sir, it is really the thought that is impaired, and not merely the thought but the personality, the life, for not only must I rack my brain to discover what I think about some point or other and this in connection with the ideas I am most passionately interested in, but my confusion is such that I am often rendered incapable of translating the simplest impressions, of expressing my own reaction to the weather, for example, however incredible this may seem. If it is cold I can still say that it is cold, but there are also times when I am incapable of saying it: this is a fact, for there is in me something damaged from the emotional point of view, and if someone asked me why I could not say it, I would answer that my inner feeling on this slight and neutral point did not correspond to the three simple little words I would have to pronounce. And this lack of correspondence, therefore, between a physiological sensation and its emotional response in the first place and next its intellectual response—insofar as it is possible to summarize and synthesize in general terms this series of swift, almost instantaneous operations which give rise to the truism *it is cold*—this lack of correspondence, since it does not select its subjects or spare me in any way, culminates, as it spreads, in the colossal troubles which correspond perfectly, alas, to the loss of personality. For it is quite clear by now, I hope, what this loss is made of. An inner feeling that no longer corresponds to the images of the sensation. Whether this sensation applies to objects that are immediate, present, and tangible, or remote, suggested, and imagined, provided by memories or constructed artificially, the result is the same, and it leads to the suppression of all inner life. An intact logic, when applied to objects that are exhausted or to an absolute loss of objects, can only be inoperative and powerless, but from another point of view this Cartesian description of the functioning of the mind is as rudimentary as it is false, for an inoperative logic of this kind *would never appear in the first place*.

The result is that without images and without feelings about the points that interest me most, simply from the point of view of my natural personality, I am overwhelmed by an immense and constant anxiety, an anxiety which takes the physical form of a kind of pain, a knot located at the point where the mind calls on itself or, more simply, I am obsessed by a terrible sensation of emptiness, incapable of summoning up any image, any representation. I also know that each time I shall try to call upon my own treasury of intellectual memories, I shall first come up against this knot, after which all comparison will be beyond me.

I insist on this representative anxiety, it expresses well that lack of normal vitality which prevents me from pursuing my ideas, and at the same time that it prevents me from voluntarily reviewing my opinions and judgments, it prevents me from analyzing anything deeply with someone else.

I have lost any point of comparison, any point of sensation for good and for evil, for good and for bad, in substance and in quality!!!!!

ANTONIN ARTAUD

TO LOUIS JOUVET

Monday evening, March 1, 1932

Dear friend,

Although the point of departure of Savoir's play seems interesting, and although I felt the particular tone you were trying to impose on its intentions and its secret spirit in your staging gave every hope of a good public reception, now that I have seen it performed by the actors I find it thin and trivial. I blame the actors first for the failure of this play, and I do not blame their professional experience or even their talent, but their spirit. Actually, and I know you won't hold it against me if I express an attitude contrary to your own, I don't share your opinion about the value of experience. I've been around long enough myself, and I've had a broad enough experience in matters of feeling, the world of the imagination and thought, the active processes of the mind, to have a right to demand that my opinion be taken into account. Well, I think that on its own merits Savoir's play doesn't hold together and that it is the duty of a good director to betray the author, if necessary, in order to give his play a production that holds together and makes an impression. In the area that particularly concerns me, I believe we would do well to give the sound effects their maximum intensity and effectiveness, provided they are placed in such a way that they don't drown anyone out and thus have a better chance of carrying. Those purely imitative sounds which the organ will never imitate perfectly won't be understood because they aren't straightforward. Since we're using dissonance, let's do it, but let's *tell* the audience we're using dissonance. They will either boo or applaud, but at least they won't be in that state of embarrassment caused by half measures and things that don't come off. At the end of the first act we wanted to show the face of war, its dirty, grim, and ominous aspect: well, the intensity and *symbolic* openness of our means must correspond to our intentions. The wind effect which you're asking us to eliminate and which today was poorly timed and drowned out the actor's cues seems to me in principle indispensable and very successful as an impression. Pierre Renoir himself came to tell me that he had found it very striking. You asked Messiaen to go in the direction of gaiety: this is an intention that I do not understand. He can put some gaiety into the harmonies of his bell-ringing or the amplification of the phonograph, but not into the interpolated sounds. I don't believe in groping and experimenting any more than I believe in experience. I might be forced to admit that experience can help me verify a hypothesis, but it will never make me give up something I have *felt* to be true. I believe only in my intuition. And on no account should we let the resistance of some, the incredulity of others, or, least of all, the fear of the audience's reaction turn us away from the idea we had or prevent us from getting as much out of it as possible. If instead of simply imitating the sound of the shell flying through the air, we underlined the anxiety and silence of the soldiers by the dramatic commentary of the organ, bursting forth with a few violent dissonances, this would be a very important element, and often the success of a work depends on the cumulative effect of a series of elements of this kind.

Your devoted friend,
Antonin Artaud

P.S. I believe that the public will always accept something that conflicts with its opinions and goes against its habits as long as it understands the intention with which it's been done. And I believe that those so-called new masterpieces which the public receives with volleys of hisses because they conflict with its attitudes must have been badly acted and badly produced; otherwise they would have succeeded. This point of view of the theatrical production of a rejected masterpiece is a point of view that no one ever considers.

TO JEAN PAULHAN

Wednesday, August 3, 1932

Dear friend,

I'm in the process of finishing the manifesto. I think it will be fine, exactly what is needed. After ten or twelve versions, my mind has finally settled on the proper form. I am wondering now whether it shouldn't appear soon, even without "The Alchemical Theater," because the investors we have approached will not take definite action until this practical and objective manifesto has appeared. And by October it would already be very late—I wonder, therefore, whether it would be possible for you to reserve the necessary number of pages, that is, six or seven, in the next, the September, issue. Is this possible? It is very important. Gide has promised me not only to do that adaptation of the apocryphal play of Shakespeare's but also to execute it *right on stage*, in close contact with the possible *mise en scène*, in other words, a real collaboration, and in addition he is to write me a letter telling me that he has a horror of the theater, but that if the theater were possible, it would have to correspond to the ideas we are talking about. I have a feeling this letter may be terribly dangerous. I haven't had a chance to stop by to see you all this time, but I find the essay by Thomas De Quincey absolutely overwhelming, and the parallels with my own conceptions are uncanny. I'll bring it back in two or three days. But just in case I am unable to stop by, please tell me the deadline for sending you the manifesto.

Your faithful friend,
Antonin Artaud

TO ANDRÉ GIDE

Paris, Sunday, August 7, 1932

Dear Mr. Gide,

I understood perfectly the reasons that prevented you from signing the text I read you. However, I believe that the tone of this text and its wording had a great deal to do with your decision. Perhaps if you had found it sufficiently convincing, these reasons would have collapsed of their own weight, at least in large measure. Well, I do not intend to publish it. The work of one night, it bears the mark of the haste in which it was composed. Besides, I think it states the question rather badly. It conveys none of the *urgency*—I insist on this word—that exists right now to create a theater which would obey certain directives, none of the necessity for this theater. I believe, in effect, that the organic terrain of the stage is the chosen place for a certain kind of poetry which manifests itself by spatial extension rather than by Speech, if we give this word the restricted Western meaning usually attributed to it—that is, the meaning of an intellectual profit directed toward the interior of words, toward whatever they have that is limited, finished, completely inventoried by the mind, and thus without possibility of expansion, that is, without real power. Consequently, I have written another text which now seems to me to answer the purpose completely. But I shall not ask you or anyone else to sign this text. Here is what I intend to do: I shall publish this text, I hope, in the September issue of the *N.R.F.*, and I shall sign it myself, directly. And after indicating the spiritual directives which this theater will follow, I shall set forth my program. In this program there will be no plays. In this way no one will be able to reproach me for their inadequacy, their poverty, or their inappropriateness. I shall say that my aim is to liberate a certain theatrical reality which belongs exclusively to the stage, to the physical and organic domain of the stage. This reality must be liberated by means of spectacle, and therefore by *mise en scène* in the broadest sense of the word, that is, as the language of everything that can be put on the stage, rather than as the secondary reality of a script, the more or less active and objective means of expansion of the script. Here, therefore, the director becomes the author, that is, the creator. And the interest that will be aroused a priori by the spectacles that I shall put on will depend on the confidence that is placed in me, the credit that will be accorded to me as creator, inventor of a theatrical reality which is absolute and which is sufficient unto itself. And why shouldn't people have complete confidence in me, why shouldn't they believe me capable of inventing and manifesting a theatrical reality which would be prodigiously appealing and which would speak like the most beautiful language? Why shouldn't these spectacles be seen to unfold as if through a kind of magic prism, for which the pretext and subjects would be provided by certain historic or sacred themes, or even certain plays, considered apart from their text and merely as themes?

ANTONIN ARTAUD

Having said this, I shall announce the creation of a committee of patronage or even of direction in which a number of writers will participate. And it is in connection with this committee that I would like to use your name. I shall also ask Paul Valéry, Valery Larbaud, Albert Thibaudet, Jean Paulhan, Gaston Gallimard, and perhaps Julien Benda. You gave me permission once before to use your name for a similar purpose. This leads me to believe that you will have no objection to authorizing me once again to put your name at the head of the list.

In addition, since we have discussed the adaptation of an apocryphal play of Shakespeare's which you and I would create together *on the stage*, I would like your permission to announce this adaptation, and since I have not yet decided around what theme I intend to begin to demonstrate this theatrical reality I am talking about, I intend to announce that the theater will begin with this adaptation. Whether circumstances at the time we begin will be favorable or not, whether or not you will be free at that time, I think that what is important in dealing with potential investors is to have a precise and concrete promise to give them for the moment, and I think the promise of this adaptation would suffice. So this is all I shall say; and in the manifesto I shall use the following text:

"For our first spectacle we shall attempt an apocryphal play of Shakespeare's as the basis for an experiment in direct staging. André Gide, who originated the project, will create this adaptation as author, but he will create it on stage, utilizing the objective language of the stage, that is, in intimate relation with the *mise en scène*. This experiment, in which the spectacle aspect will be of primary importance, will try to bring out the notion of a spectacle designed not for the eyes or the ears but for the mind. Gestures will take the place of signs, signs will take the place of words. The words that are used will be delivered, when psychological circumstances permit, in an incantatory manner. There will be no sets, properly speaking; objects will provide the sets, they will be employed to create theatrical landscapes, and we shall utilize the meaning of a certain objective humor created by unexpected displacements and combinations of objects. The movements, the attitudes, the bodies of the characters will be composed or decomposed like hieroglyphs. This language will pass from one sense organ to another, establishing analogies and unforeseen associations among series of objects, series of sounds, series of intonations. The light will not merely illuminate but will have a life of its own, it will be regarded as a state of mind. In short, in this play we shall attempt to use for the first time a physical and objective language of the stage which will seek to reach the mind by way of the sense organs, all the sense organs, with all degrees of intensity and in all directions. But, above all, the humor communicated by the words uttered will try to call into question established relationships between objects, and by carrying this dissociation to its furthest extreme, will create a physical and spatial poetry that has long been lacking in the theater."

Here, then, is what I intend to say and what *in fact* will be the substance of my program—a program which I consider it very important that you support. Since all this must appear in September, I have only a few days left to receive your consent.

May I hope that under these conditions, and after all I have told you about my program and my intentions, you will give it to me?

With this expectation believe me, dear Mr. Gide, wholeheartedly and without reservation your

Antonin Artaud

4 rue du Commerce, Paris XV

P.S. I think that in perfecting our plans for the *mise en scène* of this apocryphal play, we might stress the aspect of colorful incident. We can say that these colorful incidents, by evoking situations that are extremely human and familiar to all, accessible to all, can serve as a fundamental way of winning over the audience and leading them to consider higher things, to take seriously the poetry, and even on occasion the sublimity, that will be manifested either through the humor or directly!!!

Perhaps you might even set down your intentions in a letter, giving me some indication of the direction you plan to take in creating this adaptation. I would then append your remarks to the body of the manifesto.

ANTONIN ARTAUD

TO JEAN PAULHAN

Tuesday, August 23, 1932

Dear friend,

The Manifesto is finished: it is at least as good as "The Alchemical Theater," and as objective and concrete as it should be. I think it will have the desired effect.

Who are the writers whom I can announce as giving their support to the principles I am formulating about the reality and goal of the theater?

Before I can make use of their names I must have a letter from the *N.R.F.* granting me permission to do so. I don't want to risk a retraction, it would be too serious. André Gide has confirmed to me by letter that he will do a play especially for this theater, which I shall call "Theater of Cruelty."

1. We shall perform the story of Bluebeard, re-created in its most cruelly and philosophically significant details;

2. a tale by the Marquis de Sade, transposed and clothed with respect to its eroticism, violently *externalized* with respect to its cruelty;

3. an excerpt from the *Zohar*, which burns like fire and thus is as *immediate* as fire;

4. the Conquest of Jerusalem, with the side that is concrete and reflects in events and objects the profound metaphysical discord between prophets, king, temple, and populace;

5. *Woyzeck,* out of a spirit of reaction against my own principles;

6. romantic melodramas in which improbability will be cultivated as a concrete element of poetry;

7. Elizabethan dramas, stripped of their texts, of which we shall retain only trappings of the period, characters, plots, and situations.

I think this is enough of a program, especially in conjunction with the technical and positive part of my statement, which you will read.

Faithfully yours,
Antonin Artaud

P.S. I need an immediate answer from you concerning supporters, because I want to send this statement at once to a few investors, and to show it to a certain very highly placed political person on whom everything may depend.

TO JEAN PAULHAN

Monday, September 12, 1932

Dear friend,

Thank you for your letter and forgive me for bothering you with telegrams. I am still waiting to receive the proofs, but in the meantime here is the first sentence as I have rewritten it. I believe that it now bears my personal imprint, and that the idea of cruelty is not superimposed. Here it is:

| The term "theatrical gesture" could be replaced with "theatrical action." You have more of a feeling for language than I do, you decide which sounds *best*. | "The point is not to be constantly pulling out the butcher knife on stage but to reintroduce into each theatrical gesture the notion of a kind of cosmic cruelty without which there would be neither life nor reality." |

Cruelty has not been superadded to my thought. It has been there all along, but I had to become conscious of it. I use the word cruelty in the cosmic sense of rigor, implacable necessity, in the gnostic sense of the vortex of life which devours the shadows, in the sense of that pain outside of whose implacable necessity life could not go on. Good is willed, it is the result of an action; evil is permanent. The hidden god, when he creates, is obeying the cruel necessity of creation which is imposed even on him, and he has no choice but to create, and hence to accept, at the center of the willed vortex of good, a nucleus of evil which is more and more reduced, more and more *devoured*. And the theater in the sense of continuous creation, the entire magical action submits to this necessity. A play which did not have this will, this blind appetite for life which is capable of *getting past everything*, visible in every gesture and every act, and in the transcendent aspect of the action, would be a useless and abortive play.

I am longing to see you, too, for I am afraid that this first sentence has done me considerable harm, and it seemed to me that especially in the part dealing with theory and doctrine I had reached a point that I had never reached before.

Your friend,
A. Artaud

TO JEAN PAULHAN

[Paris] November 27, 1932

My very dear friend,
 I have read *Arden of Feversham*.
 It is a work which is far from lacking in qualities, certainly, if one takes it at face value. But I do not think it should be read literally. In it one perceives a desire to parody Shakespeare, just as a certain kind of romantic melodrama or farce in the genre of *Harnali* parodied *Hernani*. It is true that this parodic intent is sometimes not very pronounced. ─────────────
Taken literally, it is worth neither more nor less than a great many plays of the same period, in the same vein, from the same spiritual lode. It contains almost all the familiar situations, all the personages, all the characters who appear in Shakespeare or elsewhere. And aside from the story of the poisoned Crucifix, I do not see what claim it makes on our attention. Its interest seems to me primarily archaeological and retrospective. But I do not see that it has any burning element, anything that would make its performance, under the *present circumstances,* a necessity. How it might be used as an index or *reactor*. It has the qualities of fifty other similar plays, and were it not for the rich and perfect language in which André Gide has cast it, a richness and perfection which are above all grammatical and which will be almost totally invisible at the time of the performance, there would be no way to distinguish it from those fifty plays. Rather than perform *Arden of Feversham*, you might as well go directly to Shakespeare.
 With this reservation, however, that

there is in the language of the characters, in the exposition of the situations, a certain purity, a certain filtered quality which does not exist in Shakespeare and which makes *Arden of Feversham* a work of taste, a timeless and rather non literary work in which the action appears naked, detached from any doubtful contingency, without anything that is too verbal, without any literary context, with the result that the drama appears pure and unencumbered and that it can be isolated, that it has a value of its own, and that criticism, if there is any, can only address itself to the action.

Moreover, what the play does have that is localizable and literary, that could situate it in time, appears in a humorous and parodic light. In those parts where the play is not naked, not *stripped,* it has the tone of burlesque, falsity, joking, of deliberate, albeit rather subtle, distortion. I do not know the ending, but I have the impression that it can save everything, that it can recharge these attempts at parody and humor on a harsh and frenetic level in which the play would acquire a virulence that is somewhat lacking. In short, I do not find it mad enough for its sharpness and spasmodic quality, not mad enough for its overall classicism and occasional artificiality, not liberated enough for its pretensions to freedom and nonconformity, not spasmodic enough for its brusqueness and schematic quality, and I believe that with the elements it contains, the real play has yet to be created or re-created, and that it can be the object of the *mise en scène* to transform it in spirit and intention while leaving it materially untouched. ───────

The conclusion of all this is that I think that *Arden of Feversham* can be performed, and I am interested in putting it on if I am given the material means to do so. I will do it in preference to a new play of my own creation, if the fact of having a play by André Gide is likely to inspire more confidence in the investors than a spectacle of my own. ───────

Although I do not believe that the novelty and urgency of THIS spectacle are calculated to arouse the passionate interest of investors.

However this may be, I shall put on *Arden of Feversham,* but I shall ask Gide to translate the title into French and to find a title in keeping with that of the English work, but more striking. In addition, I promise to respect Gide's text scrupulously and without omitting an iota; it will be spoken by the actors just as it was written, and performed in its original order; but I must be left free to push the *interpretation* in whatever direction I find necessary, and to *add* any formal inventions inspired by the text, and thus not opposed to its spirit, but developed to the furthest degree, that I deem indispensable.

The text will not be performed "straight" but will be parodied three-quarters of the time, and the concrete images will be governed by this parody: physical enlargement and amplification of the characters, bombastic exaggeration of gestures, overall movements, etc., etc., will be left to my choice and to my free imagination!!!————————————————————————

All this will constitute MORE than *mise en scène*, it will amount to a true *theatrical adaptation* of which I shall be sole author. A new play elaborated down to the smallest detail will show through beneath Gide's text and beneath the thread of the action. And it is this new play, punctuated by Gide's spoken text, which will be performed.

Indeed, I see no other way of proceeding without going back on my promises. This means that a considerable amount of work must be done by me previous to the actual staging of the play, and previous to the moment when the play goes into rehearsal.—

I would be very much surprised if Gide did not agree with this approach, and in fact I believe it is exactly what he expected of me. One thing more. I do not want to be denied the benefit of my work of invention and interpretation, and it will be necessary to find a way of stating clearly what is Gide's responsibility and what is mine. I shall be writing Gide myself to tell him my feelings about *Arden of Feversham,* but you can tell him about all this right away. In any case, please be good enough to ask him to translate the last act too, if that's all there is left. And I don't think we have to worry about overdoing the virulence of the language, its crudity, its unclothed quality. Shakespeare and the Elizabethans went further in this direction than all of us together could possibly go.————————————————————————

Ever faithfully yours,
Antonin Artaud

TO JEAN PAULHAN

December 16, 1932

Dear friend,

I am reading Seneca, who seems to me to bear no resemblance whatsoever to the moralist preceptor of I don't know which tyrant of the Roman decadence—or else the Preceptor was this man, but he had grown old and lost his faith in magic. However this may be, he seems to me to be the greatest tragic writer in history, a man who was initiated into the Secrets and who surpassed Aeschylus in putting them into words. I weep as I read his inspired theater, and beneath the sound of the syllables I hear sizzling hideously the transparent surge of the forces of chaos. And this reminds me of something: once I am cured I intend to organize some dramatic readings—for a man who does not believe in texts in the theater this will be something—public readings at which I shall read the Tragedies of Seneca, and all potential patrons of the Theater of Cruelty will be invited. There is no better *written* example of what can be meant by cruelty in the theater than *all* the Tragedies of Seneca, but especially *Atreus and Thyestes*. Visible in the Blood, the cruelty is even more present in the mind. These monsters are wicked as only blind forces can be, and theater exists, I think, only on a level that is not yet human. Tell me what you think of this project.

A word from you would give me pleasure. I hope to be out of here in ten days—and fully recovered.

Your friend,
Antonin Artaud

In Seneca the primordial forces can be heard in the spasmodic vibration of the words. And the names which designate secrets and forces convey the *trajectory* of these forces and their uprooting and pulverizing power.

ANTONIN ARTAUD

TO ANAÏS NIN

Saturday morning [April 1933]

Dear friend,
    A few pages of *Heliogabalus* which I hope to read to you on Thursday and which I completed last night will more than explain anything about my attitude last night that may have been *upsetting*. You are certainly familiar with mental obsessions of this kind, but you cannot have experienced, I hope that you have not experienced, such horrible states of mental constriction, of exacerbated despair, in which the extreme travail and suffering of the mind is translated externally by a constant lie. A lie on several levels, the most apparent of which is the formation of an attitude—glacial, fixed, studied—in which the smile on the face corresponds to an extremely private and hardened rictus of the mind. I know that I should not need, that I *do* not need, to go on: water has power over fire. But I imagine that a statement like mine is nevertheless rather incredible: and yet it is true. I need not tell you that I was not who I was, that I was not feeling what I seemed to feel, that my stiffness did not correspond to what I would have liked to be, to what my mind regretted not being, but without being capable of modifying anything outside itself. You understand, I know, but I shall explain all this in my own voice and more fully. With details which the written word cannot convey, I mean that it is powerless to express, to clarify, to elucidate, to make real. My exterior composed itself in spite of myself, against myself, and yet I was momentarily *satisfied* with this exterior: my organism could not dream of any other modality, could not compose for itself another aspect: the best of myself was reduced to a state of inaccessible virtuality. Forgive this unexpected, ill-timed communication. A kind of moral remorse impels me to send it to you.

                                                    Antonin Artaud

I must speak to you further about this, viva voce.

"The Premature Old Age of the Cinema" (1933)

XXII

People have tried to make a fundamental distinction, a kind of division of qualities between two or three kinds of cinema.

On the one hand, there is dramatic cinema, in which chance, that is, the unforeseen, that is, poetry, is in principle suppressed. Not a single detail which does not originate from an absolutely conscious choice of the mind, which is not established with a view to a specific and certain result. The poetry, if poetry there be, is of an intellectual order; only secondarily does it draw on the particular resonance of the objects of perception at the moment they enter into contact with the cinema.

On the other hand, there is documentary cinema, the last refuge of the partisans of cinema at any cost. Here, a preponderant role is assigned to the machine and to the spontaneous and direct development of the aspects of reality. The poetry of things considered in their most innocent aspect, and as they relate to the external, is given full play.

I want, for once, to talk about cinema in itself, to study it in its organic functioning, and to see how it behaves at the moment it enters into contact with the real.

The lens which pierces to the center of objects creates its own world and it may be that the cinema takes the place of the human eye, that it thinks for the eye, that it screens the world for the eye, and that by this work of concerted and mechanical elimination it allows only the best to remain. The best—that is, that which is worth retaining, those shreds of appearance which float on the surface of memory and whose residue seems to be automatically filtered by the lens. The lens classifies and digests life, it offers the sensibility, the soul, a nourishment that is ready-made, and presents us with a world that is finished and sterile. Moreover, it is not certain that, of what is worth recording, it really lets through only the most significant and the best. For it must be noted that its vision of the world is fragmentary, that however valuable the melody it manages to create among objects may be, this melody is, as it were, a two-edged sword.

On the one hand, it is subject to the arbitrariness, the internal laws of the machine with the fixed eye; on the other, it is the result of a particular human will, a precise will which has an arbitrariness of its own.

What can be said under these conditions is that insofar as the cinema is left alone in the presence of objects it imposes an order on them, an order which the eye recognizes as valid and which corresponds to certain external habits of the memory and the mind. The question that arises here is whether or not this order would continue to be valid if the cinema tried to carry the experiment further and offer us not only certain rhythms of habitual life as the eye or ear recognizes them, but those darker, slow-motion encounters with all that is concealed beneath things, the images—crushed, trampled, slackened, or dense—of all that swarms in the lower depths of the mind.

Although the cinema does not need a language, some kind of convention in order to connect us with objects, it nevertheless does not take the place of life; these are broken pieces of objects, cutouts of views, unfinished puzzles of things which it binds together forever. And this, whatever anyone thinks, is very important, for we must realize that it is an incomplete world which the cinema presents, and from a single remote point; and it is very fortunate that this world is forever fixed in its incompleteness; for if by some miracle the objects thus photographed, thus stratified on the screen, could move, one dares not think of the figure of nothingness, the gap in the world of appearances which they would manage to create. I mean that the form of a film is final and without appeal, and although it allows a sifting and a choice of images before it presents them, it forbids the action of those images to change or to transcend itself. This is incontestable. And no one can claim that a human gesture is ever perfect, that there exists no possible improvement in its action, in its influence, in its communication. The world of the cinema is a world that is dead, illusory, and fragmented. Apart from the fact that it does not contain things, that it does not enter the center of life, that it retains only the epidermis of forms and then only what can be included in a very limited visual angle, it rules out all repetition, which is one of the major conditions of magical power, of the rending of sensibility. Life cannot be remade. Living waves, inscribed in a number of vibrations that is forever fixed, are waves that are henceforth dead. The world of the cinema is a closed

"The Premature Old Age of the Cinema" (1933)

world, without relation to existence. Its poetry exists not on the other side but on this side of images. By the time it collides with the mind, its dissociative force has been broken. There has been poetry, to be sure, around the lens, but before the filtering by the lens, the recording on film.

Besides, since the talking film, the elucidations of speech arrest the unconscious and spontaneous poetry of images; the illustration and completion of the meaning of an image by speech show the limitations of the cinema. The so-called mechanical magic of a constant drone of images has not survived the onslaught of speech, which has made this mechanical magic appear as the result of a purely physiological surprise attack on the senses. We have quickly tired of the accidental beauties of the cinema. To have one's nerves more or less pleasantly massaged by abrupt and unusual cavalcades of images whose sequence and whose mechanical appearance eluded the laws and even the structure of thought may have delighted a few aesthetes of the obscure and the unexpressed who were seeking these sensations systematically but without ever being sure that they would appear. These elements of chance and of the unexpressed were part of the dark and subtle enchantment which the cinema exerted over certain minds. All this, in addition to a few other, more precise qualities which we all went there to find.

We knew that the most characteristic and the most striking virtues of the cinema were always, or almost always, the result of chance, that is, a kind of mystery whose fatality we never managed to explain.

In this fatality there was a kind of organic emotion in which the objective and steady buzz of the projector blended, even as it contrasted, with the amusing appearance of images as precise as they were unexpected. I am not talking about alterations in rhythm imposed on the appearance of objects from the real world, but life passing at its own rhythm. I believe that the humor of the cinema arises partly from this security regarding a background rhythm on which are superimposed (in comic films) all the fantasies of a movement that is more or less irregular and vehement. For the rest, apart from that sort of rationalization of life, whose waves and patterns, such as they are, have been emptied of their fullness, their density, their range, their interior frequency, by the arbitrariness of the machine, the cinema remains a fragmentary and, as I have said, stratified and frozen, conquest of reality. All fantasies concerning the use of slow motion or speeded-up motion are applied only to a world of vibrations which is closed and which does not have the faculty of enriching or nourishing itself from its own resources; the idiot world of images trapped as if in birdlime in a myriad of retinas will never live up to the image that some persons have managed to form of it.

Therefore, the poetry which can be distilled from all this is only a poetry of contingency, the poetry of what might be, and it is not to the cinema that we must look to restore the Myths of man and of the life of today.

From *Heliogabalus, or The Anarchist Crowned* (1934)

THE BATTLE OVER, the throne won, it was time to return to Rome, to make a brilliant entrance. Not, like Septimius Severus, with soldiers armed for war, but in the manner of a real sun king, a monarch who flaunts his transitory supremacy, who won it by war, but who must erase the memory of that war.

And historians of the period never run short of epithets to describe the festivities of his coronation, their decorative and peaceful quality. Their overflowing luxury. It must be said that the coronation of Heliogabalus began in Antioch in late summer of 217 and ended in Rome in the spring of the following year, after a winter spent in Nicomedia, in Asia.

Nicomedia was the Riviera, the Deauville of the age, and it is in speaking of this sojourn of Heliogabalus in Nicomedia that the historians begin to go mad with rage.

Here are the words of Lampridius, who seems to have appointed himself the Joinville of this St. Louis of the Crusade of Sex, who carried a male member instead of cross, lance, or sword:

"During a winter which the Emperor spent in Nicomedia, since he behaved in the most disgusting manner, admitting men into a reciprocal commerce of turpitude, the soldiers soon repented of what they had done and remembered with bitterness that they had conspired against Macrinus to create this new prince; they decided, therefore, to set their hopes on Alexander, cousin of this same Heliogabalus, and the one on whom the Senate, after the death of Macrinus, had conferred the title of Caesar. For who could endure a prince who gave over to lust all the orifices of his body, when the beasts themselves are not allowed to do so? Finally, he reached the point where the only thing that occupied him in Rome was sending out emissaries entrusted with the mission of finding precisely those men best suited to his vile tastes and bringing them to the palace so that he could enjoy them.

"He enjoyed, moreover, having the fable of Paris performed; he himself would play the role of Venus, and suddenly letting his clothing fall to his feet, completely naked, one hand on his breast, the other on his genitals, he would kneel and, lifting the posterior part, he would present it to the companions of his debauch. Likewise he would do up his face as the face of Venus is painted, and would take care that his whole body was perfectly smooth, regarding it as the principal advantage that he could derive from life to be judged well qualified to satisfy the libidinous tastes of the greatest possible number."

He returned to Rome by easy stages, and along the route of the imperial escort, that immense escort which seemed to drag with it the countries through which it traveled, false emperors appeared.

Peddlers, workers, slaves who, seeing the reigning anarchy and seeing all the rules of royal heredity overthrown, thought they could be kings themselves.

"There you are," Lampridius seems to say. "Anarchy!"

Not content with turning the throne into a stage, with giving the countries through which he traveled an example of flabbiness, disorder, and depravity, he now turned the very soil of the empire into a stage, and inspired false kings. Never was a finer example of anarchy given to the world. Because for Lampridius this lifelike performance before a hundred thousand people of the fable of Venus and Paris, with the state of fever it created, with the illusions it aroused, was an example of dangerous anarchy. It was poetry and theater placed on the level of the most genuine reality.

But if we examine them closely, the accusations of Lampridius do not stand up. Exactly what did Heliogabalus do? He may have transformed the Roman throne into a stage, but in so doing he introduced theater and, through theater, poetry to the throne of Rome, into the palace of a Roman emperor, and poetry, when it is real, is worthy of blood, it justifies the shedding of blood.

For it is reasonable to assume that, so near in time to the ancient mysteries and the sprinkled blood of the Tauroboly, the personages who were brought to the stage in this manner must not have behaved like cold allegories, but that, since they signified forces of nature—I mean second nature, the one that corresponds to the inner circle of the sun, the second sun, according to Julian the Apostate, the one which is between the periphery and the center (and we know that only the third is visible)—they must have retained a force of pure element.

From *Heliogabalus* (1934)

Aside from this, Heliogabalus may have violated Roman manners and customs in any way he chose, he may have cast aside the sacred Roman toga, put on the Phoenician purple, given that example of anarchy which consists, for a Roman emperor, in adopting the costume of another country, and for a man in wearing women's clothing, covering oneself with jewels, pearls, feathers, corals, and talismans: what was anarchic from the Roman point of view was for Heliogabalus fidelity to an order, and this means that this decorum that had fallen from heaven returned there by every possible means.

*

There was nothing gratuitous in the magnificence of Heliogabalus, or in this marvelous ardor for disorder which was merely the application of a metaphysical and superior idea of order, that is, of unity.

He applied his religious idea of order like a whiff of smoke puffed into the face of the Latin world; and he applied it with the utmost rigor, with a sense of rigorous perfection in which there was an occult and mysterious idea of perfection and unification. It is not paradoxical to consider that this idea of order is also poetic.

Heliogabalus undertook a systematic and joyous demoralization of the Latin mind and consciousness; and he would have carried this subversion of the Latin world to the limit if he had lived long enough to complete it.

In any case, no one can deny Heliogabalus the logical coherence of his ideas. And no one can doubt the obstinacy with which he applied them. This emperor, who was fourteen years old at the time he took the crown, was a mythomaniac in the literal and concrete sense of the word. Which is to say that he saw the myths that existed, and applied them. He applied for once, and perhaps the only time in History, myths that were true. He threw a metaphysical idea into that confusion of poor terrestrial and Latin effigies in which nobody any longer believed, the Latin world less than any other.

He punished the Latin world for no longer believing in its myths or in any myth, and he did not bother to conceal his contempt for this race of born farmers, their faces turned toward the earth, who had never known how to do anything but watch to see what would come out of it.

*

The anarchist says:
Neither God nor master, I alone.

Heliogabalus, once on the throne, accepts no law; and he is the master. His own personal law will be the law of all. He imposes his tyranny. Every tyrant is at bottom only an anarchist who has seized the crown and who reduces everyone to obedience.

There is, however, another idea in the anarchy of Heliogabalus. Believing himself to be god, identifying himself with his god, he never commits the error of inventing a human law, an absurd and ridiculous human law through which he, as god, would speak. He obeys the divine law in which he has been initiated, and it must be acknowledged that apart from a few excesses here and there, a few pleasantries of no importance, Heliogabalus never abandoned the mystical point of view of a god incarnate, but a god who observes the millenary rite of god.

Once he has arrived in Rome, Heliogabalus banishes the men from the Senate and replaces them with women. For the Romans this was anarchy, but for the religion of the menstruae, which originated the Tyrian purple, and for Heliogabalus, who was bestowing it, it only represented a restoration of balance, a logical return to the law, since it was woman, the first born, the first arrival in the cosmic order, who was responsible for making the laws.

*

Heliogabalus finally arrived in Rome in the spring of 218 after a strange procession of sex, a spectacular orgy of festivities all through the Balkans. Now tearing along at breakneck speed in his wagon, covered with awnings, behind him the ten-ton Phallus which follows the train in a kind of monumental cage seemingly made for a whale or a mammoth; now stopping, flaunting his riches, revealing everything he can in the way of sumptuosity, largess, and also of strange displays before stupid and terrified populations. Dragged by three hundred enraged bulls who are urged on by packs of howling though chained hyenas, the Phal-

From *Heliogabalus* (1934)

lus, on an immense low platform with wheels as broad as the thighs of elephants, rides through European Turkey, Macedonia, Greece, the Balkans, and modern Austria, at the speed of a running zebra.

Then, from time to time, the music begins. The procession stops. The awnings are removed. The Phallus is mounted on its pedestal, hoisted with ropes, the head elevated. And out comes the band of pederasts, together with actors, dancers, castrated and mummified priests.

For there is a rite of the dead, a rite of the sorting of sexes, objects made from male members that have been stretched, tanned, blackened at the tips like rods hardened by fire. The members—affixed to the ends of staffs like candles impaled on nails, like the barbs of a mace; hanging like bells from arches of beaten gold; stuck on enormous plates like nails on a shield—turn in the fire among the dancing priests, which men mounted on stilts manipulate so that they dance like living creatures.

Always at the paroxysm, the height of frenzy, at the moment when the voices grow rough and pass into a procreative and feminine alto, Heliogabalus, wearing over the pubis a kind of iron spider whose legs flay his skin and draw blood with each excessive movement of his thighs, which have been dusted with saffron—his member dipped in gold, covered with gold, immovable, rigid, useless, innocuous—arrives wearing the solar tiara, his mantle laden with jewels and covered with flames.

His entrance has the quality of a dance, a marvelously timed dance movement, although there is nothing of the dancer about him. There is a silence, and then the flames rise, the orgy—a barren orgy—resumes. Heliogabalus unifies the screams, focuses the genetic and calcined ardor, the ardor of death, the rite of futility.

But these instruments, these jewels, these shoes, these garments and these fabrics, these wild recitals of music on stringed or percussive instruments, like crotalums, cymbals, Egyptian tambours, Greek lyres, sistrums, flutes, etc., these orchestras of flutes, hasosras, harps, and nebels; and also these banners, these animals, these animal skins, these feathers which fill the histories of the age, all this monstrous sumptuosity guarded at the confines by fifty thousand mounted troops who imagine that they are escorting the sun—this religious sumptuosity has a meaning. A powerful ritual meaning, as all the acts of Heliogabalus as emperor have a meaning, contrary to the verdict of history.

Heliogabalus enters Rome at dawn of a day in March 218, at a time which corresponds almost exactly to the Ides of March. And he enters it backwards. In front of him there is the Phallus, dragged by three hundred bare-breasted girls who precede the three hundred bulls, now sluggish and calm, having been given a very strong soporific in the hours before the dawn.

He enters in a variegated iridescence of feathers which flap in the wind like flags. Behind him is the gilded city, vaguely spectral. In front of him, the perfumed flock of women, the drowsing bulls, the Phallus on its wagon barded with gold, shining under the immense parasol. And on either side the double column of musicians beating crotalums, playing flutes and fifes, carrying lutes, striking Assyrian cymbals. And still farther behind, the litters of the three mothers: Julia Maesa, Julia Soaemias, and Julia Mamaea the Christian, who dozes and is aware of nothing.

The fact that Heliogabalus enters Rome at dawn at the beginning of the Ides of March represents, not from the Roman point of view but from the point of view of the Syriac priesthood, an indirect application of a principle that has become a powerful rite. Above all, it is a rite which from the religious point of view has its own meaning but which from the point of view of Roman customs means that Heliogabalus is entering Rome as a ruler, but backward, and that first he has had himself buggered by the entire Roman empire.

After the festivals of coronation, which have been marked by this profession of pederastic faith, Heliogabalus, his grandmother, his mother, and his mother's sister, the perfidious Julia Mamaea, install themselves in the Palace of Caracalla.

*

Heliogabalus has not waited for his arrival in Rome to declare open anarchy, to lend a hand to the anarchy that he encounters when it appears in the guise of theater and brings forth poetry.

Of course, he cuts off the heads of five obscure rebels who, in the name of their little democratic individuality, their totally insignificant individuality, dare to claim the royal crown. But he

From *Heliogabalus* (1934)

favors the exploit of that actor, that insurgent of genius who, now masquerading as Apollonius of Tyana, now as Alexander the Great, appears dressed in white before the populations on the banks of the Danube, wearing on his brow the crown of Skandar, which he may have stolen from the baggage of the emperor. Far from pursuing him, Heliogabalus delegates him a portion of his troops and lends him his fleet so that he can conquer the Marcomanni.

But all the ships in this fleet spring leaks, and in the middle of the Tyrrhenian Sea a fire kindled by his orders rids him of the usurper's attempt by means of a theatrical shipwreck.

*

Heliogabalus, as emperor, behaves like a thug and an irreverent libertarian. At the first somewhat solemn gathering he suddenly asks the great men of the state, the nobles, the senators in attendance, the legislators of all orders, whether they too have known pederasty in their youth, whether they have practiced sodomy, vampirism, succubus, or fornication with animals, and he puts the question, according to Lampridius, in the crudest possible terms.

One can imagine Heliogabalus rouged, escorted by his minions and his women, passing among the old graybeards, patting them on the stomachs and asking them whether they too were buggered in their youth; and the old men, pale with shame, bowing their heads under the outrage, swallowing their humiliation.

Better than this, he simulates in public, and with gestures, the act of fornication.

"Going so far," says Lampridius, "as to represent obscenities with his fingers, accustomed as he was to flinging all shame to the winds in the assemblies and in the presence of the people."

There is more here than infantilism, of course; there is a desire to demonstrate his individuality with violence, and his taste for elemental things: nature as it is.

It is easy to ascribe to madness and youth all that in Heliogabalus is merely the systematic disparagement of an order, and corresponds to a desire for concerted demoralization.

I see Heliogabalus not as a madman but as a rebel.

1. Against the Roman polytheistic anarchy.

2. Against the Roman monarchy which he has had sodomized in himself.

But in his person the two revolts, the two insurrections combine, they direct all his behavior, they govern all his actions, even the most insignificant, during his four-year reign.

His insurrection is systematic and shrewd and he directs it first of all against himself.

When Heliogabalus dresses as a prostitute and sells himself for forty cents at the doors of Christian churches or the temples of Roman gods, he is not simply pursuing the satisfaction of a vice, he is humiliating the Roman monarch.

When he appoints a dancer to head his Praetorian Guard, he is establishing a kind of incontestable but dangerous anarchy. He is flouting the cowardice of the monarchs, his predecessors, the Antonines and Marcus Aureliuses, he is expressing the opinion that it takes no more than a dancer to command a troop of policemen. He is calling weakness strength and theater reality. He is upsetting the received order, the ordinary ideas and notions of things. His is a thoroughgoing and dangerous anarchy, since he reveals himself to the eyes of all. In short, he risks his own skin. And that is the act of an anarchist of courage.

He continues his project of the debasement of values, of monstrous moral disorganization, by choosing his ministers according to the enormity of their members.

"He placed at the head of his night guards," says Lampridius, "the charioteer Gordius, and named chief steward a certain Claudius, who was a censor of morals; all other offices were distributed according to the enormity of the candidates' members. He appointed as collectors of the five-percent tax on inheritances, in succession, a mule driver, a racer, a cook, and a locksmith."

This did not prevent him from taking personal advantage of this disorder, this shameless laxity of morals, from making a habit of obscenity and from obstinately bringing into the daylight, like a maniac and a man obsessed, that which ordinarily is kept hidden.

"At banquets," Lampridius continues, "he seated himself by preference next to male prostitutes, he took pleasure in their touch, and never did he receive from anyone more willingly than from their hands the cup which they had tasted."

From *Heliogabalus* (1934)

All political structures, all forms of government seek above all to control the young. Heliogabalus, too, seeks to control Roman youth, but contrary to the rest of the world, by systematically perverting them.

"He had conceived the plan," says Lampridius, "of establishing in each town, with the title of prefects, persons who make a career of corrupting youth. Rome was to have had fourteen; and he would have done this if he had lived, determined as he was to elevate to the highest honors everything that is most vile, and men of the lowest professions."

One cannot doubt the profound contempt of Heliogabalus for the Roman world of his day.

"More than once," Lampridius remarks, "he displayed such contempt for the senators that he called them slaves in togas; the Roman people were to him merely the cultivators of a piece of land, and he took no account of the equestrian order."

His taste for free theater and poetry manifested itself on the occasion of his first marriage:

He had standing near him throughout the long Roman rite a dozen drunken energumens who screamed incessantly, "Stick it in, cram it in," to the great outrage of the newsmongers of the day, who neglect to describe the reactions of his fiancée.

Heliogabalus was married three times. The first time to Cornelia Paula, the second time to the first vestal, the third time to a woman who resembled Cornelia Paula; then he divorced her and took back his vestal, and in the end returned to Cornelia Paula. It must be noted here that Heliogabalus took the first vestal, not the way some pre-war maharaja would take the lead dancer at the Paris Opéra and marry her, but with an intention of blasphemy and sacrilege, which aroused the passionate rage of another historian, Dio Cassius.

"This man," he writes, "who should have been beaten with switches, flung into prison, and thrown down the Gemoniae, brings to his bed the guardian of the sacred fire, and deflowers her amid the silence of all."

And I maintain that Heliogabalus was the first emperor who dared to overthrow that rite of war, the guardianship of the sacred fire, and who polluted, as well he should, the temple of the Palladium.

Heliogabalus built a temple to his god, called the Eliogabalium, right in the center of Roman devotion, on the site of the insipid little temple consecrated to Jupiter Palatinus. After the temple was torn down he built a richer but smaller reproduction of the temple of Emesa.

But the zeal of Heliogabalus for his god, his taste for ritual and for theater, are nowhere better exemplified than in the marriage of the Black Stone to a bride worthy of him. He has this bride sought throughout the empire. Thus even in stone he will have performed the sacred rite, he will have demonstrated the power of the symbol. And what all history regards as another of his follies and an act of pointless childishness appears to me as the material and rigorous proof of his poetic religiosity.

But Heliogabalus, who detests war, and whose reign will not have been soiled by a single war, will not, as is suggested to him, give the Palladium as wife to Elagabalus—that bloodthirsty Palladium which, in the hands of Pallas, who should rather be called Hecate, like the night from which she issued, was the cradle of future warriors—but gives instead the Tanit-Astarte of Carthage, whose mild milk flows far from the sacrifices made to Moloch.

What does it matter that the Phallus, the Black Stone, bears on its inner face a kind of female sex which the gods themselves have chiseled? Heliogabalus wants to indicate by this staged coupling that the member is active and that it functions, and it matters little that it is in effigy and in the abstract.

*

A strange rhythm punctuates the cruelty of Heliogabalus; this initiate does everything with art and everything in pairs. I mean that he does everything on two levels. Each of his gestures is double-edged.

> Order, Disorder,
> Unity, Anarchy,
> Poetry, Dissonance,
> Rhythm, Discord,

From *Heliogabalus* (1934)

Grandeur, Childishness, Generosity, Cruelty

From the top of the newly erected towers of his temple of the Pythian god, he throws wheat and male members.

He feeds a castrated people.

Of course, there are no theorbos, no tubas, no orchestras of hasosras, accompanying the castrations which he orders, but which he orders each time like so many personal castrations and as if it were the god himself, Elagabalus, who was being castrated. Sacks of male members are thrown from the tops of the towers with the cruelest abundance on the day of the festival of the Pythian god.

I would not swear that an orchestra of hasosras or nebels with creaking strings and hard bodies is not hidden somewhere in the basements of the spiral towers to drown out the screams of the parasites being castrated; but these screams of martyred men are answered almost simultaneously by the acclamations of a rejoicing people to whom Heliogabalus is distributing the equivalent of several fields of wheat.

Good, evil, blood, sperm, rose wines, embalming oils, the most expensive perfumes, create innumerable irrigations around the generosity of Heliogabalus.

And the music that emerges from this goes beyond the ear and reaches the mind without instruments or orchestra. I mean that the vulgar noise, the thematic developments of feeble orchestras are nothing compared with this ebb and flow, this tide which comes and goes with strange dissonances, from his generosity to his cruelty, from his taste for disorder to the quest for an order inapplicable to the Latin world.

And I repeat that apart from the assassination of Gannys, which is the only crime that can be imputed to him, Heliogabalus put to death only the parasites of Macrinus, who was himself a traitor and an assassin, and he was on all occasions very economical with human blood. There is throughout his reign a striking disproportion between the amount of blood shed and the number of men actually killed.

We do not know the exact date of his coronation, but we do know the price that his largesses cost the treasury of the empire on that day. And they were of sufficient magnitude to compromise his own material security and to involve him in debt for the rest of his reign.

He doesn't stop trying to make the munificence of his largess correspond to his own idea of a king.

He puts an elephant in the place of a donkey, a horse in the place of a dog, a lion where a tiger cat would have done, the entire school of sacerdotal dancers where all that was expected was a procession of foundlings.

Everywhere amplitude, excess, abundance, immoderateness. The purest generosity and pity, which come to counterbalance a spasmodic cruelty.

While walking through marketplaces, he weeps over the poverty of the populace.

But at the same time he has the empire combed for sailors with members at the ready, to whom he gives the name of Aristocrats, prisoners and former murderers who can give as good as they get in the course of his sexual assaults, and who will season with their frightful crudities the turbulence of his feasts.

With Zoticus, he inaugurates the nepotism of the cock!

"A certain Zoticus was so powerful during his reign that all the other high officials treated him as if he were the husband of his master. Besides, this same Zoticus, abusing his right of familiarity, gave importance to all the words and actions of Heliogabalus. Aspiring to the greatest riches, making threats to some and promises to others, deceiving the whole world, and when he came from the prince, going to everyone and saying to them, 'I said this about you, here is what I heard about you; this is what will happen to you,' as is the wont of persons of this sort who, admitted by princes to too great a familiarity, sell the reputation of their master, whether he be bad or good; and thanks to the stupidity or inexperience of the emperors, who notice nothing, delight in the pleasure of divulging infamies . . ."

He weeps like the child he is over the treachery of Hierocles; but far from directing his cruelty against this lower-class charioteer, it is against himself that he turns his rage, and he punishes

From *Heliogabalus* (1934)

himself by having himself flogged until the blood flows, for having been betrayed by a charioteer.

He gives to the people everything that is important to them:

BREAD AND GAMES

Even when he feeds the people, he feeds them with lyricism; he provides them with that leaven of exaltation which is essential to all true magnificence. And the people are never touched, never scathed by his bloody tyranny, which never mistakes its object.

All whom Heliogabalus sends to the galleys, all whom he castrates or has flogged, he takes from among the aristocrats, the nobles, the pederasts of his personal court, the parasites of the palace.

He systematically pursues, as I have said, the perversion and destruction of all value and all order, but what is admirable and what proves the incurable decadence of the Latin world is the fact that he was able, for four consecutive years, and in full sight of everyone, to carry on this work of systematic destruction without anyone protesting: and his fall is no more significant than a mere palace revolution.

*

But if Heliogabalus goes from woman to woman just as he goes from charioteer to charioteer, he also goes from jewel to jewel, from robe to robe, from festivity to festivity, and from ornament to ornament.

Through the color and the touch of the jewels, the shape of the garments, the arrangement of the festivals, of the jewels which even strike his skin, his mind makes strange voyages. It is here that we see him pale, that we see him tremble in pursuit of a sudden sensation, a hardship to which he clings in the face of the terrifying flight of everything.

It is here that there is revealed a kind of superior anarchy in which his profound restlessness catches fire, and he runs from jewel to jewel, from outburst to outburst, from form to form, and from flame to flame, as if he were running from soul to soul in a mysterious interior odyssey which no one after him ever repeated.

ANTONIN ARTAUD

I see a dangerous monomania, both for others and for the one who surrenders to it, in the fact of changing one's robe every day and of placing on each robe a jewel, never the same, which corresponds to the signs of heaven. There is in this much more than a taste for expensive luxury or a propensity for unnecessary waste —there is evidence of an immense, insatiable fever of the mind, of a soul which thirsts for emotions, movements, journeys, and which has a taste for metamorphoses. Whatever the price that must be paid for them, or the risk thereby incurred.

And in the fact of inviting cripples to his table and of varying each day the form of their infirmities I denote a disturbing taste for disease and for discomfort, a taste which will expand to a pursuit of disease on the largest possible scale, that is, of a kind of perpetual contagion with the range of an epidemic. And this too is anarchy, but spiritual and specious, and all the more cruel, all the more dangerous because it is subtle and concealed.

That he spends a day eating a meal means that he is introducing space into the digestion of his food, and that a meal begun at dawn ends at sunset, after passing through the four cardinal points.

Because from hour to hour, from dish to dish, from house to house, and from orientation to orientation, Heliogabalus is in constant movement. And the end of the meal indicates that he has completed the figure, that he has closed the circle in space, and in this circle he has fixed the two poles of his digestion.

Heliogabalus carried to paroxysm the pursuit of art, the pursuit of ritual and poetry amid the most absurd magnificence.

"The fish that he had served were always cooked in a sauce that was tinted blue as sea water, and retained the color which was natural to them. For a certain period he took baths in rose wine, with roses. Here he drank with his entourage and perfumed the bathhouses with nard. He replaced the oil in the lamps with balm. Never did any woman except his wife receive his embraces more than once. He established in his house brothels for his friends, his favorites, and his servants. At supper he never spent less than a hundred sesterces. In this way he exceeded Vitellius and Apicius. He used oxen to pull fish out of the fish ponds. One day he wept over the poverty of the people as he walked through the marketplace. He used to enjoy attaching his favorites to the

From *Heliogabalus* (1934)

wheel of a windmill and, rotating it, now plunging them in the water, now bringing them up again, he would call them his dear Ixions."

Not only the Roman world but the land of Rome and the Roman countryside were thrown into disorder by him.

"It is told," says Lampridius, "that he staged mock sea battles on lakes dug by human hands and filled with wine, and that the cloaks of the combatants were perfumed with essence of pus; that he drove to the Vatican in chariots harnessed with four elephants, after having had the tombs that hindered his passage destroyed; that in the Circus, for his own personal spectacle, he had the chariots harnessed with four camels abreast."

His death was the coronation of his life; and if it was just from the Roman point of view, it was also just from the point of view of Heliogabalus. Heliogabalus died the ignominious death of a rebel, but a rebel who died for his ideas.

In the face of the general irritation occasioned by this excess of poetic anarchy, and secretly instructed by the perfidious Julia Mamaea, Heliogabalus allowed himself to be duplicated. He took into his confidence, he appointed coadjutor a bad imitation of himself, a kind of second emperor, little Alexander Severus, who was the son of Julia Mamaea.

But if Elagabalus is man and woman, he is not two men at the same time. There is in this a material duality which is for Heliogabalus an insult to reason, and which Heliogabalus cannot accept.

He rebels a first time, but instead of stirring up against the young virgin emperor those people who love him, Heliogabalus—the people who have profited from his generosity, and over whose poverty he has publicly wept—he tries to have Alexander Severus assassinated by his Praetorian Guard, who are still led by a dancer and whose open rebellion he is not aware of. It is against Heliogabalus that his own police then attempt to turn their arms; and Julia Mamaea urges them on; but Julia Maesa intervenes. Heliogabalus is able to escape in time.

Everything calms down.—Heliogabalus could have accepted the *fait accompli*, could have endured the proximity of this pale emperor of whom he was jealous and who, if he did not have the love of the people, had at least the love of the soldiers, the police, and the nobility.

But it is now, on the contrary, that Heliogabalus shows everything he is: an undisciplined and fanatical spirit, a real king, a rebel, a frantic individualist.

To accept, to submit is to gain time; it is to sanction his downfall without assuring the tranquillity of his life, for Julia Mamaea is at work, and he is well aware that she will not abdicate. Standing between absolute monarchy and her son Alexander Severus, there is only one body, one great heart, but one for which this so-called Christian woman has nothing but hatred and contempt.

A life for a life, it is a life for a life! That of Alexander Severus or his own. This, in any case, is what Heliogabalus has felt. And he decides in his own heart that it will be the life of Alexander Severus.

After this first alarm, the Praetorians have calmed down; everything has returned to order, but Heliogabalus takes it upon himself to rekindle the conflagration and the disorder, and thus to prove that he remains faithful to his methods!

Stirred up by emissaries, a band of common people—charioteers, artists, beggars, mountebanks—try to invade the part of the palace where on a certain night in February 222 Alexander Severus is sleeping right next to the room occupied by Julia Mamaea. But the palace is full of armed guards. The sound of swords being drawn, of shields being struck, of the military cymbals which rally the troops hidden in every room in the palace, is enough to put to flight a band that is almost unarmed.

It is then that the armed guard turns against Heliogabalus, whom they pursue all over the palace. Julia Soaemias has seen the comings and goings; she runs. She finds Heliogabalus in a kind of unfrequented corridor, she screams to him to flee. And she accompanies him in his flight. From all sides resound the cries of pursuers closing in, their heavy running makes the walls tremble, a nameless panic seizes Heliogabalus and his mother. They feel death all around them. They run out into the gardens, which slope down to the Tiber under the shadows of the great pines. In a remote corner, behind a thick row of fragrant box and holly

From *Heliogabalus* (1934)

oak, the soldiers' latrines extend in the open air with their trenches plowing the earth like furrows. The Tiber is too far. The soldiers too close. Heliogabalus, mad with fear, suddenly flings himself into the latrines, he plunges into the excrement. It is the end.

The troops, who have seen him, overtake him; and already his own Praetorians are seizing him by the hair. There follows a scene from the butcher's stall, a disgusting blood bath, an ancient tableau of the slaughterhouse.

Excrement mingles with blood, splashes along with blood on the swords that forage in the flesh of Heliogabalus and his mother.

Then they pull out the bodies, they transport them by torchlight, they drag them through the city before the terrified populace, before the houses of patricians, who open their windows to applaud. An immense crowd surges toward the quays of the Tiber in the wake of these deplorable masses of flesh, already bled white but smeared with their own gore.

"To the sewer!" now howls the populace which has profited from the largesses of Heliogabalus but which has digested them too well.

"To the sewer, both corpses! The corpse of Heliogabalus to the sewer!"

Satiated with blood and with the obscene sight of these two bodies—naked, ravaged, and showing all their organs, even the most private—the mob tries to stuff the body of Heliogabalus into the first sewer hole they come to. But, slender as it is, it is still too wide. They must reconsider.

To the name Elagabalus Bassianus Avitus, otherwise known as Heliogabalus, had already been added the nickname Varius, because he was formed of multiple seeds and born of a prostitute. He was later given the names Tiberian and the Dragged, because he was dragged to and thrown into the Tiber after the people had tried to cram him into the sewer; but when they reached the sewer, because his shoulders were too broad, they tried to pare him down. So they removed the skin, exposing the skeleton, which they wanted to leave intact; and they might then have added the two names the Pared and the Whittled. But after he was pared down he was evidently still too wide, and they heaved his body into the Tiber, which carried it to the sea, followed closely by the body of Julia Soaemias.

Thus ended Heliogabalus, without inscription and without a tomb, but with a hideous burial. He died as a coward, but in a state of open rebellion; and such a life, crowned by a death of this kind, needs, I think, no conclusion.

Letters and drafts from 1934–35

TO JEAN PAULHAN

June 1, 1934

Dear friend,

I note with annoyance that you understand me less and less, and on my side I no longer understand your reactions. The highest Truth is all I seek, but when people talk to me about what is true I always wonder what truth they are talking about, and to what extent the notion one may have of a limited and objective truth hides that other truth which obstinately eludes any boundary, any limit, any localization, and even in the end what is called the Real.

Here is what I can say to you—although your letter irritated me and I said to myself, what difference can it make to him whether or not it is true if it is beautiful, and if one finds in this book the notion of a truth and of the Superior Reality—the dates are correct, *all* the historical events have been based on fact but have been *reinterpreted,* a great many details are invented; the Esoteric Truths which I wanted to be true in *spirit* are frequently and deliberately FALSIFIED in form: but form is nothing; there is excess, exaggerations of images, wild statements; but then an atmosphere of madness is established in which the rational loses its footing but the spirit advances fully armed. In the last analysis a desperate sincerity underlies it, even under the apparent distortion, which is rare when it can pass for distortion. I have nothing more to say; but I am simply astonished that when confronted with a book written with my heart and with the skin of my entrails you dare, *you,* to ask me whether it is true. I think that this is either felt or not felt.

I must tell you that for the past three weeks I have been inundated with demonstrations of real enthusiasm. True or not, the character of Heliogabalus lives, I think, to the depths of his being, whether these depths be those of Heliogabalus the historical figure or those of a character who is myself. You, who have admired things I have written that are less alive, less successful, less complete, I cannot understand why this book in which I think I have realized myself with my faults, my excesses, and also with what qualities I may have, arouses your resistance. I greatly appreciated, on the other hand, the message from Daumal conveyed by Véra that many passages had touched them to the heart.

I did the lighting for Helba Huara's dance recital at the Salle Pleyel last night. Her dancing was a triumph, the huge auditorium was packed, and the lighting, which was done with pitifully small means, contributed to her success.

Your friend,
Antonin Artaud

Appeal to Youth
INTOXICATION—DISINTOXICATION

A state outside of life, a state which human medicine, that monstrous excrescence of the fixed imbecility of men, sees as hieroglyphic and can only express by a hieroglyph, made me resort one day to opium. I have not escaped from it and I never shall.

But let not medicine start up in alarm. Anyone who can read will understand that I burn with the desperate desire to escape from it, not like someone who escapes, who recovers from a temporary derangement, but like someone who leaves his room one fine day and finds himself in Eternal Life, which he thought he had lost forever.

I know therefore that I shall not escape, since I recognize in myself the fatality that caused me to be born what I am, as I am, that is to say, myself and not someone else. With that veil of differences which, although infinitesimal, are nevertheless desperately resonant when they are touched and which give back the sound of the self.

I take opium in the same way that I am myself, without recovering from myself. To stop drugging myself is to die. I mean that only death can cure me of the infernal palliative of drugs, which only a reasonable and not too prolonged or frequent absence from enables me to be what I am.

I can do nothing with opium, which is the most abominable illusion, the most formidable invention of nothingness that has ever fertilized human sensibilities. But I can do nothing unless I take into myself at moments this culture of nothingness.

It is not opium which makes me work but its absence, and in order for me to feel its absence it must from time to time be present.

This is neither a defense of disintoxication by an opium addict nor an attack on opium addiction by an ex-addict; it is the truthful memoir of a state which will be accepted and understood only by the angels and it is addressed only to those who are destined to understand and accept it.

Let this memoir be as suspicious as you like, I want it to be suspicious to those who will find it suspicious; it is not for them that I write.

As for that state outside of life to which opium does not do justice but with which it seems to have some very singular affinities, there are no words to describe it but a violent hieroglyph which designates the impossible encounter of matter with mind. A kind of inner vision in which the whirling cross of matter is cut off by the human organism; and the curve no longer occurs, for the flame of the Holy Ghost which precedes its own dove suddenly burns outside of space.

The body is there, but as if emptied of itself and its organs: the liver, the heart, the lungs, the intestines, the kidneys, function imperturbably. At most, the respiration, in its most imaginary and self-conscious aspect, may find itself slightly restricted at moments, a little labored, without expansion, without completion. The urine flows a bit heavily, is a bit light in color, too pale or too heavy. It looks a little abnormal, but analysis proves it healthy. Virility is thrown out of order: the patient is either too potent or impotent. All this happens in phases. And at times there is a Mammoth-like sensuality which would make love noisily, for the patient exceeds himself; at other times the patient is an angel, a priest, a pitiful sacristan.

From the top to the bottom of the scale of vitality the sign of this sickness is disorder, but try to regulate vitality.—But not the alteration of life, that frightful alteration without diminution in which nothing is missing and yet everything is no longer there; to say how in the channels of sense the force of life no longer diversifies, no longer ramifies, and yet continues to exist and causes the lower organs to function. And how the force of life reascends even to speech and chooses within the emission of the mind. Everything is pitiful, and nothing is missing and yet the self is no longer there.

There is in the action of opium [. . .]

TO ANDRÉ GIDE

Paris, February 10, 1935

Dear Sir and friend,

I have just finished a tragedy—*with text;* the dialogue, although condensed, is entirely written down.

This tragedy will be performed at the Comédie des Champs-Elysées in early April;—and rehearsals are starting right now.

But before the opening I'm planning to give a reading for a few friends.—All the actors will be present at this reading.

Would you do me the honor and the kindness of attending this reading? I especially need your presence, as well as that of a few friends like Jean Paulhan, for reasons which I shall explain.

The dialogue of this tragedy is, if I may say so, of the most extreme violence. And there is *nothing* among the traditional notions of Society, order, Justice, Religion, family, and Country, that is not attacked.

I am, therefore, expecting some very violent reactions on the part of the spectators. This is why I would like to prepare public opinion in advance.

There must be no incidents.

Everything that is attacked is attacked much less on the Social than on the Metaphysical level.

It is not pure anarchy.—And this is what must be understood.

Even those persons who believe themselves ideologically most free, most detached, most evolved, remain secretly attached to a certain number of notions which in this play I attack as a group.

This performance must not be an uninterrupted howl of protest.

There is no libertarian, however ideologically determined to throw the idea of family to the winds, who does not retain a deep-rooted human affection for his father, his mother, his sisters, his brothers, etc.

Well, in this play nothing is spared. And what I want everyone to understand is that I am attacking the social superstition of the family without asking anyone to take arms against a particular individual. The same for order, the same for justice. However fiercely opposed one may be to the present order, an old respect for the idea of order itself often prevents people from distinguishing between order and those who stand for order, and leads them in practice to respect individuals under the pretext of respecting order itself.

But given the ideological position I have taken, it is absolutely impossible for me to take account of all these nuances, with the result that temporarily and to speed up the action I am led to attack order itself.

These, then, are the points on which I think public opinion must be prepared.

I strike hard to strike fast, but above all to strike completely and without possibility of appeal.

Since I restrict myself to the realm of pure ideas, I do not need to take account of a whole group of human nuances which could only get in my way and which paralyze all action. And what people refuse to realize is that it is these human nuances which generally paralyze action and which prevent people from doing anything, or even trying anything.

So I have chosen to have done once and for all with all these inhibitions. But this is no reason why I should be regarded as an absolute and confirmed anarchist.

It is along these lines that public opinion must be prepared. People must hear the play first so they will have some notion of what I have in mind. And the ones who are afraid of words are the same ones who are afraid of actions, this is why nothing is ever done.—And this is why I am particularly anxious that you attend this reading; and I INSIST that you come.

After that, you can say the words that must be said; and I do not need to tell you again that what you say is always heard.

Nobody, however attached he may be to his personal ideology, or I should say to his own Mythology, would want, things being what they are, to be taken for a fool. Well, it is necessary that protesters, if any, be persuaded that by protesting they would be making fools of themselves. And this is what I had in mind.

No man of intelligence and perception has the right, without losing face, to revolt against the words of a theatrical character, since this character who says what he thinks also represents my own thinking, but represents it dramatically, that is, dynamically, that is, dialectically—and since his opinion is contingent on another speech which may temporarily destroy its effect, contingent above all on an ideal atmosphere which both distorts it and provides it with a context.

It is, therefore, to avoid the possibility that the audience will confuse ideas with people and, even further, will confuse them with forms

that I destroy the idea, for fear that respect for the idea might lead to the invention of a form which in turn would promote the continuation of bad ideas.

This is why I am counting on your presence and why I even ask you to name a day or rather an evening after dinner.

I shall await your answer before alerting my friends and my troupe.

In the meantime, I beg you to believe me your very faithfully and sincerely devoted friend,

Antonin Artaud

Hôtel des Etats-Unis, 135 Blvd. Montparnasse, Paris

The reading will take place at the home of Jean-Marie Conty, 12 rue Victor Considérant (Place Denfert-Rochereau).

TO JEAN-LOUIS BARRAULT

Paris, June 14, 1935

My dear Barrault,

You know in what honor I hold both your work and all that you are. You will understand, therefore, the spirit in which I speak to you in this letter.

There is no question of your taking the slightest offense at what I am going to say, but I do not want you to be able to harbor even the shadow of a mental reservation.

I do not believe that a collaboration is possible between us, for if I know what unites us, I see even better what divides us, which has to do with a *method of work* which, starting from two diametrically opposed points of view, leads to a result that is not the same, appearances to the contrary. I saw you work in *The Cenci*, when I asked you to rehearse the actors. You broke them, in a sense, or you put in so much of yourself that in the end things got out of hand anyway. Finally, several times in my presence you expressed a reservation about my personal way of working, based on the fact that being first of all a writer I did not push things far enough, and that in the realization of my intentions I came up against obstacles that I could not overcome through lack of work and application. But, and this is something of primary importance to me, I do not believe in watertight compartments, specifically in relation to the theater. This is fundamental to everything I have written for the past four years and more.

I won't have, in a spectacle staged by myself, so much as the flicker of an eye that does not belong to me. If in *The Cenci* everything was not regulated like this, it was because *The Cenci* deviated in part from the framework of the kind of theater I want to do, and because in the last analysis I was overwhelmed by the immensity of the task I had undertaken.

Finally, I do not believe in collaboration, especially since Surrealism, because I no longer believe in human purity. No matter how highly I regard you, I believe you to be fallible and I do not want to expose myself again even to the shadow of a risk of this sort.

I am not the man who can stand to work closely with anyone on any kind of material, and less than ever after *The Cenci*. If there are animals to be led in my play I'll lead them myself in the rhythm and attitude that I impose on them. And I'll find whatever exercises are necessary to teach them this attitude, or it will have been demonstrated that I am only a vulgar theoretician, which I do not believe.

Anyway, I repeat that you have reached the point where you must direct your own work, with your own personal way of understanding certain ideas. As for me, I plan to withdraw for a while and try to rid myself at last of the vices that paralyze me. This might go on for several months. In the meantime, see Conty, he is quite capable of finding you the little money you will need and he will be able to arrange your affairs very well. I have already spoken to him about this.

I have had a formal promise that my article on you will appear in the *N.R.F.* on the first of July, and no one finds it too laudatory.

With warm and affectionate greetings,
Antonin Artaud

DRAFT OF A LETTER TO THE INTERNATIONAL CONFERENCE OF WRITERS FOR THE DEFENSE OF CULTURE

[late June 1935]

Dear Sir,

I have just received your invitation, which was sent to an old address, and it [is] too late to send you my acceptance.

Let me say at once that I regard it as an excessive and misplaced honor to ask me to attend a conference "for the Defense of Culture." I do not believe the meeting of International Writers can expect very much from my suggestions regarding something which is not for me what it is for them.

Assuming that I see culture as a reality to be defeated, it does [not] seem to me that this reality now exists.

Moreover, I regard it as absolutely necessary, before elucidating this idea of a spirit opposed to culture, and which nothing has ever been able to touch—for only material formalists can think that gestures against culture can harm something which is above all culture and of which the changing forms of culture are merely representatives—I regard it as absolutely necessary to stress the reasons that brought about this conference, the reasons that cause people to believe that culture is in danger, and I want to say immediately that it may be good that a certain culture is in danger, however barbarous the means that have been employed to this end.

I shall never do any fascism the honor of believing that it can harm my culture or any culture by burning books glowing with that hybrid mixture which I hold responsible for our decline.

In any case, one must define what one means by culture and what aspect of culture one wants to defend: and if it is the spiritual legacy which is at the origin of the present civilization, then I reject that culture.

True culture has never had a native land, it is not human but spiritual, and it is not irrelevant to note that in this conference called together for the defense of culture an attempt is being made to justify indirectly the base and utilitarian idea of patriotism.

For me there is no legacy to be defended, no wealth to be safeguarded, insofar as these things are particularized; and the patriotism of the artisan disgusts me just as much as that of the banker.

The fact that a few contemporary thinkers have been put in jail, that the writings of ten centuries out of those regarded as civilized are being burned, is not enough to make me conclude that Barbarism threatens us or that the spirit is therefore diminished.

For inasmuch as no one is interested in the spirit, and inasmuch as culture is related to an idea of the spirit developed in man, I shall always maintain that the material lot of mankind is not an aspect of culture which should be of primary interest.

For this discussion in favor of culture seems to me above all a discussion in favor of the material comforts of man, who has always called culture that which spares him the necessity of thinking.

Besides which it takes more than protests to save a culture that is threatened by guns or force, and I do not feel personally prepared to go to war to save a culture that is everywhere based on nothing but force and guns.

The vitality which eludes what is written down and the poetry which is its violent expression, metamorphosis in perpetual action, are not related to the preservation of a culture that has led to the materialism of which we are aware.

If culture is a form of spirit, it is also a form of life, and I do not distinguish it from the sinister spectacle to which this life has unanimously led.

Culture was not born today and I cannot forgive it for the use that has been made of it here, in France, in Germany, in Italy, in the name of the more reasoned and more logical use that is made of it in Russia, for example, for it is the same culture that has flourished in all these countries. And if someone maintains that it is not the same, why bring us together for the defense of a mixture whose elements are not in accord?

Moreover, it is not true that the forms which help us to think are bound to the use of a given culture, and if all written ideas, all forms that are fixed, were to be burned, I say that true culture would not cease to survive the disappearance of all these forms, all these petrified signs.

If systems of thought are replaced, with all the more reason are the forms of life replaced, and there come moments in History when it is not useless to burn these forms of life.

True culture has never been bound up with the preservation of individual freedom, and in my opinion it is greatly underestimating culture to believe that it is weakened by the loss of a few men or the destruction of a few writings.

And I would even say that a sense of historic fatality, an understanding of the return of certain cycles and of catastrophes in which certain forms of life and thought disappear, are part of a highly evolved culture of which the organizers of this conference have never dreamed.

I would appeal to that universal culture which has always ignored the particularism of nations and which distinguishes between the destiny of the spirit contained in a given culture and the destiny of the man who has been the victim of that culture.

The poetry which eludes culture, and whose manifestations remain unscathed amid the most total absence of freedom, is a notion to which our age in its spiritual bankruptcy has long since lost the key. And I believe it important never to talk about spirit, which I regard as absolutely alien to the systematizations of culture, without combining it with the notion of pure poetic energy which has become the very flame of spirit.

The question of culture raises in my mind, it awakens the old antagonism between spirit and matter, it helps me to attempt a definition of the spirit that eludes the forms, it enables me to oppose the passing materialism, this hideous imprisonment of poetry by language, with the notion of something that endures, the preservation of a subtle quality whose persistence is capable of nourishing a hundred cultures, capable of surviving the blaze of a hundred bonfires.

And I ask that this spiritual attitude which can bring about the appearance of a concrete world of the surest and most authentic kind not be confused with some vague and sterile spiritualism that has also lost contact with the real energies.

For if everything that we manipulate which is concrete, certain, natural, and which gives us the illusion of living is powerless without the presence of a subtle virtue that must be called spirit, spirit in its turn can do nothing without the sheath of a palpable dynamism that must likewise be called material.

It is for a fitting purpose, the most urgent, toward a lost differentiation between an element originating in spirit and the same element transformable, dense, sonorous, and resistant and that . . .

DRAFT OF A LETTER TO THE DIRECTOR OF THE ALLIANCE FRANÇAISE

Paris, December 14, 1935

Sir,

In reference . . .

I wrote a screenplay for a talking film which was distinguished by the fact that it contained only one spoken line around which the whole text was written. The *N.R.F.* of October '32 published my Manifesto for the Theater of Cruelty which proposed an alternative form of theater inspired by Chinese, Hindu, and Balinese Theater, and in which stage image, gesture, and movement take precedence over the written text. Not that speech is despised, but it is taken in its concrete state, for its vibratory and sonorous value. It gives rise to gesture and gesture has given rise to it; and gesture has ceased to be conditioned by it. And in this way a kind of new poetry appears in space.

This Manifesto has practical principles. New actor founds Theater on these principles. Then there was a *Heliogabalus,* published by Denoël.

The life of Heliogabalus is theatrical. But his theatrical way of conceiving existence strives to create a true magic of the real. Indeed, I do not conceive of theater as separate from existence. Not that life appears to me as illusory and overdone, but on the contrary I am seeking to do away with the illusion of theater itself and, by poetic and technical means which are fundamental to the old art of theater as it was practiced in the beginning, to introduce into the theater the notion of reality. If dreams are the underside of life, if reality appears in dreams in a bewitching and magical form which the mind completely accepts, it is this nonillusory acceptance which I seek to force on the spectator. Thus it is that in *The Cenci* the placing of the Loudspeakers maintains a public bath of sound, and a diffused storm *as* terrible [as the] volume [of an] authentic disturbance [a] natural storm.

Lectures will principally revolve around the theater
> one on
>> traditional theater in France.

I shall seek out what has been preserved and is reappearing, the old mythical tradition of the theater in which the theater is regarded as a therapy, a way of healing comparable to certain dances of the Mexican Indians.

To go from this artistic and psychic therapy to new modern therapy inspired [by] Paracelsus, the spagyrical doctors, occultists like Jerome Cardan, Robert Fludd, etc.

from which to draw a lecture on
> *Mexican Medicine and French Middle Ages*

and on
>> Animist Spirit in France,

will show new spiritual currents which run through young consciousnesses, and which are expressed in poetry, Surrealism, medicine, Psychoanalysis and Homeopathy, Universal Myth Cure which one energetically speaks about here; in painting, Surrealism, Cubism, Picasso, Chirico, Balthus, and which are nothing else than the old animist spirit of the Mexican totems and the high magical poetry and metaphysic of the *Popol Vuh,* of the *Rabinal-Achi,* of *Ollantay,* of the Pyramids of Chichén Itzá, of the Mayan Hieroglyphs, etc., etc.

Can equally well do lecture on

Poetic and magical spirit [of the] *Popol Vuh*

compared *Zend-Avesta,* Bible, *Zohar, Sefer Yetsirah,* Vedas, Raja Yoga and will end [with]

Universal Myth Cure

seen in the light of elements, Symbols, Psychoanalysis included. All these lectures will strive to inform Mexicans about what is happening in France [from the] point of view [of] minds and of mentality, and establish liaison inner musical concordance between Mexican Metamorphoses and Metamorphoses [of the] French mentality. As unofficial as this is, point of view must please Mexico, moreover it is true and corresponds [to] profound transformation [of] youth which is evolving, which seeks intense spirituality, giving this word [its] concrete, dynamic, exalting, regenerated sense.

Antonin Artaud

Excerpts from notebooks and private papers (1935)

XXV

CÉCILE
and Imagination,
attractions are the work of the Imagination,
true reality is less mad and more reliable and more beautiful.

*

A sensibility of the flayed.

Where the body is blessed
it is there that one finds the soul.

The eagle & the serpent.

The plumed serpent,
the memory of a sorcerer writer,
a bloody garment.

When the past comes back into the light of day.

The day of resurrection.

When the gods descend to earth.

How myths are restored.

To be invited *by the Mexicans.*

Awaken love the ancient invisible magic,
the tamer of epidemics,
to heal the catastrophes of heaven.
Voyage to the land of speaking blood.

*

This is the first time that in the presence of a human being I have known the pleasure of working, seeking, and understanding as in the presence of certain favorite animals.

*

Never once came without telling me that she almost did not come,

these are not real obstacles,
it is a sickness,
the sickness of flight,
I wish I understood this desire for flight,
all the air of an obsession.

Induction,
presence of love,
if she thinks this, she can sacrifice her thought to what she
                                                    loves so she can keep it,
you can, can you not, for love change your idea of love,
what I ask you does not go against love,
but you who flee, can one count on you?

The trip to Mexico (1936)

XXVI

MAN AGAINST DESTINY

I spoke last night of Surrealism and revolution. I should have said the revolution against Surrealism, Surrealism against the revolution.

I tried to define that profound disgust, that deep-rooted anguish which never quite found its direction, out of which French Surrealism was born.

For me, the essence of Surrealism was an affirmation of life against all its caricatures, and the revolution invented by Marx is a caricature of life.

I felt that that hunger for a pure life which Surrealism was in the beginning had nothing to do with the fragmentary life of Marxism. Fragmentary, but provisionally valid. But corresponding to a real movement of history. And I said that Marx was one of the first men who experienced and felt history. But there is a world of movements in history. And if the Surrealist state of mind is a state of mind outmoded by facts, the historical movement of Marxism is also outmoded by facts.

I shall present the latest stage in our thinking on this subject: the thinking of French youth and the thinking of enlightened intellectuals.

Historical and dialectical materialism is an invention of European consciousness. Between the true movement of history and Marxism there is a kind of human dialectic which does not accord with the facts. And we think that for the last four hundred years European consciousness has been living on an enormous error of fact.

This fact is the rationalist conception of the world which in its application to our everyday life in the world produces what I shall call a *divided consciousness*.

You will understand what I mean in a moment.

You all know that one cannot grasp thought. In order to think, we have images, we have words for these images, we have representations of objects. We separate consciousness into states of consciousness. But this is merely a way of speaking. All this has no real value except insofar as it enables us to think. In order to consider our consciousness we are obliged to divide it, otherwise the rational faculty which enables us to see our thoughts could never be used. But in reality consciousness is a whole, what the philosopher Bergson calls *pure duration*. There is no stopping the motion of thought. That which we place before us so that the reason of the mind can consider it is in reality already past; and that which reason holds is merely a form, more or less empty of real thought.

That which the reason of the mind looks at can always be said to partake of death. Reason, a European faculty, exalted beyond measure by the European mentality, is always an image of death. History, which records facts, is an image of dead reason. Karl Marx wrestled with the image of facts, he tried to sense the meaning of history in its particular dynamism. But he too remained fixated on a fact: the capitalist fact, the bourgeois fact, the congestion of the machine, the asphyxia of the economy of the age caused by a monstrous abuse of the use of the machine. Out of this true fact there came, *also in history*, a false ideology.

The French youth of today, who do not tolerate dead reason, are no longer content with ideologies. They regard the materialist explanation of history as an ideology which may bring about the end of history. And when they reread Marx's *Communist Manifesto* they perceive that what is called Marxism is itself a false ideology which caricatures the thinking of Marx.

Marx started with a fact, but he refused to allow himself any sort of metaphysics. But the youth feel that the materialist explanation of the world is a false metaphysics. In the face of the false metaphysics which has come out of the materialism of Marx they demand a total metaphysics which will reconcile them with the life of today.

They blame historical materialism for the birth of a form of idolatry which, like all forms of idolatry, is religious, religious because it introduces a mystical element into the mind. French youth do not want mysticism, they want mankind to stop hallucinating the mind; they are hungry for a human truth, human without deception.

They sense life, this youth, and we sense life as a single thing, a thing which does not admit of theory. To invoke metaphysics today is not to separate life from a world which goes beyond it, it is to reintegrate into the economic idea of the world everything

The trip to Mexico (1936)

man has tried to remove from the world, and reintegrate it without hallucination.

In the eyes of youth, it is reason which created the contemporary despair and the material anarchy of the world by separating the elements of a world which a real culture would bring together.

If we have a false idea of destiny and of the way it operates in nature, this is because we have forgotten how to look at nature, how to feel life in its wholeness.

The ancients did not recognize chance, and fatality is a Greek idea whose opacity was further emphasized by crude Latin reason. In order to cure itself of chance, the so-called pagan world had wisdom. But when we invoke wisdom, how many in the modern world would still be able to say what it is?

There is a secret determinism based on the higher laws of the world; but in an age of a mechanized science lost among its microscopes, to speak of the higher laws of the world is to arouse the derision of a world in which life has become a museum.

When one speaks today of culture, governments think in terms of opening schools, grinding out books, spilling printer's ink, whereas, to let culture mature, one should close the schools, burn the museums, destroy the books, smash the printing presses.

To be cultivated is to eat one's destiny, to assimilate it through knowledge. It is to know that the books lie when they speak of god, of nature, of man, of death, and of destiny.

God, nature, man, life, death, and destiny are merely forms which life assumes when it is regarded by the thinking process of reason. Outside reason there is no destiny; and this is a high idea of culture which Europe has renounced.

Europe has dismembered nature with her separate sciences.

Biology, natural history, chemistry, physics, psychiatry, neurology, physiology, all these monstrous germinations which are the pride of the Universities, just as geomancy, chirology, physiognomy, psychurgy, and theurgy are the pride of a few separate individuals, are to enlightened minds merely a *loss of consciousness*.

Antiquity had its labyrinths, but it did not know the labyrinth of divided science.

There is in the mind a secret movement which divides knowledge and presents the bewildered reason with images of science, as if they were so many realities.

Satan, according to the ancient books of the Magians, is an image that is created. By invoking Evil, the black magicians invent it and may be said to create it. Similarly, the divided Reason invents the images of science which are taught in the Universities.

This movement is an idolatrous thing: the mind believes in what it has seen.

And to look at life through a microscope is to look at a landscape through the small end of reality.

French youth are against reason because they accuse it of coming between them and science. They are against the science which has petrified reason.

These young people feel that Europe has lost its way, and they think that it is knowingly and one may say criminally that Europe has lost its way. They lay the blame for this fatal orientation of Europe on Cartesian materialism.

They blame the Renaissance, which claimed to glorify man, for debasing the idea of man by a false interpretation of the Ancients.

They know that history is wrong when it talks about paganism, and that paganism is not what the books have made of it.

It is Europe that has invented the idolatry of the pagans, because the form of the European mind is an idolatrous one; and idolatry, as I was just saying, is precisely the separation of the idea from the form when the mind believes in what it has dreamed. The Ancients, who believed in their dreams, believed in the meaning of their dreams, they did not believe in the forms they took. Behind their dreams and at varying levels, the Ancients sensed forces, and they immersed themselves in these forces. They had an overpowering sense of the presence of these forces, and they sought throughout their entire organism, if necessary by means of a real vertigo, the means of remaining in contact with the release of these forces. The head of a European of today is a cave in which images without force shift about, images which Europe mistakes for her thoughts.

But this is to seek too far afield the critique of a thought that is dead. What paganism deified, Europe has mechanized.

We are against this rationalization of existence which pre-

The trip to Mexico (1936)

vents us from believing in ourselves, that is, from feeling human, and there exists in our idea of man an idea of the force of thought. And of the dialectical and technical wisdom of the force of thought.

Everything that science has taken away from us, everything it isolates in its retorts, its microscopes, its scales, its complicated mechanisms, everything it reduces to numbers, we aspire to win back from science, which is stifling our vitality.

Something is trying to come out of us which is not answerable to experiment. And there are many of us who reject the teachings of experiment. We do not believe in the value of experiment or in proof by experiment. This is because we do not believe in the illusions of reason and of the forms by which experiment seeks to reach our thinking.

All forms of experiment conceal reality.

When Pasteur tells us that there is no spontaneous generation and that life cannot emerge from a void, we think that Pasteur was mistaken about the real nature of the void and that a new experiment will show that Pasteur's void is not a void: and this experiment has been performed.

In our eyes history is a panorama and it is in time that we judge history, for we are cultivated people. Here people who eat potatoes have the morality of adventurers, but in the same place, five hundred years before, other people who also ate potatoes had the morality of degenerates.

It is not by experiments that we judge reality. For all this does not show us Man. A preoccupation with the external functions of Man leads one away from a profound understanding of Man. And there is a whole world in the mind. The Communist revolution ignores the internal world of thought. But it is concerned with thought, it approaches it from the viewpoint of experiment, that is, from the external world of facts.

It takes madmen and grafts onto them bizarre maladies to see what may result, it injects them with plant viruses as if it were grafting plants onto them to see what would become of the man in them. It would not be above creating a caricature of Totemism by researching experimentally the transition between Man and beast, between beast and forest.

But let us not forget that the materialism of Lenin, which is also called dialectical, claims to represent an advance over the dialectic of Hegel.

Whereas Hegel's dialectic defines the internal force of thought in three terms, Lenin's unites the terms and speaks of the dynamism of thought which it no longer separates from the facts.

There are in life three kinds of force, as taught by an old science known to all antiquity:

repulsive and dilating force,

compressive and astringent force,

rotational force.

The movement which goes from the outside in and which is called centripetal corresponds to astringent force, whereas the movement which goes from the inside out and which is called centrifugal corresponds to dilating and repulsive force.

Like life, like nature, thought goes from the inside out before going from the outside in. I begin to think in the void and from the void I move toward the plenum; and when I have reached the plenum I can fall back into the void. I go from the abstract to the concrete and not from the concrete toward the abstract.

To arrest thought from the outside and to study it with regard to what it can do is to misunderstand the internal and dynamic nature of thought. It is to refuse to perceive thought in the movement of its internal destiny which no experiment can capture.

I call poetry today the understanding of this internal and dynamic destiny of thought.

In order to recover its profound nature, to feel alive in its thought, life is rejecting the spirit of analysis in which Europe has lost its way.

Poetic understanding is internal, poetic quality is internal. There is a movement today to identify the poetry of the poets with that internal magic force which provides a path for life and makes it possible to act upon life.

Whether or not thought is a secretion of matter, I shall not take the time to discuss the subject. I shall simply say that Lenin's materialism seems in fact to be ignorant of this poetic quality of thought.

There are herbs for illnesses, and the illnesses have the color of these herbs. Between the color of the illness and the color of

The trip to Mexico (1936)

the herb, Paracelsus, who even as he cures individual men, is looking for a path for man on the road of illness (and one might say that he cures life), Paracelsus, in order to cure life, imaginatively establishes a relationship between the illness and the herb, and cures the illness.

This is the origin of alchemical medicine, which in turn is the source of homeopathy.

There are cries for the passions, and within the cries of each passion there are degrees of vibration of the passions; and in other times the world knew a harmonics of the passions. But each illness also has its cry and the form of its gasp: there is the cry of the plague victim when he runs through the street with his mind drunk with images, and the peculiar gasp of the plague victim when he is dying. And the earthquake has its own sound. But the air vibrates in a particular way when what is said to be an epidemic passes. And between an illness and a passion, between a passion and an earthquake, one can establish resemblances and strange harmonies of sound.

But the determinism of facts is not separate from a living appearance. There is not an event in history which is not associated with a color or a sound.

Ages of genius have thought, by using the relation of color or sound to the rhythm of gasps and the trembling of epidemics, to the sound made by an herb which resembles an illness, to a combination of expressions, to the modulations of a sob that expresses all the torture of humanity torn apart by destiny—ages of genius have thought by these means to rediscover the movement of history, to retrace the current of destiny.

The ancient games were based on this knowledge which by action overcomes destiny. All classical theater was a war against destiny.

But in order to tame destiny one must know nature as a whole, and in man one must know consciousness as a whole, consciousness as it is subject to the rhythm of events.

We have the idea of a unitary culture and we call this culture unitary in order to rediscover an idea of unity in all the manifestations of nature which man measures with his thought.

The 380 points of Chinese medicine which govern all the

human functions treat man as a unified whole, just as the universal cure of Paracelsus raises human consciousness to the level of divine thought.

Anyone who claims today that there are several cultures in Mexico—the culture of the Mayas, that of the Toltecs, the Aztecs, the Chichimecs, the Zapotecs, the Totonacs, the Tarascans, the Otomis, etc.—does not know what culture is, he is confusing the multiplicity of forms with the synthesis of a single idea.

There is Moslem esoterism and Brahman esoterism; there is the occult Genesis, the Jewish esoterism of the *Zohar* and of the *Sefer Yetsirah,* and here in Mexico there is the *Chilam Balam* and the *Popol Vuh.*

Who does not see that all these esoterisms are the same, and mean spiritually the same thing? They express a single idea—geometrical, mathematical, organic, harmonious, occult—an idea which reconciles man with nature and with life. The signs of these esoterisms are identical. There are profound analogies between their words, their gestures, and their cries.

Of all the esoterisms that exist, Mexican esoterism is the last to be based on blood and the magnificence of a land whose magic only certain fanatical imitators of Europe can still be unaware of.

I say we must draw out the hidden magic from an earth which bears no resemblance to the egoistical world that persists in walking on its surface and does not see the shadow that is falling on us all.

TO JEAN PAULHAN

Mexico City, March 26, 1936

My very dear friend,

Thank you for the letter and for the check. The money arrived just in time; but from now on I think my finances will be in order. I am beginning to be very much in favor with the government of Mexico.

I was invited to be a delegate to a small Conference on the Children's Theater. The proposals and suggestions I made caused a minor Scandal in the company, or rather among the rabble of Schoolteachers. They claimed that I spoke to them of things *they*

The trip to Mexico (1936)

had never thought about before in their lives. And a committee of five members was appointed to explain my ideas on the theater to this audience of professors.

By now you must have received the text of the three lectures I gave at the University of Mexico. I am giving another in a few days at the Mexican Liga de Escritores y Artistas Revolucionarios. I shall speak against Marxism and in favor of the Indian Revolution, which everyone here forgets. This population of Whites (Creoles) and half-breeds would be very happy to hear no more about the Indians. Culturally speaking, they are behind America and Europe. It is heartbreaking to come all the way to Mexico only to find this.

Nevertheless, *the Indians exist.* My ideas caused a scandal in all kinds of circles. But a great many people are coming to them independently and soon I am going to reach the Indians, most of the Indians, and there I hope to be understood.

I will be leaving very shortly for Cuernavaca, a small city two hours from Mexico City.

There they make the famous *teponextli,* a ritual drum. Then I shall try to see the tribe that flays bulls alive and is overcome with laughter (Yaqui Indians).

The Undersecretary of State for Foreign Affairs is a young man who has understood me, and all the doors of the government have been opened for me.

But this is the exoteric side. There is a strong *esoteric* world in Mexico. I made contact with that world *as early as* Havana. We shall see.

My warm regards to your wife.

For you, all my real affection,
Antonin Artaud

I am sending you a corrected text of "The Theater of the Seraphim" and of "An Emotional Athleticism." Give me your comments by return mail, so that this piece can appear as soon as possible and I can finally be free of my literary past.

This seems to be the condition for success.

Regards.

A.A.

ANTONIN ARTAUD

First Contact with the Mexican Revolution

The present world crisis has reached France after the other countries but, although this is not apparent, it has affected France more seriously. Contrary to what is happening elsewhere, modern France is suffering more acutely from the crisis in her consciousness than from the one affecting her capital and her wealth, and French youth are particularly sensitive to the effects of this crisis. Anyone who knew Paris three years ago and returned there now would not recognize it. In appearance the city has changed little, but the life of Paris, everything that made it exciting, the youth, the movement, the zest, the enjoyment, all this has changed terribly. It is above all the youth who are suffering, and there is nothing which so deeply affects the inner life of a country as the suffering of its youth.

I would not say that French youth have lost hope, I would say that they have been damaged in the very springs of hope, for they are on the point of losing confidence in the resources of life. The government is preoccupied with keeping prices up on essential commodities so that they will not be sold at a loss, thus allowing the French peasants to maintain their former standard of living, but it is not at all concerned, as is the government here, with the lives of the young people. And French youth, left to themselves—I am speaking especially of the young painters, sculptors, actors, filmmakers, etc.—are on the edge of despair.

So I need not describe my emotion when, on my arrival here, I saw the deep interest the revolutionary government of Mexico takes in the works of the young; I spoke with artists, painters, revolutionary intellectuals, and musicians; the Department of Fine Arts, under the direction of Professor Muñoz Cota, did me the honor of inviting me to its Conference on the Children's Theater as a representative of the French Republic; and I realized that the revolution in Mexico has a soul, a living soul, an exacting soul, and not even the Mexicans themselves can say how far it can lead them. This is what is so moving about the revolutionary movement in Mexico. Young Mexico forges ahead, determined to remake a world, and in reconstructing this world she shrinks from no transformation. Question the young revolutionaries of Mexico, not one will give you the same answer; this chaos of opinions is

The trip to Mexico (1936)

the best proof of the vitality of the revolution. That the life of Mexico must be socialistic, the young people are all in agreement, of course, but opinions diverge as to what means should be employed to arrive at this socialization of Mexico totally and quickly.

These very divergences possess their own force of exaltation. The consciousness of Mexico today is a chaos in which the new forces of an entire world are seething. And if the youth of France are in despair, the youth of Mexico are nowhere near despair, as I had an opportunity to observe on the occasion of this Conference on the Children's Theater at which I was asked to make a presentation on the dynamism of the Guignol.

It is true that French youth, who are now in a very restless state, are discussing the most daring ideas, sometimes almost without being aware of it. In the theater, the past few years have seen the emergence of a new concept. Abandoning the work of Jacques Copeau, for example, purely plastic effects in which production merely clothes the text and is strictly conditioned by it, the new work tends to reduce the text once again, as in the Mystery Plays of the Middle Ages, to being the servant, the slave of an order come from very far, from the very sources of language in those mythic ages when the primitive idiom uttered by man merged with the organic power of respiration. Little by little, modern French theater shows signs of rediscovering the actual necessity, the central and moving necessity of expression. This means that the theater is abandoning literature, is abandoning books and rediscovering the space of the stage, expanding in the whole perspective of space, for theater is an art in space and it was necessary at all costs to regain consciousness of the spatial value of expression. Sound, movement, light, gesture, voice, and even the shape of voice are part of this new language of theater. It is primarily because of the way it is said and the place in which it is said that a word lives, and what is most alive is the rhythmic beat of the breath, which is solar and lunar, male and female, active and passive. There is a whole technique of breathing which a young actor, Jean-Louis Barrault, fresh from Charles Dullin's Théâtre de l'Atelier, has begun to study in detail.

I expounded this technique in my presentation on the dynamism of the puppets. I had already described it in the "Manifesto of the Theater of Cruelty," which appeared in the October 1932 issue of *La Nouvelle Revue Française,* and in an article on the ternary numbers of the Cabala and their application to the art of theater which will appear in the next issue of *Revista de la Universidad* under the title "An Emotional Athleticism."

All this technique, which seems dry and repellent, actually expresses something elementary and very simple. But something which is essential. Whether or not one accepts it, it contains a profound idea of culture, and it is this essential idea of culture that forms the foundation for all the hopes of young French intellectuals today.

French youth today may be said to be in the throes of a real childbirth, and they have a revolutionary idea of culture. What I came to look for on the soil of Mexico was precisely an echo, or rather a source, a real physical source of this revolutionary force. And along with French youth I am counting on the support of Mexican youth to help us release this force and this idea.

The effort which I am asking of the youth of Mexico, which I am asking also of the Mexican revolution, will be great, and it must be terribly effective.

In short, we expect from Mexico a new concept of Revolution, and also a new concept of Man which will serve to nourish, to feed with its magical life this ultimate form of humanism that is being born in France with a spirit diametrically opposed to the spirit of the sixteenth century.

As you may be aware, on the subject of the Mexican revolution Europe is currently in a state of phantasmagoria, the victim of a kind of collective hallucination. One can almost say that Europe sees the Mexicans of today dressed in the costumes of their ancestors in the act of actually sacrificing to the sun on the steps of the pyramid of Teotihuacán. I assure you that I am scarcely joking. In any case, people heard about the vast theatrical reconstructions that took place on this same pyramid, and they believed in good faith that there was in Mexico a well-defined anti-European movement, just as they believed that modern Mexico wanted to build its revolution on the foundation of a return to the pre-Cortes tradition. A fantasy of this kind is being circulated in the most advanced intellectual circles of Paris.

The trip to Mexico (1936)

In short, people believe that the Mexican revolution is a revolution of the indigenous soul, a revolution to win back *the indigenous soul* as it was before Cortes.

This was to have been the subject of the investigation that I was asked to conduct here.

But it does not seem to me that the revolutionary youth of Mexico are very much concerned with the indigenous soul. And this is precisely where the problem arises. In coming to Mexico I dreamed of an alliance between French youth and Mexican youth with a view to bringing about a unique cultural effort, but this alliance does not seem possible as long as Mexican youth remain solely Marxist. Marxism claims to be scientific, it talks about a mass mind, but it does not destroy the notion of individual consciousness, and because it leaves this notion intact, it is in a gratuitous manner and with a romantic spirit that it addresses itself to mass consciousness. And yet the destruction of individual consciousness represents a high idea of culture; it is a profound idea of culture which gives rise to a whole new form of civilization. Not to feel oneself live as an individual means escaping that deadly form of capitalism which I call the capitalism of consciousness, since the soul is the property of all.

It is in this sense that French youth believes in a renaissance of pre-Cortes civilization. They do not want to fall back into the North American error of a civilization developing on the fringe of culture, they want first of all to arrive at that profound and central idea of culture upon which any revolution must depend.

By imposing the forms of white civilization on the Indians, one would also run the risk of destroying everything they might have preserved of their former culture, for culture and civilization are connected.

In the last analysis the problem is this:

There is in Europe an anti-European movement, I am very much afraid that there may be in Mexico an anti-Indian movement. To be concerned about the body and not about the mind is to risk losing the body too. I know perfectly well that the problem of consciousness does not exist for the Marxist youth of Mexico or, if you prefer, that it is conditioned by external elements.

But for the revolutionary youth of France, Marxism, by preserving a sense of individual conscience, is preventing the Revolution from returning to its sources, which means that it is stopping the Revolution.

What I Came to Mexico to Do

I came to Mexico in search of politicians, not artists.

And this is why:

Until now I have been an artist, which means that I have been a man without power. For there is no doubt that from a social point of view artists are slaves.

Well, I say that this must change.

There was a time when the artist was a sage, that is, a cultivated man who was also a thaumaturge, a magus, a therapeutist, and even a gymnasiarch—that combination which in carnival language is called a "one-man band" or "Protean man." The artist united in his person all the faculties and all the sciences. Then came the age of specialization, which was also the age of decadence. One cannot deny it: a society which turns science into an infinite number of sciences is a society which is degenerating.

There is a disease of the polar regions which consists in a fundamental alteration of the tissues: this disease is scurvy. For want of an essential vital principle, the cells of the organism dry out. And just as there are diseases of individuals, there are also diseases of populations. The proliferation of the products of machines has infected the organism of Europe with a collective form of scurvy.

This is the price that progress has had to pay.

Modern Mexico, which is aware of the defects of European civilization, owes it to herself to resist this superstition about progress.

And since politicians have replaced artists in the management of public affairs, this task falls to them, and not to the artists.

Modern Mexico may be said to be facing a problem of great magnitude; I came to Mexico so that I could study the solutions to this problem at first hand.

What is required, in fact, is nothing less than breaking with

The trip to Mexico (1936)

the spirit of an entire world and substituting one civilization for another.

Alexis Carrel, who also recognizes the defects of the mechanized civilization of Europe, does not hesitate, in his book *Man, the Unknown*, to stress the necessity of a revolution, and even goes so far as to suggest means to bring it about.

Mexico, which has had two or three revolutions in a century, has no reason to be afraid of another; and the next, if it takes place, will certainly be of exceptional gravity, because this time it will have to resolve fundamental problems.

However, this future revolution of Mexico—and herein will lie its originality—will not be a fratricidal revolution, for since the future of civilization is at stake, a unanimous idea animates Mexico today. This moving unanimity is what I came here to see.

The fundamental question is as follows:

The present civilization of Europe is in a state of bankruptcy. Dualistic Europe no longer has anything to offer the world but an incredible pulverization of cultures. To extract a new unity from this infinity of separate cultures is a necessity.

As for the Orient, it is totally decadent. India is lost in the dream of a liberation which has value only after death.

China is at war. The Japanese of today seem to be the fascists of the Far East. China, in the eyes of Japan, is a vast Ethiopia.

The United States has done nothing but multiply to infinity the decadence and vices of Europe.

There remains only Mexico and her subtle political structure which has not changed fundamentally since the age of Montezuma.

Mexico, that precipitate of innumerable races, appears as the diffuser of history. From this very precipitation and from this mixture of races she must extract a unique residue, from which the Mexican soul will emerge.

But in order to create a single soul, one must have a single culture, and it is here that the problem becomes momentous.

On the one hand there is culture and on the other there is civilization, and civilization and culture are in danger of moving in diametrically opposite directions. Although there may be a hundred cultures in Europe, there is only one civilization—a civilization which has its own laws. Anyone who is not provided with machines, guns, airplanes, bombs, and poisonous gases inevitably becomes the victim of his better-armed neighbor or enemy: look at the case of Ethiopia.

Modern Mexico could escape neither this necessity nor this law. But beyond this, Mexico possesses a cultural secret which the ancient Mexicans bequeathed her. Unlike the modern culture of Europe, which has arrived at an insane pulverization of forms and aspects, the eternal culture of Mexico possesses a single aspect. This is the point I wanted to make: every unified culture has a secret. With time and under the external influence of the civilization of Europe, Mexico has abandoned the knowledge and the utilization of this secret, but—and this is the sensational event of the age—there has dawned in Mexico a movement to regain this secret.

When Mexico has actually regained and revitalized its true culture, neither guns nor planes will be of any further use against her.

Please pay attention to what I am going to say, for I am not being melodramatic. Beneath its childish appearance, this statement contains a fundamental truth.

Every important cultural transformation begins with a renewed idea of man, it coincides with a new surge of humanism. People suddenly begin to cultivate man exactly as one would cultivate a fertile garden.

I came to Mexico to look for a new idea of man.

Man confronted by the inventions, the sciences, the discoveries, but as only Mexico can still present him to us, I mean with this armature on the outside, but carrying deep within him the ancient vital relations of man with nature that were established by the old Toltecs, the old Mayas—in short, all those races which down through the centuries created the grandeur of the Mexican soil.

Mexico cannot, under pain of death, renounce the new conquests of science, but it holds in reserve an ancient science infinitely superior to that of the laboratories and the scientists.

Mexico has its own science and its own culture; to develop this science and this culture is a duty for modern Mexico, and a duty of this kind is precisely what constitutes the passionate originality of this country.

The trip to Mexico (1936)

Between the now degenerated vestiges of the ancient Red Culture, such as one can find them in the last pure indigenous races, and the no less degenerate and fragmentary culture of modern Europe, Mexico can find an original form of culture which will constitute its contribution to the civilization of this age.

The task that must be accomplished in this direction is enormous, and the reason I am in Mexico today is that I have felt that this enormous task, this task of epic dimensions—let us not be afraid of big words—is being carried out in modern Mexico.

Beneath the contributions of modern science which is every day discovering new forces, there are other unknown forces, other subtle forces which do not yet belong to the realm of science but which may belong to it someday. These forces are part of the vital realm of nature as men knew it in pagan times. The superstitious mind of man gave a religious form to these profound understandings which saw man, if you will permit the expression, as the "catalyst of the universe."

Well, the conquest of modern Mexico and this contribution of capital importance which Mexico can bring us today consist precisely in the discovery of those *analogical forces* thanks to which the organism of man functions in harmony with the organism of nature and governs it. And insofar as science and poetry are a single and identical thing, this is as much the business of poets and artists as it is the business of scientists, as was clear at the time of the *Popol Vuh*.

But this time the rediscovery will be clean of all superstition, of all religious meaning, however slight.

In short, it is a question of reviving the old sacred idea, the great idea of pagan pantheism, this time in a form that will no longer be religious but scientific. True pantheism is not a philosophical system, it is merely a means of *dynamic investigation* of the universe.

This is the lesson which modern Mexico can teach us. Mexico is appropriating the forms of the mechanistic civilization of Europe and adapting them to its own spirit. What does it matter if this spirit is calculated to destroy these forms!

If it does destroy them, it will be in time, when it has already armed itself with its own strength, that is, when this spirit of the ancient synthetic culture of the Toltecs and the Mayas has regained sufficient force to allow Mexico to abandon European civilization without danger. Once again, this is not a utopia but a scientific reality that cannot be denied. If one is willing to accept the idea that man is the catalyst of the universe, one must conclude that the moral forces of man vibrate in unison with the forces of the universe, those forces which, according to the teachings of high monist philosophy, are neither physical nor mental but may assume either a mental or a physical aspect according to the sense in which one wants to utilize them.

The Cross of Palenque perfectly embodies the synthetic image of this twofold action.

Here, inscribed in stone, is the hieroglyphic representation of a single energy which, through the cross of space, that is, by passing through the four cardinal points, moves from man to the animal and to the plants.

TO JEAN-LOUIS BARRAULT

Mexico City, July 10, 1936

My dear Barrault,

Since I last wrote you, the situation has changed.

A petition signed by the most eminent intellectuals and artists of Mexico, and countersigned by several ministers and ministerial departments, has recently been sent to the President of the Republic, asking that I be given the means to carry out a Mission in connection with the old races of Indians.

This mission has to do with discovering and reviving the vestiges of the ancient Solar culture.

But I must remain alive until everything is ready; and like Bernard Palissy, I am burning the furniture and living like an ascetic and in despair.

I must have the help of my friends in Paris.

I ask you, therefore, not to wait any longer but to make an effort and send whatever you can. It does not matter whether you do it as a group or whether you send it directly to me. I am no longer ashamed to ask it of you, for my present situation is serious, but the result of all this waiting could be spectacular. They

The trip to Mexico (1936)

must have confidence in me in Paris, as official circles here have confidence in me. But they are slow. My effort is desperate. Make a desperate effort for me and above all move with urgency, with great urgency, for I am at the end of my strength, my resistance, my reserve. I cannot go on and I am counting on you.

Antonin Artaud

From *A Voyage to the Land of the Tarahumara*

The Mountain of Signs

The land of the Tarahumara is full of signs, forms, and natural effigies which in no way seem the result of chance, as if the gods, whom one feels everywhere here, had chosen to express their powers by means of these strange signatures in which the figure of man is hunted down from all sides.

Of course, there are places on the earth where Nature, moved by a kind of intelligent whim, has sculptured human forms. But here the case is different, for it is over the whole *geographic expanse of a race* that Nature *has chosen to speak*.

And the strange thing is that those who travel through this region, as if seized by an unconscious paralysis, close their senses in order to remain ignorant of everything. When Nature, by a strange whim, suddenly shows the body of a man being tortured on a rock, one can think at first that this is merely a whim and that this whim signifies nothing. But when in the course of many days on horseback the same intelligent charm is repeated, and *when Nature obstinately manifests the same idea;* when the same pathetic forms recur; when the heads of familiar gods appear on the rocks, and when a theme of death emanates from them, a death whose expense is obstinately borne by man; when the dismembered form of man is answered by the forms, *become less obscure,* more separate from a petrifying matter, of the gods who have always tortured him; when a whole area of the earth develops a philosophy parallel to that of its inhabitants; when one knows that the first men utilized a language of signs, and when one finds this language formidably expanded on the rocks—then surely one cannot continue to think that this is a whim, and that this whim signifies nothing.

If the greater part of the Tarahumara race is indigenous, and if, as they claim, they fell out of the sky into the Sierra, one may say that they fell into a *Nature that was already prepared*. And this Nature chose to think like a man. Just as she *evolved* men, she also *evolved* rocks.

This naked man who was being tortured, I saw him nailed to a rock and worked on by forms which the sun made volatile; but by I know not what optical miracle the man up there remained whole, although he was in the same light as they.

Between the mountain and myself I cannot say which was haunted, but in my periplus across the mountain I saw an optical miracle of this kind occur at least once a day.

I may have been born with a tormented body, as much a fake as the immense mountain—but a body whose obsessions are useful: and I noticed in the mountain that it is useful to have *the obsession of counting*. There was not a shadow that I did not count, when I felt it creep around something; and it was often by adding up shadows that I found my way back to strange centers.

I saw in the mountain a naked man leaning out of a large window. His head was nothing but a huge hole, a kind of circular cavity in which the sun and moon appeared by turns, according to the time of day. His right arm was stretched out like a bar but drowned in shadows and bent backward.

You could count his ribs, which numbered seven on each side. In place of the navel glittered a shiny triangle, made of what? I could not possibly say. As if Nature had chosen this piece of the mountain to expose her buried silica.

And although his head was empty, the indentations in the rock all around him gave him a precise expression which the light made more subtle from one hour to the next.

This right arm stretched forward and edged by a ray of light did not indicate an ordinary direction . . . and I was looking for what he was announcing!

It was not quite noon when I came upon this vision; I was on horseback and I was moving quickly. However, I was able to observe that what I was seeing was not sculptured forms but a certain phenomenon of light which was *superimposed* on the relief pattern of the rocks.

This figure was known to the Indians; it seemed to me by its composition and structure to obey the same principle that underlay the whole of this mountain of truncated forms. In the line of the arm there was a village surrounded by a girdle of rocks.

And I saw that the rocks all had the shape of a woman's bosom with two perfectly delineated breasts.

I saw repeated eight times the same rock which projected two shadows on the ground; I saw twice the same animal's head carrying in its jaws its effigy which it devoured; I saw, dominating the village, a kind of enormous phallic tooth with three stones

From A Voyage to the Land of the Tarahumara

at its summit and four holes on its outer face; and I saw, from their beginning, all these shapes pass gradually into reality.

I seemed to read everywhere a story of childbirth in war, a story of genesis and chaos, with all these bodies of gods which were carved out like people; and these truncated statues of human forms. Not one shape which was intact, not one body which did not look as if it had emerged from a recent massacre, not one group in which I was not forced to read the struggle that divided it.

I discovered drowned men, half eaten away by the stone, and on rocks above them, other men who were struggling to keep them down. Elsewhere, an enormous statue of Death held an infant in its hand.

There is in the Cabala a music of Numbers, and this music, which reduces the chaos of the material world to its principles, explains by a kind of awesome mathematics how Nature is ordered and how she directs the birth of the forms that she pulls out of chaos. And everything I saw seemed to correspond to a number. The statues, the forms, the shadows always presented the recurring numbers 3, 4, 7, 8. The broken-off busts of women numbered 8; the phallic tooth, as I said, had three stones and four holes; the forms that became volatile numbered 12, etc. I repeat, if someone says that these forms are natural, I shall not argue; it is their repetition which is not natural. And what is even less natural is that the forms of the landscape are repeated by the Tarahumara in their rites and their dances. And these dances are not the result of chance but obey the same secret mathematics, the same concern for the subtle relations of Numbers which governs the entire Sierra region.

This inhabited Sierra, this Sierra which exhales a metaphysical thinking in its rocks, the Tarahumara have covered with signs, signs that are completely conscious, intelligent, and purposeful.

At every bend in the road one sees trees that have *deliberately* been burned in the shape of a cross, or in the shape of creatures, and often these creatures are double and face each other, as if to manifest the essential *duality* of things; and I have seen this duality reduced to its principle in a sign in the shape ⱈ surrounded by a circle, which I saw branded with a red-hot iron on a tall pine; other trees bore spears, trefoils, or acanthus leaves surrounded by crosses; here and there, in places with steep embankments, narrow passageways between rocks, lines of Egyptian anserated crosses grew into processions; and the doors of the Tarahumara houses displayed the sign of the Mayan world: two facing triangles with their points connected by a bar; and this bar is the Tree of Life which passes through the center of Reality.

As I travel through the mountain, these spears, these crosses, these trefoils, these leafy hearts, these composite crosses, these triangles, these creatures facing each other and opposing each other to mark their eternal conflict, their division, their duality, awaken strange memories in me. I remember suddenly that there were, in History, Sects which inlaid these same signs upon rocks, carved out of jade, beaten into iron, or chiseled. And I begin to think that this symbolism conceals a Science. And I find it strange that the primitive people of the Tarahumara tribe, whose rites and culture are older than the Flood, actually possessed this science well before the appearance of the Legend of the Grail, or the founding of the Sect of the Rosicrucians.

The Peyote Dance

The physical hold was still there. This cataclysm which was my body . . . After twenty-eight days of waiting, I had not yet come back into myself, or I should say, *gone out* into myself. Into myself, into this dislocated assemblage, this piece of damaged geology.

Inert, as earth with its rocks can be—and all those crevices that run in sedimentary layers piled on top of each other. Friable, of course, I was—not in places, but as a whole—from my first moment of contact with this terrible mountain which I am sure had raised barriers against me to prevent me from entering. And since I was up there the supernatural no longer seems to me something so extraordinary that I cannot say that I was, in the literal sense of the word, *bewitched*.

To take a step was for me no longer to take a step; but to feel

From *A Voyage to the Land of the Tarahumara*

where I was carrying my head. Can you understand this? Limbs which obey one after the other, and which one moves forward one after the other; and the vertical position above the earth which must be maintained. For the head, overflowing with waves, the head which can no longer control its whirling, the head feels all the whirling energies of the earth below, which bewilder it and keep it from remaining erect.

Twenty-eight days of this heavy captivity, this ill-assembled heap of organs which I was and which I had the impression of witnessing like a vast landscape of ice on the point of breaking up.

The hold was therefore upon me, so terrible that to go from the house of the Indian to a tree located a few steps away required more than courage, required summoning the reserve forces of a truly *desperate* will. For to have come this far, to find myself at last on the threshold of an encounter and of this place from which I expected so many revelations, and to feel so lost, so abandoned, so deposed. Had I ever known joy, had there ever in the world been a sensation which was not one of anguish or of irremissible despair; had I ever been in a state other than that interstitial pain which every night pursued me? Was there anything for me which was not at the gate of death, and could there be found at least one body, a single human body which escaped my perpetual crucifixion?

It required, of course, an act of the will for me to believe that something was going to happen. And all this, for what? For a dance, for a rite of lost Indians who no longer even know who they are or where they come from and who, when you question them, answer with tales whose connection and secret they have lost.

After an exhaustion so cruel, I repeat, that I can no longer believe that I was not in fact bewitched, that these barriers of disintegration and cataclysms that I had felt rising in me were not the result of an intelligent and organized premeditation, I had reached one of the last places in the world where the dance of healing by Peyote still exists, or at least the place where it was invented. And what was it then, what false presentiment, what illusory and artificial intuition caused me to expect some sort of liberation for my body and also and above all a force, an illumination throughout the reaches of my inner landscape, which I felt at that precise minute to be beyond any kind of dimensions?

Twenty-eight days since this inexplicable torment had begun. And twelve days since I had come to this isolated corner of the earth, this tiny compartment in the vast mountain, waiting on the good will of my sorcerers.

Why was it that each time, as at this moment, I felt myself touching on a vitally important phase of my existence, I did not come to it with a whole organism? Why this terrible sensation of loss, of a void to be filled, of an event that miscarries? To be sure, I would see the sorcerers carry out their rite; but in what way would this rite profit me? I would see them. I would be rewarded for this long patience which nothing until then had been able to discourage. Nothing: neither the terrible road, nor the voyage with a body which was intelligent but dissonant and which had to be dragged, which had to be almost killed to prevent it from revolting; nor nature with her sudden storms which surround us with their nets of thunder; nor that long night filled with spasms in which I had seen a young Indian scratch himself in a dream with a kind of hostile frenzy in exactly the places where these spasms seized me—and he said, he who scarcely knew me from the day before, "Ah, let him suffer all the evil that may befall him."

Peyote, as I knew, was not made for Whites. It was necessary at all costs to prevent me from obtaining a cure by this rite which was created to act on the very nature of the spirits. And a White, for these Red men, is one whom the spirits have abandoned. If it was I who benefited from the rite, it meant so much lost for themselves, with their intelligent sheathing of spirit.

So much lost for the spirits. So many spirits that could not be utilized again.

And then there is the matter of *Tesguino*, that alcohol which requires eight days of fermentation in the jars—and there aren't that many jars or that many arms ready to grind the corn.

Once the alcohol has been drunk, the sorcerers of Peyote become useless and a whole new preparation becomes necessary. But a man of these tribes had died when I arrived at the village, and it was necessary that the rite, the priests, the alcohol, the

From *A Voyage to the Land of the Tarahumara*

crosses, the mirrors, the rasps, the jars, and all that extraordinary paraphernalia of the Peyote dance be requisitioned for the benefit of the man who had died.

For now that he was dead his double could not wait for these evil spirits to be neutralized.

And after twenty-eight days of waiting, I now had to endure, throughout one long week, an incredible comedy. All over the mountain there was a hysterical coming and going of messengers who were presumably being sent to the sorcerers. But after the messengers had left, the sorcerers would arrive in person, amazed that nothing was ready. And I discovered that I had been tricked.

They brought me priests who heal with dreams, and who speak after they have dreamed.

—"Those of *Ciguri* [Peyote dance] not good," they said. "They do not *work*. Take these." And they pushed toward me some old men who suddenly broke in two, clicking their amulets strangely under their robes. And I saw that these were not sorcerers but magicians. And I learned, moreover, that these false priests were intimate friends of death.

One day this commotion died down without protests, without arguments, without fresh promises on my part. As if all this had been part of the rite and as if the performance had lasted long enough.

I had not come to the heart of the mountain of these Tarahumara Indians to look for memories of painting. I had suffered enough, it seems to me, to be rewarded with a little reality.

However, as the daylight faded, a vision confronted my eyes.

I saw before me the Nativity of Hieronymus Bosch, with everything in order and oriented in space, the old porch with its collapsing boards in front of the stable, the flame of the Infant King glowing to the left amid the animals, the scattered farms, and the shepherds; and in the foreground other animals bleating, and to the right the dancer kings. The kings, with their crowns of mirrors on their heads and their rectangular purple cloaks on their backs, to my right in the painting, like the Magi of Hieronymus Bosch. And suddenly as I turned around, doubting to the last minute that I would ever see my sorcerers arrive, I saw them coming down the mountain leaning on huge staffs, their women carrying huge baskets, the servants armed with bundles of crosses like firewood, and mirrors that glittered like segments of sky amid all this apparatus of crosses, pikes, shovels, and tree trunks stripped of their branches. And all these people were bent under the weight of this extraordinary apparatus, and the wives of the sorcerers, like their men, were also leaning on huge staffs a head taller than they were.

Wood fires rose on all sides toward the sky. Below, the dances had already begun; and at the sight of this beauty at last realized, this beauty of glowing imaginations, like voices in an illuminated dungeon, I felt that my effort had not been in vain.

Above, on the slopes of the enormous mountain which descended toward the village in tiers, a circle had been drawn on the ground. Already the women, kneeling in front of their *metates* (stone basins), were grinding the Peyote with a kind of scrupulous violence. The priests began to trample the circle. They trampled it carefully and in all directions; and in the middle of the circle they kindled a fire that the wind from above sucked up in whorls.

During the day two young goats had been killed. And now I saw, on a branchless tree trunk that had also been carved in the shape of a cross, the lungs and hearts of the animals trembling in the night wind.

Another tree trunk had been placed near the first, and the fire that had been lighted in the middle of the circle drew from it at every moment innumerable flashes of light, something like a fire seen through a pile of thick glasses. When I approached in order to discern the nature of this burning center, I perceived an incredible network of tiny bells, some of silver, others of horn, attached to leather straps which were also awaiting the moment for their ritual use.

On the side where the sun rises they drove into the ground ten crosses of unequal height but arranged in a symmetrical pattern; and to each cross they attached a mirror.

Twenty-eight days of this horrible waiting after the dangerous withdrawal were now culminating in a circle peopled with Beings, here represented by ten crosses.

Ten, of the Number of ten, like the Invisible Masters of Peyote, in the Sierra.

And among these ten: the Male Principle of Nature, which the Indians call *San Ignacio,* and its female, *San Nicolás!*

Around this circle is a zone of moral abandonment in which no Indian would venture: it is told that birds who stray into this circle fall, and that pregnant women feel their embryos rot inside them.

There is a history of the world in the circle of this dance, compressed between two suns, the one that sets and the one that rises. And it is when the sun sets that the sorcerers enter the circle, and that the dancer with the six hundred bells (three hundred of horn and three hundred of silver) utters his coyote's howl in the forest.

The dancer enters and leaves, and yet he does not leave the circle. He moves forward deliberately into evil. He immerses himself in it with a kind of terrible courage, in a rhythm which above the Dance seems to depict the Illness. And one seems to see him alternately emerging and disappearing in a movement which evokes one knows not what obscure tantalizations. He enters and leaves: "leaves the daylight, in the first chapter," as is said of Man's Double in the *Egyptian Book of the Dead.* For this advance into the illness is a voyage, a *descent in order to* RE-EMERGE INTO THE DAYLIGHT.—He turns in a circle in the direction of the wings of the Swastika, always from right to left, and from the top.

He leaps with his army of bells, like an agglomeration of dazed bees caked together in a crackling and tempestuous disorder.

Ten crosses in the circle and *ten* mirrors. *One* beam with *three* sorcerers on it. *Four* priests (*two* Males and *two* Females). The epileptic dancer, and *myself,* for whom the rite was being performed.

At the foot of each sorcerer, *one* hole, at the foot of which the Male and Female principles in Nature, represented by the hermaphroditic roots of the Peyote plant (Peyote, we know, has the shape of the male and female sexual organs combined), lie dormant in Matter, that is, in the Concrete.

And the hole, with a wooden or earthen basin inverted over it, represents rather well the Globe of the World. On the basin, the sorcerers grate the mixture or the dislocation of the two principles, and they grate them in the Abstract, that is, in Principle. Whereas below, these two Principles, incarnated, repose in Matter, that is, in the Concrete.

And all night long the sorcerers reestablish the lost relationships with triangular gestures that strangely cut off the spatial perspective.

Between the *two* suns, *twelve* tempos in *twelve* phases. And the circular movement of everything that swarms around the fire, within the sacred limits of the circle: the dancer, the rasps, the sorcerers.

After each phase, the sorcerers were eager to perform the physical proof of the rite, to demonstrate the effectiveness of the operation. Hieratic, ritual, sacerdotal, there they stand, lined up on their beam, rocking their rasps, like babies. From what idea of a lost formality do they derive the sense of these bows, these nods, this circular movement in which they count their steps, cross themselves in front of the fire, salute one another, and leave?

So they get up, perform the bows I have mentioned, some like men on crutches, others like sawed-off robots. They step outside the circle. But once they have left the circle, before they are a yard outside it, these priests who walk between two suns have suddenly become men again, that is, abject organisms who must be cleansed, whom this rite is designed to cleanse. They behave like well-diggers, these priests, some kind of night laborers created to piss and to relieve themselves. They piss, fart, and relieve themselves with terrible thunderous noises; and to hear them one would think that they had set out to level the real thunder, to reduce it to *their need* for abasement.

Of the three sorcerers who were there, two, the two smallest and shortest, had had the right to handle the rasp for three years (for the right to handle the rasp is acquired, and in fact this right determines the nobility of the caste of the Peyote sorcerers among the Tarahumara Indians); and the third had had the right for ten years. And I must admit that it was the one most experienced in the rite who pissed the best and who farted the loudest and most expressively.

And a few moments later the same man, with the pride of this manner of crude purgation, began to spit. He spat after drinking

From *A Voyage to the Land of the Tarahumara*

the Peyote, as we all did. For after the twelve phases of the dance had been performed, and since dawn was about to break, we were passed the ground Peyote, which was like a kind of muddy gruel; and in front of each of us a new hole was dug to receive the spit from our mouths, which contact with the Peyote had henceforth made sacred.

"Spit," the dancer told me, "but as deep in the ground as possible, for no particle of *Ciguri* must ever emerge again."

And it was the sorcerer who had grown old in the harness who spat most abundantly and with the largest and most compact gobs. And the other sorcerers and the dancer, gathered in a circle around the hole, had come to admire him.

After I had spat, I fell to the ground, overcome with drowsiness. The dancer in front of me passed back and forth endlessly, turning and crying *unnecessarily*, because he had discovered that his cry pleased me.

"Get up, man, get up," he shouted each time he passed me, with diminishing effect.

Aroused and staggering, I was led toward the crosses for the final cure, in which the sorcerers shake the rasp on the very head of the patient.

Thus I took part in the rite of water, the rite of the blows on the skull, the rite of that kind of mutual cure which the participants give each other, the rite of immoderate ablutions.

They uttered strange words over my head while sprinkling me with water; then they sprinkled each other nervously, for the mixture of corn liquor and Peyote was beginning to make them wild.

And it was with these final movements that the Peyote dance ended.

The Peyote dance is contained in a rasp, in this wood steeped in time which has absorbed the secret salts of the earth. In this wand that is held out and withdrawn lies the curative power of this rite, which is so remote and which must be hunted down like a beast in the forest.

There is an out-of-the-way spot in the high Mexican Sierra where these rasps seemingly abound. They sleep there, waiting for the Predestined Man to discover them and bring them *into the light of day*.

When a Tarahumara sorcerer dies, he takes leave of his rasp with infinitely more sorrow than he feels in leaving his body; and his descendants and intimates take the rasp away and bury it in this sacred corner of the forest.

When a Tarahumara Indian believes that he is called upon to handle the rasp and distribute the cure, he goes to spend a week in the forest at Easter time every year for three years.

It is there, they say, that the Invisible Master of Peyote speaks to him with his nine advisers, and that he passes the secret on to him. And he emerges with the rasp properly macerated.

Carved out of the wood of a tree that grew in warm soil, gray as iron ore, it carries notches on its length and signs at its two extremities, four triangles with one point for the Male Principle and two points for the Female of Nature, made divine.

One notch for every year the sorcerer was alive after he had acquired the right to handle the rasp and had become a master capable of performing those acts of exorcism which pull the Elements apart.

And this is precisely the aspect of this mysterious tradition which I did not succeed in penetrating. For the Peyote sorcerers seem truly to have gained something at the end of their three years' retreat in the forest.

There is a mystery here which the Tarahumara sorcerers have until now jealously guarded. Of what they have acquired in addition, what they have *recovered,* if you will, no Tarahumara Indian who is not a member of the aristocracy of the sect seems to have the slightest idea. And as for the sorcerers themselves, on this point they are resolutely silent.

What is the singular word, the lost word which the Master of Peyote communicates to them? And why does it take the Tarahumara sorcerers three years to be able to handle the rasp, with which, it must be admitted, they perform some very curious *auscultations?*

What is it, then, which they have wrested from the forest, and which the forest *yields to them so slowly?*

In short, what has been communicated to them which is not contained in the external apparatus of the rite, and which neither the piercing cries of the dancer, nor his dance, which goes back and forth like a kind of epileptic pendulum, nor the circle, nor the fire in the middle of the circle, nor the crosses with their mirrors in which the distorted heads of the sorcerers alternately swell and disappear into the flames of the fire, nor the night wind that speaks and blows on the mirrors, nor the chant of the sorcerers rocking their rasps, that astonishingly vulnerable and intimate chant, can succeed in explaining?

They had laid me on the ground at the foot of that enormous beam on which the three sorcerers were sitting during the dances.

On the ground, so that the rite would fall on me, so that the fire, the chants, the cries, the dance, and the night itself, like a living, human vault, would turn over me. There was this rolling vault, this physical arrangement of cries, tones, steps, chants. But above everything, beyond everything, the impression that kept recurring that behind all this, greater than all this and beyond it, there was concealed something else: *the Principal.*

I did not renounce as a group those dangerous dissociations which Peyote seems to provoke and which I had pursued for twenty years by other means; I did not mount my horse with a body pulled out of itself, which the withdrawal, to which I had abandoned myself, deprived henceforth of its essential reflexes; I was not that man of stone whom it required two men to turn into a man on horseback: and who was mounted on and dismounted from the horse like a broken robot—and once I was on the horse, they placed my hands on the reins, and they also had to close my fingers around the reins, for left to myself it was only too clear that I had lost the use of them; I had not conquered by force of mind that invincible organic hostility in which it was *I* who no longer wanted to function, only to bring back a collection of outworn imageries from which the Age, true to its own system, would at most derive ideas for advertisements and models for clothing designers. It was now necessary that what lay hidden behind this heavy grinding which reduces dawn to darkness, that this thing be pulled out, and that it *serve,* that it serve precisely by *my crucifixion.*

To this I knew that my physical destiny was irrevocably bound. I was ready for all the burns, and I awaited the first fruits of the fire in view of a conflagration that would soon be generalized.

Letters from 1937

XXVIII

TO CÉCILE SCHRAMME

[Paris, February 7, 1937]

I was expecting to hear from you and I haven't.

And yet we have reached a degree of openness and simplicity where you can feel completely free and relaxed with me, and can write me anything at all with the certainty that it will touch me.

Anita tells me that you expressed a desire for fresh air and rest.

And of course Brussels is not the right place for that.

I aspire to unite myself with you, as you know. But I cannot do this as long as I am not sure of my destiny. I wrote you at some length because I sensed that you had need of help and consolation, and to show you that the solution to my own situation was now close at hand.

For I too need to rest and recover, and it would have been vital to my whole future and my career if I could have done so for these past three months that I have been hoping to without success.

In any case, the circumstances justify neither your concern nor the hesitations which I thought I noticed the morning of your departure and which were so painful for me. If I insisted that you go away it was because I felt that you needed to be alone, I mean without me, but not without the thought of me.

Antonin Artaud

TO CÉCILE SCHRAMME

[Paris, February 19, 1937]

I love you
because you have revealed human happiness to me.

Antonin Artaud

ANTONIN ARTAUD

TO CÉCILE SCHRAMME

[Sceaux, April 16, 1937]

We must face the truth.

My state is very much given over to struggle, to those kinds of unexpected battles which sometimes put us in opposition to each other: but this, unfortunately, is not all.

In these oppositions there is yourself. You simply must make up your mind to *recognize* something that threatens to make all understanding between us absolutely impossible. I write to you like this because this time I am determined to reach a solution one way or the other.

Cécile: you are a Double Being. And you cannot bring yourself to admit it. I have given you the opportunity more than once by telling you what I knew about the dark parts of your nature, those parts that one conceals from oneself, thinking that others can never touch them. Like all human beings, you are a mixture of the worst and the best, but in you this mixture is formidable because you are a lucid and intelligent being; the best is therefore extraordinary, and the worst, which partakes of an animal instinct common to a very large number of women, is no worse than in other women, *but it is more concealed.*

You have, therefore, lacked confidence in me, you have thought you could conceal from me these animal parts of your nature, believing that I would not be able to accept them because I would not be able to understand them. You have believed my love for you sufficiently selfish not to take you as you are, and to help you find your way out of things, weaknesses, passing and regrettable compromises which reduced you to despair when I reproached you for them.

The result has been that your dissimulation has poisoned our mutual understanding, where a few words from you spoken in all honesty would have cleared everything up in a moment. And it so happens that you have lied to me all along, and that you have been sufficiently oblivious to reproach me for not trusting you at the very moment when you were betraying that trust.

The result has also been that out of love for you, and because this love is very strong and very great, I have pretended to believe you, to accept explanations which my whole being honestly and sincerely rejected. In your presence I have accused my imagination, my madness, in order to put your mind at rest, when I knew that my own mind would never be at rest. And where we would have been able to reach an agreement in candor and understanding, you have provoked a state of uneasiness, obsession, and mistrust which has been all the more profound because it was not you whom I mistrusted but the repressed demon, the enemy who is not ourselves but who sometimes dominates us.

All this is to say that NOTHING inadmissible that you have managed to do has ever escaped me, and that if I have not *seen* the act, I have always noted its after-effect. And I *know* now that I have never been mistaken. Not only have you lacked confidence in my love, but you have underestimated my spirit, my sensibility, my intuition. You are not, after all, the first woman I have ever met, and it would be the first time that I imagined something that is not so. Everything I reproached you for was always justified, and if I have had occasion to reproach you incessantly it is because the struggle in you is incessant and because the evil is always mixed with good.

I shall spare you the details of your betrayals, small or great, because I do not want to argue any more, either. In any case, it is no longer possible for me to live with someone who hides from me and who denies it. And this is what I wanted to say.

You are not responsible for the nature you were born with. You want fidelity in love, and you have an ideal of love which you know satisfies the best of what you dream; unfortunately, instinct is also there to destroy your resolutions. But these resolutions represent a being toward whom you aspire within yourself and *whom you have a whole lifetime to reach*. This will not happen in a day, a month, or a year. It is up to me to help you.

I cannot help you unless you always tell the truth. And unless you do not try to conceal from me the bad sides of your nature, from the sexual and erotic point of view as well as from the point of view of moods and emotions.

You recognize yourself that you are not an angel, so why deny it when I point it out to you? I repeat, all women behave the same way when they deceive, counting on their influence to stop the mouth of the man they betray, not one of them ever imagines that the man they have to do with is not like the others, and that to keep him they would have to act otherwise.

You are an intelligent being, but you do not know *"Eternal Life."* That is to say that so far you have only a limited idea of what a human being is. And you have never had to do with someone who really sees, and whom nothing escapes. You do not know how much even in this world a spirit can grow and transform, and that life which never stops permits an eternal evolution starting at any moment. The truth is that you doubt everything at every minute—love, me, life, the infinite passion and resources of the Will and of the human consciousness.

You think you know me and you fear monotony, you are astonished that you have loved me for three months, you are trying to give me an image of yourself which *is not real* and which if you succeeded would be too perfect to be true, since you have denied everything that was imperfect.

I have confidence in your idea of absolute love and in your desire to reach it, not in your behavior, *which is weak and abandoned to the animal.*

There are terrible things in you, and the only way we can get along with each other and I can have peace is for you to recognize what is bad, what is out of focus, and what contradicts everything we owe each other.

I shall pass over the bad in behalf of the extraordinary quality that is in you and the struggle which you incessantly wage. If your pride is too strong to admit what you thrust into the darkness of yourself and later forget, so much the worse for you. As for me, I have confidence in the love of the spirit which is untainted by life.

Antonin Artaud

TO CÉCILE SCHRAMME

This Friday [April 30, 1937]

I am terribly unjust with you at times; I know it and suffer from it as much as you, I beg you to believe, for what takes place in me at these moments *has no relation* to my real attitude toward you. And in your PRESENCE the futility of my suffering appears to me with such force that I cannot regard it as real. Something false takes place in me, something inexplicable for which you will never reproach me as much as I reproach myself. In other words, I ACCUSE MYSELF; the best explanation I can find for what is inconceivable to me is the marvelous range and rapidity of your spiritual unfolding. You have become so completely and so quickly like a dream that belongs to me that I have not physically, materially, consciously had the time or the space to accustom myself to it, to lift myself to your moral eminence, which is great although I can conceive it. And I myself must now *complete* my own perfecting.

Antonin Artaud

TO RENÉ ALLENDY

Paris [June 1937]

Dear friend,

I *no longer* know what is normal or supranormal. I know what is: that is all. These distinctions between what one can discuss socially and in front of everyone and what one discusses among one's *selves,* as they say, no longer concern me.

I did not ask you whether Cécile was sick. I told you: she is sick.

Whether I love her or not is my business. If this love has been, it will be. There is no contradiction in my attitude, either apparent, or profound, or concealed.

In this love there is a sense of solidarity, of union and interreaction between beings which makes me believe that I do not have the right to dissociate myself from the fate of this person, not because of what she has done for me, but for a more mysterious reason on which you yourself have enlightened me. For you too sometimes see the truth.

If the truth is occult, it is *exclusively* for occult reasons that I have addressed myself to you.

You have made me *understand* that this creature, *because of her abominations*, was bound to me, and now you talk about putting her out of my mind. I am ready to do this if I can, just as I am ready to change my lungs in order to adopt another rhythm of respiration if that is possible.

Can I do it? This is all I ask you to tell me.

Is it inevitable? Truly? Is it me? Am I thus? For this amounts to saying that I am this creature.

All other discussions, on the social and psychological level, do not concern me. I have accepted the evidence of what you have told me only in the most secret intimacy, which it is my experience that *all* women always betray.

But before all the world I accept the evidence of what I know by clairvoyance *now*. And I shall maintain it to the point of madness before all the world. Because everything disgusts me about the stupendous obscenity of this age. I am told, for example, that Cécile is conducting a real slander campaign among all sorts of well-known people in order to make them believe that I am mad and that I have attacks. In this way, of course . . .

Affectionately yours,
Antonin Artaud

TO ANDRÉ BRETON

Friday, July 30, 1937

My dear friend,

I agree to go on living only because I think and believe that this World with which Life insults me and insults You will die before I do.

Do you know another Man whose indignation against everything that now exists is as constant or as violent and who is as constantly and as desperately in a state of perpetual fulmination?

This anger which consumes me and which I learn every day to put to better use must certainly mean something.

In my anger I am not alone, believe me: there are people

Letters from 1937

around me who speak to me and who command me as they have always spoken to and commanded those who have chosen to separate themselves from this world

and who have made the choice with a whole heart.

To agree to burn as I have burned all my life and as I burn now is also to acquire the power to burn; and I know that I was predestined to burn, this is why I believe I can say that few angers can reach where my anger will be able to rise.

If the moral fire of anger were not capable of being identified with all forms of Fire, visible or invisible, it would not be worth the trouble of living and for that matter *we would never have been able to live,* for after all, of what else are we made?

Between the anger of a furious mind and the devastating force of all fires, there is in reality no *distance.* But there is something to be found. I have found this something and this is what permits me always to speak with complete assurance.

For my faith is incarnated in *facts.*

I have told you what these facts consisted of

but I do not allow myself to write it, for these facts are my secret.

I shall give you many more details when I see you, and I beg you *not to tell anyone,* if anyone should ask you, who wrote the pamphlet that was sent to you.

You will in any case have noticed that there are 3 dates, apparently inactive,

which form a triangle.

3 being the figure of primary causation, the facts remain in the beginning stage; but starting with the 4th date (July 25, 1937)—for the 4 dates which come afterward represent the square of the perceptible, the world of reality—external events are precipitated, and it is after the 25th of July that the events of the war in China become manifestly more serious, that the disasters involving airplanes (15 dead), trains (25 dead), and burned ships follow each other more quickly.

If I say in the pamphlet that the left is politically doomed, that does not mean that the Right is going to rule, for the Right I have in mind is the Right of Man and not the stupid Reaction. The Right must be swept away *with* the left and *after* having swept away the left, so that the Natural Right, for in Nature it is the Right Hand which generally rules over the left, can come into power.

The Kings who are mentioned are not descendants of Kings humanly crowned, but Kings in Spirit to whom their power of spirit will *restore a material supremacy*. This supremacy can only be manifested by the *real servitude* of everything that heretofore has lied to the Spirit.

I know that everything I say in this letter will appear to be madness and partakes of the Nature of a Dream that the World has been dispossessed of, I know that in the presence of this Dream there will still be people who will say that the apocalypse has long since passed away and that we are in Reality.

But one need only look at the world around one to realize that Reality has already almost exceeded the Dream and that very shortly all the force of the Dream will be swept away by astonishing Realities.

For me, the only hope that remains in this world which my Spirit has already left is to watch the growth of this great Dream which alone nourishes my reality.

I know that I shall not wait any longer than the last date that I have set.

Antonin Artaud

P.S. I want to add that at the time when everything that has been my life for the past 3 months began, I thought particularly of you, I wanted to see you to rediscover everything I had had confidence in before, among the things that are, that make up Reality.

I believed that I would have things to attack, I admit, but to my great astonishment I see that you have reached *the same point as I*.

With this difference, that although you have lost faith in everything there is still one last thing in which you want to believe, whereas my absolute pessimism makes me believe that *everything today must be renounced* to permit the establishment of a world I can believe in.

And so long as I am able to imagine one thing, a single thing that must be saved, I shall destroy it in order to save myself from things, for that which is pure is always elsewhere.

TO ANNE MANSON

[September 8, 1937]

My terrestrial life is what it should be: that is, full of insurmountable difficulties which I surmount. For this is the Law.

But I perceive that you *do not wish to understand me*. And obviously there is nothing to be done. I constitute a wonderful spectacle for you, but you do not enter into the game. You regard my existence as a brilliant speculation, perhaps, but outside of the world; and you believe yourself to be in the World, but you do not notice that the World is cracking beneath your feet and that it is for you that I work, if you understand me. The Truth, my dear Anne, *and you must get this into your head*, is that by this time next year *everything that makes up for you* the life of the world WILL HAVE BLOWN UP, you understand, and that you will not EVEN RECOGNIZE YOURSELF if you go on as you are.

It is You who live in illusion and blindness and not I; I suffer, to be sure, but only a little while longer, for my haggard present life is in process of preparing something that is not a reverie but a Grand Design which the present Era has become too stupid to understand and this is why in a few months there will be nothing left of it:

A prophecy written and published 14 centuries ago, which I VERIFIED point by point and *in terms of* EVENTS for several months, foretells a future of terror for the World.

This future is at hand.

A large part of Paris will soon go up in flames. Neither earthquake, nor plague, nor rioting, nor shooting in the streets will be spared this city and this country. This is just as sure as it is sure that I was born on September 4, 1896, at 8 o'clock in the morning in Marseilles, and that you have no scruples about making deals with disgusting periodicals to write articles on disgusting subjects. In so doing, you do not cease to compromise a wonderful light which is in you and which constitutes your grandeur, but it is a grandeur that is eclipsed and a light under a bushel.

I am writing you this way because *I want* to have a high idea of you. You think too much about your personal life and not enough about the other, *which concerns you personally even more*, but this I am afraid you can understand only through the catastrophe, like the others. And it is heartbreaking. One does not complain about tennis, fishing, family, the heat, or not being in Mexico when all one has been able to derive from Mexico is an egotistical and terribly individualized pleasure, and when modern life consists of nothing but homeless starvelings, madmen, maniacs, imbeciles, and hopeless cases through the errors of modern life.

What the Spanish Anarchists are doing is quite unprecedented, but it is a human aberration. These ration cards for love and bread are the consecration of an *inhuman* disorder.

For what men today call *human* is the castration of the superhuman part of man.

It is an error in the absolute.

The Spanish Anarchists are trying *malefically* to fix the absolute of terrestrial life. It is a lie and it is a base idea. *It is not a force of love*, this idea. For what does the anarchist want? To secure the *ownership of his self* in this world.

Anarchists are disgusting proprietors and pleasure-seeking egoists.

They deserve only to be massacred. They will be. For when one encounters the Lie—! One does not argue with all the incarnations of the Lie. One destroys them to bring Man back to the Truth, and to Love, that is, to the Love of Truth!

All the same, you have strange foresight where I am concerned!

Antonin Artaud

I am leaving Galway
but write anyway
in care of General Delivery
in *Galway,*

it will be forwarded.

Give my address to *Nobody* in Paris. This is very important!

TO ANDRÉ BRETON

September 14, 1937

My dear Breton, My Friend,

It would be a great sorrow to me, the greatest no doubt among the only sorrows that I still can feel, if you were to detach yourself from me, if you were not to follow me in my new and *final* attitude. The sorrow would not be for my own sake but *for your sake*, and for the wrong—this time *irremediable*—that you would be doing yourself!

I have abandoned a great many things in the course of an abominable existence, and in the end I have abandoned everything, including the very idea of Existence. And it was in seeking NONEXISTENCE that I rediscovered the meaning of God. If I speak of God, then, it is not in order to live but in order to die.

God did not create us as Men, but it was Men who created God and polluted the escape *from* man, that is, from *the state of greatest suffering*. It is Men who are responsible for suffering and not God.

It is the state of man which *proportionately* defiles, pollutes, diminishes, and makes ridiculous the now anachronistic force of God.

This force has not made men in the sense in which Men those eternal idiots understand it, but it *became man* ALSO, *as it had to*. In order to manifest the diversity of the possible and the impossible which this force has always pondered.

Now it happens that if this force manifests itself in what the Hindus call the Triad of Brahma, Shiva, and Vishnu, and what we call the Trinity of Father, Son, and Spirit, in reality the Son-Shiva is AGAINST that Creation-Manifestation of the Father which is PRESERVED by the Holy Ghost. For the Son-Shiva is also Force, but it is the Force of Transmutation, therefore of the *destruction* of forms, it is the eternal movement *in* and *through* forms, without ever resting in any, it is therefore the very force of the Absolute. Those who seek the absolute are with the Son against the Father, but ABOVE ALL against the Holy Ghost.

For it is the Holy Ghost, the hideous dove (the Dove YONA, and YONI the vagina), which maintains the duration of life, in the contradictory delights of life.

The Father himself is not the first God, but he is the First Consciousness of the horrible Force of Nature which creates Being and causes the misery of all Beings.

The Force of *Nature* is the Law, and this Law is the *Nature of things,* which in any case makes the Law, whether one accepts it or denies it. And it is We, too, who have made the Law and who are, whether we like it or not, the custodians and accomplices of the Law.

IT IS THUS and THERE IS nothing TO BE DONE ABOUT IT.

To deny it is to deny ourselves. Until one understands this, one cannot understand life and the disorder of life or *remedy* the evil of life.

One cannot rebel against the Law, but one can rebel against the disorder of crime and the consequences of the Law.

But, for this, one must have a Science. To combat the disorder of God there is what would today be called a technique.

It is this technique that the rebellious Son came to reveal to us against his Father and to do this he took the form of christ.

Now the true christ is he who has given me his own staff, his magnetic magic wand, and he has no connection, I beg you to believe, with the christ of Christianity or the christ of Catholicism.

For listen carefully to this.

We are ourselves the force of life, but this force is not eternal, whether or not it is the Breath of God, the En-Sof mentioned in the Cabala, that which breathes is not eternal, and even the Breath of God is only for a time.

So long as this force is living, the Eternal Triad which manifested the Creatures destroys them in order to purify them by the Son-Shiva and then regenerates them by the preserving force of the Holy Ghost-Vishnu.

These forces are in equilibrium for a long time but there comes a time when they destroy each other mutually and come together to die.

Letters from 1937

The moment has come when they must die. And this explains the disorder of the Times.

Yes, my dear Breton, the Time has come, as announced by the apocalypse, when christ to punish his Church will raise up a Furious One who *will overthrow* ALL Churches and send the rite of the Initiates back under the ground.

The present Pope will be condemned to death by this Furious One, to whom the real christ speaks, and he speaks to him daily.

This christ, Jesus-christ, was a man like You and me. And he laughs a sinister laugh, I swear it, at the monstrosities that are called His Name and at the Images that are called his images. He laughs at religion and at the *external* apparatus of all religions as much as you can laugh at them, for this Man in whom the second Time, the Son Shiva of the Eternal Manifestation, was Incarnated, was a formidable Initiate, and the Men who came after him were a mere caricature of him. He was the negative force of Nature, the one that saw the evil of living and summoned the Good of Dying. And he chose to pass through a body in order to teach us to destroy bodies, and to put away attachment to bodies.

It is the Holy Ghost which protects bodies and makes us believe in the fact of living, it is the Holy Ghost which denies the Absolute. It is the Son who brings us back to the absolute. Vishnu the Holy Ghost once took the form of Krishna in India, this is why the Hindus of the Vedas say that they too possess the Incarnation of a God: but it was not the same God.

I repeat, so long as the force of manifestation is living, Brahma, Shiva, Vishnu are in equilibrium and the World lives its golden age, but there comes a time when this force of life must die. That time has come, and the Time has come when the Son and the Holy Ghost will enter into conflict and destroy each other to permit the disappearance of what is.

For if the Son Shiva the christ is going to raise up a Furious One to tear down his ridiculous Church, the Holy Ghost-Vishnu-Krishna will raise up the antichrist. Yes, it is the Holy Ghost itself which will raise up the antichrist. Incredible as that may seem.

Now just as the Furious One exists today, the antichrist exists too, and you yourself, Breton, know him. For, André Breton, this is what must be understood, it is that the *Incredible*, yes, the Incredible is the Incredible which is the truth.

He who will become the antichrist, you know him, you have shaken his hand, he is younger than me, and he loves Life as much as I hate it.

For ludicrous as this idea may seem to you, the antichrist frequents the Deux Magots. And another figure of the apocalypse has also been seen at the Deux Magots.

This is so and I swear to you that I am not joking. And that *there*, where I am now, I hardly have any desire to joke.

Jesus-christ this human personage came to establish on a spiritual level a rite of the disappearance of things, on the same principle as the Human sacrifices. Only idiots would take the point of all this to be killing, murder, or Suicide. The point, since we are alive, is to live by denying life, to look at things from the place where they rise and not from the place where they lie flat on the ground, to look at them from the place where they are going to disappear and not from the place where they are established in reality. For in the true doctrine of christ, the Holy Ghost is the established Bourgeois and christ is the eternal Revolutionary. The 2nd force of God Shiva is the revolutionary force, the 3rd force of God Vishnu is conservative.

Choose!

The rite inaugurated by christ is a rite of High revolutionary Magic out of which the priest-Men, those Eternal established Bourgeois, have made the Mass which produces Nausea.

In this rite Man, by eating the flesh of a Man who *chose* to sacrifice his own life, eats his own disappearance and affirms his contempt for the duration of things, for *their bodily structure*, and for their effigies.

If this rite is not transcendent in its immediate and real manifestation, *it does not exist*.

This rite is essential theater, and even in the secret temples of India, Brahmanism, which has no rites, has rites of essential theater.

For even in order to affirm that we do not want to Be, we need the help of beings, that is, of the created. We must touch the denied objects to invite them to destroy themselves along with us. The rite of christ takes the elements of a world denied and invites

Letters from 1937

them to disappear, but only after *inviting* them *to study each other well.*

One denies well only in the concrete.

I shall therefore call Black Magicians those who deny God the better to destroy him and who rise up against the Force of God which has forced them to exist. And I shall say to them: your Hate is justified, too, but it is misdirected.—You have a way of avenging yourselves on God, that God who forced you to live and who created the evil of existing.

It is with the brains of Men that you have risen up against God, but Man can do nothing against God, only God himself can do anything against God. The God who forces you to live is the 3rd force of God, whom the Hindus call Vishnu and the Christians the Holy Ghost. Think God with a brain of God, rise up against the Holy Ghost, the Son-Shiva—the christ is with you against the Holy Ghost.—Now the times of the Holy Ghost are numbered, for we are at the end of the world. The 3 forces of God which were in equilibrium are going to destroy each other, and in order to do this they will make war on each other and devour each other.

It will be war, all this will be the war of the Son against the Holy Ghost and the war of the christ against the antichrist. With these two primordial forces of Nature entering into conflict, it is not difficult to understand the importance of the conflict and the terrible stake involved, but above all the formidable Power of the antichrist supported by the Holy Ghost. But since the force of life is exhausted, the antichrist, who represents life and attachment to the forms of life, will be destroyed, not without destroying himself and causing the destruction of many things and many people. And there will be woe when a Life falls manifestly into corruption, woe for those who would go over to the side of the antichrist who will defend life and the enjoyment of living against the Furious One who will invite us to stop living and to feel that it is better to die.—Because it is more intelligent to follow the course of things than to rise up against it.

If you believe me I am entrusted to tell you that a formidable power will be placed at your service and at the service of everything you have ever dreamed that is beautiful, just, formidable, *incredible,* and desperate.

If you do not believe me I will have to find another just man.

But you are the most just Man whom I have so far encountered.

I embrace you.

Art.

From *The New Revelations of Being* (1937)

XXIX

I TELL WHAT I HAVE SEEN and what I believe; and whoever shall say that I have not seen what I have seen, I now tear off his head.

For I am an unpardonable Brute, and it will be thus until Time is no longer Time.

Neither Heaven nor Hell, if they exist, can do anything against this brutality which they have imposed on me, perhaps so that I may serve them . . . Who knows?

In any case, in order to lacerate me.

What exists, I see with certainty. What does not exist, I shall create, if I must.

For a long time I have felt the Void, but I have refused to throw myself into the Void.

I have been as cowardly as all that I see.

When I believed that I was denying this world, I know now that I was denying the Void.

For I know that this world does not exist and I know *how* it does not exist.

What I have suffered from until now is having denied the Void.

The Void which was already within me.

I know that someone wanted to enlighten me by means of the Void and that I refused to let myself be enlightened.

If I was turned into a funeral pyre, it was in order to cure me of being in the world.

And the world took everything I had.

I struggled to try to exist, to try to accept the forms (all the forms) with which the delirious illusion of being in the world has clothed reality.

I no longer want to be one of the Deluded.

Dead to the world, to what composes the world for everyone else, fallen at last, fallen, risen in this void which I was denying, I have a body which suffers the world and disgorges reality.

I have had enough of this movement of the moon which makes me summon what I deny and deny what I have summoned.

I must end it. I must break at last with this world which a Being in me, that Being which I can no longer call upon, since if it comes I will fall into the Void, which that Being has always denied.

It is done. I have really fallen into the Void since everything—that makes up this world—has just succeeded in making me despair.

For one does not know that one is no longer in the world until one sees that the world has left you.

The others who have died are not separated: they still turn around their dead bodies.

And I have known how the dead turn around their bodies for exactly the thirty-three Centuries that my Double has not stopped turning.

Now, no longer existing myself, I see what exists.

I really identified myself with that Being, that Being which has ceased to exist.

And that Being has revealed everything to me.

I knew it, but I could not say it, and if I can begin to say it, it is because I have left reality.

It is a real Desperate Person who speaks to you and who has not known the happiness of being in the world until now that he has left this world, now that he is absolutely separated from it.

The others who have died are not separated. They still turn around their dead bodies.

I am not dead, but I am separated.

Letters from 1940 (Ville-Evrard)

TO GÉNICA ATHANASIOU

November 10, 1940

We must not wait until next week, Génica, for I do not believe the Bohemians will wait until next week to come and find me here. It is of the utmost urgency that I get away, that I leave this corner of the world and I invite you to come with me. This world is no longer viable, it is completely contaminated. Certain persons are preventing you all by spells and other occult maneuvers from perceiving the terrifying obscenity of the evil which is upon me in order to keep you from leaping to my rescue but it is around you all. It will be overcome, but only provided I am no longer weak and I must have help. For the torment that I endure here, Génica, is UNGODLY.

I beg you in your own interest and in the interest of the inalienable purity of the Good to remain wholly pure and chaste and to remain so forever.

You must believe that the situation is very grave. It has not been so grave since the beginning of the world and the moment of the original fall into Sin. And Evil is only waiting in order to strangle us all, for a moment of weakness or merely of lack of vigilance on the part of the Pure who have defended me in this terrible business of magic and spells which are the magic and the spells of Satan.

You were born, Génica, on the side of God, and the moment is almost at hand when you must rise up in arms against Evil.

I embrace you affectionately.

Antonin Artaud

ANTONIN ARTAUD

TO GÉNICA ATHANASIOU

November 24, 1940

My very dear Génica,
   You must find *heroin* at all costs and you must risk death to get it to me here. This is where matters stand. The Initiates have real instruments of torture, as I have already told you, and they use them from a distance to mutilate me while I sleep, each night a little more. If it is difficult to procure heroin or opium, it is *solely* because of me and because they know that it is the one thing that would restore my strength and make me fit to struggle against Evil. But the most serious aspect of the affair is that all my friends, including you, have rebelled, have taken up arms in Paris, have used force to get *heroin* for me, and that they extracted it from all of you *by magic*, and that they then caused you to lose consciousness of your rebellion and that they have weighed down your shoulders
   your heads
and the backs of your necks with leaden spells in order to enslave you, for it is thus that the common people are avenged and it is the common people who are now in power and who feed on my suffering here. Search your memory and you will see that some part of the use you have made of your time eludes you. Génica, we must leave this world, but first the Kingdom of the Other World must come, and we need armed troops in great number. So that the Bohemians can enter this world in *number* as one disembarks from a ship I must have heroin so that I can open all the hidden doors and destroy the spells of Satan which are keeping them out and keeping me prisoner here.
   I count on you and I embrace you.

Antonin Artaud

Two nights ago you thought you had a dream that brought you to Marseilles, boulevard Perrier, but in reality you were having a vision from Paris of a real scene which was taking place in Marseilles, in which one of the gods of Evil went forth with his

Letters from 1940 (Ville-Evrard)

armies. These armies were cut to pieces by the Bohemians who reappear at night but some of their soldiers were loitering in Saumur, in Toulon, and in Paris in the vicinity of the Vieux-Colombier.

Letters from 1943–45 (Rodez)

XXXI

TO JACQUES LATRÉMOLIÈRE

March 25, 1943

Dear doctor and friend,
    I know that you have been sick and that you have suffered a great deal, not so much from your physical sickness as from another sickness which is a little like the one that torments me here, at any rate it has the same cause, and I can't talk about it in a letter—we'd have to have a long talk away from this place as one man to another and as friends—but this sickness has to do with the scandal of the horrible plot of which I am the victim and which you know about in the privacy of your soul and your conscience; for you have suffered from it horribly yourself. You have seen the hordes of demons which afflict me night and day, you have seen them as clearly as you see me. You have seen what filthy erotic manipulations they are constantly performing on me, and because of this and because of the revolt of your conscience which is that of a true and a great Christian, you have found yourself transported alive and awake into the midst of that occult battle which heaven has been waging against Hell for eternities in order to defend the immaculate empire of God.—But one thing has offended and unsettled your conscience: that God *in time* has not yet put an end to the appalling human depravity of a people, I mean the French people who have now passed over completely to the Antichrist and to Satan and who have kept a man locked up in an Insane Asylum for years for the sole purpose of feeding off of his seminal fluid and his excrement.—God needs all the help that can come from the good will of all just men who want no part of this government of hell.—There are, Dr. Latrémolière, certain elementary things that can be done to put a stop to this horror, this scandal, and this sin, and it is a sin and an impiety not to do them. They are in the hands of Dr. Ferdière and if I cannot obtain them from him or even see him for the past few weeks, it is not by some casual accident of circumstances, believe me, but by the calculated malice of hell. To drive out the evil and the demons one must have good food, nicotine in sufficient quantity, and one must temporarily restore heroin in large doses to an organism that has been vitiated by foul humiliations and damaged in its deepest, most vital sensibility by pain, deprivations, anxieties,

occult traumatisms of all kinds, and by harmful treatments. Without this medication which is bound to the vital energy of the person, my soul will be more and more scandalized by sin.

Antonin Nalpas

TO GASTON FERDIÈRE

March 29, 1943

My very dear friend,

    I am communicating to you in the form of a letter the reflections inspired by Ronsard's *L'Hymne des Daimons*, which you had the good idea of sending me.

    Ronsard practiced Magic and he was initiated and each verse of his poem is a reflection of this transcendental initiation. This initiation is mysterious.

Rat Vahl Vahenechti Kabhan
Krah Bahl Kaherferti Krakban

    I mean that as it presents itself in his poem I felt something which came from God and which cannot be restated by man except insofar as he has not lost communications with God. Every poem is a liberation and it is quite clear that Ronsard wrote this poem only to free himself from the infernal imprint which the Evil Spirit is constantly leaving on all things which are useful to man, and first of all his inner sensibility, the consciousness that he applies to them, and his judgment.

    As soon as one thinks, all is mystery and the more one thinks the more profound the mystery becomes but in this inner withdrawal of the thought to infinity and in infinity God has set the surest landmarks everywhere so that no good thought will be lost and so that man need not be lost in the use of his own thought, but may always draw from it an exalting Act of Faith. I do not know and I do not believe that Ronsard toward the end of his life fell into Averroism which seems to affirm the Eternity of the World, for if the World is eternal it is *like* an idea of God, and eternal like him who in comparison with this idea is a little more than an eternal being. And it is possible that the idea of God may at times have eluded Ronsard as the Manifestation of a precise essence, but it never eluded him as an integral and precise idea of the world which can only be an unusual manifestation of it. For the World and the things in it cannot, Mr. Ferdière, be understood or accepted without God, because when you consider them carefully, they are nothing but mystery and because every mystery in order to exist has need of this infinite extension which is God. Nothing has meaning and what is meaning were there not an Infinite and sublime Producer of the Mystery itself. Of the inexplicable unfathomability of all meaning whose Virtue and whose Essence are the very nature of God.

You received from God—you, as you existed at the beginning of time before the Worlds—a Major Elective Faculty which is the faculty of perceiving and promoting the essential virtues of things by an exhaustive and discriminative movement, the faculty of making them equal to their divine essence, of transporting them and keeping them there by means of that sense of the Infinite which struck you on the forehead and which magnetizes your forehead. And your interest in occult science can be effective, valid in your eyes, and worthy only if it enables you wholly to regain this Power, which can remain effective and complete only if it remains in the service of God, for outside of him it is lost, since to withdraw from him is to deny the Power by denying him.

Ronsard's *L'Hymne des Daimons*, if one reads it carefully, traces the History of the development and evolution of the Power in the spheres, and of all the dangers of the loss of the Power, and of the secret struggle of heaven against the evil allurements of the Power, and of the forms, living for a moment but condemned, which follow one another perpetually but are brought to a standstill at last, as Ronsard says, by the thunderbolts of the Last Judgment.

Daimons are provisional and non-living entities which are animated by imitation and are like the doubles of the true movements and the true orders of the creator in the spheres. For space is indeed peopled with beings, but these beings are all Angels of greater or lesser dimension, and each has a position that is lesser or greater, but each is infinite, absolute, and total in relation to the Eternal.

In the past what philosophers like Plotinus, Iamblichus, Porphyry, or Philo have called daimons is simply the self-animating evolution of an Angel who is learning to exist by loving, and who is animated by loving the soul of all life. For even the doubles of things must find their way back to the soul of their Power and their Movement. God has given Movement and the Soul but each being in its turn must earn the right to exist and in order to exist, to live its own life to the furthest limits set at its beginning and thus to participate in the creation of its soul. In order to understand one's own life one must seek it at the source and thus become one's own creator. But although one can do this only because God has given the Being a little of his own spirit of Life, the being in its turn in order to become a Being must recover the breath of this life, must live it and thus deserve it to infinity, and in so doing, it is its own *Animator*.

And the Animation of every Being is the Angel. His own personal Angel, and every created being has one.

There are Beings who have lost themselves in the Angel as a result of their own love of God, others who have not risen to the sphere of absolute sacrifice of the Angel; the fire of God which consumes itself must spare something from the limit of consummation. For the Angels are a hurricane and for the hurricane to blow there must be trees, air, and earth; there are Beings who need to love and others who need to be Loved. For there is in the Kingdom of God an infinite and inexorable battle of Love between the one who wants to love more than he is loved and the one who, wishing to love but also to be loved, is defeated by the one who wants to love the most. Which means that in the ante-eternal battle of the things the Beings are defeated by God, who is the One who wants to love the most. And the resolution and solution of this battle is the divine spirit of Eternal Pity, which by actions and by grace renders the Beings incapable of loving as much as God.

      Taentur Anta Kamarida
      Amarida Anta Kamentür

And Magic, Dr. Ferdière, is everywhere, but it is authentic and powerful only in the form of this sublime love of the creatures which lives only in the sacred and which is founded on the Evangelical Morality of Jesus Christ which is the absolute sacrifice of the self. I believe that Ronsard who was a Catholic and very Christian had a mission on earth as a poet and this sacred Mission was to translate into a language that speaks to the heart the wealth of the things of the Infinite, which are magical and mysterious in their essence. And as such he was, like all true poets, and more than other men, horribly tormented by demons. He saw them as I see them and he tried to take action to rid himself of them. But here lies the temptation that creeps into all the acts of man, because the demons of Evil which are lustful come to us only by way of the betrayed forces of the atmosphere in which they are whirled and amid which they are mingled with the *daimons*, which are those forces in fermentation and in the act of becoming creatures. This means that the demons are merely false daimons and thus false forces. And the remnant of all these forces in the Void of which they are only the hideous image. And all this is implicitly contained in Ronsard's poem. I believe that the "Samsara" of the Hindu Tradition is the domain of the false forms and the false forces, but it is not a domain and it is even the flight from and the Negation of a domain, and woe be to him who might be tempted to elevate to creatures the forms that he sees there, to believe in them would be to be swallowed by them.

And this, Mr. Ferdière, is exactly what sorcerers have done. Ronsard in his poem, which merely translates the evolution of his soul and his consciousness at the point where magic touches the evolutive forces of the atmosphere and of space, Ronsard completely escaped this danger of mistaking daimons for definitive and arrested, and thus immortal, entities, since he describes them as dissolving and, where they had been neuter and inert, as gradually becoming harmful and mischievous in the manner of the demon. But he did not describe that aspect of the primitive nature of the *daimon* (as it now is, and no longer of the *demon*) which is to regain the substance of the Angel and to reascend to the Angel after numerous ultra-substantial and dis-substantial evolutions which partake of the most secret mystical nature of the consciousness of the mind. There is in Ronsard's poem something volatile and frozen which shows that when he wrote it Ronsard had not lost contact with the meaning of the divine harmony, and this harmony is perceptible in his meter, and in the peculiar scansion of his alexandrines. The World, Mr. Ferdière, is nothing but temptation, but temptation for the mind of the just man is merely the perception of the dissolvent forces of things we have been put in the world to struggle against, that is, to help God win back his domain over the Void. The demons have taken the Void, of which Sin is merely the libidinous form, and God has taken Eternal Life, whose immortality he sublimates. But Ronsard was not tempted for long to struggle as a non-believer and in an areligious spirit with the magical forces of the atmosphere whose malice toward us becomes infernal in proportion as we have not divested ourselves above all of an intoxicated egotism and threatens, but for the warning of heaven, to make us into the slaves—at first involuntary and then little by little convinced and participating—of hell. But the censure of God is there and the warnings of heaven are not lacking. And one cannot be lost except with one's absolute and total consent. And Ronsard received these warnings.

Antonin Nalpas

N.B. There is a book which I have thought about often while writing this letter. It is Ramón Lull's *Livre de l'ami et l'aimé.* For there is one thing I have thought about much, and that is the amazing struggle in each of us which momentarily opposes mind and soul only to merge them and the better to prove to them afterward that they are but a single and identical thing because they both come from a single thing, the Being which is in us and which is us. Since Being, with respect to what it has that is personal and singular, comes from a universal cause which is God. Many Angels have remained Beings for a time and in time before abandoning themselves to the Universal Consummation of God, similarly a time passed before the two united but once opposed fires of mind and soul were given over to the universal consummation of the Being of all Beings in God, resolving first of all this secret and profound opposition which separates the faculties of the self the better to unite them in a common love—and it cannot be the love of God in itself which is expressed by the forgetting of the self—with that respect of one's self which is respect for the Spirit of God in oneself.

A.N.

TO GASTON FERDIÈRE

October 18, 1943

My very dear doctor and friend,

I have taken a great many Surrealist photographs over the years. I took some with Eli Lotar. And even in a studio with electric lights and all the necessary elements, it takes hours of preparation to develop a poetic image, especially an expressive one, out of a group of inanimate objects.—And in the present case to carry out the idea of dressing a cane in cabbage leaves presents numerous technical obstacles; and then there is something that annoys me in this poem, and that is all the subconscious eroticism which it conceals and which it is the duty of all of us to destroy instead of lending it a hand. And for nothing in the world would I want this eroticism to appear in a photograph. The truth is that the consciousness of the child is ignorant of sexuality; when he does perceive it, it is because someone introduces it to him by means of images, bad example, or words. And we incur a grave responsibility when we put the consciousness of the child on that path. A great many songs written for children are similarly based on erotic myths, more or less concealed, and when we encounter one of these it is our duty to destroy it instead of emphasizing it, for actually the erotic perception of things is itself merely a surface covering, and when one probes a little deeper their sexual foundation disappears, for sexuality is only an unfortunate accident in nature, an accident which is largely the work of that god of darkness who is king and master of our unconscious and who is called Chance, but who is neither so innocent nor so irresponsible as everyone believes. What I am telling you here, Dr. Ferdière, is discussed at length in the Cabala. For although I know little about Freud's Psychoanalysis, or Jung's, I have studied the Cabala very closely in the *Zohar* and the *Sefer Yetsirah,* and by their light as well as by that of several early Christian writers I have found an explanation of things which has satisfied me completely.—For like you I have asked myself a great many questions about the nature of everything that exists and I have always found the world very immoral and very unjust and above all very shameful.—You know that many works signed with my name are alas filled with blasphemies, but as I have already told you, behind each blasphemy there was a reservation, for it has always seemed impossible to me that God should be the cause of the world that we see.

I have always felt that there was a Mystery behind all this and it took me 20 years of meditation, sufferings, and ordeals to succeed in understanding this Mystery and to arrive at an idea of things as they present themselves in reality.

When I did understand it I came back, quite simply, to the Religion of my fathers. And since then, as in the past two months, during which I have taken communion three times a week, every erotic thought has left me, and my conscience has found peace.

The Cabala, Dr. Ferdière, has taught me many things about the origins of Evil and the antecedents of reality! And all these things were said by Christ in his brief stay on earth, they were said for him in appropriate language and indeed with some details that are terribly illuminating. But what Jesus Christ said on all these points no longer appears in the texts of the Gospels as we know them, because the truths that Jesus Christ uttered on this subject, although they inflamed human consciousness on Palm Sunday, were no longer admitted five days later, and this is why Jesus Christ was crucified on Holy Friday! Because in this interval of five days all those evil powers that drive our hearts to despair, everything that makes life so ugly and makes it appear to us in its entirety as a receptacle of crimes, of immorality, of disgrace, of egotism, of madness, and of slaughter, all these evil influences changed human consciousness so that it no longer accepted the truth of God. This Truth was, however, collected in full in the true text of the Gospels as they were known by the first Christians. And this is why in the first two or three centuries that followed the death of Christ this Truth preached by the first

Apostles and their immediate successors won over all human hearts. And it was at this time that conversions were innumerable and that Christianity was established. Since then, and in proportion as it has grown away from the Teaching of the Church, the Christian idea has declined in human hearts. In the true Gospel of Christ, and in the *Zohar* which in its original text contains the actual word of the Father, one finds a description of the world as it was before the fall of Adam and one understands the origin of Evil, suffering, injustice, and iniquity and that it is not at all, but absolutely not the fault of God but that of man. And that man has become miserable and rejected only insofar as he has betrayed the original and angelic conception of things, and insofar as he has adopted sexuality.—Jesus Christ did not say, "Increase and multiply." He said, "Increase and multiply as the Angels, for only then shall you attain a Number capable of acting on the heart of God." Each time a sexual act is committed something is tainted in universal existence.

Because the universal unconscious is communal and there is an undeniable interreaction of all human acts. Eroticism is a transaction of darkness and in committing it we make the darkness rise in the light of Life.

In order to find a little Love around me on this earth, Dr. Ferdière, I had to come to Rodez. I have suffered horribly from human wickedness in all the Asylums I have stayed in from 1937 to 1943. Only here have I found friends who have opened their hearts to me.

There is not an employee of this Asylum who does not give me a smile or an affectionate word when he meets me, who is not ready to do anything he can to help me. And one needs this in order to live, Dr. Ferdière, the soul atrophies in an atmosphere of indifference, egotism, or enmity.

You yourself are a great mind and a great heart and I know that you too have gone to the bottom of things and that you have perceived the Truth. This truth is that the Universal Principle of Infinity, which is God and which is a Being, is very pure, very chaste, and very good and that it cannot help us to live if we betray it on any point whatsoever.

The song of Roudoudou is innocent in appearance, but at bottom it is not innocent at all. I think I understand rather well what it means and what it refers to. I also know atavistically where it comes from. I see rather clearly the idea of primitive onanism which is concealed beneath these words, just as the idea of sexual procreation is stated in the song:

> I don't know where it comes from
> it's one of those ancient adages
> it says that since the world began
> babies are born under cabbages.

In the occult tradition one learns that the cabbage is the form that the void assumes to manifest itself to human consciousness. I am not inventing this, I have read it in books on occultism and magic. Now according to these books it would appear that Satan, chance born of nonexistence, may have used this form to create the feminine sexual organ, etc., etc.

Well, Dr. Ferdière, it is the duty of those of us who want no part of Evil to go beyond all these painful and destructive Myths. For further than and beyond all these baneful, degrading, and depressing libidinous images, the esoteric books teach us that the cane is the will of God, and that the woman he summoned before Him is Nature, before all else.

As for the leaves of the cabbage, they represent the Void, that is, nothing at all, since it was with nothing at all that God made everything. But in this Nothing at all he placed figures and Numbers 3–7 with 10—and up to 12, the number of maturity in forms and in the middle he threw the sign of the cross.

I thought about all this while composing this photograph. Unfortunately the objects did not lend themselves to the project and I am not at all satisfied with the result. But I do not see how to do better with these objects.

I am now going to make a second request. That nothing that will appear in this number of the "Méridien" series on Humor will cease at any moment to be *edifying*, that nothing will be found in it which is blasphemous or verges on blasphemy, or which from the point of view of eroticism or sexuality might lure the consciousness into a taste for these things, or which would show that the one who wrote, photographed, painted, or drew chose them in his will or in his heart, for this in all *conscience* would prohibit me from collaborating on the issue.

I tell you all this, Dr. Ferdière, because I know that you cannot wish it.

Because you know all too well that eroticism is at the source of many mental illnesses and because your heart, which sees beyond this accidental and transient symbolism, wants the heart of the child to be pure and not to sink into sin; and I remember reading an article by you in a magazine which did me good, for beyond the sexual thing you had been able to show the exalted and chaste poetic idea which underlies the greatest myths, and by your article you had succeeded in destroying the sexual idea which was trying to cling to them.

And in the article that you are going to write on this song I know that this is what you will do again, because this is what people need most urgently.

With my very profound affection,
Antonin Artaud

TO GHYSLAINE MALAUSSÉNA

January 9, 1944

Yes, my child, as you said Sunday to your mother with so much energy and enthusiasm I am not sick, but I have taken advantage of these six and a half years of confinement to meditate on my sins and my shortcomings and to correct them and get rid of them. As a matter of fact, your mother has known all this deep in her heart for a very long time. But for a very long time all of our hearts have been closed, Ghyslaine, and we can no longer say what we feel and think in the Truth of our consciences, and our Lives are like *borrowed costumes*. However the Medical Director of this Asylum, who is a very intelligent man, invited me to his house for Christmas and said to me, "All this is only a test, Mr. Artaud, a test, but this test will end." And in effect he promised me liberty soon.

—That is why, my child, you must not speak to me of sickness. This is very painful to me. Because it is not true. But there were in my attitude and my behavior toward everyone a great many things to be perfected. I believe that now this has been done. For it was above all a matter of conscience. And the explanation of all my miseries is that until my trip to Ireland I was thinking outside of God. God gave me the strength to look inside myself and to rid myself of Evil, for as you know I returned to him in Dublin. And here at Rodez there is in the asylum a chapel and a Chaplain. I took communion this morning to celebrate Epiphany, and I thought especially of you, Ghyslaine, at the moment of this communion.—And God has given you the strength to find your soul too, for things in this world are heavy and difficult and we do not always know where our soul is or what it wants. And whether it will be able to apply itself to all the tasks of this life. But all we need is a light from Above to illuminate for us its real aspirations and its true capacities. In return, God does not ask much of us, do you know that? One little thought, one little true prayer. And that we do not forget him behind all the burdens of this life; then He intervenes and supports us.

—Tell your mama that I received her package, that I thank her with all my heart, and that I shall write her this week. But I have been in bed for 3 days with a bout of flu and a very high fever and the Chaplain of the Asylum came and served communion to me in bed this morning at my request and as I said above to celebrate Epiphany.

I embrace you, my dear Ghyslaine, with all my great and profound affection.

Nanaqui
Antonin Artaud

P.S. Give Serge a kiss for me. I know that he too has asked for my return.
He will see me again.

Letters from 1943–45 (Rodez)

TO GASTON FERDIÈRE

February 5, 1944

My very dear friend,

I am very happy that you liked my drawings, because it is over twenty years since I have done any drawing and I had never made any attempt at imaginative drawing, and scarcely two weeks ago I did not believe myself capable of expressing my ideas in that manner. And it was at the urgent instigation of F. Delanglade who is a real friend and a *very great* one that I tried my hand at it.

I shall make you a gouache since you like this means of expression. If I was silent for a moment when you mentioned it to me it was not because I did not want to follow your suggestion, on the contrary. It was because not having touched a paintbrush for years I was simply wondering whether I could succeed in creating something that would please you enough . . . But as I have told you and written you several times: I know that with Will one can do anything; and I shall make this effort for you, since you believe in me.

As a result of close confinement, solitude, isolation, I had lapsed into a stupor and I shall never tire of telling you the astonishing good that you and F. Delanglade have done me in showing your faith in and admiration for my writing and my work.

You have not only helped me to live, you have *invited* me *to live* when I was atrophying.

Yes, I must move around, go out, see people and things. It is not good to remain perpetually staring at oneself, living in one's mind, as I did for six years because I no longer had friends around me.—That was an excellent idea that F. Delanglade had of taking me out twice with him in Rodez. In my present state, what will do me the most good is to reestablish contact with the things my confinement has made me forget.

When one is shut up, one ends by imagining that the outside world does not exist. And consciousness is affected by this. It eventually loses the sense of the concrete, the objective, and consequently of the true, and runs the risk of dwelling thoughtlessly on false images, false impressions. And, in time, of believing them. For in us false beliefs are merely the immoderate enlargement and distortion of accurate feelings and perceptions which have taken on a disproportionate value because consciousness has wrongly dwelled on them too long.

It was the confinement and the harmful treatments I underwent at the beginning which put me in that condition of a hunted animal that I was in when I arrived here. And the idea of my Return to Life will always be connected with the idea of the Good you have done me.

Antonin Artaud

TO EUPHRASIE ARTAUD

[June 22, 1944]

My very dear Mama,

I received your letter of June 6 and I thank you for your holiday wishes.—Yesterday, June 21, I received a letter from Marie-Ange and she is also sending me a little money, but I have not felt the lack of it. Besides, I do not need much here. I have a pass which allows me to go anywhere I wish in the town of Rodez and most notably I have been to the cathedral, a wonder of the Middle Ages in which it is a great pleasure to pray and to which I made a special visit on the occasion of Holy Week.—I prayed for my whole family: you first, of course, then Marie-Ange, her children, and Fernand.—I do not know when we shall see each other again but it is about time life became a little more convenient for all of us and that we did not have to be separated by circumstances. Above all it is about time life was kinder to all of us: for too many years now it has been almost impossible for all of us, and GOD cannot like this. As for myself, I have been outside of the world for 7 years, since 1937, and I cannot see when it will be over, but the whole world is suffering: I am confined but everyone all over the earth lacks something: food or something else. God will provide! I knew that you had been exhausted and I prayed for your recovery. We shall all see better days. There are a few people here among the personnel at the Asylum who are very kind to me. This helps me to keep from despairing too much, for it has been too many years that I have been deprived of too many things, but God will provide and they will come back.

I embrace you with all my heart.

Nanaqui
Antonin Artaud

TO JACQUES LATRÉMOLIÈRE

January 6, 1945

My dear friend,

When I arrived here two years ago you received me with a great deal of kindness: Dr. Ferdière, who had known me for years, had told you of my odyssey and like him you wanted to make amends in your heart for the injustice that had been done me in treating me like a madman and abusing me on account of a gesture, an attitude, a manner of talking and thinking which were in life proper to the man of the theater, the poet and the writer I used to be. What is a poet, if not a man who visualizes and expresses his ideas and his images more intensely and with more real happiness and life than other men and who, by means of cadenced speech, gives them a quality of fact.—By his general attitude behavior and manner at every instant, the man who is here and who I am is the same in every respect as the one who in 1913, in his classrooms at school, started to write verse. When I have discovered a line of poetry I recite it out loud to test and feel its rhythm and its overall sound pattern. And all the poets in the world have always done the same, and there is not a coal seller or a grocer who has figured in the life of one of these poets who has not judged him in his heart to be a maniac or a madman.—An honorable and even *Christian* doctor like yourself cannot fall into the error of believing an unfair report that was given him about me concerning a way of life which is not the same as everyone else's, because I am not a hack, a deliveryman, a roofer, a road worker, a bank clerk or a civil servant.—I came to see you to read two of my poems, "Israfel" and "Annabel Lee," and when I read

them to you I declaimed them in a loud voice with all my heart.—
This too, if someone had heard me read them to you *without
knowing that you were listening,* could have been taken for mad
by an ill-disposed person whose vices, vulgarity, and stupidity
prevent him from rising above the most small-minded denseness
in the world.—I am disgusted with living, Mr. Latrémolière, because I see that we are in a world *where nothing has stuck,* where
anything may be held up to ridicule and accused of unreason
according to the state of mind of the moment and the unconscious
of the accuser, of which this self-styled judge is totally unaware.
It was you yourself who last August put an end to the electric-
shock treatments which were so terrible for me, because you
realized that this was not a treatment I should have to undergo,
and that a man like myself did not need to be treated but on the
contrary, helped in his work. Electric shock, Mr. Latrémolière,
reduces me to despair, it takes away my memory, it dulls my
mind and my heart, it turns me into someone who is absent and
who knows he is absent and sees himself for weeks in pursuit of
his being, like a dead man alongside a living man who is no longer
himself, but who insists on the dead man being present even though
he can no longer enter into him. After the last series I remained
throughout the months of August and September absolutely incapable of working, thinking, *and feeling that I was alive.* Each
time it brings on those horrible splittings of the personality which
I wrote about in the correspondence with Rivière, but which at that
time was a perceptual knowledge and not a living agony as with
electric shock.

I have a great deal of affection for you and you know it, but if
you do not stop these electric-shock treatments at once I shall no
longer be able to keep you in my heart.—For this iniquitous
treatment is separating me from everything and from life itself.—
Put yourself in my place for a moment, Dr. Latrémolière, as a
writer and a thinker who never stops working, and see what you
would think of humanity and of everything if people were permitted to deal with you as they do with me.—Dr. Ferdière personally invited me to come here to take me away from the atmosphere of Insane Asylums and so I could be near a friend. If here,
too, they are going to regard me as a sick man *because they do
not understand me,* it was not worth the trouble of coming to

Rodez. Personally I believe, Mr. Latrémolière, that you have understood me very well and have *accepted* me in your heart, but that you are not always really there with your whole personal self and your whole representative consciousness. Such is life. Love, intelligence, the most extraordinary affective intuition represent us, and then one day all this is changed and swept aside, and all we have left is the shadow of the eternal discriminator who imagines that he is still judging with the same consciousness as before but no longer has it.—If the man in you who understood and loved me and showed me that he did last August, because he is your irreducible personal self, if this man, I say, had been wholly present these last few days, never in the world would you have agreed to inflict on me once again the torments of drugged sleep and the horrible mental torpor of electric shock.

Mr. Latrémolière, I no longer believe in the demons of hell as I did two years ago when I arrived here, because I no longer want my brain to be encumbered by all those phantasms of illumination and sacred Mysticism, for I have learned that the human being which we are in this world understands nothing about them and cannot approach them on the level of the earth and of life because the man whom we are and who I am is not equal to these problems.—Not wanting to think about them I long ago stopped seeing anything at all beyond the paper I write on, people, trees, the houses I live in, and the blue sky overhead.—You said to me one day, "You can't say that you don't have temptations, I have them myself." Well, what I cannot bear is to observe that I who am now a man of fifty still sometimes have temptations. But I fight them off like harmful physical sensations and not like demons of the occult.—For I don't believe in them any more, but I do believe that there are on earth some very bad people who desire the reign of evil and who are organized in sects to bring it about and who, by committing their abominations and their crimes, are keeping life at the level of baseness, hatred, war, despair, shame.—And I know that it is the practice of the sins of all the criminals of this ill will that is the source of temptation for us who want to be pure and good.—I know it because it was for trying to denounce them as a body that I was accused of madness, and when Dr. Ferdière or you reproach me for conjuring, it is because you can no longer see the opposing conjurations which were made against you by the whole army of evil to prevent you from judging me with your mind and your heart; my story, Dr. Latrémolière, is a nameless iniquity and a crime which people do not want to let you see and which they are sealing up in your own mind in order to reverse your judgment of me.

    I hope that Heaven will help you to understand everything I am trying to tell you, but if Dr. Ferdière refuses to continue to treat me like a sick person because I am leading here the same life that, as I said, I have lived since 1913, I am going to ask my family to come and get me.

Very affectionately yours,
Antonin Artaud

TO MARIE-ANGE MALAUSSÉNA

January 30, 1945

My very dear Marie-Ange,

    I received your letter of January 18 and it gave me great joy.—But I do not believe that it is last October since I wrote Mama and you, or acknowledged receipt of your money order, or else at least one of my letters must have been lost.—The publisher has just issued a new edition of 1,725 copies of my book *The Theater and Its Double* of which the first edition of 300 copies appeared in 1938 and has since gone out of print. The publisher sent me 15 copies to distribute to my relatives and friends. I sent a copy to Mama the day before yesterday and I would be delighted to send one to you if this book represented my present ideas. But I no longer see things the same way since in Dublin in September 1937 I returned to the faith of my childhood and since I have found in this asylum a chapel and a chaplain who are helping me fulfill all my religious duties. This book may not have anything in it that is very specifically antireligious, but it was written in a period of disbelief and estrangement from God and this can be felt in more than one passage and in the troubled times we are living in we need a literature that is passionate and energetic and when I have perfected a sample of a literature of this kind, capable of uplifting the heart and soul of the reader, I shall send you this, and you will be grateful to me because you will find it beneficial for yourself and your children.—I have only one regret as I read today this book written 8 years ago, and that is to see that all the literary dynamism I had at my disposal was not placed at the service of more exalting ideas. But this will come.

I have not yet received the package you mentioned, but I thank you for thinking of me.—I mentioned rye bread because I understand one can get it without coupons, and the thing I have missed most for several years is pastries or cookies but I am not forgetting that you have two children who both need sweets and I beg you to make sure they have everything they need before you think of me.—I wonder too whether Mama and Fernand have everything they need.—Tell Fernand when you see him that in spite of my silence I think about him and that I pray for him often.—Kiss little Serge and Ghyslaine for me and give Georges my most affectionate wishes.—As for you, My dear Marie-Ange, you can be sure that whatever happens to me I shall never forget you and that you can always count on my unalterable affection and all my love.

Nanaqui
Antonin Artaud

P.S. I have written to Mama in the same mail.

TO HENRI PARISOT

September 7, 1945

My dear Henri Parisot,

At least three weeks ago I wrote you two letters telling you to publish *A Voyage to the Land of the Tarahumara,* and enclosing a letter with which to replace the *Supplement to the Voyage,* in which I was idiotic enough to say that I had been converted to Jesus christ, whereas christ is the thing that I have always most abominated, and this conversion was merely the result of a terrible spell which caused me to forget my own nature and to swallow in the name of communion, here at Rodez, a terrifying number of hosts intended to keep me for as long as possible and if possible eternally in a being which is not my own. This being consists in rising to heaven in spirit instead of descending further and further into hell in the body, that is, into sexuality, which is the soul of all life. Whereas christ carries this being off into the empyrean of clouds and gases where he has been dissolving since eternity. The ascension of the so-called Jesus christ 2000 years ago was merely a rise into an infinite vertical in which he one day ceased to be and in which all that remained of him fell back into the sexual organs of all men as the basis of all libido. Like Jesus christ there is also the one who never descended to earth because man was too small for him and who remained in the abysses of the infinite like a so-called divine immanence who tirelessly, and like a buddha of his own contemplation, waits until the BEING is sufficiently perfect to come down and enter his body, which is the base calculation of a coward and a sluggard who did not want to suffer being, all of being, but let it be suffered by another only to banish this other, this sufferer, and send him to hell when this hallucinate of suffering would have transformed the reality of HIS suffering into a paradise, all prepared for that ghoul of sloth and villainy known as god and Jesus christ. I am one of these sufferers, I am this principal sufferer into whom god means to descend after I am dead but I have 3 daughters who are other sufferers, and I hope that you are also one in your soul, Henri Parisot, for next to god and christ there are angels who claim the same right as he and have always claimed to take over the consciousness of every creature born, although they believe themselves to belong to the inborn.—So you see it was not Jesus christ I went to find among the Tarahumara but myself, me, Antonin Artaud, born September 4, 1896, in Marseilles at 4, rue du Jardin des Plantes, of a uterus I had nothing to do with then or even before I was born, because that is not how one is born, being copulated and masturbated nine months by the membrane, that shining membrane that devours without teeth, as it says in the UPANISHADS, and I know that I was born otherwise, out of my works and not out of a mother, but the MOTHER wanted to take me and you see the result in my life.—I was born only out of my own pain, and may you do the same, Henri Parisot. And it would seem that the uterus found this pain good, 49 years ago, since it chose to take it for its own and to take nourishment from it with no pretense of maternity. And this Jesus christ is the one born of a mother who also wanted to take me for his own, and this long before time and the world, and the only reason I went to the mountains of Mexico was to rid myself of Jesus christ, just as I hope one day to go to Tibet to purge myself of god and of his holy spirit. Will you follow me there? Publish this letter *in place* of the supplement, and please send me back the supplement.

Affectionately,
Antonin Artaud

TO HENRI PARISOT

September 17, 1945

Dear Sir,

I received your letter telling me that you understand how heavily my situation weighs on me. And I told you to publish the *Voyage to the Land of the Tarahumara*, and I have written you a letter to be published in place of the supplement which I sent you in 1943. All this is very well but, dear friend, we still cannot rest. There is something else at the moment on earth and in Paris besides literature, publishing, and magazines. There is an old matter which everyone is talking about privately but which no one in ordinary life is willing to talk about publicly, although it is happening publicly all the time in ordinary life, something which, through a kind of nauseating mass hypocrisy, no one is willing to admit that he has noticed, that he has seen and experienced. This matter is a kind of mass spell-casting in which the whole world more or less participates off and on, while pretending not to be aware of it, and trying to hide from themselves the fact that they participate in it, now with their unconscious, now with their subconscious, and more and more with their full consciousness. The purpose of this spell-casting is to prevent a plan of action which I undertook years ago, which is to get out of this stinking world and to have done with this stinking world. The fact that I was committed eight years ago and that I have been confined for eight years is clearly the result of the general ill will which is determined at all costs to prevent Antonin Artaud, writer and poet, from realizing in life the ideas that he expresses in books, because they know that Antonin Artaud has at his disposal means of action which they want to prevent him from using when he wishes, together with a few souls who love him, in order to get out of this vile world, which suffocates both others and himself with its stupidity, this world which cheerfully accepts its own suffocation. People are stupid. Literature, exhausted. There is nothing left, there is no one left, the soul is insane, there is no love, there isn't even hate, all bodies are sated, everyone's consciousness resigned. Even anxiety is gone, passed into the hollows of the bones, there is nothing left but the vast complacency of these sluggards, these bovine souls, these slaves of an imbecility which oppresses them and with which they do not cease to copulate night and day, slaves as dull as this letter in which I am trying to express my exasperation with a life governed by a pack of nonentities who have chosen to impose on everyone their hatred of poetry, their love of bourgeois ineptitude in a world that has been completely taken over by the middle class, with all its verbal droning about the Soviets, anarchy, communism, socialism, radicalism, republics, monarchies, churches, rites, rationing, quotas, the black market, the resistance. This world outlives itself every day, whereas something else is happening and whereas every day the soul is summoned at last to be born and to exist. But you do not believe this, Mr. Parisot. This is what I think, and what I think and what I do, I already tried in Marseilles in 1917, during the other war, and all the beggars, workers, and pimps of Marseilles supported me and a cab driver wanted to drive me around for nothing, and a man in the crowd handed me a revolver to defend myself from the police, and it was for provoking an insurrection of this kind in Dublin that I was deported. This is no reason to pretend I am mad in order to get rid of me and to put me to sleep with electric-shock treatments to make me lose the medullar memory of my energy. All this is my own personal affair and does not interest you, I sense it, for people read the memoirs of dead poets but while they are alive no one would give them a

Letters from 1943–45 (Rodez)

cup of coffee or a glass of opium to console them. But it's not to ask you to feel sorry for me that I'm writing you, but simply to warn you that since my situation is untenable, things are going to go smash, although you do not believe it, for I cannot allow groups of spell-casters recruited from all classes of society to be posted at certain points in Paris in order to influence and command my consciousness—me, Artaud, at the mercy of launderers, cleaners, druggists, grocers, wine sellers, storekeepers, bank employes, bookkeepers, tradesmen, policemen, doctors, university professors, civil servants, even priests, especially priests, friars, monks, lay brothers, that is, incompetents, all functionaries of the spirit, a spirit which the Catholics call the Holy Ghost and which is nothing but the anal and vaginal discharge of all the masses, all the anointments, all the sacraments, all the benedictions, all the elevations, all the extreme unctions, not to mention the ablutions and the nard ritually burned by Brahmans, the gyrations of dervishes, the rose windows inChristed because encrusted of cathedrals, the lotus positions of buddhas, and the intranatural invocations of lamas. All this is much worse and much more sinister right now than the Nominalist controversy, and while I am in an insane asylum I do not want to be restrained, confined, and prevented from seeing my five first-born daughters: Neneka Chilé, Catherine Chilé, Cécile Schramme, Anie Besnard, Yvonne Nel-Dumouchel, plus several others beginning with Sonia Mossé, Yvonne Gamelin, Josette Lusson, Colette Prou (hacked to death with an ax in a cell of the hospital in Le Havre by a guard hired by the police while I was forcibly restrained with my feet tied to a bed), and I want it all the less since these magic spells are usually the work of groups of French people in Paris who meet at certain hours of the day or night in certain out-of-the-way streets in the vicinity of Notre-Dame-des-Champs, the Porte d'Orléans or the Porte de Versailles, the Cimetière Montmartre, Père-Lachaise, Les Invalides, avenue de la Motte-Picquet, Parc Monceau, the Champs-Elysées, etc. etc. When these magic spells are cast, traffic is stopped by the police for an hour on the street where they are to occur and this happened two weeks ago on the avenue de la Motte-Picquet, it happened the day before yesterday on rue de Prony at about four o'clock in the afternoon, it happened last night at about eleven o'clock (thus Sunday, September 16) on the Place de la Concorde, on the Champs-Elysées, near the Ministère de la Marine. The French people have forgotten, because they are under a spell, that I have answered these spells with piles of bodies right in Paris, and that the streets where these bodies have fallen have also been closed off by the police to allow the ditch-diggers and road repairmen to collect the dead and clean up the street, but this everyone has deliberately forgotten so they can indulge in the luxury of believing that life is going on as usual, and the populations of Paris and of the earth are beginning to be terribly depleted, Henri Parisot, but all those who have lost a relative or a friend are under orders to say nothing and not to complain, in the hope that this monstrous affair can be hushed up, while I suffer constantly from colic and diarrhea, and this is the least of it. I beg you to read and reread this letter several times with the greatest attention, for then you will understand the fate that bourgeois France imposes on a rebel writer.

Antonin Artaud

TO HENRI PARISOT (incomplete letter)

September 20, 1945

My dear friend,

All I remember translating, in the summer of 1943, was a fragment of this "Jabberwocky" which you talk about and which in fact I do not like. For I have always felt that this piece of writing lacked a soul, although it is full of an infinity of psychological tricks, the first of which is choosing to create within the body of the poem to be made and not yet made this kind of mental vacuum in which language speaks alone, and it is not a trick, it is a fact, which when it is done makes an impression, but it is by the trick of the mental that the author of "Jabberwocky" tried to give rise to the fact, the anal sexual fact of the infantile desire to speak, and not the anal infantilism which one day began to speak in all naïveté in his poem. I shall not command my desires and my inclinations, but neither do I want them to direct me, I want *to be* those desires and those inclinations, and this of course is difficult in a world which has never ceased to be under the command of the mind, and this to the imperilment of the soul and the loss of every body. This is the law which I have always imposed on myself, but I do not find it in "Jabberwocky," for anal sexual desire is a terrible appetite, a desolation of not being, a despair of not being able to take and of not being taken oneself, of not being able to penetrate or be penetrated, not with ill will but with good will, for the characteristic of this formidable desire is love, love, by electivity.—And I accuse the author of "Jabberwocky" of wanting to penetrate a void which did not want to be possessed.

Because it was a mind void and not a soul void, and because what makes the soul is the sorrow of love which is rejected and wants to be, wants to be love because it will be taken and accepted, accepted and not refused by the soul of its soul. And where I do not feel either love or soul my own soul retracts and refuses to give itself. "Jabberwocky" has never seemed to me anything but an artifice of style, because the heart is never in it, a sort of marginal success, outside the rhythm of the litany of the heart, and one cannot write like this, one does not have the right to write like this, a poem that is outside the heart, outside the spasm and the sob of the heart, a poem that has not been *suffered* like:

> Dites-moi où, dans quel pays
> Est Flora la belle Romaine,
> La royne Blanche comme un lys
> Qui chantait à voix de sirène,

or

> Advis m'est que j'ai regretté
> La belle qui fut Hëaulmière

or "Une Charogne," "Une Martyre," "Un Voyage à Cythère," of Baudelaire.

When Baudelaire no longer curses, no longer swears, no longer rails, no longer blasphemes, as in these poems of imprecation, of horrible internal uprooting, in which the soul eats its tetanus in expiation of the *sublime* cults and of the sins which have raised it from the grave, when he no longer belches hate, or the memory of I know not what ancestral reprobation, when his soul wanders off under the tamarind trees or hangs on the breasts of his mistress, even then a trace of this uterine anguish, horror of horror of his agonies, hovers in the consciousness of a verse. And this is seen. A poem that does not come out of suffering bores me, a poem made of the superfluities of existence has always done more than bore me, it exasperates me.—I do not like luxury feelings, I do not like poems of nourishment but poems of hunger, I know very well how "Jabberwocky" was written and it is not the poem of an idiot and it never verges on idiocy, of course, but [. . .]

TO HENRI PARISOT

September 22, 1945

My dear friend,

    I haven't done a translation of "Jabberwocky." I tried to translate a piece of it, but it bored me. I've never liked this poem, which has always seemed to me affectedly childish; I like spontaneous poems, not artificial languages. When I write or read I want to feel my soul stretch, as in Baudelaire's "Une Charogne," "Une Martyre," or "Un Voyage à Cythère." I don't like surface poems or surface languages, works which speak of happy leisure hours and felicities of the intellect, the intellect in question was based on the anus, but without putting any soul or heart into it. The anus is always terror, and I cannot accept the idea of someone losing a bit of excrement without coming painfully close to losing his soul, and there is no soul in "Jabberwocky." Everything that is not a tetanus of the soul or does not proceed from a tetanus of the soul, like the poems of Baudelaire and Poe, is not true and cannot be accepted as poetry. "Jabberwocky" is the work of a eunuch, a sort of hybrid mongrel who pulverized his consciousness in order to produce writing, where Baudelaire produced bedsores of aphasia or paraplegia and where Poe produced mucous membranes like prussic acid, alcoholic acid, and this to the point of poisoning and madness. For when Poe was found dead one morning on a sidewalk in Baltimore, it was not because of an attack of delirium tremens brought on by alcohol, but because a few bastards who hated his genius and despised his poetry poisoned him to prevent him from living and from offering the extraordinary, terrifying solace that is revealed in his verses. It is permissible to invent one's language and to make the language speak with an extra-grammatical meaning, but this meaning must be valid in itself, that is, it must come out of anguish—anguish that old servant of pain, that vagina like a buried iron collar which produces its verses out of its malady, being, and does not let you forget it. "Jabberwocky" is the work of an opportunist who wanted to feed intellectually on someone else's pain, although he himself was satiated from a well-served meal. And this has never been seen in his poem and no one has ever said it. But I say it because I have felt it. When one digs out the caca of existence and of language, the poem must smell bad, and "Jabberwocky" is a poem which its author has been careful to protect from the uterine existence of suffering in which every great poet has been immersed and from which when he is delivered he smells bad. There are in "Jabberwocky" passages of fecality, but it is the fecality of an English snob who forces the obscene in himself into curls and corkscrews as if with hot tongs, a kind of dilettante of the obscene who is very careful not to be obscene himself, like Baudelaire in his terminal aphasia or Poe in his gutter the morning he was found dead of a seizure brought on by prussic acid or potassium cyanide. "Jabberwocky" is the work of a coward who was not willing to suffer his work before writing it, and this can be seen. It is the work of a man who ate well, and this comes through in his writing. I like the poems of the starving, the sick, the outcast, the poisoned: François Villon, Charles Baudelaire, Edgar Allan Poe, Gérard de Nerval, and the poems of the executed criminals of language who suffer ruin in their writing, and not of those who pretend to be ruined the better to show off their consciousness of and their skill in both ruin and writing. Those who are ruined do not know it, they bleat or bellow with pain and horror. To abandon language and its laws only to twist them and to deprive the sexual flesh of the glottis which provides an outlet for the seminal pungencies of the soul and the complaints of the unconscious is all very well, provided the sex is aware of itself as an orgasm of rebellion, desperate, naked, uterine, and also piteous, naïve, astonished at being reproved, and provided this work does not appear as a success based on deprivation in which the style reeks in each of its discordances of the stale smell of a satiated mind, because the man himself is satiated, nevertheless his deprivation as in "Jabberwocky" is provoked as an additional form of nourishment. I like poems that reek of hunger and not of well-cooked meals. And I have something else against "Jabberwocky." For years I have had an idea of the consumption, the internal consummation of language by the unearthing of all manner of torpid and filthy necessities. And in 1934 I wrote a whole book with this intention, in a language which was not French but which everyone in the world could read, no matter what their nationality. Unfortunately, this book has been lost. It was printed in a very limited edition, but abominable influences on the part of people in the government, the church, or the police caused it to disappear, and there is only one copy left, which I do not own but which is in the hands of one of my daughters, Catherine Chilé. She was a nurse in 1934 at the Hôpital Saint-Jacques, where she was working toward her degree as a doctor. I see her around me all the time and I know that right now she is making a desperate effort to get to Rodez, but I no longer know exactly where she is, I mean how far she has come in this journey to reach me. I do not think all this will seem imaginary to you now that you have seen the hordes of murderous spirits which whirl around me to keep me from working, and around you to keep you from existing.

I ask you to publish this letter, which André Breton would certainly have been delighted to publish twenty-five years ago in *La Révolution Surréaliste*. Today it will not even cause a scandal, but there are enough magic spells passing through the air and through everyone's minds to insinuate that his ideas are weak and that it would take a critic of a different stamp from myself to deal with "Jabberwocky." But I am sure that a reader of my posthumous works (think of it!) a few years from now will understand—for one must have the perspective of time or of bombs to judge the situation correctly.

Having written a book like *Letura d'Eprahi Falli Tetar Fendi Photia o Fotre Indi*, I find it unbearable that present society, *from which you suffer constantly, as do I,* allows me no more

Letters from 1943–45 (Rodez)

latitude than to translate another book done in its imitation. For "Jabberwocky" is nothing but a sugar-coated and lifeless plagiarism of a work written by me, which has been spirited away so successfully that I myself hardly know what is in it.

Here are a few attempts at language which must be similar to the language of that old book. But they can only be read rhythmically, in a tempo which the reader himself must find in order to understand and to think:

> **ratara ratara ratara**
> **atara tatara rana**
>
> **otara otara katara**
> **otara ratara kana**
>
> **ortura ortura konara**
> **kokona kokona koma**
>
> **kurbura kurbura kurbura**
> **kurbata kurbata keyna**
>
> **pesti anti pestantum putara**
> **pest anti pestantum putra**

but this is worthless unless it gushes out all at once; pieced together one syllable at a time, it no longer has any value, written here it says nothing and is nothing but ash; to bring it to life in written form requires another element which is in the book that has been lost.

Forthcoming events will make all this clear.

Antonin Artaud

TO HENRI PARISOT

October 6, 1945

Dear Sir,

I am writing you in pencil because I have no ink and I can't have any, for here the other inmates overturn my ink bottles on my books and my writings.

ANTONIN ARTAUD

I did not go to Mexico on a voyage of initiation or for a pleasure trip, the kind that is recounted later in a book that one reads by the fireside; I went there to find a race of people who could follow me in my ideas. If I am a poet or an actor it is not in order to write or recite poems but in order to live them. When I recite a poem I don't do it to be applauded but to feel the bodies of men and women, I said *bodies*, tremble and turn in unison with my own, turn from the obtuse contemplation of the seated Buddha, thighs locked and sex disinterested, to the soul, that is to the bodily and physical materialization of a total being of poetry. I want the poems of François Villon, Charles Baudelaire, Edgar Allan Poe, or Gérard de Nerval to come true, I want life to escape from the books, magazines, theaters, and churches which imprison and crucify it in order to hold on to it, and to pass on to the level of that internal magic of bodies, that uterine decantation from soul to soul which, body after body and driven by hunger for love, liberates a buried sexual energy on which the religions have heaped excommunication and interdiction and which the hypocritical religiosity of the age distills in its secret sex parties out of hatred for poetry. Sex is solemn, Henri Parisot, because poetry is even more solemn. The harmonies of the generative tone of "Une Martyre," "Une Charogne," or "La Belle Hëaulmière" are a well in which the uterine hunger of the soul mourns a love that has not been born, in which the fecality of the supernatural body of the soul writhes to death because it has not been born. This century no longer understands fecal poetry, the intestine malady of herself, Madam Death, who since the age of ages has been sounding the depths of her dead woman's column, her dead woman's anal column, in the excrement of an abolished survival, the corpse too of her abolished selves, and who for the crime of not having been able to exist, for never having been able to be a creature, had to fall, the better to sound the depths of her own being into this abyss of foul matter and indeed so pleasantly foul in which the corpse of Madam Death, Madam Fecal Uterine, Madam Anus, hell upon hell of excrement, in the opium of her excrement, foments hunger, the fecal destiny of her soul, in the uterus of her own center. The soul, says the buried body of being, is that focal point of the survival of life which falls, fecal as excrement, and is piled up in its excrement. With my own eyes I

Letters from 1943–45 (Rodez)

have seen falling from a great many coffins I know not what black matter, I know not what immortal urine from these forms mute of life which, morsel by morsel, drop by drop, destroyed themselves. The name of this matter is caca, and caca is the raw material of the soul, whose puddles I have seen in so many coffins spread before my eyes. The breath of the bones has a center and this center is the abyss of Kah-Kah, Kah the corporeal breath of shit, which is the opium of eternal survival. All the shit that has come from the accumulation of so many coffins is an opium wrung from the soul which had not probed deeply enough into the abyss of its own fecality, the focal center of its fecality. The soul loves until death, until the immortal odor of its death, and there is no dead body or tomb that one can accuse of smelling bad. The odor of the eternal ass of death is the oppressed energy of a soul whom the world refused to let live.

**pho ti ti ananti phatiame
fa ti tiame ta fatridi**

I'm down to my ass, says the man of life to signify that he is at the bottom of his death, that the silver on the mirror of his soul is an abyss penetrated for him. And this soul is poetry, and lost poetry is a soul which no one wants any part of today. I don't even know whether the Tarahumara wanted any part of this soul, green humus of decomposition which out of humus and virus creates acid, the acid of survival in life. To live is eternally to survive oneself while ruminating one's excremental self, with no fear of one's fecal soul, hunger-making force of burial. For all humanity wants to live, but it does not want to pay the price, and this price is the price of fear. If one is to exist, there is a fear that must be overcome, and this means carrying fear, the entire sexual coffer of the shadow of fear, into oneself, as the unified body of the soul, the whole soul from infinite time, without recourse to any god behind one. And without forgetting any part of oneself. And when spells are cast day after day all over Paris to prevent me from weeding out my soul, from having access to its buried orifice, which every religion has had the intolerable conceit to declare forbidden, no one can continue to tell me, no one can come here and tell me that I am mad to seek this *physical* solace of the soul, which is the magical substance of poetry. For this is what I am accused of and this is why I have been confined for eight years, and why I have been put in a straitjacket, poisoned, and *put to sleep with electricity*, it is *for having tried to find the fundamental substance of the soul* and to isolate it in essential fluids. These spell-casters are not merely all of Paris, today they are the whole world, all of which is under the universally respected orders of the hate-filled masters of the Himalayas. Who are merely the subconscious of all villainy and all crime, of the obscenities and crimes of every man, which with the whole body of each man are going to the Himalayas, believing that there they can escape the anger that has been rising in me for the past forty-nine years. I blame the men of this age for causing me to be born by the most infamous magical maneuvers into a world I wanted no part of, and for trying by similar magical maneuvers to prevent me from making a hole in this world in order to leave it. I need poetry to live, and I want to see it around me. And I do not accept the fact that the poet who I am was committed to an insane asylum because he wanted to realize his poetry in its natural state. Still less do I accept the fact that groups of spell-casters, in which the entire population of Paris participates in shifts night and day, station themselves at certain prearranged hours in the streets or on the boulevards in order to hurl at me torrents of hate which each one, with skirts raised or pants unbuttoned, draws from the depths of his sexuality, and that I have to hear people say that I am exaggerating or that I am raving when I condemn these infamous maneuvers which everyone in Paris has seen. There was an orgy of this kind the day before yesterday at about eleven o'clock on the boulevard de la Madeleine, near the Café des Mathurins; there was a whole series in front of the Eglise Notre-Dame-des-Champs a few weeks ago, at which times the boulevard du Montparnasse was closed to traffic for half an hour or a quarter of an hour. There was one two weeks ago on the avenue de la Motte-Picquet, in which the promoters of the obscene gathering had hidden in a café almost directly across from the Taverne Labrunie, from which they conducted their spells with the help of a group of Parisian men and women on the sidewalk. Among these spells of stupid and criminal venomousness, there was one that was altogether sensational last night near the post office on the avenue de Ségur. It took place between eleven o'clock and midnight. The result for me was a death agony, and a rat that got inside a hunk of bread which I had beside me on a table and devoured it from within, covering my books with rat droppings. Part of this spell is the work of a small group of people sitting around tables at the Dôme, who know the occult measurement from my perineum to my brain, and who indulge in the luxury of tasting me from a distance with their tongues with all the thick-lipped libido of greedy gluttony at their disposal, tasting me like the fetus of a newborn child. The only defense against such a hideous and vile action is the crushing power of force and this is what I resorted to in a square in Dublin one day in September of 1937. The Irish are fanatical Catholics, and the foundation of Catholicism is tasting god the self in the mass with all the obscene pressure, all the obscene phallic weight of a tongue that prays, prays as if with the breath of its lungs it could lustfully force its white saliva to a foaming climax.

This is what the hypocritical Tartuffe in every Christian does on an astral plane in his soul, and what he unctuously conceals behind the joined hands of his life. And this is what certain people at the Dôme or on the avenue de Ségur did, no longer hypocritically and on an astral plane, but openly and on a physical plane.

I was not alone in Dublin, one against a thousand. I was alone with a special cane that the whole world was able to see in Paris in May, June, July, and August 1937, then the *Voyage to the Land of the Tarahumara* appeared. I used to walk with this cane to the Café des Deux Magots, the Dôme, the Coupole, and all over Paris. I showed it to André Breton and to several other friends, who examined it closely. It had come to me from a friend whom you know. René Thomas, who then lived at 21 rue Daguerre, and who had received it from the daughter of a Savoyard sorcerer who is mentioned in the prophecy of St. Patrick. The cane is also mentioned in the prophecy of St. Patrick, which is published at length in the dictionary of hagiography, which I read for the first time in 1934 in the Bibliothèque Nationale. This cane has 200 million fibers, and it is inlaid with magical signs, representing moral forces and an anti-natal symbolism which should in fact be condemned because it prevented the principle of the cane, the wand all-powerful in itself, from being as effective as possible, but this symbolism does not deny the principle of the fire, since it comes from it and criminally tried to divert this power toward an idea of the predestination of beings who, no matter what evil they have done, are incapable of not one day being saved. However this may be, the only use I made of this cane in Ireland was to impose silence on the pack that was after me, and the only reason I was put in prison and deported was because I realized myself that it was worthless as a means of defense and that I myself was becoming very bad, that is, inept, stupid, and insipid of soul the more I used it. According to legend this cane actually belonged to Lucifer, who believed himself to be god, and was only his vampire. It passed through the hands of Jesus-christ, and then through St. Patrick's.

I have planted and empowered another which I am expecting momentarily, and I have ceased to work on it here. When it is ready the battle will resume, and I already told you that just as I went to Mexico in 1936, I am now planning to undertake a long trip to the Himalayas.

Antonin Artaud

TO HENRI PARISOT

October 9, 1945

Dear Sir,

Yes, I shall be very happy to let you publish the last letters I wrote you. But two days ago I wrote you a new letter which I would like you to add to the *Voyage to the Land of the Tarahumara*. I think it will interest you because of everything that is in it. I am working on two books: *Surrealism and the End of the Christian Era,* and more importantly, *Measure without Measure,* in which I try to find a new language: to be that big clumsy puppy who walks with his legs apart carrying his heart perpetually between his thighs, rather than the crane who sweeps her bottom from side to side to show it off.

> orka ta kana izera
> kani zera tabitra

For the indefinite is a press

> ora bulda nerkita

which crushes even itself until it forces out the very blood of the infinite, not as a state, but as a being.
Tell me whether you received my last letter.

Yours,
Antonin Artaud

P.S. There is at this moment a matter of absurd possession which fills the entire earth. It is being conducted by a number of sects of initiates which I know very well and which I have been pursuing for at least thirty years, that is, since a certain day in the spring of 1915 when I was knifed in the back by two pimps in the Cours Devilliers in Marseilles, in front of the Église des Réformés. I was then nineteen years old. I was just passing the drugstore at the corner of the Cours Devilliers and the boulevard de la Madeleine when I noticed two suspicious-looking characters who were prowling around me as if they were about to attack me; I did not know them and one of them smiled at me as if to say, "You have nothing to fear from us, you are not the one we are looking for." Then I saw his face change, and in place of the man who was smiling at me I saw in the same body a mask of bestiality which struck me because it seemed not to belong to this man, and I felt a terrible twisting spasm pass over him. "Who am I and what do I want?" he seemed to say to himself suddenly. "This man is not my enemy, I do not know him, and I am not going to hurt him." And he walked away. I was starting to walk up the boulevard de la Madeleine when I felt the air behind me shake as if something were being torn; and I thought, "It is the soul of the pimp which is being torn," and before I had time to turn around I felt the blade of a knife tear the back of my heart from behind near the top of the shoulder blade, less than an inch from the spinal column. And I was sure that before the blow a body had fallen behind me, and I fell to the ground myself, but I thought, "This is not yet my last hour, the blood will go away, it will stop flowing," and so thinking I got up with a terrible pain which, indeed, gradually subsided. The pimp on the ground said to me, "It was not me, I would not have struck you for anything in the world. I know you, although you have forgotten me, and I know who you are; I tried to avoid the blow they tried to force me to give you, and if my body delivered it in part, it was because I was suddenly possessed, but my soul was not in the blow, and I fell trying to tear it out of my body." I answered him, "I know very well who wanted to strike me down, and it is an angel, but it is not you. It is an old story which goes back to before the beginning," and as I talked to him I remembered that story of a forgotten crime in which Jesus-christ is a moral ape and Lucifer the toady of god. "This story," I told him, "will take us far, and it is far from over," and indeed it has brought me all the way to the asylum of Rodez, where I now find myself in the shadow of the most Catholic cathedral on earth, which casts over me night and day indefeasible waves of spells. After thirty years I still carry on my back the scar of that knife wound whose moving force overcame the man who delivered it with his body but not with his soul.

    This possessed pimp is not unique, and the whole world is now in the same state. But no one is willing to believe it, for the initiates have a way of entering people's bodies in order to deny those who accuse them, and to have them put in prison or in insane asylums. I have spent my life for the past thirty years locating throughout the world all the sects which act upon people's consciousness, and I believe I know them all. They exist in Afghanistan, in Turkestan, in Tibet, among the bonzes of the lamaseries, among the Indian Moslems, but the most formidable are the sects of those who still do not admit that they are initiates but who work night and day in secret anyway, finding their support in the mystery of the human body. These sects say that they are of the mind, and the minds of the bodies on which they work claim to be the masters of these bodies and to control from within the self and the body of the man or woman who bears them.

Which is the most tetanizing and epilepticizing idea I have ever heard. It is the Christian Catholic religion which is at the source of this state of things. For it is this religion which has chosen to be mind and not body or, as in the intrinsic religion of Jesus-christ, it sees in the principle of the body a void which becomes full, and gradually fills the solid part which is merely its emanation. Which means that there is at the base of each living body an unfathomable abyss, an angel who gradually fills it from the cellars of eternity and who wishes by submersion to take its place. It was for trying to divulge these things that I have been everywhere declared mad and finally in 1937 imprisoned, deported, attacked on shipboard, locked up, poisoned, straitjacketed, put into a coma, and that I have not yet succeeded in regaining my freedom. When the angels I mentioned rise up inside certain bodies, the most violent spells are unleashed on me and on certain men of my acquaintance, and yet all over the earth I still know a great many who have wanted no part of this state of things. And there is at the source of these spells an old matter concerning narcotics which goes back to before the flood and well before the creation. It was not for nothing that the English, many years ago, burned the opium fields of China and that all over the world prohibitions have been placed on the free use of opium, heroin, morphine, and all plants that allegedly cause convulsions like peyote, curare, agar-agar, and beriberi. It was to prevent people from ever returning to an old pre-genital notion of being, which all the sects and religions have buried. For life is not this distilled boredom in which our soul is made to marinate for seven eternities, it is not this infernal vise in which our consciousness vegetates, and which must have music, poetry, theater, and love in order to break out occasionally, but to such a slight extent that it is not even worth talking about. Man on the earth is bored to death, and this boredom is buried so deeply within him that now he no longer knows it. He goes to bed, he sleeps, he gets up, walks around, eats, writes, swallows, breathes, shits, like a machine running dry, like someone resigned to being buried in the earth of landscapes and whom the landscape has subjugated like a serf who has been bound hand and foot to the executioner's block of a bad body, and subjected to *assigned readings,* good morning,

ANTONIN ARTAUD

good evening, how are you, nice day isn't it, the rain will do the earth good, what's on the news, can you come for tea, backgammon, cards, bowling, checkers, and chess, but this isn't what it is about, I mean that this is not what defines the obscene life in which we live. What defines it is that all our perceptions and impressions have been distilled for us, and that we are only able to experience them one drop at a time, breathing the air of the landscape from above or from the edges and experiencing love from the outside of the basket, without being able to take the whole basket. And it is not that love has no soul, it is that the soul of love no longer exists. With me it is the absolute or nothing, and here is what I have to say to this world which has neither soul nor agar-agar. It is that there is in the surrealism of trance, in the state of trance, a slime which has been dried up by the religions and by their rites which for seven eternities have been served by all the bourgeois and all the cowards of the earth and of life. And this slime is regenerative, it is not called the poetry of poets, or the music of harmonies, it is not a name but the very body of the soul, a soul which christ has banished from life in order to conserve it in his paradise (here lies), and which the sects of the initiates of the earth have diverted toward secret centers in order to parcel it out one drop at a time every day to whomever they please. What resembles this soul most closely is opium, agar-agar, heroin, beriberi. Peyote and cocaine are like perverted derivatives of it. But alcohol is the eternal drunkenness of this soul; that is, its drying up. This is why the delirium tremens of alcohol has never ceased to be permitted along with the hysteria and epilepsy which attend it generation after generation, whereas armies of cops, doctors, nurses, and nuns rise up against the so-called addictive drugs. Those who take drugs do so because they have in them a congenital and predestined deficiency—or because, poets of their self in life, they have felt in advance of other men what has always been lacking in life. For opium, since eternity, has intoxicated only because of the spell that has been cast on it. And which consists of having scraped from it the sudden attack of a power

**potam am cram
katanam anankreta**

Letters from 1943-45 (Rodez)

**karaban kreta
tanamam anangteta
konaman kreta
e pustulam orentam
taumer dauldi faldisti
taumer oumer
tena tana di li
kunchta dzeris
dzama dzena di li**

kama the train disappeared into Ule, saw the kroule of Thule ravished.

There is in opium the secret of an immortal leaven, dried out by unleavened bread, and the alcohol of consecrated wines, violated also in dark orgies in the Caucasus and in the Himalayas.

**talachtis talachti tsapoula
koiman koima nara
ara trafund arakulda**

which is a rhythm of exorcism against the drying out of opium by conspiracies and consecrations. This drying out of opium is true, for having come from a soul of life, from a body in the eternal rise of life, it cannot help but give the leap without the tomb, that atomic tomb of the body in which by its fall to the internal mortuary the force that it brought is lost. Why is it lost, when it is ever increasing, and when the force provided by opium, far from lowering the body, raises it, and in so doing causes it to rush ahead of itself, opens before it the gulf of immortal survival, which the hatred of I know not what spirit of the tomb blocks off in the marrow of the intoxicated person? The reverse heightening which opium provides is not a laziness about living, but the force to live a little more, that is, to go beyond oneself. This is something which the intoxicated do not do: they seem instead to be seeking to overcome themselves. Why? Because opium itself has been changed by the ancient loss of a soul which the English tried, twenty or thirty years ago in China, to finish burning to death.—It was this soul that they tormented in Chaucer, burned at the stake in Joan of Arc, and tried to exterminate in China because they belonged to the race of whites, and because opium is black and they wanted to exterminate the black. The rising of the gorge of the breath, the excess spittle of the back taste which always rises from below, and sinks lower and lower, the fundament of a force that rises from even further down, this trembling of a somber clitoris, this spurting of a bloody erection which is not lost but endlessly re-creates itself, it is all this that opium contains in itself when it is not denatured. I say therefore that if opium intoxicates it is because it is denatured—and that it was denatured by dark maneuvers, out of hatred for its secret surrealism.

Unlike peyote, opium does not make you see things in a hallucinatory manner, it makes you do things, without magic, but rendering always more magically acceptable the difficulty of encountering things in the ordinary course of life. The table I eat on is of unfinished wood, without opium I see it as a dirty yellow, whereas actually it is not. Opium restores it to what it is on the floor of its forest, a servant full of pity, Brueghel red, blood of the torments that all matter has endured before being able to support me. This is one stage, but there is another stage with opium. It is that the body of soft flesh and white wood cast on me by I know not what father-mother will in opium be transformed, transformed *in reality*. And perhaps I shall no longer have need of a table but shall be able to plant forests in order to liberate so much matter buried in the earth of eternity. Forests of bodies which are souls and of souls at last become beings, because they will be flame bodies. Nothing is lost, but everything creates itself and it was in opium that life was created one day, but hate has denatured it. I know in what secret centers this hate was always distilled. I have already given you abundant examples of them. But the earth on which I outlive myself has never been a thing hallucinated out of dreams which it rejects in reality. And I believe that it is about to explode. This letter must be added to the preceding ones in the book in which they will be collected.

Antonin Artaud

Letters from 1943–45 (Rodez)

TO HENRI PARISOT

November 27, 1945

My very dear friend,

I thank you for the great joy you have given me in publishing *Voyage to the Land of the Tarahumara*. For I felt very strongly when I received and saw this little book that its publication was not merely the idea of a publisher who publishes a book but that of a *friend* who likes what I do and who was concerned that Antonin Artaud, relegated by the majority of French people to insane asylums, continue to be regarded as alive, thinking and writing, and that he be able to manifest publicly what he thinks, as the letters that follow *Voyage to the Land of the Tarahumara* bear witness.

Of these letters you were able to publish only one following the *Voyage*, but you have been generous enough to ask me to collect all the others in a special book. I thank you with all my soul, and you cannot know how anxious I am that they all appear, especially the one I wrote you after my letter of September 7, 1945, which you appended to the text of the *Voyage*, and the long twenty-page letter in which I relate the principal events of my life, from the knife wound I received in front of the Eglise des Réformés in Marseilles, up to the assassination attempt which I survived on the *Washington* on my way back from Ireland, for I want the minds of the last friends whom I can have on this earth, and who are my last readers, to be illuminated and I want them to understand that I have never been either mad or sick, and that my confinement is the result of a horrible secret plot in which every sect of *initiates*—Christian, Catholic, Mohammedan, Jewish, Buddhist, Brahman—together with the lamas of the Tibetan lamaseries, has participated.

This confinement was therefore a matter of religion, of initiation, of bewitchment, of black magic, and also and above all of white magic, whatever anyone may say.

And now my freedom has been given back to me by the head physician here, who has finally been convinced that he too had been deceived on my account, whereas he wanted only to be a friend to me and he was forced by magic to consider me from the viewpoint of a doctor. There is a woman in Rodez, a middle-class woman who is a practicing Catholic, who went to see him about me, although she did not know me from Adam or Eve, and who in the space of five minutes and without his knowing it *put* him *to sleep* and put a spell on him in his office in order to change his mind about me. He really slept, that is, he remained unconscious for a good five minutes, and when he recovered consciousness he did not remember what had been done to him during those five minutes, but he was no longer the same and had another self which, seeing me struggle against the evil spirits and the demons with the breathing system which I have invented and which I mentioned briefly in "An Emotional Athleticism," was at times no longer able to understand that what I was doing here was merely the continuation and extension of my idea about theater into the physical world—this doctor, who has a complete set of my books in his library and who, especially liking my way of reciting Baudelaire or Poe or especially Gérard de Nerval, suddenly could not understand the extension of this recitation to a tone of rhythmic and incantatory psalmody, could no longer understand or endure it, whereas it is the foundation of my whole theater and of the peyote dance whose description he apparently read with enthusiasm in *A Voyage to the Land of the Tarahumara*. The reason for this is very simple, it is that these incantations, when I do them—and very often I cannot keep from doing them—cast out the evil spirits, and that the evil spirits, which are hundreds of thousands of men living and breathing all over the earth, do not want to be cast out either from my body or from yours, or from that of Dr. Ferdière, or from that, among others, of René de Solier, who, it seems, has complained about my system of breathing and chanting. Was it to you that he complained? And was it he who complained, or was it the spirits who possessed him that day and spoke through his mouth, his being, and his body? These spirits do not want to be cast out because my body is good, because my pain is good for them, and because it is while I am suffering from poison, from comas, from bad food, and from the deprivation of opium that the beings of evil spirits seize my forces in the cadaver which I am, the walking cadaver which I am and which has been wandering through life like a living dead man, ever since the knife wound I received in 1916 in Marseilles in front of the Eglise des Réformés at the

Letters from 1943–45 (Rodez)

orders of initiates and by the hand of a pimp who did not even know me. All this, my dear Henri Parisot, because, just as I went up into the mountains of Mexico at fifteen thousand feet, among the Tarahumara, to put an end to *certain magic practices* that I have always been the victim of, I and the few friends on earth who have always really loved me, I intend also to go to Tibet to finish killing magic by exterminating, with the cane I have prepared, which will replace the one I had in Ireland, all those evil beings who create spells and who cast them on the minds that love me and follow me *in order to asphyxiate them.* In 1936 I knew all this, but I forgot it in the ordinary life of the moment and I believed myself to be a simple writer and, suffering from the attempt to disintoxicate myself on horseback among the Tarahumara from the heroin that I had taken, I did not really understand what I was suffering from and that I was suffering from a monstrous horde of spell-casting jackals gathered from all corners of the earth around my struggling mind in order to dissolve and exterminate it. For I want to be sempiternal, that is, a self that moves and creates itself at every instant, and not eternal, that is, having an absolute self which governs me always from the height of its eternity by the spirit of all the doubles which do not wish to advance, but to be preserved forever in their inalienable jelly of the contemplative buddhas of I know not what eternal spirit which has never existed, when it is always the actual body of our immediate being in sempiternal time and space that exists, and not the doubles of the past, entitled eternity.

What going to Tibet means to me is first of all destroying the Tibet of the soul, the Himalaya of the soul in my body, and making my body a Himalaya where the spirits of hate can never again reach me. All the souls that love me will also be other Himalayas beside my own and I shall help them exist against the hate which has tried to destroy them and which has never ceased to humiliate them.

This is the whole truth of my story and of my life.

Yours,
Antonin Artaud

Two letters from 1946

XXXII

Letter about Lautréamont

Yes, I have some secrets to tell you about the unthinkable Comte de Lautréamont, about those extravagant coercive letters, all those grim threatening decrees of iron which he sent with such elegance, and such congratulations even, to his father, his banker, his publisher, or his friends. For these letters are, of course, extravagant, with the strident extravagance of a man who walks around with his lyricism in his left or right side, like an avenging and shameless wound.

He cannot write a simple ordinary letter that does not make us feel the epileptoid trepidation of the Word which, no matter what the meaning, does not want to be used without trembling.

Frog of the infinitely small, the recluse of this word, the Poetry which Lautréamont transforms, in each letter, into a naval cannon in order to repel the principle of beef.

A letter, not of two francs, but of twice the untouchable price of the poetry of Baudelaire added to that of Lautréamont, informs a publisher of the price, not in postage stamps, but in postmarks, as he puts it, for *the* postage for the *Supplement to the Poems of Baudelaire*. And although this *the*, which lays bare with the relentless hollowness of a surreptitious humor the firm vignettes of the stamps with which the price of the book will be paid, and lays them bare by the splinter, the shard of the existence of a small idea, although this *the* like a base, like the note of a black organ under the pedal of a huge foot, may not be felt as such by the reader, this is because the latter is merely the echoing apprentice of a whore and the incarnate substance of a pig.

Something like the totem abyss of the unredeemably filthy and established bestiality (for the idea of beauty has become established, as Arthur Rimbaud says). The beast who wants to keep between his impure thighs the thirty pieces of silver paid on account to the poet, not for his poems not yet written and to be written but for that rosy bleeding pouch that beats all night and on Sunday goes for a walk on the fortifications like every bourgeois, that pouch of leaping influx which in the breast of a great poet does not beat the same as elsewhere, for it is here that every bourgeois slakes his thirst, at this heart which strictly and obstinately, jealously and aggressively has always stiffened its attitude and hardened its intractable position. For the hypocritical and contemptuous bourgeois, sanctimonious, oblivious, potbellied with contemptuous assurance, is in reality none other than that thieving antiquity, that monkey, that old monkey of Ramayana, ancient underhanded filcher of any pulsation of instant poetry, just as it is about to burst forth. "But that isn't done, no, that isn't done," he says to the Comte de Lautréamont. We don't hear it with that ear (and the ear is that anal cave into which every bourgeois, sated and stuffed with *antistrophe,* smuggles poetry). Stop. Come back to normal.

Your heart beats with horror, but this cannot be seen. I, too, have a heart of flesh which has always had need of you. Why? None of your business.

But Lautréamont does not let himself be stopped. "Let me," he tells his publisher, "begin again on a higher level." The higher level of death, no doubt, which on that ambiguous day carried him away. For no one has ever paid enough attention, and I insist on this, to the *remorse,* the evasive flatness of the death of the unthinkable Comte de Lautréamont.

This death was too innocuously flat not to make one want to look more closely into the mystery of his life. For exactly what did poor Isidore Ducasse die of, a genius who undoubtedly could not be reduced to the world, and of whom one is forced to conclude that the world wanted no part, any more than it had wanted any part of Edgar Allan Poe, Baudelaire, Gérard de Nerval, or Arthur Rimbaud.

Did he die of a long or a short illness? And was he found dead in his bed at dawn? History tells us simply, simply and sinisterly, that the death certificate was signed by the owner of the hotel and the waiter who brought him his meals.

For a great poet this is a little brief and a little thin, and there is something so shabby about it, so evasively commonplace and shabby, that in certain respects it smells of the unspeakable, and the shoddiness of a burial so commonplace and so vulgar does not go with the life of Isidore Ducasse, although it goes all too well, I think, with everything that is simian about that surreptitious hatred with which middle-class stupidity gets rid of every great name.

But by what filthy whore of rooted imbecility was I told one

Two letters from 1946

day that if the Comte de Lautréamont had not died at twenty-four, at the beginning of his life, he would have been *locked up* too, like Nietzsche, van Gogh, or poor Gérard de Nerval?

And this because although the attitude of Maldoror may be acceptable in a book, it is not acceptable until after the death of the poet, and a hundred years after, when the compelling explosives of the green heart of the poet have had time to calm down. For during his lifetime they are too strong. This is why society stopped the mouths of Baudelaire, Poe, Gérard de Nerval, and the unthinkable Comte de Lautréamont. Because people were afraid that their poetry would escape from their books and overthrow reality . . . And they stopped the mouth of Lautréamont when he was still a young man so as to rid themselves at once of the mounting aggressiveness of a heart which everyday life upsets catastrophically and which would eventually have taken everywhere the cynical and exceptional cunning of its inexhaustible flayings.

"And beyond the red light," says poor Isidore Ducasse, "she allowed him for a modest consideration to look inside her vagina . . ."

It is not an event to have found this sentence in *Maldoror*, any more than it is an event that it is there, for the whole book is made up of horrible sentences of this kind. Yes, in *Maldoror*, everything is horrible: the calf of an unhappy abortionist or the passing of a last bus. Everything is like that sentence in which the Comte de Lautréamont sees, although I believe it was the miserable Isidore Ducasse who saw it, the unthinkable Comte de Lautréamont sees, I say, a rod moving across the closed blinds in a bedroom of the most sinister *claque* (*claque*, vulgar slang word for brothel or bordello) and learns from the mouth of this rod that it is not a rod but a hair fallen from the head of its master, a munificent client whose money gave him the right to grind some poor creature in the epidermis of a pair of sheets, which may have been clean before the fact but are always nauseating afterward.

And I say that there was in Isidore Ducasse a spirit which always wanted to drop Isidore Ducasse in favor of the unthinkable Comte de Lautréamont, a very beautiful name, a very great name. And I say that the invention of the name Lautréamont, although it may have provided Isidore Ducasse with a password to clothe and introduce the unusual magnificence of his product, I say that the invention of this literary patronym, like a suit of clothes one can't afford, brought about, by its rising above the man who produced it, one of those foul collective obscenities in which the history of letters abounds and which in the end caused the soul of Isidore Ducasse to flee from life. For it was certainly Isidore Ducasse who died, and not the Comte de Lautréamont, and it was Isidore Ducasse who gave the Comte de Lautréamont the means to survive, and it would take little, I would even say that it would take nothing to convince me that the impersonal unthinkable Count of heraldic Lautréamont was in relation to Isidore Ducasse a kind of indefinable assassin.

And I believe that it was this that in the final analysis and on the last day poor Isidore Ducasse died of, although in history the Comte de Lautréamont survived him. For it was certainly Isidore Ducasse who found the name Lautréamont. But when he found it he was not alone. I mean that there was around him and his soul that microbic flocculation of spies, that slobbering, acrimonious mob of all the most sordid parasites of being, all the ancient ghosts of non-being, that scrofula of born profiteers who at his deathbed told him: "We are the Comte de Lautréamont and you are only Isidore Ducasse and if you do not acknowledge that you are only Isidore Ducasse and that we are the Comte de Lautréamont, author of *Maldoror*, we will kill you." And he died in the early morning, at the edge of an impossible night. Sweating and watching his death as if from the orifice of his coffin, like poor Isidore Ducasse in front of the rich Lautréamont. And this is not called the revolt of things against the master, but the orgy of the dubious unconscious of all against the consciousness of one.

I insist on this point, that Isidore Ducasse was neither a hallucinator nor a visionary but a genius who never ceased all his life to see clearly when he examined and probed the fallow ground of the as yet unutilized unconscious. His own, and nothing more, for there are no points in our bodies where we can make contact with the consciousness of all. And in our bodies we are alone. But this the world has never admitted, and it has always wanted to keep in its possession a means of looking more closely into the consciousness of all the great poets, and everyone

Two letters from 1946

has wanted to be able to look inside everyone else, in order to find out what everyone else was doing.

And one day some people, not highborn kinsmen, as in Poe's "Annabel Lee," but ignoble scabs of being, the mange of those itching with envy, came to say to Isidore Ducasse, over his bed and his head, and the head of his deathbed: You are a genius, but I am that genius that inspires your consciousness, and it is I who write your poems through you, before you, and better than you. And so it was that Isidore Ducasse died of rage because he wanted, like Poe, Nietzsche, Baudelaire, and Gérard de Nerval, to preserve his inherent individuality instead of becoming, like Victor Hugo, Lamartine, Musset, Pascal, or Chateaubriand, a funnel for the thinking of everybody.

For the operation is not to sacrifice one's self as a poet and at that moment as a madman to the whole world, but to allow oneself to be penetrated and violated by the consciousness of the whole world in such a way that one is in one's body merely the slave of the ideas and reactions of everybody.

And the name Lautréamont was only a preliminary means, against which Isidore Ducasse was not perhaps sufficiently on guard, of turning to the advantage of the general consciousness the superindividualistic works of Isidore Ducasse, poet driven mad by truth.

I mean that in the limbo of death where he is, other consciousnesses and other selves than his own rejoice obscenely, no doubt, having participated in the creative emulsion of his poems and his cries, and take dark pleasure in the idea of driving this poet mad in order to suffocate and kill him.

TO HENRI PARISOT (LETTER KNOWN AS "COLERIDGE THE TRAITOR")

Dear Henri Parisot,

My soul (today I no longer have one and I no longer believe it exists) has always been gloomy. It has been gloomy in ignorance because I am a complete innocent.

This is why you were right to ask me for something on Coleridge. Not that I think Coleridge belongs to that line of accursed poets, outcasts capable of *transuding* at will, of ejecting that little black mucus, that waxen fart of horrible pain from the bleeding tourniquet, which at the furthest pitch of horror escaped from Baudelaire or his real shadow Edgar Allan Poe, Gérard de Nerval, Villon perhaps; in the case of Lautréamont, I think the fart belongs to Isidore Ducasse and the tourniquet to Lautréamont. I mention Lautréamont *second*. For it was because he, I mean Isidore Ducasse, wanted to be the Comte de Lautréamont, that he died.

And for Coleridge, too, the question arose of being and saying what he saw he was, and it was because he tried to say it completely that he died, I say that he too died between twenty and twenty-four, and that nothing was left of the Samuel Taylor Coleridge who was preparing to outclass Dante but the author of "The Rhyme of the Ancient Mariner," "Christabel," and "Kubla Khan." Which some people will say is not bad and represents one of the greatest poets of the English language. That may be, and so much the worse for the English language, but it is also true that the English *language* had given the vulnerable, truthful, intrinsic heart of Samuel Taylor Coleridge, his heart which up to a certain point still quivered, one of those tourniquet turns of flesh, one of those foul turns which tongues of flesh can never refrain from giving the heart of the budding poet—I mean that Mr. Satisfied Coitus, with the complicity of Mrs. Erotic Orgasm, rose up one day against this poet being born
and, with a flick of the tongue, diverted him and turned him away from himself,
for this is how it is done.

I mean that I once read among the youthful poems of Samuel Taylor Coleridge a short unfinished poem in which Samuel Taylor Coleridge took up the old unfinished and in a certain sense abortive work of Euripides, and undertook consciously and determinedly to flagellate the idolatrous as it deserves, to drive the occult down to its level, to avenge man of all divinity, to carry the occult into the light of day, to do what is said, I mean what every

Two letters from 1946

mind precisely because it is mind, and not body, and precisely because it is not life, and has never belonged to the living, has always pretended should not be done, which is precisely to practice the occult publicly, to carry the occult world into the light of day in order to reveal clearly of what nothingness it is made.

For that which is secret gathers together and takes root and darkens all the more for being named, unclothed, and revealed.

This is why we must unclothe the virgin male, and this is the work that Samuel Taylor Coleridge had undertaken between twenty and twenty-four,
after which he stopped short.

He too fell victim to the buried and disguised fable, hidden with a triple key.

Why triple?

And why a key?

The one with which they forever hid Samuel Taylor Coleridge from himself, for there is beneath every history of this world I know not what idiotic prejudice in favor of mystery, Key, Trinity, Holiness; and number has never yet outgrown figures, any more than the extinguished pipe of Coleridge's ancient mariner has outgrown counting the sun by years, and the years, on I know not what mode of trinitarian gravitation that enslaves this humanity, which up to the present has never been able to rise to the effort of thinking, if only once in a century,
and will now never rise to the effort of thinking one last time for all time, *that it has never been at ease.*

This being the case, I cannot regard "The Rhyme of the Ancient Mariner," "Christabel," and "Kubla Khan" as anything but the remains of a senseless loss which poetry suffered some hundred and fifty years ago when it rediscovered the fiery cord, the stout mariner's rope at the priest's throat which, in the middle of this diversion of reality toward a remote poetic *potentiality,* this dislocation of the real world in favor of an occult erotic reality, and all the more occult because it is obscene, and all the more obscene because it is true, this fiery cord leads, I say, to the true author of the misdeed, who is the priest, and the INITIATE.

But this, the occult told Samuel Taylor Coleridge, this *you will never tell.*

For myself, I love only poetry.

Yes, for the obscenity of the thing is that the bourgeois tongue, the erotic flick of the tongue of Mrs. Obscene Lower-Middle-Class, has never loved anything but poetry.

I mean poetry poetry, poetic poetry with a capital P, a polite belch on top of the blood-red depths, the depths repressed into poematics, the poematics of the blood bath of reality.

For *after* means "poematic," *after* will come the time of blood. Because *-ema,* in Greek, means blood, and because po-ema must mean
after:
blood,
blood after.

Let us first make *poem,* with blood.
We will eat the time of blood.
And forward the po-em in the form of a song. And *without* blood.

For that which was made with blood, we, we have made a poem of it.

And what does the Gregorian chant (rape carved out of an emulsion of blood) come from?

What do certain Tibetan mantras come from?

They come from having wanted to avoid blood, from having distilled blood forever, and in this blood the true reality and

Two letters from 1946

having made of it
what is called
today
poetry,
absence of cruelty in time.

And forward the flick of the erotic tongue, and chaste, chaste, the orgasms of the middle class.

This world of war and of black markets, how many children did it force each year, how many children has it *pierced* in the body, in the double fat of this organic membrane, whose suffering it has never admitted or the blood it has taken, in order to fornicate foully its children,
basely its little children.

Behind the cruelty of the thing, but forward the poem without blood, but in the form of a song.

Thus Samuel Coleridge had seen clearly. Thus he had seen that the priest, the initiate, the guru, the scholar, with the complicity of the fashionable doctor, of the yogi under his folding screens, do not cease to flagellate in secret the true heart of the suffering poet, in order to prevent the mucus of blood.

Yes, under the tourniquet of pain there is a blood which flows, an hour for the thawed clot of the shadows, and which is, itself, this veritable child without sex, born outside the slimy parturitions of sex which was only the throat and the nail of a primitive strangulation,
and for not having been believed in the face of the senseless mucus he brought, Gérard de Nerval hanged himself from a street lamp, and for not being able to possess his own mucus, the Comte de Lautréamont died of rage; and what, in the face of all this, did Samuel Taylor Coleridge do?

The mucus that they stole from him he transformed into opium, and he took laudanum until he was dead.

And, under the cover of opium, he wrote music-poems.

He set adrift a ship and a crime. The ship in the ice floes of the Pole under the sun of a latter-born crime.

For the strange thing about "The Rhyme of the Ancient Mariner" is this crime which nothing can explain and which, if one reads the poem carefully, was born *after* and not *during* his thought.

And I have searched in these three poems of Coleridge for darkness, but I have never really found it.

And one day I knew that it was this darkness, this darkness of the poem itself, that Coleridge must have renounced.

And that he lived to regret it.

Lived merely to regret it, provided it was expressed in lovely music.

For in the end Samuel Taylor Coleridge forgot everything.

And in "Kubla Khan," had his memory returned to him? I do not think so. I think that the guile of the liturgical mind, which turns the howling of the damned into rites to be droned at matins, while the cock crows in the fresh morning, went so far as to clothe the remains of that *other* soul of Samuel Taylor Coleridge, of so many minds, and nullified *beings,* that even the formidable find which this poem concealed was merely an out-of-date Eden, the Eden of all those who gave themselves to God and not to man, for it is man who must be avenged, who must now avenge himself. And Coleridge had remembered a story, the story of a mind which had experienced a solace, but which experienced it
ritualized
above humanity.

In that kind of eternal state which has never detached itself from limbo,

Two letters from 1946

has not been able to enter into reality.

When Samuel Taylor Coleridge had, between twenty and twenty-four, been aware, had been aware of the real world.

The human world *without mortality*.

Coleridge had seen himself as immortal, and he was about to take measures to live, I mean the necessary measures to survive even to our own time, when I know not what clothed priest, what guru of a Bardo that has never existed except without a sex, toward which by artifice he diverts every recently dead man of this humanity, deceived him about the price of mucus. Diverted him toward the horrible suffering which only his age-old and premeditated magic had fabricated but which in fact had not existed.

I believe that Samuel Taylor Coleridge was weak, and that he was afraid, and perhaps that Samuel Taylor Coleridge also saw what he really was.

And that he was not the man to give this mucus in order to live, to live in immortality, and that no doubt the crime of the ancient mariner is that of Coleridge himself, and that the bird is this human soul which Coleridge killed in order to live. I think that soon, very precisely, yes, very precisely, I shall know it.

Paris, November 17, 1946

Antonin Artaud

Van Gogh, the Man Suicided by Society (1947)

XXXIII

Introduction

One can speak of the good mental health of van Gogh who, in his whole life, cooked only one of his hands and did nothing else except once to cut off his left ear,

in a world in which every day one eats vagina cooked in green sauce or penis of newborn child whipped and beaten to a pulp,

just as it is when plucked from the sex of its mother.

And this is not an image, but a fact abundantly and daily repeated and cultivated throughout the world.

And this, however delirious this statement may seem, is how modern life maintains its old atmosphere of debauchery, anarchy, disorder, delirium, derangement, chronic insanity, bourgeois inertia, psychic anomaly (for it is not man but the world which has become abnormal), deliberate dishonesty and notorious hypocrisy, stingy contempt for everything that shows breeding,

insistence on an entire order based on the fulfillment of a primitive injustice,

in short, of organized crime.

Things are going badly because sick consciousness has a vested interest right now in not recovering from its sickness.

This is why a tainted society has invented psychiatry to defend itself against the investigations of certain superior intellects whose faculties of divination would be troublesome.

Gérard de Nerval was not mad, but society accused him of being mad in order to discredit certain very important revelations that he was about to make,

and besides being accused, he was also struck on the head, physically struck on the head on a certain night so that he would lose memory of the monstrous facts which he was about to reveal and which, as a result of this blow, were pushed back within him onto a supranatural level, because all society, secretly in league against his consciousness, was at that moment powerful enough to make him forget their reality.

No, van Gogh was not mad, but his paintings were bursts of Greek fire, atomic bombs, whose angle of vision, unlike all other paintings popular at the time, would have been capable of seriously upsetting the spectral conformity of the Second Empire bourgeoisie and of the myrmidons of Thiers, Gambetta, and Félix Faure, as well as those of Napoleon III.

For it is not a certain conformity of manners that the painting of van Gogh attacks, but rather the conformity of institutions themselves. And even external nature, with her climates, her tides, and her equinoctial storms, cannot, after van Gogh's stay upon earth, maintain the same gravitation.

All the more reason why on the social level institutions are falling apart and medicine resembles a stale and useless corpse which declares van Gogh insane.

In comparison with the lucidity of van Gogh, which is a dynamic force, psychiatry is no better than a den of apes who are themselves obsessed and persecuted and who possess nothing to mitigate the most appalling states of anguish and human suffocation but a ridiculous terminology,

worthy product of their damaged brains.

Indeed, the psychiatrist does not exist who is not a well-known erotomaniac.

And I do not believe that the rule of the confirmed erotomania of psychiatrists admits of a single exception.

I know one who objected, a few years ago, to the idea of my accusing as a group this way the whole gang of respected scoundrels and patented quacks to which he belonged.

I, Mr. Artaud, am not an erotomaniac, he told me, and I defy you to show me a single piece of evidence on which you can base your accusation.

As evidence, Dr. L., I need only show you yourself,

you bear the stigma on your mug,

you rotten bastard.

You have the puss of someone who inserts his sexual prey under his tongue and then turns it over like an almond as a way of showing contempt for it.

This is called feathering one's nest or having one's way.

If in coitus you have not succeeded in chuckling from the glottis in a certain way that you know, and in rumbling at the same time through the pharynx, the esophagus, the ureter, and the anus,

you cannot say that you are satisfied.

Van Gogh, the Man Suicided by Society (1947)

And through your internal organic thrills you have fallen into a rut which is the incarnate evidence of a foul lust,

and which you have been cultivating year after year, more and more, because socially speaking it does not come under the jurisdiction of the law,

but it comes under the jurisdiction of another law whereby it is the whole damaged consciousness that suffers, because by behaving in this way you prevent it from breathing.

You dismiss as delirious a consciousness that is active even as you strangle it with your vile sexuality.

And this was precisely the level on which poor van Gogh was chaste,

chaste as a seraph or a maiden cannot be, because it was in fact they

who fomented

and nourished in the beginning the vast machinery of sin.

And perhaps, Dr. L., you belong to the race of iniquitous seraphim, but for pity's sake, leave men alone,

the body of van Gogh, untouched by any sin, was also untouched by madness which, indeed, sin alone can bring.

And I do not believe in Catholic sin,

but I do believe in erotic crime which in fact all the geniuses of the earth,

the authentic madmen of the asylums, have guarded themselves against,

or if not, it was because they were not (authentically) mad.

And what is an authentic madman?

It is a man who preferred to become mad, in the socially accepted sense of the word, rather than forfeit a certain superior idea of human honor.

So society has strangled in its asylums all those it wanted to get rid of or protect itself from, because they refused to become its accomplices in certain great nastinesses.

For a madman is also a man whom society did not want to hear and whom it wanted to prevent from uttering certain intolerable truths.

But, in this case, confinement is not its only weapon, and the concerted gathering of men has other means of overcoming the wills it wants to break.

Besides the minor spells of country sorcerers, there are the great sessions of world-wide spell-casting in which all alerted consciousness participates periodically.

Thus on the occasion of a war, a revolution, or a social upheaval still in the bud, the collective consciousness is questioned and questions itself, and makes its judgment.

This consciousness may also be aroused and called forth spontaneously in connection with certain particularly striking individual cases.

Thus there were collective magic spells in connection with Baudelaire, Poe, Gérard de Nerval, Nietzsche, Kierkegaard, Hölderlin, Coleridge,

and also in connection with van Gogh.

This may take place in the daytime, but generally, it is more likely to take place at night.

Thus strange forces are aroused and brought up into the astral vault, into that kind of dark dome which constitutes, over all human respiration, the venomous hostility of the evil spirit of the majority of people.

It is thus that the few rare lucid well-disposed people who have had to struggle on the earth find themselves at certain hours of the day or night in the depth of certain authentic and waking nightmare states, surrounded by the formidable suction, the formidable tentacular oppression of a kind of civic magic which will soon be seen appearing openly in social behavior.

In the face of this concerted nastiness, which has as its basis or fulcrum on the one hand sexuality and on the other hand the mass, or other psychic rites, it is not delirium to walk around at night in a hat with twelve candles on it to paint a landscape from nature;

for how else could poor van Gogh have managed to have light, as our friend the actor Roger Blin pointed out so justly the other day?

As for the cooked hand, that is heroism pure and simple;

as for the severed ear, that is straightforward logic,

and I repeat,

a world which, day and night, and more and more, eats the uneatable,

in order to carry out its evil designs,
has nothing to do on this point
but to shut up about it.

Post-Scriptum

Van Gogh did not die of a state of delirium properly speaking,

but of having been bodily the battlefield of a problem around which the evil spirit of humanity has been struggling from the beginning.

The problem of the predominance of flesh over spirit, or of body over flesh, or of spirit over both.

And where in this delirium is the place of the human self?

Van Gogh searched for his throughout his life, with a strange energy and determination,

and he did not commit suicide in a fit of madness, in dread of not succeeding,

on the contrary, he had just succeeded, and discovered what he was and who he was, when the collective consciousness of society, to punish him for escaping from its clutches,

suicided him.

And this happened to van Gogh the way this always generally happens, during an orgy, a mass, an absolution, or some other rite of consecration, possession, succubation or incubation.

Thus it wormed its way into his body,
this society
absolved,
consecrated,
sanctified
and possessed,
erased in him the supernatural consciousness he had just achieved, and, like an inundation of black crows in the fibers of his internal tree,
overwhelmed him with one final surge,
and, taking his place,
killed him.

For it is the anatomical logic of modern man that he has never been able to live, has never thought of living, except as one possessed.

The Man Suicided by Society

Pure linear painting had been driving me mad for a long time when I encountered van Gogh, who painted neither lines nor forms but things of inert nature as if in the throes of convulsions.

And inert.

As if under the terrible staggering blow of that force of inertia which the whole world talks about cryptically and which has never been so obscure as it is now that the whole earth and all of life have combined to elucidate it.

Now, it is with a bludgeon stroke, truly with a bludgeon stroke, that van Gogh never ceases striking all forms of nature and all objects.

Carded by van Gogh's nail,

the landscapes show their hostile flesh,

the anvil of their eviscerated folds,

which one knows not what strange force is in the process of transforming.

An exhibit of the paintings of van Gogh is always a date in history,

not in the history of painted things, but in history pure and simple.

For there is nothing, no famine, no epidemic, no volcanic eruption, no earthquake, no war which grates on the monads of the air, which wrings the neck of the menacing figure of *fama fatum*, the neurotic destiny of things,

like a painting by van Gogh—brought out into the light of day,

restored directly to sight,

hearing, touch,

smell,

on the walls of an exhibit—

in short, launched afresh into current reality, reintroduced into circulation.

The latest van Gogh exhibit at the Orangerie does not have all the very great paintings of the unfortunate painter. But among those that are there, there are enough rotating processions studded with clumps of carmine plants, enough sunken roads with

overhanging yews, enough violet suns whirling over haystacks of pure gold, enough *Père Tranquille* and enough self-portraits,
  to remind us what a sordid simplicity of objects, people, materials, elements,
    van Gogh drew on for these kinds of organ peals, these fireworks, these atmospheric epiphanies, in short, this "Great Lifework" of an incessant and untimely transmutation.

  These crows painted two days before his death did not, any more than his other paintings, open the door for him to a certain posthumous glory, but they do open to painterly painting, or rather to unpainted nature, the secret door to a possible beyond, to a possible permanent reality, through the door opened by van Gogh to an enigmatic and sinister beyond.
  It is not usual to see a man, with the shot that killed him already in his belly, crowding black crows onto a canvas, and under them a kind of meadow—perhaps livid, at any rate empty—in which the wine color of the earth is juxtaposed wildly with the dirty yellow of the wheat.
  But no other painter besides van Gogh would have known how to find, as he did, in order to paint his crows, that truffle black, that "rich banquet" black which is at the same time, as it were, excremental, of the wings of the crows surprised in the fading gleam of evening.

  And what does the earth complain of down there under the wings of those *auspicious* crows, auspicious, no doubt, for van Gogh alone, and on the other hand, sumptuous augury of an evil which can no longer touch him?
  For no one until then had turned the earth into that dirty linen twisted with wine and wet blood.

   The sky in the painting is very low, bruised,
   violet, like the lower edges of lightning.
   The strange shadowy fringe of the void rising after the flash.
   Van Gogh loosed his crows like the black microbes of his suicide's spleen a few centimeters from the top *and as if from the bottom of the canvas,*
     following the black slash of that line where the beating of

their rich plumage adds to the swirling of the terrestrial storm the heavy menace of a suffocation from above.

And yet the whole painting is rich.

Rich, sumptuous, and calm.

Worthy accompaniment to the death of the man who during his life set so many drunken suns whirling over so many unruly haystacks and who, desperate, with a bullet in his belly, had no choice but to flood a landscape with blood and wine, to drench the earth with a final emulsion, both dark and joyous, with a taste of bitter wine and spoiled vinegar.

And so the tone of the last canvas painted by van Gogh—he who, elsewhere, never went beyond painting—evokes the abrupt and barbarous tonal quality of the most moving, passionate, and impassioned Elizabethan drama.

This is what strikes me most of all in van Gogh, the most painterly of all painters, and who, without going any further than what is called and is painting, without going beyond the tube, the brush, the framing of the *subject* and of the canvas to resort to anecdote, narrative, drama, picturesque action, or to the intrinsic beauty of subject or object, was able to imbue nature and objects with so much passion that not one of the fabulous tales of Edgar Allan Poe, Herman Melville, Nathaniel Hawthorne, Gérard de Nerval, Achim von Arnim, or Hoffmann says more on a psychological and dramatic level than his unpretentious canvases,

his canvases which are almost all, in fact, and as if deliberately, of modest dimensions.

A candlestick on a chair, an armchair of braided green straw,
a book on the armchair,
and there the drama is revealed.
Who is about to enter?
Will it be Gauguin or some other ghost?

The lit candle on the straw-bottomed chair seems to indicate the line of luminous demarcation that divides the two antagonistic individualities of van Gogh and Gauguin.

The aesthetic object of their disagreement would not, perhaps, be of great interest in itself, but it would necessarily indicate a

Van Gogh, the Man Suicided by Society (1947)

profound human division between the two natures of van Gogh and Gauguin.

I believe that Gauguin thought that the artist must look for symbol, for myth, must enlarge the things of life to the magnitude of myth,

whereas van Gogh thought that one must know how to deduce myth from the most ordinary things of life.

In which I think he was bloody well right.

For reality is frighteningly superior to all fiction, all fable, all divinity, all surreality.

All you need is the genius to know how to interpret it.

Which no painter before poor van Gogh had done,

which no painter will ever do again,

for I believe that this time,

today, in fact,

right now,

in this month of February 1947,

reality itself,

the myth of reality itself, mythic reality itself, is in the process of becoming flesh.

Thus, no one since van Gogh has *known* how to move the great cymbal, the superhuman, the *perpetually* superhuman tone, according to the repressed order with which the objects of real life ring,

when one has known how to open one's ear enough to understand the rise of their tidal wave.

It is thus that the light of the candle rings, that the light of the lit candle on the green straw-bottomed chair rings like the breathing of a loving body in the presence of the body of a sleeping invalid.

It rings like a strange criticism, a profound and surprising judgment whose sentence van Gogh may well allow us later to assume, much later, on that day when the violet light of the straw-bottomed chair will have finished submerging the whole painting.

And one cannot help noticing that fraction of lavender light that consumes the crossbars of the large ominous chair, the old splay-legged chair of green straw, although one cannot notice it at once.

ANTONIN ARTAUD

For the focus of this light is as if placed elsewhere and its source is strangely obscure, like a secret whose key only van Gogh would have kept on his own person.

If van Gogh had not died at thirty-seven? I do not call in the Great Mourner to tell me with what supreme masterpieces painting would have been enriched,
for after *The Crows*, I cannot persuade myself that van Gogh would ever have painted again.
I think that he died at thirty-seven because he had, alas. reached the end of his dismal and revolting story of a man strangled by an evil spirit.
For it was not because of himself, because of the disease of his own madness, that van Gogh abandoned life.
It was under the pressure of the evil influence, two days before his death, of Dr. Gachet, a so-called psychiatrist, which was the direct, effective, and sufficient cause of his death.
When I read van Gogh's letters to his brother, I was left with the firm and sincere conviction that Dr. Gachet, "psychiatrist," actually detested van Gogh, painter, and that he detested him as a painter, but above all as a genius.
It is almost impossible to be a doctor and an honest man, but it is obscenely impossible to be a psychiatrist without at the same time bearing the stamp of the most incontestable madness: that of being unable to resist that old atavistic reflex of the mass of humanity, which makes any man of science who is absorbed by this mass a kind of natural and inborn enemy of all genius.

Medicine was born of evil, if it was not born of illness, and if it has, on the contrary, provoked and created illness out of nothing to justify its own existence; but psychiatry was born of the vulgar mob of creatures who wanted to preserve the evil at the source of illness and who have thus pulled out of their own inner nothingness a kind of Swiss guard to cut off at its root that impulse of rebellious vindication which is at the origin of genius.
There is in every lunatic a misunderstood genius whose idea, shining in his head, frightened people, and for whom delirium was

the only solution to the strangulation that life had prepared for him.

Dr. Gachet did not tell van Gogh that he was there to straighten out his painting (as Dr. Gaston Ferdière, head physician of the asylum of Rodez, told me he was there to straighten out my poetry), but he sent him to paint from nature, to bury himself in a landscape to escape the pain of thinking.

Except that, as soon as van Gogh had turned his back, Dr. Gachet turned off the switch to his mind.

As if, without intending any harm but with one of those seemingly innocent disparaging wrinklings of the nose where the whole bourgeois unconscious of the earth has inscribed the old magic force of a thought one hundred times repressed.

In so doing, it was not only the evil of the problem which Dr. Gachet forbade him,
but the sulphurous insemination,
the horror of the nail turning in the gullet of the only passage, with which van Gogh,
tetanized,
van Gogh, suspended over the chasm of breath,
painted.

For van Gogh was a terrible sensibility.

To be convinced of this, one need only look at his face, the always panting and also in certain respects spellbinding face of a butcher.

Like the face of an old-time butcher, become wise and now retired from business, this badly lighted face pursues me.

Van Gogh has represented himself in a very large number of canvases and, no matter how well lighted they were, I have always had that painful impression that the lighting had been faked, that van Gogh had been deprived of a light indispensable for carving out and tracing his path within himself.

And of course it was not Dr. Gachet who was able to point out this path to him.

But, as I have said, there is in every living psychiatrist a repulsive and sordid atavism that makes him see in every artist, every genius he comes across, an enemy.

And I know that Dr. Gachet left the impression on history, with regard to van Gogh, whom he was treating and who ultimately committed suicide while at his house, that he was his last friend on earth, a kind of providential consoler.

And yet I am more convinced than ever that it was to Dr. Gachet of Auvers-sur-Oise that van Gogh was indebted on that day, the day he committed suicide at Auvers-sur-Oise,
was indebted, I say, for abandoning life—
for van Gogh was one of those natures whose superior lucidity enables them in all circumstances to see farther, infinitely and dangerously farther, than the immediate and apparent reality of facts.
I mean that he saw farther in his consciousness than consciousness usually contains.
In the depths of those almost lashless butcher's eyes, van Gogh devoted himself relentlessly to one of those operations of somber alchemy which took nature as their object and the human body as their vessel or crucible.
And I know that Dr. Gachet always found that this tired him.
Which was not in him the result of a simple medical concern,
but the admission of a jealousy as conscious as it was unacknowledged.

The truth is that van Gogh had arrived at the stage of illuminism where the mind in disorder falls back before the invading discharges of matter
and which to think is no longer to use oneself up,
and is no longer,

and where there is nothing left to do but *gather the body together*, I mean

PILE UP BODIES.

It is no longer the world of the astral, it is the world of direct creation which is thus recovered beyond consciousness and the brain.

Van Gogh, the Man Suicided by Society (1947)

And I have never seen a body without a brain that may have been tired by inert supports.

Supports of the inert—these bridges, these sunflowers, these yews, these olive harvests, these haymakings. They no longer move.

They are frozen.

But who would have been able to dream them more solid beneath the carver's blow to the quick which has unsealed their impenetrable trembling.

No, Dr. Gachet, a support has never tired anyone. These are forces of a madman which lie in repose without causing movement.

I, too, am like poor van Gogh, I no longer think, but I direct, every day at closer hand, formidable internal ebullitions, and I would like to see any medical science whatsoever come and reproach me for tiring myself.

History tells us that someone owed van Gogh a certain sum of money: van Gogh had already been fretting about it for several days.

It is a tendency of lofty natures, always one notch above reality, to explain everything in terms of bad conscience,

to believe that nothing is ever due to chance and that everything bad that happens is the result of an ill will that is conscious, intelligent, and concerted.

Which psychiatrists never believe.

Which geniuses always believe.

When I am sick, it is because I am under a spell, and I cannot believe I am sick if I do not also believe that someone has an interest in robbing me of my health and is profiting by my health.

Van Gogh also believed that he was under a spell, and he said so.

And as for myself, I believe pertinently that he was, and some day I shall tell where and how.

And Dr. Gachet was that grotesque Cerberus, that sanious and purulent Cerberus, in sky-blue jacket and gleaming linen, placed before poor van Gogh to rob him of all his sound ideas. For if this way of seeing which is sound were to become universal, society could no longer exist, but I know which heroes of the earth would find their freedom there.

Van Gogh was unable to shake off in time this type of vampirism of a family selfishly concerned that the genius of van Gogh the painter stick to painting, without at the same time demanding the revolution indispensable to the bodily and physical blossoming of his visionary personality.

And there took place between Dr. Gachet and Theo, van Gogh's brother, how many of those stinking confabulations that families have with the head physicians of insane asylums regarding the *patient* they have brought them.

"Keep an eye on him, make sure he forgets all those ideas. You understand, the doctor said so, you must forget all those ideas: they're hurting you, if you keep on thinking about them you'll stay shut up for the rest of your life."

"But no, van Gogh, come to your senses, look, it's chance, and then it never does any good to want to look into the secrets of Providence this way. I know Mr. So-and-so, he's a very fine man, it's your persecution complex that makes you believe again that he is thus secretly performing magic."

"He promised you he would pay you this sum, and he'll pay it. You can't go on this way, insisting on attributing this delay to ill will."

These are examples of those smooth conversations of good-natured psychiatrists which seem harmless enough, but which leave on the heart the trail of a little black tongue as it were, the harmless little black tongue of a poisonous salamander.

And sometimes it takes no more than this to drive a genius to suicide.

There are days when the heart feels the deadlock so terribly that it takes it like a blow on the head with a piece of bamboo, this idea that it will not be able to go on any longer.

For it was, in fact, after a conversation with Dr. Gachet that van Gogh, as if nothing were the matter, went back to his room and killed himself.

I myself spent nine years in an insane asylum and I never had the obsession of suicide, but I know that each conversation with a psychiatrist, every morning at the time of his visit, made me want

Van Gogh, the Man Suicided by Society (1947)

to hang myself, realizing that I would not be able to cut his throat.

And Theo may have been very good to his brother financially, but this did not prevent his believing him to be a raving, hallucinated visionary, and from doing everything he could, instead of following him in his delirium,

to calm him down.

If he died of regret, afterward, what does it matter?

What van Gogh cared about most in the world was his idea of a painter, his terrible, fanatical, apocalyptical idea of a visionary.

That the world should be organized under the command of its own womb, should resume its compressed, anti-psychic rhythm of a secret festival in the public square and, in front of the whole world, should be returned to the extreme heat of the crucible.

This means that the apocalypse, a consummated apocalypse, is brooding right now in the paintings of old martyred van Gogh, and that the world needs him in order to lash out with head and feet.

No one has ever written, painted, sculpted, modeled, built, or invented except literally to get out of hell.

And I prefer, to get out of hell, the landscapes of this quiet convulsionary to the teeming compositions of Brueghel the Elder or Hieronymus Bosch, who are, in comparison with him, only artists, whereas van Gogh is only a poor dunce determined not to deceive himself.

But how is one to make a scientist understand that there is something unalterably deranged about differential calculus, quantum theory, or the obscene and so inanely liturgical ordeals of the precession of the equinoxes—by means of that shrimp-pink quilt which van Gogh puffs up so gently at a chosen spot on his bed, by means of the minor insurrection—Veronese green, liquid blue—of that boat in front of which an Auvers-sur-Oise washerwoman rises from her work, also by means of that sun screwed in behind the gray angle of the village steeple, pointed, over there, behind; in the foreground, that enormous mass of earth which, like a musical introduction, seeks to form itself into a frozen wave.

o vio profe,
o vio proto
o vio loto
o théthé

What is the use of describing a painting by van Gogh! No description attempted by anyone else could be worth the simple alignment of natural objects and hues to which van Gogh gives himself,
    as great a writer as he was painter, and which gives, in relation to the work described, the impression of the most astounding authenticity.

What is drawing? How does one do it? It is the act of working one's way through an invisible wall of iron which seems to lie between what one feels and what one can do. How is one to get through this wall, for it does no good to use force? In my opinion, one must undermine the wall and file one's way through, slowly and with patience.

September 8, 1888
In my painting The Night Café, *I have tried to express that the café is a place where one can ruin oneself, go mad, commit crimes. I have tried by contrasting pale pink with blood red and maroon, by contrasting soft Louis XV and Veronese greens with yellow greens and hard pure greens, all this in an atmosphere of an infernal furnace, of pale sulphur, to express as it were the evil power of a dive.*
    And yet in the guise of Japanese gaiety and the good fellowship of Tartarin . . .

July 23, 1890
Perhaps you will see this sketch of the garden of Daubigny—it is one of my most studied paintings—I am enclosing with it a sketch of old stubble and the sketches for two twelve-inch canvases representing vast stretches of wheat after a rain.
    Daubigny's garden, foreground of green and pink grass. To the left a green and lavender bush and the stump of a plant with

Van Gogh, the Man Suicided by Society (1947)

whitish foliage. In the middle a bed of roses, to the right a wattle, a wall, and above the wall a hazel tree with violet leaves. Then a hedge of lilacs, a row of rounded yellow linden trees, the house itself in the background, pink, with a roof of bluish tile. A bench and three chairs, a dark figure with a yellow hat, and in the foreground a black cat. Pale green sky.

How easy it seems to write like this.

Well, try it then, and tell me whether, not being the creator of a van Gogh canvas, you could describe it as simply, succinctly, objectively, permanently, validly, solidly, opaquely, massively, authentically, and miraculously as in this little letter of his.
(For the distinguishing criterion is not a question of amplitude or crampedness but one of sheer personal strength.)
So I shall not describe a painting of van Gogh after van Gogh, but I shall say that van Gogh is a painter because he recollected nature, because he reperspired it and made it sweat, because he squeezed onto his canvases in clusters, in monumental sheaves of color, the grinding of elements that occurs once in a hundred years, the awful elementary pressure of apostrophes, scratches, commas, and dashes which, after him, one can no longer believe that natural appearances are not made of.

And what an onslaught of repressed jostlings, ocular collisions taken from life, blinkings taken from nature, have the luminous currents of the forces which work on reality had to reverse before being finally driven together and, as it were, *hoisted* onto the canvas, and accepted?

There are no ghosts in the paintings of van Gogh, no visions, no hallucinations.
This is the torrid truth of the sun at two o'clock in the afternoon.
A slow generative nightmare gradually becoming clear.
Without nightmare and without result.
But the suffering of the prenatal is there.

It is the wet gleam of a meadow, of the stalk of a slip of wheat which is there to be extradited.
And for which nature will one day answer.
As society will also for his untimely death.

A field of wheat bowing under the wind, and above, the wings of a single bird like a suspended comma: what painter, who would not be strictly a painter, would, like van Gogh, have had the boldness to attack a subject of such disarming simplicity?

No, there are no ghosts in van Gogh's paintings, no drama, no subject, and I would even say no object, for what is the motif?
If not something like the iron shadow of the motet of an ancient indescribable music, the leitmotiv of a theme that has despaired of its own subject.
It is nature, naked and pure, seen as she reveals herself when one knows how to approach her closely enough.
Witness this landscape of molten gold, of bronze fired in ancient Egypt, in which an enormous sun leans on roofs so tottering with light that they are as if in a state of decomposition.
And I know of no other painting—apocalyptic, hieroglyphic, phantasmal, or pathetic—which gives me this sensation of occult strangeness, of a cadaver of useless hermeticism, head opened, which would give up its secret on the executioner's block.
When I say this I am not thinking of *Père Tranquille*, or of that funambulatory autumn lane down which there walks, last, a bent old man with an umbrella hanging from his sleeve like a ragpicker's hook.
I am thinking again of those crows with their wings the black of polished truffles.
I am thinking again of his wheatfield: ear of wheat upon ear of wheat, and all is said,
with, in the foreground, a few little poppy blossoms cautiously scattered, tartly and nervously applied, and thinly sown, knowingly and furiously punctuated and shredded.
Only life knows how to offer such epidermic denudations which speak under an unbuttoned shirt, and one does not know why the glance is drawn to the left rather than to the right, toward that little mound of wavy flesh.

Van Gogh, the Man Suicided by Society (1947)

But it is thus and it is a fact.
But it is thus and this is made fact.

Occult, too, his bedroom, so charmingly rural, and sown as it were with an odor that should be bottled of that wheat that one sees trembling in the fields in the distance, behind the window that would hide it.

Rural, too, the color of the old quilt, the red of mussels, sea urchins, shrimps, mullet, the red of scorched pimento.

And it was certainly van Gogh's fault if the color of the quilt on his bed was in reality so effective, and I doubt whether any weaver could have transplanted its indescribable stamp the way van Gogh was able to transfer from the back of his mind onto his canvas the red of that indescribable glaze.

And I do not know how many criminal priests, dreaming in the head of their so-called Holy Ghost, of the ocher gold, the infinite blue of a stained-glass window dedicated to their strumpet "Mary," have known how to isolate in the air, to draw from the cunning niches of the air those homey colors which are an event in themselves, in which every stroke of van Gogh's brush on the canvas is worse than an event.

One time this takes the form of a tidy room but with an aura of balm or aroma which no Benedictine will ever find to perfect his salutary liqueurs.

Another time it takes the form of a simple haystack crushed by an enormous sun.

This room brought to mind the Great Work with its white wall the color of clear pearls on which a rough bath towel hangs like an old peasant charm, unapproachable and comforting.

There are certain light chalk whites which are worse than ancient tortures, and nowhere does the old operative scruple of poor great van Gogh appear as clearly as in this canvas.

For all this is truly van Gogh, the single-minded concern for the stroke silently and movingly applied. The plebeian color of things, but so right, so lovingly right that no precious stones could attain its rarity.

For van Gogh will prove to have been the most genuine painter of all painters, the only one who did not try to go beyond painting as the strict means of his work and the strict framework of his means.

And at the same time the only one, absolutely the only one, who absolutely transcended painting, the inert act of representing nature, in order to make a whirling force, an element torn right out of the heart, gush forth in this exclusive representation of nature.

Under the guise of representation he welded an air and enclosed within it a nerve, things which do not exist in nature, which are of a nature and an air more real than the air and nerve of real nature.

I see, as I write these lines, the blood-red face of the painter coming toward me, in a wall of eviscerated sunflowers,
    in a formidable conflagration of cinders of opaque hyacinth and of fields of lapis lazuli.

All this amid a seemingly meteoric bombardment of atoms which would appear a particle at a time,
    proof that van Gogh conceived his canvases like a painter, of course, and only like a painter, but one who would be
    for *that very reason*
    a formidable musician.

Organist of a suspended tempest which laughs in limpid nature, this nature which is pacified between two storms but which, like van Gogh himself, shows that it is ready to move on.

After seeing this, one can turn one's back on any painted canvas, it has nothing more to tell us. The stormy light of van Gogh's painting begins its somber recitations the very moment one has ceased looking at it.

Only a painter, van Gogh, and nothing more,
    no philosophy, no mysticism, no ritual, no psychurgy or liturgy,
    no history, no literature or poetry,
    these sunflowers of bronzed gold are painted; they are painted as sunflowers and nothing more, but in order to understand a

sunflower in nature, one must now go back to van Gogh, just as in order to understand a storm in nature,
a stormy sky,
a field in nature,
it is henceforth impossible not to go back to van Gogh.

It was stormy like this in Egypt or on the plains of Semitic Judaea,
perhaps it was dark like this in Chaldaea, in Mongolia, or in the mountains of Tibet, which as far as I know have not moved.
And yet when I look at this field of wheat or stones, white as a buried bone yard on which weighs this old violet sky, I can no longer believe in the mountains of Tibet.

Painter, nothing but a painter, van Gogh adopted the techniques of pure painting and never went beyond them.
I mean that in order to paint he never went beyond the means that painting offered him.
A stormy sky,
a chalk-white field,
canvases, brushes, his red hair, tubes, his yellow hand, his easel,
but all the lamas of Tibet gathered together can shake out of their skirts the apocalypse they will have prepared,
van Gogh will have given us a whiff of its nitrogen peroxide in advance, in a painting which contains just enough of the sinister to force us to reorient ourselves.
One day for no reason he decided not to go beyond the subject,
but after one has seen van Gogh, one can no longer believe that there is anything more impossible than to go beyond the subject.
The simple subject of a lighted candle on a straw-bottomed chair with a violet frame says more in the hands of van Gogh than all the Greek tragedies, or the plays of Cyril Tourneur, Webster, or Ford, which until now, moreover, have never been performed.

It is literally true that I saw the face of van Gogh, red with blood in the explosion of his landscapes, coming toward me,

ANTONIN ARTAUD

     kohan
     taver
     tensur
     purtan

  in a conflagration,
  in a bombardment,
  in an explosion,
    avengers of that millstone which poor van Gogh the mad wore around his neck all his life.
    The millstone of painting without knowing why or for what.

  For it is not for this world,
  it is never for this earth that we have always worked,
  struggled,
    troated of horror, of hunger, of poverty, of hatred, of scandal, and of disgust,
  that we were all poisoned,
  although by these things we may have all been bewitched,
  and that we have finally committed suicide,
    for are we not all, like poor van Gogh himself, suicided by society!

  Van Gogh renounced storytelling in his painting, but the amazing thing is that this painter who is only a painter,
    and who is more of a painter than other painters, since he is the one for whom the material, painting itself, is of primary importance,
    with the color caught just as it is when squeezed out of the tube,
    with the impress of the separate hairs of the brush in the paint,
    with the touch of the paint itself, as if distinct in its own sunlight,
    with the *i*, the comma, the tip of the point of the brush itself twisted right into the paint, applied roughly, and splashing in sparks which the painter smooths and reworks all over the canvas,
    the amazing thing is that this painter who is nothing but a

painter is also, of all painters born, the one most likely to make us forget that we are in the presence of painting,
  painting intended to represent the subject he has selected,
  and who presents to us in front of the fixed canvas the enigma pure, the pure enigma of the tortured flower, of the countryside slashed, plowed, and harried on all sides by his intoxicated brush.

His landscapes are old sins which have not yet recovered their primitive apocalypses, but which will not fail to recover them.

Why do the paintings of van Gogh give me this impression of being seen as if from the other side of the grave, from a world in which his suns, in the end, will have been all that turned and shone with joy?

For is it not the entire history of what was once called the soul that lives and dies in his convulsionary landscapes and in his flowers?

The soul which gave its ear to the body, and van Gogh gave the ear back to his very soul's soul,
  giving it to a woman to flesh out the grisly illusion.

One day the soul did not exist,
neither did the mind,
  as for consciousness, no one had ever thought of it,
  but where, for that matter, was thought, in a world made up solely of warring elements no sooner destroyed than recomposed,
  for thought is a luxury of peacetime.

And what is, better than the incredible van Gogh, the painter who understood the phenomenal nature of the problem, in whom every real landscape is as if latent in the crucible where it is going to be reborn?

Thus, the old van Gogh was that king against whom, while he slept, was invented the curious sin called Turkish culture,
  example, vessel, motive, of the sin of humanity, which has never been able to do anything except eat raw artist to stuff its respectability.

By which it has served only to consecrate ritually its cowardice!

For humanity does not want to go to the trouble of living, of entering into that natural friction of the forces that make up reality, in order to extract from them a body that no storm will ever be able to pierce.

It has always preferred to settle simply for existence.

As for life, it is in the genius of the artist that humanity is in the habit of seeking it.

Now van Gogh, who cooked one of his hands, was never afraid of the struggle to live, that is, to separate the fact of living from the idea of existing.

and everything can certainly exist without taking the trouble to be,

and everything can be without taking, like van Gogh the madman, the trouble to radiate and to glow red.

This is what society stole from him in order to complete the Turkish culture, that surface honesty whose source and support is crime.

And so it was that van Gogh died a suicide, because the consciousness of society as a whole could no longer endure him.

For although there may have been neither mind, nor soul, nor consciousness, nor thought,

there was fulminate,
mature volcano,
medium's stone,
patience,
inflamed ganglion,
cooked tumor,
and the skin of a flayed man.

And king van Gogh drowsed, incubating the next warning signaling the insurrection of his health.

Why?

Because good health is a plethora of deep-seated evils, of a formidable ardor for living corroded by a hundred wounds, which must nevertheless be brought to life,

which must be led to perpetuate themselves.

Anyone who does not smell cooked bomb and compressed vertigo is not worthy of being alive.

This is the solace which poor van Gogh in a burst of flame made it his duty to reveal.

Van Gogh, the Man Suicided by Society (1947)

But the evil which was watching injured him.

The Turk, beneath his honest face, crept delicately to van Gogh to pluck the praline from him,

to break off the (natural) praline that was forming.

And van Gogh lost a thousand summers there.

He died of this at thirty-seven,

before living,

for every imitator lived before him on strengths that he had assembled.

And this is what must now be given back, to enable van Gogh to rise from the dead.

In comparison with a humanity of cowardly imitators and cowering dogs, the painting of van Gogh will prove to have been the painting of a time when there was no soul, no mind, no consciousness, no thought, nothing but the first rudiments by turns enchained and unchained.

Landscapes undergoing strong convulsions, of frenzied traumatisms, as of a body that fever torments to restore it to perfect health.

The body under the skin is an overheated factory,

and, outside,

the patient glistens,

he shines,

from all his pores,

burst open.

Like a landscape

by van Gogh

at noon.

Only perpetual war explains a peace which is only a passing phase,

just as milk that is ready to be poured explains the pan in which it was boiling.

Beware of the beautiful landscapes of van Gogh, tempestuous and peaceful,

convulsed and pacified.

This is health between two bouts of brain fever which will pass.

This is fever between two bouts of an insurrection of good health.

One day the painting of van Gogh, armed both with fever and with health,
will return to scatter the dust of an imprisoned world which his heart could no longer endure.

Post-Scriptum

I am returning to the painting of the crows.

Who has already seen, as in this painting, the earth become equivalent to the sea?

Van Gogh is of all painters the one who strips us most profoundly, right down to the woof, but he does so as one would cleanse oneself of an obsession.

The obsession of causing objects to be other than they are, of daring to risk the sin of *the other,* for the earth cannot be the color of a liquid sea, and yet it is as a liquid sea that van Gogh flings his earth as if with a hoe.

And he has infused his painting with the color of the dregs of wine, and it is the earth which smells of wine, which even splashes amid the waves of wheat, which rears a dark cockscomb against those low clouds that are gathering in the sky on all sides.

But, as I have already said, the funereal aspect of all this is the luxuriousness with which the crows are treated.

This color of musk, of rich nard, of truffles from some magnificent dinner.

In the violet billows of the sky, two or three old men's faces of vapor chance an apocalyptic grimace, but van Gogh's crows are there urging them to greater decency, I mean to less spirituality,

and what did van Gogh himself mean by this painting with its brooding sky, painted almost at the precise moment that he rid himself of existence, for this painting has a strange, almost stately color of birth, marriage, departure,

I hear the wings of the crows striking cymbal blows loudly over an earth whose torrent it seems that van Gogh can no longer contain.

Then death.

The olive trees of Saint-Rémy.

Van Gogh, the Man Suicided by Society (1947)

The solar cypress.

The bedroom.

The olive harvest.

Les Aliscamps.

The café at Arles.

The bridge where one feels like dipping one's finger in the water, in a gesture of violent regression to a state of infancy forced on one by the astounding hand grip of van Gogh.
The water is blue,
not the blue of water,
but the blue of liquid paint.
The suicided madman passed this way and he gave the water of painting back to nature,
but who will give it back to him?

A madman, van Gogh?
Let someone who once knew how to look at a human face look at van Gogh's self-portrait, I am thinking of the one in a soft hat.
Painted by van Gogh the extra-lucid, this redheaded butcher's face which inspects and spies on us, which also scrutinizes us with a glowering eye.
I know of no psychiatrist who could scrutinize a man's face with such overwhelming force or so dissect its inviolable psychology as at a carving board.
The eye of van Gogh is that of a great genius, but in the way I see him dissecting me from the depths of the canvas from which he has arisen, it is no longer the genius of a painter that I feel at this moment living in him, but the genius of a certain philosopher whom I have never encountered in life.
No, Socrates did not have this eye, the unhappy Nietzsche may have been the only man before him to have had this look that undresses the soul, that releases the body from the soul, that lays bare the body of man, beyond the subterfuges of the mind.

The look of van Gogh is suspended, screwed in, it is glazed behind his unusual eyelids, his thin smooth eyebrows.

It is a look that penetrates immediately, it transfixes, in this face which is rough-hewn like a piece of squared-off timber.

But van Gogh has caught the moment when the pupil is about to pour itself out in the void,

when this look, fired at us like the bomb of a meteor, takes on the expressionless color of the void and of the inertia that fills it.

Better than any psychiatrist in the world, this was how the great van Gogh located his illness.

I penetrate, I persist, I inspect, I seize, I force open, my dead life conceals nothing, and nothingness moreover has never hurt anyone, what forces me to return within is this desolating absence which passes and submerges me at times, but I understand it clearly, very clearly, I even understand what nothingness is, and I can say what is in it.

And van Gogh was right, one can live for the infinite, can be satisfied only with the infinite, there is enough of the infinite on the earth and in the spheres to satiate a thousand great geniuses, and if van Gogh was unable to fill to overflowing his desire to irradiate his whole life with it, it is because society forbade it to him.

Flatly and consciously forbidden.

One day the executioners came for van Gogh, just as they came for Gérard de Nerval, Baudelaire, Poe, and Lautréamont.

Those who one day said to him:

That's enough now, van Gogh, to the grave, we've had enough of your genius; as for the infinite, the infinite is for us.

For it was not because he sought the infinite that van Gogh died,

that he found himself forced to suffocate from poverty and asphyxiation,

it was because he found himself denied the infinite by all that rabble which, even in his lifetime, thought to withhold the infinite from him;

and van Gogh could have found enough of the infinite to last his whole life if the brutish consciousness of the masses had not

Van Gogh, the Man Suicided by Society (1947)

wanted to appropriate it to nourish their own orgies, which have never had anything to do with painting or poetry.

Besides, one does not commit suicide by oneself.
No one has ever been born by oneself.
No one dies by oneself either.
But, in the case of suicide, there must be an army of evil beings to cause the body to make the gesture against nature, that of taking its own life.
And I believe that there is always someone else at the moment of extreme death to strip us of our own life.

So it was that van Gogh doomed himself, because he was through with life and because, as we gather from his letters to his brother, with the birth of his brother's son,
he felt he was one mouth too many to feed.

But above all, van Gogh wanted at last to rejoin that infinite for which, he says, one embarks as on a train for a star,
and one embarks on the day when one has decided to have done with life.
Now, in the death of van Gogh, the way it happened, I do not believe that this is what happened.
Van Gogh was dispatched from the world first by his brother, when he announced the birth of his nephew, next by Dr. Gachet, when, instead of recommending rest and solitude, he sent him to paint from nature on a day when he knew quite well that van Gogh would have done better to go to bed.
For one does not oppose so directly a lucidity and a sensibility of the stamp of the martyred van Gogh's.
There are consciousnesses which, on certain days, would kill themselves over a simple contradiction, and to do this it is not necessary to be a madman, a registered and classified madman; on the contrary, it is enough to be in good health and to have reason on one's side.
I, in a similar situation, shall no longer tolerate someone telling me, as has so often happened, "Mr. Artaud, you're raving," without committing a crime.
And this is what they told van Gogh.

And this is what gave the final twist to the knot of blood in his throat that strangled him.

Post-Scriptum

Regarding van Gogh, magic, and spells: Are all those people who have been filing past the exhibit of his works at the Orangerie for the last two months sure they remember everything they did and everything that happened to them on every evening of the months of February, March, April, and May 1946? And was there not a certain evening when the atmosphere of the air and the streets became as if liquid, gelatinous, unstable, and when the light of the stars and of the celestial vault disappeared?

And van Gogh, who painted the café at Arles, was not there. But I was in Rodez, that is, still on the earth, whereas all the inhabitants of Paris must for one night have felt very close to leaving it.

And was it not true that they had all participated in concert in certain generalized filthinesses during which the consciousness of Parisians left its normal level for an hour or two and passed onto another level to one of those massive unfurlings of hate that I have been many times something more than a witness to during my nine years of confinement? Now the hate has been forgotten, like the nocturnal expurgations that followed it, and the same persons, who so repeatedly laid bare their base swinish souls for all to see, now file by van Gogh, whom during his lifetime they or their fathers and mothers so effectively strangled.

But did there not fall, on one of the evenings I speak of, on the boulevard de la Madeleine, at the corner of the rue des Mathurins, an enormous white rock that might have come from a recent volcanic eruption of the volcano Popocatepetl?

Letter to Pierre Loeb
(April 23, 1947)

XXXIV

Ivry, April 23, 1947

Dear friend,
The time when man was a tree without organs or function,
but possessed of will,
and a tree of will which walks
            will return.
It has been, and it will return.
For the great lie has been to make man an organism,
        ingestion,
        assimilation,
        incubation,
        excretion,
thus creating a whole order of hidden functions which are outside
the realm of the
        deliberative will;
the will that determines itself at each instant;
for it was this, that human tree that walks,
a will that determines itself at each instant,
without functions that were hidden, underlying, governed
        by the unconscious.
Of what we are and what we want
little actually remains,
an infinitesimal dust floats on the surface,
and the rest, Pierre Loeb, what is it?
An organism to be ingurgitated,
heavy with flesh,
and which excretes
and in whose field
like an iridescence, remote,
a rainbow of reconciliation with God,
those lost atoms,
ideas,
rise to the surface,
float,
accidents and hazards in the unity of an entire body.
What was Baudelaire,
what were Poe, Nietzsche, Gérard de Nerval?
BODIES

that *ate,*
digested,
slept,
snored once a night,
shat
between 25 and 30,000 times
and in exchange for 30 or 40 thousand meals,
40 thousand sleeps,
40 thousand snores,
40 thousand sour and bitter morning mouths
have to show some 50 poems apiece,
really it is not enough,
and the balance between *magical* production and *automatic* production is very far from being maintained,
it is abominably broken,
but the *human reality*, Pierre Loeb, is not that.
We are those 50 poems,
the rest is not us but the nothingness that clothes us,
laughs at us at first,
lives off us later.
But this void is not nothing,
it is not something,
it is some people.
I mean some men.
Animals without will or thought of their own,
that is, without pain of their own,
without inner acceptance of the wish of their own pain,
and who have found no other way to live
than to fake humanity.
And who have turned the tree-body,
but pure will which we were,
into this alembic of shit,
this cask of fecal distillation,
cause of plague,
and of all diseases,
and of this aspect of hybrid weakness,
of congenital taint
which characterizes *man born.*

Letter to Pierre Loeb (April 23, 1947)

One day man was virulent,
he was nothing but electric nerves,
flames of a perpetually burning phosphorus,
but this passed into fable
because the animals were born in it,
the animals,
those deficiencies of an innate magnetism,
that hole of hollows between two mighty bellows,
who were not,
were nothingness
and became something
and the magic life of man fell,
man fell from his magnetic rock,
and inspiration which was the foundation
became chance, accident,
rarity,
excellence,
excellence perhaps
but confronting such a pile of horrors
that it would have been better never to have been born.
This was not the Edenic state,
this was the state of manual labor,
worker,
work
without flaws, without waste
in an indescribable rarity.
Why was this state not maintained?
For the reasons that
the organism of animals, made for and by animals,
which succeeded this state *for centuries,*
    is going to collapse.
For exactly the same reasons.
These more ineluctable than those.
More ineluctable, the collapse of the organism of animals,
than the collapse of extraordinary labor
in the effort of the unique and very unfindable will.
For in reality tree-man,
man without functions or organs justifying his humanity,

that man has continued
under the clothing of the illusory of the other,
the illusory clothing of the other,
he continued in his will,
but a hidden will,
without compromises or contact with the other.
And that which has fallen is that which tried to surround him and imitate him
        and soon
        with a great blow,
        like a bomb,
        will reveal its inanity.
For a screen had to be created between the first of the tree-men and the others,
but for the others it took time, centuries of time for the men who began to reach their bodies,
like the one who did not begin and never ceased reaching his body,
but in the void
and there was no one
and there was no beginning.
        So?
        So.
So the deficiencies arose between man and the barren labor of filling in the void also.
Soon this work will be finished.
And the carapace will have to give way.
The carapace of the present world.
Built upon the digestive mutilations of a body torn apart by ten thousand wars,
and evil,
and disease,
and poverty,
and the scarcity of provisions, objects, and substances of the first necessity.
The maintainers of the profit system,
of social and middle-class institutions,
who have never worked
but have *piled up* the stolen wealth grain by grain, for thousands

Letter to Pierre Loeb (April 23, 1947)

of millions of years,
and store it in certain caverns with forces *prohibited by all humanity*,
with a certain number of exceptions,
will find themselves forced to give up their energies
and to fight for that,
and they will not be able to avoid the fight
for it is their eternal *cremation* which is at the end of the war,
that one, the apocalyptic war which is coming.
This is why I believe that the conflict between America and Russia, even if it were reinforced with atomic bombs, is not much compared to and opposed to this other conflict which will
                suddenly
                ignite
between the maintainers of a digestive humanity
on the one hand,
on the other
the man of pure will and his very rare adepts and followers,
but who have power
                sempiternal
                on their side.

From *Artaud le Mômo* (1947)

XXXV

The Return of Artaud, le Mômo

The anchored mind,
screwed into me
by the psycho-lubricious
thrust
of heaven
is the one that thinks
every temptation,
every desire,
every inhibition.

**o dedi
a dada orzoura
o dou zoura
a dada skizi**

**o kaya
o kaya pontoura
o ponoura
a pena
poni**

It's the spider-web sanctuary,
the onouric tuft
of where-ere the sail,
the anal plate of anayou.

(You're not taking anything away, god,
because it's me.
You've never taken anything like this away from me.
I'm writing it here for the first time,
I'm finding it for the first time.)

Not the membrane of the vault,
not the omitted member of this fuck,
born of devastation,

but meat gone bad,
beyond membrane,
beyond where it's hard or soft.

Already gone through hard and soft,
extended this bad meat like a palm,
pulled, stretched out like the palm of
                a hand
bloodless from holding itself stiff,
black, purple
from straining toward the soft.

But what is it in the end, you, the madman?

Me?

This tongue between four gums,

this meat between two knees,
this piece of hole
for madmen.

But not for madmen at all.
For respectable people,
who refine a frenzy to belch everywhere,

and who from this meaty belch
made the page,

listen well:
made the page
from the beginning of the generations
in the palmate bad meat of my holes,
my own.

What holes, and made of what?

Of soul, of mind, of me, and of being;
but in the place where no one gives a damn,
father, mother, Artaud, and the-same.

From *Artaud le Mômo* (1947)

In the humus of the wheeled web,
in the breathing humus of the web
of this void,
between hard and soft.

Black, purple,
stiff,
contemptible
and that's all.

Which means that there's a bone,
where
         god
pounced on the poet,
to ravage the ingestion
of his verses,
like mental farts
which he pulls out of his cunt,

which he would pull from the bottom of time,
to the bottom of his cuntish hole,

and it's not a cuntish turn
that he plays on him this way,
it's the turn of the whole earth
against someone who has balls
in his cunt.

And if you don't understand the image,
—and this is what I hear you say
in a circle,
that you don't understand the image
which is at the bottom
of my cunt's hole,—

it's because you don't know the bottom,
not of things,
but of my cunt
mine,

although from the bottom of time
you all plashed there in a circle
the way one slanders a madman,
plots to death an incarceration.

    ge re ghi
    regheghi
    geghena
    e reghena
    a gegha
    riri

Between the ass and the shirt,
between the jism and the putting below,
between the member and the false leap,
between the membrane and the blade,
between the sword and the ceiling,
between the sperm and the explosion,
'tween the angle and the shaft,

between the ass and the violent hands
    of all
on the high-pressure trap
of a death rattle of ejaculation
is not a point
or a rock

burst dead at the foot of a leap

or the severed member of a soul
(the soul is nothing more than an old saying)
but the staggering suspension
of a breath of estrangement

raped, shorn, sucked dry
by all the insolent rabble
of all the shit-eaters
who had no other grub
    in order to live

From *Artaud le Mômo* (1947)

    than to gobble
    Artaud
    mômo
    there, where one can stiffen sooner
    than me
    and the other can get a bigger hard-on
    than me
    in myself
if he was careful to place his head
on the curve of that bone
located between anus and sex,

    of that weeded bone that I say

in the filth
of a paradise
whose first dupe on earth
was not the father or the mother
who in this cave remade you
    but
    I
screwed into my madness.

And what possessed me
to also roll my life there?
    ME,
    NOTHING, *nothing*.
Because me,
    I'm there,
    I'm there
and it's life
that rolls its obscene palm there.

    All right.
    And what else?

    What else? What else?
    Old Artaud
    is buried

in the chimney hole
which he has had in his cold gum
since that day when he was killed!

    And what else?
    What else?
    What else!
He is this unframed hole
which life wanted to frame.
Because it's not a hole
    but a nose
that always knew too well how to sniff
the wind of the apocalyptic
    head
which they suck on his tight ass,
and how good Artaud's ass is
for the pimps in penitence.

And you too have the gum,
the right gum buried,
    god,

your gum has been cold too
for an infinity of years
since you sent me your innate ass
to see if I was going to be born
    in the end
since the time you waited for me
    scraping
      my absentee's belly.

    menendi anenbi
    embenda
    tarch inemptle
    o marchti rombi
    tarch paiolt
    a tinemptle
    orch pendui
    o patendi

From *Artaud le Mômo* (1947)

>a merchit
>orch torpch
>ta urchpt orchpt
>ta tro taurch
>campli
>ko ti aunch
>a ti aunch
>aungbli

Insanity and Black Magic

Insane asylums are conscious and premeditated repositories of black magic,

and this isn't just because doctors promote magic by their ill-timed and hybrid methods of treatment,
it's because they practice it.

If there had been no doctors
there would never have been any sick people,
no dead skeletons
sick people to be butchered and flayed,
for it was with doctors and not with sick people that society began.

Those who live, live off the dead.
And death too must live;
and there's nothing like an insane asylum to tenderly incubate death, and to keep the dead in an incubator.

It began 400 years before Jesus Christ, this therapy of slow death,
and modern medicine, in collusion with the most sinister and debauched magic, subjects its dead to electric shock or insulin therapy so that every day it may drain its stud farms of men of their selves,
and may present them thus empty,

thus fantastically
available and empty,
to the obscene anatomic and atomic solicitations
of the state called **Bardo**, delivery of the **barda** of living to the exigencies of the non-self.

Bardo is the pang of death into which the self falls with a splash,
and there is in electric shock a splash state
through which every traumatized person passes,
and which causes him at that instant no longer to understand, but horribly and desperately to misunderstand what he was, when he was he, what, law, me, king, thee, what the hell, and THAT.

I went through it myself and I won't forget it.

The magic of electric shock sucks out a death rattle, it plunges the shocked person into that death rattle with which one leaves life.

But, the electric shocks of Bardo were never an experiment, and to give the death rattle in the electric shock of Bardo, as in the Bardo of electric shock, is to dismember an experiment sucked by the phantoms of the non-self, and which man will never recapture.

Amid this palpitation and this respiration of all the others who crowd around the one who, as the Mexicans say, scraping a hole in the bark of his rasp, *flows lawlessly in every direction.*

Mercenary medicine lies every time it claims to have cured a sick person by the electric introspections of its method,
I personally have seen only people terrorized by the method,
incapable of recovering their selves.

Anyone who has gone through the electric shock of Bardo, and the Bardo of electric shock, never again rises out of its darkness, and his life has been lowered by a notch.
I have known breath after breath these moleculations of the death rattle of those who are really dying.

From *Artaud le Mômo* (1947)

What the Tarahumara of Mexico call the spittle of the rasp, the cinder of the coal without teeth.

Loss of a flap of that first euphoria that one had one day on feeling oneself living, swallowing, and chewing.

Thus electric shock, like Bardo, creates phantoms, it transforms all the pulverized states of the patient, all the facts of his past into phantoms which cannot be utilized for the present and which do not cease to besiege the present.

And so, I repeat, Bardo is death, and **death is only a state of black magic which has not existed for long.**

To create death artificially this way as modern medicine undertakes to do is to promote a reflux of nothingness which has never profited anyone,
but on which certain predestined profiteers of man have been battening for a long time.

In fact, since a certain point in time.

Which?

The point when it was necessary to choose between renouncing one's humanity and becoming an obvious madman.

But what guarantee do the obvious madmen of this world have of being cared for by those who are authentically alive?

> **farfadi**
> **ta azor**
> **tau ela**
> **auela**
> **a**
> **tara**
> **ila**
>
> **END**

ANTONIN ARTAUD

A white page to separate the text of the book, which is finished, from all the swarming of Bardo which appears in the limbo of electric shock.
And in this limbo a special typography, which is there to render god repulsive, to force into retreat the verbal words to which one wanted to attribute a special value.

Antonin Artaud
January 12, 1948

you're leaving,
says the foul intimacy of Bardo,
and you're still there,

    you're no longer there
    but nothing leaves you,
    you have kept everything
    except yourself
and what do you care since
the world
is there.

The
world,
but it's no longer me.
And what do you care,
says Bardo,
    it's me.

From *Artaud le Mômo* (1947)

P.S. — I have to complain of meeting in electric shock dead people whom I would not have wished to see.

The same ones,
whom this idiotic book called
    Bardo Todol
has been drawing out and presenting for a little over four thousand years.

Why?

All I ask is:
Why? . . .

Indian Culture and Here Lies (1947)

XXXVI

Indian Culture

I came to Mexico to make contact with the Red Earth
and it stinks the same way as it is fragrant;
it smells good the same way as it stank.

Caffre of urine from the slope of a hard vagina,
which resists when one takes it.

Urinary camphor of the mound of a dead vagina,
which slaps you when you stretch it,

when one aims from the top of the Watchtower of the Clown,
nailed tomb of the horrible father,

the hollow hole, the acrid hollow hole, end of the cycle of the red lice,
cycle of the solar red lice,
all white in the network of the veins of one of the two.

Which two, and which of the two?
Who, both?
in the time
seventy times accursed
when man
        crossing himself
was born son
of his sodomy
on his own ass
grown hard.
Why two of them,
and why born of TWO?

Horrible clown of papa monkeysee,
foul parasitical clown dough, in hollow mamaloaf pulled out of the fire!

For the round suns that pass
are nothing next to the clubfoot,

of the vast articulation
of the old gangrenous leg,
old gangrenous ossuary leg,
ripening a shield of bones,

the warlike, underground uprising
of the shields of all the bones.

What does this mean?

It means that papa-mama no longer buggers the inborn pederast,
the foul butt-end of Christian orgies,
interloper between Je and Chri,
contracted into
          Jeje-Chrichri,

and it means that war
will replace the father-mother
where the ass made a barrier
against the nourishing plague
of the Red Earth buried
beneath the body of the warrior
          who died
for refusing to go through
the periplus of the snake
who bites his own tail in front
while papa-mama
bloody his behind.

And when one looks closely
into the swollen slice of the leg,
of the blotchy old femur
there fall
          it stinks
          and it stank;
and there rises again the old warrior
of the insurgent cruelty,
the unspeakable cruelty
of living and having no being

that can justify you;
and there fall
into the anchored hole
of the earth seen from above, and broached,
all the flashing tips of the tongue,
and which one day believed themselves souls,
although they were not even wills;

there rise
all the flashes
of the flogging of my dead hand,
against the lifted tongue,

and the sexes of will,

discarded words, at best,
which could not lay hold of being;

but fall better than rejected
suns,
into the cave where they were killing each other
papa-mama
and pederast,
the son from before it stank.

When the solar donkey believed itself good!

And where was the sky in its round?

Some place where one was,
          outside,
all silly
from feeling the sky
          in one's cunt,

without anything that could keep out the void,
where
no bottom
and no balance,

and no surface,
or up,
and where everything pulls you back to the bottom,
when your whole body is straight.

HERE LIES

I, Antonin Artaud, am my son, my father, my mother,
     and myself;
leveler of the idiotic periplus on which procreation is
 impaled,
the periplus of papa-mama
     and child,
soot of grandma's ass,
much more than of father-mother's.

Which means that before mama and papa
who had neither father nor mother,
    they say,
and indeed where would they have got them,
     them,
when they became that single
     spouse
whom neither wife nor husband
could see sitting or standing,
before that improbable hole
that the mind invents for us,
         to make us
a little more disgusted with ourselves,
being this unusable body,
made out of meat and crazy sperm,
this body hung, from before the lice,
sweating on the impossible table
of heaven
its callous odor of atoms,
its alcoholic smell of abject
detritus

Indian Culture and Here Lies (1947)

ejected from the snooze
of the fingerless Inca

who for idea had an arm
but for hand had only a dead
palm, having lost its fingers
killing kings.

And so SAYI before all that,
was the miser bitch,
was this railer

cause of the belly
puffing up to the sky

and who walked along,
the hideous one,
7 times 7 years,
7 quadrillion years,
following the piteous
arithmetic
of ancient necromancy,

until from bloody breasts
ejected
from the hollow ash
which drops from the firmament
finally burst forth from her this child
cursed by man
and by hell itself,

but which god
uglier than Satan
chose
to outdo man

and he called it being
this child

that had a sex
between his teeth.

Because another child
was true,
was real,

without grand-dam
to choose him
with all the strength in her belly,

with her whole smelly
dog's ass,

he came out alone
from the bloodied hand
of the fingerless Inca.

Here working the iron cymbals
I take the low road of gouges
in the esophagus of the right eye

under the tomb of the stiff plexus
which turns sharply under the road
to release the child of right.

> **nuyon kidi**
> **nuyon kadan**
> **nuyon kada**
> **tara dada i i**
> **ota papa**
> **ota strakman**
> **tarma strapido**
> **ota rapido**
> **ota brutan**
> **otargugido**
> **ote krutan**

For I was Inca but not king.

> **kilzi**
> **trakilzi**
> **faildor**
> **bara bama**
> **baraba**
> **mince**

etretili
                TILI
            pinches you
in the *falzourchte*
of all gold,
in the rout
of all body.

And there was no sun nor anyone,
not a being in front of me,
no, not a being who knew my name.

I had only a few faithful who never stopped dying for me.

When they were too dead to live,
I could see only those full of hate,
the ones who had ogled their places,
fighting beside them,
too cowardly to struggle against them.

But who had seen them?

            No one.
Myrmidons of the Infernal
            Persephone,
microbes of every hollow gesture,
clownish mucus of a dead law,
cysts of those who violate their own kind,
tongues of the covetous
forceps

ANTONIN ARTAUD

    scraped on its own
                urine,
    latrines of a bony death,
    always screw-cut by the same
    dismal
                vigor,
    the same fire,

                whose cave
    innovator of a terrible
                nucleus,

    placed in the enclosure
    of mother life,

    is the viper
    of my eggs.

    For it is the end which is the beginning.
                And this end
                is the very one
                that eliminates
                all means.

    And now,
                all of you, beings,
    I have to tell you that you have always made me shit.
                Go form
                a swarm
                of the pussy
                of infestation,
                crab lice
                of eternity.

    Never again shall I meet beings who swallow the nail of life.

And one day I met the beings who swallowed the nail of life,
—as soon as I had lost my mother breast,

and the being twisted me under him,
and god poured me back to her.
                    (THE BASTARD.)

This is how they
pulled out of me
papa and mama
and the frying of je in
Chri
at the sex (center)
of the great strangling,
from which they pulled this cross
                    breeding of the coffin
(dead)
and of matter,
which gave life
to Jeezus-cry
when out of the dung of
          my dead *self*
was drawn
the blood
that gilds
          every usurped life
          outside.

This is why:
the great secret of Indian culture
is to bring the world back to zero,
always,

but rather
          1) too late than sooner,

2) which means
sooner
than too soon,

3) which means that later can come back only if
sooner has eaten too soon,

4) which means that at the same time
later
is that which precedes
both too soon
and sooner,

5) and that however quick sooner may be
too late
which does not say a word
is always there,

   which dismantles
   all the sooners
   point by point.

Commentary

They came, all the bastards,
after the great dismantling,
revealed from bottom to top.

    1) time om-let

        (*whisper this:*)

    You didn't know this
    that the state of
        EGG
    was the state
    anti-Artaud
    par excellence

and that to poison Artaud
there's nothing
like whipping up
a good omelette
in the spaces
aiming for the gelatinous
point
that Artaud
looking for the future man
has fled
like a horrible plague
and it is this point
that they replace in him,
nothing like a good omelette
stuffed with poison, cyanide, capers,
sent through the air to his cadaver
to disjoint Artaud
in the anathema of his bones
HUNG ON THE INTERNAL CADASTRE.

and 2) **palaoulette pulling**
largalalouette titling yourself

3) **tuban titi tarftan** from the head and from
the head aiming at yourself

4) **lomunculus of the frontal punch**
and of the forceps whoring yourself

he sways to the stinking owner,
that arrogant capitalist
of limbo
swimming toward the regrafting
of the father-mother onto the child's sex
in order to drain the whole body,
wholly of its matter
and to replace it with, who?
The one whom being and nothingness
made,
the way one makes peepee.

ANTONIN ARTAUD

AND THEY ALL GOT THE HELL OUT.

No, there is still the terrible piercer,
the piercer-crime,
that terrible,
old usurper's nail,
deviation on behalf of the false son-in-law
from the pain sawed from the bone,

Isn't it clear that the false son-in-law,
is Jeezy-cry,
already known in Mexico
long before his flight to Jerusalem on an ass,
and the crucifixion of Artaud on Golgotha.
Artaud
who knew that there is no mind
but a body
that remakes itself like the meshing of a dead man's teeth,
in the gangrene
     of the femur
     within.

      dakantala
      dakis tekel
      ta redaba
      ta redabel
      de stra muntils
      o ept anis
      o ept atra

from the pain
    sweated
in
    the bone.—

Indian Culture and Here Lies (1947)

*All true language
is incomprehensible,
like the chatter
of a beggar's teeth;
or the clap (whorehouse)
of a toothy femur (bloody).*

From the pain mined from the bone
something was born
which became what was mind
to marinate in the driving pain,
of pain,
            that womb,
a concrete womb

            and the bone,
            the bottom of the bedrock
            that became bone.

Moral

Never tire yourself more than necessary, even if you have to found a culture on the fatigue of your bones.

Moral

When the bedrock was eaten by the bone,
that the mind was gnawing from behind,
the mind opened its mouth too wide
and received in the back
            of the head
a blow that dried up its bones;

            then,

> THEN,
> then
> bone by bone
> the sempiternal matching returned
>
> **and turned the electric atom**
> **before melting point by point.**

Conclusion

For me, plain
Antonin Artaud,
no one has influence over me
who is no more than a man
or
>> god.

I don't believe in father
>> or mother,

don't have
papa-mama,

nature,
mind
or god,
satan
or body
or being,
life
or nothingness,
nothing that is outside or inside
and above all not the mouth of being,
sewer hole drilled with teeth
where he's always watching himself
the man who sucks his substance
from me,
to take from me a papa-mama,

Indian Culture and Here Lies (1947)

and remake himself an existence
free of me
on my corpse
removed
from the void
itself,

and sniffed
                from time
                to time.

I say
                from on top
                of time

as if time
were not fried,
were not this mixed fry
of all the friable
of the threshold,
gone to sea again in their coffin.

To Have Done with the Judgment of God, a radio play (1947)

XXXVII

kré		**puc te**
kré	Everything must	**puk te**
pek	be arranged	**li le**
kre	to a hair	**pek ti le**
e	in a fulminating	**kruk**
pte	order.	

I learned yesterday
(I must be behind the times, or perhaps it's only a false rumor, one of those pieces of spiteful gossip that are circulated between sink and latrine at the hour when meals that have been ingurgitated one more time are thrown in the slop buckets),
I learned yesterday
one of the most sensational of those official practices of American public schools
which no doubt account for the fact that this country believes itself to be in the vanguard of progress.
It seems that, among the examinations or tests required of a child entering public school for the first time, there is the so-called seminal fluid or sperm test,
which consists of asking this newly entering child for a small amount of his sperm so it can be placed in a jar
and kept ready for any attempts at artificial insemination that might later take place.
For Americans are finding more and more that they lack muscle and children,
that is, not workers
but soldiers,
and they want at all costs and by every possible means to make and manufacture soldiers
with a view to all the planetary wars which might later take place,
and which would be intended to *demonstrate* by the overwhelming virtues of force
the superiority of American products,
and the fruits of American sweat in all fields of activity and of the superiority of the possible dynamism of force.

ANTONIN ARTAUD

Because one must produce,
one must by all possible means of activity replace nature wherever it can be replaced,
one must find a major field of action for human inertia,
the worker must have something to keep him busy,
new fields of activity must be created,
in which we shall see at last the reign of all the fake manufactured products,
of all the vile synthetic substitutes
in which beautiful real nature has no part,
and must give way finally and shamefully before all the victorious substitute products
in which the sperm of all the artificial insemination factories
will make a miracle
in order to produce armies and battleships.
No more fruit, no more trees, no more vegetables, no more plants pharmaceutical or otherwise and consequently no more food,
but synthetic products to satiety,
amid the fumes,
amid the special humors of the atmosphere, on the particular axes of atmospheres wrenched violently and synthetically from the resistances of a nature which has known nothing of war except fear.
And war is wonderful, isn't it?
For it's war, isn't it, that the Americans have been preparing for and are preparing for this way step by step.
In order to defend this senseless manufacture from all competition that could not fail to arise on all sides,
one must have soldiers, armies, airplanes, battleships,
hence this sperm
which it seems the governments of America have had the effrontery to think of.
For we have more than one enemy
lying in wait for us, my son,
we, the born capitalists,
and among these enemies
Stalin's Russia
which also doesn't lack armed men.

To Have Done with the Judgment of God (1947)

All this is very well,
but I didn't know the Americans were such a warlike people.
In order to fight one must get shot at
and although I have seen many Americans at war
they always had huge armies of tanks, airplanes, battleships
that served as their shield.
I have seen machines fighting a lot
but only infinitely far
      behind
them have I seen the men who directed them.
Rather than a people who feed their horses, cattle, and mules the last tons of real morphine they have left and replace it with substitutes made of smoke,
I prefer the people who eat off the bare earth the delirium from which they were born
I mean the Tarahumara
eating Peyote off the ground
while they are born,
and who kill the sun to establish the kingdom of black night,
and who smash the cross so that the spaces of space can never again meet and cross.

And so you are going to hear the dance of **TUTUGURI**.

TUTUGURI
THE RITE OF THE BLACK SUN

And below, as if at the foot of the bitter slope,
cruelly despairing at the heart,
gapes the circle of the six crosses,
      very low
as if embedded in the mother earth,
wrenched from the foul embrace of the mother
      who drools.

The earth of black coal
is the only damp place
in this cleft rock.

ANTONIN ARTAUD

The Rite is that the new sun passes through seven points before
   blazing on the orifice of the earth.

And there are six men,
one for each sun,
and a seventh man
who is the sun
            in the raw
dressed in black and in red flesh.

But, this seventh man
is a horse,
a horse with a man leading him.

But it is the horse
who is the sun
and not the man.

At the anguish of a drum and a long trumpet,
strange,
the six men
who were lying down,
rolling level with the ground,
leap up one by one like sunflowers,
not like suns
but turning earths,
water lilies,
and each leap
corresponds to the increasingly somber
            and *restrained*
            gong of the drum
until suddenly he comes galloping, at vertiginous speed,
the last sun,
the first man,
the black horse with a
            naked man,
            absolutely naked
            and *virgin*
            riding it.

To Have Done with the Judgment of God (1947)

After they leap up, they advance in winding circles
and the horse of bleeding meat rears
and prances without a stop
on the crest of his rock
until the six men
have surrounded
completely
the six crosses.

Now, the essence of the Rite is precisely
        THE ABOLITION OF THE CROSS.

When they have stopped turning
they uproot
the crosses of earth
and the naked man
on the horse
holds up
an enormous horseshoe
which he has dipped in a gash of his blood.

The Pursuit of Fecality

There where it smells of shit
it smells of being.
Man could just as well not have shat,
not have opened the anal pouch,
but he chose to shit
as he would have chosen to live
instead of consenting to live dead.

Because in order not to make caca,
he would have had to consent
not to be,
but he could not make up his mind to lose
              being,
that is, to die alive.

There is in being
something particularly tempting for man
and this something is none other than
      CACA.
     (*Roaring here.*)

To exist one need only let oneself be,
but to live,
one must be someone,
to be someone,
one must have a BONE,
not be afraid to show the bone,
and to lose the meat in the process.

Man has always preferred meat
to the earth of bones.
Because there was only earth and wood of bone,
and he had to earn his meat,
there was only iron and fire
and no shit,
and man was afraid of losing shit
or rather he *desired* shit
and, for this, sacrificed blood.

In order to have shit,
that is, meat,
where there was only blood
and a junkyard of bones
and where there was no being to win
but where there was only life to lose.

  o reche modo
  to edire
  di za
  tau dari
  do padera coco

At this point, man withdrew and fled.

To Have Done with the Judgment of God (1947)

Then the animals ate him.

It was not a rape,
he lent himself to the obscene meal.

He relished it,
he learned himself
to act like an animal
and to eat rat
daintily.

And where does this foul debasement come from?

The fact that the world is not yet formed,
or that man has only a small idea of the world
and wants to hold on to it forever?

This comes from the fact that man,
one fine day,
stopped
        the idea of the world.

Two paths were open to him:
that of the infinite without,
that of the infinitesimal within.

And he chose the infinitesimal within.
Where one need only squeeze
the spleen,
the tongue,
the anus
or the glans.

And god, god himself squeezed the movement.

Is God a being?
If he is one, he is shit.
If he is not one
he does not exist.

But he does not exist,
except as the void that approaches with all its forms
whose most perfect image
is the advance of an incalculable group of crab lice.

"You are mad Mr. Artaud, what about the mass?"

I deny baptism and the mass.
There is no human act,
on the internal erotic level,
more pernicious than the descent
of the so-called jesus-christ
onto the altars.

No one will believe me
and I can see the public shrugging its shoulders
but the so-called christ is none other than he
who in the presence of the crab louse god
consented to live without a body,
while an army of men
descended from a cross,
to which god thought he had long since nailed them,
has revolted,
and, armed with steel,
with blood,
with fire, and with bones,
advances, reviling the Invisible
to have done with **GOD'S JUDGMENT**.

THE QUESTION ARISES . . .

What makes it serious
is that we know
that after the order
of this world
there is another.

To Have Done with the Judgment of God (1947)

What is it like?

We do not know.

The number and order of possible suppositions in
    this realm
is precisely
infinity!

And what is infinity?

That is precisely what we do not know!

It is a word
that we use
to indicate
the opening
of our consciousness
toward possibility
beyond measure,
tireless and beyond measure.

And precisely what is consciousness?

That is precisely what we do not know.

It is nothingness.

A nothingness
that we use
to indicate
when we do not know something
from what side
we do not know it
and so
we say
consciousness,
from the side of consciousness,
but there are a hundred thousand other sides.

ANTONIN ARTAUD

Well?

It seems that consciousness
in us is
linked
to sexual desire
and to hunger;

but it could
just as well
not be linked
to them.

One says,
one can say,
there are those who say
that consciousness
is an appetite,
the appetite for living;

and immediately
alongside the appetite for living,
it is the appetite for food
that comes immediately to mind;

as if there were not people who eat
without any sort of appetite;
and who are hungry.

For this too
exists
to be hungry
without appetite;

well?

Well

To Have Done with the Judgment of God (1947)

the space of possibility
was given to me one day
like a loud fart
that I will make;
but neither of space,
nor possibility,
did I know precisely what it was,

and I did not feel the need to think about it,

they were words
invented to define things
that existed
or did not exist
in the face of
the pressing urgency
of a need:
the need to abolish the idea,
the idea and its myth,
and to enthrone in its place
the thundering manifestation
of this explosive necessity:
to dilate the body of my internal night,

the internal nothingness
of my self

which is night,
nothingness,
thoughtlessness,

but which is explosive affirmation
that there is
something
to make room for:

my body.

And truly
must it be reduced to this stinking gas,
my body?
To say that I have a body
because I have a stinking gas
that forms
inside me?

I do not know
but
I do know that
                space,
                time,
                dimension,
                becoming,
                future,
                destiny,
                being,
                non-being,
                self,
                non-self,
are nothing to me;

but there is a thing
which is something,
only one thing
which is something,
and which I feel
because it wants
TO GET OUT:
the presence
of my bodily
suffering,

the menacing,
never tiring
presence
of my
body;

To Have Done with the Judgment of God (1947)

however hard people press me with questions
and however vigorously I deny all questions,
there is a point
at which I find myself compelled
to say no,

NO

then
to negation;

and this point
comes when they press me,

when they pressure me
and when they handle me
until the exit
from me
of nourishment,
of my nourishment
and its milk,

and what remains?

That I am suffocated;

and I do not know if it is an action
but in pressing me with questions this way
until the absence
and nothingness
of the question
they pressed me
until the idea of body
and the idea of being a body
was suffocated
in me,

and it was then that I felt the obscene

and that I farted
from folly
and from excess
and from revolt
at my suffocation.

Because they were pressing me
to my body
and to the very body

**and it was then
that I exploded everything
because my body
can never be touched.**

Conclusion

—And what was the purpose of this broadcast, Mr. Artaud?

—Primarily to denounce certain social obscenities officially sanctioned and acknowledged:
1. this emission of infantile sperm donated by children for the artificial insemination of fetuses yet to be born
and which will be born in a century or more.

2. To denounce, in this same American people who occupy the whole surface of the former Indian continent, a rebirth of that warlike imperialism of early America that caused the pre-Columbian Indian tribes to be degraded by the aforesaid people.

3.—You are saying some very bizarre things, Mr. Artaud.

4.—Yes, I am saying something bizarre,
that contrary to everything we have been led to believe, the pre-Columbian Indians were a strangely civilized people

To Have Done with the Judgment of God (1947)

and that in fact they knew a form of civilization based exclusively on the principle of cruelty.

5.—And do you know precisely what is meant by cruelty?

6.—Offhand, no, I don't.

7.—Cruelty means eradicating by means of blood and until blood flows, god, the bestial accident of unconscious human animality, wherever one can find it.

8.—Man, when he is not restrained, is an erotic animal,
he has in him an inspired shudder,
a kind of pulsation
that produces animals without number which are the form that the ancient tribes of the earth universally attributed to god.
This created what is called a spirit.
Well, this spirit originating with the American Indians is reappearing all over the world today under scientific poses which merely accentuate its morbid infectious power, the marked condition of vice, but a vice that pullulates with diseases,
because, laugh if you like,
what has been called microbes
    is god,
and do you know what the Americans and the Russians use to make their atoms?
They make them with the microbes of god.

—You are raving, Mr. Artaud.
You are mad.

—I am not raving.
I am not mad.
I tell you that they have reinvented microbes in order to impose a new idea of god.

They have found a new way to bring out god and to capture him in his microbic noxiousness.

ANTONIN ARTAUD

This is to nail him through the heart,
in the place where men love him best,
under the guise of unhealthy sexuality,
in that sinister appearance of morbid cruelty that he adopts whenever he is pleased to tetanize and madden humanity as he is doing now.

He utilizes the spirit of purity and of a consciousness that has remained candid like mine to asphyxiate it with all the false appearances that he spreads universally through space and this is why Artaud le Mômo can be taken for a person suffering from hallucinations.

—What do you mean, Mr. Artaud?

—I mean that I have found the way to put an end to this ape once and for all
and that although nobody believes in god any more everybody believes more and more in man.

So it is man whom we must now make up our minds to emasculate.

—How's that?
    How's that?
No matter how one takes you you are mad, ready for the straitjacket.

—By placing him again, for the last time, on the autopsy table to remake his anatomy.
I say, to remake his anatomy.
Man is sick because he is badly constructed.
We must make up our minds to strip him bare in order to scrape off that animalcule that itches him mortally,

    god,
    and with god
    his organs.

To Have Done with the Judgment of God (1947)

For you can tie me up if you wish,
but there is nothing more useless than an organ.

When you will have made him a body without organs,
then you will have delivered him from all his automatic reactions
    and restored him to his true freedom.

Then you will teach him again to dance wrong side out
as in the frenzy of dance halls
and this wrong side out will be his real place.

Last letters

TO FERNAND POUEY

Ivry, December 11, 1947

Dear Sir,

When in discussing my *"attempt"*
               at doing a broadcast
                  on the Radio,
the question of my fee *"as performer"* came up,
I told you:
I place the matter in your hands,
reluctant, in an endeavor where it was a matter for me of opening up a new path, to enter into petty discussions about money, and into demands for more or for less,
I simply thought that you would want to do the maximum on your end
and not thinking that you would have permitted that I be paid less than any of my actors.
Despite one's attempts to be *"detached,"*
one must eat,
clothe oneself,
get around,
that's why the sum of 3190 francs that was allotted me *suffocated me!*
This said,
allow me to go back over the work that has been done.
I believe it is a mixture of the best and the worst.
I did a great deal of work in Radio before the war
with Paul Deharme
on educational programs
and the work done with your people had very little connection with this means of expression
still,
it is *very important*,
that the Director
Mr. Guignard,
the technicians
and generally speaking
all the people

ANTONIN ARTAUD

I worked with
understand
WHAT were my original intentions and desires.
Listening to it at one go, people will have the impression of a work that is chaotic and disconnected;
a kind of random and epileptic
choppiness,
in which the wandering sensibility of the listener must also take at random
what suits him.

————*Well*, THIS IS NOT SO!!
To put an end to the judgment of our actions
        by destiny
        and by a ruling
        force
        is to express
        one's will
        in a rather new
        way
in order to indicate that the rhythmic order of things and of the destiny of things has changed its course,
there are in the broadcast that I did
        enough elements that are
        grating,
        throbbing,
        discordant,
        dissonant
so that they need only be *arranged* in a new order to prove that the desired end has been achieved,
my function was to provide you with elements.
Have I provided them?
Some are bad,
some, I believe, are excellent,
I hope that you will find that intelligent technician who will know how to give the elements I have provided all the unusual values I was hoping for.

                                          Cordially yours,
                                          Antonin Artaud

Last letters

TO FERNAND POUEY

[January 16, 1948]

Dear Sir,

Regarding
the opening section of
To Have Done with the Judgment of God
we can cut from
"to make and manufacture soldiers"
to
"In order to fight one must get shot at and although I have seen many Americans at war."
The general sequence is as follows:
 1. opening section
 2. sound effects
    which dissolve into the passage read by Maria Casarès
 3. *dance of Tutuguri*, text
 4. sound effects (xylophonics)
 5. The Pursuit of Fecality
    (read by Roger Blin)
 6. sound effects and bangings by Roger Blin and me
 7. The Question Arises (section read by Paule Thévenin)
 8. sound effects and my scream on the stairs
 9. concluding section
 10. final sound effects.

If you're doing something on
Artaud le Mômo
I'd like to point out that Paule Thévenin reads one of the poems very well,
the shortest,
"Center-Mother and Boss-Darling."
I was very happy, about this broadcast,
excited to see that it could provide a small-scale model for what I want to do in the *Theater of cruelty*.
This is why I want to thank you especially,

ANTONIN ARTAUD

but didn't you begin your own career with some form of rhythmic dancing between theater and poetry?

Cordially,
Antonin Artaud

TO WLADIMIR PORCHÉ
DIRECTOR OF THE RADIO STATION

February 4, 1948

Sir,
You will permit me to be somewhat more than revolted and *outraged*
by the decision that has just been made at the last moment to cancel my radio broadcast:
To Have Done with the Judgment of God,
on which I had WORKED for over 2 weeks and which had been announced in all the newspapers for over a month.
And you are not unaware of the curiosity with which this broadcast had been awaited by the great majority of the public
who looked to it for a kind of deliverance,
counting on an auditory experience that would save them at last from the monotony of ordinary broadcasts.
You had ample time, therefore, well before last Sunday afternoon when you decided to take this measure against it, [to become aware] of the particularly favorable atmosphere that surrounded the airing of this broadcast.
I examine it in vain to see how it might have offended any fair-minded person
who had not taken a position
in advance
as is the case here.
I, the author, like everyone else, listened to the whole program on tape,
determined not to let anything pass

> that might infringe on
> taste,
> morals,
> good manners,
> *honorable intentions*,
> or furthermore that might
> exude
> boredom,
> familiarity,
> routine,

I wanted a fresh work, one that would make contact with certain organic points of life,
a work
in which one feels one's whole nervous system
illuminated as if by a miner's cap-lamp
with vibrations,
consonances
which invite

> man
> TO EMERGE
> WITH
> his body

to follow in the sky this new, unusual, and radiant Epiphany.
But the glory of the body is possible
> only if
> nothing

in the spoken text
happens to shock,
happens to damage
this sort of desire for glory.
Well I am looking.
And I find
1. The Pursuit of Fecality,
a text studded with violent words, terrible language,
yes, there are violent words, terrible language,
but in an atmosphere *so outside life* that I don't believe that at that point there can still be an audience capable of being scandalized by it.
Everyone down to the last coal-seller must realize

that we have had enough of indecency
—physical, as well as physiological,
and DESIRE a fundamental
> change
> OF THE BODY.

The only other thing is the opening attack on American capitalism.

But one would have to be very naïve, Wladimir Porché, to be alive at this time and not to realize that American capitalism like Russian communism are both leading us to war,

so with voices, drum, and xylophonics I am alerting separate individualities so that they may form a body.

I am,
Antonin Artaud

TO FERNAND POUEY

Ivry-sur-Seine, February 7, 1948

Very dear Fernand Pouey,

I have learned of your admirable attitude toward my Radio Broadcast.
Forgive me for the trouble I am causing you
> and
> thank you

for defending me so wholeheartedly.

I know that your job was at stake and that you were willing to risk it,

but I do not understand how an incompetent, scarcely out of university, like Wladimir Porché, can take it upon himself to cancel the broadcast of a *document* that was ANNOUNCED several weeks ago

and consequently

listened to

by dozens of technicians who judged its value

and DECIDED

Last letters

                        that it should be broadcast.
This constitutes an act of arbitrary autocracy
which must not be tolerated.
I have written Wladimir Porché a letter
explaining to him
in detail
simply and very clearly
the intention I had in writing my texts
and composing this broadcast.
As for the attitude of the unsophisticated listener,
the truth is that
                      never

has a broadcast been ANTICIPATED with greater curiosity and impatience by the great mass of the public who were specifically waiting for this broadcast to help them form an attitude to confront certain aspects of life.

This broadcast is a long protest against the fundamental eroticism of material things against which the whole world subconsciously wants to react, and against the social, political and ecclesiastical (religious), and therefore ritualistic arbitrariness of the law.

And the social body has had enough of all ritual. You will have to ask Wladimir Porché for this letter so it can be reprinted in the Press.

                                                Devotedly,
                                           Antonin Artaud

TO RENÉ GUILLY

                                       [February 7, 1948]

Sir,

I thought I was dreaming this morning when I read your article in *Combat*.
Amazed that such a thing was allowed to be printed.

ANTONIN ARTAUD

But then I have a much higher opinion of this famous mass audience than you do.
I believe them to be infinitely less steeped in prejudice than you think.
Those people who crowded around their radios Monday evening and awaited, with a curiosity and impatience never seen before, the broadcast entitled *To Have Done with the Judgment of God* were in fact members of this mass audience,
hairdressers,
laundresses,
tobacconists,
ironmongers, carpenters, printers,
in short, all people who earn their living by the sweat of their elbows,
and not certain capitalists of dung
grown rich in secret
who go to mass every Sunday and who desire above all the respect of ritual and of the law.
It is these people, together with certain prematurely rich pimps of Montmartre, who have this nauseating fear of words,
whom my broadcast would have terrified.
However this may be,
one must regard it as a sin
and a crime
to forbid a human voice that was addressing itself for the first time in this age to the best in man
to speak out.
2. Books, texts, magazines are tombstones, René Guilly, tombstones that must be pulled up at last.
We shall not live eternally surrounded by the dead
                       and by death.
If there are prejudices somewhere,
they must be destroyed,
                   the *duty*.
I repeat
                THE DUTY
of the writer, of the poet
is not to shut himself up like a coward in a text, a book, a magazine from which he never comes out

but on the contrary to go
into the world
                        to jolt,
                        to attack
                        the mind of the public,
                        otherwise
                        what use is he?
And why was he born?
3. However that may be,
I am not a choirmaster,
never having learned how to sing,
let alone
how to conduct singing.
The most I attempted in this radio broadcast,
I who had never touched an instrument in my life,
was a few vocal xylophonics over the instrumental xylophone
and the effect was successful.
I mean that this broadcast was a search for a language which the humblest road-mender or coal-seller would have understood,
a language which conveyed by means of bodily transmission the highest metaphysical truths.
Which you yourself recognized, and for this reason there was shame and infamy in prohibiting it.
This is what I wanted to say to you, René Guilly.

                                                Antonin Artaud

TO FERNAND POUEY AND RENÉ GUIGNARD
                        Ivry-sur-Seine, February 17, 1948

Very dear friends,

    I think that what certain people like Georges Braque found so overwhelming and exciting about the Radio Broadcast *To Have Done with the Judgment of God* are the parts where sound effects and xylophonics accompany the poems read by Roger Blin and

Paule Thévenin. We must not spoil the effect of the xylophonics by the logical, dialectical, and argumentative quality of the opening section. I have written you a special delivery letter pointing out certain cuts to be made which would leave only a few lines at the beginning and end of the "Introduction."
I beg you to make these cuts,
I beg you
both of you
to MAKE SURE that these cuts are carefully made.
There must be nothing left in this Radio Broadcast that might disappoint,
tire,
or bore
an enthusiastic audience which was struck by the freshness of the sound effects and xylophonics
and which even Balinese, Chinese, Japanese, and Singhalese theater do not have.
I am counting on the two of you
to take care of these cuts since they have not been made and I clasp your hands fondly.

Antonin Artaud

TO PAULE THÉVENIN

Tuesday, February 24, 1948

Paule, I am very sad and desperate,
my body hurts all over,
but above all I have the impression that people were disappointed in my radio broadcast.
Wherever the *machine* is
there is always the abyss and the void,
there is a technical intervention that distorts and annihilates what one has done.
The criticisms of M. and A.A. are unjust but they must have been based on some weakness in the transitions,
this is why I am through with Radio,

Last letters

and from now on will devote myself
exclusively
to the theater
as I conceive it,
a theater of blood,
a theater which with each performance will have done
something
bodily
to the one who performs as well as to the one who comes to see others perform,
but actually
the actors are not performing,
they are doing.
The theater is in reality the *genesis* of creation.
This will happen.
I had a vision this afternoon—I saw those who are going to follow me and who are still not completely embodied because pigs like those at the restaurant last night eat too much. There are some who eat too much and others like me who can no longer eat without *spitting*.

Yours,
Antonin Artaud

Writings about Artaud

THE LITERATURE ON ARTAUD, most of it in French, is quite large. In my opinion, the single most brilliant critical analysis is in two essays by Jacques Derrida—"La Parole soufflée" and "Le Théâtre de la Cruauté et la clôture de la représentation," which were published in his collection of essays *L'Ecriture et la différence* (Paris: Editions du Seuil, 1967), pp. 253–92 and 341–68. The first essay originally appeared in *Tel Quel*, No. 20 (Winter 1965), pp. 41–67; the second in *Critique*, No. 230 (July 1966), pp. 595–618.

ALSO RECOMMENDED:

Maurice Blanchot, "Artaud," *La Nouvelle Revue Française*, No. 47 (November 1956), pp. 873–81; and "Artaud," in *Le Livre à Venir*, 2nd ed. (Paris: Gallimard, 1959), pp. 45–52.

Naomi Greene, "Antonin Artaud: metaphysical revolutionary," *Yale French Studies*, No. 39 (1967), pp. 188–97; and her *Antonin Artaud: Poet Without Words* (New York: Simon and Schuster, 1970).

Jerzy Grotowski, "Il n'était pas entièrement lui-même," *Les Temps Modernes*, No. 251 (April 1967), pp. 1887–88.

Stephen Koch, "On Artaud," *Tri-Quarterly*, No. 6 (Spring 1966), pp. 29–37.

Guy Scarpetta, "Brecht et Artaud," *La Nouvelle Critique*, nouvelle série, No. 25 (June 1969), pp. 60–68.

Eric Sellin, *The Dramatic Concepts of Antonin Artaud* (Chicago: University of Chicago Press, 1968).

Philippe Sollers, "La Pensée émet des signes," in *Logiques* (Paris: Editions du Seuil, 1968), pp. 133–49. This essay first appeared in *Tel Quel*, No. 20 (Winter 1965), pp. 12–24.

Philippe Sollers, ed., *Artaud* (Paris: U.G.E. ["10/18"], 1973). Texts by Xavière Gautier, Pierre Guyotat, Julia Kristeva, Marcellin Pleynet, Guy Scarpetta, Sollers, and others.

Paule Thévenin, "Entendre/Voir/Lire," *Tel Quel*, No. 39 (Autumn 1969), pp. 31–63, and No. 40 (Winter 1969–70), pp. 67–99.

Alain Virmaux, *Antonin Artaud et le Théâtre* (Paris: Seghers, 1970). Also his "Artaud and Film," *Tulane Drama Review*, No. 33 (Fall 1966), pp. 154–65.

A definitive edition of Artaud's writings, the Gallimard *Oeuvres complètes*, has been underway since 1956, but there is no authoritative biography. Since understanding Artaud's writings often depends on knowing something about Artaud's life and the sequence of his various careers, a minimum amount of necessary biographical information has been included in the notes.

About the early part of Artaud's life, before the period covered in the notes:

He was born on September 4, 1896 (around 8 a.m.), in Marseilles, at 4, rue du Jardin des Plantes. Baptized Antoine-Marie-Joseph, he was the first child of Antoine-Roi Artaud (a shipbuilder) and Euphrasie Artaud née Nalpas; his mother was descended from a Greek family that had settled mostly in Smyrna. In 1901 he was stricken with severe meningitis and almost died. A brother was born on May 30 and died on June 2. A sister was born on January 13, 1905, and died on August 21. In all, the Artauds had nine children, only three of whom lived to adulthood: Antonin, his younger sister Marie-Ange, and his younger brother Fernand.

As a child, Artaud made several trips with his family to Smyrna to visit his mother's relatives; during a vacation there in 1906, he almost drowned. Throughout his childhood, ever since the near-fatal attack of meningitis, he suffered from terrible headaches and other severe neurological pain. He was first confined in a mental hospital—La Rougière, near Marseilles—in 1915. He was released after several months, and spent the summer with his parents in the country. In 1916 he was drafted and sent to Digne, but his father exerted influence to have him released from military service because of his poor health and he was discharged after nine months. Between 1917 and 1920, mental crises necessitated his confinement in various hospitals—first at Saint-Dizier, near Lyons; then at Lafoux-les-Bains (in Le Gard); then at Divonne-les-Bains (in Ain). Finally his parents sent him to the clinic run by Dr. Dardel near Neuchâtel, Switzerland, where he lived almost two years. His health much improved, he left Dr. Dardel's clinic and returned to Marseilles at the end of 1919. In March 1920, at the age of twenty-three, he left Marseilles to live in Paris.

For biographical material on Artaud, the most valuable sources are the notes at the end of each volume of the Gallimard *Oeuvres complètes*, which are the work of the editor, Paule Thévenin, Artaud's literary executor.

OTHER SOURCES:

The special Artaud issue of *K: Revue de la Poésie*, Nos. 1–2 (June 1948), especially "Lettre à Roger Blin" by Charles Dullin (pp. 21–24) and "Artaud de son vivant" by Alain Cuny (pp. 25–28).

Writings about Artaud

The special Artaud issue of *Les Cahiers de la Compagnie Madeleine Renaud–Jean-Louis Barrault*, Nos. 22–23 (May 1958), especially "Parce que je l'ai beaucoup aimé . . ." by Arthur Adamov (pp. 128–29). Reedited, with deletions and some new material, as issue No. 69 (1969).

La Tour de Feu, Nos. 63–64 (December 1959), a special issue entitled "Antonin Artaud, ou la santé des poètes"; and No. 69 (April 1961), entitled "De la contradiction au sommet, ou pour en finir avec Artaud." Reprinted together as No. 112 (December 1971).

Georges Charbonnier, *Essai sur Antonin Artaud* (Paris: Seghers, 1959).

Paule Thévenin, "Letter on Artaud," *Tulane Drama Review*, No. 27 (Spring 1965), pp. 99–116. This is a translation of "Antonin Artaud dans la vie," *Tel Quel*, No. 20 (Winter 1965), pp. 25–40. See also her "Le Bouquet de violettes de Jean Paulhan," *La Nouvelle Revue Française*, No. 197 (May 1969), pp. 909–21.

Otto Hahn, *Portrait d'Antonin Artaud* (Paris: Le Soleil Noir, 1968).

Daniel Joski, *Artaud* (Paris: Editions Universitaires, 1970).

Jean-Louis Brau, *Antonin Artaud* (Paris: La Table Ronde, 1971). The best of the book-length biographical studies so far.

Two last recommendations. The "case of Artaud," though discussed only briefly, is implicit throughout the argument of Michel Foucault's *Histoire de la folie* (Paris: Plon, 1961; revised edition, Gallimard, 1972); in English in an abridged version as *Madness and Civilization* (New York: Pantheon, 1965). For an even more far-reaching and original theoretical use of Artaud, in which his consciousness is developed as a paradigm for the analysis of modern society (though, again, Artaud is only briefly mentioned), see the book by Gilles Deleuze and Félix Guattari, *Capitalisme et Schizophrénie: L'Anti-Oedipe* (Paris: Editions de Minuit, 1972), translated as *Anti-Oedipus* (New York: Viking, 1976), and an earlier essay by Deleuze, "Le Schizophrène et la mort," *Critique*, Nos. 255–56 (August–September 1968).

S.S.

Notes

THE FRENCH ORIGINALS of nearly all the texts translated in the present volume are to be found in Antonin Artaud, *Oeuvres complètes* (Paris: Gallimard, 1956–76). In the notes below, the Gallimard volumes are referred to as *G*, followed by a roman numeral. Volumes I through XIII, plus revised editions of Volumes I through III and a Supplement to Volume I, plus new printings (adding more texts) of Volumes VI, VII, and VIII, had appeared by 1976; these contain most of what Artaud had written through 1946. The page references to Volumes I through III are to the revised editions.

Some texts which are not yet included in the *Oeuvres complètes* are to be found only in rare, mostly out-of-print magazines and booklets. And there are still many letters, drafts of prose texts and poems, and notes that have never been printed. Presumably all this material will eventually be included in the *Oeuvres complètes*. At least two volumes are still to come.

For the notes below, we have drawn on many printed sources, some of them mentioned in the preceding pages. For information—date of composition, publication history, biographical context, textual variations—the prime source is, of course, the notes to the Gallimard volumes. It should be mentioned, however, that no existing work on Artaud in French or in English is free of factual errors of both a biographical and a bibliographical nature.

The task of annotating Artaud's writings is a vast one, and these notes cannot be considered to be complete. Beyond furnishing the necessary biographical and bibliographical information, we have restricted the notes to what seemed most helpful—assuming a certain amount of general information about literature and the other arts, favoring information that could be hard for the reader to track down. The density and relative obscurity of allusion and quotation in some of Artaud's later writings have necessitated more elaborate notes than those required for writings from the first part of his career (roughly, the 1920's). Artaud's allusions to other poets, to cinema and the modern theater, to the history of literary magazines and movements (particularly the Surrealist movement) are treated more cursorily—since these are all relatively well-documented subjects, about which there is an ample literature in English.

S.S. and D.E.L.

May 1976

I. Five early poems

"Le Navire mystique": *G* I, 191. Written in 1913, when Artaud was seventeen, around the time that he was discovering the poetry of Baudelaire and Poe, this poem was first printed in the Marseilles magazine *La Criée*, No. 15 (August 1922). It is the earliest of Artaud's poems that has been published. (In 1910, while a student at the Collège du Sacré-Coeur in Marseilles, Artaud founded a literary review in which he printed his first poems under the pseudonym Louis de Attides.) Artaud published poems and essays in *La Criée*, edited by Léon Franc, between 1922 and 1924.

"Verlaine boit": *G* I, 201. First published in the magazine *Action*, 2nd year, numéro hors série (the date must be late 1921 or early 1922), along with his poems "La Bouteille et le verre," "Mystagogie," and the seven brief "Madrigaux."
    Action was edited by Georges Gabory, André Malraux, and Paul Dermée; Artaud was recommended to Gabory by the poet Max Jacob (1876–1944), whose prose poem, *Le Cornet à Dés* (1917), was—with the works of Rimbaud and Lautréamont—one of the principal texts of initiation for French poets just after the First World War. (See Artaud's letter to Jacob in Section III of this book.) Artaud had already published two poems, "L'Antartique" and "Pendule," in *Action*, 2nd year, No. 10 (November 1921). Two more poems, "Bar marin" and "Aquarium," appeared in *Action*, 3rd year, March–April 1922.

"Jardin noir": *G* I, 214. This is an earlier version of a poem which appeared in a magazine of literature and the arts called *Images de Paris*, 3rd year, No. 34 (September–October 1922). Artaud has another poem, "Square," in the same issue, and his poem "Orgue allemand" appeared in *Images de Paris*, 4th year, Nos. 42–43 (June–July 1923).

"Le Poème de Saint François d'Assise": *G* I, 207–9. First published in *La Criée*, No. 18 (November 1922); probably written in the summer of that year. (Artaud sent the poem to Génica Athanasiou in a letter dated August 3, 1922.)

"Amour": *G* I, 256. Artaud's first book, *Tric Trac du Ciel*, was a collection of poetry; it was published by the art historian and dealer

Daniel-Henry Kahnweiler (Editions de la Galerie Simon) on May 4, 1923, illustrated with woodcuts by Elie Lascaux, in an edition of 112 copies. The book consists of a seven-line prefatory poem ("Orgues tournants . . .") followed by eight poems, of which "Amour" is the fourth. The entire sequence may be found in *G* I, 252–61.

Demain (see note to Section III) and *Mercure de France* are the other magazines that published Artaud's early poetry. *Demain*, No. 81 (August–September 1920), contains a poem written in 1915, "En Songe," as well as a prose text, "Esquisse d'un nouveau programme d'enseignement." "La Marée," "Marine," and "Soir" appeared in *Mercure de France*, No. CLX (December 15, 1922).

II. Two early essays

"LE GRAND MAGASIN EMPOISONNEUR": *G* II, 228–29. This essay, not published during Artaud's lifetime, was probably written in 1922. It may be a reply to an article by Edouard Toulouse, "Le Grand Magasin educateur," which appeared in *Demain*, No. 83 (January–March 1923).

"LES VALEURS PICTURALES ET LE LOUVRE": *G* II, 234–35. Divisionism, one of the bases of Neo-Impressionist and Pointillist painting, was a method of juxtaposing small patches of pure color on a canvas according to a systematic division of hues. Edouard Detaille (1848–1912) was a popular painter of military scenes. This essay was first published in Lugné-Poë's magazine, *Le Bulletin de "l'Oeuvre,"* early in 1921. Artaud met Aurélien-Marie Lugné-Poë (1869–1940), the actor and director, soon after he came to live in Paris in March 1920. (They were introduced by Louis Nalpas, Artaud's maternal uncle and an important film producer.) Through this contact, Artaud made his debut as a stage actor on February 17, 1921: a one-line role, as a bourgeois awakened during the night, in Henri de Régnier's *Les Scrupules de Sganarelle,* directed by Lugné-Poë, at the Théâtre de l'Oeuvre.

It was in 1921—Artaud was twenty-five—that he started writing prolifically, reviews as well as poetry. He wrote on current theater productions; these early theater chronicles may be found in *G* II, 169–

82. He also drew, and looked a great deal at painting. His writings from the early 1920's on painting (and literature) may be found in *G* II, 213–63.

III. Letters from 1921–23

TO MADAME TOULOUSE (LATE JULY 1921): *G* I Supp., 11–12. Madame Toulouse was the wife of Dr. Edouard Toulouse, the director of the sanatorium in Villejuif (a suburb of Paris). When Artaud left Marseilles for Paris in March 1920, his parents (on the advice of Dr. Dardel) placed him in Toulouse's care. Artaud lived with Dr. and Madame Toulouse until the end of the year; then he moved into Paris and took a room in a *pension de famille* on the rue Faustin-Hélie in the 16th arrondissement (Passy).

Dr. Toulouse, himself a writer, printed many poems and essays by Artaud during late 1920 and 1921 in *Demain*, the small magazine, both scientific and literary, which he had founded in 1912 and of which he was the editor. At his request, Artaud edited a collection of Toulouse's psychiatric writings, entitled *Au Fil des Préjugés*, which was published in 1923 by Editions du "Progrès civique." For the brief preface which Artaud wrote for this book, see *G* I, 242–43.

In 1921, Dr. Toulouse was appointed staff psychiatrist at the Sainte-Anne Hospital in Paris. There is an interview with Madame Toulouse about Artaud in *La Tour de Feu*, No. 112, pp. 126–31.

TO MAX JACOB (OCTOBER 1921): *G* III, 115–17. Artaud met Max Jacob in 1920. It was probably Jacob (according to some, it was Elie Lascaux) who introduced Artaud to the painter André Masson. Artaud started frequenting Masson's studio on the rue Blomet, where he met more painters (Jean Dubuffet, Joan Miró) and writers (Michel Leiris, Armand Salacrou, Georges Limbour); Daniel-Henry Kahnweiler, who published Artaud's first book, was Masson's dealer.

Firmin Gémier (1865–1933) was a celebrated actor, of particular interest to Artaud because Gémier had played the title role in the original Paris production of *Ubu Roi* in 1896. Artaud met Gémier through his mother's brother, Louis Nalpas, in 1920—about the same time that he met Lugné-Poë. The Société des Cinéromans, of which Nalpas was artistic director, was producing Abel Gance's *Mater Dolorosa;* Gémier had the leading role. (This was, of course, the silent version; Artaud played a small role in the sound version of *Mater Dolorosa*, made in 1933.) As the letter indicates, it was Gémier

Notes

who introduced Artaud to the director and actor Charles Dullin (1885–1949).

TO YVONNE GILLES (OCTOBER 1921): *G* III, 118–19. Artaud met Yvonne Gilles, a young painter, in the hospital at Divonne-les-Bains in 1917.

Dullin played the role of the Prophet in *Le Simoun* by Henri René Lenormand, which opened at the Comédie Montaigne-Gémier on December 21, 1920.

As the letter indicates, Artaud joined Dullin's Atelier in 1921. (The Atelier was Dullin's theater between 1921 and 1940.) In February 1922, Artaud had his first role, Anselme, in a production of Molière's *L'Avare*, which played in Lyons as well as at the Théâtre du Vieux-Colombier in Paris (revived on October 18). In March he played the Moorish king Galvan in Alexandre rnoux's *Moriana et Galvan* and Sottinet in Regnard's *Le Divorce*. Artaud also designed the costumes for three productions of the 1922 season: Lope de Rueda's *Les Olives* (March 2); Francisco Sánchez de Castro's *L'Hôtellerie*, in which he played A Blind Man (April 1); and Calderón's *Life Is a Dream*, in which he played Basilio (June 20). In the other play presented on the April 1 program, Calderón's *Visits of Condolence*, Artaud played Don Luis.

TO YVONNE GILLES (JUNE 1922): *G* III, 122. Artaud had the role of Basilio, King of Poland, in Dullin's production of Calderón's play, which opened at the Théâtre du Vieux-Colombier on June 20 (not June 22), 1922. Dullin played Segismundo, Basilio's son.

Since the beginning of 1922 Artaud had been living in the Hôtel de Vintimille at 5, rue de Vintimille in the 9th arrondissement.

TO GÉNICA ATHANASIOU (AUGUST 17, 1922): *Lettres à Génica Athanasiou* (Paris: Gallimard, 1969), hereafter abbreviated as *LGA*, pp. 41–43. Artaud met Génica Athanasiou (1897–1966), an actress in Dullin's company, in the autumn of 1921. (Her real name was Eugénie Tanase.) She had come to Paris in 1919 from her native Bucharest, and succeeded in joining Dullin's company the following year. She and Artaud played together in a number of Dullin's productions; for instance, she was Estrella in Calderón's *Life Is a Dream*, Dame Claude in Molière's *L'Avare*, and Moriana in Arnoux's *Moriana et Galvan*. She was apparently the first and certainly the most important woman in Artaud's life. They were together for six years.

"Nanaqui," the diminutive of the Greek name Antonaki, was his

Notes

mother's pet name for Artaud when he was a child. Artaud spoke Greek as a child with his grandmother (Neneka Chilé) in Smyrna.

Artaud had arrived in Marseilles on July 18 to see his family. (Génica Athanasiou spent most of the summer in the Pyrenees.) Sometime during the first three days of this trip, Artaud visited the Colonial Exposition and saw the Cambodian dances being performed in front of a gigantic pasteboard Angkor temple. Toward the end of his stay he became ill; and after leaving Marseilles on August 8 he spent a few days in Hyères, and then at Cavalaire (from where this letter was written), before returning to Paris.

TO YVONNE GILLES (NOVEMBER 1922): *G* III, 123. In *Antigone*, a half-hour play freely adapted from Sophocles by Jean Cocteau, Artaud played the role of Tiresias (Génica Athanasiou had the title role, and Dullin was Creon). Arthur Honegger wrote the music; the sets were by Picasso and the costumes by Coco Chanel. The play was presented on December 20, 1922, to great acclaim. On the same night, Artaud played the role of Marco Fongi in the first French production of Pirandello's three-act comedy, *The Pleasure of Honesty*.

On November 3, 1922, Artaud had played the role of Apoplexy in *La Mort de Souper*, Roger Semichon's adaptation of a sixteenth-century morality play in verse by Nicole de La Chesnaye, and Génica Athanasiou had played the role of Colic.

Artaud published two essays on Dullin's work, one in *Action*, 2nd year, numéro hors série, probably late 1921 or early 1922, entitled "L'Atelier de Charles Dullin," and the other in *La Criée*, No. 17 (October 1922), entitled "Le Théâtre de l'Atelier." See *G* II, 171–72 and 175–77.

TO GÉNICA ATHANASIOU (MAY 6, 1923): *LGA*, 44. "Naky" is another version of "Nanaqui."

Artaud continued to work in Dullin's Atelier through the early part of 1923: he played the evil marionette Pedro Urdemalas in Jacinto Grau's *Monsieur de Pygmalion*, which opened on February 13 (Génica Athanasiou was Pomponina); and the elder Charlemagne in the play that followed it on March 20, Alexandre Arnoux's *Huon de Bordeaux* (Génica Athanasiou was Esclarmonde). The first role was a personal triumph for Artaud, but as Charlemagne he had some bad reviews. *Huon* was the last of Dullin's productions in which Artaud participated. For Dullin's view of Artaud's work, see Dullin's letter to Roger Blin, quoted by Paule Thévenin in *Les Cahiers de la Compagnie Madeleine Renaud–Jean-Louis Barrault*, Nos. 22–23 (May 1958), pp. 20–21.

TO GÉNICA ATHANASIOU (OCTOBER 24, 1923): *LGA*, 117–18. It is not clear how long before 1923 Artaud started using opium.

It should be mentioned that Artaud's vision of a radical theater antedates his work with Dullin. According to the actor Alain Cuny, Artaud at the age of twenty—in Marseilles—was already thinking about creating a "spontaneous theater," which would perform in factories. *Cf.* Alain Cuny, "Artaud de son vivant," *K*, Nos. 1–2 (1948), pp. 25–28.

IV. From *Bilboquet* (1923)

"Bilboquet" is a word in printers' slang and means job printing such as is done by a small firm: stationery, visiting cards, marriage and death announcements. *Bilboquet* was a small magazine, containing prose and poems, written entirely by Artaud; two issues appeared, neither bearing Artaud's name. The first issue is dated February 2, 1923, and has an editorial statement signed "Eno Dailor." (Artaud had used the pseudonym "Eno" to sign a poem, "En Songe," written in 1915, published in *Demain* in 1920.) The second issue, with neither date nor pseudonym, appeared later the same year.

"IL N'Y A PAS ASSEZ DE REVUES . . .": *G* I, 265–66. Editorial statement in No. 1.

"RIMBAUD & LES MODERNES": *G* I, 270–71. From No. 2. In 1897, the year before his death, Mallarmé published a collection of his non-verse writings (including an essay on Rimbaud) called *Divagations*.

Marcel Raval and Paul Fierens were co-contributors of poems in some issues of the magazines that printed the early poems of Artaud. In 1923 Fierens was a regular reviewer for *Les Nouvelles Littéraires*. In that magazine, in December 1925, he published a review of Artaud's second book, *L'Ombilic des Limbes*, which Artaud judged to be "d'une imbécilité noire" (see letter to Génica Athanasiou, December 15, 1925: *LGA*, 224).

"UN PEINTRE MENTAL": *G* I, 272. From No. 2. Artaud discovered the work of Klee (along with that of Chagall and Derain) at the 1921 Salon d'Automne. No. 2 also contained a hostile review of Raymond Radiguet's *Diable au Corps*, which had just appeared; it is to be found in *G* I, 278–79.

Notes

V. *Correspondence with Jacques Rivière* (1923–24)

Correspondance avec Jacques Rivière: G I, 29–58. Rivière edited *La Nouvelle Revue Française* for six years, between 1919 and 1925. It was under his editorship that the magazine, founded in 1909, became the most important literary periodical in France, perhaps in all Europe. (After Rivière's death in 1925 at the age of thirty-nine, Jean Paulhan—who was to prove such a generous friend to Artaud—became editor.)

Tric Trac du Ciel, Artaud's book of poetry, had just appeared when Rivière rejected his poems for publication in the *N.R.F.* Artaud's preface to Maeterlinck's *Douze Chansons* also appeared in 1923; it may be found in *G* I, 244–50.

The Artaud-Rivière letters were published in the *N.R.F.*, No. 132 (September 1, 1924), under the title "Une Correspondance." (In the *N.R.F.*, the writers referred to by initials in the January 29, 1924, letter were mentioned by name: "as Toulet exists, or Jean Epstein, or Jules Supervielle, or Eugène Marsan." What Artaud refers to at the end of this letter as "this prose" is probably a first version of "Paul les Oiseaux," the fifth text of *L'Ombilic des Limbes.*)

The letters were published in book form as *Correspondance avec Jacques Rivière* in October 1927, in the collection "Une Oeuvre, Un Portrait," new series, by Editions de la Nouvelle Revue Française, with a portrait of Artaud by Jean de Bosschère. Six hundred and twenty copies were printed.

VI. Two essays from 1924

"L'EVOLUTION DU DÉCOR": *G* II, 9–15. Originally published in the magazine *Comoedia,* April 19, 1924. This is Artaud's first important text on the theater; he illustrated it with two sketches.

By the word "Odéonian," Artaud refers to the traditions of the Comédie Française, one of whose theaters in Paris was at the Place de l'Odéon.

"EXPOSITION PICASSO": *G* II, 264–65. Originally published under the rubric "Lettre de Paris" in *La Criée,* No. 27 (June 1924).

•

During this period, Artaud's career as a stage actor was advancing rapidly. In 1923 he joined the theater company led by Georges Pitoëff

Notes

(1886–1939) and Ludmilla Pitoëff (1896–1951). When the Pitoëffs re-created their staging of Shaw's *Androcles and the Lion,* Artaud played Retiarius to Georges Pitoëff's Caesar. It opened on May 18, 1923. Artaud's next roles were in Ferenc Molnár's *Liliom,* directed by the Pitoëffs, in which he played one of the two detectives and one of the four policemen. *Liliom* opened on June 8, 1923, at the Comédie des Champs-Elysées, and was not a success. After it closed on June 30, Artaud went to Marseilles to see his parents. He returned to Paris in September. During the winter of 1923-24 Artaud left the Hôtel de Vintimille. He lived for a while at 10, rue Nouvelle, then in a hotel on the avenue Montaigne located opposite the Théâtre des Champs-Elysées. His first role in the fall season was that of the First Mystic in Alexander Blok's *La Petite Baraque,* directed by Jacques Hébertot, which opened on November 22, 1923. When the Pitoëffs revived their staging of Andreyev's *He Who Gets Slapped,* on December 26, 1923 (it played until February 1924), Artaud took the role of the clown Jackson (formerly played by Michel Simon). In the revival of their production of Pirandello's *Six Characters in Search of an Author* on March 4, 1924, Artaud played the Prompter. In the new production by the Pitoëffs of Karel Čapek's *R.U.R.,* directed by Théodore Komisarjevsky, Artaud had the leading role (Marius); it opened later that month, on March 26.

In the spring of 1924, Artaud began his career as an actor in films. In April he played the role of Monsieur II in Claude Autant-Lara's first film, *Faits Divers,* a small avant-garde production. Soon after, he was given a role in the commercial cinema—that of the traitor Jacques Morel in Luitz-Morat's *Surcouf, le roi des corsaires,* a big spectacle film produced by the Société des Cinéromans (his uncle Louis Nalpas was the artistic director). Génica Athanasiou, who had been in Rumania visiting her ailing mother through most of the fall of 1923, was away from Paris once again, ill; Artaud, alone, had become close to Maria Panthès, a young pianist friend of Kahnweiler's and of the Pitoëffs. In July 1924 he left for Brittany, the location of most of the outdoor scenes for *Surcouf.* The shooting lasted until the end of August.

On September 7, 1924, Artaud's father died in Marseilles. Artaud went home for the funeral and did not return to Paris until early October. After his father's death, Artaud's mother left Marseilles and came to live in Paris.

In October 1924 Artaud joined the Surrealist movement and frequented its headquarters on the rue de Grenelle, in the company of André Breton, Louis Aragon, André Masson, Robert Desnos, Paul

Eluard, Max Ernst, Michel Leiris, Roland Tual, Raymond Queneau, Pierre Naville, and the other active members. On January 25, 1925, the Surrealists met to discuss their Research Bureau, which they decided to entrust to Artaud.

VII. *The Umbilicus of Limbo* (1925)

L'Ombilic des Limbes: G I, 59–96. This is Artaud's second book—thirteen texts in various genres: poems, letters, prose declamation, art criticism, a play. It was published in the collection "Une Oeuvre, Un Portrait," with a portrait of Artaud by André Masson, by Editions de la Nouvelle Revue Française in July 1925. Seven hundred and ninety-three copies were printed. The book was originally to be titled *L'Opium Pendu, ou la fécalité de l'esprit social.*

The third text, the untitled poem that begins "Avec moi dieu-le-chien . . . ," had been published earlier that year in the special Surrealist issue of the magazine *Le Disque Vert,* No. 3, 3rd year, 4th series (June 1925), as one of a group of six poems.

The fifth text, "Paul les Oiseaux, ou la Place de l'Amour," is perhaps the earliest, and by April 1924 had already gone through several drafts. It was inspired by the life of Paolo Uccello in Marcel Schwob's *Les Vies Imaginaires* (1896). Artaud mentions his acting in *Surcouf;* he made the screen tests for that role in April 1924.

The screenplay referred to in the sixth text, a letter, has not been identified.

The painting described in the eighth text, "Un ventre fin . . . ," is André Masson's *Homme.*

The ninth text, "Poète noir," was one of the six poems published in 1925 in *Le Disque Vert.* The others were "L'Arbre," "La Rue," "La Nuit opère," "Vitres de son," and "Avec moi dieu-le-chien . . ."

The last text, the playlet *Le Jet de Sang,* appears to have been written, according to the evidence of an extant manuscript, on January 17, 1925. It is usually said that Artaud was parodying a one-act play by Armand Salacrou, *La Boule de Verre,* which had just appeared in the magazine *Intentions,* 3rd year, Nos. 28–30 (December 1924); and the manuscript is titled *Le Jet de Sang ou la Boule de Verre.* According to Eric Sellin, Artaud's playlet is in great part a satire or imitation of Apollinaire's *Les Mamelles de Tirésias* (written 1913; produced 1917; published 1918).

Sometime between 1923 and 1925 Artaud wrote a short play in four acts, *Samouraï ou le Drame du Sentiment,* influenced by Dullin's taste for Japanese drama. The text can be found in *G* II, 89–98.

VIII. From *The Nerve Meter* (1925)

Le Pèse-Nerfs: G I, 99–123. First published by Leibowitz on August 1, 1925, in the collection "Pour vos Beaux Yeux," edited by Louis Aragon. The cover was designed by André Masson. Seventy-five copies were printed. The same text, followed by the *Fragments d'un Journal d'Enfer,* with a frontispiece by Masson, was published by the magazine *Les Cahiers du Sud* (Marseilles) on March 9, 1927, in an edition of 553 copies.

Most, but not all, of *Le Pèse-Nerfs* is translated here. The remaining texts—"Lettre de ménage," "Deuxième Lettre de ménage," and "Troisième Lettre de ménage"—are to be found in *G* I, 124–30. These letters were originally written to Génica Athanasiou.

The translation follows, as far as possible, Artaud's somewhat erratic punctuation. In the text that begins "Je suis imbécile . . ." there was—in the original edition, as in that published by *Les Cahiers du Sud* in 1927—a big space between the possessive pronoun and the adjective in the third line of the third paragraph. Four pages of the original text were deleted by Artaud in the *Cahiers du Sud* edition; these pages are to be found in *G* I Supp., 175–78.

IX. *Fragments of a Diary from Hell* (1925)

Fragments d'un Journal d'Enfer: G I, 133–44. This text first appeared in the magazine *Commerce* (Cahier VII), Spring 1926. *Commerce* was edited by Paul Valéry, Léon-Paul Fargue, and Valery Larbaud. A year later, in March 1927, it was published in book form by *Les Cahiers du Sud,* along with *Le Pèse-Nerfs:* see note to Section VIII. The complete text is translated here.

The poet André Gaillard (1894–1929), to whom the text is dedicated, was one of the founders of *Les Cahiers du Sud;* he was born and died in Marseilles.

In January 1925, *Surcouf* had its première. Artaud had counted on the film establishing him as a cinema actor and was terribly disappointed when his role was barely noticed by the critics. By this point the money he had earned from *Surcouf* had run out and he was

Notes

living on a stipend from Dr. Toulouse for various editorial projects. Seeking new film roles, Artaud approached Abel Gance, who was starting to prepare his *Napoléon* (he would not begin to shoot until June 1926). Artaud was promised the role of Marat. Finally, in early May 1925, he was hired to play the role of Cecco in *Graziella*, a film inspired by the story by Lamartine of the same name written in 1849. Artaud left on May 30 for Procida, near Naples, where the director Marcel Vandal was filming most of the exteriors. The shooting lasted eight days, and Artaud was able to visit Rome and Pompeii before returning to Paris. The interior scenes of *Graziella* were shot in a studio in Paris in July.

In August 1926, Artaud had the part of the street urchin Gringalet in *Le Juif Errant*, directed by Luitz-Morat; the film was shot in the Basque countryside.

X. More prose texts from 1925

The first four texts were all published in *La Révolution Surréaliste*, the magazine edited by Pierre Naville, Benjamin Péret, and, starting with the fourth issue, André Breton. Artaud, who had joined the Surrealist movement in October 1924, first appeared in the magazine in issue No. 2 (January 15, 1925). Issue No. 3 (April 15, 1925) was a special one which Artaud edited and for which he wrote most of the contents; it was entitled "1925: Fin de l'ère chrétienne." Artaud also contributed to issue No. 5 (October 15, 1925), to No. 7 (June 15, 1926), No. 8 (December 1, 1926), and No. 11 (March 15, 1928).

"*SÛRETÉ GÉNÉRALE:* LA LIQUIDATION DE L'OPIUM": *G* I, 319–24. From issue No. 2. Jean-Pierre Liausu had, in the November 1924 issue of *Comoedia*, undertaken a campaign against cocaine.

"ENQUÊTE / On vit, on meurt. Quelle est la part de volonté en tout cela? Il semble qu'on se tue comme on rêve. Ce n'est pas une question morale que nous posons: / LE SUICIDE EST-IL UNE SOLUTION?": *G* I, 317–18. From issue No. 2.

"A TABLE": *G* I, 328–29. From issue No. 3.

"LETTRE AUX ÉCOLES DU BOUDDHA": *G* I, 342–43. This is one of the five manifestoes contained in issue No. 3. The others were: "Lettre aux Recteurs des Universités européennes," "Adresse au

Pape," "Adresse au Dalaï-Lama," and "Lettre aux médecins-chefs des asiles de fous." All five were unsigned and obviously were meant to be taken as written collectively by the Surrealist group; but Artaud's authorship of four of these "letters" seems indisputable. In the case of "Lettre aux médecins-chefs des asiles de fous," however, it is now thought that the idea was Artaud's but that the text was written by someone else in the group, perhaps his friend the poet Robert Desnos (1900–1945). "Lettre aux Recteurs des Universités européennes," "Adresse au Pape," and "Adresse au Dalaï-Lama" may be found in G I, 335–36 and 338–41; "Lettre aux médecins-chefs" may be found in G I Supp., 185–86.

"L'Activité du Bureau de Recherches surréalistes": G I, 344–47. From No. 3.

The two remaining texts in this section were both published in the N.R.F., No. 147 (December 1, 1925).

"Manifeste en langage clair": G I, 354–57. The poet and playwright Roger Vitrac (1899–1959), to whom Artaud dedicated this text, was a member of the Surrealist group from 1924 to 1929, and a co-founder, with Artaud and the essayist and historian Robert Aron, of the Alfred Jarry Theater. See notes to Section XV.

"Position de la chair": G I, 351–53. Following this text in the same issue was "Héloïse et Abélard"; see Section XII.

XI. *Eighteen Seconds*, a screenplay (1925–26)

Les Dix-huit Seconds: G III, 11–16. This screenplay, written in 1925 or 1926, was not published in Artaud's lifetime. It first appeared in *Les Cahiers de la Pléiade*, No. 7, Spring 1949.

Artaud's other screenplays, all short, are: *Deux Nations sur les confins de la Mongolie . . .*, *La Coquille et le Clergyman*, *Vols*, *Les 32*, *L'Avion solaire* (fragment), *La Révolte du Boucher*, and *Le Maître de Ballantrae* (based on the novel by Robert Louis Stevenson). The texts may be found in G III, 17–76.

La Coquille et le Clergyman was published in the *N.R.F.*, No. 170 (November 1927), and was the only one of Artaud's screenplays ever to be filmed. See Section XIV.

The last three screenplays mentioned were all written in 1929. *La Révolte du Boucher* was published in the *N.R.F.*, No. 201 (June 1930).

XII. From *Art and Death* (1925–27)

L'Art et la Mort is a collection of texts dating from the period in which Artaud belonged to the Surrealist movement: many of them were published in *La Révolution Surréaliste*. The book did not come out, however, until after Artaud's formal break with the movement. It was published in Paris by Robert Denoël on April 17, 1929, with a frontispiece by Jean de Bosschère, in an edition of eight hundred copies. The book's title is the same as the title of a lecture (the text of which has been lost) that Artaud delivered at the Sorbonne on March 22, 1928.

"QUI, AU SEIN . . .": *G* I, 147–53. This is the only text in *L'Art et la Mort* not previously published in a magazine. It was probably written sometime in 1927. Artaud's lengthy footnote was originally written as a separate text titled "L'Eperon malicieux, le Double-Cheval," and was published in *Botteghe Oscure* (Cahier VII), 1952.

"LETTRE À LA VOYANTE": *G* I, 154–60. This first appeared in *La Révolution Surréaliste*, No. 8 (December 1, 1926), just after Artaud was excluded from the Surrealist group in November. He dropped the dedication to Breton when the text was published in 1929 in *L'Art et la Mort*.

"HÉLOÏSE ET ABÉLARD": *G* I, 161–65. First published in the *N.R.F.*, No. 147 (December 1, 1925). As Jean-Louis Brau remarks in his biography of Artaud, it is plausible to see in this text, as well as in the one which follows it, "Le Clair Abélard," a parable about the Athanasiou-Artaud couple.

"LE CLAIR ABÉLARD": *G* I, 166–69. First published in *Les Feuilles Libres*, No. 47 (December 1927–January 1928).

"UCCELLO LE POIL": *G* I, 170–72. First published in *La Révolution Surréaliste*, No. 8 (December 1, 1926). Because he had broken off relations with Génica Athanasiou by that time, Artaud dropped the dedication when the text was published in 1929 in *L'Art et la Mort*.

The first five of the eight texts which make up *L'Art et la Mort* are translated here. The three remaining texts—"L'Enclume des forces," "L'Automate personnel," and "Le Vitre d'Amour"—are to be found in *G* I, 173–88. These were first published in *La Révolution Surréaliste*, No. 7 (June 15, 1926); in *Cahiers d'Art*, 2nd year, No. 3 (September 1927); and in *La Revue Européenne*, No. 29 (July 1, 1925).

"L'Automate personnel" is a response to Jean de Bosschère's portrait of Artaud. Bosschère (1878–1953), a Surrealist writer and artist, did the frontispieces for several of Artaud's books and the sets for the Alfred Jarry Theater. Artaud wrote an article about Bosschère's book *Marthe et l'Enragé*, which was published in the *N.R.F.*, No. 168 (September 1, 1927)—it may be found in *G* II, 266–68—and a short note on Bosschère's *Satan l'Obscure*, published in the *N.R.F.*, No. 247 (April 1, 1934), to be found in *G* II, 285.

XIII. "In Total Darkness, or The Surrealist Bluff" (1927)

"A LA GRANDE NUIT OU LE BLUFF SURRÉALISTE": *G* I, 363–72. Privately printed by Artaud in June 1927 in an edition of 500 copies, this pamphlet was a response to the pamphlet "Au grand jour," which appeared in Paris early in 1927, signed by Aragon, Breton, Eluard, Benjamin Péret, and Pierre Unik, in which the exclusion of Artaud and of the poet and critic Philippe Soupault from the Surrealist group was made public and the signatories announced their adherence to the French Communist Party. The article Artaud refers to in his first footnote has been lost; it was titled "Les Barbares" (see the letter from Paulhan in *G* I Supp., 210–11). Roger Vitrac was excluded only from the local branch of the group (in December 1924) after an argument with Eluard.

Martinez Pasqualis (1727–79) was a theosophist and mystic of Jewish origin, born either in Spain or in Portugal.

XIV. On *The Seashell and the Clergyman*

La Coquille et le Clergyman is the only one of Artaud's screenplays which was made into a film, though he himself did not direct it. Its director, Germaine Dulac (1882–1942), was a member of the brilliant generation of independent filmmakers in the 1920's in France. Although less interesting than, say, Louis Delluc, Jean Epstein, Léon Poirier, and Marcel L'Herbier, she should not be judged simply by the film she made from Artaud's script. Her *La Fête Espagnole* (1919, scenario by Delluc) and *La Souriante Madame Beudet* (1923) are worth seeing.

"LE CINÉMA ET L'ABSTRACTION": *G* III, 88–89. First published in *Le Monde Illustré*, No. 3645 (October 29, 1927). This text was evidently written when Artaud still had confidence in the director. (Artaud, of course, had originally hoped to make the film himself or at least to collaborate in the *mise en scène* as well as to play the part of the Clergyman. And he had written the main woman's role for Génica Athanasiou; it was at the very end of their relationship. On this point Dulac acceded, and Athanasiou did get the part.) It was shot in late July and August 1927. After Dulac finished the film, Artaud disavowed it entirely. When *La Coquille et le Clergyman* had its première at the Studio des Ursulines in Paris on February 9, 1928, Artaud arrived with Robert Desnos and a number of other friends to protest; they attempted to stop the screening and were thrown out of the theater.

"CINÉMA ET RÉALITÉ": *G* III, 22–25. This is the preface Artaud wrote when his screenplay of *La Coquille et le Clergyman* was published in the *N.R.F.*, No. 170 (November 1, 1927). The screenplay is to be found in *G* III, 25–31.

XV. On the Alfred Jarry Theater

The Théâtre Alfred Jarry—named after the author of *Ubu Roi*—was founded in 1926 by Artaud, Roger Vitrac, and Robert Aron. It was partly subsidized by Artaud's friends Dr. René Allendy and his wife Yvonne. Madame Allendy became business manager (raising money, etc.) and later, with Aron, administrative director. Artaud was the director and set designer of all of the plays.

The Alfred Jarry Theater's first production was an evening of three short plays—*Ventre Brûlé, ou la Mère Folle* by Artaud (the next has been lost), *Les Mystères de l'Amour* by Vitrac, and *Gigogne* by Aron under the pseudonym Max Robur—on June 1 and 2, 1927, at the Théâtre de Grenelle. (Génica Athanasiou played the role of Léa in *Les Mystères de l'Amour*.) In a text called "Le Théâtre Alfred Jarry en 1930" (*G* II, 51–63), Artaud describes *Ventre Brûlé* as "a lyric work, which humorously denounces the conflict between the cinema and the theater."

The second production, at the Comédie des Champs-Elysées on

January 14, 1928, consisted of two "forbidden" works. The first was a screening of Pudovkin's film *Mother* (1926), whose commercial release in France had been stopped by the government. The second was Act III of Paul Claudel's hitherto unperformed play *Le Partage de Midi*, put on without the author's permission. Génica Athanasiou played the role of Yzé. (The entire play was not produced until 1948, when it was done—with Claudel's permission—by Jean-Louis Barrault.)

The third production was Strindberg's *Dream Play* at the Théâtre de l'Avenue on June 2 and 9, 1928. Robert Aron resigned after the scandal connected with the première (see below). Génica Athanasiou did not have a part in this production; indeed, she and Artaud were barely on speaking terms, because of her love affair with the film director Jean Grémillon.

The fourth and last production was Vitrac's three-act play *Victor, ou les Enfants au Pouvoir*. It was performed at the Comédie des Champs-Elysées on December 24 and 29, 1928, and January 5, 1929. The painter Giorgio di Chirico attended all three performances.

In the program notes for *Victor* was an announcement of the next production of the Alfred Jarry Theater, scheduled for early June 1930: Vitrac's four-act "drame bourgeois" *Le Coup de Trafalgar*. Artaud wanted very much to direct this play and tried throughout 1930 and 1931 to get important people in the Paris theater world, notably Dullin and Louis Jouvet, to help him—without success. Finally, it was the company Le Rideau de Paris, directed by Marcel Herrand and Jean Marchat, which put on *Le Coup de Trafalgar* at the Théâtre de l'Atelier four years after Artaud had wanted to do it; the play had its première on June 8, 1934, and was the only commercially successful production Vitrac had during his lifetime. In the *N.R.F.* (July 1934) Artaud attacked Herrand's *mise en scène* as a betrayal of the ideas shared by him and Vitrac, and the ten-year friendship between the two men ended. *G* III contains twenty-four letters from Artaud to Vitrac, written between 1928 and 1934.

"Le Théâtre Alfred Jarry": *G* II, 19–22. First published, in a fragmented form, in the *N.R.F.*, No. 158 (November 1, 1926). It was in November that Artaud was excluded from the Surrealist movement.

"Théâtre Alfred Jarry—Ière Année.—Saison 1926–27": *G* II, 23–26. This is a second version of the manifesto that appeared in the *N.R.F.*, No. 158. It was privately published in 1926 as an eight-page brochure.

"Manifeste pour un théâtre avorté": *G* II, 28–33. This text was published in *Les Cahiers du Sud*, No. 87 (February 1927).

"*Le Songe* de Strindberg . . .": *G* II, 40–42. This text was included in the program distributed at the performances of Strindberg's *Dream Play* which Artaud directed and in which he played a small role, that of Theology. (This was the very first French production of Strindberg's play. Artaud omitted the Prologue as well as the sixth, twelfth, and fourteenth scenes.) The first performance took place on June 2, 1928, at the Théâtre de l'Avenue, before a mainly invited audience that included Paul Valéry, Abel Gance, André Gide, Arthur Honegger, François Mauriac; the Swedish Ambassador to France (who left during the performance), Prince George of Greece, and the Duchesse de La Rochefoucauld; the Surrealists were excluded and threatened to disrupt the evening. Both this and the second performance, on June 9 in the same theater, were in fact interrupted by a demonstration by some of the Surrealists. See Artaud's letter of June 7, 1928, to Yvonne Allendy in Section XVI.

XVI. Letters from 1927–30

to génica athanasiou (september 16, 1927): *LGA*, 275. Artaud and Génica Athanasiou broke up at the end of 1927.

to abel gance (november 27, 1927): *G* III, 143–44. Artaud had already acted in Gance's *Napoléon* (shot in 1926 and 1927), in which he played Marat. He did not get the part he was asking for in the Epstein film.

to rené allendy (november 30, 1927): *G* I Supp., 81–85. It might be mentioned that Dr. Allendy was the author of a book, published in 1921, called *Symbolisme des Nombres, essai d'arithmosophie*, and was particularly interested in the researches in alchemy, astrology, and the Cabala pursued by Paracelsus in the sixteenth century. Artaud borrowed many books about the Orient from Allendy.

to yvonne allendy (june 7, 1928): *G* III, 150–52. The play referred to is Artaud's production of Strindberg's *Dream Play*, whose second performance was to take place on June 9, under threat of disruption by Breton and some of the other Surrealists. The Surrealists did demonstrate, and Aron called the police. See notes to Section XV.

Notes

TO YVONNE ALLENDY (MARCH 26, 1929): *G* III, 162–64. Franco-Film was the company which had produced *Tarakanova*.

Artaud mentions two of the best American films of the late silent period. *Lonesome* (1928)—Artaud calls it by its French title, *Solitudes*—was directed by Paul Fejos. *Underworld* (1927) is by Josef von Sternberg; Artaud refers to it as *Les Nuits de Chicago*, as it is known in France.

In 1929 Artaud lived on the quai d'Auteuil in the 16th arrondissement.

TO YVONNE ALLENDY (JUNE 5, 1930): *G* III, 207–9.

The Allendys had known the Futurist poet and ideologue Filippo Tommaso Marinetti (1876–1944) at least since 1924.

Carl Dreyer's *La Passion de Jeanne d'Arc*, in which Artaud played the role of the monk Massieu, and Léon Poirier's *Verdun, Visions d'Histoire*, in which he played the Intellectual, were both made in 1928. Marcel L'Herbier's *L'Argent* (based on Zola's novel), in which he played the secretary Mazaud, was shot in 1928 and released in 1929; Raymond Bernard's *Tarakanova*, in which he played the romantic lead (a young gypsy), was shot in Nice in February and April 1929. Artaud did not succeed in making a film of *The Monk*, the famous English Gothic novel, but he did do a free translation of the novel; it was published in 1931. Seven of the photographic *tableaux vivants* that Artaud composed to illustrate scenes from *The Monk* are to be found in *G* VI. They were done to interest a producer in backing a film of *The Monk;* one of them was used for the cover of the original edition of Artaud's translation. See first note to Section XIX.

TO RENÉ ALLENDY (JULY 12, 1930): *G* III, 209–12. Artaud made two trips to Berlin in 1930, in July–August and again in October, to play a secondary role, an apprentice beggar, in G. W. Pabst's film *L'Opéra de quat'sous*, the French version of his film based on *Die Dreigroschenoper* by Brecht and Kurt Weill. The film was not released until 1932.

The Professor Sachs mentioned in the letter is the psychoanalyst and pupil of Freud, Hanns Sachs; he was a friend of Dr. Allendy.

Walter Ruttmann (1887–1941), the German film director, made mostly documentary films—the most famous of which are *Berlin, Symphonie einer Grosstadt* (1927) and *Melodie der Welt* (1929). Known for his left-wing sympathies, he rallied to the Nazis after 1933 and made several documentaries for Goebbels.

Les 32 is one of Artaud's screenplays which was not published during his lifetime. See note to Section XI.

XVII. Questions and answers on the cinema

"Réponse à une enquête": *G* III, 79–81. Not published during Artaud's lifetime; undated, but probably written in late 1924 or early 1925, while Artaud was still a member of the Surrealist movement.

"Antonin Artaud": *G* III, 345–48. This interview appeared in *Cinémonde*, August 1, 1929. Artaud names only a few of his film roles. The name of the monk in Carl Dreyer's film is usually given as Jean Massieu. Jean Epstein's *Finis Terrae* (1929), a story that takes place in a Breton fishing village, used as actors the inhabitants of the two Breton islands where the film was shot.

XVIII. Excerpts from notebooks and private papers (1931–32)

"C'est qui est vrai . . ." (early 1931): *G* VIII, 68.

"Ne plus disposer . . ." (early 1931): *G* VIII, 68.

"Tous les problèmes . . ."(probably november 1931): *G* VIII, 74–75.

"Sentiments métaphysiques . . ." (probably december 1931): *G* VIII, 76.

"Je suis malheureux . . ." (probably december 1931): *G* VIII, 76–77.

"Notre Occident . . ." (probably december 1931): *G* VIII, 77–78.

"La blessure . . ." (probably february 1932): *G* VIII, 79.

"A la poursuite étrange . . ." (probably february 1932): *G* VIII, 79–84.

"Il s'agit de . . ." (probably february 1932): *G* VIII, 84. Two of the five brief paragraphs are translated here. By "him" Artaud may be referring to Soulié de Morant, from whom he was receiving acupuncture treatments at the time.

"LA SEULE VÉRITABLE POÉSIE . . ." (PROBABLY FEBRUARY 1932):
G VIII, 85–86.

"L'OUBLI TOTAL . . ." (PROBABLY MARCH 1932) : *G* VIII, 86.

XIX. Letters from 1931

INCOMPLETE DRAFT OF A LETTER, ADDRESSEE UNKNOWN: *G* VI, 406–8. René Guénon (1886–1951) was a French writer who wrote on Hindu and Islamic metaphysics and mysticism. A convert to Islam, he was initiated into the Sufi sect in 1912, and lived in Cairo under his Arab name, Abd el Wahed Yahia, from 1930 until his death. On January 26, 1932, Artaud wrote Jean Paulhan that he wanted to do "an important essay on René Guénon" for the *N.R.F.* (see *G* V, 70–71). This essay was never written.

Artaud's free translation of Monk Lewis's *The Monk* (1794) was published by Denoël et Steele in April 1931; it takes up the whole of *G* VI ("Le Moine, de Lewis, raconté par Antonin Artaud"). Artaud's knowledge of English was less than excellent, and he is known to have used an unpublished French translation, which he constantly compared with the original.

The Monk was much admired by Breton, and it may have been he who brought the book to Artaud's attention. As early as 1929, Artaud had thought of doing *The Monk* as a film or a play.

The reference to *The Golden Ass* (real title, *Metamorphoses*) suggests that Artaud accepted the controversial theory that Apuleius' book is actually a hermetic text written for initiates of the cult of Isis.

TO LOUIS JOUVET (APRIL 15, 1931) : *G* III, 224–26. Until 1934, Jouvet (1887–1951) worked mainly at the Comédie des Champs-Elysées. The "talking pantomime" is *La Pierre Philosophale*, which Artaud had written just prior to April 1932. Published in *Les Cahiers de la Pléiade*, No. 7 (Spring 1949), it can be found in *G* II, 99–106.

TO JEAN-RICHARD BLOCH (APRIL 23, 1931) : *G* V, 63–65. Bloch (1884–1947) was a Communist, and a friend of Aragon's; he wrote novels, plays, and essays. His *Destin du Théâtre*, in which he describes the evolution of the modern French theater and attempts to prophesy its future, was published in 1930 by Gallimard. Artaud participated in a debate entitled "Le Destin du théâtre" at the Salle d'Iéna on December 8, 1931.

Notes

TO LOUIS JOUVET (APRIL 27, 1931) : *G* III, 231–32.

DRAFT OF A LETTER TO RENÉ DAUMAL (JULY 14, 1931) : *G* III, 246–50. Daumal (1908–44) wrote poems, articles, stories, a novel (*Le Mont Analogue*), and translated many Hindu texts. His interest in Oriental religion followed his study of the works of René Guénon; he knew and was strongly influenced by Gurdjieff. In the 1920's he was on the fringe of the Surrealist movement.

Between 1930 and 1935, Artaud made numerous trips to Germany, where he saw productions by Adolphe Appia, Vsevolod Meyerhold, Max Reinhardt, and Erwin Piscator. It was during a trip in 1924 that he first came in contact with the new movements in German theater and cinema; he was particularly enthusiastic about the work of Reinhardt and about two films, Robert Wiene's *The Cabinet of Dr. Caligari* (for the performance of Conrad Veidt) and F. W. Murnau's *Nosferatu*. It was also in 1924 that Artaud appeared briefly in the filmed section (directed by Jean Painlevé) of a Paris production of the German Expressionist Yvan Goll's play *Mathusalem*.

UNFINISHED LETTER TO JEAN PAULHAN (AUGUST 5, 1931) : *G* IV, 302–3. Paulhan was the editor of the *N.R.F.* Artaud's essay "Le Théâtre Balinais" was scheduled to appear in the October issue of the magazine. He discovered the Balinese theater at the Colonial Exposition in Paris in 1931.

TO JEAN PAULHAN (SEPTEMBER 23, 1931) : *G* III, 259–60.

TO LOUIS JOUVET (OCTOBER 20, 1931) : *G* III, 263–66. Artaud gave a lecture entitled *La Mise en scène et la Métaphysique* at the Sorbonne on December 10, 1931. The text is to be found in Section XX. See his letter to Paulhan of January 22, 1932, in Section XVI. In 1932 he was Jouvet's assistant in his production at the Théâtre Pigalle of Alfred Savoir's *La Pâtissière du Village*. See his letter to Jouvet of March 1, 1932, in Section XXI.

No trace of a play called *Roi des Enfants* has been found. For *Le Coup de Trafalgar*, see notes to Section XV.

In 1931 Artaud, who had been living at 178, quai d'Auteuil, moved to the Hôtel Saint-Charles, 45, rue Pigalle.

Notes

XX. For *The Theater and Its Double* (1931–36)

Le Théâtre et son Double, Artaud's most famous book, appeared in February 1938 in the "Metamorphoses" series published by Gallimard. It is a collection of Artaud's writings on the theater from 1931 on: essays published in the *N.R.F.*, manifestoes, letters, etc.

Artaud first thought of collecting these texts in book form in 1935, when he had just finished writing *Les Cenci* and was looking for a theater in which to do the play. (For more on this play, see the note in Section XXIV to Artaud's letter to Gide.) Toward the end of 1935, he was pressing Paulhan to prevail on Gaston Gallimard to publish the book. After the failure of *Les Cenci*—which lasted seventeen days at the Théâtre des Folies-Wagram in May—Artaud began making plans to leave for Mexico. Shortly before his departure, he wrote some additional texts for the collection. On the boat to Mexico, he wrote Jean Paulhan (January 25, 1936) that he had found a title for the book. After his return from Mexico, and before his trip to Ireland, he corrected the proofs. By the time *Le Théâtre et son Double* appeared, Artaud was interned in the Sainte-Anne Hospital in Paris.

"Sur le théâtre balinais": *G* IV, 64–81. The first part of this text, which ends with the words "et qui était le plus bel ornement de l'une des premières pièces jouées par le Théâtre Alfred Jarry," was published in the *N.R.F.*, No. 217 (October 1, 1931), under the title "Le Théâtre Balinais, à l'Exposition Coloniale." The second part consists of notes and extracts from letters (to Paulhan et al.). Artaud must have seen the Balinese dancers in May or July 1931; he was away from Paris during the entire month of June for the shooting of Raymond Bernard's *Les Croix de Bois*.

Arjuna is one of the five brothers known as the Pandavas, who are the joint heroes of the Hindu epic the *Mahabharata*.

"La Mise en scène et la Métaphysique": *G* IV, 40–57. This is the text of a lecture Artaud gave at the Sorbonne on December 10, 1931. The original manuscript bears the title "Peinture." It was subsequently published in the *N.R.F.*, No. 221 (February 1, 1932).

The René Guénon quote comes from his book *Orient et Occident* (1924).

Lot and His Daughters was painted by Lucas van Leyden around 1509 and is now in the Musée du Louvre.

Notes

"Les Frères Marx": *G* IV, 165–68. First published under the title "Les Frères Marx au cinéma du Panthéon" in the film column of the *N.R.F.*, No. 220 (January 1, 1932).

"Le Théâtre de la Cruauté (Premier Manifeste)": *G* IV, 106–19. First published in the *N.R.F.*, No. 229 (October 1, 1932). The French text, starting from the second paragraph of the concluding section ("Themes") to the end, is in italics.

The attribution of *Arden of Feversham* to Shakespeare, first advanced in 1770 and widely accepted in the nineteenth century, has since been discredited.

Léon-Paul Fargue (1874–1947), the poet, began as a disciple of Mallarmé and joined the Surrealists for a while. He was one of the original editors of the magazine *Commerce*, founded in 1924.

The *Zohar* (the word means radiance) is the masterpiece of Spanish Cabalism. It was mostly written by Moses de León in the last quarter of the thirteenth century in Castile; the main part of the work is in pseudo-epigraphical form: a collection of the dialogues and lectures of Rabbi Simeon ben Yohai and his pupils in the second century.

"A Tale by the Marquis de Sade . . ." According to Paule Thévenin, Artaud was thinking of Pierre Klossowski's *Château de Valmore*. This is an adaptation of Sade's *Eugénie de Franval* (1788), one of the eleven stories which comprise *Les Crimes de l'Amour*.

"En finir avec les chefs-d'oeuvre": *G* IV, 89–100. This text, written toward the end of 1933, was first published in *Le Théâtre et son Double* in 1938.

The Isawas are a Moslem sect of Dervishes founded in Morocco about 1500.

"Un Athlétisme affectif": *G* IV, 154–64. Written in late 1935 for the projected collection of his texts on the theater, just before Artaud left for Mexico; not published until the book came out in 1938. For the concluding part of this essay (before the "N.B."), Artaud used the last paragraph of "Le Théâtre de Séraphin," which was written about the same time. (See end of notes to this section.)

The Ka denotes the vital force of a person. In ancient Egypt the offerings at the tomb were specifically made to a person's Ka; to die was described as "to go to one's Ka."

"Théâtre oriental et théâtre occidental": *G* IV, 82–88. Also written in late 1935 for the projected book of theater texts.

Notes

Seven of the fifteen texts that constitute *Le Théâtre et son Double* are translated here. These are presented in the order in which Artaud wrote them, between 1931 and 1935, rather than as arranged (non-chronologically) by Artaud for the book finally published in 1938. The order of the fifteen texts that make up the book is:
"Préface: Le Théâtre et la culture"
"Le Théâtre et la peste"
"La Mise en scène et la Métaphysique"
"Le Théâtre alchimique"
"Sur le théâtre balinais"
"Théâtre oriental et théâtre occidental"
"En finir avec les chefs-d'oeuvre"
"Le Théâtre et la Cruauté"
"Le Théâtre de la Cruauté (Premier Manifeste)"
"Lettres sur la cruauté"
"Lettres sur le langage"
"Le Théâtre de la Cruauté (Second Manifeste)"
"Un Athlétisme affectif"
"Les Frères Marx"
"Autour d'une mère"

Le Théâtre et son Double is the only one of Artaud's works so far that has had a proper existence in English: in a translation by Mary Caroline Richards that is complete (though without notes) and widely available. It was published by Grove Press in 1958.

Of the texts not translated in this volume, the earliest is "Le Théâtre alchimique," which can be found in *G* IV, 58–63. Artaud wrote it at the request of the poet Jules Supervielle for the Buenos Aires magazine *Sur*. From the correspondence with Supervielle, we know that it was written between February and May 1932 (although Artaud dated the text "Paris, September 1932"); it came out in *Sur*, No. 6 (Autumn 1932). It had not been published in French before its appearance in 1938 in *Le Théâtre et son Double*.

Next comes "Le Théâtre et la peste"—*G* IV, 19–39—which was first a lecture given by Artaud at the Sorbonne on April 6, 1933 (Anaïs Nin was in the audience), and then was published in the *N.R.F.*, No. 253 (October 1, 1934).

"Le Théâtre de la Cruauté (Second Manifeste)"—*G* IV, 146–53 —was first published by Editions Denoël as a sixteen-page pamphlet in 1933. In this text Artaud announced that the first production of the Theater of Cruelty would be *La Conquête du Mexique*, about which he writes at some length. A "scenario" (description of the action; no dialogue) for *La Conquête du Mexique* may be found in *G* V, 21–29. Artaud was particularly attached to this never realized project; he read the scenario aloud more than once—most notably, at the reading organized by Lise and Paul Deharme on the evening of January 6, 1934, when he also recited from Shakespeare's *Richard II*.

"Le Théâtre de Séraphin": *G* IV, 175–82. This text was destined for inclusion in *Le Théâtre et son Double;* Artaud lists it in his proposed table of contents in letters to Paulhan on December 29, 1935, and January 6, 1936, and in a letter from Mexico written on March 26, 1936, Artaud tells Paulhan he is mailing him a revised version of the text. It is not known why it was omitted when the book was published in 1938.

The manuscript carries the date "Mexico, April 5, 1936" (and is dedicated to Paulhan), but Artaud must have written it at least six months earlier. It was first published in 1948, after Artaud's death, by Bettencourt (in the collection "L'Air du Temps"), in an edition of 250 copies.

The Théâtre de Séraphin is the name of a Chinese shadow and marionette theater established in Paris in 1781 by an Italian named Serafino. It continued to be run by his descendants, and was in the middle of the nineteenth century located first in the Galerie de Valois at the Palais Royal and then in the Bazar Européen on the boulevard Montmartre. It ceased operating in 1870. "Le Théâtre de Séraphin" is the title of a nineteen-page section of Baudelaire's book *Les Paradis artificiels* (1860). (It is the third chapter of Part Two, "Le Poème du haschisch.")

XXI. Letters from 1932–33

TO JEAN PAULHAN (JANUARY 22, 1932): *G* III, 298–306. The Sorbonne lecture referred to is "La Mise en scène et la Métaphysique." (See note to previous section.) *L'Age d'Or*, by Buñuel and Dali, came out in 1928; Cocteau's *Le Sang d'un Poète* appeared in 1930. This letter was never sent.

TO JEAN PAULHAN (JANUARY 30, 1932): *G* V, 73–76. Artaud wrote a review of this production of Passeur's *Les Tricheurs* at the Théâtre de l'Atelier; it may be found in *G* II, 186–90. The notes on *Les Tricheurs* that Artaud wrote for himself are to be found in *G* II, 159–65.

Artaud did not obtain the position of monthly film critic for the *N.R.F.*

TO GEORGE SOULIÉ DE MORANT (FEBRUARY 17, 1932): *G* I Supp., 127–33. Charles Georges Soulié de Morant (1878–1955), who wrote under the name George Soulié de Morant, was an expert on acupuncture and the author of a novel, *Bijou-de-Ceinture*, and a book on the history of Chinese art. He went to China at the age of twenty, and at one time was the French consul in Shanghai. After returning to France, he published translations of Chinese medical documents and wrote on acupuncture. Artaud was treated by Soulié de Morant in February 1932.

TO GEORGE SOULIÉ DE MORANT (FEBRUARY 19, 1932): *G* I Supp., 134–42. According to Paule Thévenin, *Nunc salmavat* is a faulty contraction of *nunc me salvat* (now he/she saves me). Another hypothesis: that Artaud, with his limited Latin, was making up a verb (*salmo/-are*) and meant either *nunc salmavit* (now he sang praises) or *nunc salmabat* (now he was singing praises).

TO LOUIS JOUVET (MARCH 1, 1932): *G* III, 324–27. The play is *La Pâtissière du Village* by Alfred Savoir (1883–1934), the Polish-born French dramatist. Artaud was Jouvet's assistant for this production, which had its première at the Théâtre Pigalle on March 8, 1932. During this time—winter 1931–32—Artaud was also pleading with Dullin, without success, to permit him to direct a production of Büchner's *Woyzeck* in the Tuesday series at the Atelier. Another unrealized project of the period was an opera which Artaud planned to write with Edgard Varèse, to be called "Il n'y a plus de firmament"; some sketches and notes of Artaud's have survived and may be found in *G* II, 107–24.

TO JEAN PAULHAN (AUGUST 3, 1932): *G* V, 116–17. The manifesto in question is the "Premier Manifeste" of the "Théâtre de la Cruauté." For "Le Théâtre alchimique," see notes to previous section.

Shakespeare's "apocryphal play" is *Arden of Feversham*; see Artaud's November 27, 1932, letter to Paulhan in this section. Thomas De Quincey's essay is "On the Knocking at the Gate in Macbeth," which Paulhan had given Artaud to read; the *N.R.F.* was to publish a translation of it in No. 242 (November 1, 1933).

TO ANDRÉ GIDE (AUGUST 7, 1932): *G* V, 118–22. Gide's answer to Artaud's letter is reproduced in *G* V, 340–41.

Notes

TO JEAN PAULHAN (AUGUST 23, 1932): *G* V, 132–33. Most of this letter is another version of the closing passage of the "Premier Manifeste" in *Le Théâtre et son Double*.

TO JEAN PAULHAN (SEPTEMBER 12, 1932): *G* V, 154–55. Artaud used the third paragraph of this letter, with a few minor changes, as the "Deuxième Lettre" (misdated November 14, 1932) in the section "Lettres sur la cruauté" in *Le Théâtre et son Double*. *Cf. G* IV, 122.

TO JEAN PAULHAN (NOVEMBER 27, 1932): *G* V, 186–90. Duvert's *Harnali ou la Contrainte par cor* was a theatrical parody of *Hernani*, the famous play by Victor Hugo.

TO JEAN PAULHAN (DECEMBER 16, 1932): *G* III, 334–35. Sometime in 1933 Artaud wrote what he described as an adaptation of Seneca's play *Atreus and Thyestes*, which he called *Le Supplice de Tantale;* the manuscript has been lost. His surviving notes for this work may be found in *G* II, 203–9. There is no Seneca play called *Atreus and Thyestes*, though he did write an *Agamemnon* and a *Thyestes*. Artaud must have meant these plays, and may also have been thinking of the tragedy by Crébillon père, *Atrée et Thyeste* (1707), based on Seneca, and the tragedy by Voltaire, *Les Pélopides ou Atrée et Thyeste* (1770).

"Out of here . . .": Artaud spent part of this month in a clinic, being disintoxicated.

TO ANAÏS NIN (APRIL 1933): *G* VII, 180–81. Artaud was introduced to Anaïs Nin by René and Yvonne Allendy. Madame Allendy died in August 1935.

Undertaken on commission, Artaud's translation (in collaboration with Bernard Steele) of Ludwig Lewisohn's novel *The Case of Mr. Crump* was published in 1932 by Denoël et Steele under the title *Crime Passionel*. Between November 1931 and October 1932 Artaud lived at 4, rue du Commerce, in the 15th arrondissement. From there he moved to a new room nearby, at 42, rue Rouelle, where he lived until September 1933.

XXII. "The Premature Old Age of the Cinema" (1933)

"LA VIELLESSE PRÉCOCE DU CINÉMA": *G* III, 102–7. First published in *Les Cahiers Jaunes*, No. 4, "Cinéma '33" (1933). Artaud had given a lecture at the Studio 28 on June 20, 1929, "sur les possibilités et les impossibilités du film parlant."

Artaud had many film roles in the early 1930's. In 1931 he played in Raymond Bernard's *Faubourg Montmartre* (shot from January to March) and in Marcel L'Herbier's *La Femme d'Une Nuit*, both resounding critical and box-office failures; in Bernard's *Les Croix de Bois* (shot in June–July 1931), a mediocre patriotic film which had its première in March 1932; and, again, in Léon Poirier's *Verdun, Souvenirs d'Histoire*, the sound version of *Verdun, Visions d'Histoire* (Artaud played the Intellectual).

In 1932, he starred in Serge de Poligny's *Coups de Feu à l'Aube*, playing the leader of a gang of assassins. The film was shot in Berlin between April and August 1932.

In 1933, Artaud had a role in the sound version of Gance's *Mater Dolorosa*.

In 1934, he was in Fritz Lang's *Liliom* (he had played in the Pitoëff stage production of *Liliom* in June 1923) and in Henri Wullschleger's *Sidonie Panache*, which was produced by Louis Nalpas, Artaud's uncle. Artaud was in Algeria for the first time—in Laghouat —for the shooting of the Wullschleger film.

XXIII. From *Heliogabalus, or The Anarchist Crowned* (1934)

Héliogabale, ou l'Anarchiste couronné: *G* VII, 114–37. Published by Denoël et Steele in April 1934, illustrated with six drawing by André Derain. Although he would probably never have written this book had it not been commissioned (like the translation of Ludwig Lewisohn's *The Case of Mr. Crump*) by Robert Denoël, the project ended by deeply involving Artaud, both as a poet and as a scholar of magical-religious systems. For a list of the many books which he is known to have consulted while writing *Héliogabale*, see *G* VII, 379–82.

The narrative of *Héliogabale* is divided into three parts: "Le Berceau de sperme"; "La Guerre des principes"; "L'Anarchie." The section translated here is the second half of "L'Anarchie." The whole text may be found in *G* VII, 11–137.

Notes

At the end of *Héliogabale,* Artaud added three factual notes: "Le Schisme d'Irshu," "La Religion du soleil en Syrie," and "Le Zodiaque de Ram": *G* VII, 139–43.

Heliogabalus was born in A.D. 204 in Emesa (Homs) in Roman Syria. Originally named Varius Avitus Bassianus, he was the son of Julia Soaemias and Varius Marcellus. His mother was the elder daughter of Julia Maesa, the sister-in-law of the emperor Septimius Severus. Through his mother's family, he was the hereditary high priest of the patron deity of Emesa, Elah-Gabal, and was called by the name of his god, though the name was never official. (The Latinized form of the god's name is Elagabalus, but because this god or Baal was regarded as a sun-god, the name was transcribed by Roman historians as Heliogabalus [from *helios,* sun]. When Artaud refers to Elagabalus he means the god and when he refers to Heliogabalus he means the man, but originally both the god and the man were known as Elagabalus.)

In 217, Heliogabalus' cousin Caracalla, Severus' son and successor, was murdered (at the age of twenty-nine) by the treachery of Macrinus, the prefect of the Praetorian Guard—the emperor's personal troops. Caracalla was replaced as emperor by Macrinus. Julia Maesa, Caracalla's aunt and Heliogabalus' grandmother, returned to Emesa—from where she instigated a revolt against Macrinus in the name of Heliogabalus. After Macrinus was murdered the following year, the Senate in Rome then acknowledged Heliogabalus, who assumed the name of Marcus Aurelius Antoninus when he was acclaimed emperor in 218 in Emesa. He was fifteen years old. Heliogabalus reached Rome with his mother and grandmother in 219, imposed the worship of his Baal upon the Roman world, and remained emperor until he and his mother were murdered in 222. According to Lampridius, he was known for his beauty and his stature.

Artaud's main source was the life of Heliogabalus, purportedly written by the late Roman historian Aelius Lampridius, in the *Scriptores Historiae Augustae* (often referred to as the *Historia Augusta*). This is a 500-page collection of biographies of Roman emperors and usurpers from 117 to 284 (from Hadrian to Diocletian, with a gap for the years 244–49), written by six authors, which was modeled on Suetonius' *Lives of the Twelve Caesars.* Lampridius, who wrote under the reign of Constantine the Great (337–61), states that his biography of Heliogabalus—one of the three he contributed to the *Scriptores Historiae Augustae*—was commissioned by Constantine. Though the col-

Notes

lection has never enjoyed great authority among scholars, it is the only near-continuous account for the history of the emperors of the second and third centuries. The *Scriptores Historiae Augustae* is published in the "Loeb Classical Library" series, the Latin text with an English translation by David Magie (Harvard University Press, 1924); the biography of Heliogabalus is in Vol. II, pp. 104–77.

"Not, like Septimius Severus . . ." Lucius Septimius Severus was emperor from 193 to 211, and had a distinguished military career. He was succeeded by his son, Marcus Aurelius Antoninus, known as Caracalla. Caracalla's mother, Julia Domna, was the second wife of Septimius Severus and the sister of Julia Maesa (Heliogabalus' maternal grandmother). Julia Domna, who hated her son, was in Antioch when Caracalla was murdered in the uprising led by Macrinus. (Macrinus was not related to the royal house.) Macrinus banished her from Antioch and she starved herself to death, vexed at having to return to private life.

"They had conspired against Macrinus . . ." Marcus Opellius Macrinus, born in 164, was a native of Africa and was Prefect of the Praetorian Guard under Caracalla. He had Caracalla assassinated in April 217 and banished Caracalla's aunt, Julia Maesa, to her native city, Emesa. After he became emperor, he cut the soldiers' pay; the army then regretted having backed Macrinus against Caracalla. Julia Maesa organized the revolt against Macrinus in the name of her grandson Heliogabalus, who was already known to many soldiers as high priest of the temple of Elagabalus and as cousin of Caracalla; Julia Maesa claimed that he was Caracalla's illegitimate son. When the army went over to Heliogabalus, Macrinus fled and was murdered in 218.

"Alexander, cousin of this same Heliogabalus . . ." That is, Alexianus—son of Heliogabalus' aunt, Julia Mamaea. (Heliogabalus' grandmother had two daughters, Julia Soaemias and Julia Mamaea, by Julius Avitus, a Syrian of consular rank.) In 221, Julia Maesa induced Heliogabalus to adopt her other grandson, Alexianus, as Caesar. When he became emperor in 222—after Heliogabalus' death —he took the name Marcus Aurelius Severus Alexander. He was thirteen years old at the time. His grandmother was virtual ruler of Rome until her death in 226. Afterward his mother assumed power and functioned as regent. He and his mother were murdered by the army in 235.

"Blood of the Tauroboly . . ." A rite of purification and initiation associated with the worship of the Magna Mater, in great vogue

Notes

in Rome in the second and third centuries. The neophyte stood in a pit covered with perforated boards on top of which a bull was slaughtered.

"Religion of the menstruae . . ." Artaud is referring to the belief in a primordial sexual duality. While the feminine principle has been vanquished by the masculine principle, the feminine continues to have its partisans among gods and humans. Heliogabalus himself was taken by Artaud to embody the antagonism between—and union of—the feminine and the masculine. Hence, his homosexuality and his wish to become a woman. Hence, the scandalous privileges he accorded to women, at least to the women of his own family. According to Lampridius IV, 2, Heliogabalus made his mother a member of the Senate (the first and only woman senator in the entire history of Rome); in XII, 3, Lampridius says it was his grandmother, Julia Maesa. While Heliogabalus apparently did not, as Artaud claims, banish men from the Senate, he did (according to Lampridius) establish another—women's—Senate on the Quirinal Hill. Thus the "religion of the menstruae" means the religion of women. Artaud says it "originated the Tyrian purple," because he interprets purple as a feminine color, taking it to derive from (menstrual) red. This is not, of course, the usual association with purple; and the Tyrian or Phoenician purple was, traditionally, bestowed only on emperors.

"Stringed or percussive instruments, like crotalums . . ." The crotalum is a kind of castanet used in ancient religious dances; the tambour is a barrel-shaped drum; the sistrum is an ancient Egyptian rattle used in the worship of Isis; the hasosra is a long straight silver trumpet; the nebel is a stringed instrument, probably a large harp, used by the Hebrews and ancient Greeks.

"The three mothers . . ." The most important of the three was Julia Maesa. After Caracalla's death, it was Julia Maesa who led the revolt against the usurper Macrinus; she spread the story that her grandson Heliogabalus was Caracalla's natural son, assisted in the proclamation of Heliogabalus and accompanied him to Rome, becoming "mater castrorum et senatus." It was she who persuaded Heliogabalus to adopt her other daughter's son—Severus Alexander—and give him the title of Caesar, and then conspired in the overthrow and murder of Heliogabalus. Next in importance was Julia Soaemias, Heliogabalus' mother, who assisted her mother in deposing Macrinus and making her son emperor. She was described by Latin historians as not as intelligent or powerful as her mother but equal in depravity to her son. According to Dio's *Roman History*, Heliogabalus was killed in his mother's arms and her body dragged through the streets with his.

"Julia Mamaea the Christian . . ." Julia Mamaea (*d.* 235)—the younger daughter of Julia Maesa, Severus Alexander's mother, and Heliogabalus' aunt—was not a Christian.

"Masquerading as Apollonius of Tyana . . ." Apollonius of Tyana (in Cappadocia, modern Turkey) was a neo-Pythagorean sage and thaumaturge, born at the beginning of the Christian era, died *c.* A.D. 98; biographers of the third century compared his virtuous life to that of Christ. Artaud dedicated *Héliogabale ou l'Anarchiste couronné* to him. In a letter to Jean Paulhan on January 26, 1932 (*G* V, 70–71), Artaud says he is thinking of writing two essays, one on Apollonius of Tyana and one on Dante; neither of them was ever written, but part of the inspiration for *Héliogabale* came from the reading Artaud did for his proposed essay on Apollonius.

"The crown of Skandar . . ." Skandar or Iskandar is the Turkish form of the name Alexander (the Great). Both Caracalla and Severus Alexander sought legitimacy in the image of Alexander the Great. Artaud identified Alexander as the last of the great mythological heroes. For the legend of the crown, see Thévenin's note, *G,* VII, 418. Artaud was relying on *De l'Etat Social de l'Homme* (1822) by the French writer Antoine Fabre d'Olivet (1768–1825), a book which influenced many passages in *Héliogabale*.

"So that he can conquer the Marcomanni . . ." A West German (Suebic) tribe, first mentioned by Julius Caesar. The Marcomannic Wars (166–72 and 177–80) actually took place under Marcus Aurelius.

"Another historian, Dio Cassius . . ." Artaud is referring to Cassius Dio (*c.* 155–240), who wrote a *Roman History* (in Greek); he came from Nicaea, in North Africa. The section on Heliogabalus is to be found toward the end, in Books 79 and 80—in Vol. IX, pp. 408–79, of the edition published in the "Loeb Classical Library" series, the Greek text with an English translation by Earnest Cary (Harvard University Press, 1927). Dio was living in Rome during Heliogabalus' brief reign; and his *Roman History*, which begins with the founding of Rome, ends in 229, during the reign of Heliogabalus' successor, Severus Alexander.

"Thrown down the Gemoniae . . ." The Gemoniae were a flight of steps from the Aventine Hill to the Tiber, down which the dead bodies of criminals were thrown.

"Temple of the Palladium . . ." The Palladium was the ancient

Notes

sacred image of Pallas (Athena) said to have been sent from heaven by Zeus to Dardanus, the founder of Troy, and to have been rescued by Aeneas from the fires of Troy and brought by him to Italy. At the time of Heliogabalus it was housed in a round building—not a temple—east of the Forum, where the Vestal Virgins celebrated the worship of Vesta, the Roman hearth-goddess. The building had a sacred eternal fire.

"The Black Stone . . ." Elagabalus, the patron-god of Emesa, was worshipped in the form of a conical black stone, supposed to have fallen from heaven. Heliogabalus brought the sacred stone to Rome with him and built two temples for the god, one on the Palatine Hill—the so-called Eliogabalium—and the other outside the city, near the modern Porta Maggiore. His plan was to unify all cults (including, according to Lampridius, those of the Jews, Samaritans, and Christians) and to make Elagabalus the chief deity of Rome. Desiring to unite his god and Vesta (as the representative of the Roman state), he transferred to the Eliogabalium the fire of Vesta and the sacred objects kept in her temple, such as the Palladium. He further symbolized the union between the two deities by his own marriage with a Vestal Virgin. Because his combining of these two cults aroused the greatest indignation in Rome, Heliogabalus divorced the Vestal and chose a new consort for his god: the Carthaginian deity Caelestis, frequently identified with the Magna Mater, whose image he had brought to Rome and placed in the Eliogabalium.

"That bloodthirsty Palladium . . ." Athena's most conspicuous functions were those associated with war.

"Tanit-Astarte . . ." Tanit, the great goddess or Magna Mater of Carthage, was another name for Caelestis—whom Heliogabalus married to his god. Astarte (called Ishtar by the Babylonians) was the Greek name for Astoreth, the goddess of fertility and reproduction among the Canaanites and Phoenicians. There is no apparent basis for Artaud's conflating the two goddesses.

"The Pythian god . . ." Apollo—so named because Apollo's earliest adventure was the slaying of Python, a formidable dragon which guarded the precincts of Delphi.

"Apart from the assassination of Gannys . . ." Gannys was a foster-son of Julia Maesa (Heliogabalus' grandmother), the consort of Julia Soaemias (Heliogabalus' mother), and Heliogabalus' foster-father and guardian; he was supposed to have been a eunuch. According to Dio, it was Gannys who had caused the army to revolt against Macrinus, and who—accompanied by Julia Maesa and Julia Soaemias—commanded Heliogabalus' troops in the final battle against Macrinus. The same year, 218, Heliogabalus had Gannys executed. Heliogabalus, Dio says, "was forced by Gannys to live temperately and prudently. And he himself was the first to give Gannys a mortal blow with his own hand, since no one of the soldiers had the hardihood to take the lead in murdering him" (Dio, LXXX, 6).

"With Zoticus, he inaugurates . . ." Aurelius Zoticus, an athlete from Smyrna, was brought to Rome by order of Heliogabalus and became one of the emperor's lovers; he was known for his beauty and the size of his genitals. Zoticus' father had been a cook.

"The treachery of Hierocles . . ." Hierocles, originally a slave from Caria and a chariot-driver, was another one of Heliogabalus' lovers. Jealous of Zoticus, Hierocles had a drug administered to him which made him impotent. Heliogabalus banished Zoticus—first from Rome, then from Italy—which saved his life. Hierocles became Heliogabalus' favorite and was killed with Heliogabalus and his mother.

"Vitellius and Apicius . . ." Aulus Vitellius (A.D. 15–69), emperor in A.D. 69, was notorious for his gluttony. Apicius is the proverbial name of several Roman gourmets, to one of whom is wrongly ascribed the *De Re Coquinaria* (the so-called *Roman Cookery Book*), which was probably written in the fourth century. For descriptions of Heliogabalus' orgiastic and inventive relation to food, see Lampridius, XIX–XXXII.

XXIV. Letters and drafts from 1934–35

TO JEAN PAULHAN (JUNE 1, 1934): *G* VII, 184–85. This letter is written in response to the following letter from Paulhan:

[Paris, May 28, 1934]
Monday

My dear friend,

Heliogabalus charms and disturbs me: it is very compelling, very striking and well done, without ceasing to be natural. (Is it *true*, and were you concerned with its being true—I mean literally, rigorously true in the part that has to do with truth, or not? This is what I would most like to know.)

I am very much interested in what you tell me about St. Augustine. Of course, I'll try not to keep you waiting too long for the proofs.

Your friend,
Jean P.

Notes

Véra was the wife of René Daumal. Helba Huara was a Peruvian dancer.

"APPEL À LA JEUNESSE / INTOXICATION-DÉSINTOXICATION": *G* VIII, 25–27. Draft of an essay, or part of an essay, not published anywhere until 1971, when it was included in Volume VIII of the *Oeuvres complètes*. The editor dates it from the end of 1934.

TO ANDRÉ GIDE (FEBRUARY 10, 1935): *G* V, 240–43. In 1935 Artaud wrote the four-act play *Les Cenci*, based on works of Shelley and Stendhal. Shelley's five-act tragedy *The Cenci*, written in 1819, had been translated into French in 1887. In 1837 Stendhal had published his translation into French of the original documents in the Cenci family archives in Rome. The text for Artaud's play may be found in *G* IV, 183–271. *Les Cenci*, the only production of the Théâtre de Cruauté, was first performed on May 6, 1935, at the Théâtre des Folies-Wagram and ran until May 22. The music and sound effects were by Robert Désormière (it was the first time stereophonic sound was used in the theater); the sets and costumes were by Balthus. Artaud directed (his assistant was Roger Blin, who had two minor roles) and took the leading role of the father, Cenci. This was the last time that Artaud performed as an actor in the theater.

A dossier on *Les Cenci* was published in *The Drama Review*, No. 54, Vol. 16, No. 2 (June 1972), pp. 90–145. It contains translations of Artaud's production notes, the text of the play, letters by Artaud relating to the production, photographs, and the reviews. For the French text of the production notes see "Notes de mise en scène d'Antonin Artaud pour *Les Cenci*," in *Les Cahiers de la Compagnie Madeleine Renaud–Jean-Louis Barrault*, No. 51 (November 1965); the French text of Artaud's articles on the play are to be found in *G* V, 45–60, the reviews in *G* V, 302–12.

TO JEAN-LOUIS BARRAULT (JUNE 14, 1935): *G* V, 261–63. It was probably in 1932, when he was a student at Dullin's Atelier, that Barrault first met Artaud. Barrault had originally accepted the role of Bernardo in *Les Cenci* but had to back out—because he could not get free of his commitments to Dullin, according to one account; according to another, because of a quarrel with Iya Abdy, the actress who played Beatrice. The reviews were all bad, with one important exception: a review by the poet and novelist Pierre-Jean Jouve in the *N.R.F.*, No. 261 (June 1, 1935), reprinted in Virmaux's *Antonin*

Artaud et le Théâtre, pp. 305–9, and partially translated in *The Drama Review*, No. 54, Vol. 16, No. 2 (June 1972), p. 141. *Les Cenci* closed on May 22, and Artaud abandoned the idea of any further productions. (He had thought of doing *Macbeth* or his own *La Conquête du Mexique* next.)

After the failure of *Les Cenci*, Barrault proposed that he and Artaud work together. Artaud did agree to help Barrault stage his first work as a director, a mime drama adapted from Faulkner's novel *As I Lay Dying* called *Autour d'une Mère*, which was presented June 4–7, 1935; Génica Athanasiou had one of the major roles. Artaud also wrote a review in the *N.R.F.*, No. 262 (July 1, 1935), later included, as the second of "Deux notes," in *Le Théâtre et son Double*, hailing Barrault's production and the emergence of a new young director. See "Autour d'une mère": *G* IV, 168–71. (This is the article to which Artaud refers at the end of this letter.)

In this letter, Artaud explains his reasons for refusing to continue working with Barrault. Still, he ranked Barrault's work much higher than that of Jacques Copeau, Dullin, and Gaston Baty when he wrote on the French theater the following year during his stay in Mexico. *Cf.* "Le Théâtre français cherche un mythe," an article which appeared in *El Nacional Revolucionario* on June 28, 1936, in *G* VIII, 254–56 (retranslated there from Spanish).

"Au Congrès International des Ecrivains pour la Défense de la Culture" (late june 1935) : *G* VIII, 328–33. This is a draft of a letter that was never sent; it was not published until 1971, in Volume VIII of the *Oeuvres complètes*. The Congress, held in Paris, was organized by the French Communist Party; its closing session was on June 26, 1935.

Au Secrétaire général de l'Alliance Française (december 14, 1935) : *G* VIII, 349–52. This is a draft of a letter that Artaud wrote on the eve of his departure for Mexico, presumably to Monsieur Dalbis, director of the Alliance Française in 1935. Artaud was preparing his curriculum vitae for Dalbis, and on the top margin of the letter is written "Dalbis [con] Alliance Française." Artaud hoped to be invited to give a series of lectures at the Alliance Française in Mexico City. One was given, "Le Théâtre d'après-guerre à Paris," on March 18, 1936 (text in *G* VIII, 209–27).

Paracelsus (1493–1541) was the Swiss alchemist and physician who made great contributions to chemistry and medicine. He elaborated a mystical neo-Platonic theosophy.

Notes

"Spagyrical" comes from "spagyric," a word coined by Paracelsus, which means the science of alchemy.

Jerome Cardan (1501–66) was an Italian physicist, mathematician, mechanician, philosopher, and astrologer, who wrote extensively about mathematical, magical, scientific, and alchemistic subjects.

Robert Fludd (1574–1637) was the prolific English Hermetist-Cabalist philosopher, whose major works were written between 1617 and 1621. He was inspired by Agrippa, Paracelsus, neo-Platonism, Cabala, Hermeticism, Rosicrucian theories, and allegorical interpretations of the Scriptures; and engaged in famous controversies with Kepler, Mersenne, and Gassendi.

Popol Vuh, or Book of the Community, is the sacred book of the ancient Quiché Maya (a branch of the Maya, in the highlands of Guatemala), first written down in the middle of the sixteenth century from oral traditions then current among the Quiché. It is an epic account of the cosmology, mythology, and traditions of the Quiché, and gives the chronology of their kings down to 1550.

The *Rabinal-Achi* is a dance drama of the Rabinal tribe—a branch of the Maya, in the highlands of Guatemala—who were conquered and absorbed by the Quiché. It represents a war between the Quiché and the Rabinal. Like the *Popol Vuh*, the *Rabinal-Achi* is an authentic document from Mayan culture before the Spanish conquest; it was first transcribed in the Quiché language in 1850, in Rabinal (the town in Guatemala), where it had continued to be performed.

Ollantay, one of the most precious ancient Peruvian documents, is a three-act drama in octosyllabic verse, transmitted orally for generations by the Incas. The form we have, which dates from the late fifteenth century, was recorded in the early sixteenth century by a Spanish priest—in the original Inca language (Quechua) but in Latin characters. The play recounts the adventures and victories of Ollantay, a great Inca warrior. A French translation was published in 1878.

The *Zend-Avesta* is the collection of sacred writings (attributed to Zoroaster) of the Parsees, Persian Zoroastrians who fled to India in the seventh and eighth centuries to escape Mohammedan persecution.

For the *Zohar*, see the note to "Le Théâtre de la Cruauté (Premier Manifeste)" in Section XX.

The *Sefer Yetsirah*, or Book of Creation, is an enigmatic text written by a Jewish neo-Pythagorean around the third century A.D. The treatise describes, with astronomical, astrological, and anatomical details, how the cosmos was built; it may also have been intended as a manual of magical practices.

Notes

Raja Yoga (it means "King Yoga") is, according to one of the late *Upanishads* (the *Yogatattva*), one of the four kinds of Yoga—along with Mantra, Laya, and Hatha Yoga. It is a technique of mental, rather than bodily, discipline.

The production of *Les Cenci* was financed mainly by money from Artaud's editor, Robert Denoël; his wife, Cécile Bressant, played the role of Lucretia. Iya Abdy, who was Beatrice Cenci, also put money into the play.

After the failure of *Les Cenci* in May, Artaud decided to take a trip to Mexico. He moved again during the summer of 1935—from the Hôtel des Etats-Unis on the boulevard Montparnasse, which had apparently become too expensive for him, to the rue Victor Considérant, also in the 14th arrondissement.

During 1935 he had his last film roles: Savonarola in Gance's *Lucrèce Borgia* (Edwige Feuillère had the title role), and the librarian Cyrus Beck in Maurice Tourneur's *Koenigsmark*.

XXV. Excerpts from notebooks and private papers (1935)

"Cécile . . .": *G* VIII, 101. The reference is to Cécile Schramme, a young woman from an upper-middle-class Brussels family whom Artaud met in the autumn of 1935. When he returned from Mexico in late 1936 and saw her again, he proposed; their engagement was announced, then broken off shortly after. See note to Section XXVIII.

"Une sensibilité . . .": *G* VIII, 101–2.

"C'est la première fois . . .": *G* VIII, 103.

"Jamais une fois . . .": *G* VIII, 104.

All these notes may be dated from October–December 1935. Throughout this period Artaud was busy raising money for his trip to Mexico.

XXVI. The trip to Mexico (1936)

Artaud left for Mexico from Antwerp on the S.S. *Albertville* on January 9, 1936. He reached Havana on January 30 and, during his brief

Notes

stop there, submitted several articles to Cuban magazines. (Only one has been found so far: "L'Eternelle Trahison des Blancs," published for the first time in *G* VIII, 2nd printing [1973], 452–56.) In Havana a black sorcerer gave him a small sword which he came to regard as a talisman.

Artaud arrived on February 7 in Veracruz, virtually penniless. (He had boarded the ship with only three hundred francs, almost all borrowed from friends—mostly from Barrault and Paulhan.) From there he took a train to Mexico City. Although the aim of the trip was to visit the Tarahumara Indians (in the state of Chihuahua), he first had to spend several months in Mexico City, where he gave lectures and, from May to August and in October and November, wrote for magazines and the daily newspaper *El Nacional Revolucionario*. For a while he stayed with a doctor, Elías Nando, who procured medicines for him.

"L'HOMME CONTRE LE DESTIN": *G* VIII, 184–95. This was a lecture delivered at the University of Mexico on February 27, 1936, the second in a series of three. (The first lecture was "Surréalisme et révolution," given on February 26; the text is to be found in *G* VIII, 176–83. The third lecture was "Le Théâtre et les dieux," given on February 29; the text is to be found in *G* VIII, 196–206.) A Spanish translation of the lecture, "El hombre contra el destino," was published in four installments in *El Nacional*.

"The ancient books of the Magians . . ." The Magians were the ancient Persian priestly caste.

"An old science known to all antiquity . . ." Artaud is referring to astrology, and to its three forms of energy—cardinal, fixed, and mutable.

For the *Zohar*, see the note to "Le Théâtre de la Cruauté (Premier Manifeste)" in Section XX. For the *Sefer Yetsirah* and the *Popol Vuh*, see the note to the letter to the director of the Alliance Française (December 14, 1935) in Section XXIV.

The *Book of Chilam Balam of Chumayel* is the chronological story of the deeds of the ancient Yucatán Maya, as written down in Maya (but with Latin characters) by converted Indians whom the Spanish had taught to write.

TO JEAN PAULHAN (MARCH 26, 1936): *G* VIII, 359–60. On March 18 Artaud had given a lecture on "Le Théâtre d'après-guerre à Paris" at the Alliance Française in Mexico City; it was attended by the French Ambassador. It is likely that Artaud had read his essay "Le

Théâtre de Séraphin" (to be found here in Section XX) to the Conference on the Children's Theater. He refers to this conference at greater length in "Premier Contact avec la Révolution mexicaine" (text in this section), which is almost certainly the lecture he delivered at the Liga de Escritores.

"Premier Contact avec la Révolution mexicaine": *G* VIII, 235–41. This essay appeared in Spanish translation in *El Nacional* on June 3, 1936. It may have been first delivered as a lecture; see the note to the letter to Jean Paulhan (March 26, 1936) in this section. The original French text has been lost.

The essay "Un Athlétisme affectif" did not appear in *Revista de la Universidad*. It was first published in 1938, in *Le Théâtre et son Double*.

"Ce que je suis venu faire au Mexique": *G* VIII, 257–63. First published in Spanish translation in *El Nacional* on July 5, 1936. The original French text has been lost.

"The Cross of Palenque . . ." Palenque—near the modern town of that name (Santo Domingo de Palenque) in the southern Mexican state of Chiapas—was one of the great centers of Mayan culture, in the late classic period (A.D. 600–900). The Cross, actually a large bas-relief which shows (among other things) a child adoring a cross, was in a temple in Palenque; it is now in the National Museum of Anthropology in Mexico City. The cross was an important Mayan symbol.

to jean-louis barrault (july 10, 1936): *G* VIII, 366–67. According to Roger Blin, Barrault (who had recently earned some money from a film, *Drôle de Drame*) paid for Artaud's ticket to Mexico. The steamship company gave a 50 percent discount.

Bernard Palissy (*c.* 1510–89) was the greatest French ceramicist of his day—noted for a distinctive type of rustic pottery—who rediscovered the secret of the manufacture of Italian enamels through sixteen years of experiment. For his scientific use of the experimental method, he is considered one of the most original minds of the sixteenth century. His heroic struggle against misery, hunger, sickness, and slander is recounted in his *Discours Admirables: De l'art de terre* (1580). Artaud is referring to the passage where Palissy writes: ". . . il me survint un autre malheur, lequel me donna grande fascherie, qui est que, le bois m'ayant failli, je fus contraint . . . brusler les tables et plancher de la maison, afin de faire fondre le seconde composition."

Notes

By August, Artaud had finally obtained some money and was able to leave Mexico City. He reached the Tarahumara region on horseback, accompanied by a guide, and stayed until early October. Around October 15 he was in Mexico City, and began the return trip to France at the end of the month; he boarded the S.S. *Mexique* at Veracruz on October 31 and disembarked at Saint-Nazaire on November 12.

XXVII. From *A Voyage to the Land of the Tarahumara*

A text entitled "D'un Voyage au Pays des Tarahumaras" appeared in the *N.R.F.*, No. 287 (August 1, 1937). It consists of two parts: "La Montagne des Signes" and "La Danse du Peyotl," both of which are translated here in their entirety.

"LA MONTAGNE DES SIGNES": *G* IX, 43–48. Artaud wrote this text while still in Mexico, and published it in a first version, translated into Spanish, in *El Nacional* on October 16, 1936.

"LA DANSE DU PEYOTL": *G* IX, 49–62. Written shortly after Artaud's return to France, at the end of 1936 or at the beginning of 1937.

"The Magi of Hieronymus Bosch . . ." Artaud is describing a Bosch painting called *The Epiphany* (or *The Adoration of the Magi*), now in the Philadelphia Museum of Art. The description is not accurate.

After Artaud had given the manuscript to Jean Paulhan, the editor of the *N.R.F.*, he wrote Paulhan on May 27 or 28, 1937, requesting that it be published anonymously. "Mon nom doit disparaître," he wrote in his letter. "D'un Voyage au Pays des Tarahumaras" was therefore published with three asterisks in place of the author's name when it appeared in the *N.R.F.* Another account of his trip, "La Race des hommes perdus," was published in the magazine *Voilà*, No. 354 (December 31, 1937), under the pseudonym John Forester. (The editor of *Voilà* was Florent Fels.)

In book form, the text has a complicated publishing history. In October 1943, the publisher Robert-J. Godet contacted Artaud—by then interned in the asylum in Rodez—about the possibility of bringing out the material written in 1936–37 as a small book. Artaud gave his consent and between November 20 and December 10, 1943, wrote another text: "Supplément au Voyage au Pays des Tarahumaras."

(Artaud's final version, written in January 1944, is a good example of his Rodez style, with its heavy use of capital letters.) The project dragged on, however, and was eventually taken over by the editor who was the original intermediary between Artaud and Godet, Henri Parisot. (Parisot probably met Artaud through Breton, whom he had known since the early 1930's.) See Artaud's letter of December 10, 1943, to Parisot in *G* IX, 134–37.

The book entitled *D'un Voyage au Pays des Tarahumaras* was finally published in November 1945 in Parisot's series "L'Age d'Or" (Editions Fontaine), in an edition of 725 copies. But it was no longer the same book that Godet had planned to publish. On September 7, a week before the manuscript went to the printer, Artaud wrote Parisot that he wished to withdraw the "Supplément" written in January 1944 at Rodez, dismissing the conversion to Christ expressed in that text as a bewitchment induced by shock therapy. He asked that this letter be substituted for the "Supplément." The book published in 1945 under the title *D'un Voyage au Pays des Tarahumaras* thus contained three texts: "La Montagne des Signes," "La Danse du Peyotl," and "Lettre à Henri Parisot." The first two texts are translated here; the Parisot letter is translated as part of Section XXXI.

In June 1947, Artaud agreed to a new edition of *D'un Voyage au Pays des Tarahumaras* by another publisher, Marc Barbezat, to which he added several new texts written between 1945 and 1947, as well as "Le Rite du Peyotl chez les Tarahumaras," written at Rodez in 1943. The latter was first published in Barbezat's magazine *L'Arbalète*, No. 12 (Spring 1947). But the book was not published as planned. It did not appear until November 1955, and under the title *Les Tarahumaras* (Editions de l'Arbalète). This final edition of this material in book form includes the "Supplément" written in January 1944 and a poem, "Tutuguri" (dated February 16, 1948).

The complete Tarahumara cycle, consisting of material written by Artaud over a period of twelve years (1936–48), is to be found in *G* IX, 9–137, under the title *Les Tarahumaras*. It includes all the texts mentioned above, plus three other texts about the Tarahumara which appeared as articles in *El Nacional* in October and November 1936 ("Le Pays des Rois-Mages," "Une Race-Principe," and "Le Rite des Rois de l'Atlantide") and six letters, five of them written to Paulhan in early 1937 and one to Parisot in late 1943.

XXVIII. Letters from 1937

TO CÉCILE SCHRAMME (FEBRUARY 7, 1937): *G* VII, 197–98. See note to Section XXV.

TO CÉCILE SCHRAMME (FEBRUARY 19, 1937): *G* VII, 199.

TO CÉCILE SCHRAMME (APRIL 16, 1937): *G* VII, 208–12. Artaud wrote from a clinic in Sceaux, which he had entered on April 14 to be treated for opium addiction. (He left on April 29.) It was his second attempt at disintoxication since his return from Mexico; between February 25 and March 4 he had been in a clinic in Paris (Jean Paulhan paid the bills). These were only the most recent of numerous cures which Artaud underwent during the 1930's.

TO CÉCILE SCHRAMME (APRIL 30, 1937): *G* VII, 217–18. In May Artaud went to Brussels, where he was supposed to give a lecture announced for May 18 under the title "Paris sous l'oeil des Aztèques—Antonin Artaud à Bruxelles." (Another title given was "La Décomposition de Paris.") He stayed with the Schramme family. For the account of Artaud's convulsive public appearance the night of the lecture, see *G* VII, 439. His prospective father-in-law was horrified by the scandal, the engagement was broken off, and Artaud returned to Paris on May 20.

TO RENÉ ALLENDY (JUNE 1937): *G* VII, 224–25.

TO ANDRÉ BRETON (JULY 30, 1937): *G* VII, 240–43. The "pamphlet" is *Les Nouvelles Révélations de l'Être*.

"The events of the war in China . . ." The Sino-Japanese War had broken out on July 7, 1937.

The reconciliation between Artaud and Breton took place in November–December 1936, just after Artaud's return from Mexico. See the interview Breton gave about Artaud in *La Tour de Feu*, Nos. 63–64 (December 1959), pp. 5–7. Breton, born the same year as Artaud (1896), died in 1966.

TO ANNE MANSON (SEPTEMBER 8, 1937): *G* VII, 274–77. Anne Manson was a young journalist Artaud met in 1937 when mutual friends suggested she consult him for names and addresses of people to look up during her trip to Mexico.

Notes

TO ANDRÉ BRETON (SEPTEMBER 14, 1937): *G* VII, 286–93. Artaud wrote from Ireland, where he had gone on August 14. The letter is postmarked Paris. He had sent it to Anne Manson in Paris, asking her to mail it to Breton, because he didn't want anyone to know where he was. But Artaud had already sent Breton a number of letters directly from Ireland since his arrival a month earlier.

"The En-Sof mentioned in the Cabala . . ." The *Zohar* distinguishes between two worlds, which both represent God. The first, the En-Sof, is a primary world, the most deeply hidden of all, which remains insensible and unintelligible to all but God.

According to the testimony of many friends, Anaïs Nin among them, Artaud was in an extremely agitated state before his departure for Ireland. Information about his stay there is scant. All that is known with certainty is that he disembarked at Cobh on August 14, he was in Galway on August 17, in Kilronan in the Aran Islands on August 23 (from where he wrote to Anne Manson and to Breton), and again in Galway, at the Imperial Hotel, on September 5. On September 8 he went to Dublin; his last letter from Dublin, dated September 21, is to Jacqueline Breton. On September 23 he sought refuge in a Jesuit college; the director refused to receive him. Artaud made a great deal of noise and became violent (brandishing the cane, with thirteen knots, mentioned often in his letters, that he now carried and to which he attributed magical properties) and the police were called. Artaud was jailed and then, either despite or because of the intervention on his behalf by the French counsul in Dublin, he was expelled from Ireland. He was put on the ferry *Washington* at Cobh on September 29. When the boat reached France the following day, he was confined in a hospital in Le Havre.

XXIX. From *The New Revelations of Being* (1937)

Les Nouvelles Révélations de l'Etre: G VII, 149–51. These pages could be regarded as the prologue to this little book, published on July 28, 1937, by Editions Denoël without the author's name. It was signed "Le Révélé." The main part of the text, not translated here, is based on notions adapted from astrology, the Cabala, and tarot. Artaud had been reading intensively in the Cabala, as well as in the *Egyptian Book of the Dead*, throughout 1935. More recently, he had been learning to read the tarot deck under the guidance of his friend Manuel

Notes

Cano de Casto, whose drawings and commentaries accompany Artaud's text in the 1937 edition. Artaud's text is to be found in *G* VII, 145–74. It is the last work Artaud wrote for publication before his breakdown.

Artaud mentions several times in *Les Nouvelles Révélations de l'Etre* the "cane of St. Patrick" to which he attached such importance and whose possession probably inspired his decision to go to Ireland.

He left for Ireland two weeks after the book appeared. After traveling about Ireland for almost a month, he came to Dublin—where he was arrested and eventually ordered out of the country. (See last part of the notes to Section XXVIII.) Artaud was put on a boat bound for France on September 29, reportedly became violent during the voyage, and was placed in irons by the captain. When the boat docked at Le Havre on the following day, he was taken to a public hospital. This was the beginning of nine years of continuous confinement in various mental institutions.

After seven days in Le Havre, Artaud was transferred to the Quatre-Mares Hospital in Sotteville-lès-Rouen. It was not until December, when he had been in Rouen for more than a month, that his whereabouts were discovered—by his mother, who had been searching for him since his disappearance. Artaud was in a state of complete collapse and did not recognize her. Madame Artaud tried to have him released or at least moved to a hospital in Paris, where she and his friends could visit him. On April 12, 1938, he was transferred to the public asylum of Sainte-Anne in Paris; Roger Blin and Robert Desnos went to see him. Meanwhile, in February of that year, *Le Théâtre et son Double* was finally published by Gallimard, in an edition of 400 copies.

XXX. Letters from 1940 (Ville-Evrard)

After approximately ten months in Sainte-Anne, Artaud was pronounced incurable and transferred to the asylum of Ville-Evrard (in Seine-et-Marne), near Paris, from which these letters were written. This was the fourth institution Artaud had been locked up in since his return from Ireland. He entered Ville Evrard on February 27, 1939, and was put in the drug-addict ward. His head was shaved, and he had to wear hospital clothing. He was there for four years.

Notes

TO GÉNICA ATHANASIOU (NOVEMBER 10, 1940): *LGA*, 307–8. Artaud addresses her as "vous," as he had done since early 1928.

TO GÉNICA ATHANASIOU (NOVEMBER 24, 1940) · *LGA*, 309–10.

During these years Artaud became terribly thin and his physical health deteriorated alarmingly. Finally, through the efforts of his mother, Desnos, and Eluard, he was moved from Ville-Evrard to a much more humanely run hospital, where patients got something better than the starvation rations allotted to asylum inmates by the government of the German Occupation. This was the psychiatric hospital in Rodez (in Aveyron, 610 kilometers south of Paris), in the unoccupied zone. Artaud left Ville-Evrard on January 22, 1943, and was admitted to Rodez on February 11.

XXXI. Letters from 1943–45 (Rodez)

TO JACQUES LATRÉMOLIÈRE (MARCH 25, 1943): *G* X, 18–20. Dr. Latrémolière was one of the psychiatrists at the hospital at Rodez, where Artaud spent three years. It was he who administered the electric-shock treatments to Artaud. This letter and seven others from Artaud to Latrémolière written between February 15 and July 31, 1943, and on January 6, 1945, were first published in the second Artaud issue of the magazine *La Tour de Feu*—No. 69 (April 1961)— in the body of an article by Latrémolière called "J'ai parlé de dieu avec Antonin Artaud." This article, with a new preface by Latrémolière, is reprinted in *La Tour de Feu*, No. 112 (December 1971), pp. 75–106.

Artaud signs the letter Antonin Nalpas: Nalpas is his mother's name.

TO GASTON FERDIÈRE (MARCH 29, 1943): *G* X, 24–31. Dr. Ferdière, a friend of Desnos and other writers, was the director of the hospital at Rodez. Artaud had first met him in 1934 or 1935 at Desnos' apartment in Paris. A cultivated man and a poet, Ferdière took a special interest in Artaud. But his therapeutic methods—Artaud was subjected to electric shock more than sixty times while at Rodez—continue to shock. This letter was first printed in *La Tour de Feu*, Nos. 63–64 (December 1959), a special issue devoted to Artaud, with considerable material about his stay at Rodez; besides three letters from

Notes

Artaud to Ferdière (of which this is one), it contains an article by Ferdière entitled "J'ai soigné Antonin Artaud" (pp. 28–37). *Cf.* also the interview with Ferdière in *Planète + Plus* (special issue on Artaud), No. 7 (February 1971), pp. 103–9.

Ronsard's *L'Hymne des Daimons* is a poem of 428 lines in rhymed couplets. It appeared in 1555, in the first edition of *Les Hymnes* of Ronsard, which also contains hymns to Henri II, Justice, Philosophy, Heaven, Stars, Death, and Gold. *L'Hymne des Daimons* is an "esoteric" poem, in which Ronsard describes the hierarchy of spirits (demons in the larger sense), their manners, habits, and powers. Ronsard drew on the eleventh-century treatise on demons by the Byzantine Michael Psellus and on neo-Platonic works by Marsilio Ficino, Agrippa, and Paracelsus.

"That Ronsard toward the end of his life fell into Averroism . . ." It was not at the end of his life but in 1569 that Ronsard expressed pantheistic ideas, derived from the works of Jerome Cardan, that could loosely be called Averroistic. Ronsard (*b*. 1524) died in 1585.

The second line of glossolalia at the beginning of the letter, "Krah Bahl Kaherferti Krakban," was crossed out by Artaud.

Iamblichus (*c*. 250–325), the neo-Platonist philosopher, was a student of Porphyry. His extant writings include a life of Pythagoras and a defense of ritualistic magic known as *De Mysteriis*. Julian the Apostate was a student of Iamblichus.

"The 'Samsara' of the Hindu Tradition . . ." Samsara, a Sanskrit term which refers to the phenomenal universe, is the antithesis of Nirvana (which means Reality, Liberation, Buddhahood).

Ramón Lull (1232/35–1313) was a Spanish philosopher who taught at the Sorbonne and, according to legend, was also an alchemist and magician. He wrote on logic, philosophy, pedagogy, history, science, and poetry in his native Catalan, in Arabic, and in Latin; over 290 works are attributed to him. The book Artaud refers to as *Livre de l'ami et l'aimé* was written in Catalan (original title: *Libre d'amic e amat*) and was translated into French during Lull's lifetime; it was first printed in 1586. Influenced by Sufi mysticism, the work is a dialogue between God (*l'aimé*) and a person who loves God (*l'ami*); it is divided into 365 moral metaphors, one for each day of the year, according to Lull, "each one sufficient to contemplate God for an entire day."

TO GASTON FERDIÈRE (OCTOBER 18, 1943) : *G* X, 134–40. Eli Lotar was the photographer whose nine photo-collages illustrated the brochure

Notes

Artaud published in 1930 called "Le Théâtre Alfred Jarry et l'Hostilité publique." The photographs are of *tableaux vivants* devised by Artaud, not of real theater productions. Only three persons (Artaud, Roger Vitrac, and Josette Lusson) posed for the photographs, but Lotar, using the device of superimposition favored by "Surrealist" photographers, has a single person figuring, in different poses, as many as nine times in the same photograph. The text of Artaud's brochure is in *G* II, 49–86; eight of Lotar's nine photographs are to be found following page 64.

The photograph with cabbage leaves and cane, described in the first paragraph (and discussed again toward the end of the letter), is not one of those he composed with Lotar, but a photograph he did in 1943 for Dr. Ferdière.

For the *Zohar*, see the note to "Le Théâtre de la Cruauté (Premier Manifeste)" in Section XX; for the *Sefer Yetsirah*, see the note to the letter to the Director of the Alliance Française in Section XXVI.

"Jesus Christ did not say . . ." "Increase and multiply," God's injunction to Adam and Eve (Gen. 1:28) and to Noah and his sons (Gen. 9:1,7), was interpreted by the Church Fathers (on the basis of II Cor. 9:10) to mean that one ought to increase one's good works and multiply the number of the faithful in the Church.

"Roudoudou" is a French nursery rhyme.

> Roudoudou n'a pas de femme,
> Il en fait une avec sa canne,
> Il l'habille en feuilles de chou,
> Voici la femme à Roudoudou.

The verses Artaud quotes in the letter are another nursery rhyme.

"While composing this photograph . . ." For more on the photograph inspired by "Roudoudou" that Artaud had just finished when he wrote this letter, and for a reproduction of it, see Ferdière's article "La Femme à Roudoudou—Un photomontage d'Antonin Artaud," *Le Figaro Littéraire*, September 2, 1961, p. 4.

Méridien, a journal published at Rodez from May–June 1942 to January–February 1944, had planned to do a special issue on humor under the editorship of Dr. Ferdière; Ferdière was to have written an article on "Roudoudou" and Artaud was to have done translations of Lewis Carroll (see note to the letter to Henri Parisot, September 20, 1945, in this section). This issue never appeared.

Dr. Ferdière planned to edit and publish from Rodez—under the imprint "Editions du Méridien"—a series of texts with the general title "Humor." No. I in the projected series was *La Place de l'Etoile*,

Notes

Antipoème by Robert Desnos, which was published in November 1945. (Desnos had been arrested by the Nazis in February 1944, sent to Buchenwald in April, and died of typhus at another camp in June 1945, shortly after the camp's liberation.) At the beginning of Desnos's book was a list of forthcoming titles in Ferdière's series: No. II was *Le Surréalisme et la fin de l'ère chrétienne (Essai)*" by Artaud and No. III was *L'Humour dans les comptines et les formulettes enfantines* (Étude)" by Ferdière. The title of Artaud's text recalls the title of the special issue of *La Révolution Surréaliste*, No. 3 (April 15, 1925), called "1925: Fin de l'ère chrétienne," which Artaud had edited and for which he had written most of the contents. (See the notes to Section X.) Though Ferdière's series never went beyond Desnos' book, what appears to be a surviving fragment of Artaud's text was published in the magazine *84*, No. 16 (December 1950), pp. 11–20, under the title "Je n'ai jamais rien étudié . . ."

"And in the article that you are going to write on this song . . ." Artaud is referring to what he calls "the song of Roudoudou," which Ferdière was going to discuss in his article for *Méridien* as well as in his projected study of nursery rhymes.

It was soon after getting this letter that Ferdière retrieved from his celebrated patient a copy of *Les Nouvelles Révélations de l'Etre* that Artaud had dedicated to Hitler. The dedication reads:

> To Adolf HITLER
> in memory of the *Romanisches café* in Berlin one afternoon in May 1932
> and because I pray to GOD
> to give you the grace to remember again all the marvels with which HE that day GRATIFIED (RESUSCITATED)
> YOUR HEART
> kudar dayro Tarish Ankhara
> Thabi
>
> Antonin Artaud
>
> December 3, 1943

In this copy, in black ink, Artaud also added several passages and made a few changes in the text. For the French original of the dedication, as well as the alterations made in this copy, see *G* VII, 430–33.

Notes

TO GHYSLAINE MALAUSSÉNA (JANUARY 9, 1944): *G* X, 178–80. The letter is written to Artaud's niece, the daughter of his sister Marie-Ange Malausséna. At Ville-Evrard, Artaud had been visited by his mother, and his sister with her two children, Serge and Ghyslaine. It is not clear whether they were able to visit him after he was moved to Rodez. From a letter to Henri Parisot dated December 4, 1945 (to be found in *G* IX, 236–37), we know that Raymond Queneau wanted to come see Artaud in Rodez around Christmas 1943 and bring him food.

TO GASTON FERDIÈRE (FEBRUARY 5, 1944): *G* X, 196–97. Frédéric Delanglade was a minor Surrealist painter who lived in the town of Rodez during the war and befriended Artaud. In late 1943, when Artaud had first been approached with the plan to publish *D'un Voyage au Pays des Tarahumaras*, he had wanted Delanglade to do the illustrations. In a letter to Anie Besnard written on January 31, 1945 (*G* XI, 39–40), Artaud says that Delanglade has done a portrait of him.

TO EUPHRASIE ARTAUD (JUNE 22, 1944): *G* X, 240–41. The letter is to Artaud's mother; Marie-Ange and Fernand are Artaud's younger sister and brother.

TO JACQUES LATRÉMOLIÈRE (JANUARY 6, 1945): *G* XI, 11–15. Artaud had freely translated Poe's "Israfel" in May 1944; it may be found in *G* IX, 151–53. "Israfel" is one of many poems by Poe that Artaud worked on while at Rodez, but in late 1946 or early 1947 he burned most of his Poe adaptations in the fireplace of his room in Ivry—dissatisfied with their "tonality" (according to Paule Thévenin). Besides his "Israfel," only fragments of Artaud's version of "Annabel Lee" survive; these may be found in *G* IX, 271–73.

TO MARIE-ANGE MALAUSSÉNA (JANUARY 30, 1945): *G* XI, 31–33. The recipient was Artaud's sister. The first edition of *Le Théâtre et son Double* was 400, not 300, copies. When it was republished in May 1944, 1525—not 1725—copies were printed.

TO HENRI PARISOT (SEPTEMBER 7, 1945): *G* IX, 63–65. Artaud's correspondence with Parisot, who was a friend of Breton and Eluard, begins with a letter from Rodez dated December 10, 1943 (*G* IX, 134–37). As Artaud requested, this letter of September 7, 1945, was included in *D'un Voyage au Pays des Tarahumaras*—the collection of Artaud's writings about the trip he made to Mexico in 1936. (For the complicated history of this book, see the notes to Section XXVII.) Parisot received the letter just as the book was about to go to the printer. The account Artaud gives here of how he came to be arrested in Dublin is probably not true. In any case, it was in September, not in December, 1937, that Artaud was arrested and deported.

TO HENRI PARISOT (SEPTEMBER 17, 1945): *G* IX, 179–83. "My five first-born daughters . . ." Neneka Chilé is the maiden name of Artaud's maternal grandmother. Catherine Chilé, her sister, was Artaud's paternal grandmother. (Artaud's mother and father were first cousins.) Cécile Schramme was the young Belgian woman to whom Artaud was engaged in early 1937, after his return from Mexico. (See the notes to Sections XXV and XXVIII.) Anie Besnard was a young woman whom Artaud befriended in the late 1920's and who remained devoted to him. Yvonne Nel-Dumouchel was the maiden name of Yvonne Allendy; she had died in 1934.

"Plus several others beginning with . . ." Sonia Mossé, who had been killed in a concentration camp, was a friend of Cécile Schramme. Yvonne Gamelin has not been identified. Josette Lusson was the actress who had posed for the photomontages that Artaud devised with the photographer Eli Lotar in 1930 (see the note to the October 18, 1943, letter to Ferdière in this section); her photograph was on the cover of Artaud's translation of *Le Moine* (see photographs at the beginning of *G* VI), published in 1931. Colette Prou was an actress and friend of Artaud. The anecdote is fictitious: she was not murdered.

TO HENRI PARISOT (SEPTEMBER 20, 1945): *G* IX, 225–27. This is a first (and very different) version of the letter which follows, dated September 22. It was Dr. Ferdière who suggested to Artaud that he translate Lewis Carroll. On August 28, 1945, Parisot had written asking if he could publish Artaud's translation of the "Jabberwocky" poem in his magazine *Les Quatre Vents*. Parisot had asked for it again in a letter of September 15, 1945.

"Dites-moi où . . ." Artaud's first quotation is from the first Ballade (called "Ballade des dames du temps jadis") in Villon's *Le Testament*. The ballad is in three eight-line stanzas, with a four-line envoi. Artaud quotes the first two lines of the first stanza and mistakenly (perhaps because of the rhyme) follows them with the first

Notes

two lines of the third stanza. All four lines are partly modernized and incorrectly remembered.

"Advis m'est que . . ." The second quotation is the first two lines of Villon's fourth Ballade (usually known as "Les Regrets de la belle Hëaulmière"); Artaud has modernized the spelling and made some errors. There are eighteen Ballades in *Le Testament*.

"Une Charogne," "Une Martyre: dessin d'un maître inconnu," and "Un Voyage à Cythère" are three poems from Baudelaire's *Les Fleurs du Mal*.

TO HENRI PARISOT (SEPTEMBER 22, 1945): *G* IX, 184–89. As Artaud explains, he had not translated the "Jabberwocky" poem but, rather, had translated Chapter VI of *Through the Looking Glass*, which contains the first verse of "Jabberwocky." It is this "fragment" which is discussed in this letter. It was published under the title "L'Arve et l'Aume: Tentative anti-grammaticale contre Lewis Carroll" in Marc Barbezat's magazine *L'Arbalète*, No. 12 (Spring 1947), and may be found in *G* IX, 156–73. (*Cf.* also the "Post-Scriptum"—*G* IX, 174—which Artaud wrote on March 23, 1947.)

Artaud's other Carroll translation, "Le Chevalier Mate-Tapis" (an adaption of Carroll's "Ye Carpette Knyghte"), was published in *Les Cahiers du Sud*, No. 287 (premier semestre, 1948), and is dedicated to Ferdière. It may be found in *G* IX, 154–55. In a letter to Barbezat dated March 10, 1947, Artaud states: "J'ajoute que j'ai toujours *détesté* Lewis Carroll."

"One of my daughters, Catherine Chilé . . ." The maiden name of Artaud's paternal grandmother.

Of course, Artaud never wrote a book called *Letura d'Eprahi Falli*, etc. (For a description of this "book," see Artaud's letter to Peter Watson, July 27, 1946, in *G* XII, 230–39.) But the sample of the language of that imaginary book which Artaud gives at the end of this letter is partly decipherable and many words reflect his preoccupations. Eric Sellin has pointed out pesti (*peste,* plague), koma (coma), kurbura (*courbature,* ache), and kana (cane). Many words are variations on (or imitations of) Greek and, more often, Latin words—or use Greek and Latin word endings.

TO HENRI PARISOT (OCTOBER 6, 1945): *G* IX, 190–6. "Kah the corporeal breath of shit . . ." The allusions to excrement ("Kah-Kah") and the Egyptian Ka may not be the only pertinent ones. Artaud was acquainted with Charles Fossey's *La Magie Assyrienne: Etude suivi de textes magiques* (Paris, 1902), and Naomi Greene argues that this book, which translates numerous ancient Assyrian incantations into French, may be Artaud's source for many of the incantatory words that appear in his late writings. Some of these magic syllables, used in ancient Assyrian rituals designed to cure sickness, denote parts of the body: ka (mouth), eme (tongue), ma (womb).

For several months before his departure for Ireland in August 1937, Artaud was being lodged in the building at 21, rue Daguerre, in the 14th arrondissement where René Thomas (a press agent and illustrator), Anie Besnard, and several painters and actors had studios.

For the sources of "the prophecy of St. Patrick" and the cane, see Thévenin's notes in *G* IX, 280–82.

TO HENRI PARISOT (OCTOBER 9, 1945): *G* IX, 197–206. There is no evidence that Artaud ever began the two books he says he is "working on." The French word translated as crane (*grue*), in the ninth line of the letter, means whore as well as the bird and the machine.

TO HENRI PARISOT (NOVEMBER 27, 1945): *G* IX, 207–12. The five letters Artaud wrote Parisot between September 17 and November 27, 1945, were published in book form as *Les Lettres de Rodez* by Guy Lévis Mano (GLM) in February 1946, in an edition of 666 copies, plus twenty-five copies reserved for Les Amis de GLM. A further letter to Henri Parisot, dated December 6, 1945, was intended for publication in *Suppôts et Suppliciations*. (See the notes to Section XXXVI.)

René de Solier was a poet and art critic. Artaud read his book of poems, *La Larderie*, which appeared in 1945. In June 1945 Solier had asked Artaud to collaborate with him on a magazine to be called *Le Fesse-Nombril.*

Artaud started writing again in 1943—translations of Lewis Carroll and Poe, and a new text for the "Tarahumara cycle" called "Le Rite du Peyotl chez les Tarahumaras," which he wrote between November 20 and December 10. There was, of course, a stream of letters: to Dr. Ferdière, Dr. Latrémoliere, and another doctor at Rodez, Jean Dequeker, and to Georges Bataille (the letter has been lost), Paulhan, Barrault, Gide, Michel Leiris, Robert Desnos, Roger Blin, Alain Cuny, Henri Parisot, Anne Manson, Gaston Gallimard, and many others. He also drew and painted. In one of the Rodez drawings Artaud depicts himself as the King of the Incas.

Dr. Ferdière, as Dr. Toulouse had once done, encouraged Artaud to translate. In April 1944 Artaud did a translation of "The Burning Babe" by Robert Southwell, which he titled "Le Bébé de feu." Artaud's translation—it is to be found in *G* IX, 149–50—is reasonably exact, though his verse form is very free as compared with Southwell's rhymed couplets. Artaud prefaces his translation with the following lines about Southwell:

> Poète anglais mort vierge
> coupé en tranches en 1595
> sur l'ordre de Henri VIII

Presumably Artaud says Southwell died a virgin because the poet was a member of the Society of Jesus. Southwell, who was born around 1561, was arrested in 1592 for refusing to renounce the Catholic faith, and remained in prison until his death three years later; he was "examined," that is, tortured, thirteen times, and finally hanged (not cut in pieces). Elizabeth I, not Henry VIII, was monarch in 1595. Artaud's translation was dedicated to Adrienne André, a young ward supervisor at the asylum to whom Artaud had become attached. Dr. Ferdière sent the translation to the editor Pierre Seghers, who published it in his magazine *Poésie 44*, No. 20 (July–October 1944).

Starting in early 1944, Artaud was able to leave the asylum and walk around Rodez, and he made the acquaintance of several writers who lived in the area; he usually ate with Dr. and Madame Ferdière or Dr. and Madame Dequeker. After the Liberation in 1944, he was visited by the painter Jean Dubuffet and the novelist-poet Henri Thomas. On May 10, 1944, *Le Théâtre et son Double* was reissued by Editions de la Nouvelle Revue Française in an edition of 1525 copies.

XXXII. Two letters from 1946

"LETTRE SUR LAUTRÉAMONT" (1946). This text was written sometime in 1946 (probably before his release from Rodez in March) for the Lautréamont issue of *Les Cahiers du Sud*, No. 275 (August 1946). (It is on pp. 6–10.) This issue was entitled "Lautréamont n'a pas Cent Ans," and also included articles by Bachelard, Ponge, and Reverdy. The addressee of the "Lettre" was probably the playwright Arthur Adamov, who had already published extracts from letters he received from Artaud in 1945 in the magazine he edited, *L'Heure Nouvelle*, No. 2. Artaud meant to include it in the book he was working on at the time of his death, called *Suppôts et Suppliciations*—which has

Notes

never been published. The "Lettre" was reprinted in the magazine *Change*, No. 7 (1970), pp. 50–54. It should be noted that the present translation, done from the text in *Change*, undoubtedly perpetuates certain errors in the French original, which cannot be corrected until the definitive form of the text becomes available with the publication of *Suppôts et Suppliciations* in the Gallimard *Oeuvres complètes*. (See the notes to Section XXXVI.)

In the fourth paragraph, Artaud is paraphrasing the beginning of a letter sent by Ducasse to a Monsieur Verboeckhoven on February 21, 1870. By the *Supplément aux poèmes de Baudelaire*, Artaud must mean the *Complément aux Fleurs du Mal de Charles Baudelaire* (first edition, 1869) published in Brussels by Edition Michel Lévy. It contains the poems that Baudelaire was forced to drop from *Les Fleurs du Mal*.

"That old monkey of Ramayana . . ." The 96,000-line Indian epic, the *Ramayana* (literally, the goings of Rama), is divided into seven parts. (The oldest sections of the poem date from before 350 B.C.; it took its final form around A.D. 250.) Parts four and five recount the role played by the Vanara (monkey) people in helping the hero, Rama, in his great adventure. It is not clear which incident Artaud has in mind.

"'And beyond the red light,' says poor Isidore Ducasse . . ." Artaud is alluding to a passage in the Chant Troisième of *Les Chants de Maldoror*, which begins: "Une lanterne rouge, drapeau de vice . . ."

"Not highborn kinsmen . . ." Artaud is quoting a phrase from the third stanza of Poe's "Annabel Lee." (His nine attempts at translating this phrase can be found in *G* IX, 271–72.) For Artaud's translations of Poe see the note in this section to the January 6, 1945, letter to Latrémolière.

On February 26–27, 1946, Adamov and the critic Marthe Robert came to Rodez to discuss with Dr. Ferdière the possibility of releasing Artaud. Ferdière agreed, on two conditions. Artaud's financial security must be assured; and a private clinic must be found in or near Paris where he would live and be cared for.

A committee of Artaud's friends was formed in Paris, headed by Jean Paulhan and consisting of Adamov, Balthus, Barrault, Gide, Picasso, Pierre Loeb, Henri Thomas, and Dubuffet (acting as treasurer), to organize an auction of works of art and manuscripts to guarantee Artaud an income for life. Marthe Robert and Adamov

Notes

asked Paule Thévenin, who was to be Artaud's literary executor and the editor of the *Oeuvres complètes* but who at this time did not know him, to find a private clinic where Artaud could live. She chose the *maison de santé* in Ivry-sur-Seine, a suburb southeast of Paris, run by Dr. Achille Delmas. (James Joyce's daughter Lucia had been at Ivry, under Delmas' care, between April 1936 and September 1939.)

Dr. Ferdière's two conditions having been met, Artaud was released on March 19, 1946—to live first in Espalion, some thirty kilometers from Rodez, for a short trial period. He left for Paris on May 25, accompanied by Ferdière. Some friends met them at the station when they arrived the following morning. After a brief celebration, Artaud was taken to the clinic in Ivry-sur-Seine, where he was to live "voluntarily." Dr. Delmas greeted Artaud cordially and gave him the keys to the clinic's front gate as a mark of Artaud's special status in the institution.

As part of the effort undertaken by Artaud's friends to raise money for him, a "séance consacrée à l'oeuvre d'Antonin Artaud" was held in Paris on June 7 at the Théâtre Sarah-Bernhardt. The evening started with a homage to Artaud delivered by Breton, just returned from his wartime exile in the United States; this was followed by readings of Artaud's work by, among others, Adamov, Barrault (*Les Cenci*), Roger Blin (*Les Nouvelles Révélations de l'Etre*), Maria Casarès, Alain Cuny, Dullin, Jouvet, Madeleine Renaud, and Jean Vilar (*Les Pèse-Nerfs*). On June 13, at 3 p.m., an auction of manuscripts and works of art to raise money for Artaud was held at the Galerie Pierre. Among the distinguished donors were Paulhan (chairman of the organizing committee), Dubuffet, Braque, Picasso, Giacometti, Sartre, and Simone de Beauvoir. (For a fuller list of the donors, see the Brau biography, pp. 223–24.) The proceeds of the "evening" and of the auction amounted to a fairly large sum of money; but Artaud lived only until March 1948. The amount left at his death—some 300,000 francs—was the subject of a violent quarrel between Artaud's family and the members of the "Société des amis d'Artaud."

LETTER TO HENRI PARISOT (NOVEMBER 17, 1946). Parisot had done translations of Coleridge's "Rhyme of the Ancient Mariner," "Christabel," and "Kubla Khan," and had asked Artaud to write a preface. Artaud's letter, the response to Parisot's request, was not ready in time for publication. (The volume appeared in early 1947.) Artaud's letter was first printed, after his death, in *K Revue de la Poésie*, Nos.

Notes

1–2 (June 1948), under the title "Coleridge le traître." It was reprinted in March 1949 in a small book called *Supplément aux Lettres de Rodez, suivi de Coleridge le traître*, edited by Parisot and published by Guy Lévis Mano in an edition of one thousand copies plus twenty-five copies reserved for Les Amis de GLM. In addition to the Coleridge letter, Parisot included three other texts in this book: a last, previously unpublished letter from the 1945 series that Artaud wrote him from Rodez, dated December 9, 1945; a text included with this letter called "L'Evêque de Rodez"; and an undated letter from Artaud to Guy Lévis Mano. The December 9, 1945, letter and the text "L'Evêque de Rodez" have been grouped together, under the title *L'Evêque de Rodez*, in *G* IX, 213–22. Neither the letter to Guy Lévis Mano, which Artaud intended to publish in *Suppôts et Suppliciations*, nor the Coleridge letter has yet appeared in the Gallimard *Oeuvres complètes*. The present translation undoubtedly contains some errors, but these cannot be corrected until a definitive text is published in the *Oeuvres complètes*.

"Because -*ema* in Greek means blood . . ." The Greek word for blood is *haimo*.

During the summer of 1946, Artaud came in to Paris every day to see friends. He hoped to work again in the theater; among his numerous projects was an adaptation of Euripides' *Bacchae*, which he wanted to stage at the Théâtre du Vieux-Colombier. Paule Thévenin reports that Artaud wrote incessantly during this period—even while riding in the Métro or in automobiles; she learned to decipher and transcribe his almost illegible handwriting. On August 12, 1946, he wrote to Gaston Gallimard regarding the projected publication of his *Oeuvres complètes*. Artaud's "Préambule" was first published in 1956, when Volume I of the *Oeuvres complètes* finally appeared; it may be found in *G* I, 9–15. In the autumn he wrote "Histoire entre la Groume et Dieu," which was first published in the magazine *Fontaine*, No. 57 (1946), pp. 673–77. It subsequently appeared, along with a text called "Apoème," by Artaud's friend the poet and essayist Henri Pichette (*b.* 1924) in a small book, *Xylophonie contre la Grande Presse et son petit public*, privately published in 1946 in an edition of fifty copies.

After spending October in the South of France, Artaud returned to Ivry and asked to be moved to a dilapidated two-room pavilion dating from the eighteenth century, on the edge of the clinic property. He lived there until his death.

Notes

XXXIII. *Van Gogh, the Man Suicided by Society* (1947)

Van Gogh le suicidé de la société: G XIII, 9–64. The great van Gogh exhibition (173 works) at the Orangerie in Paris opened in late January 1947 and ran through March. Artaud's text was inspired by reading an article by a psychiatrist describing van Gogh as a degenerate. (This article, which appeared on January 31 in the weekly paper *Arts*, is reprinted in G XIII, 302–4.) Artaud visited the exhibition on the morning of February 2, and wrote the main portion of his text ("Le Suicidé de la société") the following week, between February 8 and 15. Revisions were made and additional material was written during the next few months. One of the later sections, the second "Post-Scriptum," incorporates many ideas expressed in letters Artaud wrote Breton on the occasion of the opening of the International Surrealist Exhibition in March. The whole text was published by K on September 25, 1947, in an original edition of 630 copies. The book contains reproductions of seven works by van Gogh, plus a van Gogh self-portrait on the cover. *Van Gogh* is the only one of Artaud's books to have received a literary prize—the Prix Sainte-Beuve for the best essay published in 1947; it was awarded on January 16, 1948.

Greek fire was a combustible mixture (including niter, sulphur, and naphtha) hurled at an enemy's ships, fortifications, etc., much used by the Byzantines.

"Thiers, Gambetta, and Félix Faure . . ." Louis Adolphe Thiers (1797–1877), the leader of the Liberals against Napoleon III, liquidated the Paris Commune and was the first President (1871–73) of the Third Republic. Léon Gambetta (1838–82), a statesman opposed to Napoleon III, was Premier in 1881–82. Félix Faure (1841–99) was President of the Republic from 1895 to 1899.

There is every reason to think that the "Dr. L." castigated in the text is Dr. Jacques Latrémolière, one of the psychiatrists at Rodez, even though Paule Thévenin insists—in G XIII, 307–8—that Artaud was referring to another doctor, whose name she does not divulge. Latrémolière recognized himself as "Dr. L." in *La Tour de Feu*, No. 69 (1961).

Père Tranquille is a mistranscription of Père Tanguy, referring to *Portrait of Père Tanguy*, a painting done by van Gogh in autumn 1887 and one of two portraits he did of Julien-François Tanguy. (The second portrait, done in late 1887, was not included in the Orangerie exhibition.) When Paule Thévenin (to whom Artaud dictated his text) pointed out her faulty transcription of the name, Artaud decided to let it stand.

Notes

"These crows painted two days before his death . . ." *Wheatfield with Crows* was painted shortly before July 9, 1890, at Auvers-sur-Oise. Van Gogh shot himself on July 27 and died on July 29.

"Dr. Gachet, a so-called psychiatrist . . ." Van Gogh spent the last months of his life at Auvers-sur-Oise, seventy miles from Paris, under the care of Dr. Gachet.

"What is drawing? . . ." In the paragraphs in italics Artaud is giving excerpts from three of van Gogh's letters to his brother Théo. The first, and undated, letter (#237 in the standard edition of van Gogh's letters) was written from The Hague in 1882 or 1883. The second letter (#534) was written from Arles. The third letter (#651) was written from Auvers-sur-Oise. "In my painting *The Night Café* . . ." Van Gogh did this painting in September 1888. "The good fellowship of *Tartarin* . . ." Tartarin is a comic character, a prodigious braggard, created by Alphonse Daudet (1840–85) in two books, *Aventures Prodigieuses de Tartarin de Tarascon* (1872) and *Tartarin sur les Alpes* (1885).

"The soul which gave its ear to the body . . ." When van Gogh cut his ear off in Arles, he gave it to a prostitute.

From "The olive trees of Saint-Rémy" to "the bridge where . . ." This list refers to seven of van Gogh's best-known paintings. Les Aliscamps is a park in Arles, on the site of an ancient Roman cemetery. (Van Gogh did two paintings titled "Les Aliscamps" in late October 1888.) Many of the descriptive passages in Artaud's text are in fact descriptions and evocations of paintings by van Gogh. More than twenty paintings are described, most of which are identified in the notes to *G* XIII.

In the same month that Artaud saw the van Gogh exhibition he made an extraordinary public appearance. Friends organized an evening at the Théâtre du Vieux-Colombier, on January 13, for Artaud to read from his works and talk. It was called "Tête-à-tête, par Antonin Artaud." Gide, Breton, Paulhan, Henri Michaux, Audiberti, Blin, Adamov, Camus, Adrienne Monnier, and many other friends and admirers attended. Artaud was on stage for three hours: declaiming his new poems, explaining his trips to Mexico and Ireland, denouncing electroshock and psychiatrists—talking, trembling, screaming, humming, singing, chanting. By all accounts, this spectacle of Artaud's Passion was terribly painful to watch. Gide wrote a short article about it which first appeared in Camus' newspaper *Combat* (March 19, 1948) and was reprinted in the special Artaud issue of the magazine *84*, Nos. 5–6 (1948); it can be found in Virmaux's *Antonin Artaud et le théâtre*, pp. 309–10. A contrasting view of the evening is given by Barrault, who refused to attend, in an interview in *Planète + Plus*, February 1971, pp. 51–57.

XXXIV. Letter to Pierre Loeb (April 23, 1947)

"LETTRE À PIERRE LOEB." This letter was first printed in the magazine *Les Lettres Nouvelles*, No. 59 (April 1958), pp. 481–86, and was reprinted in Georges Charbonnier's *Essai sur Antonin Artaud* (Paris: Seghers, 1959), pp. 202–6. Artaud had known the art dealer Pierre Loeb since 1924, when Loeb had his Pascin exhibition; his gallery on the rue Bonaparte started exhibiting the Surrealist group the following year. After the war, Loeb's gallery was on the rue des Beaux-Arts. From July 4 to 20, 1947, the Galerie Pierre had an exhibition of Artaud's drawings (mostly portraits), and on July 19 a reading of Artaud's recent poems was held there. The catalogue for the exhibition, entitled *Portraits et Dessins*, was prefaced by Artaud with a poem, known as "Le Visage humain," that begins:

> Le visage humain
> est une force vide, un
> champ de mort.
> La vieille revendication
> révolutionnaire d'une forme
> qui n'a jamais corres-
> pondu à son corps, qui partait
> pour être autre chose
> que le corps
>
> .   .   .   .   .
>
> [que] le visage humain
> n'a pas encore trouvé sa face . . .

For the whole poem, see Charbonnier's *Essai sur Antonin Artaud*, pp. 52–53.

XXXV. From *Artaud le Mômo* (1947)

Artaud le Mômo is a small book which was published by Bordas in an edition of 355 copies on September 15, 1947, illustrated with eight drawings by Artaud. It contains five texts, all written between July

Notes

and September 1946. Artaud had returned to Paris, after his nine years of incarceration, in May 1946.

Mômo is Marseilles patois; it means simpleton, village idiot. It is also possible that Artaud was thinking of the Greek god Momos (Momo in Italian), who was the god of ridicule, a personification of fault-finding, a licensed grumbler who objects to everything the gods do. In Latin and in several modern languages, the name came to mean—more generally—any captious or irascible critic, someone impossible to please.

"LE RETOUR D'ARTAUD, LE MÔMO": *G* XII, 11–20. The first text in the book published by Bordas, though not the earliest of the five texts. It was written in August–early September 1946, reworked between September and January 1947, and was one of the poems that Artaud read aloud on January 13, 1947, at the Théâtre du Vieux-Colombier.

"ALIÉNATION ET MAGIE NOIRE": *G* XII, 55–65. The last of the five texts in *Artaud le Mômo*. The major portion of the text, from the beginning through *farfadi / ta azor / tau ela / auela / a / tare / ila*, was written in the first two weeks of July 1946. The word END after this passage ("ces syllabes que j'invente," as Artaud elsewhere described it) and the note dated January 12, 1948, were added by Artaud on that date to a copy of the book, for inclusion in a possible re-edition. The rest of the text was added between April and August 1947, when Artaud was correcting the proofs for *Artaud le Mômo*.

The *Bardo Todol* is the book more commonly known in English as the *Tibetan Book of the Dead*; the Tibetan title means "Liberation by Hearing on the After-Death Plane." The book, compiled in Tibet from Sanskrit texts in the eighth century A.D., was used as a breviary and read or recited on the occasion of death. It is meant to be a guide for the dead person during the period of *Bardo* existence, an intermediary state of forty-nine days' duration between one's death and rebirth, and suggests a yogic method of attaining Nirvanic liberation from the cycle of reincarnation.

The other three texts in *Artaud le Mômo*, not translated here, are: "Centre-Mère et Patron-Minet" (*G* XII, 21–25), "Insulte à l'Inconditionée" (*G* XII, 27–31), and "L'Exécration du père-mère" (*G* XII, 33–53). The second text, "Centre-Mère et Patron-Minet," written by July 28, 1946, is the only one to have been published before its appearance in the book—in the magazine *Troisième Convoi*, No. 3

Notes

(November 1946). It was also among the poems read aloud at the Théâtre du Vieux-Colombier during the evening of January 13, 1947.

XXXVI. *Indian Culture* and *Here Lies* (1947)

Ci-gît, précédé de la Culture Indienne: G XII, 67–100. These two texts (translated here in their entirety) were printed together as a small book in an edition of 450 copies by the publisher K on December 15, 1947. They were both written on one day, November 25, 1946, and dictated a few days later, with some changes, to Paule Thévenin. Both texts contain many puns and plays on words, which are impossible to convey fully in translation. The repeated portmanteau word "jiji-cricri" (also "Jizo-cri," "Jizi-cri," "ji en cri," "Jizo-cri," "ji et cri," etc.) is a play on the words meaning "Jesus Christ," "I cry," and "I cry there." Among the other words that Artaud plays with are "cafre" and "camphre," "om" (the Vedic syllable), "homme," and "omelette," "gendre" and "gendron," "d'eux" and "deux," "motrice" and "matrice," "fond du" and "fonder."

"LA CULTURE INDIENNE": *G* XII, 59–74. Artaud read "La Culture Indienne" at the Théâtre du Vieux-Colombier on January 13, 1947.

"CI-GÎT": *G* XII, 75–100. The passage translated as "like the chatter / of a beggar's teeth; / or the clap (whorehouse) / of a toothy femur (bloody)" reads in the original:

> comme la claque
> du claque-dents;
> ou le claque (bordel)
> du fémur à dents (en sang).

Artaud is playing on some of the meanings of the word "claque," which refers to a short, sharp noise and is also a slang term for death. As the shortened form of "claque-dents," it is slang for whorehouse, but also refers to a pauper, a miserable wretch, or one whose teeth are chattering.

Much of what Artaud wrote in 1947 was given to two small literary magazines: *84*, edited by Marcel Bisiaux, and *K*. Between 1946 and his death in early 1948 Artaud was not able to work in the theater; but, preoccupied by the idea of remaking one's body, he continually returned to the idea of theater. The two key texts on the theater from 1947 were both published posthumously, in the magazine *L'Arbalète*, No. 13 (Summer 1948): "Aliéner l'acteur," dated May 12, 1947 (pp. 7–14), and "Le théâtre et la science" (pp. 15–24). Another remarkable text from this period is a letter Artaud wrote on June 4, 1947, to a new friend, the young poet Jacques Prével; it was published after Artaud's death (in 1949, by Jacques Haumont) under the title *Lettre contre la Cabbale*.

In July, Artaud's physical condition suddenly worsened. From then on, his visits to Paris became increasingly rare and most of the time he stayed in his quarters in Ivry. A maid and the gardener brought in his meals; a local barber came every day to shave him; friends from Paris visited frequently. While continuing to write, he had to resort more and more to dictation. From his bed he dictated to Paule Thévenin in late 1947 and early 1948 the principal texts for a book entitled *Suppôts et Suppliciations* which was to be published by K. This book has never been published. Extracts were printed after Artaud's death in various magazines—in *84*, Nos. 5–6 (1948); in *Les Temps Modernes*, No. 40 (February 1949); in *84*, Nos. 8–9 (1949); and in *La Nef*, Nos. 71–72 (December 1950–January 1951). Besides this material, Artaud also planned to include (among other older texts) a letter to Jean Dubuffet written November 29, 1945, the already published *Lettre sur Lautréamont* (1946), and the undated letter to Guy Lévis Mano which was published in 1949 in the book called *Supplément aux Lettres de Rodez*. (*Suppôts et Suppliciations* has been announced as forthcoming in the Gallimard *Oeuvres complètes*.)

The violent intestinal pains from which Artaud had long suffered became worse, and he was taking even larger doses of opium, laudanum, and chloral. In February 1948, Paule Thévenin took Artaud for an examination at the Salpêtrière Hospital in Paris. The diagnosis was cancer of the rectum, inoperable and incurable. Although Artaud was never told he was dying of cancer, there seems to be no doubt that he knew it.

XXXVII. *To Have Done with the Judgment of God*, a radio play (1947)

Pour en finir avec le jugement de dieu: G XIII, 67–104. In the fall of 1947, Artaud was approached by Fernand Pouey, the director of the literary and dramatic programs of the French Radio, to create a broadcast for the program "La Voix des poètes." The program was rehearsed and then recorded between November 22 and 29, a period in which, despite his terrible physical state, Artaud traveled in from Ivry to Paris every day to supervise the direction of the recording. He provided the sound effects himself (improvised on drums of various sizes and pitch, a xylophone, and gongs, plus an extraordinary range of voice effects), and read the introduction and the conclusion ("Vous délirez, Monsieur Artaud . . .") and engaged in a dialogue in glossolalia with Roger Blin. Besides Artaud, the cast consisted of Maria Casarès, who read "Tutuguri"; Roger Blin, who read "La Recherche de la fécalité"; and Paule Thévenin, who read "La Question se pose de . . ." The program was scheduled for 10:45 p.m. on February 2, 1948. The day before, the director-in-chief of the French Radio, Wladimir Porché, banned it.

The oldest stratum of the text is probably "Tutuguri," which existed, at least in note form, in 1936, before Artaud returned from Mexico. The present version was written in October 1947 under the title "Tutuguri, le rite du soleil noir." It was promised to Marc Barbezat, the editor of the magazine *L'Arbalète*, but when Artaud decided to insert it in *Pour en finir avec le jugement de dieu*, he wrote a second version of the same text for publication by K, which he sent to him on February 12, 1948. With the exception of "Tutuguri" and "La Question se pose de . . ." (the latter written in early October 1947), everything else in Artaud's "sound play" was written in November 1947, for the projected broadcast.

Pour en finir avec le jugement de dieu was published by K on April 30, 1948, in an edition of 2,000 copies. The present translation follows the definitive text published in 1975 by Paule Thévenin in Vol. XIII of the Gallimard edition, but stops where the K edition stops. Not translated is a poem dated November 19, 1947, and entitled "Le Théâtre de la Cruauté," which Artaud intended for the broadcast but never recorded because of time limitations. This was to be the final section (after the "Conclusion"). It was first published in the magazine *84*, Nos. 5–6 (1948) and is to be found in *G* XIII, 105–15. There is also a "Post-Scriptum" (*G* XIII, 116–17) as well as a second "Post-Scriptum" (*G* XIII, 118), which concludes the published work. The second "Post-Scriptum," a kind of farewell, reads:

> Qui suis-je?
> D'où je viens?
> Je suis Antonin Artaud
> et que je le dise

Notes

> comme je sais le dire
> immédiatement
> vous verrez mon corps actuel
> voler en éclats
> et se ramasser
> sous dix mille aspects
> notoires
> un corps neuf
> où vous ne pourrez
> plus jamais
> m'oublier.

XXXVIII. Last letters

TO FERNAND POUEY (DECEMBER 11, 1947): *G* XIII, 123–25. Pouey was the radio producer who commissioned Artaud to do a radio "play." This letter, as well as the ones which follow, were first printed —in imperfect transcriptions, and out of order—along with the text of Artaud's play/poem in the book published by K in 1948.

TO FERNAND POUEY (JANUARY 16, 1948): *G* XIII, 126–27. "Centre-Mère et Patron-Minet" ("Center-Mother and Boss-Darling") is the second text included in *Artaud le Mômo*.

TO WLADIMIR PORCHÉ (FEBRUARY 4, 1948): *G* XIII, 130–32. Porché was the director-in-chief of the French Radio. The letter was written on February 4; the program had been scheduled for February 2; Porché canceled it on February 1.

TO FERNAND POUEY (FEBRUARY 7, 1948): *G* XIII, 133–34. Pouey stood by Artaud and urged Porché to let the program go on the air. Aided by the clamor in the newspapers about Porché's decision, Pouey got permission to do a private studio broadcast of the poem on February 5. It was acclaimed by the small invited audience of fifty people (which included Barrault, Jouvet, Cocteau, Queneau, Eluard, René Clair, Paulhan, Roger Vitrac, René Char, Jean Vilar, and Claude Mauriac), but Porché would not reverse his decision.

TO RENÉ GUILLY (FEBRUARY 7, 1948): *G* XIII, 135–37. Guilly was one of the writers and journalists invited to the first studio broadcast of *Pour en finir avec le jugement de dieu* and asked to give their opinion as to whether it should be publicly broadcast. His article in the news-

Notes

paper *Combat* on February 7 is given in *G* XIII, 354–56. It provoked a response from the critic Maurice Nadeau, in *Combat* on February 8–9, defending Artaud (see *G* XIII, 356–57 for the text).

TO FERNAND POUEY AND RENÉ GUIGNARD (FEBRUARY 17, 1948) : *G* XIII, 140–41. Guignard was in charge of the program on which Artaud's play was to be done. The day before writing this letter, Artaud rewrote the first part of his poem "Tutuguri."

TO PAULE THÉVENIN (FEBRUARY 24, 1948) : *G* XIII, 146–47. "M." is the critic Marthe Robert; "A.A." is the playwright Arthur Adamov. There had been one more private studio broadcast on February 23; the reaction of the second invited audience—which included Robert and Adamov—was less enthusiastic than that of the first. Porché again refused to change his mind.

A little before 8 a.m. on March 4, the gardener who brought Artaud his breakfast each morning in his room at the clinic in Ivry found him sitting at the foot of his bed, dead. The diagnosis made at the autopsy confirmed that Artaud died of cancer. He was buried in the cemetery in Ivry on March 8. He was fifty-two years old.